ARLIDGE AND PARRY ON FRAUD

AUSTRALIA
Law Book Co.
Sydney

CANADA AND USA
Carswell
Toronto

HONG KONG
Sweet & Maxwell Asia

NEW ZEALAND
Brookers
Wellington

SINGAPORE and MALAYSIA
Sweet & Maxwell Asia
Singapore and Kuala Lumpur

ARLIDGE AND PARRY ON FRAUD

Third Edition

By

Jacques Parry, Barrister

with

Anthony Arlidge Q.C.
Joanne Hacking, Barrister
Josepha Jacobson, Barrister

LONDON
SWEET & MAXWELL
2007

First Edition 1985
Second Edition 1996
Third Edition 2007

Published by
Sweet & Maxwell Limited of 100 Avenue Road,
Swiss Cottage, London NW3 3PF
http://www.sweetandmaxwell.co.uk
Typeset by LBJ Typesetting Ltd of Kingsclere
Printed and bound in Great Britain by
William Clowes Ltd, Beccles, Suffolk

No natural forests were destroyed to make this product;
only farmed timber was used and re-planted.

British Library Cataloguing in Publication Data

A CIP catalogue record for this book
is available from the British Library

ISBN 978-0-421-89210-1

To my mother

PREFACE

Since the second edition of this book was completed, the law of deception has been holed below the waterline by the House of Lords' decision in *Preddy* [1996] A.C. 815, given emergency repairs by the Theft (Amendment) Act 1996 and finally sunk by the Fraud Act 2006. Good riddance, many will say. The new law of "fraud by false representation", coupled with the new offence of obtaining services dishonestly (with or without deception), is certainly much simpler; but that is more of an advantage for prosecutors than for the general public. The new law has defects which its architect, the Law Commission, appears to have underestimated or overlooked. They arise partly from the perverse decision to abandon the concept of deception in favour of that of false representation—thus reintroducing a degree of technicality which the Criminal Law Revision Committee wisely discarded in 1966—and partly from the retention of a requirement of causation, but in the form of mens rea rather than actus reus. These changes may mean that the Act not only fails to achieve its aims but creates new difficulties of its own.

The courts will probably manage to work around (or, more likely, ignore) these problems. More worrying is that the new fraud offence can consist in a dishonest "abuse of position", without false representation or even non-disclosure. It has to include *some* such conduct if it is to be an adequate replacement for conspiracy to defraud, as the Law Commission intended (though the Government has absurdly insisted on retaining conspiracy to defraud alongside the new offences). But the drafting of the relevant provision is so open-ended that it is impossible to tell what kinds of "position" are caught. Arguably the prosecution need only prove that the defendant was in some kind of financial relationship with someone else, and did something which the other person did not expect and which the jury think was dishonest.

If the Act is construed in this way, it will be nothing new. It already happens, for example, in cases charged as conspiracy to defraud. But the Law Commission itself, in a consultation paper published in 1999, had mounted a powerful attack on this aspect of the law. Rather than simply making it criminal to do things that a jury would regard as dishonest (the Commission argued), the proper approach was to identify the ways in which the law would be inadequate if conspiracy to defraud were abolished, and to extend the law only as far as necessary to remedy those defects. In its final report, however, the Commission described this approach as "no longer realistic", because it is "bound to be always lagging behind developments in technology and commerce". This may be a valid objection; but it is impossible to judge from the report whether it is valid, because it is not subjected to even the most cursory critical scrutiny. One would expect a serious law reform body to develop reasoned criteria for identifying the kinds of dishonest conduct that *ought* to be criminal; to apply those criteria to the kinds of conduct that were previously criminal only as conspiracy to defraud; and, where the conclusion is that some such conduct ought to be criminal, to examine possible ways of making it criminal which would *not* be soon overtaken by developments—for example by framing the law in terms of legal concepts rather than particular technologies or commercial techniques, and learning from mistakes such as the one exposed in *Preddy* (which had nothing to do with developments since 1968, and arose because the Criminal Law Revision Committee overlooked the legal nature of transfers between bank accounts). To judge from its report, the Law Commission did none of these things. It simply rejects, without argument or evidence, the approach that it had previously advocated, and embraces one that it had shown to be untenable. One is left wondering what happened between 1999 and 2002 to prompt such a Damascene conversion.

It is true that some influential voices would have preferred the Commission to go even further, and to recommend an offence defined in terms of dishonest conduct and little else. Almost the only point on which the report agrees with the consultation paper is that the requirement of dishonesty cannot be allowed to "do all the work". The recommendations are presented as a judicious compromise between that extreme and the minimalist stance of the consultation paper. But, in the case of fraud by abuse of position, dishonesty will certainly be doing *most* of the work; and the additional element of abuse of position is so ill-defined that there may not be much practical difference between the offence ostensibly rejected and the one we now have. Moreover the Commission's refusal to recommend a "general dishonesty offence" was soon exposed as mere posturing by its recommendation (also implemented by the Fraud Act) that fraudulent trading be extended to non-corporate businesses, without otherwise clarifying its scope. Thanks to *Kemp* [1988] Q.B. 645, fraudulent trading relies as heavily on the element of dishonesty as conspiracy to defraud does; so this change dramatically expands the area in which dishonesty does all the work. And the Commission has now abandoned its plan, announced in 1994 but never seriously pursued, to overhaul the law of dishonesty as a whole. It seems untroubled by the fact that, since *Hinks* [2001] 2 A.C. 241, theft is an offence of doing something dishonest (not necessarily unlawful) in relation to someone else's property.

The upshot is that, teething troubles aside, the Fraud Act is unlikely to make much practical difference. A much more far-reaching change is section 43 of the Criminal Justice Act 2003, which, if brought into force, will enable serious fraud trials to be conducted by a judge alone. It is ironic, to put it charitably, that the Government should be trying to make juries optional in fraud cases at the same time as reforming the substantive law in a way which ensures that dishonesty—that is, the standards of ordinary people—will in most cases continue to be the sole or main issue. The justification offered is not that juries cannot understand complex cases, but that long trials may be too "burdensome" for them. That may well be true; but in that case it is not clear why the new procedure is reserved for fraud trials—which, because dishonesty continues to do most of the work, are more likely than other trials to require the input of non-lawyers.

There have been many other changes since 1995. There are new offences of income tax evasion, social security fraud, cheating at gambling and operating a cartel. The extra-territoriality provisions of the Criminal Justice Act 1993 finally came into force in 1999, by which time they had been rendered largely unnecessary by developments in the case law, as well as being overtaken by the Criminal Justice (Terrorism and Conspiracy) Act 1998. This edition also takes account of the Financial Services and Markets Act 2000, the changes made to the law of evidence by the Criminal Justice Act 2003, the new procedure for two-stage trials under the Domestic Violence, Crime and Victims Act 2004, the Criminal Procedure Rules 2005 (including the mystifying amendments of April 2007) and the Companies Act 2006.

I am indebted to a number of people for assistance with individual chapters. In alphabetical order, they are: Anthony Arlidge Q.C. (Chapter 28), Jonathan Fisher Q.C. (Chapter 16), Joanne Hacking (Chapters 16, 17 and 23 to 26), Christina Hughes (Chapter 27), Josepha Jacobson (Chapter 20) and Stephen Robins (Chapters 8, 14 and 15). They are not responsible for the errors that remain, and neither they nor their employers (if any) should be assumed to agree with any of the views expressed.

I have tried to state the law as at May 1, 2007, except that I have included coverage of certain provisions not yet in force at that date and (for the benefit of practitioners still dealing with cases arising under the old law) of certain provisions already repealed.

Jacques Parry

May 2007

CONTENTS

Chapter 3: Gain and loss

Chapter 4: False representations and deception

Chapter 6: Abuse of position

Chapter 7: Conspiracy to defraud

Chapter 8: Fraudulent trading

Chapter 19: Corruption

Chapter 20: Cartels

Chapter 21: Inchoate fraud

Chapter 27: Evidence

Chapter 28: Presenting a fraud case

TABLE OF CASES

Table of Cases

Table of Cases

TABLE OF STATUTES

2006 Police and Justice Act (c.48) .... 21–025—21–027, 21–031, 21–036, 21–040, 21–041, 22–090, 22–092, 22–093, 22–132

2006 Police and Justice Act—*cont.*
s.38(2) 21–027
Armed Forces Act (c.52) 22–006

TABLE OF STATUTORY INSTRUMENTS

TABLE OF ABBREVIATIONS

ACSA 2001	Anti-terrorism, Crime and Security Act 2001
CA 1985	Companies Act 1985
CA 2006	Companies Act 2006
CAA 1981	Criminal Attempts Act 1981
CDA 1998	Crime and Disorder Act 1998
CEMA 1979	Customs and Excise Management Act 1979
CJA 1987	Criminal Justice Act 1987
CJA 1993	Criminal Justice Act 1993
CJA 2003	Criminal Justice Act 2003
CLA 1977	Criminal Law Act 1977
CMA 1990	Computer Misuse Act 1990
CPIA 1996	Criminal Procedure and Investigations Act 1996
CPR 2005	Criminal Procedure Rules 2005
DVCVA 2004	Domestic Violence, Crime and Victims Act 2004
EA 2002	Enterprise Act 2002
FA 2006	Fraud Act 2006
FCA 1981	Forgery and Counterfeiting Act 1981
FSA 1986	Financial Services Act 1986
FSMA 2000	Financial Services and Markets Act 2000
GA 2005	Gambling Act 2005
IA 1986	Insolvency Act 1986
PACE	Police and Criminal Evidence Act 1984
PBCPA 1889	Public Bodies Corrupt Practices Act 1889
PCA 1906	Prevention of Corruption Act 1906
PCA 1916	Prevention of Corruption Act 1916
PFIA 1958	Prevention of Fraud (Investments) Act 1958
PJA 2006	Police and Justice Act 2006
SSAA 1992	Social Security Administration Act 1992
TA 1968	Theft Act 1968
TA 1978	Theft Act 1978
VATA 1994	Value Added Tax Act 1994

Chapter 1

STATUTORY FRAUD: AN OVERVIEW

Previous editions of this book began by remarking that fraud was a concept but not (in English law) a criminal offence. That is no longer true: fraud is now an offence as well as a concept.[1] Section 1(1) of the Fraud Act 2006 ("FA 2006") provides: 1–001

> "A person is guilty of fraud if he is in breach of any of the sections listed in subsection (2) (which provide for different ways of committing the offence)."

The offence is triable either way, and is punishable on conviction on indictment with 10 years' imprisonment.[2]

The sections listed in s.1(2) are 1–002

- s.2 (fraud by false representation),
- s.3 (fraud by failing to disclose information), and
- s.4 (fraud by abuse of position).

THE ELEMENTS OF THE OFFENCE

The drafting of FA 2006, s.1(1) makes it clear that there is a single offence, created by s.1—*not* three offences created by ss.2, 3 and 4. Those sections merely provide for different ways of committing the single offence under s.1. A statement of offence should therefore cite s.1, while the particulars of offence should allege facts falling within s.2, 3 or 4. Since there is only one offence, a count can in theory allege breaches of more than one section without duplicity, but it would seem to be good practice to charge breaches of different sections in different counts. Difficulties may arise if the jury are agreed that the defendant is in breach of one of ss.2 to 4, 1–003

[1] For the concept of fraud at common law (which is not identical to the statutory offence) see below, Ch.7.
[2] FA 2006, s.1(3).

but are divided about which one;[3] but these difficulties could equally arise if the alternatives are charged in the same count.

1–004 Two elements of the offence are common to all three ways of committing it, namely

- dishonesty, and
- intent to make a gain, cause loss to another or expose another to a risk of loss.

Dishonesty is not defined in FA 2006. "Gain" and "loss" are defined by s.5. Both these elements are broadly shared by other, previously existing offences, and authorities on them in the context of those other offences will in most cases[4] be equally relevant to the new offence. They are examined in Chs 2 and 3 respectively.

1–005 The other elements required by FA 2006, ss.2 to 4 are examined in Chs 4 to 6.

- Section 2 deals with fraud by false representation, and broadly replaces eight offences of deception created by the Theft Acts 1968 and 1978. Although the deception offences are repealed with effect from January 15, 2007, the new law is not retrospective. Conduct before that date will therefore have to be charged under the old law,[5] and Ch.4 examines the old law as well as the new.
- Whereas s.2 deals with positive misrepresentation, s.3 deals with pure non-disclosure. This was a grey area under the old law, but the courts never had to resolve the matter because non-disclosure nearly always amounts to implied misrepresentation anyway. For the same reason, s.3 adds little to s.2.
- Section 4 deals with abuse of position. Some examples of it would fall within previously existing offences, such as theft or corruption. Others would previously have amounted to no offence at all (unless two or more persons were involved, in which case they would be guilty of conspiracy to defraud at common law).[6] Section 4 seems to have been aimed primarily if not exclusively at breaches of fiduciary duty, but the drafting is open to a much wider reading.

In construing these provisions it will often be helpful to refer to the Law Commission report on which they are based.[7]

[3] cf. below, para.4–196.
[4] Certain provisions relating to the requirement of dishonesty apply only to theft: see below, paras 2–065 *et seq.*
[5] Subject to the transitional provisions: below, para.1–006.
[6] See below, Ch.7.
[7] Law Com. No.276, *Fraud*, Cm.5560 (2002).

COMMENCEMENT AND TRANSITIONAL PROVISIONS

The provisions creating the new fraud offence came into force on January 15, 2007.[8] Nothing done before that date can be charged as fraud under FA 2006. With effect from the same date, para.1 of Sch.1 to FA 2006 repeals the provisions of the Theft Acts 1968 and 1978 relating to the eight deception offences. This calls for transitional provision, because there would otherwise be a lacuna in the case of a deception before January 15, 2007 which results in an obtaining of property, services, etc. on or after that date. Paragraph 3 of Sch.2 therefore provides: **1–006**

> "(1) Paragraph 1 of Schedule 1 does not affect any liability, investigation, legal proceeding or penalty for or in respect of any offence partly committed before the commencement of that paragraph.
>
> (2) An offence is partly committed before the commencement of paragraph 1 of Schedule 1 if—
>
> (a) a relevant event occurs before its commencement, and
>
> (b) another relevant event occurs on or after its commencement.
>
> (3) 'Relevant event', in relation to an offence, means any act, omission or other event (including any result of one or more acts or omissions) proof of which is required for conviction of the offence."

The definition of "relevant event" is virtually identical to the definition of the same expression in the Criminal Justice Act 1993, s.2(1) for the purpose of the rules governing liability for frauds committed outside England and Wales.[9] In the context of the deception offences, however, it is clear that there will always be two relevant events: (a) the deception, and (b) the obtaining of property or services, or the securing of some other event, by means of the deception. The effect is that the life of the deception provisions is extended so as to catch a person who obtains something on or after January 15, 2007 by means of a deception committed before that date. **1–007**

[8] SI 2006/3200 (c.112).
[9] See para.22–021.

Chapter 2

DISHONESTY

Central to the new fraud offence is the requirement that the relevant act **2–001** or omission must be done or made "dishonestly". This requirement is shared with many other offences, including the majority of those created by the Theft Act 1968 ("TA 1968"). There are also a number of offences defined in terms of the common law concept of fraud[1] (which is not coterminous with the new offence), and dishonesty is an element of these offences too. It means the same in every case.[2] In this chapter we analyse that meaning.

"Dishonesty" is a deceptively simple name for a complex concept. It **2–002** embraces at least three, and arguably four, distinct elements. The defendant's conduct must fail to conform

- to generally accepted standards of honest conduct (as they are, and as the defendant believes them to be); *and*
- to the limits of what he is legally entitled to do (at least as he believes those limits to be, and arguably also as they actually are).

[1] e.g. conspiracy to defraud (below, Ch.7) and fraudulent trading (Ch.8). Forgery was another example until it was redefined by the Forgery and Counterfeiting Act 1981, which does not require dishonesty: see Ch.11.
[2] *Ghosh* [1982] Q.B. 1053.

2–003 It is only comparatively recently that the relevance of generally accepted standards has been recognised. Previously, dishonesty in the context of criminal law had meant little more than the absence of any supposed legal justification for the defendant's conduct. In recent years, however, such importance has been attached to those standards that the courts have tended to refer to them even where the real issue is not what ordinary people consider dishonest but what the law itself allows. In accordance with this approach, we discuss first the element of non-conformity with accepted standards, and then the relationship between dishonesty and legal rights.

DISHONESTY AND ACCEPTED STANDARDS

DISHONESTY AS A JURY QUESTION

2–004 A person's conduct is not dishonest unless it falls short of the standards of honesty accepted by ordinary people. Since the standards of ordinary people are not always as stringent as those of the law, conduct is not necessarily dishonest merely because it is unlawful. In the context of fraudulent trading Maugham J. said that

> "the words 'defraud' and 'fraudulent purpose' . . . are words which connote actual dishonesty involving, according to current notions of fair trading among commercial men, real moral blame".[3]

2–005 The requirement of "moral blame" was recognised in *Wright*,[4] where the defendant obtained money on behalf of another person with a written authority signed by that person. The signature purported to have been witnessed by a third party, but the third party's signature had in fact been forged by the defendant. His conviction of obtaining the money by false pretences was quashed. The "intent to defraud" which had to be established was said to be "really synonymous with dishonesty". If he intended to pay the money over to the person entitled to it, it was arguable that he did not act dishonestly. The issue should not have been withdrawn from the jury.

2–006 But the courts have sometimes appeared to assume that conduct which the defendant knows to be unlawful is automatically dishonest. In *Draper*[5] it was held that, although forgery then required an intent to defraud, even a "perfectly honest motive" was no defence. This case followed *Welham v DPP*,[6] where the House of Lords had defined the requisite intent without reference to any requirement of dishonesty going beyond the disregard of

[3] *Re Patrick & Lyon Ltd* [1933] Ch. 786 at 790.
[4] [1960] Crim. L.R. 366.
[5] [1962] Crim. L.R. 107.
[6] [1961] A.C. 103.

legal rights. Similarly in *Hagan*[7] the defendant, a priest and a trustee of certain trusts existing for the benefit of the parish, obtained trust funds by forging the signatures of his co-trustees. He claimed that this was not dishonest because he used the money for church (though not parish) purposes. Convictions of obtaining money on a forged instrument[8] were affirmed: the requirement of intent to defraud was satisfied by the act of obtaining the money by deception. The court said that there was no reason to import a further element of dishonesty, and that to do so would amount to "an unwarrantable gloss upon the statutory provision".

There was a similar lack of consistency in the context of larceny. The definition of the offence required that the property be taken "fraudulently and without a claim of right made in good faith",[9] which implied that not every taking without a claim of right was fraudulent; and in *Williams*[10] it was said that the requirement of fraud was not redundant. However, the court went on to define it as meaning that the taking must be intentional, under no mistake, and with knowledge that the thing taken was the property of another person.[11] If that were all it meant, it *would* be redundant. But Lord Goddard C.J., giving the judgment of the court, also said: 2–007

> "It is one thing if a person with good credit and with plenty of money uses somebody else's money which may be in his possession and which may have been entrusted to him or which he may have had the opportunity of taking, merely intending to use those coins instead of some of his own which he has only to go to his room or to his bank to obtain. No jury would then say that there was any intent to defraud or any fraudulent taking. It is quite another matter if the person who takes the money is not in a position to replace it at the time but only has a hope or expectation that he will be able to do so in the future . . ."[12]

This passage was relied upon in *Cockburn*,[13] where the manager of a shop was charged with stealing from the till. He claimed that he had intended to replace the money before it was missed, and he had apparently had good reason for expecting to be able to do so. His conviction was nevertheless affirmed. The court pointed out that the passage quoted above did not appear in the official report of *Williams* and had probably been deleted by Lord Goddard himself when he came to revise the judgment. The court described it as "an extremely dangerous and most misleading statement" and hoped that it would in future be disregarded, adding that a taking 2–008

7 [1985] Crim. L.R. 598.

8 Forgery Act 1913, s.7. The offences were committed before the enactment of the Forgery and Counterfeiting Act 1981, which does not expressly require an intent to defraud: see below, Ch.11.

9 Larceny Act 1916, s.1(1).

10 [1953] 1 Q.B. 660.

11 [1953] 1 Q.B. 660 at 666.

12 [1953] 2 W.L.R. 937 at 942.

13 [1968] 1 W.L.R. 281.

might be technically larcenous even if it attracted no moral obloquy and did no harm at all.

2–009 This view was in turn criticised by a full Court of Appeal in *Feely,* and the need for dishonesty in the ordinary sense was reaffirmed.

> "It is possible to imagine a case of taking by an employee in breach of instructions to which no one would, or could reasonably, attach moral obloquy; for example, that of a manager of a shop, who having been told that under no circumstances was he to take money from the till for his own purposes, took 40p from it, having no small change himself, to pay for a taxi hired by his wife who had arrived at the shop saying that she only had a £5 note which the cabby could not change. To hold that such a man was a thief and to say that his intention to put the money back in the till when he acquired some change was at the most a matter of mitigation would tend to bring the law into contempt. In our judgment a taking to which no moral obloquy can reasonably attach is not within the concept of stealing either at common law or under the Theft Act 1968."[14]

2–010 *Feely* was concerned not with larceny but with its replacement, theft. The definition of theft requires not "fraud" but "dishonesty". The Criminal Law Revision Committee, which drafted the Bill that became TA 1968, does not seem to have intended that this change of terminology should mark any change of substance.

> "'Dishonestly' seems to us a better word than 'fraudulently'. The question 'Was this dishonest?' is easier for a jury to answer than the question 'Was this fraudulent?'. 'Dishonesty' is something which laymen may easily recognize when they see it, whereas 'fraud' may seem to involve technicalities which have to be explained by a lawyer."[15]

It is not clear whether this was intended to mean that the requirement of fraud did involve "technicalities" which the Committee thought unnecessary—i.e. that a requirement of dishonesty would be satisfied in circumstances where one of fraud might not—or only that the term "dishonesty" would be less likely to confuse a jury by hinting at the existence of requirements which did not in fact exist. What was certainly *not* intended was that dishonesty should be harder to prove than the old requirement of fraud had been.

2–011 In *Feely,* however, following the House of Lords' decision in *Brutus v Cozens*[16] that the meaning of an ordinary English word in a statutory provision is a question of fact, the court disapproved the practice of directing the jury that particular conduct is as a matter of law dishonest. The jury must be asked to decide this for themselves.

> "We do not agree that judges should define what 'dishonestly' means. This word is in common use whereas the word 'fraudulently' which was used in

[14] [1973] Q.B. 530 at 539.
[15] *Eighth Report: Theft and Related Offences*, Cmnd 2977, para.39.
[16] [1972] A.C. 854.

section 1(1) of the Larceny Act 1916 had acquired as a result of case law a special meaning. Jurors, when deciding whether an appropriation was dishonest, can be reasonably expected to, and should, apply the current standards of ordinary decent people. In their own lives they have to decide what is and what is not dishonest. We can see no reason why, when in a jury box, they should require the help of a judge to tell them what amounts to dishonesty."[17]

This principle is equally applicable not only to those offences that expressly require dishonesty[18] but also (and despite the court's emphasis on the difference between "dishonestly" and "fraudulently") to conspiracy to defraud,[19] fraudulent trading[20] and presumably all other offences requiring an element of "fraud".

The effect of *Feely* at first seemed clear enough: the jury were to be asked **2–012** whether they thought the defendant's conduct dishonest according to their own standards of honesty, which could be taken as representative of "the current standards of ordinary decent people". But it began to be suggested that this "objective" test did not adequately represent the ordinary meaning of dishonesty, and that a more "subjective" test was required—in other words, that the standards to be applied by the jury were not their own standards but those of the defendant himself. A number of cases proposed different ways of incorporating this approach.[21] It was even suggested that the test might vary from one offence to another.[22]

In *Ghosh*[23] the Court of Appeal made a fresh start, holding that the test **2–013** of dishonesty is the same whether the offence charged is theft, deception or conspiracy to defraud—or, presumably, any other offence requiring dishonesty or fraud. It was therefore necessary to consider afresh what that test should be. The test laid down by the court is an amalgam of the objective and the subjective. It is objective in the sense that it is ordinary people's standards that must be applied, not the defendant's. But it is also subjective, in the sense that his conduct must not only *be* dishonest according to those standards: he must *know* that it is.

"In determining whether the prosecution has proved that the defendant was acting dishonestly, a jury must first of all decide whether according to the ordinary standards of reasonable and honest people what was done was dishonest. If it was not dishonest by those standards, that is the end of the matter and the prosecution fails. If it was dishonest by those standards, then the jury must consider whether the defendant himself must have realised that what he was doing was by those standards dishonest. In most cases, where the actions are obviously dishonest by ordinary standards, there will be no doubt about it. It will be obvious that the defendant himself knew that he was acting dishonestly. It is dishonest for a defendant to act in a way which he knows

[17] [1973] Q.B. 530 at 537–538.
[18] *Melwani* [1989] Crim. L.R. 565; *Clarke* [1996] Crim. L.R. 824.
[19] *Landy* [1981] 1 W.L.R. 355.
[20] *Lockwood* [1986] Crim. L.R. 244.
[21] *Boggeln v Williams* [1978] 1 W.L.R. 873; *Landy* [1981] 1 W.L.R. 355.
[22] *McIvor* [1982] 1 W.L.R. 409.
[23] [1982] Q.B. 1053.

ordinary people consider to be dishonest, even if he asserts or genuinely believes that he is morally justified in acting as he did."[24]

2–014 The *Ghosh* direction is not appropriate where the only issue is one of fact and, if that issue is determined against the defendant, his conduct was "obviously dishonest by ordinary standards".[25] Even in the minority of cases where this is not so, the issue will usually be whether ordinary people *would* consider the defendant's conduct dishonest, not whether he *knew* they would. There is no need for a *Ghosh* direction unless the defence raises the latter issue.[26] Thus it may not be essential where the defendant admits deception but claims that it was justifiable in the circumstances,[27] or that he intended to repay the money he obtained.[28] Even where it ought to have been given, and was not, a conviction will not necessarily be unsafe.[29]

2–015 In a case of fraud by false representation[30] or false accounting,[31] the issue of dishonesty is distinct from that of whether the defendant knew that the representation or account was, or might be, untrue or misleading. A proper direction on the latter is therefore no substitute for the *Ghosh* direction on the former.[32] But this is subject to the exception for "obviously dishonest" conduct. If the only issue is whether an alleged misrepresentation was false,[33] or whether the defendant knew it might be false, and there is no suggestion that he might have acted honestly despite making a representation that he knew to be false or possibly false, the *Ghosh* direction is unnecessary.

2–016 In *Atkinson*[34] the direction was held to be unnecessary even though the jury had been directed that they could infer dishonesty if they were sure that the defendant had known that some of the representations she was making were *likely* to be false. This seems to go too far. The defendant in that case was a pharmacist who submitted large numbers of prescription forms for payment, some of which contained false information which resulted in her being overpaid. Assuming she did not know that any individual form was wrong, but only realised that errors were likely to have crept in, it was surely arguable that her conduct was not dishonest. This might depend, for example, on how many errors she thought there were

[24] [1982] Q.B. 1053 at 1064.

[25] *Price* (1990) 90 Cr.App.R. 409; *Squire* [1990] Crim. L.R. 341; *Timson* [1992] Crim. L.R. 58. See Andrew Halpin, "The Test for Dishonesty" [1996] Crim. L.R. 283.

[26] *Roberts* (1987) 84 Cr.App.R. 117; *Price* (1990) 90 Cr.App.R. 409; *Mendez* [1990] Crim. L.R. 397.

[27] *Ravenshad* [1990] Crim. L.R. 398; *Buzalek* [1991] Crim. L.R. 130.

[28] *Green* [1992] Crim. L.R. 292.

[29] cf. *O'Connell* (1992) 94 Cr.App.R. 39, where the proviso was applied.

[30] Below, Ch.4.

[31] Below, Ch.12.

[32] *Feeny* (1991) 94 Cr.App.R. 1; *Lamb* [1995] Crim. L.R. 77.

[33] The facts of *Ghosh* itself are only briefly reported, but it appears to have been such a case: the defendant denied deception.

[34] [2004] EWCA Crim 3031; [2004] Crim. L.R. 226; see below, para.12–023.

likely to be, and how difficult it would be to eliminate them all, and how much money she thought they might involve.[35]

It has been said that it is wrong to give the first limb of the direction without the second.[36] If the judge does attempt the complete direction it is advisable to use the exact words of *Ghosh*.[37] In *Green*[38] the judge got the two limbs the wrong way round, and the result was so confusing that the Crown did not seek to support the convictions. **2–017**

THE OBJECTIVE TEST

If the defendant's conduct is not what ordinary people would regard as dishonest then he does not act "dishonestly" for the purposes of the criminal law, even if he knows that his conduct is unlawful. In theory the implications of this rule might be alarming. For example, surveys sometimes suggest that most people do not think small-scale tax evasion is morally wrong.[39] Does it follow that small-scale tax evasion is not dishonest for the purposes of the criminal law? **2–018**

It might be argued that, although the court in *Ghosh* spoke mostly of "ordinary standards" and "ordinary people", it began the passage quoted above with a reference to "the ordinary standards of reasonable and honest people". Perhaps, then, the question is not to be determined on the basis of one person, one vote: only "reasonable and honest" people count. Arguably a person who considers tax evasion to be morally permissible is unreasonable, dishonest or both, even if most other people agree with him. But the issue is one of fact. It would be wrong to direct the jury that people who condone tax evasion are themselves dishonest and can therefore be disregarded. That would be to usurp what is, according to *Feely,*[40] the function of the jury. Even if it is right that the jury should take account only of the views of reasonable and honest people, it must be for them to decide whether a particular view should be disregarded as unreasonable or dishonest. By the law of averages, the jury's view is likely to coincide with the view most commonly held. If most people think that tax evasion is not dishonest, most juries will think so too. And in that case, according to *Ghosh,* it will not *be* dishonest.[41] **2–019**

[35] In the court's view, the argument that a *Ghosh* direction was required in these circumstances assumed that the judge had in effect said recklessness was enough, which in the court's view he had not (though he clearly had). It is not clear why the description attached to the state of mind described by the judge should affect the question whether that state of mind is necessarily dishonest.

[36] *Small* (1988) 86 Cr.App.R. 170; *Brennen* [1990] Crim. L.R. 118.

[37] *Ravenshad* [1990] Crim. L.R. 398; *Hyam* [1997] Crim. L.R. 439.

[38] [1992] Crim. L.R. 292.

[39] MORI poll for the *Sunday Times*, October, 1985, quoted by M. Levi, *Regulating Fraud* (1987) at 65.

[40] [1973] Q.B. 530; above, para.2–009.

[41] This may undermine the new statutory offence of fraudulently evading income tax (below, para.16–019): see David Ormerod, "Summary Evasion of Income Tax" [2002] Crim. L.R. 3 at 19–20.

2–020 In practice, however, acquittals on this basis seem to be rare. Even in theory it is immaterial that many people would have done what the defendant did: what matters is whether they would think it dishonest to do it.[42] In *Sinclair,*[43] where it was held to be fraudulent for a director to take dishonest risks with company assets, a passage in the judgment suggested that the crucial factor in determining whether it was dishonest to take a given risk was whether it was a "normal" business risk. On an application for leave to appeal, it was argued that this was a novel proposition, and the court disowned it.

> "The court welcomes the opportunity to make it clear that no such test was intended, and, indeed, the normality of the transaction is not the test and was never intended so to be. The distinction is between honesty and dishonesty . . ."[44]

Moreover the question for the jury, strictly speaking, is not whether *they* think the defendant's conduct dishonest but whether they think most *other* people would.[45] An acquittal by magistrates on this basis may be perverse.[46]

2–021 Even where the defendant admits that what he did was unlawful and that he knew it was, *Feely* and *Ghosh* allow him to seek an acquittal on the basis of *any* circumstances which the jury might be persuaded to see as justifying his conduct. A defendant charged with obtaining a job by misrepresentation, for example, is entitled to argue that his conduct was not dishonest because he was capable of doing the job well and intended to do so.[47] But most of the reported cases have involved essentially the same extenuating circumstance: the defendant's intention to replace the property that he appropriates or obtains by deception. Such a defendant cannot rely on the defence that he did not intend permanently to deprive the owner of the property unless his intention was to return the *same* property, rather than replace it with other property of the same value; but he may be able to argue that his conduct was not dishonest.

2–022 A typical example is the shop assistant who takes money from the till and is charged with theft. Sometimes he will be able to claim that he thought the owner would consent if he knew the circumstances, in which case dishonesty will be ruled out by TA 1968, s.2(1)(b).[48] But in other cases it will be clear to him, either from the circumstances in which the money is

[42] "In my judgment, to deliberately set out to cheat H.M. Commissioners of Customs and Excise of large sums for VAT must be regarded by all commercial men (even those who wish they could get away with such an act) as requiring real moral blame": *Re L. Todd (Swanscombe) Ltd* [1990] B.C.L.C. 454 at 458, *per* Harman J.

[43] [1968] 1 W.L.R. 1246; below, para.7–016.

[44] [1968] 1 W.L.R. 1246 at 1251–1252.

[45] The survey referred to at fn.39 above found that only 35% of adults thought it morally wrong to evade tax by accepting payment in cash, but that the proportion who thought this practice morally acceptable to *most* people was only 37%. This tends to suggest that many people think their own moral standards are unusually low!

[46] *DPP v Gohill* [2007] EWHC 239.

[47] *Clarke* [1996] Crim L.R. 824.

[48] Below, para.2–073.

entrusted to him or from his express instructions, that the owner would not consent. It does not follow that the appropriation is dishonest, because there may be no risk of the owner suffering any real loss. For example (to adapt the case put in the "missing passage" in *Williams*),[49] it might not be dishonest for an assistant to take money out of the till, even though he knew that his employer would not allow it, if he had the money with which to replace it in his jacket in the rest room and intended to substitute that money as soon as he had the chance; nor if he intended to go to the bank and cash a cheque during his lunch hour. He might, of course, be run over on the way to the bank, or the bank might collapse before he got there; but the risk is negligible. For all practical purposes it is certain that the owner will suffer no loss, and in the absence of any risk of loss it is arguable that the law of dishonesty is out of place.

On the other hand there are sound reasons for regarding even conduct **2–023** such as this as dishonest. The usual reason for imposing a strict rule against borrowing from the till is to ensure that employees caught embezzling the takings cannot excuse their conduct by pleading an intention to repay. If the excuse is accepted, the reason for the rule is undermined. Moreover, it may be revealing to compare this scenario with the obtaining of property by misrepresentation. If it is not dishonest to take someone else's money without his consent but with the intention of paying it back, it is hard to see why the same principle should not apply where the victim is deceived into handing the money over. Yet few would say that it is justifiable to obtain money by deception merely because the deceiver intends to repay it. An entrepreneur who secures financial backing by misrepresenting the nature of his business is likely to be regarded as dishonest even if he is sure that his backers are getting a good investment. It can hardly make any difference that the victim is exploited behind his back and not to his face.

In any event it will rarely be plausible for the defendant to claim that he **2–024** was *certain* he could repay the money. Usually he will know that there is some risk of his being unable to do so. Exposing another person to a risk of financial loss is an established form of criminal fraud.[50] A defendant who takes even a slight risk with another's property, knowing that the other would not allow that risk to be taken if he knew the true position, will almost inevitably be found to have acted dishonestly. His belief that the risk would not materialise ought not to be a defence. Admittedly the view was expressed in *Feely* that on the facts of that case the issue of dishonesty should have been left to the jury without explanation. But there is no reason why the jury's attention should not be drawn to considerations such as those suggested above, as long as it is made clear that the ultimate decision is theirs.

[49] [1953] 2 W.L.R. 937 at 942; above, para.2–007.
[50] Below, paras 7–008, 7–016.

DISHONESTY NOT EXCLUDED

2–025 Two situations are expressly mentioned in TA 1968 only to make it clear that in these cases, on a charge of theft, the requirement of dishonesty *may* be satisfied. Whether it *is* satisfied therefore depends on the *Ghosh* test. These provisions do not apply to other offences of dishonesty, though it may be possible to reason by analogy from them.

No view to gain

2–026 TA 1968, s.1(2) provides:

> "It is immaterial whether the appropriation is made with a view to gain, or is made for the thief's own benefit."

Thus the jury is not precluded from finding the defendant's conduct dishonest merely because he intended someone else to benefit rather than himself, or because he intended that no-one should benefit but only that someone should suffer loss. The definitions of some offences (though not of theft) expressly provide that the defendant must intend *either* to make a gain *or* to cause loss, and that an intent to make a gain for another is sufficient.[51]

Willingness to pay

2–027 TA 1968, s.2(2) provides:

> "A person's appropriation of property belonging to another may be dishonest notwithstanding that he is willing to pay for the property."

Thus it is not *in itself* a defence to a charge of theft that the defendant intends the owner of the property to receive its value in full. Similarly it may be dishonest to draw unauthorised cheques on another person's account even if they are used for the payment of debts owed by that person, so that he receives a benefit (namely the payment of his debts) corresponding to his loss.[52] In *Wheatley v Commissioner of Police of the British Virgin Islands*[53] the defendant, a government official, awarded his business associates a government contract to build a wall, and was convicted of stealing the contract price. The Privy Council rejected the argument that this was not dishonest because the wall was built and the price was not excessive. The British Virgin Islands provision corresponding to TA 1968, s.2(2) showed that the prospect of loss is not determinative of dishonesty. It seems to have been assumed that corruption is one form of dishonesty.

[51] See below, Ch.3.
[52] *Sobel* [1986] Crim. L.R. 261.
[53] [2006] UKPC 24; [2006] 2 Cr.App.R. 21 (p.328).

THE SUBJECTIVE TEST

The issue of dishonesty typically arises where the defendant has appropriated property, or obtained it by misrepresentation, and claims that he intended to replace it or reimburse the owner for it. The issues in such a case are: (1) Did he have the intention that he claims to have had? and (2) If so, would most people think that he therefore did not act dishonestly? There is no suggestion that his own standards of honesty are different from other people's. The two-tiered concept of dishonesty set out in *Ghosh* is an unnecessary complication. **2–028**

The importance of *Ghosh* lies rather in its application to the less typical case where the defendant claims that what he did was not dishonest *even if most people would think it was,* because he does not subscribe to the general consensus. The jury may of course disbelieve him, and, if there is no apparent reason for his allegedly unconventional point of view, probably will. But if there may be a genuine difference of opinion, the second limb of the *Ghosh* test comes into play: his conduct is dishonest not only if he knows it is, but also if most other people would think so *and* (while he may disagree with them) he knows that they would think so.[54] He is not entitled to an acquittal merely because he personally thinks he has done nothing wrong. It would be absurd if the law were otherwise. The public should not be at risk from the huckster who constructs his own private standard of honesty and justifies himself by it. People doing business expect those with whom they deal to comply with standards that are generally accepted, and it is the function of the law to curb those who seek to profit by flouting those standards. The defendant's own evaluation of his conduct therefore cannot be a defence. **2–029**

On the other hand, a person is not dishonest under the *Ghosh* test if he is so cocooned from the views of ordinary people that he not only disagrees with them but does not even *realise* that he disagrees. To describe such a person as dishonest would not accord with the ordinary meaning of that word. But the scope of this defence is limited. The only defendant likely to invoke it is the professional or business person who asserts that his activities are acceptable in the circles in which he moves. If outsiders disagree, that is because they are outsiders and therefore ill-informed. The point is not that professionals and business people have lower ethical standards than people in other walks of life, but that the way in which things are normally done in a particular profession or business is sometimes regarded by those in that field as, by definition, the right way to do them. In **2–030**

[54] Dicta of Lords Hoffmann and Hutton in *Twinsectra Ltd v Yardley* [2002] UKHL 12; [2002] 2 A.C. 164 at [20] and [36] seemed to imply that there is a similar requirement in the civil law of dishonest assistance in breach of trust. But in *Barlow Clowes International Ltd v Eurotrust International Ltd* [2005] UKPC 37; [2006] 1 W.L.R. 1476 these dicta were explained as meaning only that the defendant's knowledge of the *transaction* must be such as to make his participation contrary to ordinary standards of honest behaviour: he need not know what those standards are.

the context of fraudulent trading Maugham J. laid down a requirement of "actual dishonesty involving, according to current notions of fair trading *among commercial men,* real moral blame".[55] But since *Ghosh* this appears too lenient. There is no special standard of dishonesty for commercial cases.[56] It is not a defence that business people would think what was done was acceptable, only that ordinary people would (or the defendant thought they would). Tampering with a car's odometer would still be dishonest even if all second-hand car dealers thought it was not.[57]

2–031 It is of course legitimate to adduce evidence of the commercial background, and of what is and is not common practice in the trade or market in question, so that the jury can reach a more informed judgment. It is also important to distinguish the issue of what was actually done from that of whether it was dishonest to do it. The question whether certain accounts are misleading, for example, is a question of fact, and evidence of normal accounting practice will be highly relevant in determining what impression the accounts are likely to give. But, once the jury find that the accounts are in fact misleading, it is for them, not accountants, to decide whether it is dishonest to draw up accounts in that way. Professional opinion may be relevant in so far as the jury choose to attach importance to it, or if it lends credibility to the defendant's assertion that he did not realise non-professionals might disapprove. The more reputable the body of opinion, the more likely it is to turn the scales. But it is not in itself decisive.

DISHONESTY AND LEGAL RIGHTS

THINGS THE DEFENDANT HAS A RIGHT TO DO

2–032 The *Ghosh* test involves asking whether, applying the accepted standards of society, there is any *moral* justification for the defendant's conduct. Paradoxically, the courts have paid far less attention to the question of how, and indeed whether, the position is affected by the fact that the defendant's conduct is justifiable in law.

2–033 Where the defendant has dealt with another's property in a way which is objectively lawful, the legal justification for his conduct is usually that he acted with the other's consent. The question whether such consent can ever be a defence to a charge of theft, and if so in what circumstances, has been examined in a number of cases, including four appeals to the House of Lords. For the most part, the discussion in these cases has centred on the argument that consent can sometimes negative the element of appropriation.[58] But it is also arguable that consent, if not vitiated by deception or

[55] *Re Patrick & Lyon Ltd* [1933] Ch. 786 at 790 (italics supplied).

[56] *Lockwood* [1986] Crim. L.R. 244.

[57] *A fortiori* it is no defence that the conduct in question is common practice in an organisation if that practice was instituted by the very people whose honesty is in question. "Actions which are basically dishonest are not rendered honest by repetition": *Adams (Grant)* [1995] 1 W.L.R. 52 at 63.

[58] See below, paras 9–120 *et seq*.

otherwise, can negative the element of dishonesty. In most of the cases this is not recognised to be a separate issue, usually because any consent that may have been given was clearly vitiated by deception. Even where the dishonesty issue is not addressed directly, however, the law is sometimes stated in a way which has implications for that issue.

In *McHugh (Eileen)*[59] a company director appealed against convictions of stealing funds from her company by drawing cheques on its account. It was said that a number of propositions could be derived from the authorities,[60] including the following: **2–034**

> "The question whether the company or its creditors or its liquidator has a civil remedy against the actor, or against those who derived benefit from the transaction is immaterial."[61]

In other words a director can commit theft by disposing of the company's assets without even incurring liability for breach of fiduciary duty, provided only that the jury think it was a dishonest thing to do. Several of the propositions advanced in *McHugh* were rejected by the House of Lords in *Gomez,*[62] but not this one.

In *Mazo*[63] the defendant accepted substantial amounts of money from her 89-year-old employer, ostensibly by way of gift. It was conceded by the Crown, and the court agreed, that the convictions could only be upheld on the basis that the employer had insufficient mental capacity to make valid gifts. The court did not expressly state whether this was because the acceptance of a valid gift could not be an appropriation or because it could not be dishonest. But it relied on the dictum of Viscount Dilhorne in *Lawrence v Metropolitan Police Commissioner* that **2–035**

> "a person is not to be regarded as acting dishonestly if he appropriates another's property believing that, with full knowledge of the circumstances, that other person has in fact agreed to the appropriation."[64]

Viscount Dilhorne was plainly saying that, although there is still an appropriation in these circumstances, the appropriation is not dishonest. So

[59] (1989) 88 Cr.App.R. 385.

[60] In particular, *Lawrence v Metropolitan Police Commissioner* [1972] A.C. 626; *Morris* [1984] A.C. 320 and *Tarling (No.1) v Government of the Republic of Singapore* (1978) 70 Cr.App.R. 77. It is not clear which of these cases was regarded as authority for the proposition quoted, or why. Earlier authorities which did support the proposition (though none of them settled the point conclusively) include *Bonner* [1970] 1 W.L.R. 838; *Gilks* [1972] 1 W.L.R. 1341 and *Turner (No.2)* [1971] 1 W.L.R. 901. See Glanville Williams, "Theft, Consent and Illegality" [1977] Crim. L.R. 127, 205, 327; J.C. Smith, "Civil Law Concepts in the Criminal Law" [1972] B.C.L.J. 197. In *Lally* [1989] Crim. L.R. 648 it was unsuccessfully argued that the defendant could not properly be convicted of obtaining social security benefits by deception unless and until there had been an adjudication that he was not entitled to them—though the argument appears to have been, not that he *was* entitled to them, but that in the absence of an adjudication the prosecution could not prove that he was not.

[61] (1989) 88 Cr.App.R. 385 at 393.

[62] [1993] A.C. 442.

[63] [1997] 2 Cr.App.R. 518.

[64] [1972] A.C. 626 at 632.

the court in *Mazo* presumably thought, like Viscount Dilhorne, that the acceptance of a valid gift cannot be dishonest. In *Hopkins*[65] the suggestion that the acceptance of a valid gift cannot be an appropriation was doubted, but it was apparently not argued that the validity of the gift might negative the element of dishonesty.

2–036 In *Hinks*[66] the point might have been resolved by the House of Lords, but the opportunity was missed. Karen Hinks befriended a man of limited intelligence and induced him to give her large sums of money. She was charged with theft. The prosecution alleged that the man lacked the mental capacity to make the gifts, but the evidence of this was weak. The judge rejected a submission of no case, and directed the jury that the only question was whether the defendant had acted dishonestly in accepting the money. The man's alleged incapacity was relevant only as going to that question. The judge made no attempt to explain the criteria that, in law, would determine whether the gifts were valid.[67]

2–037 In the Court of Appeal it was argued that the jury should have been directed to acquit unless they were satisfied that the gifts were legally invalid, because the acceptance of a valid gift is neither an appropriation nor dishonest. Both limbs of the argument were rejected, but the judgment fails to draw a clear distinction between them; and, in relation to the dishonesty point, the reasons given are obscure. Counsel's submission on the dishonesty point was said to encounter "very serious difficulties in the form of *Lawrence*".[68] But it is not clear what the court thought those difficulties were. In *Lawrence* the victim's apparent consent was clearly procured by deception, and the transfer of title to the money was clearly voidable for fraud. The only issue was whether the victim's apparent consent prevented the defendant's conduct from being an appropriation. It was not suggested, and was plainly not arguable, that even if Lawrence appropriated the money he did not do so dishonestly. The submission in *Hinks* that the acceptance of a *valid* gift cannot be dishonest was in no way inconsistent with *Lawrence*.

2–038 The judgment in *Hinks* continues: "That is emphasised when one turns to consider the [appellant's] submission . . . in relation to appropriation." The court then considered the appropriation issue, but did not explain how the authorities on that issue undermined the submission on the dishonesty point. When the court returned to the dishonesty issue, its conclusion was:

> "[A]s it seems to us, the two concessions made by prosecuting counsel during the hearing of the appeal in *Mazo*, namely that there cannot be theft if there was a valid gift, and that a direction to the jury is necessary as to the validity of gifts were wrongly made and led that Court into error. At page 521c,[69] where the Court cites the passage from Lord Dilhorne's speech in *Lawrence*, relating

[65] [1997] 2 Cr.App.R. 524.
[66] [2001] 2 A.C. 241.
[67] See *Re Beaney* [1978] 1 W.L.R. 770.
[68] [2000] 1 Cr.App.R. 1 at 7.
[69] i.e. [1997] 2 Cr.App.R. 518 at 521c.

to dishonesty, it does so as impliedly excluding valid gifts from the ambit of theft. For our part, we are unable to read that passage in Lord Dilhorne's speech as bearing that implication. The authorities, as it seems to us, make clear the importance of maintaining a distinction in relation to theft between the two quite separate ingredients of appropriation and dishonesty. Belief or lack of belief that the owner consented to the appropriation is relevant to dishonesty. But appropriation may occur even though the owner has consented to the property being taken."[70]

This passage is hard to understand. Since appropriation and dishonesty are "quite separate ingredients" of the offence, the fact that consent does not negative appropriation does not mean that it cannot negative dishonesty either. And, even if *Lawrence* did not support the proposition accepted in *Mazo* (which it does), it would not follow that that proposition is wrong. The judgment in *Hinks* does not explain why it is wrong.

The Court of Appeal's decision on the appropriation issue was affirmed by a majority in the House of Lords. The question certified for consideration by the House related only to that issue. Lord Steyn, with whom Lords Slynn and Jauncey agreed, thought it inappropriate to consider whether the trial judge had correctly dealt with the issue of dishonesty.[71] Lord Slynn added that this should not be read as an approval of the judge's directions on that issue.[72] **2–039**

On the other hand, the appeal was dismissed. Lord Steyn said: **2–040**

"My Lords, for my part the position would have been different if I had any lurking doubt about the guilt of the appellant on the charges for which she was convicted. In the light of a fair and balanced summing up and a very strong prosecution case, the jury accepted the prosecution case and rejected the appellant's account as untruthful. They found that she had acted dishonestly by systematically raiding the savings in a building society account of a vulnerable person who trusted her. Even if one assumes that the judge ought to have directed more fully on dishonesty I am satisfied that the convictions are entirely safe."[73]

His Lordship may have meant that, since a properly directed jury would inevitably have found the gifts to be invalid, it was immaterial whether the acceptance of a valid gift could properly be found dishonest. However, as he had just pointed out,[74] the House had not seen transcripts of evidence. The majority cannot have been satisfied that the gifts were invalid. Their decision that the convictions were safe must therefore imply that it was immaterial to *any* of the issues before the jury, including that of dishonesty, whether the gifts were valid. This is arguably part of the *ratio decidendi*. But it is difficult to see how a decision can be a binding precedent on a point which the court has expressly declined to consider.

[70] [2000] 1 Cr.App.R. 1 at 9.
[71] [2001] 2 A.C. 241 at 253.
[72] [2001] 2 A.C. 241 at 243.
[73] [2001] 2 A.C. 241 at 253–254.
[74] [2001] 2 A.C. 241 at 253.

2–041 It is therefore submitted that the point is still open, in the House of Lords at least.[75] The proposition that the acceptance of a valid gift may be dishonest is supported by the decision of the Court of Appeal in *Hinks*. Against this judgment must be set Viscount Dilhorne's clear dictum in *Lawrence*, the view taken in *Mazo,* the incoherence of the Court of Appeal's reasoning in *Hinks*, and the speeches of the minority in the House of Lords. Lords Hutton and Hobhouse did not accept that the artificially restricted scope of the certified question made it inappropriate to consider the dishonesty issue. They both considered it at some length, and both would have decided it in the appellant's favour. Lord Hutton agreed with the majority that the acceptance of a valid gift could be an appropriation, but thought it could not be dishonest. Lord Hobhouse thought that the two issues could not be considered in isolation from one another: the question was whether the acceptance of a valid and indefeasible gift could be a dishonest appropriation. In his view it could not.

OBJECTIONS TO *HINKS*

2–042 Assuming that the point is still open, it is submitted with respect that Lords Hutton and Hobhouse were right, and the Court of Appeal wrong. The main reasons for this view may be summarised as follows.

2–043 First and most fundamentally, it would be absurd that there should be such a direct conflict between the civil and the criminal law as the Court of Appeal was apparently willing to contemplate. It cannot be a crime to take the benefit of a gift, contract, will or other transaction which is unimpeachable in civil law. This might be possible if the civil and criminal law were entirely separate systems; but they are not. TA 1968 takes the civil law of property, gift, contract and so on as its starting point, and builds the rules of criminal law upon it. It does not attempt to set up a self-contained set of rules. Such an attempt would make no sense, because it would make the law internally inconsistent.

2–044 This is not an abstract, theoretical principle. It is fundamental to the coherence of the law. The price for infringing it is the creation of insoluble dilemmas for the courts.[76] For example, the civil case of *Smith v Hughes*[77] decided that, in the absence of misrepresentation or breach of warranty, a seller of goods is entitled to the contract price even if he knew, when he

[75] In *Wheatley v Commissioner of Police of the British Virgin Islands* [2006] UKPC 24; [2006] 1 W.L.R. 1683 Lord Hutton's reasoning in *Hinks* was cited in support of the contention, rejected by the Privy Council, that the defendant's conduct was not dishonest. But his conduct was not lawful on any view: he had, for reward, abused his position as a government official to award government contracts to his associates. The Board pointed out at [11]: "In this instance, there is no dissonance between the criminal and the civil law, since the contracts made by the . . . appellant, contrary to his authority . . ., were plainly voidable at the suit of the Government". This perhaps implies that the Board might have been more sympathetic to the argument if his conduct had been otherwise lawful.

[76] See J. Beatson and A.P. Simester, "Stealing One's Own Property" (1999) 115 L.Q.R. 372.

[77] [1871] L.R. 6 Q.B. 597.

made the contract, that the goods would not meet the buyer's needs. Some jurors might think it dishonest for the seller to demand the price in these circumstances. On the view taken by the Court of Appeal in *Hinks*, it would follow that the seller commits theft if he demands the price and the buyer pays it. What if the buyer declines to pay, and the seller sues for the price? The civil court will have to choose between depriving the seller of his rights in civil law and assisting him in the commission of a crime.

Lord Steyn, while declining to consider the dishonesty issue, was **2–045**
undaunted by the prospect of the law becoming self-contradictory.

> "The purposes of the civil law and the criminal law are somewhat different. In theory the two systems should be in perfect harmony. In a practical world there will sometimes be some disharmony between the two systems. In any event, it would be wrong to assume on a priori grounds that the criminal law rather than the civil law is defective. Given the jury's conclusions, one is entitled to observe that the appellant's conduct should constitute theft, the only available charge. The tension between the civil and the criminal law is therefore not in my view a factor which justifies a departure from the law as stated in *Lawrence* and *Gomez*."[78]

But it is improbable that Parliament intended to create a law of theft which would directly contradict the civil law. Moreover, there is plenty of evidence in TA 1968 itself that that was not Parliament's intention.

Perhaps the clearest pointer is s.2(1), which provides that a person's **2–046**
appropriation of property is not dishonest if he believes that he has in law the right to deprive of the property the person to whom it belongs, or that he would have that person's consent if that person knew of the appropriation and its circumstances.[79] This provision is primarily aimed at the case where the defendant's belief is mistaken; but it would seem to apply equally where the belief is correct. It would be absurd if the law were more lenient in the former case than the latter. Hinks could not properly have been

[78] [2001] 2 A.C. 241 at 252–253. Part of this passage was cited in the Law Commission's report on fraud, in support of the Commission's conclusion that the objective lawfulness of a person's conduct should not in itself be a defence to a charge of the new fraud offence (Law Com. No.276, *Fraud*, Cm.5560, paras 7.59 *et seq.*) The report goes on: "The criminal law should be free standing, particularly where the civil law is complex and, perhaps, to some extent unpredictable. Thus, we do not think that the absence of a civil wrong should be a defence in itself . . . . If this results, in a very small number of cases, in a want of congruence between criminal and civil sanctions then that would be unfortunate but a price worth paying to avoid the criminal courts becoming embroiled in arguments over civil liability." Since the Commission has a statutory duty to further the "systematic development and reform" of English law, "including in particular . . . the elimination of anomalies" (Law Commissions Act 1965, s.3(1)), this readiness to accept internal contradictions in the law is surprising. Sir John Smith, who acted as the Commission's consultant, commented: "I thought the passage of Lord Steyn's speech in *Hinks* quoted . . . was breathtaking. I am surprised to find it supported and extended. . . . As the dissenting judges . . . said, the criminal courts must take the civil law as they find it. So surely must the Commission when it is dealing with a criminal reference. The Commission has not, so far as I am aware, been invited to recommend the abolition or modification of the principle of caveat emptor as exemplified in *Smith v Hughes*." Letter to the Law Commission, June 27, 2001.

[79] See below, paras 2–065 *et seq.*

convicted if she had mistakenly believed that her benefactor consented to her taking the money and that she therefore had a legal right to take the money. Nor, *a fortiori*, could she have been convicted if she had been correct in so believing.[80] How then can it make a difference that, while the gifts were valid and Hinks was legally entitled to accept the money, she did not know this? Such a distinction might perhaps make sense if dishonesty were an aspect of mens rea alone, to be assessed entirely on the basis of what the defendant knows or believes the position to be; but it is not. As *Ghosh* makes clear, dishonesty is not just a state of mind. The conduct in question must *in fact* be dishonest according to the moral standards of ordinary people. If it is morally justifiable according to those standards, dishonesty is automatically negatived. It is irrelevant that the defendant may have *thought* that others would regard his conduct as dishonest. It must equally be irrelevant whether he realises that his conduct is *legally* justifiable, if in fact it is. The view taken by the Court of Appeal in *Hinks* can be reconciled with s.2(1) only on the basis that the law pays greater attention to moral standards than to legal rules. That cannot be right.

2–047 Further evidence against the Court of Appeal's interpretation may be found in the rule that property cannot be stolen unless it "belongs to another". That expression is given an artificially wide meaning by TA 1968, s.5; but even s.5 does not go so far as to deem property to belong to a person who has ceased to have any right to it or any right of action in respect of its loss. It follows that, if the defendant acquires indefeasible title to the property *before* appropriating it, his appropriation of it cannot be theft. Assuming that the gift was valid, Hinks could not have been guilty if the donor had put the money in her letter-box (thus completing the gift) and she had subsequently picked it up and kept it. As Lord Hobhouse said in his dissenting speech:

> "If . . . the transferee has already had validly transferred to him the legal title to and possession of the chattel without any obligation to make restoration, a later retention of or dealing with the chattel by the transferee, whether or not 'dishonest' and whether or not it would otherwise amount to an appropriation, cannot amount to theft. However much the jury may consider that his conduct in not returning the chattel falls below the standards of ordinary and decent people, he has not committed the crime of theft. The property did not belong to another."[81]

On the Court of Appeal's view, the law draws a distinction between that situation and the case where title passes only at the moment of appropriation. Such a distinction would be irrational. The gravamen of the defendant's conduct is the same in either case, namely taking advantage of the

[80] "If belief in such a right or such consent can prevent the defendant's conduct from amounting to theft (whatever the jury may think of it), how can it be said that his knowledge that he has such a right or the actual consent of the person to whom the property belongs is irrelevant—or the fact that the transferor has actually and validly consented to the defendant having the relevant property? Yet it is precisely these things which the judgment of the Court of Appeal would wholly exclude." [2001] 2 A.C. 241 at 266, *per* Lord Hobhouse.

[81] [2001] 2 A.C. 241 at 265.

fact that the donor has acted with limited understanding of the situation. Whether the defendant does this at the time of the donor's act or later is surely beside the point.

Yet another clue is to be found in the provisions that define "stolen goods". TA 1968, s.24(3) provides that "no goods shall be regarded as having continued to be stolen goods after . . . the person from whom they were stolen . . . [has] ceased . . . to have any right to restitution in respect of the theft". If Hinks was legally entitled to keep the money, but nevertheless stole it, it follows that she stole goods which never became "stolen goods" at all. But s.24(3) clearly assumes that goods which are stolen become stolen goods immediately after the theft: the only question is when they *cease* to be stolen goods. This is apparent from the words "having continued to be". The idea that goods might be stolen without *ever* becoming "stolen goods" clearly did not occur to those who drafted the Act. That would be entirely understandable, if they never intended that the Act should criminalise the lawful obtaining of property. **2–048**

For these reasons it is submitted with respect that the view assumed to be correct in *Mazo*, and the speeches of Lords Hutton and Hobhouse in *Hinks*, are to be preferred to the Court of Appeal's decision in *Hinks*. The law cannot coherently regard a person as acting dishonestly if he is doing what the law gives him a right to do. **2–049**

WHAT IS A RIGHT?

It may be objected that this conclusion is inconsistent with the House of Lords' decision in *Gomez*[82] that it can be dishonest to appropriate property with the owner's consent, or otherwise in such circumstances that the appropriation is not wrongful as a matter of civil law. In such circumstances, the defendant in one sense has a "right" to do what he does, because he commits no wrong by doing it. Yet it is now settled, by *Gomez*, that this does not prevent his act from being an offence of dishonesty. **2–050**

However, the concept of a legal "right" to do something is an ambiguous one. The proposition argued above, that it cannot be dishonest to do what one has a legal right to do, can be reconciled with *Gomez* if the word "right" is given a restricted meaning. Sir John Smith apparently supported this approach. **2–051**

> "There are many cases where the civil law authorises or even requires D to appropriate P's property with the intention of permanently depriving P of it. If, in such a case, D is aware of the law, it is submitted that he cannot be considered to be acting dishonestly and he commits no offence, however evil his motive might be. Suppose, however, that D is unaware of the civil law which authorises or requires him to act as he does and he proceeds in a furtive manner evincing a dishonest intention. He now falls literally within the terms of the Act unless 'dishonestly' is interpreted to include the objective element at

[82] [1993] A.C. 442.

> one time[83] discerned by Arlidge and Parry. The court would, it is submitted, have to find some means of avoiding the conviction of D for doing no more than the civil law expressly authorised or required him to do.[84]
>
> An express authority or right in the strict sense must, however, be distinguished from a mere liberty or power. D has a liberty under the civil law to do an act if the performance of that act does not amount to a civil wrong. There is no reason why the criminal law should not curtail such liberties in appropriate cases . . ."[85]

So Smith's argument is that the defendant cannot be guilty of an offence of dishonesty if the civil law gives him "an express authority or right in the strict sense" to do what he does, but may be guilty if the law gives him only a "liberty or power" to do it.

2–052 It is clear that the exercise of a *power* may be dishonest. A power is simply the ability to bring about a change in existing legal relations. The exercise of a power may or may not be a legal wrong, such as a breach of contract or of fiduciary duty. In other words, a person may have a power to do something, but no right to exercise that power. Smith gives the examples of a mercantile agent in possession of goods with the owner's consent, and of an unpaid seller of goods who has exercised his right of lien or retention or stoppage *in transitu.* Such persons have a power to pass title, in the sense that a sale by them (even if dishonest) is legally effective:[86] the buyer acquires title. There is no reason why a person who unlawfully exercises such a power should not be guilty of an offence. Indeed, this possibility is expressly recognised by TA 1968, s.4(2)(a), which provides that land can be stolen by a person who is authorised to sell or dispose of it and deals with it in breach of the confidence reposed in him.[87]

2–053 The more difficult distinction is that between "an express authority or right in the strict sense" and a "mere liberty". A person has a liberty to act in a particular way if he commits no legal wrong by doing so. Smith gives the example of a co-owner who appropriates the joint property without the other co-owner's consent.[88] Such an appropriation is not unlawful per se; yet it can be theft,[89] because (Smith suggests) the co-owner has only a liberty and not a "right in the strict sense". As examples of the latter, Smith cites the right of a bailee to sell uncollected goods,[90] and the right of an unpaid seller of goods to re-sell them if they are perishable or if the buyer fails to pay or tender the price within a reasonable time of the seller's giving notice of his intention to re-sell.[91] But what is it about these rights that makes them rights "in the strict sense", while the right of a co-owner

[83] And still.
[84] In the previous edition, Smith had added: "and this seems the neatest solution".
[85] J.C. Smith, *The Law of Theft* (8th edn, 1997), paras 2–25 and 2–26 (footnotes omitted).
[86] Factors Act 1889, s.2(1); Sale of Goods Act 1979, s.48(2).
[87] Below, para.9–006.
[88] *The Law of Theft* (8th edn, 1997) para.2–104.
[89] *Bonner* [1970] 2 All E.R. 97. The appropriation in that case was a breach of contract, but this was not regarded as crucial—rightly, according to Smith.
[90] Torts (Interference with Goods) Act 1977, Sch.1.
[91] Sale of Goods Act 1979, s.48(3).

to deal with the joint property is a right only in some looser sense? Three possibilities suggest themselves.

One explanation is that these examples of rights "in the strict sense" are *statutory* rights. But it would make little sense to distinguish between those rights that are conferred by statute and those conferred in other ways. If two people enter into a contract which expressly confers on one of them the right to deal with the property of the other, this must surely qualify as a right in the strict sense. **2–054**

An alternative distinction is between rights *expressly* conferred (whether by statute, contract, deed or otherwise) and those conferred only by implication. Indeed, Smith appears to have regarded "express authority" as synonymous with "right in the strict sense". But this too would be an odd place to draw the line. A right implicitly conferred normally has the same effect as one expressly conferred. The only difference lies in the drafting of the statute or instrument that creates it. **2–055**

A third possibility is that a right can be a right in the strict sense even if it is non-statutory, or implied, or both; and that the distinction lies not in the kind of source from which the right derives, but in whether it derives from any particular source at all. If a person relies upon a statutory right, express or implied, he can point to the statute as the source of his entitlement. If he relies upon a contractual right, express or implied, he can point to the contract. But if he cannot point to any particular source at all, and his claim to be entitled to do what he does is based only on the absence of anything that prohibits him from doing it, he does not have a "right in the strict sense" but only a liberty. A mere liberty is a right that comes from nowhere in particular. It exists only because there is nothing to take it away. **2–056**

This last explanation seems the least unattractive of the three, and it may be the only way to avoid the anomalies inherent in the Court of Appeal's decision in *Hinks* without falling foul of *Gomez*. But it is a distinction of language, not of legal substance. According to conventional legal analysis a person has a right to do something (sometimes called a "privilege" or "liberty") if he is not under a legal duty to refrain from doing it—in other words, if his doing it would not be a legal wrong.[92] There is no difference in substance between a liberty that is conferred expressly or by implication, by common law or statute or agreement, and one that exists only because it has never been taken away. In either case its effect is the same: its holder can act in the manner in question without committing a wrong. Whether it amounts to a "right" to do the thing in question, for the purposes of a particular rule about such rights, does not depend on the legal character of the entitlement. It depends on the kinds of liberty to which the rule applies. **2–057**

We have argued for a rule that it cannot be "dishonest", within the meaning of TA 1968, to do what one has a legal right to do. That rule is not to be found in the express words of the Act. But one of the main arguments for the proposed rule is that it is implicit in s.2(1)(a) of the Act, which, on a **2–058**

[92] W.N. Hohfeld, *Fundamental Legal Conceptions as Applied in Judicial Reasoning* (1919).

theft charge, precludes a finding of dishonesty where the defendant believed he had a legal right to do as he did. The argument is that, where the defendant's *belief* that he has a particular kind of entitlement would lead to his acquittal under s.2(1)(a), he must also be acquitted if he *does in fact* have that kind of entitlement. So, for the purposes of our proposed rule, a legal "right" to do something must include *at least* those kinds of entitlement that qualify as "rights" within the meaning of s.2(1)(a). And it is submitted with respect that Sir John Smith's distinction between liberties and rights, if understood in the third sense suggested above, is a workable explanation of what counts as a "right" within the meaning of s.2(1)(a). The law would therefore be coherent if the same distinction applied for the purposes of our proposed rule about *actual* rights.

2–059 Our proposed rule, therefore, is as follows. It cannot be "dishonest" for a person to do what he has a legal right to do. For the purposes of this rule a legal right to do something is a positive entitlement which derives, expressly or by implication, from a particular and identifiable source, and not from the mere absence of any prohibition or sanction. The source of the right may be a legislative provision, a contract or any other source of private rights and obligations. Arguably the law should go further, and say that it cannot be dishonest to do what one has a mere liberty to do; but since *Gomez* it seems unlikely that the courts would accept such a rule.

DISHONESTY IN FRAUD

2–060 The discussion above relates primarily to theft, with which most of the relevant case law is concerned. But dishonesty is now an element of the new fraud offence. Is it possible to commit *fraud* by doing something which one has a legal right to do? It seems that the issue can only arise in the case of fraud by abuse of position, as defined by s.4 of the Fraud Act 2006. This is because the other two forms of the offence are defined in such a way that, even if they did not require dishonesty, they would necessarily involve an act or omission which is unlawful in civil law. Fraud by false representation is the tort of deceit, and fraud by failing to disclose information expressly requires a breach of a legal duty of disclosure.[93] Fraud by abuse of position is arguably a different matter. Its definition does not on the face of it relate to any civil law concepts at all, and the Government resisted Parliamentary attempts to confine it to breaches of fiduciary duty. But the Government's position (and, on this point, the Law Commission's) seems to have been based on a curiously limited notion of the scope of fiduciary law. Read

[93] It seems to be possible to commit either of these forms of the offence without committing a legal *wrong*. Fraud by false representation, unlike the tort of deceit, does not require that the representee should believe the representation or act on it; and fraud by failing to disclose information apparently does not require a legal wrong or even an intention to commit one (see below, paras 5–004 *et seq*.). But a person can never have a *right* to make a false representation with the intention of thereby making a gain or causing a loss, or to withhold information which he has a "legal duty" (albeit in a loose sense) to disclose.

literally, s.4 could apply to all manner of lawful conduct; but it does not appear to be *aimed* at any conduct that would not be a breach of fiduciary duty.[94]

It is arguably implicit in the drafting of s.4 of the Fraud Act that the section is not confined to conduct which is unlawful in civil law. This is because s.3 of the Act expressly requires a breach of a legal duty of disclosure. The absence of a corresponding requirement in s.4 therefore suggests that in *that* section the civil law is *not* intended to be material. On the other hand, dishonesty in the Fraud Act is plainly intended to mean the same as dishonesty in TA 1968. If, as we have argued, dishonesty in theft incorporates an element of unlawfulness, the fact that Parliament adopted the same concept in the Fraud Act suggests that unlawful conduct is similarly intended to be an element of the fraud offence. It will often be possible to charge the same conduct either as theft or as fraud by abuse of position. It cannot have been Parliament's intention that the position in civil law should be irrelevant to a fraud charge where it would be a defence to a theft charge. **2–061**

There is an extraordinary passage in the Law Commission's report in which the Commission appears to envisage that wholly lawful conduct might amount to fraud. It appears in the discussion of whether claim of right[95] should be a defence—that is, whether it should be possible for a person to be convicted of the offence even though he *thought* he had a legal right to act as he did.[96] If this were a defence, the Commission argued, **2–062**

> "a 'Robin Hood' defendant could seek to exploit legal 'loopholes' in order to redistribute property in a way, not amounting to theft, which she believes to be morally right, but which she knows most reasonable, honest people would consider dishonest. She may then argue that she genuinely believed that she had a legal right to act as she did, despite knowing that most reasonable, honest people would categorise her actions as dishonest. If there were a complete 'belief in a claim of right' defence, such a defendant would have to be acquitted. Under the *Ghosh* test, however, it would be for the jury to decide whether her exploitation of legal loopholes was in fact dishonest, on the ordinary standards of reasonable, honest people."[97]

If it were a complete defence that this defendant *thought* she had a legal right to act as she did, it would *a fortiori* have to be a complete defence that she *did* have such a right. So it would follow from the Commission's argument that a person might commit fraud by exploiting what are *in fact* legal "loopholes". The Commission did not explain what constitutes a "loophole", and gave no examples. Assuming that s.4 is aimed at the abuse of fiduciary positions, it is hard to see how such a situation might arise; but, if it did, the Commission would apparently be content to see the exploiter

[94] See below, paras 6–067 *et seq*.
[95] Or, as the Commission prefers to call it, "belief in a claim of right".
[96] See below, paras 2–063 *et seq*.
[97] Law Com. No.276, para.7.69.

of loopholes convicted of fraud. The Commission did not explain how this view was to be reconciled with its rejection of a "general dishonesty offence" as insufficiently certain. It is submitted that the passage is an aberration and should be disregarded.

THINGS THE DEFENDANT BELIEVES HE HAS A RIGHT TO DO

2–063 It is, oddly, easier to say when dishonesty is negatived by the defendant's *beliefs* about his legal position than when it is negatived by his *actual* position (of which he may or may not be aware). A person who believes that he has a legal right to act as he does is not acting "fraudulently" in the ordinary sense of the word, and the law has generally accepted "claim of right" as a defence to a charge of certain offences involving fraud. According to Stephen J.,

> "Fraud is inconsistent with a claim of right made in good faith to do the act complained of. A man who takes possession of property which he really believes to be his own does not take it fraudulently, however unfounded his claim may be."[98]

2–064 In the law of larceny, the defence was not confined to a defendant who thought the property was his own: it was sufficient if for any reason he thought he was entitled to take it,[99] and even if he must have known he was not entitled to take it in the way he did.[100] His belief did not have to be correct, or even based on reasonable grounds.[101] The principle was thus an exception to the rule that ignorance of the law is no defence. It was also applied in the law of false pretences,[102] but not in forgery[103] (though the Forgery and Counterfeiting Act 1981 brings forgery into line on this point).[104] Stephen J.'s assertion notwithstanding, it appears to have been regarded as a special rule applying to offences of fraudulently taking or obtaining *property*, rather than an aspect of the concept of fraud and thus applicable to all fraud offences.

CLAIM OF RIGHT IN THEFT

2–065 Claim of right is preserved, in its application to the offence of theft, by TA 1968. Section 2(1) provides that it is not dishonest to appropriate property in the belief that one has a legal right to do so, or that the owner

[98] *History of Criminal Law*, vol.3, p.124.
[99] *Clayton* (1920) 15 Cr.App.R. 45.
[100] *Boden* (1844) 1 C. & K. 395; *Hemmings* (1864) 4 F. & F. 50; *Skivington* [1968] 1 Q.B. 166.
[101] *Bernhard* [1938] 2 K.B. 264; *Hancock* [1963] Crim. L.R. 572.
[102] *Williams* (1836) 7 C. & P. 354, as explained by Pollock C.B. in *Hamilton* (1845) 1 Cox C.C. 244 at 247; followed in *Strickland* (1850) 14 J.P. 784.
[103] *Wilson* (1847) 1 Den. 284; *Parker* (1910) 74 J.P. 208; *Smith* (1919) 14 Cr.App.R. 101.
[104] Forgery and Counterfeiting Act 1981, s.10(2); below, para.11–032.

would consent if he knew the circumstances, or that the owner cannot be traced.

It is arguable that s.2(1) adds little to the *Ghosh* test. Before *Ghosh* it was said to be "extremely important" to direct the jury on s.2(1)(a) in an appropriate case.[105] Since the development of the *Ghosh* test, however, this seems to be less important: a defendant who holds one of the beliefs specified in s.2(1) is unlikely to be regarded as acting dishonestly according to the standards of ordinary people. In *Woolven*[106] it was said that a *Ghosh* direction "seems likely . . . to cover all occasions when a s.2(1)(a) type direction might otherwise have been desirable". **2–066**

In *Wootton*,[107] however, s.2(1) was thought still to have some importance. The defendants were charged with the theft of some pottery from their place of work. They were sometimes paid in kind with pottery items. Their defence was that they had, or thought they had, a right to take the pottery in lieu of accrued wages. The court accepted that this was a clear claim of right, distinct from the argument that what they did was not dishonest according to ordinary standards. The jury should have been directed in accordance with s.2(1)(a). In view of what was said in *Woolven*, the omission was regarded as less important than it might otherwise have been, but it was one of the reasons given for allowing the appeals. This approach is clearly preferable to the view that s.2(1) is subsumed within the *Ghosh* test. While it may be unlikely that a defendant falling within s.2(1) would be regarded as acting dishonestly under *Ghosh*, ordinary people do not always think highly of those who stand on their legal rights (let alone those who stand on what they wrongly and without justification *believe* to be their legal rights). A defendant is entitled to an acquittal if the jury think he may have believed one of the things mentioned in s.2(1). It is irrelevant that they might think his conduct was dishonest (according to ordinary standards) even if he did believe one of those things.[108] **2–067**

In *Attorney-General's Reference (No.2 of 1982)*[109] it was said that s.2(1) applies only if the belief is an honest one. This adds nothing. The defendant cannot secure an acquittal merely by *claiming* to have believed one of the things mentioned, because the jury may be satisfied that in truth he believed no such thing; but that is to say only that the belief must be held, not that it must be held honestly. The whole purpose of s.2(1) is to preclude certain conduct from being treated as dishonest. It is meaningless to say that a belief does not count for this purpose unless it is honestly held. **2–068**

105 *Falconer-Atlee* (1974) 58 Cr.App.R. 348 at 359.

106 (1983) 77 Cr.App.R. 231 at 236. This was a deception case, so s.2(1)(a) strictly did not apply anyway: see below, para.2–090.

107 [1990] Crim. L.R. 201.

108 "Section 2(1) is cutting down the classes of conduct which the jury are at liberty to treat as dishonest": *Hinks* [2001] 2 A.C. 241 at 266, *per* Lord Hobhouse.

109 [1984] Q.B. 624.

Belief in right to deprive

2–069 TA 1968, s.2(1)(a) provides that a person's appropriation of property belonging to another is not to be regarded as dishonest "if he appropriates the property in the belief that he has in law the right to deprive the other of it, on behalf of himself or of a third person". It need not be reasonable for him to believe this. The reasonableness of the belief goes only to the question whether he did in fact hold it.[110] Moreover the question is not whether he would, in law, have such a right if the facts were as he supposes them to be: it is whether he believes that he does have such a right. He may think so because he is mistaken about the facts or the law, or both.[111]

2–070 He must, however, believe that he has a right to deprive the other of the property he appropriates. If he appropriates property in lieu of money that he is owed, or of other property to which he is entitled, he is not entitled to an acquittal unless he believes he has a right to do this. Otherwise, he cannot rely on the statutory defence and has to fall back on the *Ghosh* test. In *Feely,*[112] for example, the defendant had taken £30 from the till in defiance of his employers' express instructions; but his employers owed him £70. When the deficiency came to light he put an IOU in the till. If he really intended from the start that the £30 should be deducted from the £70, his employers stood to lose nothing, and it would be arguable that he was not dishonest. The issue should therefore have been left to the jury. But it would have been equally wrong to direct the jury that if that was his intention he was not dishonest as a matter of law. He would not be *entitled* to an acquittal under s.2(1)(a).

2–071 In *Wood*[113] the court went further than this, and implied that the only kind of "right" which will satisfy s.2(1)(a) is a proprietary right. This cannot be correct. Under the law of larceny it was sufficient if the defendant took property in the belief that the owner owed him money: he did not have to believe that he had a proprietary interest in the property taken, only that he had a right to take it.[114] There is no reason to suppose that s.2(1)(a) is more limited in scope (though it may be of less importance now that its role has largely been taken over by the *Ghosh* test). What the court presumably meant is that the claim of right principle which underlies s.2(1)(a) applies only to offences *against property*, such as theft and obtaining property by deception, and not to the charges of false accounting[115] and procuring the execution of a valuable security by deception[116] with which *Wood* was

[110] *Holden* [1991] Crim. L.R. 478.

[111] In *Lightfoot* (1993) 97 Cr.App.R. 24 at 28 it was said that the defendant's knowledge of the law, whether the criminal law or the law of contract, is irrelevant. But this should not be taken out of context. The point was that, *if* the defendant's conduct is dishonest, it is immaterial whether he knows the law. His knowledge or ignorance of the law may be relevant to the question of whether his conduct *is* dishonest. See below, paras 2–075 *et seq*.

[112] [1973] Q.B. 530.

[113] [1999] Crim. L.R. 564.

[114] *Bernhard* [1938] 2 K.B. 264; *Skivington* [1968] 1 Q.B. 166.

[115] Below, Ch.12.

[116] Below, para.4–151. This offence was abolished by the Fraud Act 2006.

concerned. If this is right, the principle presumably does not extend to the new fraud offence, since it is not an element of that offence that the defendant should appropriate or obtain property.

If *Wood* goes too far in requiring a belief in a proprietary right, what kind of "right" must the defendant believe that he has? Is it sufficient that he believes he is legally free to deprive the owner of the property, in the sense that he incurs no civil liability by doing so? This is connected with questions we have discussed above: whether there are certain kinds of legal right which, as a matter of law, it cannot be "dishonest" to exercise, and, if so, what kinds of right these might be. Sir John Smith's distinction between a mere liberty and a "right in the strict sense", it is suggested, is applicable both to the rule we propose (that it cannot be dishonest to exercise a legal right) and also to s.2(1)(a). It seems that the absence of any civil remedy for the defendant's conduct is not in itself a defence: he must at least have some positive entitlement to act as he does. It must follow that he does not believe he has a "right" to deprive the owner of the property, within the meaning of s.2(1)(a), merely because he believes that by doing so he incurs no civil liability. If the fact that he incurs no such liability is not itself a defence, there is no reason why his belief in that fact should be a defence either. Section 2(1)(a) must be construed as requiring a belief in the existence of the kind of right that, if it existed, would be a defence.[117] 2–072

Belief that consent would be given

TA 1968, s.2(1)(b) provides that a person's appropriation of property belonging to another is not to be regarded as dishonest 2–073

> "if he appropriates the property in the belief that he would have the other's consent if the other knew of the appropriation and the circumstances of it".

It has been said that the belief must be "an honest belief in a true consent, honestly obtained".[118] This assertion is doubly[119] puzzling, because the defendant need not believe that consent *has* been given at all—only that it *would* be if the circumstances were known. It is not enough that he thinks he could have got consent, if he thinks he would have had to use deception to get it: he must believe that the person to whom the property belongs would have consented if he had known all the circumstances, including the defendant's true motives.[120] The chief importance of s.2(1)(b) in the context of fraud lies in its implications for the case where the defendant believes (rightly or wrongly) that the owner of the property *has* consented to what the defendant does.[121]

[117] For a discussion of what kind of entitlement might have this effect, see above, paras 2–050 *et seq*.
[118] *Att-Gen's Reference (No.2 of 1982)* [1984] Q.B. 624 at 641.
[119] See above, para.2–068.
[120] *Lawrence* [1971] 1 Q.B. 373 at 377.
[121] See below, paras 2–084 *et seq*.

Belief that owner not traceable

2–074 TA 1968, s.2(1)(c) provides that, except where the property came to him as trustee or personal representative, a person's appropriation of property belonging to another is not to be regarded as dishonest

> "if he appropriates the property in the belief that the person to whom the property belongs cannot be discovered by taking reasonable steps".

For present purposes this provision is notable only for the exception: the defence is not available to a person who obtains property as a trustee or personal representative. Such a person cannot safely keep the property for himself, or dispose of it for his own purposes, even if the person beneficially entitled to it cannot be traced. If he does so, s.2(1)(c) does not apply, and his conduct may be found to be dishonest under the *Ghosh* test.

Belief that the property does not belong to another

2–075 TA 1968 does not expressly provide that it is not dishonest to appropriate property which belongs to another, in the belief that it does not; but this is clearly implied. In *Small*[122] the defendant was charged with theft of a car. He claimed that he thought it had been abandoned. The jury were directed that such a belief would be a defence only if there were reasonable grounds for it. The conviction was quashed, on the ground that if the defendant thought the car had been abandoned the second limb of the *Ghosh* test was not satisfied, even if that belief was unreasonable. The conclusion was right, but the reasoning was unnecessarily circuitous. If Small thought the car was abandoned, the appropriation would not be dishonest by anyone's standards. The first limb of the *Ghosh* test would not be satisfied, and there would be no need to consider the second. In *Wood*,[123] on essentially similar facts, the judge gave a standard *Ghosh* direction but did not tell the jury to acquit if they thought the defendant might have believed that the property was abandoned. The Court of Appeal held that he should have so directed them, and added that the *Ghosh* direction was positively unhelpful in these circumstances. The only issue was whether the defendant had believed what he said he had believed. If he did not believe it, the appropriation was plainly dishonest on any view.

2–076 In fraud cases this issue has sometimes arisen where the property in question is alleged to have belonged to someone other than the defendant by virtue of TA 1968, s.5(3).[124] That subsection provides:

> "Where a person receives property from or on account of another, and is under an obligation to the other to retain and deal with that property or its proceeds in a particular way, the property or proceeds shall be regarded (as against him) as belonging to the other."

[122] (1988) 86 Cr.App.R. 170.
[123] [2002] EWCA Crim 832.
[124] See below, paras 9–039 *et seq*.

Must the prosecution prove not only that he *was* under such an obligation, as required by s.5(3), but also (as an aspect of the element of dishonesty) that he *knew* he was? The courts have sometimes confused the two issues. It has been said that the obligation required by s.5(3) cannot be implied in order to give an agreement "business efficacy" unless both parties understand that it is implied.[125] If this is right, and the defendant enters into the agreement in person, the necessary obligation cannot be implied *on this basis* without his knowing that it is. But in other cases he may be subject to the necessary obligation without knowing it. It may be implied by law or by custom, or it may have been undertaken by an agent on his behalf. In such a case he should in principle have a defence.

In *Wills*,[126] for example, the defendant was a financial consultant. His assistants obtained money from clients in such circumstances that he was obliged to forward it to a named insurance company. It therefore belonged to the clients by virtue of s.5(3). He did not forward it to the insurance company, but used it for the general purposes of the business. His conviction of theft was quashed because there was no evidence that he had known of the obligation to forward the money. The fact that his assistants had known of it was not enough. **2–077**

> "Whatever may be the position in civil law of knowledge by an agent being imputed to the principal, for the purposes of the criminal law it is necessary for the prosecution to prove that the principal had knowledge of the nature and extent of the obligation to deal with property in a particular way before section 5(3) of the 1968 Act can apply."[127]

The issue was not in fact whether s.5(3) applied—clearly it did, because the requisite obligation did in fact exist—but whether the necessary mens rea had been proved. In effect the court held that it had not.

Similarly in *Boakye*[128] the defendant was convicted of conspiracy to steal money paid by the Manpower Services Commission to an employment agency called MACMA, on the basis that the money belonged to the MSC under s.5(3). The conviction was quashed because the indictment alleged that the money belonged to MACMA, not the MSC, and no amendment had been sought. But it was also said that the conviction could not have stood even if the indictment had been correct, because there was no evidence that the defendant knew of the arrangements between the MSC and MACMA that were relied upon as bringing the money within s.5(3). **2–078**

In other cases, however, the courts have failed to recognise any separate requirement of knowledge that the property belongs to another. In *Wain* the defendant was alleged to have stolen money he had collected for charity. It was said that **2–079**

> "Whether a person in the position of the appellant is a trustee is to be judged on an objective basis. It is an obligation imposed on him by law. It is not

[125] *McHugh (Christopher)* (1993) 97 Cr.App.R. 335; below, para.9–074.
[126] (1991) 92 Cr.App.R. 297.
[127] (1991) 92 Cr.App.R. 297 at 301.
[128] March 12, 1992.

> essential that he should have realised that he was a trustee, but of course the question remains as to whether he was acting honestly or dishonestly in using the money for his own purposes. That is a matter of fact for the jury."[129]

This seems to imply that the defendant could have stolen the money even if he did not realise that in law it belonged to the charity,[130] and thought he was only under a personal obligation to pay the charity a sum equivalent to that which he had collected. The judgment does not explain how this could be the case. It does not in fact appear to have been argued that the defendant did not realise he was a trustee: the issue was whether he was.

2–080 In *Lightfoot* the court firmly rejected any requirement that the defendant must be aware of the legal position.

> "There is a clear distinction between the defendant's knowledge of the law and his appreciation that he is doing something which, by the ordinary standards of reasonable and honest people, is regarded as dishonest. His knowledge of the law, whether the criminal law or the law of contract, is irrelevant. Some dishonest behaviour falls foul of the criminal law; much does not. The fact that a man does not know what is criminal and what is not, or that he does not understand the relevant principles of the civil law, if any, cannot save him from conviction if what he does, coupled with the state of his mind, satisfies all the elements of the crime of which he is accused."[131]

This appears to overlook the fact that, if the defendant does not understand the relevant principles of the civil law, that lack of understanding may in itself prevent his conduct from being dishonest by ordinary standards. Where a person's conduct would be entirely proper if the facts and the law were as he believes them to be, it cannot be dishonest merely because he is mistaken.

2–081 In *Clowes (No.2)*[132] the defendant was convicted of stealing funds paid to the Barlow Clowes group for investment in gilts. Phillips J. had directed the jury that the funds appropriated by Clowes were in law the property of the investors, and that the issue for the jury was whether he had acted dishonestly. The Court of Appeal rejected an argument that the judge should not have determined the ownership of the funds himself, and an argument that his determination of that issue was wrong in law. It was further argued that, even if the funds did belong to the investors, the direction had undermined Clowes' defence that he had *believed* he was entitled to use the funds as he did. This argument too was rejected.

> "Now in one sense it might be argued that whether he was dishonest depended upon whether he knew that in law he was a trustee of the investors' funds and had appropriated their funds. Where, as here, the question of law was open to

129 [1995] 2 Cr.App.R. 660 at 666.
130 *Lewis v Lethbridge* [1987] Crim. L.R. 59, where it was held on comparable facts that the obligation was purely personal, was overruled.
131 (1993) 97 Cr.App.R. 24 at 28.
132 [1994] 2 All E.R. 316.

argument among lawyers it could have been very difficult, if not impossible, to make a jury sure that Clowes, a layman, had reached such a conclusion of law.

However, dishonesty is an ingredient of many offences and does not necessarily depend upon a correct understanding by an accused of all the legal implications of the particular offence with which he is charged. The test is that laid down by this court in *R. v. Ghosh* . . ."[133]

The passage from *Lightfoot* quoted above was cited with apparent approval.

At first sight this looks like an emphatic rejection of what was said in **2–082** *Wills* and *Boakye* (neither of which was cited). But the judgment must be read in the light of the summing-up. Phillips J. had said:

"Mr Clowes has told you that he believed that each transfer that he authorised was a proper transfer. He has told you that he believed that the contracts authorised him to take over the funds as a mini merchant bank and invest them as he pleased . . . If Mr Clowes genuinely held these beliefs, he was not dishonest in authorising the transfers and he was not guilty of theft . . .

You can only convict Mr Clowes of theft if you are sure he knew very well he could not use investors' funds in the way that he did."[134]

And the Court of Appeal cited with apparent approval a passage from the Australian case of *Stephens*:

"The real question for the jury was whether the applicant had fraudulently converted the money. For him to be guilty of fraud knowledge that he was not entitled to treat the money as his own was a necessary element . . . He would not have been guilty of fraudulent conversion if he had not had that knowledge and belief . . ."[135]

Thus, it seems, the defendant need not be proved to have known that the **2–083** property he appropriated *belonged to another*; but, if he claims to have thought he was entitled to appropriate it, the prosecution must prove that he knew he was not. The difference is not great. Despite the court's reference to the *Ghosh* test, it is clear both from the summing-up and from the reference to *Stephens* that if the defendant believed he was entitled to do what he did then he must be acquitted, even if the jury might think it dishonest to act as he did. In one sense this is a claim of right. It does not strictly fall within TA 1968, s.2(1)(a), because that refers to a belief that the defendant has the right to deprive of the property the person to whom it belongs: it assumes that he knows the property *does* belong to another. This is hardly surprising, since another requirement of the offence is that he should intend permanently to deprive the other of the property. He cannot intend to deprive another of property unless he knows that there is (or might be) another who has an interest in the property.

[133] [1994] 2 All E.R. 316 at 330–331.
[134] [1994] 2 All E.R. 316 at 332–333.
[135] (1978) 139 C.L.R. 315 at 336–337, *per* Jacobs J.

Belief that consent has been given

2–084 Nor does TA 1968 expressly provide for the defendant who knows that the property belongs to someone else but believes that that person has, with full knowledge of the circumstances, consented to the appropriation. The omission is surprising, particularly since such a defence is expressly conferred in the case of other offences of taking[136] and damaging[137] property; but it is clearly implied. In *Lawrence v Metropolitan Police Commissioner* Viscount Dilhorne said:

> "Section 2(1) provides, inter alia, that a person's appropriation of property belonging to another is not to be regarded as dishonest if he appropriates the property in the belief that he would have the other's consent if the other knew of the appropriation and the circumstances of it. A fortiori, a person is not to be regarded as acting dishonestly if he appropriates another's property believing that with full knowledge of the circumstances that other person has in fact agreed to the appropriation."[138]

2–085 Similarly in the course of his summing-up in *Clowes*[139] Phillips J. said "You are not guilty of theft if you take someone else's property in the mistaken belief that he has authorised you to do so." In *Kell*[140] this was regarded as being the effect either of the *Ghosh* test or of s.2(1)(a). The *Ghosh* test would normally suffice, because an appropriation in such circumstances could hardly be dishonest on any view. But such a belief, like those expressly referred to in s.2(1), must in principle be a complete defence, whether or not the jury agree that it ought to be.

2–086 It is also arguable that such a belief will fall within s.2(1)(a) in any event, because if the owner did consent to the defendant's depriving him of the property then the defendant would have a "right" to do so. But he probably does not have a "right" to do so within the meaning of s.2(1)(a) unless he is positively *entitled* to do so: it is not sufficient that he incurs no civil liability by doing so.[141] It is doubtful whether the owner's consent to part with the property would be sufficient entitlement for this purpose. To say that a person has "the right to deprive" another of property implies that he is entitled to deprive the other *without* the other's consent.

Appropriations by company directors

2–087 In *Attorney-General's Reference (No.2 of 1982)*[142] it was argued that an appropriation by a company director of his company's property, even if dishonest in the ordinary sense of the word, cannot be dishonest within the meaning of TA 1968, because whatever a director does with the company's

[136] e.g. TA 1968, ss.11(3), 12(6).
[137] Criminal Damage Act 1971, s.5(2)(a).
[138] [1972] A.C. 626 at 632.
[139] [1994] 2 All E.R. 316 at 332.
[140] [1985] Crim. L.R. 239.
[141] See above, paras 2–050 *et seq*. and 2–072.
[142] [1984] Q.B. 624.

property is in law done by the company itself. TA 1968, s.2(1)(b), which provides that an appropriation is not dishonest if done in the belief that the owner *would* consent if he knew the circumstances, applies *a fortiori* to an appropriation done in the belief that the owner *has* consented. The argument was rejected, partly on the ground that the "belief" referred to must be an honest belief[143] and partly because the argument was in any event self-contradictory.

> "The essence of the defendants' argument is the alleged identity, in all respects, and for every purpose, between the defendants and the company. It is said, in effect, that their acts are necessarily the company's acts; that their will, knowledge and belief are those of the company, and that their consent necessarily implies consent by the company. But how then can the company be regarded as 'the other' for the purposes of [s.2(1)(b)]? One merely has to read its wording to see that it cannot be given any sensible meaning in a context such as the present, where the mind and will of the defendants are also treated in law as the mind and will of 'the other'."[144]

It is true that the wording of s.2(1)(b) did not literally apply to the facts 2–088 of the case. The fraudulent director does not believe that the company *would* consent to his depredations *if* it knew the circumstances: he believes (rightly or wrongly) that, through him, it *does* know the circumstances and it *does* consent. One might expect such a case to be covered by s.2(1)(a), which applies where the defendant thinks he has a "right" to deprive the owner of the property. But, even if a director's fraudulent disposals of company property are in theory made with the company's consent, he has no "right" to make them because to do so is a breach of his duty to the company. So he cannot rely on s.2(1)(a). Apart from the *Ghosh* test, s.2(1)(b) is his only hope. According to s.2(1)(b), he would be entitled to an acquittal if he knew that the owner did not consent, but thought that the owner would consent if he knew the circumstances. It would be anomalous if the position were different where he knows that the owner does know the circumstances and does consent. Section 2(1)(b) must surely be read, *a fortiori*, as implicitly applying in this case too.

If that is right, the question is whether a company defrauded by one of its 2–089 own directors can be said to consent to what he does. In the *Attorney-General's Reference* this question was answered in the negative, on the ground that for this purpose the fraudulent director cannot be regarded as the company's *alter ego*. The authority cited for this proposition was *Belmont Finance Corporation Ltd v Williams Furniture Ltd*.[145] In that case an action was brought in a company's name in respect of the allegedly fraudulent misuse of the company's funds by its shareholders and directors. At first instance the action was dismissed on the ground that, on the facts alleged, the company must itself have been a party to the conspiracy. This

143 See above, para.2–068.
144 [1984] Q.B. 624 at 642.
145 [1979] Ch. 250.

decision was reversed on appeal. With the agreement of the other members of the court, Buckley L.J. said:

> "[I]f the allegations in the statement of claim are made good, the directors of the plaintiff must then have known that the transaction was an illegal transaction. But in my view such knowledge should not be imputed to the company, for the essence of the arrangement was to deprive the company improperly of a large part of its assets. As I have said, the company was a victim of the conspiracy. I think it would be irrational to treat the directors, who were allegedly parties to the conspiracy, notionally as having transmitted this knowledge to the company . . ."[146]

In the *Attorney-General's Reference* the court added:

> "There can be no reason, in our view, why the position in the criminal law should be any different."[147]

Yet in *Moore v I. Bresler Ltd*,[148] which was not referred to in *Belmont*, a company was held criminally liable for a fraud of which it was itself the victim.

CLAIM OF RIGHT IN OTHER OFFENCES

2–090 TA 1968, s.2(1) applies only to theft,[149] and not to other offences requiring dishonesty or fraud. It could be argued that this precludes any corresponding defence in the case of other offences. But the Criminal Law Revision Committee did not intend to draw any such distinction.

> "The partial definition in clause 2(1) is not repeated in clause 12(1).[150] It would be only partly applicable to the offence of criminal deception, and it seems unnecessary and undesirable to complicate the Bill by including a separate definition in clause 12(1)."[151]

Section 2(1) is confined to theft because theft is what it is designed for, and most of it has no direct application to any other offence. But the *principle* represented by s.2(1)(a), at least, was intended to extend to obtaining property by deception as well.

> "Owing to the words 'dishonestly obtains' a person who uses deception in order to obtain property to which he believes himself entitled will not be guilty; for though the deception may be dishonest the obtaining is not . . ."[152]

146 [1979] Ch. 250 at 261.
147 [1984] Q.B. 624 at 641.
148 [1944] 2 All E.R. 515.
149 TA 1968, s.1(3).
150 Clause 12(1) of the original Bill became TA 1968, s.15(1), which created the now-superseded offence of obtaining property by deception.
151 *Eighth Report: Theft and Related Offences* (Cmnd 2977, 1966) para.88.
152 *Eighth Report: Theft and Related Offences*, para.88.

In *Woolven*[153] the court accepted that claim of right was a defence to obtaining property by deception, but thought it unnecessary to direct the jury to this effect because it was implicit in the *Ghosh* direction. However, a jury may feel that deception is inherently dishonest, and that it is therefore dishonest to obtain property by deception—even property to which one thinks one is entitled. In *Talbott*[154] the defendant, an actor, obtained housing benefit by telling the local authority that she rented her home from a woman named Deva. Deva was in fact her own stage name: she did not want her real landlord to know that she was claiming benefit. Her defence was that her circumstances entitled her to benefit, and that the identity of her landlord was immaterial. The assessment officer gave evidence that it was not immaterial, at least in the sense that the benefit would not have been paid had he known that the details supplied were false;[155] and the court regarded this as conclusive. But even if the defendant did obtain the benefit by deception,[156] she arguably did not obtain it *dishonestly* if she thought she was entitled to it anyway. The point was not mentioned, probably because deception is usually (and wrongly) regarded as dishonest per se. Had the charge been one of *stealing* the benefit, as it could have been,[157] the prosecution would have avoided the need to prove all the elements of obtaining by deception; but the issue of dishonesty could scarcely have been overlooked, and s.2(1)(a) might have been successfully invoked. The choice of a deception charge should not have been allowed to deprive the defendant of what was essentially the same defence. **2–091**

Indeed, where money is obtained by deception, it may actually be easier to establish a claim of right than where the money is simply appropriated without consent. This is because, even where the defendant is owed money, he is unlikely to suppose that he is legally entitled to help himself to any *particular* money. In the absence of such a belief, the existence of the debt is not a defence in itself, but is only one factor to be considered in applying the *Ghosh* test. Where the money is obtained by deception, on the other hand, this difficulty does not arise, because the particular money (or payment instrument) that changes hands is selected by the victim, not the defendant. The claim of right would appear to be available, on a charge of theft or (under the old law) of obtaining property by deception, if a creditor obtains by deception the payment of a debt which he believes to be legally due. He may not be entitled to any particular money in advance of the deception; but, if he can induce his debtor to pay him any money, he can plausibly claim (despite the deception) to be entitled to *that* money. **2–092**

In the context of deception a claim of right can take two forms. The defendant may think he is *already* entitled to the thing he obtains. For example, he deceives his debtor into paying the debt. Alternatively, he may **2–093**

153 (1983) 77 Cr.App.R. 231.

154 [1995] Crim. L.R. 396.

155 cf. below, para.4–179.

156 It is submitted that in principle she would lack mens rea if she thought she would still have obtained the benefit even if the assessment officer had known the truth: below, para.4–195.

157 Below, paras 9–120 *et seq*.

think he is entitled to it by virtue of the very transaction that the deception enables him to secure. For example, he misleads another into buying property, but believes that the deception does not invalidate the contract and that he is therefore legally entitled to the purchase price. Authority on this latter situation is lacking, but in principle it seems to amount to a claim of right. A charge of theft would be defeated by TA 1968, s.2(1)(a); and it is not obvious why the position should be different in the case of a charge (under the old law) of obtaining property by deception.

2–094 However, the claim of right defence may not extend to all offences of dishonesty. In *Wood*[158] the defendant claimed income support and housing benefit without declaring income from his practice at the Bar. He was charged with false accounting[159] and procuring the execution of a valuable security by deception.[160] His defence was that, since the local authority had incorrectly assessed his housing benefit, he had a right to obtain by deception other benefits for which he was not eligible. He appealed on the ground that the *Ghosh* direction was inadequate: the jury should have been told that he was entitled to an acquittal if he thought he was entitled to withhold information for the purpose of obtaining money which he thought he should have been granted. The court accepted that such a belief might negative dishonesty, but held that the *Ghosh* direction dealt adequately with the point. This is consistent with the pre-1968 case law. The claim of right principle seems always to have been confined to offences which *consisted in* the taking or obtaining of property, such as larceny and obtaining by false pretences. It did not apply where getting property was not an element of the offence. In *Boden,*[161] for example, a charge of assault with intent to rob was withdrawn from the jury because the defendant was trying to get money he was owed; but he had no such defence to the charge of simple assault. False accounting and procuring the execution of a valuable security by deception are closely analogous to obtaining property by deception, but it seems that the claim of right principle does not strictly apply to them. The defendant must take his chance with the jury's interpretation of the *Ghosh* test.

2–095 This suggests that claim of right is not in itself a defence to the new fraud offence either, because, even where the fraud is directed at the obtaining of property, the obtaining of the property is not itself an element of the offence. It was certainly the Law Commission's intention that claim of right should not be a complete defence.[162] The Commission argued that, where a person thinks he has a legal right to act as he does, he will nearly always be entitled to an acquittal under one or other limb of the *Ghosh* test. It conceded that, unlike TA 1968, s.2(1)(a), *Ghosh* will not provide a *complete* defence in such a case, and that in rare cases the outcome might therefore

[158] [1999] Crim. L.R. 564.
[159] TA 1968, s.17(1); below, Ch.12.
[160] TA 1968, s.20(2) (now repealed); below, para.4–151.
[161] (1844) C. & K. 395.
[162] See Law Com. No.276, paras 7.59 *et seq.*

depend whether the charge is theft or fraud; but it saw no need to eliminate this anomaly.[163] A further anomaly would be that claim of right is a complete defence to the old offence of obtaining property by deception,[164] but not to fraud—even if the fraud alleged is the making of a false representation (or failing to disclose information) with the intention of obtaining property.

DISHONESTY AGAINST WHOM?

The late Professor D.W. Elliott drew attention to an important feature of the notion of dishonesty. **2–096**

> "A transaction may have many. . . qualities—it may be describable as quick, deft, clumsy, kind, cruel, generous. Some descriptions of quality require no object, external to the doer—such descriptions as quick, deft, clumsy. An act can be described as quick even if no-one other than the actor is involved. Other descriptions necessarily imply a focus for the quality, some external entity affected by the quality of the act. One cannot be kind, cruel or generous in the abstract . . . Dishonesty appears to be of the latter class, in that it cannot exist in the abstract and needs a focus."[165]

Are there any restrictions on who (or what) that "focus" may be? Elliott argued that, in the case of theft at least, the focus must be the alleged victim, the person to whom the property appropriated belongs. Elliott put the case of a person who, having his mother's authority to sell her cottage, procures a buyer by misrepresenting the state of the drains. He has, it seems, appropriated the cottage,[166] and he intends permanently to deprive his mother of it. A jury might well think his conduct dishonest by the standards of ordinary decent people, and so might he. Has he therefore stolen the cottage? Elliott argued that he has not, because dishonesty vis-à-vis a third party is not enough. The son is guilty of fraud by false representation, and apparently also of stealing the price, but not of stealing the cottage.

In principle this conclusion must be right, but it is hard to reconcile with **2–097** the authorities. Elliott's main targets were the cases[167] holding that the directors of a company may be convicted of stealing the company's property even if they own all the shares or have the consent of all the other shareholders. He argued that, if the only natural persons prejudiced by the

[163] The Commission added: "In the light of our conclusion, . . . it is possible that at some point in the future we may re-visit the interaction between s.2(1)(a) and *Ghosh*, in the context of the law of theft." Since the Commission has now abandoned its plan to review the law of dishonesty in general, this possibility seems remote.

[164] *Woolven* (1983) 77 Cr.App.R. 231.

[165] "Directors' Thefts and Dishonesty" [1991] Crim. L.R. 732 at 734.

[166] The owner's consent does not prevent the disposal of the property from being an appropriation: below, paras 9–120 *et seq*.

[167] *Att-Gen's Reference (No.2 of 1982)* [1984] Q.B. 624; *Philippou* (1989) 89 Cr.App.R. 290.

directors' actions are persons outside the company such as its creditors, the directors are not stealing from the company. But these cases were unanimously approved by the House of Lords in *Gomez*.[168] They can perhaps be explained as turning on the peculiar characteristics of a limited company; but Elliott's principle has found little favour in other areas either. It was held under the old law that a person could be convicted of obtaining property or other benefits by deception even if the person from whom he obtained them was not the person vis-à-vis whom he was dishonest.[169] The courts may similarly hold that a person can be guilty of fraud by abuse of position even if the person whose financial interests he is expected to safeguard is not the person vis-à-vis whom he is dishonest, though s.4 of the Fraud Act 2006 does not appear to be aimed at such a case.

2–098 A requirement of dishonesty has even been included in the new offence of agreeing to operate a cartel, created by the Enterprise Act 2002.[170] It appears to have been inserted in "an attempt to incorporate into the elements of the . . . offence some sense of an awareness of the prohibited nature of the cartel activity".[171] If that was the intention, it is regrettable that the legislation does not say so. In the context of activity which is harmful to society in general rather than identifiable victims, the concept of dishonesty is out of place.

DISHONESTY AND LEGAL CERTAINTY

2–099 Glanville Williams identified two different functions that the requirement of dishonesty serves in different offences.

> "In theft and obtaining by deception, dishonesty is merely a limit on liability. As a philosopher would say, it is a necessary but not a sufficient condition. For theft you must appropriate property belonging to another, etc.; for obtaining you must obtain property by deception, etc. The requirement of dishonesty is an extra. In the case of conspiracy to defraud there appears to be no other requirement, apart from the agreement. Anything that the jury labels (and is allowed to label) as dishonest becomes punishable as the object of a conspiracy to defraud."[172]

2–100 The Law Commission adopted this distinction in a consultation paper published in 1999.

> "[W]here dishonesty is the main determinant of liability, it acts as a *positive* element in the offence. The conduct requirements of such an offence are very

[168] [1993] A.C. 442.

[169] *Metropolitan Police Commissioner v Charles* [1977] A.C. 177; *Lambie* [1982] A.C. 449; below, paras 4–055 *et seq*.

[170] Below, Ch.20.

[171] C. Harding and J. Joshua, "Breaking Up the Hard Core: the Prospects for the Proposed Cartel Offence" [2002] Crim. L.R. 933 at 937.

[172] *Textbook of Criminal Law* (2nd edn, 1983) at 707–708.

general, and occur frequently in commerce or indeed in everyday life. Thus dishonesty 'does all the work' in such offences. It turns what would otherwise not be even prima facie unlawful (say, making a gain or causing prejudice) into a crime.

Dishonesty may also feature, as an 'element', in offences in which the conduct requirements are much more substantial. In such offences, the conduct requirements describe conduct which may be considered prima facie criminal (subject, of course, to the proof of mental elements). The requirement of dishonesty, though in form an element of the offence which must be proved like any other, in effect provides the defendant with a defence. It operates primarily to *exempt* from criminal liability conduct which one would prima facie expect to be criminal—for example, obtaining property by deception with the intention of permanently depriving the owner of it. In these cases we refer to it as a *negative* element."[173]

As the Commission accepted, this distinction is not logically watertight. **2–101** The formal role of dishonesty is the same in all offences of which it is an element: it excludes from the scope of the offence certain conduct that would otherwise be included. The point is that the *function* served by a requirement of dishonesty may differ according to the type of conduct that it excludes. In some offences (such as fraud by false representation) the only conduct it excludes is conduct that, because of the other elements of the offence, one might have expected to be unlawful. In others (such as conspiracy to defraud) this is not the case. The other elements of the offence do exclude certain conduct—for example, in conspiracy to defraud the requirement of conspiracy excludes fraud committed by a person acting alone—but they do not ensure that the *only* conduct caught is conduct which is prima facie culpable. In the former kind of offence, dishonesty is an additional requirement which prevents certain kinds of wrongful conduct from being criminal. In the latter kind, it is all that prevents *legitimate* conduct from being criminal. As the late Professor Edward Griew put it, the requirement of dishonesty "does all the work".

Because dishonesty is defined in terms of the moral standards of the **2–102** community rather than any objective legal distinctions, it is arguably questionable whether the latter kind of dishonesty offence meets the minimum standards of certainty required by human rights law. Section 6 of the Human Rights Act 1998 makes it unlawful for a public authority (including a court) to act in a way which is incompatible with a Convention right. One such right is that conferred by Art.7 of the European Convention on Human Rights, the right not to be held guilty of an offence on account of an act which did not constitute an offence at the time when it was committed. Article 7 embodies the principle of legal certainty. That principle was explained by the European Court of Human Rights in *S.W. v United Kingdom*:

"The guarantee enshrined in Article 7 . . . is an essential element of the rule of law . . . . It should be construed and applied, as follows from its object and

[173] Law Commission Consultation Paper No.155, *Legislating the Criminal Code: Fraud and Deception*, paras 3.15–3.16.

purpose, in such a way as to provide effective safeguards against arbitrary prosecution, conviction and punishment.

Accordingly, as the Court held in its *Kokkinakis v Greece* judgment[174] . . . Article 7 is not confined to prohibiting the retrospective application of the criminal law to an accused's disadvantage: it also embodies, more generally, the principle that only the law can define a crime and prescribe a penalty (*nullum crimen, nulla poena sine lege*) and the principle that the criminal law must not be extensively construed to an accused's detriment, for instance by analogy. From these principles it follows that an offence must be clearly defined in the law. In its aforementioned judgment the Court added that this requirement is satisfied where the individual can know from the wording of the relevant provision and, if need be, with the assistance of the courts' interpretation of it, what acts and omissions will make him criminally liable. The Court thus indicated that when speaking of 'law' Article 7 alludes to the very same concept as that to which the Convention refers elsewhere when using that term, a concept which comprises written as well as unwritten law and implies qualitative requirements, notably those of accessibility and foreseeability . . ."[175]

2–103 It is arguable that the principle of legal certainty is infringed when a person is convicted of an offence which is defined in such a way that the element of dishonesty "does all the work", and his conduct was otherwise lawful, because he could not have known whether a jury would regard that lawful conduct as dishonest. Dominic Grieve MP, the Shadow Attorney-General, made a similar point in debate on the clause that became s.4 of the Fraud Act 2006:

> "The difficulty of the present wording of the clause is that, other than leaving the matter to a judge on a ruling of no case to answer, the case is pretty much open to the jury. The old saying, when I was first at the Bar, was that perhaps we should get rid of all forms of criminal code and simply present facts to a jury, which would be allowed to say on its verdict 'in order', 'out of order' or 'totally out of order'. There is a sense that that is what we are doing with the clause: a set of facts is put to a jury and it is asked, 'Is it in order, out of order or totally out of order,' and on that depends guilt or innocence. That worries me."[176]

2–104 In *Hashman v United Kingdom*[177] the European Court of Human Rights held that binding a person over "to be of good behaviour" was a violation of the right to freedom of expression conferred by Art.10 of the Convention. That right may be interfered with, but only in a manner "prescribed by law". The law prescribing such an interference must satisfy the "quality of law" tests developed by the Court; and one element of "quality of law" is that of legal certainty. A requirement to be of good behaviour did not satisfy the test, because a person subject to it could not tell what he might

[174] A 260–A, para.52 (1993).
[175] *S.W. v United Kingdom* A 335–B, paras 34–35 (1995).
[176] *Hansard*, SC Deb.B, col.12 (June 20, 2006). Whether this is a valid criticism of s.4 depends how the section is construed: see below, paras 6–067 *et seq*.
[177] [2000] Crim. L.R. 185.

and might not lawfully do. The Court contrasted such a requirement with a bind over to keep the peace, which in *Steel v United Kingdom*[178] it had held to be sufficiently certain. The difference was that the law on breach of the peace "describes behaviour by reference to its effects", i.e. according to whether its natural consequences would be to provoke others to violence. The Court similarly distinguished its decision in *Chorherr v Austria*[179] that the offence of "causing a breach of the peace by conduct likely to cause annoyance" was sufficiently certain: the requirement that the conduct be likely to cause annoyance was an adequate indication of the kind of conduct that was prohibited.

> "Conduct which is 'wrong rather than right in the judgment of the majority of contemporary fellow citizens',[180] by contrast, is conduct which is not described at all, but merely expressed to be 'wrong' in the opinion of a majority of citizens."[181]

This proposition would be equally true if "dishonest" were substituted for "wrong". The Government had in fact relied on the requirement of dishonesty under the Theft Acts as an example of law which is sufficiently certain despite being defined in terms of the standards of ordinary people. The Court said that this was distinguishable from a requirement to be of good behaviour, because it was "but one element of a more comprehensive definition of the proscribed behaviour".[182] This appears to be another way of expressing the distinction between a rule which excuses prima facie unlawful conduct on the ground that it is not "dishonest" and a rule which criminalises prima facie lawful conduct on the ground that it is. In most of the offences under the Theft Acts, the requirement of dishonesty falls into the former category.[183] It is revealing that the example chosen by the Government was dishonesty in the Theft Acts, rather than in the law of fraud generally. The requirement of dishonesty in conspiracy to defraud[184] or fraudulent trading[185] is not just "one element of a more comprehensive definition": it is the essence of the offence. **2–105**

Whether an offence of the latter kind provides the necessary certainty is debatable. The fact that offences in which dishonesty "does all the work" are arguably non-compliant was one of the reasons given by the Law Commission for declining to propose any such offence in its consultation paper in 1999. In its final report in 2002 the Commission noted that, of **2–106**

[178] 1998–VII, p.2742.
[179] (1994) 17 E.H.R.R. 358.
[180] This was said to be the kind of conduct that a person could be bound over not to engage in: *Hughes v Holley* (1988) 86 Cr.App.R. 130.
[181] *Hashman v United Kingdom* [2000] Crim. L.R. 185 at [38].
[182] *Hashman v United Kingdom* [2000] Crim. L.R. 185 at [39].
[183] The offence of theft seems to be an exception, since the requisite appropriation of another's property need not be wrongful at all: below, paras 9–120 *et seq*. But the Court was probably unaware of this.
[184] Below, Ch.7.
[185] Below, Ch.8.

those who commented on the consultation paper, a majority had agreed that such an offence might be non-compliant, while a substantial minority had disagreed.[186] Some respondents pointed out that a number of vaguely-defined offences had been held in Strasbourg to be sufficiently certain. The Commission concluded that

> "general dishonesty offences (such as conspiracy to defraud) could perhaps be found to be compatible with the requirements of article 7. We nonetheless remain of the view that they offend against the principle of maximum certainty."[187]

2–107 The Joint Committee on Human Rights, in its report on the Bill that became the Fraud Act 2006, expressed the view that "conspiracy to defraud is a general dishonesty offence and as such is not compatible with the common law and ECHR requirements of legal certainty".[188] It is not clear how a common law offence can be incompatible with the common law, but in relation to the ECHR it is respectfully submitted that the Committee's concerns were justified. Moreover, since the decisions in *Gomez*[189] and *Hinks*[190] have effectively converted the offence of theft into another "general dishonesty offence", these concerns are equally applicable to theft. The Law Commission seems unconcerned by this. Its Ninth Programme of Law Reform[191] does not include plans to complete the comprehensive review of the law of dishonesty which it announced in 1994.[192]

186 Law Com. No.276, para.5.31.
187 Law Com. No.276, para.5.33.
188 Para 2.25.
189 [1993] A.C. 442; below, para.9–123.
190 [2001] 2 A.C. 241; below, para.9–125.
191 Law Com. No.293.
192 In its Eighth Programme of Law Reform (Law Com. No.274) the Commission had questioned "whether the conceptual problems, which many think still exist [in the law of theft] . . . are in urgent need of being addressed", and did not consider it "the prime aspect of the law of dishonesty requiring reform". The Ninth Programme states at para.1.18 that "the Commission hopes to review the law governing burglary and robbery . . ., which has hitherto been left untouched by the Commission's proposals to reform the law of theft, fraud and deception." The Commission has not in fact made any proposals to reform the *offence* of theft at all.

Chapter 3

GAIN AND LOSS

In addition to the requirement of dishonesty, the mens rea of each form of the offence under s.1 of the Fraud Act 2006 ("FA 2006") includes a requirement that the defendant intend, by means of the conduct or omission in question, **3–001**

"(i) to make a gain for himself or another, or
(ii) to cause loss to another or to expose another to a risk of loss."

Certain other offences similarly require either "a view to gain for [the defendant] or another" or "intent to cause loss to another". These offences include false accounting[1] and procuring the execution of a valuable security by deception[2] (which is abolished by FA 2006, but may still be charged in respect of deceptions before January 15, 2007).

THE INCHOATE NATURE OF THE FRAUD OFFENCE

In ordinary usage a person is not defrauded unless he suffers loss, or (perhaps) another makes a gain. A person who dishonestly tries to make a gain or cause a loss, but fails to do so, has not committed fraud but only tried to do so. The old law of deception reflected this. If the intended victim saw through the intended deception, or for any other reason it failed to secure the desired effect, there was at most an attempt. Under FA 2006, by contrast, a person can commit the offence of fraud by acting (or omitting to act) dishonestly and with intent to make a gain or cause a loss or risk of loss, even if no gain, loss or even risk of loss actually results. Gain and loss **3–002**

[1] TA 1968, s.17; below, Ch.12.
[2] TA 1968, s.20(2); below, paras 4–151 *et seq.*

are not part of the actus reus of the offence, but only of the mens rea. As the Law Commission acknowledged, the result is that fraud is effectively an inchoate offence. It includes what a non-lawyer would call attempted fraud.

3–003 The Law Commission's justification for this change was that

> "It may sometimes be debatable . . . whether a loss has actually been caused or a gain made, whilst it is clear beyond doubt that the defendant *intended* to bring about one or both of those outcomes. We think it would be unfortunate if, in such a case, it had to be determined whether there had in fact been gain or loss within the meaning of the Act, when that question had little bearing on the gravity of the defendant's conduct or the appropriate sentence."[3]

The Commission omitted to explain why, in circumstances where it is not clear whether anyone has actually been defrauded, a conviction of attempt or conspiracy would not suffice. Moreover the argument is undermined by the fact that, under the Criminal Justice Act 1993, s.2(1A) (inserted by FA 2006, though not recommended by the Commission), liability for cross-border fraud sometimes *will* turn on whether gain or loss actually occurred.[4] Presumably the difficulty of determining that question is not insuperable.

INTENDED CAUSATION

3–004 Since there is no need to prove actual gain, loss or risk of loss, it follows that, even if one of those things did occur, there is no need to prove that it was caused by the defendant's act or omission. In this respect fraud is wider than the old deception offences, which required the securing of specified results *by* deception.[5] It does not follow that causation is now irrelevant. Sections 2 to 4 of FA 2006 require not merely an intent to make a gain or cause a loss or expose another to a risk of loss, but an intent to do so *by* making the false representation, *by* failing to disclose the information, or *by means of* the abuse of position (as the case may be). The Law Commission acknowledged this.

> "The requirement of intent to make a gain or cause a loss . . . implies a requirement of *intended* causation (as distinct from *actual* causation). The defendant's intention must be to make a gain or cause a loss *by means of* his or her conduct."[6]

3–005 So it must be proved not only that the defendant intended to make a gain, cause a loss or expose another to a risk of loss, but also that he

[3] Law Com. No.276, *Fraud*, Cm.5560, para.7.54.

[4] See below, para.22–030. In fact s.2(1A) of the 1993 Act distinguishes between the occurrence of a loss and the occurrence of a risk of loss—which is an even more subtle distinction than that between the occurrence of a gain, a loss or a risk of loss and the occurrence of none of those things.

[5] Below, paras 4–166 *et seq*.

[6] Law Com. No.276, para.7.56.

intended the gain, loss or risk to occur as a *result* of his conduct. This could make the offence wider in some circumstances and narrower in others. Suppose an applicant for a loan gives a false answer to a question in the application form, but the question is included purely for purposes of market research: the lender does not take account of the answer when deciding whether to grant the loan. If the applicant obtains the loan, he arguably does not obtain it *by* making the false representation.[7] But he would be guilty of fraud if he *thought* that the representation would be taken into account.[8] Conversely, if he thought (albeit wrongly) that it would *not* be taken into account, he would not be guilty of fraud because he would not intend to make a gain *by* making the representation. The Law Commission thought that this requirement of intended causation would rarely create any difficulty; but it raises much the same issues, and is capable of creating much the same problems, as the requirement of actual causation under the old law.[9] They are merely shunted from actus reus to mens rea.

"GAIN" AND "LOSS"

FA 2006, s.5 defines "gain" and "loss" for the purposes of ss.2 to 4. It provides, in part: **3–006**

> "(2) 'Gain' and 'loss'—
>
> (a) extend only to gain or loss in money or other property;
> (b) include any such gain or loss whether temporary or permanent;
>
> and "property" means any property whether real or personal (including things in action and other intangible property).
>
> (3) 'Gain' includes a gain by keeping what one has, as well as a gain by getting what one does not have.
>
> (4) 'Loss' includes a loss by not getting what one might get, as well as a loss by parting with what one has."

For the purposes of the offences under the Theft Act 1968 ("TA 1968") that require a view to gain or intent to cause loss, TA 1968, s.34(2)(a) similarly provides that **3–007**

> "'gain' and 'loss' are to be construed as extending only to gain or loss in money or other property, but as extending to any such gain or loss whether temporary or permanent; and

[7] But arguably he does: below, para.4–178.

[8] Lord Kingsland proposed the insertion of a requirement that the representation be "material". The Attorney-General pointed out that, if the defendant intends to make a gain or cause a loss by making the representation, he obviously thinks that it is material; and, if he thinks it is, there is no reason why he should escape liability because someone else might think it is not. *Hansard*, HL Vol.673, col.1420 (July 19, 2005).

[9] See below, paras 4–166 *et seq*.

(i) 'gain' includes a gain by keeping what one has, as well as a gain by getting what one has not; and
(ii) 'loss' includes a loss by not getting what one might get, as well as a loss by parting with what one has . . ."

TA 1968, s.4(1) further provides that

> "'Property' includes money and all other property, real or personal, including things in action and other intangible property."[10]

GETTING WHAT ONE IS ENTITLED TO

3–008 These definitions do not say that "gain" includes getting what one does not have, and keeping what one has: they say that it includes *a gain by* doing those things. They do not say that "loss" includes parting with what one has, and not getting what one might get: they say that it includes *a loss by* doing those things. To that extent they are circular. It may be arguable that the getting of a thing by D from V would be neither a gain to D nor a loss to V, because D was entitled to the thing all along. This argument has not found favour with the courts. In *Parkes*[11] it was rejected by a trial judge on the ground that "getting hard cash as opposed to a mere right of action is getting more than one already has". Whether this is true in a particular case would seem to depend on the relative value of the cash and the right of action, the likelihood of the action's succeeding, and its likely cost. A bird in the hand may be worth two in the bush, but not necessarily a hundred.

3–009 However, *Parkes* was approved in *Attorney-General's Reference (No.1 of 2001)*.[12] The defendants submitted a false invoice to the trustees of a trust fund set up for their support in connection with criminal proceedings against their daughter. The trial judge had ruled that there was no case to answer on a charge of false accounting, because the defendants were entitled to the money in any event. It was held that the ruling was wrong, and that there was clear evidence that the defendants were acting with a view to gain.

> "Even if they had a valid claim to some of the money in the Trust Fund on the basis that the money should never have gone into the fund, and even recognising that they were beneficiaries under the trust, makes no difference, because none of that relates to what they were doing at the material time. They were dishonestly making use of a false invoice to substantiate a claim for expenses, and thus to extract from the trustees a cheque . . ."[13]

[10] TA 1968, s.4(1) appears among the provisions dealing with the offence of theft, but s.34(1) applies it for the purposes of TA 1968 generally.
[11] [1973] Crim. L.R. 358.
[12] [2002] EWCA Crim 1768; [2003] 1 W.L.R. 395.
[13] [2002] EWCA Crim 1768; [2003] 1 W.L.R. 395 at [28].

It therefore seems that a person who intends to get money or other property has a view to gain by definition, even if he is (or thinks he is) entitled to the thing he intends to get. This goes only to dishonesty.[14]

KEEPING WHAT ONE HAS

Since "gain" includes "a gain by keeping what one has", a person can intend to make a gain by covering up a fraud or other misconduct for which he would otherwise have to account.[15] And, since "gain" extends to any gain, "whether temporary or permanent", it is immaterial that he has no intention of keeping the proceeds indefinitely and is concerned only to conceal the position for the time being. In *Eden*[16] a sub-postmaster submitted accounts showing payments in excess of the value of the corresponding vouchers. His defence to charges of false accounting was that he had incompetently got into a muddle and falsified the returns in order to conceal the true position. On appeal it was said that a conviction would have been in order if the jury had been properly directed. Intent to make a temporary gain was sufficient, including "putting off the evil day of having to sort out the muddle". That would be an intent to make a gain by (temporarily) keeping money that the defendant had but should not have had. **3–010**

In *Golechha*[17] a bank had agreed to discount bills of exchange accepted by the second defendant. The bank would credit the first defendant's current account with the discounted value of each bill when it was presented, and would debit the account with the full value of the bill when it matured. The defendants so arranged matters that whenever one bill matured another one was presented, thus keeping the account in balance. The prosecution's case was that some of the later bills were false and were presented in order to preserve the discounting facility and enable the defendants to maintain a credit balance on which they could draw. They argued that, even if their purpose in presenting the false bills was to ensure that the account remained in credit, that object could not be described as a "gain . . . in money or other property" because a liability brought about by fraud is unenforceable and is therefore not a chose in action at all.[18] At the trial Rougier J. had pointed out the "inherent paradox" in this argument, that "any attempt to secure a conviction . . . would be defeated by the very dishonesty which was the key feature in the charge". But he found it unnecessary to decide the point, because in his view the obtaining of the credit was the means, not the end. The defendants' purpose was not just to **3–011**

[14] See above, Ch.2.
[15] *Lee Cheung Wing* (1992) 94 Cr.App.R. 355.
[16] (1971) 55 Cr.App.R. 193; cf. *Wines* [1954] 1 W.L.R. 64.
[17] [1989] 1 W.L.R. 1050.
[18] cf. *Thompson* (1984) 79 Cr.App.R. 191 at 196. It was apparently also argued that the credit balance obtained by the first defendant would not have been "property" even if not obtained by fraud. As summarised by the court, this argument is incomprehensible.

obtain the credit, but to use it for commercial purposes; and that purpose clearly was a view to gain.

3–012 The Court of Appeal, however, thought it immaterial whether an intention to obtain a credit was "a view to gain", because there was no evidence that the defendants' intention in presenting the false bills was to obtain a credit, as distinct from inducing the bank to forbear to sue on the earlier bills. This latter intention would not be a view to gain.

> "[W]hile it may well be that the three falsified bills were falsified with a view to securing [the bank's] forbearance from enforcing their rights on the earlier bills, this did not and could not constitute falsification with a view to gain (that is gain by keeping money or other property). It was designed simply to postpone the enforcement of an obligation.
>
> If it be accepted for present purposes that the learned judge's construction of the words 'with a view to gain' was correct, and that it is therefore legitimate to see how funds sought to be obtained on the strength of a falsified bill would be used by the defendant, that cannot avail the prosecution in a case where all that the defendant had in view was the forbearance to enforce an existing indebtedness. If the desired forbearance is obtained, this neither gives to the defendant nor allows him to retain anything on which he can draw or which he can convert into cash or goods. Such a case is quite distinct from one in which the object in view is to obtain an advance."[19]

3–013 On the basis of the report it is hard to see why the evidence did not justify Rougier J.'s approach. But, even if it did not, the court's conclusion is (with respect) baffling. If a creditor enforces his debt, the debtor has to hand over money or other property. If the debtor induces the creditor not to enforce the debt, he is thereby enabled to keep money or other property that he already has. And an intention to make a gain by keeping what one has is a view to gain. The judgment does not appear to deal with this point. An intention to induce one's creditor not to enforce a debt is clearly a view to gain.[20]

OTHER FORMS OF GAIN AND LOSS

3–014 Getting what one does not have, and keeping what one has, are only two of the ways in which a person can make a gain. Parting with what one has, and not getting what one might get, are only two of the ways in which a person can suffer a loss. For example, a person clearly makes a gain if his property appreciates in value, and makes a loss if it depreciates. There is no need to argue that he will eventually make a gain or a loss if and when he comes to sell the property.

[19] [1989] 1 W.L.R. 1050 at 1059.

[20] *Golechha* was distinguished in *Cummings-John* [1997] Crim. L.R. 660, where the defendant by deception induced a secured creditor to allow its security to be postponed to a new security. Since the property on which the loans were secured was not worth enough to pay off both loans, the result was that the first creditor lost its security altogether. The defendant's intention was plainly to cause loss to the first creditor.

Although "gain" and "loss" extend only to gain or loss in money or other property, and therefore do not include the obtaining of a service per se, it may be arguable that the obtaining of a service is a gain if the obtainer avoids having to pay for it. The Law Commission said: 3–015

> "It is debatable whether the fraud offence would be committed where by deception D obtains, for nothing, a service which would otherwise have had to be paid for, and which costs the supplier nothing to supply. Arguably it depends whether, had D not been able to get the service for nothing, he or she would have (a) paid for it, or (b) done without it. In the former case there would be an intent to make a gain, by keeping the money that D has; in the latter, arguably not. But it is equally arguable that D has an intent to make a gain even in the latter case, on the basis that the deception makes the difference between getting the service for nothing and having to pay for it. We think it unlikely that many defendants would escape liability as a result of this case not being expressly covered."[21]

The dishonest obtaining of a service is now a separate offence under FA 2006, s.11.[22]

RISK OF LOSS

For the purposes of the fraud offence, though not for false accounting or the old offence of procuring the execution of a valuable security by deception, an intent to cause loss to another is not required: an intent to expose another to a *risk* of loss is sufficient. "Risk" is not defined, but the idea seems clear enough. For example, the offence can be committed by a person who uses misrepresentation for the purpose of inducing others to invest in his enterprise, even if he is confident that they will get a good return on their investment: even if they do not lose their money, he knows that they will be at risk of losing it. This is consistent with the authorities on conspiracy to defraud at common law. For the purpose of that offence a person is defrauded if his financial interests are unlawfully put at risk.[23] This rule has been justified on the basis that "Interests which are imperilled are less valuable in terms of money than those same interests when they are secure and protected".[24] This seems to imply that a person who is exposed to a risk of loss automatically suffers an actual loss, namely the extent to which his interests are thus made less valuable. So it may be that the words "or to expose another to a risk of loss" in FA 2006 add nothing of substance. They do however avoid the need to explain to a jury how it is that a risk of loss counts as a loss. 3–016

[21] Law Com. No.276, para.8.15, fn.16.

[22] See below, Ch.10.

[23] *Sinclair* [1968] 1 W.L.R. 1246; *Allsop* (1976) 64 Cr.App.R. 29; *Wai Yu-Tsang* [1992] 1 A.C. 269; below, paras 7–008 and 7–016.

[24] *Allsop* (1976) 64 Cr.App.R. 29 at 32.

GAIN AND LOSS AS ALTERNATIVES

3–017 Intent to cause loss, or to expose another to a risk of loss, will usually be inseparable from intent to make a gain. They are two sides of the same coin. But they are alternatives. It is clearly possible to defraud another by causing him loss without making any corresponding gain, for example out of spite. More surprisingly, it is theoretically possible to commit the fraud offence by acting with intent to make a gain, even if the making of the gain would not cause loss to another or expose another to a risk of loss. It is difficult to imagine circumstances in which this might actually occur. The Law Commission's justification for the rule was not that it would catch any cases which might not otherwise be caught,[25] but that it was pragmatically desirable.

> "In our view, . . . the law should take a robust and realistic line on this issue. It may be that, where a person's dishonest conduct has genuinely caused no harm whatsoever to anyone else, that conduct is not appropriately described as fraud. However, for every case where this is truly so, there will be many where the loss to others is hard to identify but is none the less real. [In] the Guinness fraud . . . it was clear that there were many losers, but it would have been very hard to bring evidence of these widely dispersed losses. Similarly, in cases of insider dealing it is clear that market participants suffer as a result of the insiders' actions, but the losses are indirect and diffuse. The fact that the defendant has dishonestly made a gain is not itself the *reason* for criminalising the defendant's conduct. It is, however, the obvious and visible symptom of conduct which, on closer inspection, proves to be anti-social in less obvious ways."[26]

INTENT

3–018 The meaning of a requirement of intention has been the subject of much discussion in other areas of the criminal law, but is now reasonably clear. A person intends to cause loss to another if it is his purpose to cause it; he may also be found to have intended to cause loss if he knows that loss is virtually certain to result from what he does.[27]

3–019 During the passage of FA 2006, Lord Kingsland tabled an amendment which would have replaced the "intends . . . to cause loss to another or to expose another to a risk of loss" limb with a requirement that the defendant knows that his conduct "will, in the ordinary course of events, cause loss to another or expose another to a risk of loss". He explained that fraudsters do not act for the purpose of causing loss, though they may know that in achieving their purpose they will cause loss or expose others to a risk

[25] In its consultation paper on corruption the Commission had argued that fraud, unlike corruption, requires the causing of loss rather than the making of gain: Consultation Paper No.145, *Legislating the Criminal Code: Corruption*, paras 1.17–1.30.

[26] Law Com. No.276, para.7.49.

[27] *Maloney* [1985] A.C. 905; *Hancock* [1986] A.C. 455; *Woollin* [1999] A.C. 82.

of loss; that this must be what the Bill meant by the requirement of an intention to cause loss or expose another to a risk of loss; and that it would be better to say it clearly rather than rely on the case law on the meaning of "intention".

The Attorney-General pointed out that there was no reason why a person who intends to cause loss[28] should escape liability merely because he is not sure that he will succeed. But he gave a further reason for resisting the amendment: **3–020**

> "If the effect of the amendment is that it can be said that the offender's knowledge is such that in the normal course of events his behaviour would lead to loss by another, but that is certainly not what he intended—he may intend something other than that—is it right to make him criminally liable in those circumstances? I suggest that it is better to keep the hurdle at a height which puts the intention as the relevant state of mind."[29]

This seems to mean that the offence is not meant to catch a person who knows that his conduct will certainly cause loss, unless that is his purpose (which the Attorney seemed to equate with intention). This would be a surprising interpretation. There is no reason why "intends" should not have the meaning it normally has in criminal law. On that basis, a jury can be directed that they may infer an intention to cause loss or a risk of loss if satisfied that the defendant knew that loss or a risk of loss was virtually certain to result from his conduct.

"VIEW TO GAIN"

In relation to false accounting and the old offence of procuring the execution of a valuable security by deception, the alternative to intent to cause loss is not (as in FA 2006) intent to make a gain, but "a view to gain". There must be a difference between a view to gain and an intent to make a gain. Had the draftsman intended to require the same mental element in relation to both gain and loss, he would have used the same word. The Oxford English Dictionary defines "with a view to" as "with the aim or object of attaining, effecting or accomplishing something". If that is right, view to gain is narrower than intent to gain. A person can intend something which is not his aim or object, if he knows that it is virtually certain to result from what he does. In the context of fraud, however, the difference seems almost entirely theoretical. People who commit fraud do so in order to make a gain. That is why FA 2006 requires intention in relation to both gain and loss.[30] **3–021**

There is, however, some authority that view to gain is *wider* than intent to gain. In *Zaman*[31] the defendant was in possession of a quantity of clothing bearing unauthorised "designer" labels. He was convicted under the Trade **3–022**

[28] Presumably meaning a person whose *purpose* is to cause loss.
[29] *Hansard*, HL Vol.673, col.141 (July 19, 2005).
[30] See Law Com. No.276, para.7.54, fn.29.
[31] [2002] EWCA Crim 1862; *The Times*, July 22, 2002.

Marks Act 1994, s.92 of having the goods in his possession with a view to their sale by himself or another, and with a view to gain for himself or another. His case was that the goods had been left with him as security for a debt, and he had no intention of selling them himself. The trial judge accepted the prosecution's argument that he would be acting "with a view to" the sale of the goods by another if that was something that he had in his contemplation—"not necessarily something that he wanted or intended to happen but something which might realistically occur"—and this interpretation was upheld on appeal. This is effectively a requirement of recklessness rather than intention (let alone purpose).[32] It does not accord with the ordinary meaning of the words in question. Having an event in contemplation is not the same as acting with a view to that event. The court thought it important that the conduct prohibited might also amount to aiding and abetting an offence committed by the eventual seller of the goods: having another's offence in contemplation is sufficient mens rea for a conviction of aiding and abetting that offence. But the actual sale of the infringing goods is not an element of the offence of which Zaman was convicted. The offence is essentially inchoate. It is natural that its mens rea should be narrower than that of aiding and abetting a sale. It is submitted with respect that the decision is wrong. In any event it is not a binding authority on the same expression in TA 1968. The court seems to have been partly influenced by the fact that the definition of the offence uses the words "with a view to" not only in relation to gain but also in relation to the sale of the goods. In the offences under TA 1968 that use the same expression, this reasoning would not apply. Another difference is that, as the court pointed out,[33] the offences under TA 1968 also require dishonesty.

3–023 A different view was taken in *Dooley*.[34] The defendant downloaded indecent photographs of children from a file-sharing service to his computer, and moved most of them to a folder where other users could not access them. But a few of them were found in the folder to which they were downloaded, and to which other users did have access. The defendant claimed that this was because they took a long time to download, and he had not got round to moving them once the download was complete. He was charged with possessing them with a view to their being distributed, contrary to the Protection of Children Act 1978, s.1(1)(c). The judge ruled that it was sufficient if he downloaded them in the knowledge that they were likely to be seen by other users. The fact that he did not *want* other users to access them would be a defence if the offence required an *intent*

[32] The appellant had not argued that "with a view to" was *narrower* than "with intent to", but (perhaps unwisely) that they meant the same.

[33] The court remarked that, because the offences under TA 1968 require dishonesty, "it is not usually material to differentiate between 'with a view to gain' or [*sic*] 'intent to cause loss' ": [2002] EWCA Crim 1862 at [16]. This seems to mean that if the defendant is dishonest there will usually be no difficulty in proving both a view to gain *and* an intent to cause loss. If so, it is true; but it is true even if "view to gain" is given its ordinary meaning. There is no need to give it an artificially wide one.

[34] [2005] EWCA Crim 3093; [2006] 1 W.L.R. 775.

that they be distributed; but "with a view to" was wider than "with the intention of". This interpretation was consistent with *Zaman* (which was not cited) but was rejected on appeal.

> "One can envisage circumstances where a person foresees X as a likely consequence of doing Y, but does not do Y with a view to X. To take a far fetched example, a general may foresee the likelihood of his soldiers being killed in battle, but he surely does not send his troops into battle with a view to their being killed."[35]

In the court's opinion, a person can act with a view to X even if that is not his primary purpose, but it must be *one* of his reasons for acting as he does.[36] It is submitted that this is clearly right, and that it applies equally to the requirement of a view to gain. A person does not act with a view to gain unless the prospect of making a gain is at least one of his reasons for acting as he does.

[35] [2005] EWCA Crim 3093; [2006] 1 W.L.R. 775 at [17].

[36] The court surprisingly thought that this requirement was satisfied on the facts, but allowed the appeal because defending counsel had not appreciated the implications of the ruling when the defendant pleaded guilty on the basis of it.

Chapter 4

FALSE REPRESENTATIONS AND DECEPTION

Of the three ways in which the offence under s.1 of the Fraud Act 2006 **4–001**
("FA 2006") can be committed, the first is by making a false representation. FA 2006, s.2(1) provides:

"A person is in breach of this section if he—

(a) dishonestly makes a false representation, and

(b) intends, by making the representation—

(i) to make a gain for himself or another, or

(ii) to cause loss to another or to expose another to a risk of loss."

4–002 The requirement of dishonesty was examined in Ch.2, and that of intention to make a gain or cause a loss or a risk of loss in Ch.3. In this chapter we consider the remaining element, namely the making of a false representation.

4–003 The concept of false representation is closely related to that of deception, which was an element of eight offences under the Theft Act 1968 ("TA 1968") and the Theft Act 1978 ("TA 1978"). These offences have been abolished with effect from January 15, 2007, but much of the case law on the element of deception is likely to be relevant to fraud by false representation. Our discussion of what constitutes a false representation therefore makes extensive use of authorities on the old law.

4–004 Also relevant to the new law is the old requirement that the property, services or other benefit obtained by the defendant be obtained *by* the deception. The new offence requires that the defendant intend to make a gain or cause a loss or a risk of loss *by* making the false representation.[1] The authorities on the causation requirement under the old law are therefore examined at the end of the chapter. And, although the other elements of the old offences are unlikely to be directly relevant to the new law,[2] those other elements are also examined for the benefit of practitioners dealing with cases arising under the old law.

REPRESENTATION

4–005 FA 2006, s.2 provides, in part:

"(3) 'Representation' means any representation as to fact or law, including a representation as to the state of mind of—

(a) the person making the representation, or

(b) any other person.

(4) A representation may be express or implied."

These provisions replace TA 1968, s.15(4), which provided:

". . . 'deception' means any deception (whether deliberate or reckless) by words or conduct as to fact or as to law, including a deception as to the present intentions of the person using the deception or any other person."

[1] Above, para.3–004.

[2] But authorities on them may be relevant in other contexts—particularly *Preddy* [1996] A.C. 815, below, para.4–104.

TA 1968, s.15(4) is repealed with effect from January 15, 2007, since all the offences under TA 1968 and TA 1978 that were defined in terms of "deception" are abolished by FA 2006.[3]

FALSE REPRESENTATIONS AND THE CIVIL LAW

FA 2006, s.2(3) provides that "'Representation' means any representation . . .", but does not say what a representation is. Though circular, this is understandable, since the term is a familiar one in civil law. Various remedies may be available to a person who enters into a transaction with another person, or otherwise acts to his detriment, on the basis of a mistaken belief induced by the other. This situation is commonly described, in statute[4] as well as case law, in terms of misrepresentation. The law relating to it was often relevant to the old law of deception, and will often be relevant to the new law of fraud by false representation. But it cannot necessarily be assumed that the expression "false representation" in FA 2006 simply incorporates the civil law concept. There are at least two reasons for this.[5] **4–006**

First, the legal meaning of the word "representation" is wider than its ordinary meaning. The Oxford English Dictionary defines it as **4–007**

> "The action of placing a fact, etc., before another or others by means of discourse;[6] a statement or account, *esp.* one intended to convey a particular view or impression of a matter in order to influence opinion or action".

In this sense, a representation is not just a statement but an *express* statement. In the civil law of misrepresentation, by contrast, a representation can certainly be implied rather than express.

Less obviously, a representation in the legal sense need not be a *statement* at all. It is sufficient that D has led V to believe that something is true, without in any real sense asserting it to be true. In *Scott v Brown, Doering, McNab & Co* an agreement to buy shares at prices in excess of their real value, thus creating a false market, was held to be an indictable conspiracy. A.L. Smith L.J. said: **4–008**

> "Test it in this way. Suppose a purchaser induced to purchase shares . . . by means of the fictitious premium created by [the parties to the agreement] solely for the purpose of inducing such purchaser and others to buy, could he

[3] There are other offences which refer to deception or its cognates, such as those that involve doing something which is "misleading, false or deceptive" (see below, para.12–012), but TA 1968, s.15(4) never applied to them.

[4] e.g. the Misrepresentation Act 1967.

[5] A third reason, arguably, is that the concept of representation varies between different civil law contexts: see John Cartwright, *Misrepresentation, Mistake and Non-Disclosure*, 2nd edn (2007), para.2.02. Also, a representation of law is sufficient for the fraud offence but arguably insufficient in civil law.

[6] "Discourse" is defined as "A spoken or written treatment of a subject, in which it is handled or discussed at length".

or not have successfully sued either or both for a false and fraudulent misrepresentation? I say that he could."[7]

A purchaser of shares does not assert to anyone, let alone to persons with whom he is not dealing and does not intend to deal, that he thinks the shares he is buying are worth the price he pays. If an officious bystander were to ask an honest purchaser why he is buying those shares at that price, the answer would probably be "Mind your own business" rather than "Because I think they are worth it, of course". But this is immaterial, because no statement is required. It is sufficient that a false impression is deliberately created.[8]

4–009 The point becomes clearer if the representee is wholly unaware of the conduct that constitutes the representation. If D conceals dry rot in a property before selling it to V, he may be liable on the basis of a fraudulent misrepresentation that the property does not suffer from dry rot.[9] The concealment constitutes the representation. But it cannot be regarded as an *assertion* made to V, because V does not know that it has occurred. Indeed it is the fact that V does not know about it that makes it fraudulent. D clearly makes no representation in the ordinary sense of the word. He does not assert that there is no dry rot. But this does not matter: he is liable because his conduct is meant to, and does, induce V to assume that there is no dry rot.

4–010 On these facts, does D make a false representation within the meaning of FA 2006, s.2? "Representation" is an ordinary English word, and FA 2006 does not expressly give it the technical meaning that it has in civil law. Arguably, therefore, its meaning is a matter for the jury.[10] If the jury are not told what it means, they are likely to give it its ordinary meaning. In *that* sense, D probably makes no representation. A jury would be more likely to accept that the concealment of the dry rot was a deception than that it was a false representation. The Law Commission's decision to formulate the new law in terms of false representation rather than deception may therefore have narrowed the scope of the offence.[11]

[7] [1892] 2 Q.B. 724 at 734.

[8] In April 2003 Charles Ingram and two others were convicted of conspiracy to procure the execution of a valuable security (a cheque for £1m) by deceiving the presenter of a television quiz programme. Ingram cheated by choosing his answers with the covert help of a co-defendant, who coughed whenever the correct answer was mentioned. The alleged representation was that he did not receive any assistance. But it would be odd to say that he *asserted* (even by implication) that he was not receiving assistance. The presenter did not seek an assurance to that effect, and was doubtless surprised to learn that Ingram had implicitly offered one. The reality is that Ingram simply cheated, and failed to confess that he had cheated. He made a representation only in the technical legal sense, by *giving the impression* that he was answering the questions unaided.

[9] *Gordon v Selico Co Ltd* [1986] 1 E.G.L.R. 71 (where the point was conceded). See also *Ormrod v Huth* (1845) 14 M. & W. 651; *Horsfall v Thomas* (1862) 1 H. & C. 90.

[10] cf. *Brutus v Cozens* [1973] A.C. 854.

[11] The Commission thought that "For most practical purposes, . . . the distinction is immaterial", but it went on to define fraudulent misrepresentation as "an assertion of a proposition which is untrue or misleading . . .": Law Com. No.276, *Fraud*, Cm.5560, paras 7.16, 7.17. Clearly one can deceive without making an assertion in any ordinary sense of that word.

The second reason to be cautious in applying the civil law of misrepresentation is that in the civil law nothing actually turns on the narrow question of whether a false representation has been *made*. The question is always whether the aggrieved party is entitled to relief from the consequences of his mistake. The representee has no remedy unless he has relied on the representation, and he obviously cannot rely on it until it is made. Fraud by false representation, on the other hand, is committed simply by making a false representation dishonestly and with the necessary intent. This makes it necessary to determine what constitutes the *making* of a representation. For example, V can rescind his purchase of property because D concealed the dry rot. But at what point did D "make" the representation that there was no dry rot? When he concealed the dry rot? When he put the property on the market? When V viewed the property? When contracts were exchanged? The civil law does not have to decide, because it is concerned with the situation that arises once V has acted in reliance on the impression created by D. The same was true of the old law of deception. But the new offence consists in the making of the representation itself. On this point, the civil law is unlikely to be of any help. **4–011**

FALSE REPRESENTATIONS AND DECEPTION

False representation is also not the same as deception. The Larceny Act required a "false pretence", which was broadly the same as a representation. In 1966 the Criminal Law Revision Committee proposed to replace this requirement with one of deception. **4–012**

> "The word 'deception' seems to us . . . to have the advantage of directing attention to the effect that the offender deliberately produced on the mind of the person deceived, whereas 'false pretence' makes one think of what exactly the offender did in order to deceive. 'Deception' seems also more apt in relation to deception by conduct."[12]

The proposal was implemented in TA 1968. The Oxford English Dictionary defines "deception" as "the action of deceiving", and "deceive" as "to cause to believe what is false".[13] The Committee's purpose seems to have been not just to use more everyday language but to shift the emphasis. False pretence, or misrepresentation, is what the defendant *does*; deception is the *effect* of what he does ("the effect . . . deliberately produced on the mind of the person deceived"). This additional element—the victim's *belief* in the truth of the proposition falsely represented by the defendant to be true—made little practical difference, because even under the old law it had **4–013**

[12] *Eighth Report: Theft and Related Offences*, Cmnd.2977, para.87.

[13] cf. Buckley J. in *Re London and Globe Finance Corp Ltd* [1903] 1 Ch. 728 at 732: "To deceive is, I apprehend, to induce a man to believe that a thing is true which is false, and which the person practising the deceit knows or believes to be false." This dictum was approved in *DPP v Ray* [1974] A.C. 370.

to be proved that the defendant had obtained property *by* false pretences. The necessary causal link between the false representation and the obtaining would not exist if the intended victim was not taken in. But the new offence requires no such link. The offence can be committed *merely* by making a false representation with the necessary intent.[14]

4–014 The concept of deception had a practical advantage over that of false representation. It avoided the artificiality of describing a person as having made a false representation even though he has made no assertion and therefore has not made a representation in the ordinary sense of the word. While this terminology is consistent with the civil law,[15] it is not particularly transparent. Under the old law, the concealer of dry rot could be charged on the basis that he had induced the purchaser to believe that there was no dry rot. Under the new law, the case has to be put on the basis that he *represented* that there was no dry rot. This may achieve the same result—if it is explained to the jury what the law regards as a representation,[16] and they understand the explanation—but it is an extra complication. In *Landy*, suggesting how an indictment for conspiracy to defraud should have been drawn, the Court of Appeal said that particulars of the kind it recommended "would have avoided such terms as 'falsely representing' . . . which are imprecise and likely to confuse juries".[17] Indictments for deception were occasionally drawn without an allegation of false representation, and some trials were probably made slightly less puzzling for juries as a result. It is difficult to see how the law is improved by withdrawing this option.[18]

THE PROPOSITION REPRESENTED

FACT OR LAW

4–015 As FA 2006, s.2(3) makes clear, the proposition represented may be one of fact or of law. In this respect the criminal law arguably diverges from the civil law of misrepresentation.[19] So it may be fraud for a trader to add a percentage to a bill on the pretext that the law requires the customer to pay

[14] But the necessary intent includes an element of causation: above, para.3–004.

[15] See above, para.4–008.

[16] Assuming that such explanation is permissible: see above, para.4–010.

[17] [1981] 1 W.L.R. 355 at 362.

[18] In its consultation paper the Law Commission had argued not only that a false representation was no longer required, but that this was an improvement on the old law of false pretences. The majority of those who commented agreed with this analysis: Law Com. No.276, para.7.15. The only reason given for reverting to a requirement of false representation was that in cases of credit card fraud it is sometimes difficult to establish that the merchant *believed* that the defendant had authority to use the card, because he will normally be indifferent on that point: see below, paras 4–055 *et seq.* But the Commission's approach does not even solve that problem, because it must still be proved that the defendant intended to make a gain or cause a loss *by* representing that he has authority: see above, para.3–004.

[19] *Chitty on Contracts*, 29th edn (2004), para.6–011; but cf. John Cartwright, *Misrepresentation, Mistake and Non-Disclosure*, 2nd edn (2007), paras 3.20 *et seq.*

VAT, or for a seller of goods to tell the buyer that he has no redress in respect of defects. But what on the face of it is a bald statement of law may sometimes be no more than a statement of opinion.[20] In any event the prosecution must prove that the defendant *knew* that the proposition he represented was, or might be, untrue or misleading. Where the proposition is one of law, this may be harder to prove.

PROMISES

A representation is a proposition of existing fact (or law). A promise is not a representation, and a broken promise is not a false representation;[21] so it is wrong to allege in an indictment that the defendant falsely represented that something would happen. But a promise may be accompanied by an implied representation that its maker intends to keep it. FA 2006, s.2(3) expressly states (as did TA 1968, s.15(4)) that a representation as to a person's state of mind will suffice.[22] A person who orders goods or services normally makes an implied representation that he intends to pay for them, and thus commits fraud if he does not intend to do so.[23] But it must be proved that he did not intend to keep the promise at the time when he made it, or at some later time when he represented that he still intended to keep it. A dishonest decision to break a promise might, however, amount to fraud by non-disclosure, on the basis that the defendant had a legal duty to disclose that decision.[24] And the breaking of a promise might in some circumstances amount to fraud by abuse of position.[25] **4–016**

A less clear case is that of the defendant who does hope to carry out his promise if possible, but knows that he will probably be unable to do so—for example, the trader who is on the brink of insolvency but continues to order goods in the hope that something will turn up. There is no misrepresentation as to his intentions, since, like any honest debtor, he intends to pay if he can. The misrepresentation, if any, is as to the likelihood of his being able to pay. The prosecution must show that he misled his suppliers as to their prospects of being paid. An alternative approach would be to allege a false representation as to *his own assessment* of those prospects; but it comes to much the same thing, since it must be proved in either case that **4–017**

[20] For statements of opinion, see below, para.4–020.

[21] But cf. *Warwickshire County Council v Johnson* [1992] Crim. L.R. 644, where a branch manager was held to have published a "misleading" advertisement within the meaning of the Consumer Protection Act 1987, s.20(1), by failing to honour a promise to "beat any . . . price by £20".

[22] It had been held in *Dent* [1955] 2 Q.B. 590 that it was not a "false pretence" for a person to make a promise which he had no intention of keeping.

[23] *Re Shackleton, ex p. Whittaker* (1875) L.R. 10 Ch. App. 446; *DPP v Ray* [1974] A.C. 370; *Harris* (1975) 62 Cr.App.R. 28; *Waterfall* [1970] 1 Q.B. 148.

[24] See below, Ch.5. It is not clear whether non-disclosure in these circumstances could amount to deception under the old law: see below, para.4–052.

[25] See below, Ch.6.

he knew he might not be able to pay. It is probably not enough that he is not *sure* he will be able to pay, since he probably does not represent that he is. No-one expects a trader to go out of business as soon as he sees the slightest risk of insolvency.[26] Only when the risk becomes serious can it be said that creditors have been defrauded.

4–018 One advantage of relying on a representation that the defendant *intended* to act in a particular way[27] is that, if that proposition can be proved to have been false, it follows inevitably that the defendant must have *known* it was false. Recklessness becomes irrelevant.

PREDICTIONS

4–019 The position is similar in the case of predictions of future events. Admittedly a prediction is a statement of a sort, and may be true or false.[28] *Chitty on Contracts* suggests that a statement as to the future is not inherently incapable of being a misrepresentation for the purposes of the law of contract, provided that it is reasonable for the representee to rely on the statement rather than on his own judgment.[29] But such a statement would not be fraudulent unless its maker knew that it was or might be untrue; and, if he knows this, he is making a false representation about an existing fact, namely that *he believes* that the prediction will come true.[30] For practical purposes, therefore, a representation of existing facts is required. A person who draws a cheque without funds to meet it, for example, may be guilty of fraud by false representation. But the proposition he falsely asserts is not that the cheque will be honoured: it is that the existing state of facts is such that in the ordinary course of events the cheque can be expected to be honoured.[31]

OPINIONS

4–020 The hallmark of a proposition of fact (or law) is that it can, at least in principle, be demonstrated to be true or false. A statement which could never be proved or disproved is not a representation but a mere expression

[26] There are a number of offences directed specifically at debtors who put their creditors at risk: see below, Ch.15.

[27] Or a representation that he believed a forecast to be accurate, or that he held a particular opinion: see below, paras 4–019, 4–020.

[28] A.R. White, "Trade Descriptions about the Future" (1974) 90 L.Q.R. 15.

[29] 29th edn (2004), para.6–010.

[30] That is not to say that the making of a prediction is fraudulent if the person making it is not certain that it will come true: it depends how certain a reasonable person would understand him to be. A tipster is not expected to be certain that all his tips will be winners. What he must not do is pretend to have inside knowledge that he does not have, or otherwise to be more confident than he is.

[31] *Gilmartin* [1983] Q.B. 953.

of opinion.[32] It may however be accompanied by an implied representation that the person expressing the opinion does in fact hold it, or has reasonable grounds for holding it. In *Levine*[33] a tea and coffee service made of poor quality metal covered with a transparent film of silver was described as "the best silver plate". This was held not to be a false pretence, although no-one with any knowledge of plate would have agreed with it. It is not fraud to puff inferior goods. But if there is an accepted scale of quality, so that it can be objectively determined whether the goods merit the description they are given, the question becomes one of fact. On the facts of *Levine* it would be sufficient if the expression "best silver plate" were regarded in the trade as denoting a certain minimum content of silver.[34] There would then be a representation that the goods offered met that standard.

A similar problem arises where the defendant puts a specific and inflated value on his wares or services. He may do this either by comparing his price with that charged by others (for example, describing as "worth £100" goods that can be bought elsewhere for a fraction of that sum), or by charging an exorbitant amount where no fixed price has been agreed. Ultimately the question is the same in each case: is he describing only his own, subjective assessment of the value of what he provides? Or is he asserting that an informed buyer might be willing to pay the sum asked? Usually the latter interpretation will be more natural,[35] and there will therefore be a representation of fact. **4–021**

In *Bassett* the defendants were convicted of obtaining money by the false pretences that they had done necessary repairs on the victim's roof, that they had done the work in a proper and workmanlike manner, and that £35 was a fair and reasonable sum to charge. The Court of Appeal rejected the argument that the last of these allegations related to a matter of opinion. It was **4–022**

[32] *Chitty on Contracts*, 29th edn (2004), para.6–010 suggests that even a statement of opinion may be a misrepresentation for the purposes of the law of contract, if it is reasonable to rely on it; but it is hard to see how this can be so, since it is by definition impossible to determine whether such a statement is false. John Cartwright, *Misrepresentation, Mistake and Non-Disclosure*, 2nd edn (2007), para.2.02 argues that a statement of opinion may be a misrepresentation for the purpose of liability in negligence; but the point is surely that such liability does not require a *representation* at all.

[33] (1876) 10 Cox C.C. 374.

[34] At the time when the case was decided this would not have been sufficient, since the false pretence had to relate to the type of goods offered and not merely to their quality: *Bryan* (1857) Dears. & B. 265; *Lee* (1859) 8 Cox C.C. 233; *Williamson* (1869) 11 Cox C.C. 328. But in *Ardley* (1871) L.R. 1 C.C.R. 301 it was held a false pretence to describe 6-carat gold as 15-carat, because it was a misrepresentation as to an objective fact. It was immaterial that the item in question was of the type it was stated to be, viz. a gold chain. This is clearly the law today.

[35] cf. *Mirror Group Newspapers v Northants C.C.* [1997] Crim. L.R. 882, where an advertisement for "a £50 watch" was held to be misleading within the meaning of the Consumer Protection Act 1987, s.20(1), because no similar watches were on sale at that price at that time.

> "really part and parcel of the real false pretence alleged, which was that they had done necessary repairs to the roof and that those repairs could be measured by this sum of £35. In other words, it was all one false pretence . . ."[36]

This implies that there might not have been a false pretence about the price if the repairs had been necessary, even though the price was unreasonable. But they are separate representations, and should be separately considered. On principle the charging of an exorbitant price ought to be sufficient, provided that the defendant can be regarded as having made a representation that the price was not grossly in excess of the going rate.

4–023 In *Silverman*[37] it was said that the charging of an excessive price could amount to a deception where there was a situation of "mutual trust" in which the customer had depended on the defendant for fair and reasonable conduct. Under the new law, the fact that the defendant had been in a position of trust might make him guilty of fraud by abuse of position[38] or by failing to disclose information.[39] For the purposes of fraud by false representation, however, there must be a representation of fact (or law). If all that the defendant asserts is that his wares or services are worth the price he asks, and this is purely a matter of opinion, the existence of a relationship of trust cannot turn that expression of opinion into a representation of fact. Presumably what the court meant was that the relationship of trust was relevant in determining whether the customer was entitled to infer from the defendant's conduct that his charges were objectively reasonable.

4–024 It may sometimes be better to rely not on a representation that the price *is* fair or competitive, but on a separate representation that the defendant *thinks* it is. If he does not think so, such a representation will be false, and he will inevitably know that it is false. It may be debatable whether he can be regarded as making any such representation, but it is a question of fact.

WAYS OF REPRESENTING A PROPOSITION

4–025 TA 1968, s.15(4) provided that a representation may be "by words or conduct". The Fraud Bill originally said the same, but was later amended: FA 2006, s.2(4) provides instead that "A representation may be express or implied." There is no substantive difference between the two formulations, but the distinction drawn is not quite the same because a representation may be implied by words as well as by conduct.

[36] (1967) 51 Cr.App.R. 28 at 31.
[37] (1988) 86 Cr.App.R. 213.
[38] Below, Ch.6.
[39] Below, Ch.5.

WORDS

Express representations

An express statement of a proposition will normally amount to a representation, but only if a reasonable person would have inferred from it that the proposition stated is true. Statements are made for many reasons, and not always with a view to their being accepted as literally true.[40] It has been held in Australia, for example, that it is not deception to make a false allegation in a statement of claim.[41] The function of such a document is to provide information about the nature of the claim, not about the facts of the case. **4–026**

Representations implied from words

A representation may be implicit in words which do not amount to an express representation. Thus the making of a promise may carry an implied representation that the maker intends to keep it, or has reason to believe that he will be able to do so. The making of a prediction may carry an implied representation that the maker expects it to come true, or has reason to believe that it will. The expression of an opinion may carry an implied representation that the person expressing it genuinely holds it, or has reasonable grounds for holding it. **4–027**

A false representation may be implicit in words which are too vague to be literally false—for example, where an advertisement for sheet music was cunningly worded so as to suggest that what was being offered was some kind of musical contraption, although a careful reader would have realised that that could not be so.[42] A motor dealer's warning that a car's odometer reading "may not be correct" can imply that he does not know it to be false.[43] **4–028**

Alternatively, express representations which are true in themselves may be misleading because of what is left out. **4–029**

> "If by a number of statements you intentionally give a false impression and induce a person to act upon it, it is not the less false, although if one takes each statement by itself there may be a difficulty in shewing that any specific statement is untrue."[44]

Thus in *Kylsant*[45] a prospectus saying, truthfully, that dividends had been regularly paid over a number of years was held to be "false in a material

[40] cf. Criminal Justice Act 2003 s.115, which defines a hearsay statement in terms of whether the statement was made for the purpose of causing another person to believe the matter stated: below, para.27–057.
[41] *Jamieson* (1993) 116 A.L.R. 193.
[42] *Lawrence* (1909) 2 Cr.App.R. 42.
[43] *King* [1979] Crim. L.R. 122.
[44] *Aaron's Reefs Ltd v Twiss* [1896] A.C. 273 at 281, *per* Lord Halsbury L.C.
[45] [1932] 1 K.B. 442.

particular" because it did not mention that the dividends had not been paid out of current income. This is an example of a situation to which the terminology of deception is better suited than that of false representation. The investors were deceived because the defendant, without actually saying so, gave the impression that the dividends had been paid out of current income. On a charge of fraud by false representation, however, a jury would have to consider whether, by making express representations which were true, the defendant had also made an implied representation which was false. This is unnecessarily confusing.

4–030 It may also be sufficient if an express statement is neither true nor false, but meaningless. In *Banaster*[46] a mini-cab driver picked up a foreign passenger at Heathrow Airport, claiming to be "an airport taxi", and told him that the "correct fare" for a ride to Ealing was £27.50. There was in fact no such thing as an airport taxi, nor was there any scale by which the "correct" fare might be determined. It was held that, even if the defendant had said nothing that was positively false, the jury had been properly directed that they might find in his words the implication that it was "all official". It is not entirely clear what, on this reasoning, was the false proposition that the defendant represented to be true. Perhaps it was that he was not just entitled to pick up passengers at the airport, but was a member of a privileged class of drivers who were individually authorised to pick up passengers and were subject to supervision by the airport authorities. Alternatively, it may have been simply that £27.50 was roughly what most taxi-drivers would charge.

An objective test?

4–031 Under the law of deception, it was sufficient if the defendant intended the victim to draw a particular inference from the words used, and that inference was untrue. It was immaterial whether that was what the words used *objectively meant*—that is, what a reasonable person in the victim's position would have understood them to mean. The latter question, where it arises, is a question of law for the judge;[47] but in a deception case it did not arise. The question was whether the alleged victim was in fact led to believe in the truth of a proposition which was false, and if so whether the defendant intended this to happen or knew that it might happen. These were jury questions.

4–032 In *Adams (Junior)*[48] the defendant submitted a car hire application form. One of the questions read: "Have you (a) Been convicted during the past 5 years in connection with any motor vehicle. (b) Ever been disqualified from driving. (c) Any prosecution or police enquiry pending?" The defendant's answer to this question was "No". If this meant that he had never been disqualified, it was untrue. But it was argued that the form was ambiguous,

[46] (1979) 68 Cr.App.R. 272.
[47] *Cross* [1987] Crim. L.R. 43.
[48] [1994] R.T.R. 220.

and that the answer "No" could be construed as relating only to part (a) of the question. The judge ruled that the completed form bore the meaning contended for by the prosecution. It was held on appeal that the point should have been left to the jury.

Here too the substitution of the requirement of false representation for that of deception creates an unnecessary problem. The problem was anticipated in *Adams*, where the judgment was worded as if the old law required a false representation. **4–033**

> "Where the central question is whether the defendant has made a representation or not, and, if so, whether it is false, then both aspects of that question are questions of fact for the jury. This is clearly so where the alleged representation is oral. It must equally be so in our judgment where the representation is contained in writing. The question is not in truth as to the meaning of the representation, still less as to the legal effect of the document. The question is simply whether a representation to the effect alleged in the indictment has been made at all."[49]

In his commentary on the case, Sir John Smith argued that there were two questions for the jury: (1) Did the defendant know that the hire company would or might take him to be asserting that he had never been disqualified? and (2) Did the hire company in fact take him to be so asserting, and let him have the car when they would not have done so if they had known that the assertion was false? Asking whether he made a *representation* to the effect alleged was an extra complication. **4–034**

> "Suppose that the jury, though answering the two above questions in the affirmative, say that they, being the reasonable reader, would not have taken the writer to be asserting that he had never been disqualified. Are we really to say that there is no obtaining by deception (because no representation) although the writer intended to (or knew he might) deceive and the reader was deceived as intended (or foreseen)? The implication of the decision seems to be that we must say that. If that is right, there are three questions. An additional question must be inserted between those posed above:—Would a reasonable reader of the document have taken him to be so asserting?"[50]

[49] [1994] R.T.R. 220 at 224. The point seems to have been overlooked again in *Patel* [2006] EWCA Crim 2689; [2007] 1 Cr.App.R. 12 (p.191), where the defendant was alleged to have falsely represented in a job application form that she had never been convicted of an offence. This representation was technically true, because she had been given a conditional discharge in respect of the offence of which she had been found guilty, and she was therefore deemed by statute not to have been convicted of that offence. But it was not suggested that she had known that the representation was true. Since she was charged with the old offence of obtaining a pecuniary advantage by deception, the case could have been put on the basis that she was *deceiving* her prospective employer into believing that she had never been found guilty of an offence. Under the new law it would have to be argued that she made a *false representation* to that effect—which was less obviously the case.

[50] [1993] Crim. L.R. 525. This commentary was approved in *Page* [1996] Crim. L.R. 821, but on a different point—viz. Smith's argument that, where there is an issue as to the legal effect of a document, that issue is for the judge (as in *Spens* [1991] 1 W.L.R. 624: construction of City Code on Take-overs and Mergers); but, where the issue is as to the meaning of a document as (a) understood or intended by the person making it and (b)

4–035 The court may or may not have been right to say that the question, under the old law, was whether the defendant had made a representation to the effect alleged.[51] But that is certainly the question under the new law: FA 2006 says so. If Smith is right about the way in which that question must be answered, FA 2006 has turned what was only a potential problem (easily avoided by reinterpreting *Adams*) into a real one. Suppose D makes a statement to V which he knows to be ambiguous. If it means *x*, it is true. If it means *y*, it is false. He knows that V may understand it to mean *y*. If Smith is right, D is not making a false representation unless a reasonable person in V's position would understand the statement to mean *y*. But is Smith right?

4–036 In general, the law does regard a statement as meaning what a reasonable person would understand it to mean. And it is arguable that this is true even where the maker of the statement intends it to be understood in the sense that is objectively wrong.[52] But it would be remarkable if this were the law; and it seems that it is not. In *Smith v Chadwick* no less an authority than Lord Blackburn said:

> "[I]f with intent to lead the plaintiff to act upon it, [the defendants] put forth a statement which they know may bear two meanings, one of which is false to their knowledge, and thereby the plaintiff putting that meaning on it is misled, I do not think they can escape by saying he ought to have put the other. If they palter with him in a double sense, it may be that they lie *like* truth; but I think they lie, and it is a fraud."[53]

That is as one would expect. If D hopes that V will understand the statement to mean *y*, because D would not get what he wants if V understood it to mean *x*, it is submitted that D has made a representation of *y* within the meaning of FA 2006, s.2.

understood by the person reading it, the issue is for the jury. In *Page* the question of false representation did not arise, because the truth or falsity of statements made by the defendants depended on the meaning of undertakings given to them by a third party. It was held, applying Smith's distinction, that the question was not what the undertakings meant in law but what the defendants understood them to mean. It was therefore a jury question.

[51] In *Naviede* [1997] Crim. L.R. 662 the defendant was alleged to have obtained a credit agreement for his company by the deception that the company's main business was trade finance, whereas in fact it was property financing, which was riskier. His case was that property financing was actually a kind of trade finance, so the representation was true. The jury were directed that they were not concerned with whether there was any legal distinction between the two kinds of business. The only question was whether the bank had understood the representation as including property financing or as being confined to traditional stock financing, and whether the defendant had intended the bank so to understand it. On appeal this direction was held to be right. It was not suggested that it was relevant whether it was *reasonable* for the bank so to understand it.

[52] John Cartwright, *Misrepresentation, Mistake and Non-Disclosure*, 2nd edn (2007), para.5.09 suggests that the test is the same in the tort of deceit (which requires a fraudulent representation) as where the representee seeks rescission of a contract. Cf. the rule that contributory negligence is not a defence to an action in deceit: ibid., para.5.31.

[53] (1884) 9 App. Cas. 187 at 201. The question did not arise for decision. The plaintiff's action for deceit failed because there was no evidence that he had understood the defendants' statement in the sense in which it was false rather than an alternative sense in which it was true.

This may also be so if D is indifferent whether V understands the statement to mean *x* or *y*, because D expects to get what he wants even if V understands it to mean *x*. But in this case there is a further difficulty: it is doubtful whether D intends to make a gain, or to cause a loss or expose another to a risk of loss, *by* making the representation of *y*.[54] He thinks that a representation of *x* would also suffice.[55] **4–037**

CONDUCT

Non-verbal conduct may similarly carry an implied representation as a matter of convention. A person may be regarded as having represented a proposition to be true if it is reasonable for another person to infer from his conduct that that proposition is true.[56] The same must be true, it is submitted, if a reasonable person would *not* have inferred that, but the defendant knew that the person with whom he was dealing would or might infer it. This is another case which is easier to explain as a deception than as a false representation. **4–038**

Drawing a cheque

Identifying the representation (if any) that can be implied from a person's conduct is not always easy. An example that has been much discussed is the drawing of a cheque. The important issue, for a person considering whether to accept a cheque, is whether it will be honoured. There is no representation that the cheque will be honoured, because that is not a proposition of existing fact. But there is usually an implied representation that the circumstances are such that in the ordinary course of events the cheque can be expected to be honoured on first presentation[57] (or, in the case of a post-dated cheque, on presentation on or after the date shown).[58] **4–039**

The traditional wording alleges a representation that the cheque is a "good and valid order" for the amount for which it is drawn. If this means simply that the cheque can be expected to be honoured, it is unobjectionable shorthand. But a cheque is *valid* if it satisfies the requirements of the **4–040**

[54] Above, para.3–004.

[55] See below, para.4–178.

[56] This assumes that "representation" is to be understood in its civil law sense, i.e. as not requiring an *assertion*: see above, para.4–008.

[57] *Hazelton* (1874) L.R. 2 C.C.R. 134; *Page* [1971] 2 Q.B. 330; *Charles* [1977] A.C. 177; *Gilmartin* [1983] Q.B. 953. There is no representation that there are sufficient funds in the account to cover the cheque, since it would not normally be reasonable for the payee to infer that that is true: *Hazelton* (1874) L.R. 2 C.C.R. 134; *Page* [1971] 2 Q.B. 330. The drawer may have an overdraft facility, or he may have reason to expect that he will be allowed to overdraw, or that sufficient funds will be paid into the account before the cheque is presented. Nor is there a representation that the drawer has the bank's authority to draw a cheque on it for the amount in question, because the customer is not the bank's agent for this purpose and does not need its authority to draw cheques on it. It is the bank that needs his authority to honour them: *Charles* [1977] A.C. 177 at 182, *per* Lord Diplock.

[58] *Gilmartin* [1983] Q.B. 953.

Bills of Exchange Act, even if it has no *value* because there is no prospect of its being honoured. The expression "a good and valid order" is too ambiguous to be used without risk of misunderstanding. To avoid confusion, an indictment should spell out the precise representation alleged.

4–041 There is also a more specific representation that the drawer has an account at the bank on which the cheque is drawn.[59] If this is false then the circumstances are plainly *not* such that the cheque can be expected to be honoured, but it may be simpler to rely on the more specific representation if it is false. There will seldom be any difficulty in proving that the defendant knew he had no account at that bank, unless he used to have an account there and it is not clear whether he knew that it had been closed.[60]

Exploiting an unconscious assumption

4–042 There may be an implied representation even if it does not occur to the victim to consider whether the representation is true or false, and he might be surprised to learn that he is relying on a representation at all. He may simply be lulled into a false sense of security, in which he assumes that everything is as it should be. Thus there will usually be a false representation where a person presents a money order or cheque which is not made out to him as if it were,[61] or purports to sell goods which he has no right to sell,[62] or sells his own goods as if they were his employer's.[63] It is immaterial that the other party to the transaction may not have been consciously aware that any such representation had been made.[64]

4–043 This approach makes it possible to regard almost anything done with dishonest intent as carrying an implied false representation, if the intended victim is aware that the thing is being done at all. In *Williams (Jean-Jacques)*[65] a schoolboy bought obsolete Jugoslavian banknotes which were worthless except as collectors' items. He took them to a bureau de change and said to the cashier either "Will you change these notes?" or "Can I cash these in?" The cashier paid him over £100 for notes which had cost him only £7. The Court of Appeal upheld a conviction of theft,[66] and criticised the recorder's ruling that there was no evidence of a false representation. By his words and conduct the defendant impliedly represented that he believed the notes to be valid currency in Jugoslavia.

[59] *Jackson* (1813) 3 Camp. 370; *Parker* (1837) 2 Mood. 1; *Maytum-White* (1957) 42 Cr.App.R. 165; *Page* [1971] 2 Q.B. 330.

[60] *Walne* (1870) 11 Cox C.C. 647; cf. *Cosnett* (1901) 65 J.P. 472.

[61] *Story* (1805) Russ. & Ry. 81; *Davies* [1982] 1 All E.R. 513.

[62] *Sampon* (1885) 52 L.T. 772.

[63] *Rashid* [1977] 1 W.L.R. 298; *Doukas* [1978] 1 W.L.R. 372.

[64] A.T.H. Smith, "The Idea of Criminal Deception" [1982] Crim. L.R. 721 at 723.

[65] [1980] Crim. L.R. 589.

[66] In the light of *Hinks* [2001] 2 A.C. 241 (below, para.9–125) it would seem that the cashier's consent to the defendant's taking of the £100 did not prevent that taking from being an appropriation for the purposes of the theft charge, even if the bureau de change had no grounds for rescinding the transaction. But it may still be arguable that, if there were no grounds for rescinding the transaction, the defendant's acceptance of the £100 in pursuance of that transaction could not be dishonest: above, paras 2–032 *et seq*.

It is submitted that the recorder was right. A person offering to sell something to a dealer does not represent that he believes the thing to be of a particular type merely because he knows that the dealer does not knowingly deal in things of other types: *caveat emptor*.[67] Williams merely took advantage of the cashier's incompetence, by omitting to point out that he knew the notes were worthless. He was under no legal duty to point this out, and therefore would not be guilty of fraud by failing to disclose information under FA 2006, s.3. But it seems that he would be guilty of fraud by false representation under s.2. **4–044**

In *Thompson*[68] the defendant programmed the computer of a bank in Kuwait to credit his accounts with sums to which he was not entitled. He then came to England and wrote to the bank requesting it to transfer these funds to his accounts in England. It was held that he had procured the transfer by deception. The "only proper construction" to be put on his letters was that they contained the implied representations alleged, namely that the sums were genuine and accurate credits and that he was entitled to receive payment of those sums. The letters are not quoted in the judgment, so the court must have thought that their precise terms were immaterial. Apparently the request for the transfer *in itself* carried an implied representation that Thompson was entitled to the funds. Again the conclusion is questionable. If the bank staff assumed that he was entitled to the funds, this was presumably because the bank's records said so, not because he asked for the transfer. **4–045**

Similarly, in *Hamilton* the defendant paid forged cheques into bank accounts and withdrew cash. The false representation alleged was that the balance in the account was a genuine credit balance and he was entitled to withdraw the sum in question. It was held that this representation could be inferred. **4–046**

> "By identifying the account he represented that he was the person to whom the bank was indebted in respect of that account, and by demanding withdrawal of a stated amount he necessarily represented in our view that the bank was indebted in that amount to him . . ."[69]

But the cashiers presumably paid him the money because their records said that he was entitled to it. Had the records not said so, the cashiers would not have paid it merely because *he* said so. Since they would not have relied on a representation to that effect if it had been express, it is difficult to see why it should be implied.[70]

[67] *Smith v Hughes* (1871) L.R. 6 Q.B. 597.
[68] [1984] 1 W.L.R. 962.
[69] (1990) 92 Cr.App.R. 54 at 59.
[70] The judgment went on: "We think it is worth noting that any implied representation by the customer is concerned with the actual state of his account with the bank as he considers it to be, and not with the state of the bank's records of the account at the time." This is puzzling for two reasons. First, the representation alleged was that the balance *was* genuine—that is, that the bank's records reflected the true position—not that the defendant *believed* it to be genuine. His knowledge that it was not genuine was a matter of mens rea, not actus reus. Secondly, it is not clear why the cashier should be assumed to be interested whether the customer thinks the bank's records are correct. But see below, para.4–176.

4–047 *Greenstein*[71] concerned a variation on the practice of stagging (applying for new issues of shares with the intention of immediately selling at a profit). Knowing that the issues would probably be oversubscribed and that the shares would be allotted in proportion to the number applied for by each applicant, the defendants applied for shares far in excess of the number for which they could pay. With each application they enclosed a cheque for the full amount. The issuing house sent a "return" cheque for the difference between that amount and the price of the shares allotted. The return cheque was generally cleared in time for the original cheque to be honoured on first presentation. Convictions of obtaining property by deception were upheld. The representation normally implied in the drawing of a cheque, namely that the cheque could be expected to be honoured on first presentation,[72] was true. Nearly 90 per cent of the cheques were so honoured. However, they were not "valid orders" because they could not be honoured unless the return cheques were cleared first. The court's reasoning emphasises that the defendants did not have the bank's authority to write the cheques, but this is now revealed as a bad point.[73] And it is difficult to see how a cheque with a 90 per cent chance of being honoured on first presentation can be said not to be a "valid order". Applicants could have been required to give an express representation that they expected their cheques to be honoured even if they were allotted all the shares for which they were applying. But no such representation was requested, and it is submitted that there was no basis for inferring one.

4–048 In *Norris v Government of the USA*[74] it was held that a secret agreement to fix prices could be a conspiracy to defraud. This conclusion could have been reached on the ground that it is possible to defraud without making false representations.[75] But Auld L.J. (with whom Field J. agreed) cited with approval an article which argued that

> "in many situations today third parties who deal with undertakings that are in fact parties to cartel agreements will proceed on the *assumption* that they are dealing with undertakings that are lawfully engaged in normal competition with each other; and the cartelists will know that that is so and will, in effect act in a dishonest and therefore criminal manner, if the existence of the cartel is kept secret. They will then be dishonestly taking advantage of third parties' mistaken assumption that they are dealing with undertakings that are engaged in lawful competition with each other."[76]

On this basis the alleged agreement was treated as intended

> "financially to prejudice the conspirators' customers by dishonestly deceiving them into paying higher prices than they otherwise would have done for the

[71] [1975] 1 W.L.R. 1353.
[72] See above, para.4–039.
[73] See above, fn.57.
[74] [2007] EWHC 71.
[75] *Scott v Metropolitan Police Commissioner* [1975] A.C. 819; below, para.7–012.
[76] Sir Jeremy Lever Q.C. and John Pike, "Cartel Agreements, Criminal Conspiracy and the Statutory Cartel Offence" (2005) 26 E.C.L.R. vol.2 at 70–77, vol.3 at 164–172.

> conspirators' products, the vehicle for the deceit being the cloak of secrecy under which they agreed and sought to maintain to conceal the agreement".[77]

It seems to follow that the operation of a dishonest price-fixing agreement is not only a conspiracy to defraud (and an offence under the Enterprise Act 2002, s.188)[78] but also fraud by false representation.

4–049 Cases such as these suggest that, where a person's intentions are dishonest, *any* dealings by that person with the target of his intended dishonesty are likely to be regarded as carrying an implied misrepresentation, if only as to his own state of mind. It is questionable whether the criminal courts' readiness to let juries find such representations is an accurate reflection of the civil law.

Non-disclosure

4–050 Failing to disclose a fact is not, without more, a representation that the fact does not exist. FA 2006, s.3 therefore provides for a separate form of the fraud offence, consisting in failure to disclose information which there is a legal duty to disclose.[79] But non-disclosure can in some circumstances count as a false representation. This may be because the defendant's positive conduct is such as to give a particular impression unless he fails to correct it.[80] As we have just seen, a person who deals with another and fails to disclose that his intentions are dishonest is likely to be regarded (in effect) as representing that they are honest. This may be so even if he is under no legal duty to disclose the truth. So he may be guilty under FA 2006, s.2 though not under s.3. This is a potential trap for prosecutors. Where the defendant behaved as if the facts were otherwise than he knew them to be, and the alleged victim was aware of that behaviour, and there is any risk that the prosecution may fail to establish a legal duty to disclose, it may be prudent to include an allegation that that behaviour amounted to fraud by virtue of s.2.

4–051 Moreover, in certain circumstances non-disclosure may count as false representation even if unaccompanied by positive conduct.

Breach of duty to disclose

4–052 Where there is a legal duty to disclose, a deliberate failure to disclose may for some purposes[81] be regarded as a fraudulent misrepresentation. Lord Blackburn said in *Brownlie v Campbell*:

> "[W]here there is a duty or an obligation to speak, and a man in breach of that duty or obligation holds his tongue and does not speak, and does not say the

[77] [2007] EWHC 71 at [68], *per* Auld L.J.
[78] Below, Ch.20.
[79] See below, Ch.5.
[80] e.g. *Firth* (1990) 91 Cr.App.R. 217; below, para.5–020.
[81] Though not those of the tort of deceit: *Banque Keyser Ullmann SA v Skandia (UK) Insurance Co Ltd* [1990] 1 Q.B. 665 at 777–781, CA; [1991] 2 A.C. 249 at 280, *per* Lord Templeman, and at 281, *per* Lord Jauncey of Tullichettle.

> thing he was bound to say, if that was done with the intention of inducing the other party to act upon the belief that the reason why he did not speak was because he had nothing to say, I should be inclined myself to hold that that was fraud also."[82]

This appears to be true not only of a duty to disclose in the strict sense, where non-disclosure is a legal wrong per se, but also where breach of the "duty" is remediable only by rescission of a contract or other transaction.[83] The point is academic as far as fraud by false representation is concerned, because such a case will fall within FA 2006, s.3 anyway; but it might arise if the prosecution rashly chooses to rely only on s.2. It might also arise in a case brought under the old law. Non-disclosure in breach of a duty to disclose (in either sense) can probably amount to deception.

Failure to correct a previous representation

4–053 Where a person enters into a contract in reliance on a representation which was true (or believed to be true) when made, but which the representor knows to be false by the time the contract is made, the representor is liable for fraudulent misrepresentation.[84] In *DPP v Ray*[85] a majority of the House of Lords similarly held that a diner in a restaurant had deceived the waiter by continuing to sit at his table after deciding to leave without paying the bill. The prosecution put its case in two ways. The first was that a person who makes a representation which later becomes false, or turns out to have been false all along, has a duty to correct it.[86] By entering the restaurant and ordering a meal the defendant represented that he intended to pay. When this ceased to be true, it was his duty to say so, and his failure to say so was a deception. The second argument was that, by remaining at the table and maintaining the demeanour of an honest customer who intended to pay, he was guilty of a positive misrepresentation. Of the majority, Lords Morris and Pearson appeared to accept the second argument, and Lord MacDermott the first.[87] Under the law of deception there may have been no practical difference between the two. Under the new law, the first argument would suggest that the case is one of fraud by failing to disclose information under FA 2006, s.3, and the second that it is fraud by false representation under s.2.[88]

[82] (1880) 5 App. Cas. 925 at 950.

[83] *Banque Keyser Ullmann SA v Skandia (UK) Insurance Co Ltd* [1990] 1 Q.B. 665 at 773–774, 782–783, CA; *HIH Casualty and General Insurance Ltd v Chase Manhattan Bank* [2003] UKHL 6; [2003] 1 All E.R. (Comm.) 349 at [21], *per* Lord Bingham.

[84] *With v O'Flanagan* [1936] 1 Ch. 575; *Spice Girls Ltd v Aprilia World Service BV* [2002] EWCA Civ 15; [2002] E.M.L.R. 27 at [51].

[85] [1974] A.C. 370.

[86] cf. *Traill v Baring* (1864) 4 De G.J. & Sm. 318; *With v O'Flanagan* [1936] Ch. 575 at 583, *per* Lord Wright M.R.

[87] But Lord Hodson, who dissented, appears to have thought that the majority were accepting the prosecution's first argument.

[88] But Ray would probably be charged today with making off without payment: TA 1978, s.3.

In *Rai* the defendant secured a local authority grant to install a downstairs bathroom in his house for his elderly mother. Two days later, his mother died. He did not inform the local authority, and the work was done. A conviction of obtaining services by deception was upheld. 4–054

> "The learned judge held, . . . in his ruling, that by simply sitting there doing nothing and allowing the work to be done, the appellant was committing a straightforward deception, because, as he was aware, the local authority were still of the mind that the mother would occupy the premises. He was living there at all material times. In the judgment of this Court, that, against the background of it being his home and he having made the application, was conduct sufficient to amount to conduct within the terms of section 15(4) of the 1968 Act. . . . [O]n a common-sense and purposive construction of the word 'conduct', it does, in our judgment, cover positive acquiescence in knowingly letting this work proceed as the appellant did in the present case."[89]

This suggests that the defendant was guilty of positive representation (and would today be guilty of fraud by virtue of s.2) rather than mere non-disclosure. But it is not clear why the court attached any significance to his conduct in continuing to occupy the house. The reason why the local authority thought his mother was still alive was not that he was still living there, but that he had not told them she was dead.

Representations to which the representee is indifferent

Under the old law of deception, difficulties arose in cases where it was immaterial to the putative representee whether the proposition supposedly represented by the defendant was true or false. These difficulties do not arise in quite the same form under the new law, because there is no requirement that the victim be *deceived* at all: it is sufficient that a false representation is made. Indeed, this was the main reason given by the Law Commission for framing the offence in terms of false representation rather than deception.[90] But the Commission's solution does not avoid the difficulty. Indeed it arguably makes it worse. 4–055

The difficulty arises mainly in cases where a purchaser of goods or services authorises their provider (the "merchant") to charge the price to an account. Suppose first that he pays by cheque. If the merchant accepts the cheque without insisting that it be backed by a cheque guarantee card, he does so in reliance on the purchaser's implied representation that it is a good cheque (in the sense that it is likely to be honoured). If the cheque is backed by a cheque card, however, the position is quite different. There is still an implied representation that the cheque is good; but this representation is true. By relying on the card, the merchant creates a contract between himself and the bank on which the cheque is drawn, under which the bank is obliged to honour the cheque. Arguably it follows that the drawer of the 4–056

[89] [2000] 1 Cr.App.R. 242 at 246.
[90] Law Com. No.276, para.7.16.

cheque makes no false representation even if he knows that there are insufficient funds in the account, because the bank will have to honour the cheque anyway. He is defrauding the bank, but is not deceiving the merchant.

4–057 In *Charles*[91] this argument was rejected. Charles drew a number of cheques in payment for gaming chips, and backed each one with a cheque card, with the result that his account became overdrawn in a sum far in excess of his agreed limit. The House of Lords dismissed his appeal against a conviction of obtaining the increased overdraft by the implied representation that he was authorised to use the card to back cheques of that amount. It was held to be immaterial that the manager of the gaming club was, as he made clear in his evidence, wholly indifferent to the state of Charles's account. The crucial point was that he would not have accepted the cheques had he *known* that Charles had no authority to back them with the card.

> "[T]he witness [*sc*. the manager] made clear that the accused's cheques were accepted only because he produced a cheque card, and he repeatedly stressed that, had he been aware that the accused was using his cheque book and cheque card 'in a way in which he was not allowed or entitled to use [them]' no cheque would have been accepted. The evidence of that witness, taken as a whole, points irresistibly to the conclusions (a) that by this dishonest conduct the accused deceived [the manager] in the manner averred in the particulars of the charges and (b) that [the manager] was thereby induced to accept the cheques because of his belief that the representations as to both cheque and card were true."[92]

4–058 From the manager's point of view it makes sense to distinguish between the case where he does not know whether the customer has authority to use the card and the case where he knows that the customer has no such authority. In the former case he is legally entitled to payment; in the latter he is not. But it is questionable whether this means that the customer can properly be regarded as representing that he does have authority. The merchant *does not care* whether the customer has authority, as long as the merchant does not know that he does not. The customer is regarded as making an implied representation as to a matter which in itself is of no interest to the representee. This reasoning is very strained.

4–059 In *Lambie*[93] a similar issue arose in relation to the dishonest use of a credit card. The defendant used a credit card to buy goods in a Mothercare shop when she had already exceeded her credit limit, and was charged with obtaining a pecuniary advantage by deception.[94] The manageress gave evidence that she had made no assumption as to the state of the account, and had been concerned only to ensure that Mothercare would be paid. The Court of Appeal quashed the conviction.[95] *Charles* was distinguished

[91] [1977] A.C. 177.
[92] [1977] A.C. 177 at 193, *per* Lord Edmund-Davies.
[93] [1982] A.C. 449.
[94] TA 1968, s.16. The relevant paragraph of s.16(2) was para.(a), which was replaced by TA 1978, ss.1 and 2; but the offence was committed in 1977.
[95] [1981] 1 W.L.R. 78.

on the ground that, where a merchant has made arrangements with a bank for the acceptance of the bank's credit cards, he has bought from the bank the right to sell goods to card-holders without regard to the position as between each customer and the bank. In the case of a cheque card no such arrangements have been made.

The House of Lords restored the conviction. Lord Roskill, with whom the other members of the House agreed, said: **4–060**

> "My Lords, . . . the Court of Appeal . . . laid too much emphasis upon the undoubted, but to my mind irrelevant, fact that [the manageress] said she made no assumption about the respondent's credit standing with the bank. They reasoned from the absence of assumption that there was no evidence from which the jury could conclude that she was 'induced by a false representation that the defendant's credit standing at the bank gave her authority to use the card'. But . . . that is not the relevant question. Following the decision of this House in *R. v Charles*, it is in my view clear that the representation arising from the presentation of a credit card has nothing to do with the respondent's credit standing at the bank but is a representation of actual authority to make the contract with, in this case, Mothercare on the bank's behalf that the bank will honour the voucher upon presentation. Upon that view, the existence and terms of the agreement between the bank and Mothercare are irrelevant, as is the fact that Mothercare, because of that agreement, would look to the bank for payment."[96]

It is hard to see how any valid distinction can be drawn between an assumption as to Lambie's authority to use the card and an assumption as to her credit standing with the bank. Like any other card-holder, she had authority to use the card only as long as she was within her credit limit. The manageress could not make an assumption as to the one and not the other. But the case was on all fours with *Charles*. The manageress did not care whether Lambie had authority to use the card, but presumably[97] would not have accepted it if she had known that Lambie had no such authority. According to *Charles* this is sufficient. So the jury were entitled to find an implied representation that Lambie did have authority. The position is presumably the same if, instead of physically presenting a card bearing details of the account to be charged, the defendant supplies those details by post, by telephone or electronically.[98] Indeed the principle can be stated more generally. Where A obtains something by conferring on B a legal right to be paid by C, he may be regarded as representing that he has C's authority to do this—even if B has no interest in whether that is the case. **4–061**

But the *Charles/Lambie* solution only works on the basis that the merchant, though otherwise uninterested in whether the customer has authority to use the card, would not accept the card if he *knew* that the customer does *not* have such authority. It is apparently permissible to **4–062**

[96] [1982] A.C. 449 at 459–460.

[97] See below, para.4–062.

[98] But there are serious difficulties in treating a communication made to a computer as an implied representation: below, para.4–077.

assume this if there is no evidence on the point. In *Lambie* the manageress had not been asked what she would have done if she had known that the respondent was over her credit limit, but the House of Lords was prepared to assume that she would have refused to accept the card. Where there *is* evidence on the point, however, the case cannot be left to the jury if that evidence precludes the *Charles/Lambie* solution. As the Law Commission pointed out in 1994:

> "Unfortunately shop assistants, and others whose business it is to accept such payments, do not always perceive as clearly as lawyers the distinction between *not knowing whether* the customer has authority to use the instrument and *knowing that he does not*, and will often give evidence that they had no interest in his relationship with the bank and would still have accepted the payment in question had they known the truth. In the face of evidence to this effect a submission of no case ought to succeed."[99]

4–063 Even if a representation of authority could be inferred, under the old law of deception there were further difficulties. The prosecution had to show that the merchant was deceived into believing that the customer had authority, and that it was *by* that deception that the defendant obtained the property or services in question.[100] It was debatable whether either of these things could be true if the merchant did not care whether the customer had authority. FA 2006 is intended to avoid the problem by requiring that a false representation be *made* without also requiring that the representation be *believed*. It fails to achieve this objective, for two reasons.

4–064 First, although the offence does not require that the merchant should actually be deceived, it does require that the false representation be made with intent to make a gain, or to cause a loss or expose another to a risk of loss, *by* making the false representation.[101] The defendant must *think* that, if he gets the property (etc.), it will be at least partly because he pretended to have authority to use the card. The new offence merely moves the causation problem from actus reus to mens rea. Indeed this may make convictions harder to secure. According to *Charles* and *Lambie*, actual causation could be proved by showing that the merchant would not have accepted the card if he had known the truth. That could be assumed to be true if the defence did not raise the issue, and, even if the defence did raise the issue, would in fact be true if the merchant knew what he was doing. But that is no longer enough. It must now be shown that the defendant *knew* or *believed* that the merchant would not accept the card if he knew the truth.

4–065 The Law Commission was unconcerned by this difficulty.

> "The necessary intent will exist only if, at the time of tendering the card, the defendant believed that the retailer would not accept the card (or at any rate thought that the retailer might not accept the card) if the retailer knew that the

[99] *Criminal Law: Conspiracy to Defraud*, Law Com. No.228, HC 11, para.4.38.
[100] See below, paras 4–166 *et seq.*
[101] See above, para.3–004.

defendant was not authorised to use it. In some circumstances the defendant may plausibly, or even truthfully, claim not to have believed this—for instance where he or she has slightly exceeded the credit limit, but does not expect the card issuer to object, and assumes that the retailer would take a similar view but does not think it necessary to ask. We are not especially concerned at the possibility of an acquittal in such circumstances. The case we wish to catch is that in which the defendant has stolen the card, or forged it, or has obtained it legitimately but has been expressly requested to return it to the issuer or to stop using it. In such a case we doubt that many fact-finders would give credence to a claim that the defendant thought the retailer would still have accepted the card even if the retailer had known the truth."[102]

No evidence was cited in support of this prediction. Many people do not realise that the merchant would not be entitled to payment from the issuer if he knew that the customer had no authority to use the card. These people might expect the merchant to accept the card anyway.[103] It may be hard to prove that the defendant was not one of them, even in the kind of case that the Law Commission wanted to catch.

Secondly, the Commission was wrong to assume that it would be easier to establish a representation than a deception. The Commission said: **4–066**

"Since the merchant who accepts the card in payment does not care whether the defendant has authority to use it, it is debatable whether the merchant can be said to be *deceived*. It is clear from *Charles* and *Lambie*, however, that by tendering the card the defendant is impliedly and falsely *representing* that he or she has authority to use it for the transaction in question."[104]

The explanatory notes on FA 2006 similarly state:

"By tendering the card, [the defendant] is falsely representing that he has the authority to use it for that transaction. It is immaterial whether the merchant accepting the card for payment is deceived by the representation."

These statements are simply wrong. As Viscount Dilhorne stressed in *Charles* itself, whether a representation should be inferred in a particular case is a jury question. **4–067**

"The Court of Appeal . . . certified that the following point of law was of general public importance . . . : 'When the holder of a cheque card presents a cheque in accordance with the conditions of the card which is accepted in exchange for goods, services or cash, does this transaction provide evidence of itself from which it can or should be inferred (a) that the drawer represented that he then had authority, as between himself and the bank, to draw a cheque

[102] Law Com. No.276, para.7.57.

[103] In 2001 one of the authors conducted an informal survey at his place of work. Respondents were asked whether they thought a shop assistant would in practice be likely to accept payment by credit card if, in conversation with the customer, the assistant had learned (a) that the customer was over his credit limit, or (b) that the bank had asked him to stop using the card. A large majority of respondents thought that the card would be accepted in case (a), and half thought it would or might be accepted even in case (b).

[104] Law Com. No.276, para.7.16.

> for that amount and (b) that the recipient of the cheque was induced by that representation to accept the cheque?' With respect I do not think that this question was very happily phrased. Whether an inference can be properly drawn is a matter of law; whether it should be drawn is a question of fact for the jury. Whether or not the recipient of a cheque was induced by a representation to accept it, is also a question of fact. It would have been better if the question had been worded as follows: 'When the holder of a cheque card presents a cheque card together with a cheque made out in accordance with the conditions of the card which cheque is accepted in exchange for goods, services or cash, does this transaction provide evidence of itself from which it can be inferred that the drawer represented that he then had authority as between himself and the bank to use the card in order to oblige the bank to honour the cheque?'"[105]

The other members of the House agreed with this speech, and Lord Edmund-Davies expressly preferred Viscount Dilhorne's reformulation of the certified question.[106]

4–068 FA 2006 does not affect the position in this respect. There is no rule of law that the user of a cheque card or credit card is deemed to represent that he has authority to use it. So it is still for the jury to decide whether such a representation should be inferred on the facts of the case. According to *Charles* and *Lambie*, the use of the card is evidence from which a jury may infer that a representation of authority was made. Many judges would encourage the jury to draw that inference. But, if the alleged victim has given evidence that he had no interest in the subject-matter of the alleged representation, a jury may be reluctant to do so. Indeed, because they are likely (unless otherwise directed) to give the word "representation" its ordinary rather than its legal meaning,[107] they may be even more reluctant to infer a representation than they would have been, under the old law, to accept that the merchant was deceived. They might take the view that, even if the merchant thought the customer had authority (and was thus deceived), this was not the result of any *representation* by the customer to that effect.

4–069 In *Nabina*[108] the defendant made false statements in applications for credit cards, and used the cards to buy goods at a number of retail outlets. He was charged with obtaining each item by falsely representing that he was the legitimate holder of the credit card used. The convictions were quashed because the jury had not been directed to consider whether it could be inferred that he had made such representations. But the court also expressed "the gravest possible doubt" about whether any such inference could properly have been drawn. Suppliers of goods were generally concerned to ensure that they would receive payment when a credit card was used; but there was room to doubt whether they were interested in how the holder got the card, provided that the transaction would be honoured.

105 [1977] A.C. 177 at 186–187.
106 [1977] A.C. 177 at 194.
107 See above, para.4–010.
108 [2000] Crim. L.R. 481; see also *Stephen Parish*, [2001] Crim. L.R. 69.

It seems that the card issuers would have had no basis for not honouring the transactions. Indeed, the defendant's authority to use the cards had not even been withdrawn.[109] Formulating the offence in terms of representation rather than deception does nothing to avoid this kind of problem.

While the problem seems so far to have arisen only in the context of cheque cards and credit cards, it raises a fundamental issue: is it ever proper to infer a representation in whose subject matter the alleged representee has no interest? The civil law of misrepresentation provides relief for a person who has acted to his detriment under a mistake of fact which was caused by someone else. He has no remedy unless he relied on the belief he mistakenly held. So, even if the concept of a implied representation which is of no interest to the representee is not a contradiction in terms, the point is academic for the purposes of the civil law: such a representation could never be actionable anyway. It would therefore be remarkable if the concept not only existed in the criminal law but was sufficient for criminal liability. FA 2006 does not determine the point, because it does not explain what constitutes a "representation". Sir John Smith wrote: **4–070**

> "You cannot properly divorce the question of whether there is a representation from the question whether it matters to the 'representee'. The intelligent shopper with a credit card does not represent to the seller that he has authority to use the card because he is aware that the seller does not care whether he has authority to use it or not—he considers it none of the seller's business, as it is not. Why should he represent that, any more than that he is a Roman Catholic or a member of the Conservative party?"[110]

Representations to machines

FA 2006, s.2(5) provides: **4–071**

> "For the purposes of this section a representation may be regarded as made if it (or anything implying it) is submitted in any form to any system or device designed to receive, convey or respond to communications (with or without human intervention)."

Since deception means inducing a human being to believe a proposition which is untrue, deception of a computer or other machine[111] was a logical impossibility under the old law.[112] For example, since VAT returns are processed by computer, the submission of false returns does not involve an intent to deceive.[113] The problem does not arise if the fraud depends on the **4–072**

[109] So, even if he did represent that he was the "legitimate holder" of the cards, in a sense that was true. He was the legitimate holder unless and until the issuers chose to cancel his authority.

[110] Letter to the Law Commission, May 3, 2000.

[111] "Machine" is here used to mean any inanimate object designed to perform a function, including an electronic device such as a computer.

[112] *Davies v Flackett* [1973] R.T.R. 8; *Re Holmes* [2004] EWHC 2020; [2005] Crim. L.R. 229.

[113] *Moritz* June 17–19, 1981, Acton CC. But see now Value Added Tax Act 1994, s.72(6): below, para.16–009.

generation of false output which will then be acted upon by a person, because that person will be deceived. But if the desired outcome follows automatically and without human intervention, there is no deception. FA 2006, s.2(5) seeks to avoid this difficulty.

4–073 Section 2(5) did not appear in the Law Commission's draft Bill. The Commission reasoned that, since the obtaining of *property* by "deceiving" a machine is theft,[114] there was a lacuna only where the "deception" of the machine results in the obtaining of services; and that case was more analogous to theft than to deception.

> "[W]here a person dishonestly obtains a service by giving false information to a machine, the gravamen of that person's conduct is not the provision of the false information but the taking of a valuable benefit without paying for it.
>
> Suppose, for example, that an internet website offers valuable information to subscribers, who are supposed to gain access to the information by giving their password. If a non-subscriber dishonestly downloads the information, it hardly matters whether she does so by giving the password of a genuine subscriber (and thus impliedly representing herself to be that subscriber) or by somehow bypassing the password screen altogether. To distinguish between these two situations would be like distinguishing between the person who puts a foreign coin into a vending machine and the one who gets at the contents by opening up the machine with a screwdriver, on the basis that the former makes a 'misrepresentation' to the machine (that the coin is legal tender) whereas the latter does not. This would be absurd. Both are guilty of stealing the contents. Equally, in our view, a person who 'steals' a service should be guilty of an offence, whether it is obtained by providing false information or in any other way."[115]

4–074 The Commission therefore recommended the new offence of obtaining services dishonestly, which is created by FA 2006, s.11.[116] In the Commission's view this made it unnecessary to define the fraud offence in such a way as to catch misrepresentations made to machines. Dishonestly obtaining services from a machine would fall within what is now s.11, and dishonestly obtaining property was already theft. The Commission thought it arguable that some such cases might fall within the fraud offence too, but regarded this possibility as "somewhat academic" since it expected prosecutors to charge such cases as theft or dishonestly obtaining services anyway.[117]

4–075 Section 2(5) was inserted into the Bill at Report stage in the House of Lords. Introducing the amendment, the Attorney-General explained:

> "The Clause 11 offence should indeed be used in cases where services have been dishonestly obtained, but on one reading of Clause 2 as it stands, the

[114] e.g. *Goodwin* [1996] Crim. L.R. 262, where the defendant played gaming machines using foreign coins of the same size, shape and weight as the UK coins required. It was held that he would be guilty of stealing any coins that he might win.

[115] Law Com. No.276, paras 8.4, 8.5.

[116] Below, Ch.10.

[117] Law Com. No.276, para 8.2, fn.5.

prosecution might need to rely on a charge of theft where property has been obtained by inputting data into a machine. We consider that it would be undesirable to differentiate between cases where property is obtained fraudulently by a representation made to a machine, which in practice operates on behalf of a person, and where the representation is made directly to a person. For example, we see no need to distinguish between a credit or debit card tendered to a machine and cases where the card is tendered to a person. Indeed, in many everyday situations it is a combination of the two and, increasingly, the sales assistant takes a back seat while the customer inputs the PIN into the card machine.

The Law Commission said that its new offence would apply even if the person to whom the card is tendered is indifferent as to whether the representation to him is false, but it may not always be clear in such cases whether the representation is actually made to an indifferent sales assistant or simply to the machine. For example, on occasions the sales assistant may not even look at the card as the card owner himself inserts the card into the machine and enters the PIN. The practical difference between a person misusing a credit card before a sales assistant indifferent as to whether a representation is false and a representation being made without the presence of any assistants seems to us to be negligible.

We do not want law enforcers to face unreasonably technical choices in making charges and we consider therefore that the Bill should make it clear that a false representation should be an offence whether made to a machine or to a person. This is done by making amendments to provide expressly that representations may be implied and that a representation may be regarded as being made where it or anything implying it is submitted to any system or device, the aim being to clarify, for example, that the entering of a number into a chip-and-pin machine is a representation."[118]

The amendment was not opposed and there was no further debate on it.

The intention seems to be that dishonestly providing any input into a computer or similar device[119] in order to obtain property or services should be fraud. Such conduct will normally be attempted theft or an attempt to obtain services dishonestly, but it might be neither. It might be merely preparatory to the appropriation of the property or the obtaining of the services. It might be an attempt to obtain property with no intention permanently to deprive, or to obtain a service which falls outside FA 2006, s.11 because it is not made available on the basis that it is to be paid for. Prosecutors may be tempted to avoid such problems by charging *all* such conduct as fraud. They would be well advised to resist this temptation. FA 2006, s.2(5) does not say that dishonestly providing input into a computer is a false representation. It says (in effect) that the offence includes the making of a false representation to a computer. The prosecution must still **4–076**

[118] *Hansard*, HL Vol.679, col.1108 (March 14, 2006).

[119] The subsection applies only to systems and devices designed to receive, convey or respond to communications, not to machines generally. The insertion of a foreign coin into a gaming machine, for example (cf. *Goodwin* [1996] Crim. L.R. 262, above, fn.114), is probably not fraud because a gaming machine is not such a system or device. But even this may be debatable: when the player presses a button on the machine, is that not a communication of his decision, to which the machine is designed to respond? Frauds on gaming machines committed on or after September 1, 2007 can instead be charged under the Gambling Act 2005, s.42: below, paras 18–007 *et seq*.

prove either that the input was itself a false representation or that it implied one.[120]

4–077 There is relatively little difficulty where the input amounts to an express representation, such as information contained in an online application form. Implied representations are another matter. A person's conduct carries an implied representation if it is reasonable for another person to infer from it that a particular proposition is true, and to rely on that inference. How is this to be adapted where the putative representee is a computer? A computer infers nothing: it merely does what it is programmed to do. Suppose a person orders goods from a website, and gives the details of a credit card account which he is not authorised to use. Is this an implied representation to the computer that he is authorised to use that account? According to *Lambie*, a customer who presents a credit card to a sales assistant can be regarded as representing to the assistant that he is authorised to charge the card with the amount in question. This can be done on the basis that the assistant would not accept the card if he knew that the customer had no authority to use it. This reasoning is dubious even in the case of a human assistant; in the case of a computer it simply does not work. It is meaningless even to ask what the computer would do if it "knew" that the customer was not authorised to use the card.

4–078 The Attorney-General's explanation implies that there is some further representation to the computer which is implicit in the input of the PIN. But it is not clear what the content of this further representation might be,[121] or why it should be inferred that the customer is making it. The input of the PIN is merely a demonstration by the customer that he has information which he would be unlikely to have if he were not the authorised holder of the card (or someone trusted by the authorised holder). Suppose there were no machine, and the customer had to disclose the PIN to the assistant, who had to telephone the card issuer for confirmation that the PIN disclosed was the right one. In that case it would be clear that the *Lambie* analysis applies. If any representation is made, it is made to the assistant, and is to the effect that the customer is authorised to use the card. It makes no difference that the customer inputs the PIN directly. The effect is the same. The input of the PIN adds nothing. If an assistant is involved, the prosecution should rely on a *Lambie* representation to the assistant rather than some fictitious representation to the card machine. If no assistant is involved, there is no basis for inferring any representation at all.

4–079 The courts normally try to interpret obscure provisions in the light of their apparent rationale. But the rationale of FA 2006, s.2(5) is as obscure

[120] Since a representation may be express or implied, it might be said that there are actually three cases: submission of an express representation, submission of an implied representation, and submission of something implying a representation. But there seems to be no practical difference between the second and third.

[121] It might perhaps be said that the input of the PIN implies a representation that the customer is the person to whom the PIN was issued. But this would add nothing to the representation that he is the person to whom the *card* was issued.

as its drafting. The Government wanted to ensure that the fraud offence would apply to false representations made to computers, but seems to have had no clear idea what principle distinguishes a false representation made to a computer from any other way of getting the computer to respond in the manner desired. Where a bank's computer is programmed to transfer funds in response to certain input, it seems to be intended that a person who provides the necessary input should be guilty of the offence if the input is false. But if he simply hacks into the computer and gets it to transfer the funds without requiring the usual input, he may make no representation at all. It is not clear why the former should be fraud when the latter is not.[122] As the Law Commission pointed out, this is like drawing a distinction between inserting a foreign coin into a vending machine and getting at the contents with a screwdriver. It is debatable whether the law ought to distinguish between misleading a person into handing over his property and simply helping oneself to it; but at least there is a real difference between the two cases which is arguably significant, namely the difference between impaired consent and a complete absence of consent. There is no such significance in the difference between providing false input to a computer and manipulating the computer in other ways. A computer cannot give consent at all, whether real or impaired. *Anything* obtained from a computer is obtained without its consent. FA 2006, s.2(5) is misconceived, and is likely to cause great difficulty.

MUST THE REPRESENTATION BE COMMUNICATED?

If D posts a letter or sends an email containing false statements, but the communication never arrives, has he made a false representation within the meaning of FA 2006, s.2? The question cannot be answered by reference to the civil law, because in the civil law the mere making of a misrepresentation is not sufficient for liability. There is no liability unless the misrepresentation is relied upon, and it cannot be relied upon if it has not been made.[123] **4–080**

In *Treacy* it was held that the defendant had "made" a demand with menaces, within the meaning of TA 1968, s.21, by posting a blackmailing letter. It was immaterial whether the letter arrived. But Lord Hodson, with whom Lord Guest agreed, was influenced by the fact that the defendant's conduct (in posting the letter from England to Germany) would have fallen within the offence under the Larceny Act 1916 that blackmail replaced. He thought it unlikely that Parliament would have intended to take such conduct outside the scope of the offence. **4–081**

In the case of fraud by false representation, however, the position is the other way round. The old deception offences were committed only if the false representation came to the attention of the representee[124] and was **4–082**

[122] The latter is theft, as well as an offence under the Computer Misuse Act 1990.

[123] See above, para.4–011.

[124] Though he did not have to realise that what he knew to be happening was in fact a representation: above, paras 4–042 *et seq.*

believed and relied upon. The new offence can be committed if the false representation is received but is not believed, or is received and believed but is not relied upon. The courts may be reluctant to accept that Parliament intended to go even further, and to include the *sending* of a false representation which does not arrive. It is submitted that this is an attempt only.

MULTIPLE REPRESENTATIONS

4–083 Under the old law, an obtaining of property (etc.) was a single offence even if it resulted from a number of deceptions.[125] Under the new law, each false representation is a separate offence. Unless an exception to the rule against duplicity applies,[126] each representation therefore needs a count to itself. This may sometimes create practical difficulties.[127]

FALSITY

4–084 FA 2006, s.2(2) provides:

> "A representation is false if—
>
> (a) it is untrue or misleading, and
>
> (b) the person making it knows that it is, or might be, untrue or misleading."

This is confusing. One would expect that a representation would be false if the proposition represented to be true is in fact false. But, under s.2(2), a representation of a false proposition is not a "false" representation within the meaning of the Act if the person making it *believes* that the proposition is true (and that the representation is not misleading). The requirement of falsity is partly actus reus and partly mens rea.

UNTRUE OR MISLEADING

UNTRUE

4–085 A representation is untrue if the proposition represented is untrue. If the only representation alleged is true (and is not misleading), the offence is

[125] For the need to prove at least one of the alleged deceptions, see below, para.4–196.

[126] e.g. Criminal Procedure Rules 2005, r.14.2(2): below, para.25–003.

[127] For some possible solutions, see Ch.25. Despite examining the problem of multiple offences alongside the new fraud offence, the Law Commission does not appear to have considered this effect of its decision that the offence should be complete when the false representation is made.

not committed, even if the defendant thinks that it is untrue. In *Patel*[128] the defendant stated in a job application form that she had never been convicted of an offence. In fact she had once been given a conditional discharge for shoplifting; but that was deemed by statute not to be a conviction,[129] so the representation was technically true. The defendant did not claim to have had that rule in mind when she filled in the form, but this was immaterial. The possibility that she might be convicted of an attempt, on the basis that she *would* have been making a false representation if the position had been as she believed it to be,[130] was not discussed; but such a conviction was arguably impossible because her mistake was one of law.

The prosecution must prove that the representation is untrue, even if, **4–086** were it true, it would be easy for the defence to prove it. In *Ng*[131] the defendant attempted to obtain money by claiming that she was in a position to influence a magistrate before whom the victim was due to appear. It was held to be for the prosecution to prove that she was not in such a position, not for the defence to prove that she was.

In the absence of any evidence that the representation is true, however, **4–087** relatively slight evidence may be enough to prove that it is false. In *Mandry*[132] street traders sold scent at £1 for four bottles, claiming that it was on sale in the shops at two guineas a bottle. A police officer gave evidence that he had visited four local shops and that the scent was not on sale in any of them. In cross-examination he was asked whether he had been to Selfridges. He admitted that he had not. The jury were directed that this did not affect the prosecution's case because it was up to the defence to prove that the scent *was* on sale at Selfridges, and they had adduced no evidence to that effect. On appeal it was held that it was for the prosecution to disprove the statement, not for the defence to prove it; but the appeals were dismissed because, in the absence of any evidence that the statement was true, there was ample evidence that it was false.

MISLEADING

According to FA 2006, s.2(2) a representation is also "false" if, though **4–088** true, it is misleading. There seems to be some confusion here. Deliberately to mislead another is to deceive him—that is, to cause him to believe in the truth of a proposition which is false. This can be done by representing to him that the proposition is true. But in that case the representation is not merely misleading: it is untrue.

The words "or misleading" may perhaps be intended to catch express **4–089** representations which are literally true but are designed to give a false impression about a matter not expressly stated. So, where a person states

128 [2006] EWCA Crim 2689; [2007] 1 Cr.App.R. 12 (p.191); cf. *Deller* (1952) 36 Cr.App.R. 184.
129 Powers of Criminal Courts (Sentencing) Act 2000, s.14(1).
130 Criminal Attempts Act 1981, s.1(2), (3).
131 [1958] A.C. 173.
132 [1973] 1 W.L.R. 1232.

that *x* is true, that representation is "false" not only if *x* is untrue but also if the representation implies that *y* is true, and *y* is in fact untrue. But in that case there is an implied representation of *y*, and *that* representation is untrue. There is no need to say that the express representation of *x* is "misleading". If that were necessary, the Act would need to say that the offence can be committed by any *conduct* which is misleading, not just by making a *representation* which is false or misleading. It is submitted that the words "or misleading" add nothing.

KNOWLEDGE THAT REPRESENTATION IS OR MIGHT BE UNTRUE

4–090 Even if a representation is untrue, it is not "false" within the meaning of FA 2006 unless the person making it *knows* that it is or might be untrue.[133] This requirement roughly corresponds to the old rule that a deception must be "deliberate or reckless".[134] Like that rule, it is distinct from the element of dishonesty.[135] It is not necessarily dishonest to make a representation which one knows to be untrue, or (especially) a representation which one merely suspects may be untrue.[136]

4–091 The new wording is potentially wider than the old. The maker of a representation knows that it might be untrue if he is aware of a risk that it might be untrue. He is not *reckless* whether it is untrue unless he is aware of such a risk[137] *and*, in view of the risk as he perceives it, it is unreasonable (i.e. negligent) for him to make the representation. In debate on the Fraud Bill, Lord Kingsland pointed out that the clause was wide enough to catch a person who takes a reasonable risk.

> "[A] person selling a painting may genuinely believe that the painting is an original Renoir. There may be every reason to believe that the painting is by Renoir—for instance, the painting may have been continuously owned by a family who originally purchased it from Renoir, and an expert may have examined it and confirmed it to be a Renoir. However, no matter how strong the reasons for concluding that the painting is genuine, ordinary human experience tells us that in a situation such as this there is always some possibility, however remote, that the painting is not genuine.
>
> On the present wording of Clause 2, it would seem that the seller of the painting would make a false representation within the meaning of Clause 2 if he said, 'This is a painting by Renoir' rather than saying, 'I honestly believe that this is a painting by Renoir'."[138]

[133] Or that the representation is or might be misleading; but it is submitted that this adds nothing. See above, para.4–088.

[134] TA 1968, s.15(4).

[135] See above, Ch.2.

[136] See above, para.2–016.

[137] The "objective" form of recklessness deriving from *Caldwell* [1982] A.C. 341 did not apply to deception even before *Caldwell* was overruled in *G.* [2003] UKHL 50; [2004] 1 A.C. 1034, because a person's making of a representation cannot be dishonest if he is unaware that there is even a risk it may be untrue: *Goldman* [1997] Crim. L.R. 894.

[138] *Hansard*, HL Vol.673, cols 1421–1422 (July 19, 2005).

Depending on the circumstances, the statement "This is a painting by Renoir" might in fact be intended to be understood *only* as a representation that the maker honestly believes the painting to be by Renoir.[139] Assuming that the statement is intended to be understood literally, however, Lord Kingsland's analysis would seem to be technically correct. The honest seller is not *reckless* whether his statement is untrue because, in the circumstances as he understands them to be, the risk of its being untrue is outweighed by the inconvenience of having to include a pointless caveat to the effect that it might conceivably be untrue. Under FA 2006 there is no requirement of recklessness, so the fact that the risk is negligible does not prevent the representation from being "false" within the meaning of s.2. But it seems inconceivable that a jury might find it dishonest to take a risk which was so small that it was reasonable to take it. **4–092**

DECEPTION: THE OLD LAW

The remainder of this chapter is *directly* concerned only with the old law of deception (though the discussion of causation in the old law is indirectly relevant to the requirement under the new law that the defendant intend to make a gain, or to cause a loss or expose another to a risk of loss, *by* making the representation).[140] The old law applies to offences completed before January 15, 2007, and cases in which there is a deception before that date but the offence under the old law is not completed until later.[141] **4–093**

THE DECEPTION OFFENCES

Under the old law, dishonest deception was not an offence in itself. It became an offence only if it resulted in **4–094**

- the obtaining of property;
- the obtaining of a money transfer;
- the obtaining of services;
- the evasion of liability;

[139] Lord Goodhart pointed out that if a picture is described by an auction house as being by Renoir, it means (or at any rate used to mean) that it might be by Renoir; if it is described as being by Auguste Renoir, it means that it really is by Renoir. The Attorney-General explained that "if they use a description which is understood by people to mean 'It might be; provenance uncertain', then they will not have been dishonest in making that statement. If, on the other hand, the provenance is uncertain and they use the expression 'Auguste Renoir' knowing that people would take that to mean it was in fact by Renoir, that is fraud if they are dishonest": *Hansard*, HL Vol.673, col.1422 (July 19, 2005).

[140] See above, para.3–004.

[141] See above, para.1–006.

- the obtaining of a pecuniary advantage; or
- the execution of a valuable security.

But the definitions of some of these expressions diverged widely from their ordinary meanings, being wider in some cases and narrower in others.

OBTAINING PROPERTY

4–095 Under TA 1968, s.15(1), an offence was committed by a person who "by any deception dishonestly obtains property belonging to another, with the intention of permanently depriving the other of it". The offence was triable either way,[142] and was punishable on conviction on indictment with 10 years' imprisonment.[143]

4–096 In view of the House of Lords' decision in *Gomez*[144] that the consent of the property's owner does not negative the element of appropriation in theft (at any rate where that consent is secured by deception),[145] almost every instance of the offence under s.15 was also theft. Many of the difficulties raised by the section could be avoided if theft was charged instead.

"Property"

4–097 "Property" is defined by TA 1968, s.4(1) for the purposes of theft, and that definition also applied for the purposes of s.15:[146]

> "'Property' includes money and all other property, real or personal, including things in action and other intangible property."

This provision is discussed in the context of theft.[147] Its application to s.15 meant that the offence could be committed by obtaining anything that qualifies as property, whether tangible or otherwise. Corporeal land cannot generally be the subject of theft,[148] but this rule did not apply to s.15.

Belonging to another

4–098 The property obtained by deception had to belong to someone other than the defendant. TA 1968, s.5(1), which provides for the main cases in which property belongs to another for the purposes of theft, also applied for the purposes of s.15.[149] It provides:

> "Property shall be regarded as belonging to any person having possession or control of it, or having in it any proprietary right or interest (not being an

[142] Magistrates' Courts Act 1980, s.17(1), Sch.1.
[143] TA 1968, s.15(1).
[144] [1993] A.C. 442.
[145] And, according to *Hinks* [2001] 2 A.C. 241, even if it is not.
[146] TA 1968, s.34(1).
[147] Below, para.9–004.
[148] TA 1968, s.4(2); below, para.9–006.
[149] TA 1968, s.34(1).

equitable interest arising only from an agreement to transfer or grant an interest)."

This provision is discussed in the context of theft.[150] Subsections (2) to (5) of TA 1968, s.5, which in various circumstances deem property to belong to a person even if he has neither possession nor control of it nor any proprietary interest in it,[151] did not apply to s.15. It could thus be necessary, on a s.15 charge, to determine whether property which clearly fell within one of those subsections fell within subsection (1) as well.

Property belonging to the defendant

4–099 It was not sufficient that the defendant obtained intangible property if it had never belonged to anyone but him. In *Thompson*[152] the defendant fraudulently effected credits to his account with a Kuwaiti bank and gave instructions for the balance to be transferred to an account in England. It was held that he had thus obtained by deception funds belonging to the Kuwaiti bank. But that bank did not literally send funds to England. There was merely an exchange of telex messages, with the effect that the English bank undertook a liability to the defendant corresponding to that supposedly owed to him by the Kuwaiti bank. What he obtained by his deception was not money but, at most,[153] a chose in action against the English bank. That chose in action had never belonged to anyone else. In one sense it was not an entirely new item of property, because in effect it represented the chose in action that he had ostensibly had against the Kuwaiti bank; but, even if it had been identical to that chose in action,[154] that too had belonged not to the bank but to him.

4–100 The conviction in *Thompson* might perhaps be justified on the assumption that the English bank would eventually have received funds that did belong to the Kuwaiti bank as reimbursement for accepting the latter's liability. A defendant whose deception enabled another person to obtain (albeit innocently) property belonging to another was deemed for the purposes of s.15 to have obtained that property himself.[155] But it is more likely that settlement of the transaction would have been effected through an adjustment of the respective banks' accounts with a third bank (such as the Bank of England), in which case there would strictly be no property passing from the one bank to the other.[156] An argument along these lines would in any event need to be supported by evidence of the banking procedures involved. After 1996 the problem would normally be avoided by charging the obtaining of a money transfer instead.[157]

[150] Below, paras 9–029 *et seq.*
[151] Below, paras 9–035 *et seq.*
[152] [1984] 3 All E.R. 565; cf. *Davies* [1982] 1 All E.R. 513.
[153] The Court of Appeal thought that the original fraud had given him no valid chose in action against the Kuwaiti bank. Presumably he acquired no valid rights against the English bank either.
[154] Which it was not: see below, para.4–104.
[155] TA 1968, s.15(2).
[156] See below, para.4–104.
[157] Below, para.4–116.

Newly created property

4–101 A person did not obtain property belonging to another if the property he obtained did not exist until he obtained it and, from that moment on, belonged to him alone. If by deception he induced another to confer fresh rights upon him (as distinct from assigning to him rights already possessed by the other), he might be obtaining intangible property *from* another,[158] but he did not obtain property *belonging* to another as the section required. A person who by deception induced a freeholder to grant him a lease was not guilty of obtaining the lease by deception, because the lease did not exist until it was granted, and as soon as it was granted it belonged to the lessee.[159]

4–102 Similarly, Lord Goff of Chieveley explained in *Preddy* that a person was not guilty of obtaining a chose in action by deception if the deception induced another person to draw a cheque in his favour, thereby conferring on him a chose in action which had not previously existed.

> "[W]hen the cheque was obtained by the payee from the drawer, the chose in action represented by the cheque then came into existence and so had never belonged to the drawer. When it came into existence it belonged to the payee, and so there could be no question of his having obtained by deception 'property belonging to another.'"[160]

Earlier authorities to the effect that the offence was committed in such circumstances[161] were overruled.[162] It seems that the defendant could be charged neither with obtaining the chose in action represented by the cheque (because that did not exist until he obtained it) nor with obtaining the cheque itself (because there was no intention permanently to deprive the drawer of it).[163] *Preddy* further established that he could not be charged

[158] Indictments sometimes allege that the defendant obtained property "from" a named person, rather than that he obtained property "belonging to" that person. It would be pedantic to object to this form of words in itself, but its use undoubtedly increases the risk of the requirement being overlooked.

[159] *Chan Wai Lam* [1981] Crim. L.R. 497.

[160] [1996] A.C. 815 at 836.

[161] *Duru* [1974] 1 W.L.R. 2; *Mitchell* [1993] Crim. L.R. 788.

[162] In *Pyman* (May 24, 1994) the difficulty had been met with the ingenious argument that the chose in action belongs to the deceived *drawer*, either by virtue of TA 1968, s.5(4) (which deems property to belong to a person who by mistake transfers it to the defendant, if the defendant is under an obligation to make restoration of the property or its proceeds) or because the drawer retains an equitable interest under a constructive trust (*Chase Manhattan Bank NA v Israel-British Bank (London) Ltd* [1981] Ch. 105). The former ground is clearly unsound because s.5(4) applies only to theft, not deception. As for the latter, it would be very odd if the drawer had an equitable interest in the payee's claim against the drawer himself. But it seems that he does have an equitable interest in the funds credited to the payee's bank account when the cheque is presented; and if he owns the proceeds of the cheque once it is presented, there is a certain logic in the argument that he must also own the rights conferred by the cheque (albeit against him) in the meantime. However, the argument does not meet the fundamental difficulty, namely that the defendant does not obtain property belonging to another, as required by TA 1968, s.15(1), if he obtains property which does not belong to another until he has obtained it. *Pyman* was cited in *Preddy* but not referred to in the speeches.

[163] See below, paras 9–150 *et seq.*

with obtaining a credit balance by *presenting* the cheque that he had obtained by deception.[164] Possible charges in such a case (under the old law) include procuring the execution of a valuable security by deception,[165] obtaining a money transfer by deception,[166] and stealing the drawer's credit balance by presenting the cheque.[167]

Newly created property representing existing property

Sometimes property is obtained which, though in law newly created, is in substance no more than existing property in another form. This occurs when funds are transferred from one person's bank account to another's. It was long assumed that in this situation the transferee obtained property belonging to the transferor (namely the funds transferred) for the purposes of TA 1968, s.15. But this is not an accurate analysis of the transaction. Initially, the transferor is the owner of an item of property, namely the chose in action consisting in his right to the funds as against his bank. When the funds are transferred, that property disappears, and the transferee acquires *another* item of property—namely the chose in action consisting in his right to the funds as against his own bank. The transferor surrenders property and the transferee acquires property of the same value, but the property surrendered is distinct from the property acquired. In fact it is strictly inaccurate to speak of funds being "transferred" at all, though that terminology is difficult to avoid. In law, nothing is transferred. What happens is that property owned by one person disappears, and property owned by another person appears in its place. **4–103**

In *Preddy* the House of Lords accordingly held that a person who by deception obtained a mortgage advance consisting in the transfer of funds from an account held by the lender did not obtain property belonging to another within the meaning of TA 1968, s.15. It was immaterial for this purpose whether the funds were transferred by cheque, by telegraphic transfer, by the clearing house automated payment system or in any other way. **4–104**

> "In truth the property which the defendant has obtained is the new chose in action constituted by the debt now owed to him by his bank, and represented by the credit entry in his own bank account. This did not come into existence until the debt so created was owed to him by his bank, and so never belonged to anyone else. True, it corresponded to the debit entered in the lending institution's bank account; but it does not follow that the property which the defendant acquired can be identified with the property which the lending institution lost when its account was debited. In truth, section 15(1) is here being invoked for a purpose for which it was never designed, and for which it does not legislate."[168]

[164] See below, para.4–104.
[165] Below, para.4–151.
[166] Below, para.4–116.
[167] *Williams (Roy)* [2001] 1 Cr.App.R. 23 (p.362).
[168] [1996] A.C. 815 at 834, *per* Lord Goff of Chieveley.

The lacuna thus exposed was hastily plugged with the new offence of obtaining a money transfer by deception.[169]

4–105 The decision in *Preddy* was based on the requirement that the defendant obtain property belonging to another. It cannot be said that the transferee of funds obtains the victim's chose in action. But the victim does *lose* his chose in action, and it may be possible to regard the transferee as having *stolen* it. It is possible to appropriate property for the purposes of theft without obtaining it for the purposes of the offence under TA 1968, s.15.[170]

Obtaining

4–106 The defendant had to "obtain" the property. TA 1968, s.15(2) provided:

> "For purposes of this section a person is to be treated as obtaining property if he obtains ownership, possession or control of it, and 'obtain' includes obtaining for another or enabling another to obtain or to retain."

Obtaining ownership

4–107 The defendant obtained property if he obtained ownership of it, even without possession or control. It was of course immaterial that the title he obtained was voidable on the grounds of his fraud, but if the effect of the fraud was to render the transaction completely void he did not obtain ownership at all. It was apparently sufficient if he already had possession or control of the property, and by deception obtained ownership as well.[171] But if he obtained possession and control *by deception*, thus committing the offence, it is arguable that he did not commit it again when he subsequently obtained ownership.[172]

Obtaining possession or control

4–108 Even if the owner had no intention of parting with the ownership of the property, or if his intention to do so was nullified by the fraud, a person obtained the property if he obtained possession or control of it. Thus he committed the offence if he persuaded the owner to let him borrow goods for some temporary purpose but in fact intended to keep them for good.

Obtaining for another

4–109 A person obtained property if he obtained it for another. Thus A could be guilty of the offence if by deception he induced B to confer ownership, possession or control of B's property on C. C need not be a party to the fraud.

[169] Below, para.4–116.
[170] See below, para.9–013.
[171] cf. *Collis-Smith* [1971] Crim. L.R. 716.
[172] cf. *Atakpu* [1994] Q.B. 69; below, para.9–110.

Enabling another to obtain

Nor was it necessary that the defendant should himself obtain the property for another: it was sufficient if he enabled another to obtain it for himself. A could be guilty of the offence if by deception he enabled C to obtain ownership, possession or control of B's property, either for C himself or for D. Again C need not be a party to the fraud.[173] **4–110**

Enabling another to retain

Finally a person obtained property if he merely enabled another person to retain property which that other person already had. But the property obtained had to be property belonging to another, and in order to make sense of the section this had to be construed as meaning that the property must belong to someone who is neither the defendant nor the person enabled to retain the property. Where a person other than the defendant has sole ownership, possession and control of the property, it is literally property belonging to a person other than the defendant. But it can hardly be said that the defendant is obtaining property belonging to another if he merely enables that person to retain the ownership, possession and control that he already has. In any case the defendant does not intend thereby to deprive that person of the property. Therefore the offence was not committed if an associate of the defendant had obtained ownership, possession and control[174] of property under a voidable contract[175] and the defendant ensured by deception that the contract was not rescinded. There was no-one from whom the property could be obtained, or who could be deprived of it. **4–111**

If, however, the associate had obtained possession or control but not ownership, it was possible to commit the offence by enabling him to retain that possession or control without enabling him to obtain ownership as well. The property "belonged" not only to the associate but also to the owner. By enabling the associate to retain possession or control, the defendant "obtained" property belonging to another (the owner). And he would probably be regarded as intending to "deprive" the owner of the property by ensuring that he did not get it back.[176] Similarly if the associate had obtained ownership under a voidable contract, but not possession or control, it was in theory sufficient that the defendant enabled him to retain his ownership by dissuading the former owner from rescinding the contract. But in that case the associate's retention of ownership would doubtless have enabled him to obtain possession and control as well. **4–112**

[173] e.g. *DPP v Stonehouse* [1978] A.C. 55. Cf. the suggested explanation of *Thompson* [1984] 3 All E.R. 565, above, para.4–100.

[174] Or, in the case of intangible property, ownership only.

[175] For the purposes of the offence of theft it is arguable that property obtained under a contract which is voidable on the grounds of fraud or other mistake continues to belong to the original owner by virtue of TA 1968, s.5(4); but s.5(4) had no application to s.15.

[176] cf. *Stapylton v O'Callaghan* [1973] 2 All E.R. 782.

4–113 TA 1968, s.15(2) did not say that a person "obtained" property if he enabled *himself* to retain property which he already had. Presumably this was not sufficient. It scarcely falls within the ordinary meaning of the word, and s.15(2) appears to have been an exhaustive definition. Thus there was a curious anomaly. If A was in possession of property belonging to B, C could commit the offence by enabling A to retain possession. But if C was himself in possession of the property, it seems that he could not commit the offence by deceiving B into letting him keep it.

Intention permanently to deprive

4–114 Like theft, the offence of obtaining property by deception required an intention permanently to deprive of the property the person to whom it belonged.[177] A person who obtained property by deception with the intention of subsequently returning that same property[178] would not normally commit the offence.[179] But, as in theft, there could be a constructive intention permanently to deprive where no such intention literally existed. TA 1968, s.6 applied, with the substitution of references to obtaining for those to appropriation, as it applies to theft.[180] Thus it was sufficient if the defendant intended to return the property only on receiving payment for it, or only when all the "goodness" had gone out of it. It might be argued, for example, that if a person obtained a sub-lease of land for a period one day shorter than the unexpired portion of the head lease he intended to deprive the lessor permanently of the land.[181]

Obtaining by deception and theft

4–115 In *Gomez*[182] the House of Lords held that the obtaining of property by deception could be theft, even if title passed to the obtainer. There was at least one case which amounted to obtaining by deception but (even after *Gomez*) not to theft, namely the obtaining of land. There may have been others.[183] The requirements of property belonging to another, dishonesty and intention permanently to deprive were common to both offences, and TA 1968, s.15 was more restrictive than theft in requiring the element of deception.[184] But, whereas theft requires an "appropriation" of the property—that is, an assumption of the rights of an owner—s.15 required an obtaining of ownership, possession or control. It may have been possible for the latter to occur without the former. If A induces B by deception to

[177] See below, paras 9–132 *et seq*.
[178] Not just property of the same value.
[179] He might commit some other offence, e.g. obtaining services or evading liability: below, paras 4–121, 4–134.
[180] TA 1968, s.15(3); see below, paras 9–136 *et seq*.
[181] cf. *Chan Wai Lam* [1981] Crim. L.R. 497.
[182] [1993] A.C. 442; below, para.9–123.
[183] Russell Heaton, "Deceiving without Thieving" [2001] Crim. L.R. 712.
[184] It was also slightly more restrictive as to the circumstances in which property was regarded as belonging to another: above, para.4–098.

confer upon him the ownership of B's property, A has obtained it by deception; but this does not in itself amount to an appropriation by A.[185] He does not steal the property until he assumes a right to it by keeping it or dealing with it as owner.[186] So *Gomez* did not make s.15 entirely redundant.

OBTAINING A MONEY TRANSFER

The gap in the law exposed by *Preddy* was filled by the Theft (Amendment) Act 1996, which amended TA 1968 so as to create a new offence of obtaining a money transfer by deception. The new offence was based on recommendations by the Law Commission.[187] TA 1968, s.15A(1) provided: **4–116**

> "A person is guilty of an offence if by any deception he dishonestly obtains a money transfer for himself or another."

The offence was triable either way,[188] and was punishable on conviction on indictment with 10 years' imprisonment.[189] It applied only to things done between December 18, 1996[190] and January 14, 2007.[191]

TA 1968, s.15A(2) defined a "money transfer" as occurring when **4–117**

- a debit[192] is made to one account;
- a credit[193] is made to another; and
- the credit results from the debit or the debit results from the credit.

In *Re Holmes*[194] it was held that for this purpose a credit had to be unconditional. So the offence was committed where a conditional credit, procured by giving instructions to a computer (and thus without deception), was made unconditional by deception. It was also held that, if one account were proved to have been credited, it could be inferred that another account must have been debited. There was no need to identify the account debited. This seems inconsistent with the statutory wording.

TA 1968, s.15B(3) defined an "account" as an account kept with **4–118**

- a bank, or
- a person carrying on a business,[195] if

[185] See below, paras 9–114 *et seq.*
[186] TA 1968, s.3(1).
[187] Law Com. No.243, *Offences of Dishonesty: Money Transfers*, HC 690.
[188] Magistrates' Courts Act 1980, s.17(1), Sch.1.
[189] TA 1968, s.15A(5).
[190] Theft (Amendment) Act 1996, s.1(2).
[191] Subject to the transitional provisions of FA 2006: above, para.1–006.
[192] i.e. a debit of an amount of money: TA 1968, s.15A(3).
[193] i.e. a credit of an amount of money: TA 1968, s.15A(3).
[194] [2004] EWHC 2020; [2005] Crim. L.R. 229.
[195] All the activities which a person carries on by way of business were to be regarded as a single business carried on by him: TA 1968, s.15B(5)(a).

- in the course of the business money[196] received by way of deposit[197] is lent to others; or
- any other activity of the business is financed, wholly or to any material extent, out of the capital of or the interest on money received by way of deposit.[198]

An account falling outside this definition was not covered. Where a "transfer" of property out of such an account was in law the destruction of one chose in action accompanied by the creation of another to the same value, *Preddy* applied and there was no offence under TA 1968, s.15 *or* 15A.

4–119 It was immaterial whether the money transfer was effected on presentment of a cheque or by another method.[199] The offence thus provided a solution to the difficulty created by Lord Goff's statement in *Preddy* that it is not an offence under TA 1968, s.15 to obtain a cheque by deception.[200] The offence under TA 1968, s.15A could be charged not only where the account-holder was induced to instruct his bank directly to make the transfer, but also where he gave the defendant the power to secure the transfer by presenting a cheque.[201] However, the offence was complete only when the cheque was honoured and the funds transferred. *Presenting* a cheque obtained by deception was presumably an *attempt* to obtain a money transfer (unless the cheque was presented for cash). *Obtaining* the cheque by deception, however, was probably merely preparatory to the obtaining of the transfer. Where a cheque was obtained by a deception made before January 15, 2007 and was not presented, therefore, it is safer to charge procuring the execution of a valuable security by deception.[202]

4–120 It was also immaterial whether either of the accounts was overdrawn before or after the money transfer was effected.[203] This means that the offence did more than merely restore the law to what it was widely but erroneously believed to be before *Preddy*.[204] Even before *Preddy* it was clear that there could be no offence of obtaining property from an account if the account was overdrawn beyond any agreed overdraft facility, because there was no property to obtain. It was arguably anomalous that the state of the

[196] Including money expressed in a currency other than sterling or in the European currency unit: TA 1968, s.15B(5)(b).

[197] References to a deposit were to be read with the Financial Services and Markets Act 2000, s.22, any relevant order under that section, and Sch.2 to that Act, but disregarding any restriction arising from the identity of the person making the deposit: TA 1968, s.15B(4A).

[198] TA 1968, s.15B(4).

[199] TA 1968, s.15A(4)(b). To avoid technical objections based on variations in banking procedures, it was also immaterial whether the amount credited was the same as the amount debited, whether any delay occurred in the process by which the money transfer was effected, or whether any intermediate credits or debits were made in the course of the money transfer.

[200] See above, para.4–102.

[201] Securing a transfer of funds by presenting a cheque can also be charged as theft of the funds: *Williams (Roy)* [2001] 1 Cr.App.R. 23 (p.362); below, para.9–014.

[202] Below, para.4–151.

[203] TA 1968, s.15A(4)(e).

[204] Law Com. No.243, para.5.11.

account should make any difference, and TA 1968, s.15A removed the anomaly. The new offence could be charged without regard to the state of the account. But this created a new anomaly, between transfers secured by deception and transfers secured by (for example) drawing cheques without authority, or hacking into the bank's computer. If conduct of these latter kinds is charged as theft, the state of the account is still crucial.[205] But in some cases (such as the drawing of cheques for an unauthorised purpose by an authorised signatory) it would now constitute the new fraud offence by virtue of being an abuse of position.[206]

OBTAINING SERVICES

A person who by deception obtained something other than property could be guilty of various offences under the old law. The widest of them was known as obtaining *services* by deception, though that was a misnomer. TA 1978, s.1 provided: **4–121**

> "(1) A person who by any deception dishonestly obtains services from another shall be guilty of an offence.
>
> (2) It is an obtaining of services where the other is induced to confer a benefit by doing some act, or causing or permitting some act to be done, on the understanding that the benefit has been or will be paid for."

The offence was triable either way,[207] and was punishable on conviction on indictment with five years' imprisonment.[208]

Inducing another to confer a benefit

The effect of TA 1978, s.1(2) was that the offence was not confined to the obtaining of "services" in any normal sense. Indeed that word was used in s.1(1) only as a convenient (but misleading) label. The offence was therefore extremely wide. It extended to the dishonest procuring by deception of any act, or of the causing or permitting of any act, which was understood to be paid for.[209] **4–122**

Property

In *Sofroniou* it was said that "obtaining services is to be contrasted with obtaining property".[210] Similarly, in *Preddy*[211] Lord Goff queried whether it was right to apply the section to "services" which consist in the provision of **4–123**

[205] See below, para.9–018.
[206] Below, Ch.6.
[207] TA 1978, s.4(1).
[208] TA 1978, s.4(2).
[209] And, perhaps, which amounted to the conferring of a benefit: below, para.4–127.
[210] [2003] EWCA Crim 3681; [2004] Q.B. 1218 at [24].
[211] [1996] A.C. 815 at 840.

money, because this would result in a substantial overlap with TA 1968, s.15. But, while the section was primarily aimed at cases in which no property is obtained, it was not confined to such cases. A person who obtains property by deception is inducing another to confer a benefit on him by doing an act—namely transferring ownership, possession or control of the property. If it is understood that that act has been or will be paid for, there would appear to be an obtaining of services under the old law. Indeed the obtaining of property could sometimes fall within TA 1978, s.1 but *not* TA 1968, s.15—for example where a person obtained the *hire* of property by deception, and was not guilty under TA 1968, s.15 because he intended to return the property at the end of the hire period, and thus had no intention permanently to deprive.

4–124 It is now clear that the obtaining of a loan was within the section. It was formerly held in *Halai*[212] that the obtaining of a mortgage advance was not an obtaining of services. It was generally agreed that this was wrong, but there was no way of getting a case to the Court of Appeal so that it could be corrected. Prosecutors got round the problem by charging mortgage frauds as the obtaining of property instead, contrary to TA 1968, s.15. Once the House of Lords had decided in *Preddy*[213] that this was not permissible either, *Halai* was reversed by the Theft (Amendment) Act 1996. For good measure, that Act inserted a new s.1(3) in TA 1978, which provided:

> "Without prejudice to the generality of subsection (2) above, it is an obtaining of services where the other is induced to make a loan, or to cause or permit a loan to be made, on the understanding that any payment (whether by way of interest or otherwise) will be or has been made in respect of the loan."

4–125 This amendment applied only to offences committed after the 1996 Act came into force on December 18, 1996. But it was said in *Graham*,[214] and confirmed in *Cooke*[215] and *Cummings-John*,[216] that *Halai* was not good law even before that date. The definition in TA 1978, s.1(2) was in itself wide enough to cover the inducing of a financial institution to advance funds by way of loan, on the understanding that payment would be made in the form of interest charges, an arrangement fee or both. In *Naviede*[217] it was argued that none of the established grounds on which the Court of Appeal can depart from its own decisions existed in this case, and that the cases which purported to overrule *Halai* were themselves decided *per incuriam.* The court regarded *Halai* as distinguishable in any event (because the service relied upon in *Naviede* was not a mortgage advance but a revolving credit facility) but added that, had it been necessary, it would have decided the matter on the basis that *Halai* was no longer binding.

212 [1983] Crim. L.R. 624.
213 [1996] A.C. 815.
214 [1997] 1 Cr.App.R. 302.
215 [1997] Crim. L.R. 436.
216 [1997] Crim. L.R. 660.
217 [1997] Crim. L.R. 662.

Commercial services

The definition included the provision of commercial services such as banking[218] or hire-purchase[219] facilities, for the defendant or a third party,[220] if it was understood that they had been or would be paid for. In *Sofroniou* the defendant opened bank accounts in false names and dishonestly overdrew. It was argued that the only "service" he had obtained was the opening of the accounts, not the use of them. The court disagreed. **4–126**

> "We . . . consider that the dishonest operation of a bank or building society account over a period and a dishonest use of a credit card over a period constitutes obtaining services within the section. . . . What the bank provides in each instance is the benefit of their participation in the banking system which can in our judgment properly be described as a service or services."[221]

Under the terms of the section, however, what mattered was not whether the banks were providing the defendant with a service in the ordinary sense of the word, but whether they were doing some act or causing or permitting some act to be done. Presumably they were doing both, by honouring the defendant's transactions and permitting him to continue making them. The court acknowledged that its interpretation might logically include dishonestly inducing a bank to negotiate a single cheque, or the dishonest use of a credit card on a single occasion; but it did not have to decide the point, and did not encourage prosecutors to bring proceedings on this basis. Conversely, in *Smith (Wallace Duncan) (No.4)*[222] it was said that an agreement to provide finance at some future date could itself be a service because it might help to establish the borrower's liquidity.

Benefit: a separate requirement?

The scope of the offence was arguably restricted to some extent by the use of the words "where the other is induced to confer a benefit by doing some act" rather than simply "where the other is induced to do some act". Are there circumstances in which one person induces another to do an act but the latter does not thereby "confer a benefit" on the former? The section was concerned with people who use deception to get things they want. It has been suggested that some acts which are illegal or contrary to public policy might not be benefits even if some people think them worth paying for.[223] But this probably attaches undue significance to the word **4–127**

[218] *Shortland* [1995] Crim. L.R. 893; *Sofroniou* [2003] EWCA Crim 3681; [2004] Q.B. 1218. *Halai* [1983] Crim. L.R. 624, which decided otherwise, was said in *Sofroniou* not to have survived the Theft (Amendment) Act 1996. It is not clear how the 1996 Act affected the position in this respect, but *Halai* was plainly wrong anyway.

[219] *Widdowson* (1985) 82 Cr.App.R. 314 at 318. The services were obtained from the finance company, not the dealer: *Phillips*, January 21, 1992.

[220] *Nathan* [1997] Crim. L.R. 835.

[221] [2003] EWCA Crim 3681; [2004] Q.B. 1218 at [32].

[222] [2004] EWCA Crim 631; [2004] Q.B. 1418 at [36].

[223] J.C. Smith, *The Law of Theft* (8th edn, 1997) para.4–84.

"benefit", which seems to have been used for brevity rather than substance. The subsection would be unwieldy without it.[224] Elsewhere TA 1978 expressly excluded liabilities which are unenforceable due to the illegal nature of the consideration.[225] If the drafter had intended to incorporate a similar distinction into s.1 it seems unlikely that he would have relied on such a vague word as "benefit" to do it.[226]

Understanding as to payment

4–128 The main restriction on the scope of the offence was that it caught only the obtaining of benefits on the understanding that they had been or would be paid for. If it was understood that the benefit was provided gratuitously, there was no obtaining of "services"[227] and no offence. It was not enough that payment for the benefit *would* have been expected but for the deception. This was a curious rule. It was not clear why a person should be guilty of the offence if by deception he got something cheap, but not if by deception he got it free.[228]

The understanding

4–129 Where the person obtaining the benefit did so dishonestly, his dishonesty would often lie in the fact that he had no intention of paying for the benefit. This did not of course mean that there was no understanding that the benefit had been or would be paid for. In *Sofroniou* the court said:

> "[I]n a subjective sense the understanding may not in truth be mutual. The section is concerned with dishonest deception and the deception may well relate to the deceiver's intention and ability to pay. A dishonest person may well not have a subjective intention or understanding that he will pay. But we do consider that the section envisages a putative objective mutual understanding as to payment on the assumption that the inducement was not dishonest. We consider that an understanding which is mutual in this sense is the natural meaning of the use of the word 'understanding' in its context."[229]

[224] cf. Edward Griew, *The Theft Acts* (7th edn, 1995), para.9–06.
[225] TA 1978, ss.2(2), 3(3).
[226] In *Sofroniou* [2003] EWCA Crim 3681; [2004] Q.B. 1218 at [16] it was said that "the section only applied where there was a sufficient understanding that the benefit conferred had been or would be paid for". This is consistent with the view expressed in the text, that the word "benefit" did not exclude anything from the offence that would otherwise be included. The court also said at [24] that "Inducing someone to confer a benefit is . . . capable of wide application", which does imply that there is a separate requirement that the act done must be beneficial in character. But the point does not appear to have been discussed, and the acts secured by the defendant had on any view been beneficial to him.
[227] In *Sofroniou* [2003] EWCA Crim 3681; [2004] Q.B. 1218 at [24] it was said that "An understanding as to payment is . . . necessary, but only indirectly affects the question whether what is obtained constitutes services." But the understanding as to payment was as much a part of the definition of "services" as the conferral of the benefit.
[228] In the latter case there would seem to be an offence of obtaining an exemption from liability, contrary to TA 1978, s.2(1)(c): below, para.4–145.
[229] [2003] EWCA Crim 3681; [2004] Q.B. 1218 at [37].

Payment for the use of a bank account

In *Sofroniou* the defendant opened bank and credit card accounts in false names and used them to obtain money and goods. Most of the accounts were opened without charge,[230] and it was argued that the benefit provided was not provided on the understanding that it had been or would be paid for. The Crown argued that these words were intended merely to limit the ambit of the section to commercial transactions. It was sufficient if the bank's purpose in allowing the customer to have an account was to make a profit indirectly, for example by obtaining a higher rate of interest in the market than it paid to the customer. 4–130

The court did not accept this argument. 4–131

> "[I]n our judgment, an understanding as to payment under the section will not be satisfied unless there is an agreement or sufficient understanding that an identifiable payment or payments have been or will be made by or on behalf of the person receiving the services to the person providing them. Although it is a common understanding that banks often make charges on accounts which are in credit and charge interest on accounts which are overdrawn, this is not invariably so. Likewise, although it is common for credit card providers to make charges and to charge interest on debit balances which are not promptly paid, it is not to be assumed that every credit card provider makes a charge irrespective of when the balance is repaid; and many people are careful to pay off their balances promptly and thus avoid interest charges. It may therefore be possible to have the benefit of a credit card without ever making any identifiable direct payment to the credit card provider. . . .
>
> We do not consider that inferred indirect commercial advantages to a bank, building society or credit card provider are capable of providing the necessary ingredient as to payment. These will include the difference between interest paid by a bank to an account holder and interest earned by the bank on the same money; or a charge by the credit card provider to the seller of goods bought by means of a credit card."[231]

The convictions were nonetheless upheld. The jury had been entitled to infer that the services actually obtained by the defendant *were* provided on the understanding that he would make "identifiable payments" for them. 4–132

> "The services he obtained were not just the use of bank accounts, but of bank accounts which he dishonestly intended to overdraw. It was open to the jury to infer that the banks would charge interest on accounts overdrawn in this way. Although in different circumstances an inference that interest would be charged might not safely be drawn, it did not require direct evidence that banks invariably charge interest on substantial unauthorised overdrafts to draw such an inference in the present case."[232]

[230] One of the accounts was with American Express, and involved an annual charge of £12. In this case it was conceded that there was an obtaining of services within the meaning of the section.

[231] [2003] EWCA Crim 3681; [2004] Q.B. 1218 at [38] and [40], following *Shortland* [1995] Crim. L.R. 893.

[232] [2003] EWCA Crim 3681; [2004] Q.B. 1218 at [40].

This is questionable. The court had already said that the understanding as to payment must be "a putative objective mutual understanding . . . on the assumption that the inducement was not dishonest". The banks did not allow the defendant to use the accounts on the understanding that he would dishonestly overdraw. At most, they did so on the understanding that he could overdraw if he chose, but would have to pay charges for doing so. This was an understanding that the use of the account would be paid for only in certain circumstances, which might or might not arise. Arguably it was not an understanding that the use of the account *would* be paid for. In effect the court treated the service provided as the granting of the overdraft, rather than the overall use of the account. This was not what was alleged. Had it been alleged, it would have been arguable that, while the defendant obtained the *account* by deception, he obtained the *overdraft* by using the account. On this view, the necessary causal link would not exist. The prosecution seems to have been allowed to have it both ways.

Deception unrelated to prospect of payment

4–133 Although there had to be an understanding that the benefit had been or would be paid for, there was no need for that understanding to be unfounded. The offence could be committed even if the defendant had paid or intended to do so. A person who obtained services by using a payment instrument without authority, for example, could be regarded as deceiving the provider of the services about his authority to use it.[233] He could be obtaining the services *by* the deception although his lack of authority was of no interest to the provider, who would be paid in any event.[234] The services were provided on the understanding that they would be paid for. It was immaterial that, because of the use of the instrument, that understanding was correct. In *Naviede*[235] it was held that the section was not ambiguous on this point, and that evidence of legislative intention was therefore irrelevant.

EVASION OF LIABILITY

4–134 TA 1978, s.2(1) created several offences which could be committed by a person whose deception enabled him to evade an existing liability. It provided:

"[W]here a person by any deception—

(a) dishonestly secures the remission of the whole or part of any existing liability to make a payment, whether his own liability or another's; or

(b) with intent to make permanent default in whole or in part on any existing liability to make a payment, or with intent to let another do so,

[233] Above, paras 4–055 *et seq.*
[234] Below, para.4–177.
[235] [1997] Crim. L.R. 662.

dishonestly induces the creditor[236] or any person claiming payment on behalf of the creditor to wait for payment (whether or not the due date for payment is deferred) or to forgo payment; or

(c) dishonestly obtains[237] any exemption from or abatement of liability to make a payment;

he shall be guilty of an offence."

These offences were triable either way[238] and were punishable on conviction on indictment with five years' imprisonment.[239]

Liability

TA 1978, s.2(1) was concerned with the evasion of a "liability to make a payment". Section 2(2) provided: 4–135

"For purposes of this section 'liability' means legally enforceable liability . . ."

An obligation under an agreement could be a liability even if it was enforceable only by order of the court.[240]

TA 1978, s.2(2) went on: 4–136

". . . and subsection (1) shall not apply in relation to a liability that has not been accepted or established to pay compensation for a wrongful act or omission."

In other words a liability to make a payment was covered if it was a liability to pay compensation for a wrongful act or omission and it was either "accepted" (which presumably meant admitted) or "established" (which presumably meant that judgment had been entered). But it still had to be a liability *to make a payment.* This arguably did not include a liability for an unliquidated sum (even if "accepted") or a liability under a judgment where quantum remains to be determined.

Waiting, forgoing and remitting

TA 1978, s.2(1) created at least three offences.[241] Although there was some overlap between them,[242] each presumably applied in certain circumstances where the others—and TA 1978, s.1—did not. But it was never 4–137

[236] The "creditor" was the person entitled to enforce the liability. Where the defendant was under a contractual obligation to pay money to a third party, the third party was not the creditor unless he was entitled to enforce the obligation: *Gee* [1999] Crim. L.R. 397. At common law he could not enforce it, but under the Contracts (Rights of Third Parties) Act 1999 he might be able to do so.

[237] "Obtains" included obtaining for another or enabling another to obtain: TA 1978, s.2(4).

[238] TA 1978, s.4(1).

[239] TA 1978, s.4(2)(a).

[240] *Modupe* [1991] Crim. L.R. 530.

[241] *Holt* [1981] 1 W.L.R. 1000.

[242] *Sibartie* [1983] Crim. L.R. 470; *Jackson* [1983] Crim. L.R. 617.

clear how they differed from one another. In *Holt* the court tried to clarify the position.

> "[W]e are not sure whether the choice of expressions describing the consequences of deception employed in each of [section 2(1)'s] paragraphs, namely in paragraph (a) 'secures the remission of any existing liability', in paragraph (b) 'induces the creditor to forgo payment' and in paragraph (c) 'obtains any exemption from liability', are simply different ways of describing the same end result or represent conceptual differences. Whilst it is plain that there are substantial differences in the elements of the three offences defined in section 2(1), they show these common features: first, the use of deception to a creditor in relation to a liability, second, dishonesty in the use of deception, and third, the use of deception to gain some advantage in time or money. Thus the differences between the offences relate principally to the different situations in which the debtor-creditor relationship has arisen."[243]

The last sentence is a *non sequitur*. Section 2(1) made no mention of the circumstances in which the liability arose, but distinguished various ways in which the creditor might be induced to refrain from enforcing it—namely remission and abatement of the liability, exemption from it, waiting for payment and forgoing payment. These expressions were not defined.

4–138 In ordinary usage, a creditor *waits* for payment if he does not demand it when it is due (and irrespective of whether the due date for payment is deferred). He *forgoes* payment if he does not demand it at all, though he is still entitled to it. And the liability is *remitted* if, with his agreement, it ceases to exist. Forgoing payment is a more drastic step than waiting for payment, and remitting the liability is more drastic than both. If this is right it explains why TA 1978, s.2(1)(b) required an intent to make permanent default while s.2(1)(a) did not. The prosecution could prove *either* that the defendant intended to make permanent default (though the liability continued to exist) *or* that he induced the creditor to cancel the liability altogether, in whole or in part.

4–139 On this view, s.2(1)(a) applied where the defendant provided consideration for the release. In *Jackson*[244] it was held that a person who paid a debt with a stolen credit card secured the remission of the debt by deception. This was consistent with the view that a debt is not remitted unless it ceases to exist, because the use of a credit card so as to confer on the creditor a claim against the issuing company[245] is consideration for the discharge of the original debt. If the issuing company fails to pay the creditor he can no longer enforce the original liability against the debtor.[246]

4–140 Where the debt is paid by cheque, the creditor retains his right to claim from the debtor if the cheque is dishonoured.[247] The liability is suspended

[243] [1981] 1 W.L.R. 1000 at 1002–1003.

[244] [1983] Crim. L.R. 617.

[245] As long as the defendant produces a signature which resembles that on the card, the fact that he is not authorised to use the card will not prevent the creditor acquiring such a claim: *First Sport Ltd v Barclays Bank plc* [1993] 1 W.L.R. 1229. The same is presumably true if he is required to input a PIN rather than providing a signature.

[246] *Re Charge Card Services Ltd* [1989] Ch. 497.

[247] According to Millett J. in *Re Charge Card Services Ltd* [1987] Ch. 150, this is so even if the cheque is backed with a cheque guarantee card.

but not remitted. The payment of a debt with a bad cheque could therefore be charged under s.2(1)(b), but only if an intent to make permanent default could be proved. A possible argument to the effect that the creditor was not induced to wait for or forgo payment, but was actually paid (albeit conditionally) when he accepted the cheque, was anticipated by TA 1978, s.2(3):

> "For purposes of subsection (1)(b) a person induced to take in payment a cheque or other security for money by way of conditional satisfaction of a pre-existing liability is to be treated not as being paid but as being induced to wait for payment."

It is doubtful whether s.2(1)(b), even as reinforced by s.2(3), could properly be invoked where a cheque card or credit card was used. Did a creditor forgo payment of the original debt by accepting a claim against a third party in lieu? He was not waiting for payment of the original debt, and, at least in the case of a credit card,[248] s.2(3) did not help because the use of the card constituted full (not conditional) satisfaction. This kind of case fell more properly under s.2(1)(a), which had the additional advantage for the prosecution of not requiring an intent to make permanent default.

Section 2(1)(b) required either an intent to make permanent default on an existing liability, or an intent to let another make such default. The former could exist only if the liability in question was (or, perhaps, was believed by the defendant to be) the defendant's, since one cannot default on a liability to which one is not subject.[249] **4–141**

In *Graham* it was ingeniously suggested that a defendant who by deception induced another person to transfer funds from his bank account (as in *Preddy*) was securing the remission of part of the bank's liability to the transferor. The suggestion was rejected. **4–142**

> "We cannot regard this as a realistic way of analysing cases such as *Preddy*, since in no ordinary case could the defendant contemplate or seek to 'secure' a reduction of the liability of the lender's bank. Nor would the analysis be apt if the lender owed money to its bank."[250]

The objection seems to be that a person does not "secure" a result unless that is his intention or purpose. In the case at which TA 1978, s.2(1)(a) is aimed, the defendant's purpose is to ensure that the liability is remitted so that he (or the person subject to the liability) does not have to pay. Clearly he has no interest in reducing the bank's indebtedness to the victim of the deception.

Exemption and abatement

In the case of an existing liability it was not clear what TA 1978, s.2(1)(c) added to s.2(1)(b). Unlike s.2(1)(b), it did not require an intent to make permanent default; but nor did s.2(1)(a). Is it possible to obtain an **4–143**

[248] See above, fn.247.
[249] *Attewell-Hughes* (1991) 93 Cr.App.R. 132.
[250] [1997] 1 Cr.App.R. 302 at 314.

exemption from an existing liability without securing its remission? Is it possible to obtain an "abatement" of it—i.e., presumably, a reduction—without securing its remission in part?

4–144 In *Sibartie*[251] the defendant, while changing trains on the London Underground, "flashed" at a ticket inspector a season ticket which did not cover the journey he was making. This was held to be an attempt to obtain an exemption from liability. But, had the defendant deceived the inspector, she would not have *exempted* him from liability. She would have been under the impression that he had already paid, and that there was no liability from which he needed to be exempted. Inducing a creditor to refrain from demanding payment by pretending to have already paid is more naturally described as inducing him to forgo payment, contrary to s.2(1)(b)[252]—but that paragraph required an intent to make permanent default. Perhaps the point is that the defendant was pretending not just to have paid for the particular journey he was making, but to be "exempt" from the requirement to pay for the journey because he had a *season* ticket. But the decision seems to envisage that there could be an exemption from an existing liability without the liability itself being affected, and without the person deceived even realising that there *was* an existing liability. It is hard to see how this can be right.

Evasion of fresh liability

4–145 The chief significance of TA 1978, s.2(1)(c) probably lay in the fact that, unlike s.2(1)(a) and (b), it applied to the evasion of a fresh liability as well as an existing one,[253] and thus complemented s.1. There was no obtaining of "services" if the victim believed neither that the defendant would pay nor that he already had.[254] But if he *would* have had to pay, but for the deception, he obtained an exemption from the liability that he would otherwise have incurred. If there was an exemption from a liability where the defendant evaded payment by pretending that he had already paid,[255] the obtaining of a benefit by means of such a deception fell within s.1 *and* s.2(1)(c). Similarly, where the deception enabled the defendant to obtain a benefit at a reduced price, there was not only an abatement of a liability within s.2(1)(c) but also an obtaining of services within s.1. In this case there was an understanding that the benefit was to be paid for, albeit at a reduced rate.

OBTAINING A PECUNIARY ADVANTAGE

4–146 TA 1978, ss.1 and 2 covered most of the cases that would previously have amounted to the offence of obtaining a pecuniary advantage by deception, contrary to TA 1968, s.16. TA 1978 drastically restricted the scope of TA

[251] [1983] Crim. L.R. 470.
[252] cf. *Holt* [1981] 1 W.L.R. 1000.
[253] *Firth* (1990) 91 Cr.App.R. 217.
[254] Above, para.4–128.
[255] See *Sibartie* [1983] Crim. L.R. 470; above, para.4–144.

1968, s.16 by repealing the notoriously obscure s.16(2)(a), which set out a variety of circumstances in which a pecuniary advantage was deemed to be obtained. But the rest of TA 1968, s.16 survived until repealed by FA 2006, and, in the relatively few situations still included, was a useful alternative to the other deception offences. Under TA 1968, s.16(1) a person committed an offence if he

> "by any deception dishonestly obtains for himself or another any pecuniary advantage".

The offence was triable either way[256] and was punishable on conviction on indictment with five years' imprisonment.[257]

Even before its emasculation by TA 1978, the offence was much narrower than s.16(1) suggested, because a "pecuniary advantage" was obtained within the meaning of the section only in certain circumstances specified in s.16(2). After the repeal of s.16(2)(a), a pecunary advantage was obtained for a person only where **4–147**

> "(b) he is allowed to borrow by way of overdraft, or to take out any policy of insurance[258] or annuity contract, or obtains an improvement of the terms on which he is allowed to do so; or
>
> (c) he is given the opportunity to earn remuneration or greater remuneration in an office or employment, or to win money by betting."

The section created one offence which could be committed in various ways.[259]

A person was "allowed to borrow by way of overdraft" not only if he induced a bank to give him permission to overdraw (and whether or not he actually did so)[260] but also if he succeeded in overdrawing *without* the bank's permission because his cheques were backed with a guarantee card and therefore had to be honoured.[261] In this case it is a curious use of language to say that by using the card he induces the bank to *allow* him to overdraw. The bank has no choice. Moreover a person who uses a *stolen* cheque book and cheque card is probably not "borrowing" at all. And there are many ways of borrowing which do not involve an overdraft. Under the old law, dishonest borrowing in these other ways could usually be charged as the obtaining of property[262] or services[263] or as the evasion of a liability.[264] **4–148**

256 Magistrates' Courts Act 1980, s.17, Sch.1.
257 TA 1968, s.16(1).
258 The offence could be committed even if the policy was void due to a mistake of identity: *Alexander* [1981] Crim. L.R. 183.
259 *Bale v Rosier* [1977] 1 W.L.R. 263.
260 *Watkins* [1976] 1 All E.R. 578. This interpretation is not free from doubt. If the bank charged a fee for granting the overdraft facility there would in any case be an obtaining of services by deception: above, para.4–121.
261 *Waites* [1982] Crim. L.R. 369; *Bevan* (1987) 84 Cr.App.R. 143.
262 Above, para.4–095.
263 Above, para.4–121.
264 Above, para.4–134.

4–149 The remaining parts of TA 1968, s.16(2) dealt with various cases in which a person's deception earned him an opportunity to obtain money, but it was doubtful whether any money he obtained was obtained *by* the deception.[265] For example, a punter who by deception induced a bookmaker to accept a bet on credit did not obtain his winnings by deception but by backing the right horse.[266] The difficulty could be avoided by charging an obtaining of a pecuniary advantage, namely the *opportunity* to obtain the money. But this reasoning could not be extended indefinitely. In *McNiff*[267] the defendant obtained a provisional tenancy of a pub by deceiving the brewery. The tenancy was to take effect when he got a justices' licence. His conviction under s.16(2)(c) was quashed. By deceiving the brewery he had obtained two things: the provisional tenancy (which was not an "office or employment") and the opportunity to obtain a licence. A licence may be an opportunity to earn remuneration in the office of a licensee, but the opportunity to obtain a licence is not.

4–150 It was held in *Callender*[268] that the term "employment" in s.16(2)(c) was not confined to contracts of employment in the strict sense, but included a contract for services. It was not clear how far this went. The defendant had, by deception, obtained work as a self-employed accountant, and the court thought that this kind of work fell within the ordinary meaning of "employment". But it would be odd to speak of an odd job man being "employed" by each of his customers. It might perhaps be said that *in general* he earns remuneration in an employment (i.e. an occupation) because it is his occupation to do odd jobs, and that whenever he is engaged to do a particular job he is obtaining the opportunity to earn remuneration as part of his overall, continuing employment. But this reasoning would not apply to a person who fraudulently obtains only one or two jobs and does not earn a living at it.

PROCURING THE EXECUTION OF A VALUABLE SECURITY

4–151 Under TA 1968, s.20(2), a person committed an offence if he

> "dishonestly, with a view to gain for himself or another or with intent to cause loss to another,[269] by any deception procures the execution of a valuable security".

The offence was triable either way,[270] and was punishable on conviction on indictment with seven years' imprisonment.[271] It covered certain kinds of

[265] Below, paras 4–189 *et seq.*
[266] *Clucas* [1949] 2 K.B. 226.
[267] [1986] Crim. L.R. 57.
[268] [1993] Q.B. 303.
[269] For discussion of this requirement see above, Ch.3.
[270] Magistrates' Courts Act 1980, s.17, Sch.1.
[271] TA 1968, s.20(2).

conduct which did not amount to obtaining property by deception and do not amount to theft, such as deceiving another into drawing a cheque.[272]

Most of the difficulties surrounding the offence concerned its application to modern methods of transferring funds through the banking system. The offence was clearly committed where the defendant deceived another into drawing a cheque, but not necessarily where the other instructed his bank to transfer the funds electronically. **4–152**

> "Unless the means by which funds are to be transferred are clearly and specifically identified, it cannot be assumed that procuring the transfer would necessarily involve procuring the execution of a valuable security. The proliferation of new and sophisticated ways of transferring money means that some care is needed to identify the means by which payment was, or was to be, made in the particular case."[273]

Section 20(2) therefore could not be applied to any particular form of transfer without evidence of the banking procedures involved.[274] In *King (Hugo)*[275] it was said that the process of applying the subsection to a given document involved three stages: **4–153**

(1) What does the document do? This is a question of fact.

(2) Does it fall within the definition of a "valuable security"?

(3) In the respect in which the document is a valuable security (if it is), has the defendant procured by deception an "execution" of it?

Valuable securities

The expression "valuable security" is used in TA 1968, s.20(1), which creates an offence of suppressing documents and is discussed below,[276] as well as the now-repealed s.20(2). Section 20(3) defines it so as to include any document which **4–154**

(1) creates, transfers, surrenders or releases any right to, in or over property,

(2) authorises the payment of money or the delivery of any property, or

(3) evidences

  (a) the creation, transfer, surrender or release of any such right,

  (b) the payment of money or the delivery of any property, or

  (c) the satisfaction of any obligation.

[272] See above, para.4–102, and below, paras 9–151 *et seq.*
[273] *Graham* [1997] 1 Cr.App.R. 302 at 315.
[274] *Bolton* (1991) 94 Cr.App.R. 74.
[275] [1992] Q.B. 20.
[276] Para.11–056.

A document within this definition is a valuable security even if it is forged and therefore invalid.[277]

Documents creating, transferring, surrendering or releasing property rights

4–155 This category includes conveyances, leases, mortgage deeds, wills and so on. In *Benstead*[278] it was held to include an irrevocable letter of credit, on the ground that such a document confers on its beneficiary a right to payment and is therefore a document creating a right to property (namely money). Sir John Smith argued that the words "any document creating . . . any right to, in or over property" presuppose the prior existence of some property to which, in which or over which the document creates a new right. Otherwise, every written contract would be a valuable security. Another and perhaps better way of avoiding that conclusion might be to construe these words as referring to the creation of a *proprietary* right. A right to be paid a sum of money is not a right to, in or over property because it is a personal right. It is not a right to, in or over any *particular* property.

4–156 In *King (Hugo)*[279] this category was held to include a clearing house automated payment system ("CHAPS") order—that is, a customer's written instruction to his bank to make an instantaneous electronic transfer of funds to an account at another bank. The court thought it unnecessary to decide whether Sir John Smith's criticism of *Benstead* was correct, because in this case there *is* pre-existing property—the drawer's credit balance. The CHAPS order, once processed, creates a right over that property.[280] But this now appears to be wrong. It is clear since *Preddy*[281] that the right acquired by the payee is not a right over the paying customer's credit balance. It is an entirely separate item of property.

4–157 The argument that the document did not itself create a right, but merely instructed the bank's employees to do so, was rejected as unrealistic.

> "A credit of £X, over which the paying customer had a right before the order was processed . . . , is now available, not to him, but to the payee. To argue that the transfer is the result simply of the actions of the bank officials is analogous to arguing that a cheque (incontestably a valuable security) is not efficacious to transfer property because there has to be bank activity before a credit appears in the payee's account. In either case the activity at the bank, or banks, is simply the incidental machinery by which the document is given its practical and intended effect, just as the postman who delivers the envelope containing a cheque becomes part of that incidental machinery."

[277] *Beck* [1985] 1 W.L.R. 22.

[278] (1982) 75 Cr.App.R. 276. The Court of Appeal purported to follow *Benstead* in *Moffat* September 15, 1992; but the criticisms of *Benstead* do not apply to *Moffat*, because the contract in question was one for the sale and lease back of certain mining equipment, and clearly created rights in or over property.

[279] [1992] Q.B. 20.

[280] It was said that the order *transfers* the right to the payee as well as creating it. But, if the right belongs to the payee once it is created, there is no question of transferring it to him.

[281] [1996] A.C. 815.

If the argument were analogous to saying that a cheque is not a valuable security, this would be a powerful objection. But a cheque is a valuable security because it falls within the second of the categories in TA 1968, s.20(3), not the first. In *Manjdadria*[282] the court said that *King* might have gone to "the extreme boundaries of a valuable security", and declined to extend it to a telegraphic transfer or the computerised ledger account of the solicitors making it.

Documents authorising payment of money or delivery of property

A cheque, like any other bill of exchange, is a valuable security because it is a document authorising (and indeed ordering) the payment of money.[283] In most cases the "payment" will actually take the form of a credit to the payee's account; but *Preddy* does not cause difficulty here because the cheque authorises payment in "money" (i.e. cash).[284] **4–158**

It is less clear whether other forms of instruction to a bank to transfer funds also fall within this category. In *King* it was argued that the acts authorised by a CHAPS order are the debiting of the paying customer's account and the making of a corresponding credit to the payee's account—neither of which is "the payment of money" or "delivery of any property". The court thought the argument unrealistic—which could equally be said of the similar argument that succeeded in *Preddy*—but did not have to decide the point because it held that the CHAPS order was a valuable security on other grounds. In *Johl*[285] the court doubted whether a telex message authorising a telegraphic transfer could be a valuable security either, but held that it would not be "executed" within the meaning of s.20(2) anyway.[286] In *Weiss v Government of Germany*,[287] however, a document authorising a transfer was held to be a valuable security. *Johl* was probably distinguishable because it was concerned with a printout of a telex message, as distinct from an original document. *Weiss* was an unusual case because the transfer was in cash, via Western Union. There was therefore no difficulty in regarding it as "the payment of money". The *Preddy* problem did not arise. **4–159**

Evidential documents

The third category of the definition has received relatively little attention. In one sense, a document "evidences" an event if it is admissible evidence of that event. It cannot have been intended that, for example, a letter **4–160**

282 [1993] Crim. L.R. 73.

283 Sir John Smith argued that a cheque is a document creating a right over property, because it confers on the payee a right to diminish or destroy the drawer's bank balance: commentary to *Weiss v Government of Germany* [2000] Crim. L.R. 484. It is submitted with respect that this is wrong, because the payee acquires no *proprietary* right over the drawer's bank balance.

284 Bills of Exchange Act 1882, s.3(1).

285 July 26, 1993.

286 See below, para.4–162.

287 [2000] Crim. L.R. 484.

describing a transaction should qualify as a valuable security merely because it could be used as evidence that the transaction took place. But it was held in *King* that a CHAPS order falls within this category as well as the first. It evidences the creation and transfer of a right over property, and also the satisfaction of an obligation (namely the obligation of the bank to act upon the customer's instructions to effect the transfer).[288] The order was therefore "executed"—that is, it became a document falling within the third category—when the bank officials signed it, by way of confirmation that the funds had been transferred. In *Johl*[289] the court was prepared to assume that a letter from the paying bank confirming the transfer was a valuable security and was "executed" when signed, but did not have to decide the point because it was held that the defendant had not procured the signing of the letter.

Execution

4–161 The offence under TA 1968, s.20(2) was committed only if a person procured by deception the "execution" of a valuable security. In the primary sense of the word, a valuable security is executed when it is made. In most cases the document that constitutes the valuable security will have previously existed in a form in which it did not constitute a valuable security, and is executed when it is converted into a valuable security—for example, when a cheque form is filled in and signed.

4–162 But s.20(2) provided that the "execution" of a valuable security also included its "acceptance,[290] indorsement, alteration, cancellation or destruction in whole or in part". It was at one time thought that a valuable security was "executed" if it was honoured or otherwise given effect to,[291] but in *Kassim* this interpretation was rejected. The defendant used cheques and a credit card issued to him in a false name. The House of Lords quashed his convictions of procuring by deception the execution of the cheques and the credit card vouchers by the bank. Lord Ackner, with whose speech the other members of the House agreed, said:

> "It is . . . clear from the legislative history of section 20(2) that 'execution', which is deemed to cover the various activities detailed in the subsection, has as its object a wide variety of documents including bills of exchange and other negotiable instruments. The subsection contemplates acts being done to or in connection with such documents. It does not contemplate and accordingly is not concerned with giving effect to the documents by the carrying out [*sic*] the

[288] TA 1968, s.20(3).

[289] July 26, 1993. Edward Griew, *The Theft Acts* (7th edn, 1995) para.12–18, fn.31 is wrong in saying that the letter was held not to be a valuable security at all. (The citation given, [1994] Crim. L.R. 522, is also wrong.)

[290] "Acceptance" here has its technical meaning in the law of bills of exchange—viz. the drawee's act of writing on the bill and signing his assent to the order of the drawer: *Nanayakkara* (1986) 84 Cr.App.R. 125; *Kassim* [1992] 1 A.C. 9, overruling *Beck* [1985] 1 W.L.R. 22 on this point.

[291] *Beck* [1985] 1 W.L.R. 22; *Nanayakkara* (1986) 84 Cr.App.R. 125.

instructions which they may contain, such as the delivery of goods or the payment out of money."[292]

A valuable security was also deemed to have been executed, even if there was no valuable security in existence, if any paper or other material was signed or sealed in order that it might be made or converted into, or used or dealt with as, a valuable security.[293] The wording suggests that the intention referred to had to be that of the person signing or sealing the paper or material. In other words the offence was probably not committed by a person who, intending to use a document as a valuable security, induced another to sign it under the impression that the signature was required for some purpose which would not involve such use. But if the victim knew that the document would be used as a valuable security, it seems to have been immaterial that he did not appreciate the particular use to which it would be put, or even the particular type of valuable security into which it would be converted. **4–163**

Procuring execution

The requirement that the defendant "procure" the execution of a valuable security was construed as meaning that the execution must be part of his plan. In *Kassim* it was argued that the cheques and vouchers were cancelled or destroyed once the bank had acted on them, and that this was sufficient because cancellation and destruction were expressly included within "execution". It was held that the defendant had not *procured* the instruments' cancellation or destruction at all. **4–164**

> "This argument . . . confuses consequences with intention. What the appellant set out to achieve was a gain for himself. The dishonest means by which he intended to achieve this was not by the cancellation or destruction of the cheque. He achieved the profit he sought prior to the cheque's destruction or cancellation."[294]

Similarly in *Johl*[295] the defendant was held not to have procured the execution of a letter confirming that a mortgage advance had been paid: his object was to obtain the advance, not the letter. In *Hussain*[296] it was said to be irrelevant whether the defendant hoped or expected to get the money in the form of a valuable security rather than some other way. But in *N'Wadiche*[297] it was held that the defendant must either intend to procure the execution of a valuable security or be reckless as to that possibility. This seems right, but *Hussain* was not cited. **4–165**

292 [1992] 1 A.C. 9.
293 TA 1968, s.20(2).
294 [1992] 1 A.C. 9 at 19, *per* Lord Ackner.
295 July 26, 1993.
296 March 26, 1993.
297 [1998] Crim. L.R. 498.

CAUSATION

4–166 Each of the deception offences required two causal links. The first was inherent in the concept of deception: a person does not deceive unless he causes another person to believe that a proposition is true which is in fact false. The second arose because each of the offences consisted in the obtaining of a thing, or the procuring of some event, *by* deception. There had to be a causal link between the mistaken belief induced by the defendant and the obtaining or other event.

4–167 These two causal links were part of the actus reus of each of the deception offences. They are not part of the actus reus of fraud by false representation, because that offence is complete when the representation is made. It is immaterial whether the representation is believed, or whether the representor achieves anything by making it. But fraud by false representation is committed only if the defendant intends to make a gain for himself or another, or to cause loss to another or expose another to a risk of loss, *by* making the representation. He is not guilty unless there *would* be a causal link between the representation and the gain, loss or risk of loss if the events he intends were to occur. The requirements discussed in this section are thus equally relevant to fraud by false representation, but in relation to mens rea rather than actus reus.[298] This seems to be true of *both* the causal links required under the old law, because it is difficult to see how one might make a gain, etc. *by* making a false representation without the representee's being deceived by it.

CAUSATION OF BELIEF

4–168 Where a person made a representation which he knew to be false, under the old law there was a deception only if the representee was thereby induced to believe that the representation was true. The mistaken belief had to be caused by the representation. If it was attributable only to the stupidity or incompetence of the person mistaken, the necessary causal link was absent. In *Roebuck*[299] the defendant offered a chain to a pawnbroker, falsely claiming that it was silver. The pawnbroker tested it and accepted it as security for a loan. He relied solely on his own examination of the chain, and not on the defendant's assertion. The defendant was held to be guilty only of an attempt. The pawnbroker did believe that the chain was silver, as the defendant intended; but the belief was not caused by the false pretence. The defendant had tried to deceive him, but had failed. The position would have been otherwise if the pawnbroker had taken the statement into account in making his assessment, even if he would have reached the same conclusion on the basis of the test alone. The defendant's conduct had to be

[298] See above, para.3–004.
[299] (1856) Dears. & B. 24.

at least partially responsible for the victim's misapprehension, but it did not have to be the crucial factor.[300]

Where a person charges payment to an account (for example by presenting a credit card or otherwise providing the account details) without authority to do so, and the merchant runs a telephone or computer check and obtains clearance (for example because the card has been stolen but the theft has not yet been reported, or because the defendant is using the account details but is not in possession of the card), it might be argued that, while the merchant does believe that the user has authority to charge the payment to the account, he believes it because of the clearance—not because of the defendant's conduct. But the element of causation is established if the victim's belief is *partly* induced by the defendant, even if it is partly due to other factors for which the defendant is not responsible. Under the old law it was a question of fact whether the individual merchant relied wholly on the precautions he took (like the pawnbroker in *Roebuck*), or was also influenced to some extent by a representation on the part of the customer. **4–169**

A person could be deceived even if he had the opportunity to discover the truth and failed to do so—for example where a shop assistant accepted a credit card without seeking clearance, although clearance was a condition precedent of the shop's right to payment. "Contributory negligence" was not a defence.[301] **4–170**

OBTAINING BY DECEPTION

Once it was established that the victim had in fact been deceived, under the old law it had to be determined whether it was *by* the deception that the defendant obtained the specified thing or secured the specified event. There had to be a causal nexus between the deception and the specified outcome.[302] In the absence of such a nexus the full offence was not made out, though a charge of attempt or conspiracy might succeed.[303] This requirement was additional to that of a nexus between the defendant's words or conduct and the victim's mistaken belief. Which issue was raised by a given case might depend on how the deception was formulated. In *English*[304] a brickmaker agreed to take a lease of a brick field after inspecting it and being shown bricks which were falsely said to have been made from the earth of the field. It was argued (unsuccessfully) that he had relied on his own inspection rather than the false representation. The argument might be put in either of two ways: (a) that he believed it was a good and profitable brick field, but it was not the false representation that led him to believe this; or (b) that he believed that the defendant had been making good bricks from the field, but **4–171**

[300] See below, para.4–182.

[301] *Jessop* (1858) Dears. & B. 442.

[302] So the deception must come first: *Collis-Smith* [1971] Crim. L.R. 716; *Coady* [1996] Crim. L.R. 518.

[303] *Edwards* [1978] Crim. L.R. 49.

[304] (1872) 12 Cox C.C. 171.

it was not that belief that induced him to take the lease. On the first view there would be no deception at all, as in *Roebuck*. On the second, there might be a deception but it would not be operative.

4–172 Whether this second causal nexus was present depended primarily on the victim's attitude towards the proposition that the defendant led him to believe. There were a number of different attitudes that he might have.

Point important to victim

4–173 The point on which the victim was deceived might be one that was in itself important to him, such as the quality of goods which he was induced to buy. Normally it was self-evident that the defendant would not have obtained (for example) the purchase price if the victim had known the truth. But there could be exceptional cases where the victim had no choice in the matter: he would have had to co-operate, albeit reluctantly, even if he had known the truth. If a creditor was obliged, under the terms of the contract between him and his debtor, to accept payment by cheque (unsupported by a cheque guarantee card), it could not be said that he was induced to accept the debtor's cheque[305] by the debtor's implied representation that the cheque was good.[306] It was important to him that that representation should be true, but he would not be entitled to refuse the cheque even if he knew it was unlikely to be honoured. He would just have to present it and see.

4–174 If, however, he accepted a cheque (not backed by a cheque card) when he was not obliged to do so, it would usually be clear that he would not have accepted it had he known it was bad. If the cheque was backed by a cheque card, but the debtor was not authorised to use the card and was therefore deceiving the creditor by doing so,[307] it was a question of fact whether the creditor would have accepted the cheque had he known of the debtor's lack of authority.[308] Similar considerations would apply if he was obliged to accept payment by credit card, or in any other form which consisted in the conferral on him of a right to be paid by a third party.

Point has potentially important implications

4–175 The point on which the victim was deceived might be unimportant in itself, but might have important implications. In that case he would not necessarily refuse to co-operate if he knew the truth: it would depend whether there was a satisfactory explanation. In *Laverty*[309] the defendant changed the number plates on a stolen car and sold it. He was charged with obtaining the purchase price by a false implied representation that the car had originally been registered with the number it now bore. The conviction

[305] And therefore to wait for payment: TA 1978, s.2(3).
[306] *Andrews* [1981] Crim. L.R. 106.
[307] Above, paras 4–055 *et seq*.
[308] Clearly he would not be *obliged* to do so in these circumstances.
[309] [1970] 3 All E.R. 432.

was quashed because there was no evidence that the representation as to the car's identity had had any effect in inducing the purchaser to buy the car. The purchaser had no interest in the car's registration number as such,[310] and might still have bought the car had he known that the number had been changed. But nobody changes a car's registration number without a reason, and some of the possible reasons for doing so will be unattractive to an honest purchaser. In the absence of special circumstances it can surely be inferred that a purchaser who knew that the number had been changed would not buy the car without further enquiry. If he were given a false explanation which he accepted, the price would clearly have been obtained by deception. It ought not to make any difference that he is deceived into not demanding an explanation at all. The defendant cannot attain his objective without one deception or the other. Whichever one he uses, it is only by deception that he obtains the price.

This is a possible explanation of a curious dictum in *Hamilton*, where it **4–176** was said that by presenting withdrawal slips to bank cashiers the appellant had made implied representations about what he *believed* to be the state of the account (as against what it actually was). If that was the only deception, did it enable him to obtain the money?

> "There was no evidence that the cashiers in fact checked the bank's records before making any payments to the appellant, but it may perhaps be inferred that they did so, probably by calling up computer records on a VDU screen on their desks. If this was the case, then the argument would be that the bank was induced to make the payments, not by the alleged or any representation made by the appellant, but by the cashier's belief formed from the computer data that the payment was justified. In our view, however, it would remain open to the jury to find that the payment was induced, at least in part, by the representation which they were entitled to infer was made by the appellant."[311]

At first sight this is a surprising suggestion. The cashier pays the money because the computer says the customer is entitled to it, not because the customer seems to think so. But if the cashier learned (for example by overhearing the customer admitting it to a third party) that the customer knows he is not entitled to the money, that might give the cashier pause. The customer's state of mind, *in itself*, is of no concern to the cashier: if the cashier is satisfied that the bank's records are correct, he is unlikely to care that the customer thinks they are not. But if he knew that the customer thinks they are not, this might lead him to wonder whether they really are.

Point unimportant provided victim does not know the truth

The subject-matter of the deception might be of no interest to the victim **4–177** at all, except that he would not co-operate if he knew the truth. This would often be the case where a payment instrument such as a cheque card or

[310] He would of course be interested in the car's age, but the letter representing the date of first registration was the same in the new number as in the old one.
[311] (1990) 92 Cr.App.R. 54 at 59.

credit card was used without authority. The customer's implied representation that he had authority to use the card might be of no interest to the merchant. The merchant would be entitled to payment by the bank or card issuer anyway, as long as he did not accept the card in the knowledge that the customer did *not* have authority to use it. The main issue here, under the old law, was whether the merchant could be said to have been deceived. As we have seen, it was held that he could.[312] The absence of knowledge that the customer lacked authority, coupled with indifference whether he had it or not, was treated as a "belief" that he had it. If this "belief" was in fact mistaken, and was fostered by the customer's conduct, the merchant was deceived. Once that first (dubious) step was taken, there was little further difficulty in concluding that the property was obtained *by* the deception. Were it not for the merchant's "belief" that the customer had authority—in other words, if he knew that the customer did not—he would not accept payment in that form.

Point unimportant except for fact of deception

4–178 Sometimes the victim of a deception might be wholly indifferent to the truth or falsity of the representation (in the sense that he would still have co-operated had the defendant admitted the truth in the first place), but might have been less inclined to co-operate had he known of the deception. In *Sullivan*[313] the defendant obtained money from a number of people by advertising dartboards for sale. The false pretence alleged was that he made the dartboards himself—a pretence which, in the court's view, must have influenced the customers. This inference was questionable, since none of the customers gave evidence that they were anxious to buy dartboards from the manufacturer rather than anyone else. As long as they got dartboards of acceptable quality they probably did not care who the manufacturer was. If that is right, does it follow that the defendant did not obtain the money *by* the deception? Arguably he did, because, while the customers might have been willing to buy dartboards from someone who was not the manufacturer *and did not claim to be*, they might have been less ready to part with their money had they known that one of the statements in the advertisement was a lie. It is submitted that in that case he would not be obtaining the money *by* deception. It was suggested above that if a person can obtain property in either of two ways, and either way involves a deception, he is obtaining the property by deception whichever way he chooses.[314] But it does not follow that he obtains it by deception if one way involves a deception and the other does not, and he chooses the one that does. In this case the deception is not the means by which he obtains the property: he could equally have obtained it without deception. On this view it was not conclusive that the victim would not have co-operated had he known that

312 Above, paras 4–055 *et seq*.
313 (1945) 30 Cr.App.R. 132.
314 Above, para.4–175.

the statement was false. The question is whether he would have done so had the defendant not made a false statement at all.

In *Talbott*[315] an actress applied for housing benefit and gave her stage name as that of her landlady. The purpose of this was to conceal from her real landlord the fact that she was claiming benefit. Her defence was that, given her circumstances, she was entitled to housing benefit anyway. But the assessment officer gave evidence that she would not have got it if he had known the truth. These two propositions are not necessarily inconsistent. Perhaps she was entitled to benefit, and would have got it if she had told the truth; but she would not have got it (or not without a lot of explaining) if the lie had been immediately detected. In that case, it is submitted, she would not be obtaining the benefit *by* the deception. *Talbott* is an unusual case because the defendant appears to have been using the deception for a wholly collateral purpose. She wanted to deceive her landlord, not the local authority. Usually the defendant will have employed the deception because he thought, rightly or wrongly, that it would help him to get what he wanted. In that case there would at least be an *attempt* to obtain by deception under the old law.[316] Under the new law, the full offence will be complete. **4–179**

Point wholly unimportant

In other cases the point on which the alleged victim was deceived was of no concern to him whatsoever. Not only could the defendant have obtained the specified thing or secured the specified event without resorting to deception, but he would still have obtained or secured it even if the alleged victim had known he was lying. In such a case the required causal link was clearly absent. In *Rashid*[317] a British Rail steward was charged with the possession of articles for use in the obtaining of property by deception.[318] The articles in question were two loaves of sliced bread and a bag of tomatoes. The steward intended to sell his own tomato sandwiches and keep the proceeds. The prosecution had to establish that if he had carried out this scheme he would have obtained the proceeds by the deception that the sandwiches were British Rail's. It was held that no such inference could be drawn. The passengers would not care whose sandwiches they were buying, as long as they were fresh and reasonably priced. In *Doukas*,[319] however, which concerned a similar fraud by a wine waiter, it was held that a jury is entitled to assume that members of the public would not willingly participate in a fraud. This approach was followed in *Corboz*[320] and approved by the House of Lords in *Cooke*.[321] **4–180**

315 [1995] Crim. L.R. 396.
316 *Edwards* [1978] Crim. L.R. 49.
317 [1977] 1 W.L.R. 298.
318 TA 1968, s.25(1); see now FA 2006, s.6, below, para.21–042.
319 [1978] 1 W.L.R. 372.
320 [1984] Crim. L.R. 629.
321 [1986] A.C. 909.

4–181 This did not affect the principle applied in *Rashid*: it merely involved the making of an assumption which rendered that principle inapplicable. Where the charge was of actually obtaining something by deception, the question whether the defendant could have obtained the thing without the deception was one of fact. It depended what the particular victim would in fact have done if he had not been deceived. Inchoate offences such as going equipped[322] or conspiracy[323] are another matter. Where there is no identifiable victim, and it is therefore meaningless to ask whether the victim would have co-operated had he known the truth, it may be legitimate for the law to make assumptions as to what the intended victims' reaction would have been. But it had to be proved at any rate that the defendant *thought* the victims' reaction would (or might) be such as would suffice for the full offence.[324]

Multiple causation

4–182 The deception had to be a reason for the victim's action, but it did not have to be the only reason or even the main reason.[325] In *Whiteside*[326] it was said to be inappropriate to direct the jury to this effect where there was only one factor that could have caused the victim to act as he did; but the court was clearly wrong in thinking that there was only one such factor in that case. The defendants sold counterfeit cassettes in the street, pretending that they were genuine. That pretence would clearly be relevant to a prospective purchaser—not because he would be participating in a fraud on the copyright owner if he knew the truth and bought the cassettes anyway (which might or might not concern him), but because they would be *copies* of legitimate recordings and therefore of inferior quality. However, many purchasers would attach greater weight to the identity of the music and of the performers. The judge was clearly right to remind the jury that the likely existence of such other considerations was not a defence.

4–183 It was sometimes said that the deception must be a *decisive* factor, a *sine qua non*—that it must be proved that the defendant would not have obtained the benefit but for the deception. This was not an accurate reflection of the civil law. In *JEB Fasteners Ltd v Marks Bloom & Co* the plaintiffs alleged that they had been induced to take over a company by accounts which had been negligently prepared by the defendants. The trial judge found that the plaintiffs "relied on" the accounts, in the sense of being encouraged by them, but that the defendants' negligence did not "cause" the loss because the plaintiffs would still have taken over the company even if they had known the true position.[327] On appeal it was held that the former finding was crucial and the latter irrelevant.

322 This was the charge in *Rashid, Doukas* and *Corboz*.
323 This was the point at issue in *Cooke*.
324 The same seems to be true of the new fraud offence, which is inchoate by nature: see above, para.3–002.
325 *English* (1872) 12 Cox C.C. 171; *Lince* (1873) 12 Cox C.C. 451.
326 [1989] Crim. L.R. 436.
327 [1981] 3 All E.R. 289.

> "[I]f the plaintiffs' directors were motivated or influenced by the accounts to any substantial extent, there would be the necessary reliance on the misrepresentation they contained . . ., and the judge should have found for the plaintiffs. Nor would it necessarily follow from his finding that the plaintiffs would have taken over the company without having false accounts to consider, that the judge's conclusion was right: he had to decide what in fact caused the plaintiffs to take over the company when they did have the false accounts before them."[328]

Thing obtained from person not deceived

In most cases under the old law it was the person deceived who provided the defendant with the thing that he was charged with obtaining; but this was not necessarily so. It was sufficient, for example, if the benefit was conferred by someone acting on the instructions of the person deceived, provided that the benefit was conferred *because* of the deception. It did not matter even that the person providing the thing was well aware of the deception, as long as he would not have done so but for the deception. If a person obtained goods by using a cheque guarantee card when he had insufficient funds to meet the cheque and no agreed overdraft facility, he could be charged with obtaining a pecuniary advantage, namely the resulting overdraft.[329] The bank conferred this advantage on him by honouring the cheque. It was immaterial that the bank was not deceived, because it had no choice. It created the overdraft because it had a legal obligation to do so, and it had an obligation to do so because the payee had been deceived into accepting the cheque card. So the defendant had obtained the overdraft by deception. 4–184

Nor was it essential that there should be a legal obligation to confer the benefit. In *Beck*[330] the defendant cashed forged traveller's cheques. They were honoured by the bank that had issued them, and it was alleged that he had procured the bank's acceptance of them by deception.[331] It was argued that there was no causal nexus, because the bank was under no legal obligation to pay. It knew the cheques were forgeries but chose to honour them anyway. The argument was rejected. In legal theory the bank may have voluntarily chosen to accept the cheques, but in commercial reality it had no alternative. Had it not been for the deception, the bank would not have been put in that position. So the defendant had procured its acceptance of the cheques by deception. 4–185

In *Rozeik*[332] it seems to have been assumed that property cannot be obtained by deception unless it is the *owner* who is deceived. The defendants obtained cheques from finance companies on the basis of false 4–186

[328] [1983] 1 All E.R. 583 at 589, *per* Stephenson L.J.

[329] TA 1968, s.16(2)(b), above, para.4–148; *Waites* [1982] Crim. L.R. 369.

[330] [1985] 1 W.L.R. 22.

[331] The decision that this was an "acceptance" of a valuable security within the meaning of the Act was overruled in *Kassim* [1992] 1 A.C. 9 (above, fn.290), but this does not affect the point made in the text.

[332] [1996] 1 W.L.R. 159.

information as to the purposes for which the funds were to be used. The prosecution accepted that the managers of the relevant branches of the finance companies may have known the truth. The jury were directed to assume that the managers *had* known the truth, but to consider whether any *other* employee concerned in the processing of the applications had been deceived. This was held to be a misdirection.

> "[Counsel for the Crown] submitted that it was sufficient that any person in the chain or sequence of employees who handled each application was deceived. Each such person represented or constituted the company for the purpose of being deceived. It seems to us that that states the position far too widely. True it is that in the present case a cheque was in each instance obtained from the company, and that may have been as a result of many people being deceived. But the offences would not have been made out unless it were proved that an individual was deceived from whom the cheque could properly be said to have been obtained."[333]

4–187 But the legislation laid down no such rule. It was certainly sufficient that D obtained property from A by deceiving B. What the court appears to have meant is that it would not be sufficient that, for example, the secretary who typed the cheque was deceived, if the signatories were not:

> "[A] cheque could only be obtained from the company from an employee who had authority to provide it. The deception had to operate on the mind of the employee from whom the cheque was obtained. In no sense could a cheque be 'obtained' from the person who merely typed it out. So the judge's references to 'any' employee were fatally wide. What the Crown had to prove was that when the cheque was obtained from the company it was obtained from a person who was deceived. Although in no sense was it obtained from those who checked or typed it, the signatories of the cheques (apart from [the branch managers]) were in a different position. They had a responsibility to ensure that the cheques were not signed unless satisfied that the money should be paid. They were more than mere mechanics and in our judgment, if they were deceived, the company also was, once [the branch managers] were disregarded. That means that (1) where a manager only signed, the offence could not be made out; (2) where a manager signed with another employee, it had to be shown that that other was deceived; and (3) where two employees (other than a manager) signed, it had to be proved either that one was or that both were deceived, and that where one was, the other did not know of the fraud, since if he or she did, the company would not have been deceived."[334]

There is some confusion here. Under the old law, the issues were (1) whether *someone* was deceived, and (2) whether the property was obtained *by* that deception. If there was no offence under the old law where the only person deceived was the secretary who typed the cheque, this was not because the *company* was not deceived. It was because the obtaining of the cheque did not result from the deception of the secretary. The cheque would have been obtained even if the secretary had known the truth,

[333] [1996] 1 W.L.R. 159 at 165.
[334] [1996] 1 W.L.R. 159 at 165.

because the secretary typed whatever cheques were requested by whoever had authority to request them.

The court also gave a second reason for allowing the appeals, which was equally flawed. Since the branch managers knew the truth, the finance companies must also be taken to have known the truth (unless it was proved that the managers were parties to the fraud,[335] of which there was no evidence). It followed, the court thought, that the companies were not deceived, and that there was therefore no offence. It is the last step that is suspect. The indictment did not allege that the defendants had deceived the company. It alleged only that they had obtained the company's property by deceiving *someone.* The court declined to certify the following question: **4–188**

> "Is a company capable of being deceived if one or more of its employees is proved to have been deceived when acting in the course of their employment, but another employee, in a superior position but not proved to be a party to any offence, knows the truth of the matter?"

But this was the wrong question. It was immaterial whether the company was deceived, because that was not the deception alleged.

Remoteness

A thing was not necessarily obtained *by* deception just because the obtaining was the culmination of a chain of events in which deception played a part. It was not enough that the defendant would not have obtained the benefit had he not at some stage practised a deception. This might be so only because it was by deception that he obtained the *opportunity* to obtain the benefit. In that case the deception might in a factual sense be a cause of the obtaining, but it would not necessarily be a cause in law. The obtaining might be too remote a consequence. In *Gardner*[336] the victim was induced by the defendant's false pretences to accept him as a lodger, and twelve days later agreed to provide him with board as well. The food was not paid for. In a sense the deception contributed towards the obtaining of the food. Had it not been for the deception the defendant would not have been accepted as a lodger, and had he not already been known to the victim as a lodger she would not have agreed to provide him with food on credit. But it was held that the obtaining of the food was "too remotely the result of the false pretence". **4–189**

Thing obtained by fulfilling conditions

It was sometimes arguable that the reason the defendant was able to obtain the thing in question was not that he had deceived the victim but that he was entitled to that thing, having fulfilled the necessary conditions. In *Clucas*[337] the defendants induced a bookmaker to accept large bets by **4–190**

[335] *Att-Gen's Reference (No.2 of 1982)* [1984] Q.B. 624; above, para.2–087.
[336] (1856) Dears. & B. 40.
[337] [1949] 2 K.B. 226.

pretending to be acting as commission agents. It was held that they had obtained their winnings not by false pretences but by backing the right horse. Similarly it was held that a person who obtained a job by deception did not obtain the salary by deception but by doing the job.[338]

4–191 On the other hand, a person who deceived another into making a contract could be found to have obtained the proceeds of the contract by deception even though the immediate cause of the obtaining was his performance of the contract.[339] In *King*[340] the defendants falsely told an elderly widow that they were tree surgeons and that the trees in her garden were dangerous, and offered to remove the trees for £500. Convictions of attempting to obtain property by deception were upheld. The jury were entitled to find that if the plan had succeeded the defendants would have obtained the money by the deception, and not just by removing the trees.[341]

4–192 The difficulty could sometimes be avoided by charging the obtaining by deception of a "pecuniary advantage", namely an opportunity to earn remuneration in an office or employment, or to win money by betting.[342] Under TA 1968, s.16, Clucas could have been charged with obtaining the *bet* by deception. King could probably[343] have been charged with attempting to obtain the job.

Thing obtained after discovery of deception

4–193 Where a thing was obtained from a person who had previously been deceived, the fact that the victim had already seen through the deception was not necessarily fatal to a charge under the old law. In *Miller*[344] the defendant induced foreign tourists to ride in his vehicle by pretending "that he was a taxi-driver, that his vehicle was a taxi and that he would charge a fair and reasonable sum". It was argued that he had not obtained their money *by* deception because by the time they came to pay his extortionate charges they already suspected that he had been lying. They paid because they felt they had no choice. This was held to be irrelevant. The decision is questionable, since the defendant appears to have obtained the money by duress rather than by deception. The deception merely enabled him to create a situation in which he was able to exercise duress.[345]

338 *Lewis* (January 1922), cited in *Russell on Crime* (12th edn, 1964) vol.2, p.1186, fn.66.

339 *Abbott* (1847) 1 Den. 273; *Burgon* (1856) Dears. & B. 11; *Roebuck* (1856) Dears. & B. 24.

340 [1987] Q.B. 547.

341 The fact that the charge was one of attempt rather than the full offence, and that the question was therefore whether the defendants *intended* the deception to be a cause of the obtaining, seems to have been overlooked. Under the new law it is similarly crucial whether the defendant intends the representation to be a cause of the gain, loss or risk of loss that he intends to make or cause: see above, para.3–004.

342 See above, para.4–146.

343 i.e. assuming that he was earning money in an "employment": cf. above, para.4–150.

344 (1992) 95 Cr.App.R. 421.

345 Under the new law it would be sufficient that he made the representations with the intention of thereby making a gain. Presumably he did not know, when he made the representations, that the tourists would realise the truth before they paid. If his intention was that they should pay *either* because they still thought he was a genuine taxi-driver *or* because they were too scared to refuse, this would seem to be enough.

Intended causation under the old law

4–194 Under the new law there is no requirement that anything be obtained at all, let alone by means of the false representation; but the defendant must *intend* to make a gain, cause a loss or expose another to a risk of loss *by* making the representation. Causation is an element of the mens rea, though not of the actus reus.[346] It is arguable that under the old law it was an element of both. On this view, a person did not commit an offence of obtaining a thing by deception unless he did in fact obtain it by deception *and* knew that he was doing so.

4–195 In *Talbott*[347] the defendant gave false information about her landlord in an application for housing benefit, although she appears to have been entitled to the benefit anyway. It was argued above[348] that she did not obtain the benefit by deception unless the deception helped her to obtain it. What if for some reason it did help—that is, she might not otherwise have got the benefit—but she did not expect it to? In that case she would intend to obtain the benefit *with* deception but not *by* deception. Arguably she ought not to be guilty even under the old law, on the basis that mens rea is required in relation to every element of the actus reus. This argument could be supported by reference to the new law, under which she would clearly not be guilty because she would not intend to get the benefit *by* making the false representation. If she would have been guilty under the old law, it would follow that Parliament has changed the law so that she would no longer be guilty. This seems unlikely to have been Parliament's intention. So perhaps she would not be guilty under the old law either.

MULTIPLE REPRESENTATIONS

4–196 Because each of the deception offences required not merely deception but the securing of a particular *result* by deception, the securing of the result was a single offence even if it was achieved by means of a number of separate deceptions. Multiple representations could therefore be included in a single count without duplicity,[349] and the offence was made out even if only one representation were proved.[350] But the jury had to be satisfied that *one* of the representations alleged was proved.[351] In *Brown (Kevin)* the Court of Appeal gave this guidance:

> "Each ingredient of the offence must be proved to the satisfaction of each and every member of the jury (subject to the majority direction).
>
> However, where a number of matters are specified in the charge as together constituting one ingredient in the offence, and any one of them is capable of

[346] See above, para.3–004.
[347] [1995] Crim. L.R. 396.
[348] Para.4–179.
[349] *Linnell* [1969] 1 W.L.R. 1514.
[350] *Lince* (1873) 12 Cox C.C. 451.
[351] See J. C. Smith, "Satisfying the Jury" [1988] Crim. L.R. 335.

doing so, then it is enough to establish the ingredient that any one of them is proved; but (because of the first principle above) any such matter must be proved to the satisfaction of the whole jury. The jury should be directed accordingly, and it should be made clear to them as well that they should all be satisfied that the statement upon which they are agreed was an inducement as alleged."[352]

4–197 The court distinguished *Agbim*,[353] where the defendant submitted an expenses claim which included various allegedly false statements as to the expenditure incurred. It was held that, as long as the jury were satisfied that the claim as a whole was deceptive, there was no need for them to agree that any particular statement was false. The decision was explained in *Brown* on the basis that the deception was as to the total expenditure claimed, not the individual items.

4–198 The *Brown* direction should be given in any case where the defendant is alleged to have secured a particular result by means of multiple representations, and there is any possibility of jurors reaching differing conclusions about different representations.[354] Counsel should be invited to make submissions concerning the direction to be given, particularly (but not only) in a complicated fraud case.[355] But it is comparatively rare for a direction on the point to be required,[356] because in most cases the allegations stand or fall together. In such a case the *Brown* direction is unnecessary.[357] It may then be sufficient for the judge to say that the Crown need only prove one false representation, but that the jury must be unanimous.[358]

4–199 Moreover the need for the *Brown* direction can apparently be evaded simply by charging conspiracy to defraud. In *Hancock*[359] the defendants were charged with conspiracy to defraud investors by making 10 misrepresentations which were listed in the particulars. It was held that the alleged representations were not essential to the offence. The jury were entitled to convict if they were all sure that the defendants had agreed to defraud investors somehow, even though each of them thought that a different misrepresentation had been agreed upon. It is questionable whether this is consistent with *Brown*.

[352] (1983) 79 Cr.App.R. 115 at 119.
[353] [1979] Crim. L.R. 171.
[354] *Gray*, October 9, 1992.
[355] *Day*, *The Times*, October 3, 1991.
[356] *Phillips* (1988) 86 Cr.App.R. 18.
[357] *Mitchell* [1994] Crim. L.R. 66.
[358] *Price* [1991] Crim. L.R. 465.
[359] [1996] 2 Cr.App.R. 554.

CHAPTER 5

FAILING TO DISCLOSE INFORMATION

Under the old law it was not clear whether a failure to disclose information, not amounting to an implied misrepresentation,[1] could nevertheless be a deception.[2] Such a failure by definition cannot be fraud by false representation by virtue of s.2 of the Fraud Act 2006 ("FA 2006"). It may, however, constitute fraud by virtue of FA 2006, s.3, which provides: **5–001**

> "A person is in breach of this section if he—
>
> (a) dishonestly fails to disclose to another person information which he is under a legal duty to disclose, and
>
> (b) intends, by failing to disclose the information—
>
> (i) to make a gain for himself or another, or
>
> (ii) to cause loss to another or to expose another to a risk of loss."

A person who is in breach of FA 2006, s.3 commits the offence of fraud, contrary to FA 2006, s.1. The requirement of dishonesty is discussed in Ch.2, and that of intention to make a gain or cause a loss or a risk of loss in Ch.3. The only further requirements are that the defendant must be under a legal duty to disclose information to another person, and must fail to do so. **5–002**

[1] For circumstances in which a failure to disclose may amount to a false representation, see above, paras 4–050 *et seq*.
[2] See below, paras 5–018 *et seq*.

LEGAL DUTY TO DISCLOSE

THE LAW COMMISSION'S RECOMMENDATION

5–003 Under the Law Commission's draft Bill, it would not have been necessary to prove a legal duty to disclose. It would have been sufficient if the defendant knows that the victim "trusts" him to disclose the information, and it is reasonable in the circumstances to expect him to do so. According to the Commission, the situation envisaged was "broadly similar to the existence of a relationship which imports fiduciary duties as a matter of civil law, but . . . does not depend on the existence of such a relationship".[3] Liability would have turned on the slippery notion of "trust", and on juries' views as to what can reasonably be expected. It is remarkable that such a recommendation should have appeared in a report which rejected the idea of a "general dishonesty offence" as unduly vague. Even the Home Office was not willing to stretch the law this far. Under FA 2006, s.3, non-disclosure is not fraud unless there is a legal duty to disclose. The effect is that s.3 adds little to ss.2 and 4, because breach of a legal duty to disclose will usually involve either an implied false representation or a breach of fiduciary duty.

TWO KINDS OF DUTY

5–004 There are two senses in which a person may be said to be under a "duty" to disclose information. First, he may literally be under a legal obligation to make disclosure, in the sense that another person has a legal right that he do so, and a failure to do so is a legal wrong against that person.[4] The obligation may arise from the express or implied terms of a contract, from principles of equity[5] or from a statute.[6] Since non-disclosure is a legal wrong, it will typically be remediable in damages or equitable compensation. This is a duty of disclosure in the strict sense.

5–005 Secondly, a person is sometimes precluded from enforcing a transaction, or retaining the benefit of it, on the ground that he failed to disclose relevant information to another party before the other party entered into the transaction. An example is a contract of insurance, which is said to be *uberrimae fidei* (of the utmost good faith). The description is misleading, because the requirement of good faith is imposed not by the terms of the

[3] Law Com. No.276, *Fraud*, Cm.5560, para.7.32.

[4] See W.N. Hohfeld, *Fundamental Legal Conceptions as Applied in Judicial Reasoning* (1919). There may also be duties imposed by public law which are not owed to particular persons. Where a statute requires disclosure, there is presumably a duty to disclose within the meaning of FA 2006 even if the sanction is criminal rather than a right of civil action.

[5] For example, it seems that non-disclosure by a fiduciary to his principal is not just a ground of rescission but, at least in some cases, an equitable wrong. See below, para.6–053, fn.93.

[6] e.g. Financial Services and Markets Act 2000, s.80, which imposes a general duty of disclosure on persons submitting listing particulars.

contract itself but by a rule which governs negotiations towards certain kinds of contract.[7] Moreover the rule only allows the aggrieved party to rescind the transaction and claim restitution: he cannot claim compensation, because the non-disclosure is not itself a legal wrong.[8] Strictly speaking, there is no *duty* to disclose at all. Disclosure is merely a condition precedent to the enforceability of the transaction and the retention of benefits conferred under it.

FA 2006 does not define "a legal duty to disclose", but it seems that both kinds of duty are intended to be covered. The Law Commission explained that, for the purpose of cl.3 of its draft Bill, **5–006**

> "there is a legal duty to disclose information not only if the defendant's failure to disclose it gives the victim a cause of action for damages, but also if the law gives the victim a right to set aside any change in his or her legal position to which he or she may consent as a result of the non-disclosure. For example, a person in a fiduciary position has a duty to disclose material information when entering into a contract with his or her beneficiary, in the sense that a failure to make such disclosure will entitle the beneficiary to rescind the contract and to reclaim any property transferred under it."[9]

It is understandable that the Commission's draft Bill should have used the word "duty" in this extended sense without definition, because under the Commission's recommendations nothing would have turned on the existence of a legal duty anyway.[10] The existence of such a duty would have been only one example of a looser requirement. Under FA 2006, it has become an essential element of this form of the offence; but its introduction was not accompanied by an amendment clarifying its meaning. The explanatory notes to the Act do not mention the rejected recommendation, but cite the above passage from the Commission's report and add: **5–007**

> "For example, the failure of a solicitor to share vital information with a client within the context of their work relationship, in order to perpetrate a fraud upon that client, would be covered by this section. Similarly, an offence could be committed under this section if a person intentionally failed to disclose information relating to his heart condition when making an application for life insurance."

[7] See John Cartwright, *Misrepresentation, Mistake and Non-Disclosure* (2nd edn, 2007) paras 17.03–17.05.

[8] *Banque Keyser Ullmann SA v Skandia (UK) Insurance Ltd* [1990] 1 Q.B. 665, 771–781. On appeal the point was not decided, but Lords Templeman and Jauncey agreed with the Court of Appeal: [1991] 2 A.C. 249 at 280, 281. This might conceivably mean that the non-disclosure is an anomalous kind of wrong which, unlike most wrongs, does not sound in compensation; but the more natural conclusion is that the non-disclosure is only an event triggering a right to restitution, and is not a wrong at all. See Peter Birks, "The Concept of a Civil Wrong" in D. Owen (ed.) *Philosophical Foundations of Tort Law* (1995).

[9] Law Com. No.276, para.7.29. Contracts *uberrimae fidei* might have been a better example. It now seems that non-disclosure by a fiduciary may give the principal a right to equitable compensation rather than restitution, and may therefore be a legal wrong anyway: below, para.6–053, fn.93. Non-disclosure by a fiduciary is more likely to be charged under FA 2006, s.4 than under s.3, because a charge under s.4 would probably avoid potential difficulties about whether there is a duty to disclose.

[10] See above, para.5–003.

The Attorney-General explained in Parliament:

> "There are many occasions in the law where there is a duty of disclosure: in contracts of insurance, under certain market customs or certain contractual arrangements. In those circumstances, people may well be under a duty to make a disclosure and fail to make it. That will have consequences in law . . . for example, the ability to set aside contracts on the grounds of non-disclosure . . ."[11]

It is clear from these explanations that non-disclosure may fall within s.3 if its effect is to trigger a rule of law which has adverse consequences for the non-discloser, even if it is not a legal wrong and does not render him liable for compensation.

5–008 Indeed it seems clearer that the section is intended to apply to non-disclosure in the course of negotiations towards a transaction than that it is intended to apply to breach of a duty of disclosure in the strict sense. The Law Commission said:

> "The kind of conduct we have described as 'non-disclosure' is broadly analogous to, though in our view distinct from, that of positive misrepresentation which brings about a transfer of property or some other economic consequence. It is in the nature of the situation that the person who trusts the defendant to disclose the information in question will act, or omit to act, in reliance on the defendant's failure to do so."[12]

The Commission then contrasted this situation with abuse of position.

> "In addition to this case, however, we believe that some kinds of conduct can properly be described as fraudulent on the ground that they amount to an abuse of an existing position of trust, even if there is no question of the victim's thereby being induced to act or omit to act. The difference between this case and that of non-disclosure is that in this case the defendant does not need to enlist the victim's co-operation in order to secure the desired result."[13]

5–009 The Commission's examples include an antique dealer who buys valuable heirlooms from vulnerable people without disclosing their true value—a case which now falls outside FA 2006 unless an implied misrepresentation can be proved, because the dealer is under no legal duty to disclose the value—and a fiduciary who enters into a contract with his beneficiary without disclosing material information. The clause that became s.3 seems to have been aimed at failure to disclose information which is material to *a proposed transaction* between the defendant and the person to whom disclosure ought to be made.

5–010 The explanatory notes to the Bill at one point seemed to support this view. In relation to what is now s.4 it was said:

[11] *Hansard*, HL Vol.673, col.1412 (July 19, 2005). In the Commons, the Solicitor General similarly gave the example of non-disclosure in connection with an insurance contract: *Hansard*, SC Deb.B, col.10 (June 20, 2006).

[12] Law Com. No.276, para.7.35.

[13] Law Com. No.276, para.7.36.

> "For example, the defendant may have been given the authority to exercise a discretion on the other's behalf or to have access to the other's assets, premises, equipment or customers. Therefore the defendant does not need to secure any further co-operation from him in order to commit an offence of fraud against him."[14]

But this passage does not appear in the notes on the Act. Moreover, both versions give as an example of the application of s.3 "the failure of a solicitor to share vital information with a client within the context of their work relationship, in order to perpetrate a fraud upon that client". There is no suggestion here that the solicitor is assumed to be withholding information relevant to a proposed transaction between the solicitor and the client.

Moreover, the Law Commission's draft Bill expressly provided that the **5–011** duty to disclose information could be "under any enactment, instrument or rule of law".[15] The Commission's report explained that such a duty

> "may derive from statute (such as the provisions governing company prospectuses), from the fact that the transaction in question is one of the utmost good faith (such as a contract of insurance), from the express or implied terms of a contract, from the custom of a particular trade or market, or from the existence of a fiduciary relationship between the parties (such as that of agent and principal)."[16]

In some of these cases (such as the contract of insurance) the duty would arise before the transaction is entered into, but in others (such as a duty under the terms of a contract) it would arise from the transaction itself.

It therefore seems clear that, while the section was primarily aimed at **5–012** non-disclosure in the context of a proposed transaction between the parties, it was also intended to apply to any non-disclosure which is a legal wrong. For example, it would seem to apply to an agent who fails to inform his principal of a business opportunity because he plans to take it up himself. If a director has a fiduciary duty to disclose his own misconduct to the company,[17] a dishonest failure to do so would seem to be fraud by virtue of s.3 as well as s.4.

This interpretation could make the section alarmingly wide. There must **5–013** be many employees, for example, whose contracts of employment expressly or by implication require them to disclose certain matters to their employers. It is not clear why a failure to make such disclosure should be

[14] Notes to the Fraud Bill as introduced in the House of Lords, para.18.

[15] Under the Law Commission's recommendations a legal duty of disclosure would not have been necessary, but the Commission's draft Bill dealt separately with the case where there is a legal duty and the case where there is not.

[16] Law Com. No.276, para.7.28. This passage is cited in the explanatory notes to the Act, at para.18. Similarly the Attorney-General said in Committee that the requisite duty "could be a legal duty arising under a rule of law, a statute, an enactment, or it could arise out of a relationship, for example, a fiduciary relationship, but it could arise out of a contract as well": *Hansard*, HL Vol.673, col.1428 (July 19, 2005).

[17] See *Item Software (UK) Ltd v Fassihi* [2004] EWCA Civ 1244; [2005] I.C.R. 450; below, para.6–056.

regarded as fraud, even if it is accompanied by an intent to make a gain (which might be no more than a wish to avoid dismissal or a fine) and even if a jury can be persuaded that it is dishonest. Assuming that the offence does not extend to dishonest breaches of contract in general,[18] why should it include a dishonest breach of contract merely because the term broken is one requiring the disclosure of information? By failing to examine sufficiently closely the various ways in which a duty of disclosure can arise, the Law Commission appears to have cast its net wider than it really intended.

FAILURE TO DISCLOSE

PARTIAL NON-DISCLOSURE

5–014 FA 2006, s.3(a) is satisfied if the person subject to the duty of disclosure fails to disclose *any* information which is covered by the duty. Disclosure of *some* information is no defence if the defendant dishonestly fails to disclose other information which he is also obliged to disclose. Partial disclosure goes only to the question of whether the failure to make complete disclosure is dishonest.

NON-DISCLOSURE TO A THIRD PARTY

5–015 On a literal reading, s.3(a) might arguably be satisfied where A has a duty to disclose information to B, and dishonestly fails to disclose it to C, to whom he has no duty to disclose it. But it would be anomalous that A's liability for failing to disclose to C should turn on his duty to B. The section is clearly not aimed at such a case. The person to whom the defendant dishonestly fails to disclose the information must be the person to whom he owes a duty of disclosure.

MENS REA

IGNORANCE OF CIRCUMSTANCES

5–016 The only mental elements expressly required by FA 2006, s.3 are dishonesty and intent to make a gain or cause a loss or a risk of loss. There is no express requirement that the defendant must be aware of the circumstances that generate the duty to disclose. The Law Commission said:

> "It is perhaps unlikely that a person might be under a legal duty to disclose information despite being ignorant of the circumstances giving rise to the duty.

[18] Which may be debatable: see below, paras 6–067 *et seq.*

> On principle, however, we believe that the offence should require knowledge that such circumstances exist, or at least awareness that they might exist."[19]

The Commission's draft Bill therefore expressly provided that, to be in breach of cl.3 on the basis of a breach of a legal duty to disclose, the defendant must either know that the circumstances which give rise to the duty exist or be aware that they might exist. FA 2006 includes no such provision, but it is probably implicit in the requirement of dishonesty. Even if a person could in theory commit this form of the offence without realising that the circumstances which require disclosure might exist, it is unlikely that dishonesty could in practice be proved.

IGNORANCE OF LAW

However, the defendant clearly need not know that he is under a duty to **5–017**
disclose as a matter of law. Provided that his failure to disclose is dishonest, it is immaterial whether he knows that it is also a breach of a legal duty.

THE OLD LAW: NON-DISCLOSURE AS DECEPTION

Non-disclosure before FA 2006 came into force on January 15, 2007 may **5–018**
also be an offence in some circumstances. For example, the omission of a material particular from an account or other document counts as a falsification of the account or document for the purposes of false accounting.[20] It is not entirely clear whether a mere failure to disclose could be a deception for the purpose of the old deception offences. The question is largely academic. Even if the non-disclosure is not itself a deception, it will usually be accompanied by positive conduct which is. Any act done with dishonest intent, but with the knowledge of the victim, is likely to be regarded as a deception for the purposes of the old law, just as it is likely to be regarded as conveying an implied false representation for the purposes of the new.[21] Even in the absence of positive conduct, non-disclosure may amount to deception if there is a legal duty to disclose, or if it consists in a deliberate failure to correct a representation which has become false or has been found to be false.[22]

Outside these circumstances, the position is still unclear. When the **5–019**
Criminal Law Revision Committee proposed to replace the concept of false pretences with that of deception, it considered the possibility of defining deception so as to include the "concealment"[23] of a fact which there is no

[19] Law Com. No.276, para.7.30.
[20] Theft Act 1968, s.17(2); below, para.12–018.
[21] See above, paras 4–042 *et seq.*
[22] See above, paras 4–050 *et seq.*
[23] By this term the Committee seems to have meant passive non-disclosure as well as active concealment.

duty to disclose, but thought that this would be "too great an extension". On the other hand,

> "To provide expressly that concealment should be criminal only when there is a duty in the civil law to make disclosure would be unwelcome to criminal lawyers, who quite properly object to legislation by reference to the civil law."[24]

In the event, it was pragmatically decided that the Theft Act should be silent on the point.

5–020 There is some slight authority that non-disclosure will suffice, even if there is neither a legal duty to disclose nor a prior representation which stands in need of correction. In *Firth* a consultant was held to have committed a deception by referring patients to a hospital without stating that they were private patients. The court said:

> "If, as was alleged, it was incumbent upon [the appellant] to give the information to the hospital and he deliberately and dishonestly refrained from doing so, with the result that no charge was levied either upon the patients or upon himself, in our judgment the wording of the section . . . is satisfied. It matters not whether it was an act of commission or an act of omission."[25]

5–021 This passage suggests that the defendant was guilty of deception *simply* because he failed to disclose the true facts. The court appears to have thought it unnecessary to identify any legal duty of disclosure to which the defendant was subject. Saying merely that it was "incumbent" on him to give the information implies only that he was under a *moral* duty; and that would be required anyway, because if he had no moral duty to disclose then his failure to disclose could not be dishonest. So the dictum implies that any failure to disclose what one has a moral obligation to disclose can constitute deception.

5–022 But this proposition was unnecessary to the decision. *Firth* was a clear case of deception by positive conduct. The deception did not lie in the defendant's omission to disclose what he should have disclosed. It lay in the act of referring a patient, from which, in the absence of any express assertion about the patient's status, he knew the hospital would infer that she was an NHS patient. There were three possible interpretations of his conduct in relation to each patient: an implied representation that she was an NHS patient, an implied representation that she was a private patient, or no representation either way. The third interpretation could not be right, because the hospital had to know the patient's status, one way or the other. The defendant cannot have supposed that the hospital would be content to form its own view on this question, or to proceed without knowing the answer. He must have known that the hospital would infer *either* that the patient was an NHS patient *or* that she was a private patient. The jury concluded that he knew it would be the former, and indeed it does not

[24] *Eighth Report: Theft and Related Offences*, Cmnd.2977, para.101(iv).
[25] (1990) 91 Cr.App.R. 217 at 221.

appear to have been suggested that he thought it would be the latter. He did not just omit to correct the hospital's mistake. It was he who had *caused* the mistake, by creating a situation in which he knew a false inference would be drawn.

As a matter of ordinary usage, it is not obvious that "deception" either is or is not wide enough to include a mere omission to disclose. The most compelling argument for construing it in the narrower sense is that the wider sense would create a conflict between the criminal law and the civil. It would (under the old law) be a criminal offence to obtain a benefit by failing to disclose a fact, even where there was no legal obligation to disclose that fact. But the view that the Theft Act should be construed in such a way as to avoid conflicts with the civil law was rejected by the House of Lords in *Hinks*.[26] The majority of their Lordships there held that a person can "appropriate" property for the purposes of the offence of theft even if the "victim" has no remedy in civil law. Lord Steyn, with whose speech Lords Slynn and Jauncey agreed, dismissed the argument that consistency is essential. **5–023**

> "The purposes of the civil law and the criminal law are somewhat different. In theory the two systems should be in perfect harmony. In a practical world there will sometimes be some disharmony between the two systems. In any event, it would be wrong to assume on a priori grounds that the criminal law rather than the civil law is defective. Given the jury's conclusions, one is entitled to observe that the appellant's conduct should constitute theft, the only available charge. The tension between the civil and the criminal law is therefore not in my view a factor which justifies a departure from the law as stated in *Lawrence* and *Gomez*."[27]

In this passage Lord Steyn accepted that consistency between the civil and the criminal law is desirable, but thought that consistency with previous authority on the criminal law may be more important. In the present context the latter consideration does not arise, since there is no clear authority that non-disclosure can amount to deception where there is no duty to disclose. On the other hand it would be very odd if an obtaining of property by non-disclosure, in the absence of a duty to disclose, were theft but not (under the old law) obtaining property by deception. It looks more like the latter than the former.[28] In principle it should be neither, because that would create an intolerable conflict with the civil law. And it may still be arguable (despite *Hinks*) that this is the law, on the ground that, even if there is an appropriation or (under the old law) a deception, such conduct cannot be dishonest.[29] **5–024**

[26] [2001] 2 A.C. 241.
[27] [2001] 2 A.C. 241 at 252.
[28] The Law Commission was undisturbed by the possibility of a private individual being convicted of theft if at a car boot sale he offers a very low price for what he knows to be a valuable antique, but decided not to make such a person potentially guilty of fraud: Law Com. No.276, para.7.26.
[29] See above, paras 2–032 *et seq.*

5–025 Even if that argument is rejected, a further reason for not treating lawful non-disclosure as deception is that it would become necessary to determine exactly *what* the defendant should have disclosed. The difficulty of doing so in any particular case is probably one reason why the common law recognises no general duty to disclose everything that ought in fairness to be disclosed. It would also be necessary to consider, in the absence of guidance from the civil law, *to whom* the material facts ought to have been disclosed. If it were accepted, for example, that a person applying for a mortgage had a duty for the purposes of the old law of deception (though not the law of contract) to disclose all material facts to the lender, whether or not he was asked for them, it would also have to be decided whether this duty was satisfied by disclosure to the borrower's solicitor if he was also acting for the lender.[30]

[30] cf. *Halifax Mortgage Services Ltd v Stepsky* [1996] Ch. 207.

CHAPTER 6

ABUSE OF POSITION

Section 4(1) of the Fraud Act 2006 ("FA 2006") provides: **6–001**

"A person is in breach of this section if he—

(a) occupies a position in which he is expected to safeguard, or not to act against, the financial interests of another person,

(b) dishonestly abuses that position, and

(c) intends, by means of the abuse of that position—

(i) to make a gain for himself or another, or

(ii) to cause loss to another or to expose another to a risk of loss."

A person who is in breach of s.4 commits the offence of fraud, contrary to FA 2006, s.1. The requirement of dishonesty is discussed in Ch.2, and that of intention to make a gain or cause a loss or a risk of loss in Ch.3. The other requirements of this form of the offence are that the defendant must occupy a position in which he is expected to safeguard, or not to act against, the financial interests of another person; and he must abuse that position.[1]

[1] Under the Law Commission's draft Bill, it would also have been necessary that the defendant abuse his position *secretly*. This was defined as meaning that he must believe that the person whose interests he is expected to safeguard, and any person acting on that person's behalf, are ignorant of the abuse. The proposed rule was difficult to justify in principle: if it is fraud for an agent to transfer his principal's funds to the agent's account, it is not obvious why it should make a difference that he telephones his principal and announces what he is doing, in such circumstances that the principal cannot stop him. Moreover, as the Commission recognised, the rule would have led to an unattractive anomaly between the case where the victim already knows what the defendant is doing and the case where the victim does not yet know but the defendant intends to tell him. Under FA 2006, s.4, the fact that the victim knows what the defendant is doing is not in itself a defence, though it may go to dishonesty or even to the issue of whether the defendant was abusing his position at all.

6–002 The defendant must occupy a position in which he is expected *either* to safeguard the financial interests of another person, *or* not to act against those interests. Presumably the abuse of the position must at least[2] involve falling short of the expectation engendered by the defendant's position (or, if his position involves both kinds of expectation, at least one of them). So this form of the offence can itself take either of two forms:

- occupying a position in which one is expected to safeguard the financial interests of another person, and failing to safeguard those interests; or
- occupying a position in which one is expected not to act against the financial interests of another person, and acting against those interests.

"EXPECTED"

6–003 A person is clearly "expected" to act (or not act) in a particular way if the law says he must. In most if not all cases in which the conditions in FA 2006, s.4 are satisfied, the defendant will be under a legal duty to act (or not act) in the way described in s.4(1)(a) as a matter of fiduciary law. As we shall see, however, predicting whether the civil courts would regard a relationship as fiduciary is not always easy. That is not a reason to regard the civil law as irrelevant, because in many cases the position will be clear.[3] But it does raise the question of what mental element is required. A person may be held to have been under a duty to safeguard another's interests at a time when he thought he had no such duty. Because fiduciary law is so uncertain in scope, he may make this mistake even if he is well informed or advised about the law. Section 4 does not expressly require that he must *know* he is expected to safeguard another's interests, etc; but he must *abuse* the position in which he is expected to do so, and he must do so dishonestly. It is difficult to see how the pursuit of his own interests could be an abuse of his position, let alone a dishonest abuse, if he thought (albeit wrongly and unreasonably) that it was wholly consistent with that position. On the other hand it may be enough that he knows of the *circumstances* which, in law, require him to safeguard the other's interests—for example, the fact that the other believes he will do so—even if he does not understand their legal consequences.

6–004 In any event, under s.4 (by contrast with s.3) a legal duty is not expressly required. The choice of the word "expected" reflects the policy that the section should be free-standing, so that it can be explained and applied without reference to the civil law. A person can be expected to do something which he is not legally obliged to do.[4] But, if a legal obligation is

[2] See below, para.6–045,

[3] e.g. where the relationship is *inherently* fiduciary: below, para.6–016.

[4] cf. Theft Act 1978, s.3, which makes it an offence to make off without paying as required *or expected* for any goods supplied or service done.

not required, what is? What does "expected" mean in this context? And who must do the expecting?

To say that I expect you to do a thing is ambiguous. Sometimes it means I think you will do it, though there may be no reason why you should. Sometimes it means I think you ought to do it, though there may be no reason to think that you will.[5] In the context of s.4(1)(a), it presumably means the latter. It seems irrelevant how the alleged victim thought the defendant *would in fact* behave. Certain professions are widely distrusted. In the absence of personal connection or recommendation, a person engaging a member of such a profession may be sceptical about how much loyalty he is likely to get. And some fiduciaries, such as trustees, are not selected by their beneficiaries anyway. For the purposes of s.4(1)(a), it is submitted, a person is "expected" to safeguard another's interests (etc.) if the other thinks it incumbent on him to do so, whether or not the other thinks he actually will.[6] But again there must be an implied mental element here. If the other did think it incumbent on the defendant to safeguard the other's interests but the defendant did not know that the other thought this, it is difficult to see how the defendant's conduct could be a dishonest abuse of his position. 6–005

Since s.4(1)(a) does not say who must do the expecting, it is arguably sufficient that the defendant knows *some* people think it incumbent on him to safeguard another person's interests, even if that other does not himself think so. But one such person could hardly suffice, if his own interests are not at stake. Perhaps, by analogy with *Ghosh*,[7] it is sufficient if most right-thinking people would think so and the defendant knows they would. But the section says "*is* expected", not "would be expected by a right-thinking person". 6–006

On the other hand, if another person thinks it incumbent on the defendant to safeguard that person's interests, and the defendant knows this, the fact that others might disagree seems to go only to dishonesty. The defendant can make it clear that he is not prepared to act on the basis of the other's unreasonable expectations. If he agrees to act, he must be taken to have accepted them. 6–007

These considerations suggest that D occupies a position of the kind required if 6–008

- D has a legal obligation to safeguard, or not act against, the financial interests of another (V),
- V thinks it incumbent on D to safeguard, or not act against, V's financial interests, *or*

[5] Sometimes it seems to mean both, as in "England expects that every man will do his duty"—leaving aside the fact that one's duty is by definition what one ought to do.

[6] This interpretation would fit with the view that everyone who is subject to fiduciary duties as a matter of law is within s.4(1)(a) (below, para.6–030), since legal duties are obviously normative rather than predictive.

[7] [1982] Q.B. 1053; above, para.2–013.

- (possibly) most people would think it incumbent on D to safeguard, or not act against, V's financial interests—

provided (in each case) that D knows this.[8]

FIDUCIARY POSITION

6–009 If the word "expected" is obscure, the words "to safeguard, or not to act against, the financial interests of another person" are impenetrable. The Law Commission's explanation was as follows.

> "The essence of the kind of relationship which in our view should be a prerequisite of this form of the offence is that the victim has voluntarily put the defendant in a privileged position, by virtue of which the defendant is expected to safeguard the victim's financial interests or given power to damage those interests. Such an expectation to safeguard or power to damage may arise, for example, because the defendant is given authority to exercise a discretion on the victim's behalf, or is given access to the victim's assets, premises, equipment or customers. In these cases the defendant does not need to enlist the victim's *further* co-operation in order to secure the desired result, because the necessary co-operation has been given in advance.
>
> The necessary relationship will be present between trustee and beneficiary, director and company, professional person and client, agent and principal, employee and employer, or between partners. It may arise otherwise, for example within a family, or in the context of voluntary work, or in any context where the parties are not at arm's length. In nearly all cases where it arises, it will be recognised by the civil law as importing fiduciary duties, and any relationship that is so recognised will suffice."[9]

6–010 The explanatory notes on FA 2006 similarly state that s.4 "applies in situations where the defendant has been put in a privileged position, and by virtue of this position is expected to safeguard another's financial interests or not act against those interests", and quote the second of the two paragraphs above.[10] Two examples are given of cases that would fall within s.4: an employee of a software company who uses his position to clone software products with the intention of selling the products on, and a person employed to care for an elderly or disabled person who has access to that person's bank account and abuses his position by removing funds for his own personal use (which would be theft anyway).

LOYALTY

6–011 It is clear from these explanations that s.4 is at least primarily aimed at persons in a *fiduciary* position. The classic modern exposition of the nature of fiduciary duty is that of Millett L.J. in *Bristol & West Building Society v Mothew*:

[8] But it may be sufficient that D knows of the circumstances that generate the legal obligation, without knowing that they do generate that obligation: above, para.6–003.

[9] Law Com. No.276, *Fraud*, Cm.5560, paras 7.37, 7.38.

[10] A passage closely resembling the first paragraph appeared in the notes to the Bill as introduced in the House of Lords, but was omitted when the Bill moved to the Commons.

"A fiduciary is someone who has undertaken to act for or on behalf of another in a particular matter in circumstances which give rise to a relationship of trust and confidence. The distinguishing obligation of a fiduciary is the obligation of loyalty. The principal is entitled to the single-minded loyalty of his fiduciary. This core liability has several facets. A fiduciary must act in good faith; he must not make a profit out of his trust; he must not place himself in a position where his duty and his interest may conflict; he may not act for his own benefit or the benefit of a third person without the informed consent of his principal. This is not intended to be an exhaustive list, but it is sufficient to indicate the nature of fiduciary obligations. They are the defining characteristics of the fiduciary."[11]

When the law requires one person to do something which it is in another person's interests that he should do, that obligation usually relates only to the thing that he must do and the standard to which he must do it. For example, a builder's obligation is to construct the building in accordance with the specification, and to do so with reasonable care and skill. As long as he does not depart from the specification or fall below the required standard of work, the law leaves him free to make such additional profit from the job as he can arrange, for example by choosing suppliers who will give him discounts or commissions. Nor does the law restrict his freedom to make further agreements with his client in relation to the project. **6–012**

Sometimes, however, the law goes further. In these cases the party subject to the obligation is required not merely to act in another's interests, but to do so *without regard to his own*. He must subordinate his own interests to those of the other. In *Arklow Investments Ltd v MacLean* the Privy Council said that this concept of a duty of loyalty **6–013**

"encaptures a situation where one person is in a relationship with another which gives rise to a legitimate expectation, which equity will recognise, that the fiduciary will not utilise his or her position in such a way which is adverse to the interests of the principal."[12]

The general principle of equity is that a fiduciary who falls short of this expectation must account for any benefit he thereby receives. In an analysis now broadly accepted as accurate,[13] Deane J. observed in the High Court of Australia that this principle has been formulated in various ways; but **6–014**

"The variations between more precise formulations of the principle governing the liability to account are largely the result of the fact that what is conveniently regarded as the one 'fundamental rule' embodies two themes. The first is that which appropriates for the benefit of the person to whom the fiduciary duty is owed any benefit or gain obtained or received by the fiduciary in circumstances where there existed a conflict of personal interest and

[11] [1998] 1 Ch. 1 at 18. See also Robert Flannigan, "The Fiduciary Obligation" (1989) 9 O.J.L.S. 285; Peter Birks, "The Content of Fiduciary Obligation" (2000) 34 Israel L.R. 3 and (2002) 16 Tru. L.I. 34; Matthew Conaglen, "The Nature and Function of Fiduciary Loyalty" (2005) 121 L.Q.R. 452.

[12] [2000] 1 W.L.R. 594 at 598.

[13] e.g. *Don King Productions Inc v Warren* [2000] Ch. 291.

fiduciary duty or a significant possibility of such conflict: the objective is to preclude the fiduciary from being swayed by considerations of personal interest. The second is that which requires the fiduciary to account for any benefit or gain obtained or received by reason of or by use of his fiduciary position or of opportunity or knowledge resulting from it: the objective is to preclude the fiduciary from actually misusing his position for his personal advantage. . . . Stated comprehensively in terms of the liability to account, the principle of equity is that a person who is under a fiduciary obligation must account to the person to whom the obligation is owed for any benefit or gain (i) which has been obtained or received in circumstances where a conflict or significant possibility of conflict existed between his fiduciary duty and his personal interest in the pursuit or possible receipt of such a benefit or gain or (ii) which was obtained or received by use or by reason of his fiduciary position or of opportunity or knowledge resulting from it."[14]

6–015 These "themes" are known as the "no conflict" rule and the "no profit" rule respectively. Strictly speaking they are rules rather than duties.[15] Their primary focus is on whether the principal can obtain restitution of a gain made by the fiduciary. Where he can, the circumstances giving him a right to do so will usually include a breach of duty (that is, legally wrongful conduct) on the part of the fiduciary; but this is not necessarily the case. While the two rules often overlap, and it is not always clear which of them should be regarded as applicable to a given situation,[16] they seem to be distinct. The principal can recover a profit made by the fiduciary even if the fiduciary has acted in good faith;[17] and he can rescind a transaction involving a possible conflict between the fiduciary's duty of loyalty and his personal interest without proof that the fiduciary did in fact profit from the transaction or that it was unfair.[18] In either case the fiduciary can escape

[14] *Chan v Zacharia* (1984) 154 C.L.R. 178 at 198–199.

[15] A rule requiring restitution does of course impose a duty to make restitution, but that is a second-order duty: it does not render legally wrongful the conduct that generates the right to restitution. See Peter Birks, "Rights, Wrongs and Remedies" (2000) 20 O.J.L.S. 1. Moreover the existence of a fiduciary relationship may sometimes entitle the principal to seek restitution from someone other than the fiduciary, e.g. where the principal has unknowingly entered into a transaction with an associate of the fiduciary.

[16] For example, cases involving the poaching by a fiduciary of opportunities which he might have taken up for his principal sometimes appear to be regarded as an application of the no conflict rule (*Cook v Deeks* [1916] 1 A.C. 554; *Industrial Development Consultants Ltd v Cooley* [1972] 1 W.L.R. 443; *Bhullar v Bhullar* [2003] EWCA Civ 424; [2003] 2 B.C.L.C. 241) and sometimes of the no profit rule, on the basis that the opportunity is in a sense the principal's property (*CMS Dolphin Ltd v Simonet* [2001] 2 B.C.L.C. 704). The cases are examined by Lewison J. in *Ultraframe Ltd v Fielding* [2005] EWHC 1638 at [1332]–[1356].

[17] *Phipps v Boardman* [1967] 2 A.C. 46.

[18] *Aberdeen Railway Co v Blaikie Bros* (1854) 1 Macq. 461. The no conflict rule appears to have two aspects: the "self-dealing rule", under which the principal can rescind a transaction between the fiduciary in his fiduciary capacity and the fiduciary in his personal capacity, without showing that the transaction was unfair; and the "fair-dealing rule", under which the principal may set aside a transaction between himself and the fiduciary (or an associate of the fiduciary, such as his spouse: *Newgate Stud Co v Penfold* [2004] EWHC 2993) unless the fiduciary shows that the transaction was fair and that the principal was fully informed: *Tito v Waddell (No.2)* [1977] Ch. 106 at 224, *per* Megarry V.C. See Richard Nolan, "Dispositions Involving Fiduciaries: The Equity to Rescind and the Resulting Trust" in

liability by showing that the principal gave an informed consent to what was done.

IDENTIFYING A FIDUCIARY POSITION

Certain types of relationship are inherently fiduciary. They virtually always involve the assumption by one party (and sometimes more than one) of the fiduciary duty of loyalty in its strictest form, including the no conflict rule and the no profit rule. Examples are the relationships of trustee and beneficiary, director and company,[19] agent and principal,[20] solicitor and client, partner and firm. The majority of cases charged under s.4 are likely to fall within one of these categories. **6–016**

In addition, however, fiduciary obligations can arise in a relationship which is not inherently fiduciary, if its individual circumstances justify its being so classified.[21] Unfortunately there is no consensus as to the appropriate criteria for identifying such circumstances. Millett L.J.'s explanation of the nature of fiduciary duty[22] is sometimes misinterpreted as laying down a test for *identifying* fiduciaries;[23] but this is asking too much of it. **6–017**

> "[I]t is crucial to distinguish the *process* of identifying the existence of a fiduciary relationship from the *content* of a fiduciary obligation. Definitions of the fiduciary relationship which turn on the duty of loyalty ultimately are circular, and provide no guidance on when that fiduciary obligation should be *attached* to a relationship between the parties."[24]

Peter Birks (ed.) *Restitution and Equity: Vol.1—Resulting Trusts and Equitable Compensation*; Matthew Conaglen, "Equitable Compensation for Breach of Fiduciary Dealing Rules" (2003) 119 L.Q.R. 246. A fiduciary must similarly obtain his principal's informed consent before putting himself in a position where his duty to that principal may conflict with his duty to another principal: *Bristol and West B.S. v Mothew* [1998] Ch. 1, 18, *per* Millett L.J.; *Bolkiah v KPMG* [1999] 2 A.C. 222; *Marks & Spencer plc v Freshfields Bruckhaus Deringer* [2004] EWCA Civ 741; *Ratiu v Conway* [2005] EWCA Civ 1302; *Hilton v Barker Booth & Eastwood* [2005] UKHL 8; [2005] 1 W.L.R. 567.

19 A director does not, as such, owe any fiduciary duty to the shareholders: *Percival v Wright* [1902] 2 Ch. 421. But he may owe such a duty if the circumstances so require, for example if he acts as an agent for the shareholders: *Allen v Hyatt* (1914) 30 T.L.R. 444; *Coleman v Myers* [1977] 2 N.Z.L.R. 225; *Re Chez Nico (Restaurants) Ltd* [1992] B.C.L.C. 192; *Platt v Platt* [1999] 2 B.C.L.C. 745. Normally the point would be academic in relation to FA 2006, s.4. For example, if a director bought the company's property at an undervalue, this would be an abuse of his fiduciary position vis-à-vis the company: the prosecution would not need to show that it was also an abuse of his position vis-à-vis the shareholders.

20 But an agent may not be a fiduciary if he has no discretion as to the terms on which he can bind his principal: *R.H. Deacon & Co Ltd v Varga* (1973) 41 D.L.R. (3d) 767.

21 *Chirnside v Fay* [2006] N.Z.S.C. 68 at [75]–[76], *per* Blanchard and Tipping JJ.

22 Above, para.6–011.

23 e.g. *Button v Phelps* [2006] EWHC 53 at [58]; *Donnelly v Weybridge Construction Ltd* [2006] EWHC 2678; cf. *Ratiu v Conway* [2005] EWCA Civ 1302 at [72], where Auld L.J. (with whom the other members of the court agreed) described Millett L.J.'s dictum as a "non-exhaustive description".

24 Laura Hoyano, "The Flight to the Fiduciary Haven" in P. Birks (ed.) *Privacy and Loyalty* (1997) at 182.

6–018 Similarly, the expression "at arm's length" is sometimes repeated as if it were a *criterion* for determining whether a fiduciary relationship exists.[25] But to say that the parties are at arm's length is just another way of saying that their relationship is not fiduciary. Certainly the fact that they were at arm's length while they were *negotiating* their agreement does not mean that the agreement does not impose fiduciary duties once it comes into being. Moreover, it is important to avoid the trap of reasoning that, because the defendant's conduct would be a breach of fiduciary duty if he were a fiduciary, therefore he must be a fiduciary.[26]

6–019 It seems clear at least that where a person has *undertaken* a duty of loyalty, expressly or by implication,[27] equity will require him to honour that undertaking. Indeed it has been argued that, outside the relationships which are inherently fiduciary, fiduciary responsibility can *only* be voluntarily undertaken.[28] Lord Millett, writing extra-judicially, has said:

> "[E]very fiduciary relationship is a voluntary relationship. No one can be compelled to enter into a fiduciary relationship or to accept fiduciary obligations, any more than he can be compelled to enter into a contract or to accept contractual obligations. . . . A fiduciary relationship most commonly arises where one party voluntarily undertakes to act in the interests of another; but it can also arise where he voluntarily places himself in a position where he is obliged by equity to act in the interests of another."[29]

But a relationship which is "voluntary" only in this latter sense is hardly voluntary at all. One might as well say that liability to pay income tax is voluntary because only those who choose to earn an income are liable to pay.[30] It seems more helpful to think of fiduciary obligations as being imposed by equity in certain circumstances, irrespective of the intentions of the persons on whom they are imposed.

6–020 Blanchard and Tipping JJ., of the Supreme Court of New Zealand, have said:

[25] e.g. the Law Commission's statement that "The necessary relationship . . . may arise . . . in any context where the parties are not at arm's length": Law Com. No.276, para.7.38.

[26] *Tito v Waddell (No.2)* [1977] Ch. 106, 230, *per* Megarry V.C. *Lac Minerals Ltd v International Corona Resources Ltd* (1989) 61 D.L.R. (4th) 14, 63, *per* Sopinka J.; Laura Hoyano, "The Flight to the Fiduciary Haven" in P. Birks (ed.) *Privacy and Loyalty* (1997) at 182.

[27] An express undertaking is not necessary: *Chirnside v Fay* [2006] N.Z.S.C. 68.

[28] Laura Hoyano, "The Flight to the Fiduciary Haven" in P. Birks (ed.) *Privacy and Loyalty* (1997) at 182–3, drawing an analogy with liability for negligent misstatement under *Hedley Byrne & Co v Heller & Partners Ltd* [1964] A.C. 465. CF. N. McBride and A. Hughes, "*Hedley Byrne* in the House of Lords: an Interpretation" (1995) 15 L.S. 376, 387–389, arguing that *Hedley Byrne* liability is actually a form of fiduciary liability because it depends on an assumption of responsibility.

[29] "Restitution and Constructive Trusts" (1998) 114 L.Q.R. 399 at 404–405. See also *Henderson v Merrett Syndicates Ltd* [1995] 2 A.C. 145 at 205, *per* Lord Browne-Wilkinson.

[30] There seems to be no reason in principle why a fiduciary duty should not be imposed by statute: *Tito v Waddell (No.2)* [1977] Ch. 106 at 235, *per* Megarry V.C. Indeed some of the duties imposed on a company director by the Companies Act 2006 appear to fall into this category. Clearly a statutory duty is voluntary only in the sense, and to the extent, that a person can choose whether to create a situation in which the duty applies to him.

"It is clear from the authorities that relationships which are inherently fiduciary all possess the feature which justifies the imposition of fiduciary duties in a case which falls outside the traditional categories; all fiduciary relationships, whether inherent or particular, are marked by the entitlement . . . of one party to place trust and confidence in the other. That party is entitled to rely on the other party not to act in a way which is contrary to the first party's interests. . . .

[T]he true principle, in our view, resides in the idea that the circumstances must be such that one party is entitled to repose and does repose trust and confidence in the other. The existence of an agreement or undertaking is no more than a frequent manifestation of such a circumstance. . . .

It does not, for present purposes, matter whether one sees the fiduciary obligation as one which is imposed by reason of the nature of the relationship, or as one which, in the light of that relationship, is impliedly accepted. In some cases, essentially the traditional categories, the implied acceptance rationale may be apposite and in others, of the particular kind, the imposition rationale may be preferable."[31]

While the repose of trust and confidence may be a *justification* for imposing fiduciary obligations, however, it is not in itself an adequate criterion for determining *when* such obligations will be imposed.

The English courts have been particularly wary of the assumption that 6–021
everyone who is trusted or relied upon to act in a particular way is a fiduciary. The Privy Council pointed out in *Re Goldcorp Exchange Ltd*, in relation to an argument that the relationship between the parties was fiduciary as well as contractual:

"No doubt the fact that one person is placed in a particular position vis-à-vis another through the medium of a contract does not necessarily mean that he does not also owe fiduciary duties to that other by virtue of being in that position. But the essence of a fiduciary relationship is that it creates obligations of a different character from those deriving from the contract itself. Their Lordships have not heard in argument any submission which went beyond suggesting that by virtue of being a fiduciary the company was obliged honestly and conscientiously to do what it had by contract promised to do. Many commercial relationships involve just such a reliance by one party on the other . . . It is possible without misuse of language to say that the customers put faith in the company, and that their trust has not been repaid. But the vocabulary is misleading; high expectations do not necessarily lead to equitable remedies."[32]

Indeed, the terms of a contract between the parties may militate against 6–022
the inference that the relationship is fiduciary as well as contractual. In *Hospital Products Ltd v United States Surgical Corp*, Mason J. said:

"That contractual and fiduciary relationships may co-exist between the same parties has never been doubted. Indeed, the existence of a basic contractual relationship has in many situations provided a foundation for the erection of a fiduciary relationship. In these situations it is the contractual foundation which is all important because it is the contract that regulates the basic rights and

[31] *Chirnside v Fay* [2006] N.Z.S.C. 68 at [80], [85] and [87].

[32] [1995] 1 A.C. 74 at 98.

> liabilities of the parties. The fiduciary relationship, if it is to exist at all, must accommodate itself to the terms of the contract so that it is consistent with, and conforms to, them. The fiduciary relationship cannot be superimposed upon the contract in such a way as to alter the operation which the contract was intended to have according to its true construction."[33]

On the other hand, fiduciary obligations may be appropriately imposed on parties who are negotiating towards a joint venture but have not yet entered into a contract or partnership agreement.[34]

PERSONS WHO ARE FIDUCIARIES ONLY FOR LIMITED PURPOSES

6–023 A person may be another's fiduciary in relation only to certain matters, or certain aspects of their relationship.[35] This may be so, for example, because the scope of the fiduciary's responsibility is limited by contract, or because the principal makes it clear that he takes personal responsibility for looking after his own interests in relation to some matters.[36] Moreover it is ultimately futile to seek a single criterion for determining whether a person is a fiduciary, because the question cannot always be answered "yes" or "no": sometimes it depends on the particular rule in issue. Lord Browne-Wilkinson has pointed out that

> "The phrase 'fiduciary duties' is a dangerous one, giving rise to a mistaken assumption that all fiduciaries owe the same duties in all circumstances. That is not the case."[37]

6–024 In *Bristol & West Building Society v Mothew*, at the end of his explanation of the nature of fiduciary duty,[38] Millett L.J. said:

> "As Dr Finn pointed out in his classic work *Fiduciary Obligations* (1977), p. 2, [a fiduciary] is not subject to fiduciary obligations because he is a fiduciary; it is because he is subject to them that he is a fiduciary."[39]

In debate on the Fraud Bill, the Solicitor General described this sentence as "important", and added: "The duties create the nature of the relationship; the relationship is not of itself the cause of the fiduciary duties."[40] He did not

[33] (1984) 156 C.L.R. 41 at 97. This dictum was cited with approval by the Privy Council in *Kelly v Cooper* [1993] A.C. 205 at 215.

[34] *United Dominions Corp Ltd v Brian Pty Ltd* (1985) 157 C.L.R. 1; *Murad v Al-Saraj* [2005] EWCA Civ 959; *Chirnside v Fay* [2006] N.Z.S.C. 68 at [14] (Elias C.J.) and [91] (Blanchard and Tipping JJ.). See Gerard M.D. Bean, *Fiduciary Obligations and Joint Ventures: The Collaborative Fiduciary Relationship* (1995).

[35] *New Zealand Netherlands Society "Oranje" Inc v Kuys* [1973] 1 W.L.R. 1126 at 1130.

[36] See Paul Finn, "The Fiduciary Principle" in T.G. Youdan (ed.) *Equity, Fiduciaries and Trusts* at 49–51.

[37] *Henderson v Merrett Syndicates Ltd* [1995] 2 A.C. 145 at 206.

[38] Above, para.6–011.

[39] [1998] 1 Ch. 1 at 18.

[40] *Hansard*, SC Deb.B, col.19 (June 20, 2006).

explain this remark, and it appears at first sight to be obviously untrue. Equity does not impose duties at random. Clearly it must be the nature of the relationship that determines whether it gives rise to fiduciary duties.

The confusion seems to have arisen because Millett L.J. omitted part of what Dr Finn[41] had written. The relevant passage of Finn's book reads as follows: **6–025**

> "[I]t is meaningless to talk of fiduciary relationships as such. Once one looks to the rules and principles which have actually been evolved, it quickly becomes apparent that it is pointless to describe a person—or for that matter a power—as being fiduciary unless at the same time it is said for the purposes of which particular rules and principles that description is being used. These rules are everything. The description 'fiduciary', nothing. It has gone much the same way as did the general descriptive term 'trust' one hundred and fifty years ago.
>
> And the rules and principles evolved under the 'fiduciary' rubric? In the writer's opinion it should be recognised today that Equity has established and formalised a new and coherent head of law. As will be seen, it has evolved a series of self-contained obligations—obligations which are themselves certain and distinct, and which individually define their own 'fiduciary' for their own respective purposes. These obligations attribute no large significance to the term used to describe the persons to whom each individually applies. In some instances he is referred to as a fiduciary; in others as a confidant. The term used is not important. It is not because a person is a 'fiduciary' or a 'confidant' that a rule applies to him. It is because a particular rule applies to him that he is a fiduciary or confidant *for its purposes*."

The last three words (though italicised in the original) were omitted from Millett L.J.'s paraphrase and from the Solicitor General's adoption of it; and their omission obscures the point. Finn's point is that that part of equity known as fiduciary law is not an indivisible whole. It comprises a complex of different rules, and a person may be subject to some of these rules but not others. We cannot simply ask "Is X a fiduciary?", and, if the answer is yes, assume that the whole body of fiduciary law applies to him.

In *Re Coomber*,[42] for example, the plaintiff sought to set aside a gift of the family business by his mother to his brother. The brother had been running the business as his mother's agent since his father's death. It was argued that he was therefore in a fiduciary position in relation to her, and that a gift from her to him was therefore invalid unless made upon independent advice. The Court of Appeal thought this argument plainly fallacious. Fletcher Moulton L.J. said that it **6–026**

> "illustrates in a most striking form the danger of trusting to verbal formulae. Fiduciary relations are of many different types; they extend from the relation of myself to an errand boy who is bound to bring me back my change up to the most intimate and confidential relations which can possibly exist between one party and another where the one is wholly in the hands of the other because of his infinite trust in him. All these are cases of fiduciary relations, and the Courts

[41] Now the Hon. Justice Finn of the Federal Court of Australia.
[42] [1911] 1 Ch. 723.

have again and again, in cases where there has been a fiduciary relation, interfered and set aside acts which, between persons in a wholly independent position, would have been perfectly valid. Thereupon in some minds there arises the idea that if there is any fiduciary relation whatever any of these types of interference is warranted by it. They conclude that every kind of fiduciary relation justifies every kind of interference. Of course that is absurd. The nature of the fiduciary relation must be such that it justifies the interference."[43]

Buckley L.J. said:

"[T]here was not here any such fiduciary relation between the donor and the donee as that the gift can, on that ground, be called into question. It is not every fiduciary relation that calls this doctrine of equity into action. Between master and servant, between employer and bailiff or steward, there subsists, of course, a fiduciary relation; but there is no authority for the proposition that by reason of the existence of relations such as those a deed of gift from the one to the other can be set aside. This doctrine of equity does not rest upon the existence of a fiduciary relationship whatever be its nature. It rests upon the existence of such a fiduciary relationship as will lead the Court to infer undue influence, or knowledge in the one party concealed from the other, or other circumstances into which I need not go."[44]

6–027 Lewison J. made a similar point in *Ultraframe Ltd v Fielding* in relation to a person who was a fiduciary by virtue of being the sole signatory on a company's bank account:

"[H]e was not entitled to draw on the account for his personal benefit. By voluntarily becoming the sole signatory on that account, he took it upon himself to assume control of an asset belonging to another. That voluntary assumption must, in my judgment, carry with it a duty to use the asset for the benefit of the person to whom it belongs. That duty is properly called a fiduciary duty. However, it is important to recognise that this fact alone does not mean that wider fiduciary duties are imposed upon him."[45]

The position of such a person is analogous to that of Fletcher Moulton L.J.'s errand boy. Both are fiduciaries *only* in relation to the property entrusted to them.

6–028 Lewison J. also drew an analogy with the position of a junior employee.

"By the same token, in *Brinks Ltd v Abu-Saleh [No.3]*[46] Rimer J held that a security guard was employed in a position of trust in which he possessed valuable information; and as a result owed a fiduciary duty to his employer not to divulge that information to anyone not entitled to it. But it could not have been suggested that a security guard owed his employer the full range of directors' fiduciary duties."[47]

In *Nottingham University v Fishel*, Elias J. pointed out that

[43] [1911] 1 Ch. 723 at 728–729.
[44] [1911] 1 Ch. 723 at 730–731.
[45] [2005] EWHC 1638 at [1290].
[46] [1999] C.L.C. 133 at 148.
[47] [2005] EWHC 1638 at [1291].

"The employment relationship is obviously not a fiduciary relationship in the classic sense. . . . Its purpose is not to place the employee in a position where he is obliged to pursue his employer's interests at the expense of his own. The relationship is a contractual one and the powers imposed on the employee are conferred by the employer himself. The employee's freedom of action is regulated by the contract, the scope of his powers is determined by the terms (express or implied) of the contract, and as a consequence the employer can exercise (or at least he can place himself in a position where he has the opportunity to exercise) considerable control over the employee's decision-making powers.

This is not to say that fiduciary duties cannot arise out of the employment relationship itself. But they arise not as a result of the mere fact that there is an employment relationship. Rather they result from the fact that within a particular contractual relationship there are specific contractual obligations which the employee has undertaken which have placed him in a situation where equity imposes these rigorous duties in addition to the contractual obligations. Where this occurs, the scope of the fiduciary obligations both arises out of, and is circumscribed by, the contractual terms . . ."[48]

Even a junior employee would be liable to account for a secret profit; but, since he is not subject to the fiduciary dealing rules, an agreed rise in his salary could not be rescinded on the ground that he had failed to admit committing disciplinary offences.[49]

It is clear, then, that some persons are fiduciaries only for certain **6–029** purposes. They are subject to some fiduciary duties but not others.[50] They are subject to the duty of loyalty only in an attenuated form, in that they are obliged to abstain only from certain forms of disloyalty. In particular, they are not subject to the full rigour of the no profit rule or (especially) the no conflict rule.

THE APPLICATION OF SECTION 4(1)(A) TO FIDUCIARIES

Although the Solicitor General regarded Finn's point about the variety of **6–030** fiduciary duties as "important" in the context of the clause,[51] it seems that all fiduciaries are intended to fall within FA 2006, s.4(1)(a)[52]—including

[48] [2000] I.R.L.R. 471 at [90]–[91]; see also *Helmet Integrated Systems Ltd v Tunnard* [2006] EWCA Civ 1735; [2007] I.R.L.R. 126.

[49] cf. *Item Software (UK) Ltd v Fassihi* [2004] EWCA Civ 1244; [2005] I.C.R. 450; below, para.6–056.

[50] Indeed it is arguable that no-one is subject to *every* fiduciary duty. According to P. Finn, *Fiduciary Obligations* (1977), there are some duties that apply only to "fiduciary officers" and at least one that applies only to employees. An employee is not a fiduciary officer in Finn's sense.

[51] Above, para.6–024.

[52] If it is possible to owe a fiduciary duty to an unincorporated body, a person subject to such a duty would appear to be within s.4(1)(a), because "person" includes an unincorporated body unless the contrary intention appears: Interpretation Act 1978, s.5 and Sch.1. Where the duty arises out of a joint venture and is a duty of loyalty to the joint interest rather than that of any single person, it might perhaps be arguable that the fiduciary is not expected to safeguard, or not to act against, the financial interests of *another person*; but it seems most unlikely that such a fiduciary would be held to fall outside s.4(1)(a) on this ground.

those who are fiduciaries only in relation to certain matters or for the purpose of certain fiduciary rules. The Law Commission said in its report:

> "In nearly all cases where [the necessary relationship] arises, it will be recognised by the civil law as importing fiduciary duties, and any relationship that is so recognised will suffice."[53]

The Commission expressly said, for example, that the necessary relationship would be present between an employee and his employer.[54] Yet most employees are fiduciaries only for limited purposes.[55] Similarly, the Government was anxious to ensure that s.4 would apply to a carer who has access to a vulnerable person's bank account, although such a person will not normally be a fiduciary except in relation to that access.[56]

6–031 This does not of course mean that a person who is subject only to certain fiduciary rules can commit the offence by breaking a rule to which he is not subject. Clearly a person cannot "abuse" a position of the kind described in s.4(1)(a) without falling short of the particular expectations arising out of his occupation of that position.[57] If he is a fiduciary by virtue only of being a signatory on a company's bank account, for example, he can abuse his position by writing cheques for unauthorised purposes, but not by buying the company's property at an undervalue.

6–032 If the Law Commission is correct in saying that all fiduciaries are within s.4(1)(a), the effect seems to be that the civil law can be relied upon by the prosecution but not the defence. The existence of a fiduciary duty—*any* fiduciary duty—is sufficient, but not necessary. The importance of this would be that, where the factual nature of the relationship is agreed and in the judge's view is such as to have rendered the defendant subject to fiduciary duty as a matter of civil law, the judge could presumably rule that s.4(1)(a) is satisfied and direct the jury accordingly.

6–033 But there would be two stages in this reasoning. The judge would not only have to identify the duty to which the defendant had been subject, but also determine whether that duty is properly described as a *fiduciary* duty. In the case of many duties, the latter point is beyond doubt. A trustee's duty not to make a secret profit from the trust, for example, is a fiduciary duty on any view. In other cases, however, there is no consensus as to whether a duty imposed by equity is a fiduciary one. Examples include the duty not to exercise undue influence over another,[58] and the duty not to misuse confidential information.[59] The question "Is this duty a *fiduciary*

[53] Law Com. No.276, para.7.38.
[54] Law Com. No.276, para.7.38.
[55] See above, para.6–028.
[56] See above, para.6–027. But the Government may have fallen into the trap of assuming that, because the carer is not a fiduciary for all purposes, he is not a fiduciary at all: see below, para.6–076.
[57] See below, para.6–044.
[58] See below, para.6–039.
[59] See below, para.6–034.

duty?" may have no right answer. The meaning of a word is its use in the language. The word "fiduciary" is normally used to reflect the fact that a duty arises out of trust placed by one person in another, or perhaps that the duty can helpfully be regarded as a particular manifestation of the duty of loyalty. But it is sometimes a matter of opinion whether either of these propositions is true of a particular duty. The courts will need to decide whether a person subject only to one of these borderline duties is within s.4(1)(a). That cannot be done simply by asking whether the duty is appropriately categorised as "fiduciary".

BORDERLINE CASES

CONFIDENTIAL INFORMATION

For example, is a person within FA 2006, s.4(1)(a) merely because another person has entrusted him with confidential information, and expects him not to misuse it? Equity certainly prohibits him from misusing the information; but it is questionable whether this is a *fiduciary* duty, since equity sometimes prohibits a person from misusing information which has *not* been entrusted to him. Arguably it follows that the duty not to misuse secret information is distinct from the duty not to betray a trust.[60] The misuse of secret information by a person to whom it has not been entrusted cannot amount to the fraud offence, because it cannot be said that he occupies a position of the kind required by s.4(1)(a) merely by virtue of possessing information which he ought not to possess. But what if the information *is* entrusted to him by virtue of his position, for example as an employee? In this case the general duty not to misuse secret information overlaps with the duty not to abuse a fiduciary position. One would have thought that the dishonest misuse of such information would be the sort of conduct at which s.4 is aimed. There appears to be no suggestion in the Law Commission's report that it was meant to be excluded. **6–034**

The Government, however, seems to have intended otherwise. In debate on the Bill, Dominic Grieve MP (the Shadow Attorney-General) asked whether cl.4 would apply to the Queen's nanny, who, he said, had recounted her experiences in her memoirs.[61] The Solicitor General replied that such cases "would properly be the subject of civil law, and the civil court is where they would normally be dealt with".[62] This falls short of saying that they could not be dealt with in a criminal court. **6–035**

Earlier in the debate, however, the Solicitor General seems to have gone further. Mr Grieve had posed another hypothetical case. **6–036**

> "A person is helping his aged aunt with her affairs, in the course of which she gives him access to all her private papers. From those, he discovers that a bust

[60] *Att-Gen v Blake* [1998] Ch. 439; *Arklow Investments Ltd v MacLean* [2000] 1 W.L.R. 594.
[61] *Hansard*, SC Deb.B, col.24 (June 20, 2006).
[62] *Hansard*, SC Deb.B, col.25 (June 20, 2006).

sold out of the family 20 years before in a house sale was made by Bernini. Nobody knew about that at the time, but it is clear in the family papers to which he has been given a degree of access by his aunt. That bust is now for sale in the antique shop down the road, so he zooms down there; nobody knows that it is a Bernini bust and he buys it at a vastly discounted rate—it is the bargain of a lifetime. He does not tell his aunt; he just takes it home and puts it in his house.

Did that person abuse his position? After all, his aunt allowed him access to her papers. He took advantage of the information that he gleaned from those papers and made use of it for his own benefit. Hon. Members must understand that the aunt was not ga-ga; she just asked him to help her. To what extent would he be caught by clause 4? One might consider what he did to be morally reprehensible, but was it a crime?"[63]

6–037 The Solicitor General answered:

> "On the face of it, the particular item was no longer in the aunt's possession. She had dispensed with it. He obtained information about its value, so he decided to buy it. If there were a relationship in which he was supposed to be looking after her interests in a particular way, that relationship might produce a expectation, but it does not seem on the face of it that that is likely to happen if it were merely the case that he happens to come across the information, purchases the bust and makes some money on it. That is just a receipt of information that results in his becoming slightly wealthier. It may be immoral; perhaps he should have shared it, but I do not think that it would be unlawful unless the relationship was a more particular relationship than the one that [Mr Grieve] described."[64]

6–038 This is puzzling. The Solicitor General was adamant that s.4 should extend to a person who is given access to another's property.[65] This clearly includes the nephew in Mr Grieve's example. If the nephew had stolen the aunt's papers, he would apparently be guilty of fraud by virtue of s.4. If he is not guilty of fraud in Mr Grieve's example, therefore, this cannot be because he does not occupy a position of the kind required by s.4(1)(a). It must be because misuse of the information in the aunt's papers is somehow different from, and less reprehensible than, appropriating the papers themselves. Unless the papers are assumed to have some value independent of the information in them, it is not clear why this should be so. Since the example probably took the Solicitor General by surprise, however, it may be unrealistic to treat his response as an authoritative statement of the Government's intentions. It is submitted that a person to whom information is entrusted in confidence is a fiduciary in relation to that information; that he therefore occupies a position within s.4(1)(a); and that he can abuse that position by misusing the information.

RELATIONSHIPS OF INFLUENCE

6–039 Another borderline case is that of the person who is in a position to influence the decisions of another. Equity will allow a transaction to be rescinded if it was secured by the exercise of *undue* influence. The

[63] *Hansard*, SC Deb.B, col.12 (June 20, 2006).
[64] *Hansard*, SC Deb.B, col.21 (June 20, 2006).
[65] See below, para.6–074.

aggrieved party can prove undue influence by showing that the other was in a position of influence over him, and that the transaction was so disadvantageous to him as to call for an explanation.[66] In the case of certain types of relationship the former condition is presumed to be satisfied. These relationships include some which are inherently fiduciary in the fullest sense (such as lawyer and client), but also some which are not (such as parent and child). Does FA 2006, s.4(1)(a) apply to every parent? Does it apply to a person who, though not *presumed* to be in a position to influence another by virtue of their relationship, is in fact in such a position?

It is debatable whether such persons are, without more, properly to be **6–040** regarded as fiduciaries. The exercise of undue influence may be a kind of disloyalty, but that is arguably incidental. On this view the underlying purpose of the rule is not to ensure loyalty, but to enable a person to set aside a transaction to which he did not give a full and informed consent.[67] Even if that is right, however, it does not follow that relationships of influence are outside the section, because the section does not (expressly) require a fiduciary relationship at all. It may be arguable that a person who has influence over another occupies a position of the kind required by s.4(1)(a), even if it is not a fiduciary position. But this would be a strained reading. Unless he is also a fiduciary, a person in a position of influence is not required to refrain from disloyalty generally. He is required *only* to refrain from abusing his influence. To say that he is expected not to act against the other's financial interests, without more, would be a misuse of language. One might as well say that *everyone* falls within s.4(1)(a), because equity requires everyone to refrain from unconscionably exploiting others.

DUTIES OF GOOD FAITH

Justice Paul Finn has argued that there are broadly three levels of **6–041** concern which the law may require a person to show for the financial interests of another.[68] At the lowest level (the default), he may be free to pursue his own interests without regard to those of the other, provided only that he refrains from unconscionable exploitation. The highest level is that of fiduciary duty, which requires him (within the parameters of the fiduciary relationship) to refrain from pursuing his own interests at all. Between

[66] *Royal Bank of Scotland plc v Etridge (No.2)* [2001] UKHL 44; [2002] 2 A.C. 773.

[67] D. Hayton, "Fiduciaries in Context: An Overview" in P. Birks (ed.) *Privacy and Loyalty* at 285–286. But in *Chirnside v Fay* [2006] N.Z.S.C. 68 at [73], Blanchard and Tipping JJ. included doctor and patient among the relationships that are inherently fiduciary. Despite recent suggestions to the contrary (*National Commercial Bank (Jamaica) Ltd v Hew* [2003] UKPC 51; *R. v Attorney-General for England and Wales* [2003] UKPC 22), it seems that the exercise of undue influence is not necessarily a legal wrong, but may be merely a ground for rescission and restitution: Peter Birks and Chin Nyuk Yin, "On the Nature of Undue Influence" in J. Beatson and D. Friedmann (eds) *Good Faith and Fault in Contract Law* (1995); Peter Birks, "Undue Influence as Wrongful Exploitation" (2004) 120 L.Q.R. 34.

[68] P.D. Finn, "The Fiduciary Principle" in T.G. Youdan (ed.) *Equity, Fiduciaries and Trusts* (1989).

these extremes are rules of "good faith", which require him to have due regard to the other's interests without requiring him to give them priority over his own. Finn's examples include the rules governing contracts *uberrimae fidei*, the exercise of a mortgagee's power of sale, the treatment of minority shareholders, and the reduction of the assets of a marginally insolvent company. While there is no general rule of English contract law that each party to a contract must have due regard to the legitimate interests of the other,[69] a particular contract may include an express or implied term to that effect. An example is the implied term in a contract of employment requiring both parties to honour the relationship of trust and confidence between them.[70]

6–042 In North America there has in recent years been a tendency to approach these situations in terms of fiduciary reasoning. The English courts have mostly[71] resisted that temptation, and it is clear that under English law these situations do not in themselves attract fiduciary obligations.[72] In *Nottingham University v Fishel* Elias J. pointed out that the implied duty of trust and confidence in an employment contract is not a fiduciary duty because, while employer and employee are required to take each other's interests into consideration, neither of them is required to act *solely* in the interests of the other.[73] Whether such relationships are within s.4 therefore depends whether s.4 extends to relationships which are not fiduciary. That question is discussed below.[74]

SUPERIOR KNOWLEDGE

6–043 Courts are sometimes tempted to find a fiduciary relationship where one party to a transaction had superior knowledge, and treating him as a fiduciary will enable the court to conclude that he owed the other party a duty of disclosure.[75] But an imbalance in the information available to the parties cannot in itself give rise to a fiduciary relationship, or to fraud by virtue of s.4. It is the province of s.3.[76]

[69] For example, a party is entitled to perform his contractual obligations and claim the agreed payment even after the other party has indicated that performance is no longer required: *White & Carter (Councils) Ltd v McGregor* [1962] A.C. 413.

[70] *Malik v BCCI* [1997] I.R.L.R. 469.

[71] Not always: e.g. *Donnelly v Weybridge Construction Ltd* [2006] EWHC 2678, where Ramsey J. found a fiduciary relationship partly because the parties' agreement was expressly entered into "in the utmost good faith".

[72] See Matthew Conaglen, "The Nature and Function of Fiduciary Loyalty" (2005) 121 L.Q.R. 452 at 456–460 (distinguishing the duty to act for proper purposes from the duty to act in good faith, but arguing that neither is peculiarly fiduciary); cf. R.P. Austin, "Moulding the Content of Fiduciary Duties" in A.J. Oakley (ed.) *Trends in Contemporary Trust Law* (1997) at 159–161.

[73] [2000] I.R.L.R. 471 at [92]; see also *Imperial Group Trust v Imperial Ltd* [1991] 1 W.L.R. 589.

[74] Paras 6–067 *et seq*.

[75] P.D. Finn, "The Fiduciary Principle" in T.G. Youdan (ed.) *Equity, Fiduciaries and Trusts* (1989) at 10.

[76] Above, Ch.5.

ABUSE OF FIDUCIARY POSITION

To commit the offence of fraud by virtue of s.4, a fiduciary must commit a dishonest abuse of his fiduciary position. Broadly speaking, this seems to mean that he must commit a breach of the duty of loyalty imposed by virtue of his position. For example, a person entrusted with access to another's property can commit fraud (as well as theft) by misappropriating the property. A person entrusted with confidential information can probably[77] do so by misusing the information. A person employed to sell goods can do so by selling his own goods instead. A company director can do so by taking up for himself an opportunity that he should have secured for the company. An employee can do so by accepting or soliciting a bribe. **6–044**

It is arguable that *any* dishonest breach of fiduciary duty is, by definition, an abuse of position. On this view, for example, a fiduciary could commit the offence simply by dishonestly creating a conflict between his personal interest and his fiduciary duty, with the intention of giving priority to the former. But in that case it is not clear why s.4(1)(b) uses the word "abuse" rather than the terminology of s.4(1)(a). It could have said something like "dishonestly fails to safeguard, or acts against, the financial interests of that person".[78] Though less concise, this would have made it clear that s.4(1)(b) requires *only* a failure to meet the expectation required by s.4(1)(a). Instead, s.4(1)(b) introduces the new term "abuse". In the absence of a definition saying so, the drafter is unlikely to have intended this merely as shorthand. Arguably it implies a higher threshold. That is, "abuse" is arguably *narrower* than "dishonestly fails to safeguard, or acts against, the financial interests of that person". But, while it is certainly possible for the occupant of a s.4(1)(a) position to fall short of the standards required by that position without abusing it (because those standards are very high, and one can fall short of them despite acting in good faith), it is difficult to see how a *dishonest* failure to meet those standards, with intent to make a gain or cause a loss or a risk of loss, could fail to be an abuse. **6–045**

Conversely, in certain circumstances a dishonest breach of fiduciary duty involves neither acting against the principal's interests nor failing to safeguard them. This is because a fiduciary may not make an uncovenanted profit from his position, even if the principal could never have made that profit and is in no way disadvantaged by the fiduciary's doing so.[79] Such conduct, if dishonest,[80] would probably be an abuse of the fiduciary's position within the meaning of the Act. In other words, "abuse" seems to **6–046**

[77] See above, para.6–038.

[78] Geoffrey Cox, Q.C. M.P. seems to have assumed that "abuse of position" means no more than this. He predicted difficulties in determining whether a defendant's conduct was ultimately in the interests of his company or employer: *Hansard*, SC Deb.B, col.16 (June 20, 2006).

[79] e.g. *Phipps v Boardman* [1967] 2 A.C. 46.

[80] The absence of any intent to cause loss would not in itself be a defence, because an intent to make a gain is sufficient: FA 2006, s.4(1)(c)(i). It would go to dishonesty only.

be *wider* than "dishonestly fails to safeguard, or acts against, the financial interests of that person". If that is right, it reveals a curious anomaly. Since s.4 begins by saying what the defendant must be "expected" to do or refrain from doing, it would be odd if the prohibited conduct could be something other than a failure to meet that expectation. The difficulty arises because s.4(1)(a) does not accurately describe the nature of fiduciary duty. Had it done so, s.4(1)(b) would only have had to refer to a breach of the expectation required by s.4(1)(a).

6–047 Where a person occupies a position falling within s.4(1)(a), various things may be expected of him. Some of those things may be expected of him by virtue of his occupation of the position. That is, they may involve safeguarding the other's interests, or not acting against those interests—the very expectations that bring the position within s.4(1)(a). But he may also be expected to do things *other* than safeguarding or not acting against the other's interests. Expectations of this latter kind do not arise out of the position that brings the person within s.4(1)(a): they merely apply to the same person. A failure to meet them therefore cannot be an abuse of position within the meaning of the Act.

6–048 The practical significance of this will depend how widely the words "expected to safeguard, or not to act against, the financial interests of another person" are construed. For example, the Law Commission intended that s.4 should apply to an employee who "omits to take up a chance of a crucial contract, intending to enable an associate to pick up the contract instead".[81] But, while an employee is a fiduciary for limited purposes,[82] he does not abuse his fiduciary position merely by failing (albeit deliberately) to do his job. That is a breach of contract and no more. If it counted as an abuse of position within the meaning of s.4, the same would presumably be true of any breach of contract on an employee's part which is intended to damage the employer's interests. For example, it might be fraud for an employee to absent himself from work without good reason,[83] if a jury thought it dishonest to do so. It is submitted that the Commission's example is not an abuse of position at all.

OMISSIONS

6–049 FA 2006, s.4(1)(a) expressly provides not only for a person who is expected *not* to act *against* another's interests, but also for a person who is expected to *safeguard* those interests. If a person were expected to safeguard another's interests without also being expected not to act against them, s.4(1)(a) would be satisfied; but the point seems academic, because the situation would never arise.

[81] Law Com. No.276, para.7.39.
[82] See above, para.6–028.
[83] Pretending to be ill could presumably be fraud by false representation, contrary to FA 2006, s.2.

Much more important is s.4(2), which complements the "safeguard" limb of s.4(1)(a) in relation to the requirement that the defendant *abuse* the position described in s.4(1)(a): 6–050

> "A person may be regarded as having abused his position even though his conduct consisted of an omission rather than an act."

So a person who is expected to safeguard another's interests can commit the offence by dishonestly failing to do so. This rule is unlikely to have much direct practical effect, since the likelihood of a person being prosecuted for fraud on the basis of a dishonest omission *alone* seems remote. The only example offered by the Law Commission was that of an employee who "omits to take up a chance of a crucial contract, intending to enable an associate to pick up the contract instead".[84] Even if s.4 could theoretically apply to such a case,[85] it is hard to imagine a prosecution being brought in the absence of a positive breach of duty (such as tipping the associate off). Section 4(2) might be invoked where a fiduciary has dishonestly infringed either the self-dealing rule or the fair dealing rule[86] without disclosing the full facts to his principal. But in such a case it would normally be artificial to regard his fraud as one of mere non-disclosure. The fraud lies in the positive act of dealing, without making disclosure and obtaining consent.[87]

The significance of s.4(2) lies rather in what it says about the intended scope of s.4(1)(a). It does not sit easily with the suggestion that s.4(1)(a) is aimed only at positions of a fiduciary character. The purist view is that it is incorrect to describe a fiduciary's duty of loyalty as a duty to act in the interests of his principal.[88] The duty is more accurately described as a duty to *refrain* from positive acts of *dis*loyalty. On this view a duty to take positive action is, by definition, not a fiduciary duty. Many fiduciaries do of course have duties to act; but those duties arise from the fiduciary's position as a contractor, trustee, company director, employee etc., not from his status as a fiduciary. An express trustee, for example, is obliged to administer the trust in the interests of the beneficiaries. That is not a fiduciary duty: it is simply the duty imposed by the terms of the trust. The trustee's duty of loyalty *prohibits* him from, for example, making a secret profit from the trust. It is separate from, and ancillary to, his primary duty 6–051

[84] Law Com. No.276, para.7.39.

[85] See above, para.6–048.

[86] See above, fn.18.

[87] The fiduciary's non-disclosure might, however, be the *only* misconduct on his part if the transaction is entered into by a third party, and the fiduciary fails to disclose to the principal that the third party is the fiduciary's associate: e.g. *Re Cape Breton Co* (1885) 29 Ch. D. 795. See Richard Nolan, "Conflicts of Interest, Unjust Enrichment and Wrongdoing" in W.R. Cornish et al. (eds), *Restitution: Past, Present and Future*, and "Dispositions involving Fiduciaries: The Equity to Rescind" in P. Birks (ed.) *Restitution and Equity: Vol.1—Resulting Trusts and Equitable Compensation*; Matthew Conaglen, "Equitable Compensation for Breach of Fiduciary Dealing Rules" (2003) 119 L.Q.R. 246.

[88] Richard Nolan, "A Fiduciary Duty to Disclose?" (1997) 113 L.Q.R. 220.

as a trustee.[89] Similarly, a duty to exercise reasonable care and skill is not a fiduciary duty.[90] Nor is a contractual obligation to account.[91]

6–052 Again, it is often said that a fiduciary is under a duty of disclosure in certain circumstances, for example when there is a conflict between his own interests and those of his principal. A duty of disclosure would obviously be a duty to take positive action. On the purist view, however, a fiduciary is not (*qua* fiduciary) under a duty to disclose conflicts of interest or anything else. Non-disclosure on the part of a fiduciary is not itself a legal wrong. It merely precludes the fiduciary from arguing, by way of defence to a claim by the principal (for example, for restitution of a profit derived by the fiduciary from his position), that the principal gave an informed consent to what was done. Disclosure is not mandatory, but merely prudent.

> "[T]here are countless statements in the authorities that fiduciaries as such (I exclude contractual undertakings) have an obligation to make voluntary disclosure, but always, so far as my researches reveal, as the means of avoiding a breach of the related duties not to have a secret interest conflicting with their duty as a fiduciary and not to make a secret profit from their fiduciary position."[92]

6–053 But the purist view is not universally accepted.[93] The Canadian courts, in particular, have developed the concept of fiduciary duty beyond its traditional role in English law, and this has included recognising fiduciary duties to act. In *McInerney v MacDonald*,[94] for example, the Supreme Court of Canada held that a doctor had a fiduciary duty to make a patient's medical records available to her. The High Court of Australia, by contrast, held in *Breen v Williams* that such a duty could only arise from a contract or the law of tort: it could not be fiduciary.

> "In this country, fiduciary obligations arise because a person has come under an obligation to act in another's interests. As a result, equity imposes on the

[89] Robert Flannigan, "The Boundaries of Fiduciary Accountability" (2004) 83 Can. B. Rev. 35 at 48–49; Peter Birks, "The Content of Fiduciary Obligation" (2000) 34 Israel L.R. 3 and (2002) 16 Tru. L.I. 34. Matthew Conaglen, "The Nature and Function of Fiduciary Loyalty" (2005) 121 L.Q.R. 452 argues that the function of fiduciary duties is to safeguard other duties against the risk of breach.

[90] *Henderson v Merrett Syndicates Ltd* [1995] 2 A.C. 145.

[91] *Paragon Finance plc v Thakerar & Co* [1999] 1 All E.R. 400.

[92] *National Mutual Property Services (Australia) Pty Ltd v Citibank Savings Ltd* (May 28, 1998) at [23], *per* Lindgren J., cited by Hollingworth J. in *P. & V. Industries Pty Ltd v Porto* [2006] V.S.C. 131. See also Richard Nolan, "A Fiduciary Duty to Disclose?" (1997) 113 L.Q.R. 220.

[93] See especially Matthew Conaglen, "Equitable Compensation for Breach of Fiduciary Dealing Rules" (2003) 119 L.Q.R. 246, arguing that equitable compensation can be awarded for non-disclosure of an interest by a fiduciary: if this is right, it would seem to follow that there is a duty of disclosure in the strict sense (i.e. that non-disclosure is a legal wrong). In *Gwembe Valley Development Co Ltd v Koshy* [2003] EWCA Civ 1048 at [143] the Court of Appeal agreed that "There are arguments, both on authority and in principle" for this view, but did not have to decide the point because the case involved dishonest concealment rather than mere non-disclosure.

[94] (1992) 93 D.L.R. (4th) 415.

fiduciary proscriptive obligations—not to obtain any unauthorised benefit from the relationship and not to be in a position of conflict. If these obligations are breached, the fiduciary must account for any profits and make good any losses arising from the breach. But the law of this country does not otherwise impose positive legal duties on the fiduciary to act in the interests of the person to whom the duty is owed."[95]

The High Court of Australia reasserted this position in *Pilmer v Duke Group Ltd*.[96] Kirby J., who in *Breen v Williams* would have preferred to follow *McInerney v MacDonald*, conceded in *Pilmer* that 6–054

"*Breen* upholds the principle stated in the aphorism that fiduciary obligations are 'proscriptive' and not 'prescriptive'. This, in my view, is the fundamental reason why all members of this court in *Breen* rejected [the patient's] claim of a fiduciary obligation. Whatever the differing views which the justices held concerning the character of the relationship in question there and whether it was, or was not, a fiduciary one for some or all purposes, there was agreement that [the patient's] claim failed because it would have involved imposing on the suggested fiduciary positive obligations to act. It would have burdened him with an affirmative obligation to grant access to his notes to a patient ('prescriptive' duties). It would thus have gone further than the conventional ('proscriptive') duties of loyalty, of avoiding conflicts of interest or of misusing one's power, such as fiduciary duties have traditionally upheld."[97]

In England and Wales, authority for the existence of fiduciary duties requiring positive action is relatively scarce. In *Balston Ltd v Headline Filters Ltd*[98] Falconer J. held that a director did not commit a breach of duty by failing to disclose to his company that he intended to set up a competing business. This decision has been applied in other cases.[99] In *British Midland Tool Ltd v Midland International Tooling Ltd*, however, Hart J. said: 6–055

"A director's duty to act so as to promote the best interests of his company prima facie includes a duty to inform the company of any activity, actual or threatened, which damages those interests."[100]

A duty to inform is obviously a duty to take positive action. In *Shepherds Investments Ltd v Walters*[101] Etherton J. said he preferred Hart J.'s approach to that adopted in the *Balston* line of cases; but he also thought it material that the director in *British Midland Tool Ltd* had committed positive breaches of duty which he failed to disclose. Merely making a decision to set up a competing business at some point in the future, and failing to inform the company of that decision immediately, would not suffice.

[95] (1996) 186 C.L.R. 71 at 113, *per* Gaudron and McHugh JJ.
[96] (2001) 207 C.L.R. 165.
[97] (2001) 207 C.L.R. 165 at 214.
[98] [1990] F.S.R. 385.
[99] *Framlington Group plc v Anderson* [1995] 1 B.C.L.C. 475; *Saatchi & Saatchi Co plc v Saatchi*, February 13, 1995; *Coleman Taymar Ltd v Oakes* [2001] 2 B.C.L.C. 749.
[100] [2003] EWHC 466; [2003] 2 B.C.L.C. 523 at [89].
[101] [2006] EWHC 836.

6–056 Etherton J. also cited *Item Software (UK) Ltd v Fassihi*.[102] In that case, without discussing either the *Balston* line of cases or *British Midland Tool Ltd*, the Court of Appeal held a company director liable for failing to disclose to the company that he was acting contrary to the company's interests. Arden L.J., with whom the other members of the court agreed on this issue, regarded this obligation as an aspect of "the fundamental duty to which a director is subject, that is the duty to act in what he in good faith considers to be the best interests of his company".[103] But she then referred to this duty as the "duty of loyalty", as if loyalty involved something more than refraining from disloyal acts. In support of her view she cited Professor Robert C. Clark's observation that

> "The most general formulation of corporate law's attempted solution to the problem of managerial accountability is *the fiduciary duty of loyalty*: the corporation's directors . . . owe a duty of undivided loyalty to their corporations, and they may not so use corporate assets, or deal with the corporation, as to benefit themselves at the expense of the corporation and its shareholders."[104]

But this passage accords with the purist view, since it refers to what directors may *not* do.

6–057 Arden L.J. concluded:

> "The only reason that I can see that it could be said that the duty of loyalty does not require a fiduciary to disclose his own misconduct is that it has never been applied to this situation before."[105]

It does not appear to have been argued that the duty of loyalty cannot, by its very nature, require a fiduciary to take any positive steps at all. None of the Commonwealth authorities were cited. The decision has not been followed in Australia. The Supreme Court of Victoria has found the reasoning unsatisfactory, and has doubted whether the decision is correct even in English law.[106]

6–058 It is therefore unclear whether an omission can in itself be a breach of fiduciary duty. What *is* clear (because FA 2006, s.4(2) says so) is that it can be an abuse of position for the purposes of s.4. If the purist view is correct, it follows that s.4 cannot be confined to breaches of fiduciary duty, and that the courts will have to find some other interpretation which does not make s.4 unfeasibly wide. One alternative interpretation[107] might be that, while

[102] [2004] EWCA 1244; [2005] I.C.R. 450.

[103] [2004] EWCA 1244; [2005] I.C.R. 450 at [41].

[104] *Corporate Law* (1986) at 34 (emphasis in original).

[105] [2004] EWCA 1244; [2005] I.C.R. 450 at [44].

[106] *P. & V. Industries Pty Ltd v Porto* [2006] V.S.C. 131. See also John Armour and Matthew Conaglen, "Directorial Disclosure" [2005] C.L.J. 48.

[107] A third explanation might be that an omission can be an abuse of position even though it is not a breach of fiduciary duty, but only a fiduciary can fall within s.4(1)(a). This is consistent with the conventional view and with s.4(2), but would make the section internally incoherent. If only a fiduciary can fall within s.4(1)(a), the position required by s.4(1)(a) is a fiduciary position, and it is difficult to see how one might abuse a fiduciary position without committing a breach of fiduciary duty.

s.4(1)(a) is aimed only at persons owing a duty of loyalty to another, an omission can for this purpose amount to disloyalty. This approach would cut across the purist view of the duty of loyalty, but seems to be consistent with the Law Commission's intentions. The Commission seems to have been ignorant of the debate as to the nature of fiduciary duty, and to have assumed that every breach of duty on the part of a fiduciary is a breach of fiduciary duty.

This approach would also be consistent with an apparent trend against the purist view in recent decisions. It is noteworthy that these authorities are concerned only with non-disclosure of conflicts of interest and other matters of concern to the principal, which is arguably a special case. Perhaps non-disclosure of such matters is the *only* kind of omission that can suffice for s.4. An objection to this solution is that it would make s.4(2) redundant, since non-disclosure is the province of s.3. But, even where the alleged abuse of position consists in non-disclosure, s.4 seems to be wider than s.3, in that the defendant need not be under a legal duty to disclose. It is enough that he occupies a position in which he is "expected" to safeguard another's financial interests by making disclosure. So the prosecution will prefer, if possible, to rely on s.4 rather than s.3.[108] This does not mean that s.3 is redundant, because it applies to duties of disclosure imposed on persons who fall outside s.4 (such as persons entering into a contract *uberrimae fidei*). **6–059**

INFORMED CONSENT

A fiduciary commits no breach of duty by doing something to which his principal has given informed consent. For example, the members of a company can waive a director's duty either by provision in the articles of association or by ratifying a particular transaction.[109] Informed consent must similarly be a defence to a charge of fraud under s.4. This is not just because it prevents an abuse from being dishonest, but because it prevents the fiduciary's conduct from being an abuse at all. While the fiduciary may have failed to safeguard the principal's interests, in respect of the matter in question he was at liberty not to do so. The same must be true if a contract **6–060**

[108] This does not explain what the Law Commission had in mind when it included what is now s.4(2) in its draft Bill, because the Commission's version of s.3 was *not* confined to non-disclosure in breach of a legal duty. But the Commission does not appear to have appreciated the distinction between fiduciary duties (which, on the purist view, cannot be duties to act) and other duties owed by fiduciaries (which obviously can).

[109] *Boulting v Association of Cinematograph, Television and Allied Technicians* [1963] 2 Q.B. 606 at 636, *per* Upjohn L.J. In *Item Software (UK) Ltd v Fassihi* [2004] EWCA Civ 1244; [2005] I.C.R. 450 at [35], Arden L.J. said : "[Fiduciary] duties are imposed by law. They are not simply default rules, that is rules of law subject to contrary agreement. They are mandatory rules of law which the company and the director cannot contract out of them [*sic*]." But the authority cited for this proposition was the Companies Act 1985, s.310, which prevents *liability* for a director's breach of duty from being excluded by the company's articles or otherwise. It does not prevent a company from agreeing that certain conduct by a director should not be a breach of duty at all.

between the parties includes a term (express or implied) which permits the defendant to do things which would otherwise be breaches of fiduciary duty.

6–061 This defence is available only if the principal's consent is fully informed—that is, only if the fiduciary has made *full* disclosure. It is not enough for the fiduciary to disclose that he has an interest in a transaction if he fails to disclose the nature and extent of that interest.[110] If the principal's consent is obtained by misrepresentation or by breach of a duty of disclosure, the fiduciary could be guilty of fraud by abuse of position as well as fraud by false representation or failing to disclose information (as the case may be).

FORMER FIDUCIARIES

6–062 When a relationship imposing fiduciary duties has come to an end, certain aspects of the duty of loyalty may persist. This may sometimes be because, although a formal and inherently fiduciary relationship has ceased to exist, the factual relationship continues to be one of trust and confidence. Thus in *Longstaff v Birtles*[111] the conduct of solicitors whose retainer had been terminated was held to be a breach of a continuing fiduciary duty to their former clients. It seems clear that such conduct, if dishonest, could be an abuse of position for the purposes of FA 2006, s.4, because s.4(1)(a) is certainly not confined to *formal* fiduciary relationships.

6–063 But even if a relationship of trust and confidence no longer exists, a former fiduciary may continue to be subject to certain fiduciary duties. For example, a company director can commit a breach of duty if, on learning of an opportunity which he might have taken up for the company, he resigns and takes it up for himself.[112] An ex-employee would surely be liable to account to his former employer for a payment received by him after the end of his employment as a reward for favour shown during it. A former fiduciary may also be liable for misusing confidential information acquired

[110] *Wrexham Association Football Club Ltd v Crucialmove Ltd* [2006] EWCA Civ 237 at [39], *per* Sir Peter Gibson.

[111] [2001] EWCA Civ 1219; [2002] 1 W.L.R. 470. The decision seems inconsistent with Lord Millett's dictum in *Bolkiah v KPMG* [1999] 2 A.C. 222 at 235 that "The fiduciary relationship which subsists between solicitor and client comes to an end with the termination of the retainer. Thereafter the solicitor has no obligation to defend and advance the interests of his former client. The only duty to the former client which survives the termination of the client relationship is a continuing duty to preserve the confidentiality of information imparted during its subsistence." But in *Ratiu v Conway* [2005] EWCA Civ 1302; [2006] 1 All E.R. 571 at [75]–[77] Auld L.J. rejected an argument that *Longstaff v Birtles* was decided *per incuriam* because *Bolkiah* was not cited, on the ground that Lord Millett had been primarily concerned with the extent of the duty of confidence rather than that of fiduciary duty.

[112] This suggests that the diversion of corporate opportunities is best regarded as a breach of the no profit rule (which can continue to apply after the end of the relationship) rather than the no conflict rule (which cannot): see *Ultraframe Ltd v Fielding* [2005] EWHC 1638 at [1309], *per* Lewison J.

while he was a fiduciary; but this is arguably because the duty to respect confidential information is independent of the fiduciary relationship.[113] An ex-employee may not disclose his former employer's trade secrets, but his freedom to use information acquired during his employment is greater than that of an existing employee.[114]

Surprisingly, it seems that conduct by a former fiduciary which amounts **6–064** to a breach of a continuing fiduciary duty cannot be fraud by virtue of s.4. The wording of the section clearly envisages that the defendant will occupy the position described in s.4(1)(a) at the time when he abuses it. When the Opposition raised the issue in Parliament, the Solicitor General's response implied first that conduct after the end of the relationship can be an abuse of position[115] and then that it cannot.[116] At Report stage he tried again.

> "A defendant . . . will not be prosecutable under clause 4 if he manages to abuse the position after he ceases to occupy it, but in any event, there are limits to how he could do that. I accept that information obtained during the course of employment could be valuable, but, as I made clear in Committee, we expect breaches of confidentiality to be a matter of civil law. That will certainly be the case once the employee ceases to occupy his position, which must be right."[117]

Since this answer was given in response to an Opposition amendment, it was presumably prepared in advance of the debate, and would be admissible as evidence of Parliament's intention.[118] It is a clear statement that a person's conduct after he has ceased to occupy a position cannot be an abuse of that position for the purposes of s.4. This is remarkable. In 1997 the Law Commission was greatly exercised about the fact that an employee or ex-employee who misuses his employer's trade secrets may be guilty of no offence.[119] Its report on fraud does not explain why the employee's conduct should be criminal but the ex-employee's should not. The point appears to have been overlooked.

QUASI–FIDUCIARIES

Many public officers are fiduciaries by virtue of being employees of a **6–065** public body, or Crown servants. In *Reading v Attorney-General*, for example, an army sergeant who had accepted bribes to ensure the safe passage of contraband goods by escorting them through Cairo while in uniform was

[113] See above, para.6–034.
[114] *Faccenda Chicken Ltd v Fowler* [1986] I.R.L.R. 69.
[115] *Hansard*, SC Deb.B, col.23 (June 20, 2006).
[116] *Hansard*, SC Deb.B, cols 25–26 (June 20, 2006).
[117] *Hansard*, HC Vol.450, col.1701 (October 26, 2006).
[118] *Pepper (Inspector of Taxes) v Hart* [1990] 1 W.L.R. 204.
[119] Law Commission Consultation Paper No.150, *Legislating the Criminal Code: Misuse of Trade Secrets*.

held liable to account for the bribes to the Crown. The Court of Appeal thought that he was a fiduciary "in the wide sense in which the term is used in the relevant cases", by virtue of the authority conferred upon him by his rank and uniform (though adding that it would not necessarily be fatal to the Crown's case if he were not).[120] The House of Lords agreed.[121] Reading was a Crown servant, and it seems to have been common ground that his position was analogous to that of an employee.[122] His conduct would probably amount to fraud by virtue of FA 2006, s.4 on the basis that, by virtue of his position, he was expected to safeguard or not act against the financial interests of another person (namely the Crown). But it may be arguable that the Crown is a "person" only in a technical sense, and that s.4 should not be given a technical construction.

6–066 Some public officers, moreover, are neither employees nor Crown servants. The private law of fiduciaries does not strictly apply to them, though they may be subject to analogous rules as a matter of public law.[123] Such persons may conveniently be described as quasi-fiduciaries.[124] It may be arguable that even they are within s.4, on the ground that they serve *under* the Crown[125] and are therefore expected to show loyalty to the Crown as if they were servants of the Crown. But misconduct by such persons can be dealt with as (for example) corruption, bribery at common law, or misconduct in public office.[126] There is no need to stretch the fraud offence to cover them.

OTHER CASES

6–067 While it is clear that FA 2006, s.4 is primarily aimed at breaches of fiduciary duty, it does not actually mention fiduciaries at all. If intended simply as a plain-English description of fiduciary duty, s.4(1)(a) is not entirely apt for the purpose.[127] It is equally arguable that s.4 catches forms of dishonesty which do not involve fiduciary disloyalty or anything like it. Much of private law is concerned with situations in which a person is obliged to act in a way which will further another's financial interests. Suppose D contracts with V that he will construct a building, using materials of a quality specified in the contract. If he uses inferior materials, the building will cost more to maintain and will be worth less, so V's

[120] [1949] 2 K.B. 232.
[121] [1951] A.C. 507.
[122] Finn criticises the decision, and that in *Att-Gen v Goddard* (1929) 98 L.J.K.B. 743 (bribery of police officer): *Fiduciary Obligations* (1977) para.498.
[123] P.D. Finn, "Public Officers: Some Personal Liabilities" (1977) 51 A.L.J. 313.
[124] Law Commission Consultation Paper No.145, *Legislating the Criminal Code: Corruption*, paras 7.18 *et seq*.
[125] cf. *Barrett* [1976] 1 W.L.R. 946.
[126] See below, Ch.19.
[127] For example, it ignores the fiduciary duty to refrain from making a secret profit even if the principal suffers no loss.

financial interests will be adversely affected. Does it follow that D is expected to safeguard V's interests by adhering to the specifications, and that he commits fraud if he dishonestly fails to do so? Is *every* party to a contract expected to safeguard the other party's interests by performing his contractual obligations?

There are some clues in the Act which suggest that s.4 is not intended to be as wide as this. First, if s.4(1)(a) included everyone who is expected to act in a way which would further another's financial interests, s.3 would be redundant, because a breach of a legal duty to disclose information would be an abuse of position within the meaning of s.4. And, if s.4(1)(a) included everyone who is expected not to act in a way which would be contrary to another's financial interests, s.2 would be redundant, because the making of false representations would be an abuse of position within the meaning of s.4. If s.4 were intended to include all the conduct falling within ss.2 and 3, those sections could and presumably would have been omitted. **6–068**

Secondly, "safeguard" is a strong word.[128] It seems to imply a standard of duty higher than that routinely undertaken by everyone who undertakes contractual obligations. Arguably a person is not expected to *safeguard* another's interests merely because he is expected to do something which it is in another's interests that he should do. The alternative of being expected "not to act against" another's financial interests clearly does *not* imply a high standard; but perhaps its meaning is coloured by that of "safeguard". On this basis it might be said that a person is expected "not to act against the financial interests of another person" only where his position is analogous to that of a person expected to safeguard those interests, except that he is not expected to take any *positive* steps to safeguard those interests but only to refrain from damaging them. **6–069**

Thirdly, s.4(1)(a) does not say that the defendant must be *required* or *obliged* to safeguard another's interests, but only that he must be *expected* to do so. Apparently he need not be under a legal obligation at all.[129] If "safeguard" meant "advance" or "promote" and no more, it would scarcely have been necessary to go beyond persons who are *obliged* to safeguard. The word "expected", in combination with a wide interpretation of "safeguard", would make the offence astonishingly wide. **6–070**

Finally, the defendant must not only be expected to safeguard another's interests: he must *occupy a position* in which he is expected to do so. Even if a party to an ordinary contract is expected to safeguard the other party's interests, it may be arguable that he is expected to do so by virtue of the contract, not by virtue of any "position" that he occupies. Arguably, the requirement that the defendant occupy a position must be intended to add something to the requirement that he be expected to safeguard another's interests. Otherwise the first six words of s.4(1)(a) would be redundant. On **6–071**

[128] The Oxford English Dictionary defines it as "To keep secure from danger or attack; to guard, protect, defend".

[129] See above, para.6–004.

the other hand, those words enable s.4(1)(b) and (c) to refer to an abuse of the position mentioned in s.4(1)(a), rather than repetitively referring to a failure to safeguard the other's interests or an act done against them (as the case may be). So it is arguable that the reference to a "position" has no substantive effect, but is merely a drafting device.

6–072 The Law Commission certainly intended a narrower interpretation. This is apparent from Part 9 of its report, which discussed whether the common law offence of conspiracy to defraud needed to be retained alongside the new offence. Two examples were given of conduct which is caught by conspiracy to defraud but not by the proposed new offences: dishonestly failing to fulfil a contractual obligation,[130] and dishonestly infringing a legal right (such as a copyright). According to the Commission, these cases

> "represent a huge range of activities which is potentially criminal at common law but, in the absence of misrepresentation, wrongful non-disclosure or abuse of position, would fall outside the new offences we recommend. . . . If it is thought that certain torts, breaches of contract or equitable wrongs should be criminal, legislation can be framed with reference to the particular kinds of conduct involved."

Clearly, therefore, the Commission did not intend that every such wrong should be an abuse of position.[131] That would have meant that the new offence was virtually the "general dishonesty offence" which the Law Commission was at pains to reject, partly because it might infringe the principle of legal certainty (and therefore Art.7 of the European Convention on Human Rights).[132]

6–073 During the Bill's passage through Parliament, the Opposition repeatedly pressed the Government to explain why cl.4(1)(a) was not drafted in terms of fiduciary duty, and in what circumstances (if any) it might apply to a person who is not a fiduciary. David Heath MP summarised the concern.

> "I am a little alarmed by the paucity of examples of matters that fall outside the concept of a duty . . . This is one of the rare occasions when I can criticise the Law Commission, because its report also fails to deal with the matter. It baldly says that there may be cases and that it will be for the court to determine them and for the prosecution to demonstrate its case, but it gives no examples of what those instances might be, and why they would be of such import as to require a redefinition of what is a stand-alone offence in the provision. Someone would be required to have done nothing else besides being

[130] It is questionable whether this is caught by conspiracy to defraud either: see below, para.7–028.

[131] The Law Commission did say that "The necessary relationship will be present between . . . professional person and client" (Law Com. No.276, para.7.38), and many professionals are not fiduciaries vis-à-vis all (or any) of their clients; but the Commission was probably referring only to those professionals who *are* fiduciaries, such as solicitors. The Solicitor General said that "for there to be an abuse of position, it is required that a particular duty is owed by the individual, over and above that which people have when they enter into a normal contract to purchase property, or anything else": *Hansard*, HC Vol.447, col.538 (June 12, 2006).

[132] See above, paras 2–099 *et seq.*

subject to the ill-defined expectation and, in that context, to have acted in the dishonest way specified."[133]

In the Commons, an amendment was tabled which would have expressly confined s.4 to fiduciaries. The Solicitor General's reasons for resisting the amendment were as follows. 6–074

"[Fiduciary] obligations may not be present in a range of informal personal relationships and it would be difficult for the prosecution to prove the existence of fiduciary relationships in certain informal circumstances, even though it would be clear to the man on the Clapham omnibus or the man in the street . . . that one person occupied a position in which he was expected to safeguard the interests of another. We do not want to get ourselves into a situation where a complex legal argument about the nature of a fiduciary relationship and whether it exists is the subject of the case, rather than the court and jury looking at the relationship as a whole and taking a view as to whether those circumstances produced a relationship where there is a legitimate and proper expectation that there was a duty owed and someone was expected to safeguard or not to act against the financial interests of another person, and that position was dishonestly abused. . . .

It would be difficult in some circumstances for prosecutors to argue that a particular relationship, which members of the public may well see as a relationship where someone is expected to safeguard the interests of another, was necessarily a fiduciary relationship. While in most cases the measure would apply to circumstances where a duty clearly exists, there would be some cases where a formal legal duty may not exist. Those cases will arise particularly in personal and family relationships. . . .

Many elderly people are looked after by helpers who do not have formal power of attorney, but take various degrees of responsibility for their finances. Few abuse their position, but it would not be right that those who do so should escape prosecution for fraud just because they have no full legal or fiduciary duty to that elderly person or because the Crown Prosecution Service has a difficulty proving that fiduciary duty beyond reasonable doubt."[134]

There seem to be two different points here. First, the scope of fiduciary law is, as we have seen, not especially well defined. A requirement of fiduciary duty would lead to "complex legal argument" and might require the jury to be directed about the relevant law. There would have been obvious advantages in avoiding this, if the Act had instead been drafted so as to incorporate or restate the relevant principles of fiduciary law. 6–075

But that would not have met the Solicitor General's second point— namely that the offence was intended to catch some people who simply *are not* fiduciaries. The example given is that of a carer who misappropriates the funds of an elderly person.[135] It is not clear why the Solicitor General 6–076

[133] *Hansard*, SC Deb.B, col.23 (June 20, 2006). In the Lords the Attorney-General had been asked whether the clause would apply to an art dealer who, having been asked by a friend to make a fair offer for a collection of pictures, makes an offer which ignores what he knows to be the true value of one picture. The Attorney did not answer the question, but merely quoted the Law Commission's report: *Hansard*, HL Vol.673, cols 1430–1431 (July 19, 2005).

[134] *Hansard*, SC Deb.B, cols 19–21 (June 20, 2006).

[135] FA 2006 does not in fact need to cover this case at all, because it is plainly theft. To make the Solicitor General's point, the example needed to be modified so that the carer's fraud would not otherwise amount to any serious offence: for example, the carer rents out the elderly person's spare room and keeps the proceeds.

thought that such a person would not be a fiduciary. He seems to have been under the impression that fiduciary duties apply only within the established types of relationship that are *inherently* fiduciary.[136] At Report stage he said:

> "While in most cases the clause will apply to circumstances where a duty clearly exists, there will be some cases where a formal fiduciary duty does not exist."[137]

The word "formal" reveals the confusion. Equity looks to the substance, not the form. Fiduciary duties can arise whenever the reasons for imposing them exist, and those reasons are not confined to banks and boardrooms.[138] Perhaps the Solicitor General saw some difficulty in regarding as a fiduciary a person who is not subject to the higher-level fiduciary rules such as the no conflict rule and the no profit rule. But, as we have seen, the fact that a person is not subject to *every* fiduciary rule does not mean that he is not a fiduciary at all.[139]

6–077 In any event, the crucial point for present purposes is that the carer was the only example the Solicitor General gave of a person who, though not a fiduciary, was intended to fall within s.4. It seems reasonable to infer from this that s.4 is intended to apply, first, to fiduciaries, and secondly (in so far as they are not fiduciaries) to persons whose position is analogous to that of the carer. But in what respect must the defendant's position be analogous to that of the carer? What distinguishes the carer from the builder,[140] who is clearly intended to fall outside the section?

6–078 The Law Commission gave two examples of persons to whom s.4 would apply: someone who "is given authority to exercise a discretion on the victim's behalf" (who is clearly a fiduciary on any view), and someone who "is given access to the victim's assets, premises, equipment or customers". This latter example would include the carer even if he were not a fiduciary. Section 4 will have the scope it was apparently intended to have if the words "to safeguard, or not to act against, the financial interests of another person" are read as referring to an expectation of *loyalty*, in much the same sense as the duty of loyalty imposed by equity on a fiduciary. This would include persons who are given access to another's property or information and are expected not to misuse that access for their own purposes. Since (*pace* the Solicitor General) equity requires a person to show loyalty whenever he knows that he is expected to do so, the effect would be that s.4 applied only to persons who are fiduciaries as a matter of civil law. But there would be no need to explain fiduciary *law* to a jury—only the idea of loyalty, which permeates that law.

[136] See above, para.6–016.
[137] *Hansard*, HC Vol.450, col.1701 (October 26, 2006).
[138] cf. Robert Flannigan, "Commercial Fiduciary Obligation" (1997–98) 36 Alberta L. Rev. 905 at 909.
[139] See above, paras 6–023 *et seq.*
[140] See above, para.6–067.

This interpretation is supported by the Law Commission's statement that, although fiduciary duty would not be essential, 6–079

> "This does not of course mean that it would be entirely a matter for the fact-finders whether the necessary relationship exists. The question whether the particular facts alleged can properly be described as giving rise to that relationship will be an issue capable of being ruled upon by the judge and, if the case goes to the jury, of being the subject of directions."[141]

The Commission seems to have envisaged that there would be some cases to which s.4 *could* not apply, as a matter of law. But, if s.4 applies to relationships that are not fiduciary, it is not clear what the line of demarcation might be, or what kind of directions the judge might give. Section 4 is couched in ordinary language, and a judge cannot give directions about the meaning of ordinary words.[142] The presence or absence of an expectation of fiduciary loyalty seems the obvious place to draw the line.

[141] Law Com. No.276, para.7.38.
[142] *Brutus v Cozens* [1973] A.C. 854.

CHAPTER 7

CONSPIRACY TO DEFRAUD

An agreement to commit the offence under s.1 of the Fraud Act 2006 ("FA 2006") is a statutory conspiracy contrary to the Criminal Law Act 1977, s.1. But conspiracy to defraud another person has long been an offence at common law. The offence is now punishable with 10 years' imprisonment.[1] It is, remarkably, unaffected by FA 2006. Its usefulness was for a time severely curtailed by the House of Lords' decision in *Ayres*[2] that the 1977 Act had abolished it except in the case of agreements that did not involve the commission of any offence; but that decision was reversed by the Criminal Justice Act 1987, s.12.[3] **7–001**

Defrauding is a concept of the common law. It may be relevant to offences other than conspiracy to defraud. Statutes creating offences sometimes require that a thing be done "fraudulently" or "with intent to defraud", and such provisions are normally construed in accordance with the common law concept of defrauding. In *Scott v Metropolitan Police Commissioner*[4] Viscount Dilhorne referred to Lord Radcliffe's analysis in *Welham v DPP*[5] of the "intent to defraud" then required for forgery, and saw no reason why the same should not apply in relation to conspiracy to defraud. His analysis was in turn applied to the offence of fraudulent evasion of a Customs and Excise prohibition,[6] and the reasoning in *Welham* has been applied to the fraudulent use of an excise licence[7] and to fraudulent trading.[8] The test of dishonesty, which is not only an express **7–002**

[1] Criminal Justice Act 1987, s.12(3). At common law the punishment was at large.
[2] [1984] A.C. 447.
[3] Section 12 came into force on July 20, 1987. The position in relation to conspiracies concluded before that date is examined in the second edition of this book, at paras 2–046 *et seq*.
[4] [1975] A.C. 819.
[5] [1961] A.C. 103.
[6] *Att-Gen's Reference (No.1 of 1981)* [1982] Q.B. 848.
[7] *Terry* [1984] A.C. 374.
[8] *Grantham* [1984] Q.B. 675.

requirement of many statutory offences but also a central element of the concept of defrauding, is the same in every case.[9] The use of "fraud" and its cognates as elements of statutory offences has fallen out of favour,[10] but the difference is often one of terminology rather than substance.[11]

7–003 The common law concept of defrauding is distinct from the fraud *offence* created by FA 2006, s.1 (though that offence resembles it in some respects), and does not necessarily involve the commission of an offence at all. Conspiracy to defraud is therefore anomalous because, unlike statutory conspiracy under the Criminal Law Act 1977, it consists in an agreement to do something which itself is not necessarily criminal.

7–004 This chapter examines first the concept of defrauding, and then the element of agreement that a defrauding shall occur.

DEFRAUDING

7–005 Stephen explained the common law concept of defrauding as follows.

> "I shall not attempt to construct a definition which will meet every case which might be suggested, but there is little danger in saying that whenever the words 'fraud' or 'intent to defraud' or 'fraudulently' occur in the definition of a crime two elements at least are essential to the commission of the crime: namely, first, deceit or an intention to deceive or in some cases mere secrecy; and, secondly, either actual injury or possible injury or an intent to expose some person either to actual injury or to a risk of possible injury by means of that deceit or secrecy."[12]

The alternatives "deceit" and "mere secrecy" are well established in the modern law. It may be fraudulent either to obtain an economic benefit by deception, or simply to take it.

DISHONESTY

7–006 Dishonesty is an essential element of fraud at common law,[13] and means the same in this context as in statutory offences.[14] Its meaning is examined in Ch.2.

[9] *Ghosh* [1982] Q.B. 1053; above, Ch.2.

[10] The offence under FA 2006, s.1 is *called* "fraud", but that word does not appear in the provisions *defining* it.

[11] Examples include the redefinition of forgery in the Forgery and Counterfeiting Act 1981 (below, Ch.11), and the replacement of larceny with theft in the Theft Act 1968 (below, Ch.9).

[12] *History of Criminal Law*, Vol.2 at 121–122.

[13] *Scott v Metropolitan Police Commissioner* [1975] A.C. 819; *Tarling (No.1) v Government of the Republic of Singapore* (1978) 70 Cr.App.R. 77.

[14] *Ghosh* [1982] Q.B. 1053.

MISREPRESENTATION CAUSING LOSS

The paradigm of fraud involves misrepresentation. But misrepresentation, even if dishonest, is not enough: it must also cause the victim to suffer loss, or at least to alter his conduct.[15] In *Re London and Globe Finance Corp Ltd* Buckley J. explained: 7–007

> "To deceive is, I apprehend, to induce a man to believe that a thing is true which is false, and which the person practising the deceit knows or believes to be false. To defraud is to deprive by deceit: it is by deceit to induce a man to act to his injury. More tersely it may be put, that to deceive is by falsehood to induce a state of mind; to defraud is by deceit to induce a course of action."[16]

Thus a person who pretends to be something that he is not, merely to win the esteem of others and with no thought of financial gain, is guilty of misrepresentation but not fraud.[17]

On the other hand a misrepresentation may be fraudulent even if there is 7–008
no intention of leaving the victim financially worse off in the long run: it is sufficient that the misrepresentation induces him to take a risk that he would not otherwise have taken. Conduct involving *no* risk of loss is arguably not dishonest; but a jury is unlikely to think it acceptable to deceive another into taking a real financial risk, and if such conduct is dishonest it is fraudulent. In *Allsop* a sub-broker for a finance company put false particulars in hire-purchase application forms so that the company would accept applications which it might otherwise have rejected. His defence to a charge of conspiracy to defraud was that he expected all the transactions to be satisfactorily completed. Since he did not intend to cause the company any loss, he had no intention to defraud. The Court of Appeal disagreed.

> "Interests which are imperilled are less valuable in terms of money than those same interests when they are secure and protected. Where a person intends by deceit to induce a course of conduct in another which puts that other's economic interests in jeopardy he is guilty of fraud even though he does not intend or desire that actual loss should ultimately be suffered by that other in this context."[18]

Conspiracy to defraud requires an *intention* to defraud, because an element of intention is inherent in the requirement of agreement.[19] *Allsop* does not suggest that intention to defraud is not required: it decides that to deceive

[15] The Oxford English Dictionary defines "fraud" as "criminal deception; the using of false representations to obtain an unjust advantage or to injure the rights or interests of another". In this respect defrauding is a narrower concept than fraud by false representation, for which the representation need not have any actual effect: see above, para.3–002.

[16] [1903] 1 Ch. 728 at 732–733.

[17] *Hodgson* (1856) Dears. & B. 3; cf. *Moon* [1967] 3 All E.R. 962.

[18] (1976) 64 Cr.App.R. 29 at 32.

[19] See below, para.7–030.

someone into putting his property at risk is to defraud him. An intention to do so is therefore an intention to defraud.

7–009 *Allsop* was approved in *Wai Yu-Tsang*, and arguably extended. The chief accountant of a bank conspired with others to conceal in the bank's accounts the fact that cheques purchased by the bank had been dishonoured. The Privy Council dismissed his appeal against conviction of conspiracy to defraud the bank and its existing and potential shareholders, creditors and depositors.

> "It is suggested that [*Allsop*] was not about recklessness, and did not decide that anything less than intention in the strict sense would suffice for conspiracy to defraud. Their Lordships are however reluctant to allow this part of the law to become enmeshed in a distinction, sometimes artificially drawn, between intention and recklessness. The question whether particular facts reveal a conspiracy to defraud depends upon what the conspirators have dishonestly agreed to do, and in particular whether they have agreed to practise a fraud on somebody. For this purpose it is enough for example that, as in *Allsop* and in the present case, the conspirators have dishonestly agreed to bring about a state of affairs which they realise will or may deceive the victim into so acting, or failing to act, that he will suffer economic loss or his economic interests will be put at risk."[20]

Read literally this means that a person is defrauded not only if he is deceived into putting his economic interests at risk, but also if a state of affairs exists which *may* deceive him into doing so. This goes further than was necessary, since the appellant (like Allsop) had clearly intended that others *should* be deceived, not just that a state of affairs should exist in which they *might* be; and it is submitted with respect that it goes too far. If the putative victim's interests are not in fact endangered it can hardly be said that he has been defrauded merely because, if things had turned out differently (for example, if he had not seen through the deception), they might have been.[21]

7–010 In *Adams (Grant)*[22] the prosecution attempted to extend the concept of defrauding even further, but this time without success. The case involved an elaborate scheme for the laundering of certain sums whose source remained obscure. It was argued, and the Court of Appeal of New Zealand agreed, that the scheme was a conspiracy to defraud if the object was to prevent the company from ascertaining whether it had any interest in the sums in question, even if in fact it had no such interest. The Privy Council disagreed. On that hypothesis,[23] the company would have suffered no prejudice.

[20] [1992] 1 A.C. 269 at 279–280.

[21] But fraud by false representation can be committed in these circumstances: above, para.3–002.

[22] [1995] 1 W.L.R. 52.

[23] The Privy Council concluded that the company did have an interest in the sums, because they were secret profits for which the directors were accountable to it.

> "A person is not prejudiced if he is hindered in inquiring into the source of moneys in which he has no interest. He can only suffer prejudice in relation to some right or interest which he possesses."[24]

This proposition was said to be clear from the passage from *Wai Yu-Tsang* cited above.

LOSS WITHOUT MISREPRESENTATION

In some contexts a requirement of fraud seems inevitably to imply an element of misrepresentation. Forgery, for example, required an intent to defraud until the offence was recast by the Forgery and Counterfeiting Act 1981; but, with the exception of the special case where it is a machine that is "deceived",[25] it is hard to imagine how one might use a forged document to defraud another without deceiving anyone. In *Buono*[26] a conviction of forging valuable securities was upheld where the persons with whom the defendant dealt were not deceived because they knew that the documents were forgeries; but the documents would hardly have been forged in the first place if *everybody* likely to see them had been expected to know what was going on. It was presumably intended that the documents would be passed on to other people who *would* be deceived. **7–011**

But misrepresentation is not an essential element of the concept of defrauding. One of the Oxford English Dictionary's definitions is "an artifice by which the right or interest of another is injured, a dishonest trick or stratagem"; and Stephen's definition expressly allowed for "mere secrecy" as an alternative to "deceit" or an "intention to deceive". In *Scott v Metropolitan Police Commissioner* the defendant bribed cinema staff to let him make illicit copies of films. He appealed against a conviction of conspiracy to defraud the owners of the copyright and distribution rights. Clearly he did not intend to deceive those persons, and it was argued that he therefore did not intend to defraud them. The argument was rejected. Viscount Dilhorne, with whose speech the other members of the House agreed, pointed out that until its repeal by the Theft Act 1968 the offence of larceny had expressly required the taking to be fraudulent; yet deception was obviously not an element of that offence. Nor was it an essential element of conspiracy to defraud. In his Lordship's view, **7–012**

> "'to defraud' ordinarily means . . . to deprive a person dishonestly of something which is his or of something to which he is or would or might but for the perpetration of the fraud be entitled."[27]

[24] [1995] 1 W.L.R. 52 at 64.
[25] Above, paras 4–071 *et seq*.
[26] [1970] Crim. L.R. 154.
[27] [1975] A.C. 819 at 839.

Lord Diplock added:

> "Where the intended victim of a 'conspiracy to defraud' is a private individual the purpose of the conspirators must be to cause the victim economic loss by depriving him of some property or right, corporeal or incorporeal, to which he is or would or might become entitled. The intended means by which the purpose is to be achieved must be dishonest. They need not involve fraudulent misrepresentation such as is needed to constitute the civil tort of deceit. Dishonesty of any kind is enough."[28]

These definitions are extremely wide. It is the objective of most economic activity to obtain financial benefits which might otherwise have gone elsewhere. In the absence of misrepresentation, all that distinguishes fraud from legitimate competition is the element of dishonesty.

7–013 In *Tarling (No.1) v Government of the Republic of Singapore* the House of Lords showed some unease at the prospect of non-deceptive conduct being categorised as fraud on the basis of an ill-defined notion of dishonesty. A company chairman was alleged to have made secret profits at his company's expense, and one of the charges alleged a conspiracy to defraud by the "dishonest concealment" of what had been done. The majority thought that the breach of a fiduciary duty to disclose did not amount to fraud.

> "Breach of fiduciary duty, exorbitant profit making, secrecy . . . are one thing: theft and fraud are others . . . The highest . . . that the evidence can be put is that the participants made a secret profit . . . and that they kept it secret: it would not otherwise be a secret profit. This by itself is no criminal offence, whatever other epithet may be appropriate."[29]

This is not strictly inconsistent with the wide concept of fraud espoused in *Scott*, since that requires not just economic prejudice but also dishonesty. The majority in *Tarling* thought that, while there might have been dishonesty "in a broad and general sense",[30] there was no dishonesty in the sense required for fraud at common law. But the requirement of dishonesty is a matter for the jury, and a jury cannot be expected to apply it in anything *but* a broad and general sense. The way is therefore clear for non-disclosure to be treated as fraud at common law if a jury see fit.

7–014 In *Adams*[31] the Privy Council distinguished the passage from *Tarling* quoted above, on the basis that in *Tarling* there was no *concealment.* Emphasis was placed on a remark by Lord Keith:

> "The evidence, while clearly showing that Mr Tarling and those of his codirectors who were party to the dealings missed a number of suitable opportunities for disclosing these dealings, does not indicate that positive steps were taken to conceal them."[32]

[28] [1975] A.C. 819 at 841.
[29] (1978) 70 Cr.App.R. 77 at 110–111, *per* Lord Wilberforce. Lords Salmon and Keith agreed, at 130 and 137 respectively.
[30] (1978) 70 Cr.App.R. 77 at 138, *per* Lord Keith.
[31] [1995] 1 W.L.R. 52; above, para.7–010.
[32] (1978) 70 Cr.App.R. 77 at 137–138.

In *Adams* the defendant had taken positive and indeed elaborate steps to conceal what was happening, and the Privy Council thought that the Court of Appeal of New Zealand had therefore been wrong to quash a conviction of conspiracy to defraud by dishonestly making a secret profit. But it is not clear from *Adams* whether the crucial distinction is between positive concealment and mere non-disclosure, or between conduct which is dishonest and conduct which is not. Mere non-disclosure is arguably sufficient *if dishonest*, but concealment is more likely to be dishonest.

The authority of *Tarling* is further weakened by the enactment of FA 2006. That Act does not directly affect conspiracy to defraud at common law; but, now that Parliament has included dishonest breach of fiduciary duty or of a duty of disclosure within a statutory offence called "fraud", it may be harder to argue that such conduct is not fraud at common law. **7–015**

We have seen that a person who deceives another into taking a financial risk is regarded as intending to defraud him.[33] A similar rule applies where the victim's interests are jeopardised not by misrepresentation but by the defendant's unilateral act. In *Sinclair*[34] a company director was party to an agreement under which the company lent most of its funds to a third party so that he could acquire a majority shareholding in the company. All it received in exchange was his unsecured promise to transfer to it assets of equivalent value. This was held to be a conspiracy to defraud even if the parties to the agreement honestly believed that the third party would fulfil his promise, as long as they knew it was a risk which they had no right to take. **7–016**

The difficulty is to distinguish between those risks that are legitimate and those that are not. It is, after all, a director's job to take risks with the company's assets in search of profit. Since the element of misrepresentation is not essential, what is the hallmark of *fraudulent* risk-taking? Perhaps the solution is to be found in the concept of the fiduciary duty owed by a director to his company. In *Sinclair* the court accepted the Crown's argument that **7–017**

> "there was a duty upon a director of a company owed to the company and its shareholders—and a corresponding right vested in the company and shareholders—the duty being to use the assets of the company in what is honestly believed to be the best interests of the company: if the assets are used in the honest belief that the best interests of the company are being served by that use there is no fraud and it is irrelevant that such use incidentally brings a personal benefit to the director. If on the other hand a risk is taken in using the assets which no director could honestly believe to be taken in the interests of the company and which is to the prejudice of the rights of others, that is taking a risk which there is no right to take and is fraudulent."[35]

[33] Above, para.7–008.
[34] [1968] 1 W.L.R. 1246.
[35] [1968] 1 W.L.R. 1246 at 1249.

7–018 In *McHugh (Eileen)*[36] it was said to be immaterial whether the company has a civil remedy against the actor, or against those who derived benefit from the transaction. Since the company *will* have a civil remedy against a director who is in breach of his fiduciary duty, it would follow that it is possible for a director to defraud his company without committing a breach of fiduciary duty. That would be surprising, but would accord with the position under FA 2006: it appears to be envisaged that a person might commit the offence of fraud by abuse of position without being liable for breach of fiduciary duty. But it is questionable whether the requirements of that form of fraud could in practice be satisfied in the absence of such a breach.[37]

MISREPRESENTATION WITHOUT LOSS

7–019 *Scott*[38] shows that, although fraud often involves the use of misrepresentation so as to inflict financial loss, the element of misrepresentation is not essential: any dishonest means of inflicting financial loss will suffice. Conversely, it is established by another line of authority that the element of financial loss is not essential either, and that a person can be defrauded by being deceived into acting (or refraining from acting) in a particular way. This is certainly the case where he is under a public duty and is deceived into failing to carry it out (or to carry out what would have been his duty had he not been deceived).

7–020 In *Toshack*[39] the defendant forged a testimonial to get a master's certificate from Trinity House. His conviction of forgery (which at that time required an intent to defraud) was upheld. Similarly it is fraud to use false documents in order to gain admission to one of the Inns of Court,[40] to impersonate someone else in a driving test,[41] to conceal from one's employer (at least where the employer is a public body) misconduct which might give rise to disciplinary proceedings,[42] or to display in a car the tax disc issued in respect of a different car.[43] The principle was confirmed in *Welham v DPP*,[44] where forged documents had been used for the purpose of evading statutory credit restrictions. The House of Lords held that the necessary intent to defraud was established because the defendant had intended to deceive those responsible for enforcing the legislation into not doing so.

7–021 The *Welham* principle, that a public officer is "defrauded" if he is deceived into failing to do his duty, applies not only to forgery[45] but also to

36 (1989) 88 Cr.App.R. 385.
37 See above, paras 6–067 *et seq*.
38 [1975] A.C. 819; above, para.7–012.
39 (1849) 4 Cox C.C. 38.
40 *Bassey* (1931) 22 Cr.App.R. 160.
41 *Potter* [1958] 1 W.L.R. 638.
42 *Garland* [1960] Crim. L.R. 129.
43 *Terry* [1984] A.C. 374.
44 [1961] A.C. 103.
45 See now Forgery and Counterfeiting Act 1981, s.10(1)(c); below, para.11–038.

offences of doing an act "fraudulently",[46] fraudulent trading[47] and, it seems, conspiracy to defraud. In *DPP v Withers* the defendants obtained confidential information by deceiving both civil servants and the employees of private concerns. They were charged with conspiracy to effect a public mischief. The House of Lords held that there was no such offence, but it was agreed that in the case of the public officials a charge of conspiracy to defraud might have succeeded.[48] This was applied in *Moses*,[49] where officials of the Department of Social Security were held to have been defrauded by being deceived into issuing national insurance numbers to persons who were not entitled to them.

In *Scott*, where there was an element of financial loss and it was the necessity for a misrepresentation that was in issue, Viscount Dilhorne was careful not to rule out the converse possibility. 7–022

> "In *Welham* . . . Lord Radcliffe referred to a special line of cases where the person deceived is a person holding public office or a public authority and where the person deceived was not caused any pecuniary or economic loss. Forgery whereby the deceit has been accomplished had, he pointed out, been in a number of cases treated as having been done with intent to defraud despite the absence of pecuniary or economic loss. In this case it is not necessary to decide that a conspiracy to defraud may exist even though its object was not to secure a financial advantage by inflicting an economic loss on the person at whom the conspiracy was directed. But for myself I see no reason why what was said by Lord Radcliffe in relation to forgery should not equally apply in relation to conspiracy to defraud."[50]

The other members of the House agreed. Lord Diplock added his own formulation:

> "Where the intended victim of a 'conspiracy to defraud' is a private individual the purpose of the conspirators must be to cause the victim economic loss . . . Where the intended victim . . . is a person performing public duties as distinct from a private individual it is sufficient if the purpose is to cause him to act contrary to his public duty, and the intended means of achieving this purpose are dishonest. The purpose need not involve causing economic loss to anyone."[51]

It now appears that this distinction between private individuals and public officers is too rigid. *Welham* decides that it is fraud to deceive a public officer into failing to do his duty. It does not decide that this is the *only* form of fraud for which financial loss is not essential, and there are passages suggesting that the rule about public officers is only an example of 7–023

46 *Terry* [1984] A.C. 374.
47 *Grantham* [1984] 1 Q.B. 675 at 683.
48 [1975] A.C. 842 at 860, *per* Viscount Dilhorne, with whom Lord Reid concurred; at 862, *per* Lord Diplock; at 873, *per* Lord Simon; at 875, *per* Lord Kilbrandon.
49 [1991] Crim. L.R. 617.
50 [1975] A.C. 819 at 839.
51 [1975] A.C. 819 at 841.

a wider principle extending to private individuals too. Lord Radcliffe suggested that "defrauding" included "any deceiving of another to his injury, his detriment or his prejudice",[52] and, although he referred to some of the authorities on the deception of public officials,[53] he appears to have regarded them as an example of this wide usage and not as the sole justification for it. Lord Denning was more explicit.

> "These scholars seem to think they have found the solution. 'To defraud', they say, involves the idea of economic loss. I cannot agree with them on this. If a drug addict forges a doctor's prescription so as to enable him to get drugs from a chemist, he has, I should have thought, an intent to defraud, even though he intends to pay the chemist the full price and no one is a penny the worse off. . . .
>
> Put shortly, 'with intent to defraud' means 'with intent to practise a fraud' on someone or other. It need not be anyone in particular. Someone in general will suffice. If anyone may be prejudiced in any way by the fraud, that is enough."[54]

7–024 These wider formulations were endorsed by the Privy Council in *Wai Yu-Tsang*, and Lord Diplock's distinction between private individuals and public officers was rejected.

> "With the greatest respect to Lord Diplock, their Lordships consider this categorisation to be too narrow. In their opinion, in agreement with the approach of Lord Radcliffe in *Welham,* the cases concerned with persons performing public duties are not to be regarded as a special category in the manner described by Lord Diplock, but rather as exemplifying the general principle that conspiracies to defraud are not restricted to cases of intention to cause the victim economic loss."[55]

While it may be true that economic loss is not required, this can hardly be described as a "general principle" because it does not tell us what *is* required. If the *Welham* principle is not confined to public officers, how much further does it go? Lord Radcliffe conceded that "to defraud must involve something more than the mere inducing of a course of action by deceit",[56] and insisted that there be some "prejudice" to the victim; but if "prejudice" is not confined to economic loss on the one hand, and does not include *every* act induced by deception on the other, where is the line to be drawn? To some extent the point is academic: if a private individual is deceived into doing something that he would not otherwise have done (or not doing something that he would otherwise have done), there will nearly always be at least a risk that his response will turn out to be less advantageous for him than what he would otherwise have done. And being subject to a risk of economic loss is itself a kind of economic loss.[57]

[52] [1961] A.C. 103 at 128.
[53] [1961] A.C. 103 at 124–125.
[54] [1961] A.C. 103 at 131, 133.
[55] [1992] 1 A.C. 269 at 277.
[56] [1961] A.C. 103 at 127.
[57] Above, para.7–008.

EVASION OF PROHIBITIONS

7–025 We have seen that, although fraud typically involves both misrepresentation and financial loss, it may consist of loss without misrepresentation or of misrepresentation without loss. Is it essential to establish one or the other? Or can a scheme be fraudulent even if no-one is deceived *and* no-one suffers loss? The element of financial loss is central to the *Scott* principle, and the *Welham* principle would seem to require a misrepresentation. In *Withers* confidential information had been obtained from the Criminal Records Office by corruption rather than deception. Lord Kilbrandon thought that there was therefore no fraud "in the *Welham* sense".[58] But this interpretation of *Welham* may be too narrow. The essence of the fraud in that case lay in the evasion of statutory credit restrictions, and that objective was held to be fraudulent although no-one suffered loss. It might be argued that the deception was purely incidental, and that to regard it as crucial would be to "confuse the object of a conspiracy with the means by which it is intended to be carried out".[59] On this view the deliberate evasion of statutory restrictions is in itself fraudulent, whether effected by deception of the officials responsible or by any other means.

7–026 This reasoning is supported by *Attorney-General's Reference (No.1 of 1981)*,[60] where it was held that a person who smuggles prohibited goods into the country without encountering a customs officer, and therefore without deceiving one, may be guilty of fraudulently evading a Customs and Excise prohibition.[61] The court relied on *Scott* rather than *Welham*. But the case involved the evasion of a prohibition, not of duty: the object was not to deprive the Customs of revenue but to make a profit on the black market. Perhaps, then, the case is closer to *Welham* than to *Scott*. In any event, it suggests that it is the nature of the defendant's objective that is crucial to a finding of fraud, rather than the method by which he seeks to achieve it. Fraudulent objectives include not only the infliction of financial loss but also the evasion of statutory prohibitions.

LIMITS

7–027 In 1994 the Law Commission, recommending that conspiracy to defraud should remain an offence pending the Commission's proposed review of the whole law of dishonesty,[62] tried to identify kinds of conduct which amount to defrauding at common law but not (or arguably not) to any substantive offence, and which might therefore cease to be criminal if conspiracy to defraud were abolished.[63] Most of the Commission's examples

[58] [1975] A.C. 842 at 878.
[59] *Scott v Metropolitan Police Commissioner* [1975] A.C. 819 at 839, *per* Viscount Dilhorne.
[60] [1982] Q.B. 848.
[61] Customs and Excise Management Act 1979, s.170(2); below, para.16–015.
[62] Which never materialised, and was quietly abandoned.
[63] Law Com. No.228, *Criminal Law: Conspiracy to Defraud*, HC 11, para.4.48.

are now, or soon will be, substantive offences.[64] The remainder include the appropriation of property which cannot normally be the subject of a charge of theft, such as land; the obtaining of confidential information by industrial espionage; the appropriation of property belonging to another with no intention permanently to deprive; and the appropriation of property over which another has some sort of moral claim, but which does not belong to that other within the meaning of the Theft Act 1968 because there is no legal obligation to deal with it in a particular way.

7–028 The Commission was rightly criticised by Sir John Smith for applying Viscount Dilhorne's formulation in *Scott* as if it were a statute.[65] In the absence of any decision confirming that (for example) a dishonest failure to pay a debt is fraud at common law, it would be unwise to assume this merely because it is within the literal meaning of what Viscount Dilhorne said. Moreover, even if such conduct did amount to fraud at common law, it would be arguable that an agreement to defraud in such a way would no longer be indictable as a conspiracy to defraud because the common law has been implicitly curtailed by legislation. In *Zemmel*[66] it was held that an agreement dishonestly to induce creditors not to press for payment could not be a conspiracy to defraud in the absence of an intention to make permanent default, because Parliament had expressly excluded such conduct from the corresponding substantive offence in 1978.[67] The court declined to accept that "by a side wind the common law has suddenly reemerged to reinstate or create as a crime that which Parliament thought it right to take off the statute book as a crime".[68]

7–029 It might similarly be argued that it cannot have been Parliament's intention, when enacting FA 2006, that conduct falling outside the new fraud offence should still be indictable as conspiracy to defraud. But the possibility of abolishing conspiracy to defraud was discussed at length in the debates on the Fraud Bill, and was rejected. It would be difficult to argue that Parliament had done by implication what it chose not to do expressly.

[64] e.g. obtaining property by deception but with no intention permanently to deprive, deceiving a creditor into waiting for payment with no intent to make permanent default, and "deceiving" computers and other machines (all of which are now fraud by false representation: above, Ch.4); the making of a secret profit in breach of fiduciary duty, and breach of duty by an agent which cannot be proved to have been secured by corrupt inducements (which are now fraud by abuse of position: above, Ch.6); obtaining benefits other than property without deception (which is now obtaining services dishonestly: below, Ch.10); rigging a sporting event so as to win a bet (which from September 1, 2007 is cheating at gambling: below, Ch.18); providing assistance towards the commission of a fraud offence by a third party, when that offence is not proved to have been committed (which is to be the subject of new offences under the Serious Crime Bill).

[65] "Conspiracy to Defraud: Some Comments on the Law Commission's Report" [1995] Crim. L.R. 209.

[66] (1985) 81 Cr.App.R. 279.

[67] Theft Act 1978, s.2(1)(b); above, para.4–134. Now that dishonest false representations can be charged as fraud irrespective of the effect (if any) that they have, it may be arguable that there is no longer any reason to exclude such conduct from common law fraud. On this view, the Theft Act 1978 implicitly restricted the scope of conspiracy to defraud, but FA 2006 implicitly reversed that change.

[68] (1985) 81 Cr.App.R. 279 at 284.

Moreover it was held in *Norris v Government of the USA*[69] that the availability of conspiracy to defraud in a case of price-fixing was unaffected by the Restrictive Trade Practices Acts 1956 and 1976. The court thought it would also be unaffected by the introduction of the statutory offence under the Enterprise Act 2002, s.188,[70] which had not been in force at the material time.

AGREEMENT TO DEFRAUD

The offence consists in entering into an agreement to defraud another. The requirement of agreement seems to be the same as in the context of statutory conspiracy.[71] It is sometimes said that it must be the conspirators' *purpose* to defraud.[72] Strictly speaking this is to confuse intention, which is implicit in the requirement of agreement, with purpose, which is not.[73] **7–030**

> "Generally the primary objective of fraudsmen is to advantage themselves. The detriment that results to their victims is secondary to that purpose and incidental. It is 'intended' only in the sense that it is a contemplated outcome of the fraud that is perpetrated."[74]

Wai Yu-Tsang[75] confirms that it is sufficient if the conspirators agree to do something that will cause prejudice to others, albeit only as a side-effect of their real purpose (namely profit for themselves). The chief accountant of a bank conspired with others to conceal in the bank's accounts the fact that cheques purchased by the bank had been dishonoured. The Privy Council dismissed his appeal against conviction of conspiracy to defraud the bank and its existing and potential shareholders, creditors and depositors. The defence was that he had acted in good faith with a view to ensuring that junior staff did not hear what had happened, which might have precipitated a run on the bank. If true, this went to dishonesty; but, subject to that, it did not negative the intent to defraud. **7–031**

> "[I]t is enough . . . that . . . the conspirators have dishonestly agreed to bring about a state of affairs which they realise will or may deceive the victim into so

[69] [2007] EWHC 71.
[70] See below, Ch.20.
[71] There is one possible exception: an agreement to aid an abet an offence by a third party can be a conspiracy to defraud but probably not a statutory conspiracy. See below, paras 21–022 *et seq.*
[72] e.g. *Scott v Metropolitan Police Commissioner* [1975] A.C. 819 at 841, *per* Lord Diplock.
[73] The Oxford English Dictionary defines "purpose" as "That which one sets before oneself as a thing to be done or attained; the object which one has in view". It does not appear to recognise a looser sense including consequences which, though inseparable from the object one has in view, are not desired for their own sake. But cf. fraudulent trading, which requires that a business be carried on for a "fraudulent purpose" (below, Ch.8). Obviously this includes the case where the objective is to make a profit rather than to cause loss.
[74] *Allsop* (1976) 64 Cr.App.R. 29 at 31.
[75] [1992] 1 A.C. 269.

acting, or failing to act, that he will suffer economic loss or his economic interests will be put at risk. It is however important in such a case, as the Court of Appeal stressed in *Allsop*, to distinguish a conspirator's intention (or immediate purpose) dishonestly to bring about such a state of affairs from his motive (or underlying purpose). The latter may be benign to the extent that he does not wish the victim or potential victim to suffer harm; but the mere fact that it is benign will not of itself prevent the agreement from constituting a conspiracy to defraud."[76]

THE FUTURE OF CONSPIRACY TO DEFRAUD

7–032 The Law Commission's work on fraud originally grew out of its attempts to codify the common law of conspiracy. Conspiracy to defraud was left in place when the rest of the common law of conspiracy was abolished by the Criminal Law Act 1977, because the Commission had not had time to work out what to replace it with. The ultimate objective of the Commission's subsequent work on fraud was to devise one or more statutory offences which, without being open to the same objections as conspiracy to defraud, would make that offence redundant and enable it to be abolished. When the Commission finally produced the draft Bill that became FA 2006, it considered that this objective had been accomplished. Moreover it argued that conspiracy to defraud might be incompatible with the European Convention on Human Rights, because its definition is insufficiently precise.[77] The draft Bill therefore provided for the abolition of conspiracy to defraud.

7–033 The Government did not accept that recommendation. It refused even to include in FA 2006 a provision abolishing conspiracy to defraud which would not be brought into force for some time, on the comically far-fetched ground that this would leave "a sword of Damocles dangling over . . . the common law offence", implying that Parliament had no faith in the offence and that prosecutors therefore ought not to charge it. The Government did undertake to review the matter in three years' time; but, since FA 2006 does not apply to anything done before January 15, 2007 and fraud cases often take years to come to trial, it seems unlikely that three years will be long enough for any conclusions to be drawn.

7–034 Undue resort to common law charges has been criticised by Lord Bingham.

> "Where Parliament has defined the ingredients of an offence, perhaps stipulating what shall and shall not be a defence, and has prescribed a mode of trial and a maximum penalty, it must ordinarily be proper that conduct falling within that definition should be prosecuted for the statutory offence and not for a common law offence which may or may not provide the same defences and for which the potential penalty is unlimited. . . . I would not go to the

[76] [1992] 1 A.C. 269 at 280.

[77] See above, paras 2–099 *et seq.*

> length of holding that conduct may never be lawfully prosecuted as a generally expressed common law crime where it falls within the terms of a specific statutory provision, but good practice and respect for the primacy of statute do in my judgment require that conduct falling within the terms of a specific statutory provision should be prosecuted under that provision unless there is good reason for doing otherwise."[78]

The latter part of this dictum is prominently quoted in guidance issued by the Attorney-General on the use of conspiracy to defraud after the coming into force of FA 2006. The guidance suggests that good reasons for preferring the common law charge might be either that the case can be *more effectively* charged as conspiracy to defraud (for example because statutory conspiracies would require too many counts, and possibly severed trials) or that it can *only* be charged as conspiracy to defraud (for example, the dishonest infringement of those intellectual property rights that are not protected by specific statutory offences). **7–035**

[78] *Rimmington* [2005] UKHL 63; [2006] 2 All E.R. 257 at [30]. But cf. Lord Rodger at [52]: "[W]here Parliament has not abolished the relevant area of the common law when it enacts a statutory offence, it cannot be said that the Crown can never properly frame a common law charge to cover conduct which is covered by the statutory offence. Where nothing would have prevented the Crown from charging the defendant under the statute and where the sentence imposed would also have been competent in proceedings under the statute, the defendant is not prejudiced by being prosecuted at common law and can have no legitimate complaint."

CHAPTER 8

FRAUDULENT TRADING

In this chapter we examine two[1] parallel offences which, in combination, virtually amount to a general offence of being involved in any form of fraudulent trading. One is committed where the body that trades fraudulently is a British company, or one of certain other kinds of corporation. The other, broadly speaking,[2] is committed where there is fraudulent trading but the first offence does not apply. **8–001**

LEGISLATIVE HISTORY

The mischief with which these provisions are intended to deal was first recognised in the Greene Report, which recommended legislation to deal with directors who abused the privilege of limited liability. The problem that chiefly concerned the Greene Committee was quite narrow. **8–002**

> "Our attention has been directed particularly to the case (met with principally in private companies) where the person in control of the company holds a floating charge and, while knowing that the company is on the verge of liquidation, 'fills up' his security by means of goods obtained on credit and then appoints a receiver."[3]

[1] Technically three: see below, para.8–013.

[2] But there is no offence at all if a company which trades fraudulently is exempted from the offence under the Companies Acts: below, para.8–015.

[3] *Company Law Amendment Committee Report*, Cmd.2657 (1925–26) para.61.

But the remedy recommended was very wide, namely the imposition of both civil and criminal liability on directors who had knowingly been party to the fraudulent carrying on of business by their companies. The recommendation was implemented as the Companies Act 1928, s.75, which was consolidated as the Companies Act 1929, s.275.

8–003 In its original form the provision applied only to directors of the company, past or present. The Cohen Committee recommended its extension to *anyone* who is knowingly a party to the fraudulent carrying on of a company's business.[4] Section 275 of the Act of 1929 was duly amended by s.101 of the Act of 1947, before being consolidated as the Companies Act 1948, s.332.

8–004 In *DPP v Schildkamp*[5] the House of Lords held it to be implicit in the statutory context of s.332 of the 1948 Act that the offence could only be charged if the company had been or was being wound up. This decision was reversed by the Companies Act 1981, s.96, which enabled the offence to be charged "whether or not the company has been or is in the course of being wound up".

8–005 In the Companies Act 1985 ("CA 1985"), the criminal and civil aspects of the section were split between ss.458 and 630 respectively. The provision reversing *Schildkamp* was retained. CA 1985, s.630 was then replaced with the Insolvency Act 1986, s.213. This is drafted in essentially the same terms as CA 1985, s.458, and authorities on it are likely to be relevant to the construction of s.458; but it cannot be assumed that the two provisions will always be construed in the same way.[6]

8–006 The offence under CA 1985, s.458 was formerly punishable with seven years' imprisonment,[7] but the maximum was increased to 10 years by the Fraud Act 2006 ("FA 2006").[8] This change came into force on January 15, 2007, and applies only to offences committed on or after that date.[9]

8–007 CA 1985, s.458 has been re-enacted as s.993 of the Companies Act 2006 ("CA 2006"). CA 2006, s.993(1) provides:

[4] *Report of the Committee on Company Law Amendment*, Cmd.6659 (1944–45).

[5] [1971] A.C. 1.

[6] "[T]he severing of criminal and civil liability for fraudulent trading means that there is no question of any conclusion, in principle or on particular facts, as to civil liability affecting the basis on which criminal liability is assessed": *Re Bank of Credit and Commerce International SA (No.15)* [2005] EWCA Civ 693; [2005] 2 B.C.L.C. 328 at [129].

[7] Until 1980 it carried only two years.

[8] FA 2006, s.10(1).

[9] Where the maximum penalty for an offence is increased, the increase does not apply to offences committed before the change in the law unless there is a clear legislative intention to that effect: *R. v Penwith JJ., ex p. Hay* (1979) 1 Cr.App.R.(S.) 265. It has been suggested that the increase might apply to an offence committed after the Act making the change was *passed* (which in the case of FA 2006 was November 8, 2006), on the ground that in this case the potential offender has notice that he is at risk of a greater penalty: D.A. Thomas, [1982] Crim. L.R. 191. But this would be contrary to Art.7 of the European Convention on Human Rights, which prohibits the imposition of a heavier penalty than the one that was applicable at the time of the offence. Clearly the 10-year maximum was not "applicable" until FA 2006, s.10 came into force on January 15, 2007.

> "If any business of a company is carried on with intent to defraud creditors of the company or creditors of any other person, or for any fraudulent purpose, every person who is knowingly a party to the carrying on of the business in that manner commits an offence."

The offence is triable either way, and is punishable on conviction on indictment with 10 years' imprisonment.[10] CA 2006, s.993 is not in force at the time of writing, but is expected to be in force by October 2007. Except where it is necessary to distinguish between CA 2006, s.993 and CA 1985, s.458, this chapter is written as if CA 2006, s.993 were already in force. But offences committed before it is brought into force will need to be charged under CA 1985, s.458 even if the charge is brought after that date.

In 1982 the Cork Committee recommended the creation of a parallel offence of fraudulent trading by persons to whom the Companies Acts do not apply.[11] In 1987 the Law Commission invited views on whether the offence should, in principle, be limited to companies. It acknowledged that the restriction might be justifiable on the basis that those who carry on the business of a company are protected against personal liability (which was the original justification for creating the offence at all), but pointed out that trading under a false appearance of solvency affects creditors equally regardless of the form of business organisation involved.[12] In 2002 the Commission returned to the issue, gave short shrift to the former argument, pronounced it "anomalous and illogical" that the offence should be confined to British companies, and made the somewhat eccentric recommendation that CA 1985, s.458 should itself be extended to non-corporate traders.[13] **8–008**

Instead, FA 2006, s.9 creates a *parallel* offence. Section 9(1) provides: **8–009**

> "A person is guilty of an offence if he is knowingly a party to the carrying on of a business to which this section applies."

Broadly speaking, s.9 applies where

- a business is carried on "with intent to defraud creditors of any person, or for any other fraudulent purpose", but
- the offence under CA 2006, s.993 is *not* committed because the trader is outside the categories caught by that offence.

[10] CA 2006, s.993(3).
[11] *Insolvency Law and Practice: Report of the Review Committee*, Cmnd.8558 (1982) para.1890.
[12] Law Commission Working Paper No.104, *Criminal Law: Conspiracy to Defraud*, para.10.21.
[13] Law Com. No.277, *The Effective Prosecution of Multiple Offending*, Cm.5609, para.8.15. The fact that the recommendation appeared in a report on the problems of prosecuting multiple offences rather than the slightly earlier report on fraud (Law Com. No.276), coupled with the absence of any examination of the relationship between fraudulent trading (as extended) and the new fraud offence, suggests that the recommendation was driven more by procedural considerations than by any lacuna in the substantive law which the Commission thought might survive the introduction of the new fraud offence.

The offence is triable either way, and is punishable on conviction on indictment with 10 years' imprisonment.[14]

SCOPE OF THE OFFENCES

COMPANIES ACT 1985, SECTION 458 AND COMPANIES ACT 2006, SECTION 993

8–010 Both CA 1985, s.458 and CA 2006, s.993 apply where a *company* carries on business fraudulently. For the purposes of CA 1985 "company" normally means a company registered in Great Britain, whereas under CA 2006 it also includes a company registered in Northern Ireland.[15] A company registered outside the United Kingdom is probably not a "company" under either Act.[16]

8–011 CA 1985, s.458 also applies to certain bodies corporate which are incorporated in and have a principal place of business in Great Britain, but are not companies within the meaning of CA 1985.[17] CA 2006, s.993 may similarly be applied by regulations to certain bodies corporate which are incorporated in and have a principal place of business in the United Kingdom, but are not companies within the meaning of CA 2006.[18]

8–012 CA 1985, s.458 also applies to limited liability partnerships[19] and European Economic Interest Groupings,[20] which are bodies corporate but not companies. When CA 2006, s.993 is brought into force, the relevant regulations will presumably be amended so that CA 2006, s.993 similarly applies to such bodies.

8–013 Open-ended investment companies (a form of collective investment scheme with corporate personality)[21] are not companies within the meaning of CA 1985 or CA 2006. Moreover CA 1985, s.458 does not apply to them by virtue of CA 1985, s.718,[22] and CA 2006, s.993 cannot be extended to them under CA 2006, s.1043.[23] However, the Open-ended Investment Companies Regulations 2001,[24] reg.64 creates a separate offence which is committed if "any business of an open-ended investment company is carried on with intent to defraud creditors of the company or creditors of any other person, or for any fraudulent purpose". This offence is punishable on conviction on indictment with two years' imprisonment. With the

[14] FA 2006, s.9(6).
[15] See below, para.14–003.
[16] See below, para.14–004.
[17] CA 1985, s.718, Sch.22.
[18] CA 2006, s.1043. It remains to be seen whether CA 2006, s.993 will be so extended, since a body corporate not caught by s.993 will be caught by FA 2006, s.9 anyway.
[19] Limited Liability Partnership Regulations 2001 (SI 2001/1090) reg.4(1), Sch.2.
[20] European Economic Interest Groupings Regulations 1989 (SI 1989/638).
[21] Financial Services and Markets Act 2000, s.236.
[22] CA 1985, s.718(2)(d).
[23] CA 2006, s.1043(1)(d).
[24] SI 2001/1228.

exception of the business organisations to which the offence applies and the maximum punishment, everything said in this chapter about the offence under CA 2006, s.993 applies equally to this offence.

FRAUD ACT 2006, SECTION 9

8–014 At the time of writing, FA 2006, s.9 applies to a business which is carried on with intent to defraud creditors of any person, or for any other fraudulent purpose, by a person who is "outside the reach" of CA 1985, s.458 or the corresponding provision under the law of Northern Ireland.[25] The following are "within the reach" of CA 1985, s.458:

(a) a company within the meaning of CA 1985;

(b) a person to whom CA 1985, s.458 applies (with or without adaptations or modifications) as if the person were a company; and

(c) a person exempted from the application of CA 1985, s.458.[26]

Similar rules determine who is within the reach of the corresponding Northern Ireland provision.[27]

8–015 The effect is that FA 2006, s.9 currently applies to a fraudulent business carried on by a person to whom neither CA 1985, s.458 nor the corresponding Northern Ireland provision applies, *unless* the reason why neither of those provisions applies to that person is that the person has been exempted from one of them.[28] An exempted person is caught *neither* by CA 1985, s.458 (or the corresponding Northern Ireland provision) *nor* by FA 2006, s.9.

8–016 CA 2006 does not amend FA 2006, s.9 so that, when CA 2006, s.993 is brought into force, FA 2006 will refer to CA 2006, s.993 instead of CA 1985, s.458 and the corresponding Northern Ireland provision. There is power to make such an amendment by order under CA 2006, s.1294. Even if no such amendment is made, the references to CA 1985, s.458 and the corresponding Northern Ireland provision would seem capable of applying in relation to CA 2006, s.993 by virtue of the Interpretation Act 1978, s.17(2)(a). The effect will be that FA 2006, s.9 will apply to a fraudulent business carried on by a person to whom CA 2006, s.993 does not apply, unless s.993 does not apply because, although the person is an unregistered company to which s.993 would otherwise apply by virtue of regulations under CA 2006, s.1043, the person has been exempted from s.1043 by direction pursuant to s.1043(1)(c).

[25] FA 2006, s.9(2). The corresponding Northern Ireland provision is the Companies (Northern Ireland) Order 1986 (SI 1986/1032) (N.I. 6) Art.451.

[26] FA 2006, s.9(3).

[27] FA 2006, s.9(4).

[28] sc. under CA 1985, s.718(2)(c) or the corresponding Northern Ireland provision.

ELEMENTS OF THE OFFENCES

8–017 In the remainder of this chapter we examine those elements of the fraudulent trading offences that do not relate to the kind of business organisation involved. Except where otherwise stated, the discussion is equally applicable to each of the offences.

CARRYING ON BUSINESS

8–018 In proceedings for any offence of fraudulent trading it must be shown that a business has been carried on with intent to defraud creditors or for a fraudulent purpose. This could be construed as meaning that the *entirety* of the business in question must be carried on fraudulently, or as meaning that it is sufficient if *some part* of the business is carried on fraudulently. The former view initially prevailed. In *Re Murray-Watson Ltd*,[29] Oliver J. held that s.993's predecessor was aimed at the carrying on of a business and not at the execution of individual transactions in the course of carrying on that business. This would have narrowed the scope of the section significantly. A person who participated in one fraudulent transaction would not be guilty of the offence if the rest of the company's business was carried on legitimately.

8–019 In *Re Gerald Cooper Chemicals Ltd*, however, Templeman J. held that it did not matter that only one creditor was defrauded, and by one transaction, provided that the transaction could properly be described as a fraud on a creditor perpetrated in the course of carrying on business.[30] Oliver J. subsequently abandoned his interpretation,[31] and the Court of Appeal rejected an argument that a single transaction could be sufficient only in special circumstances.[32] In *Morphitis v Bernasconi*[33] the point was resolved in favour of Templeman J.'s view. Chadwick L.J., with whom the other members of the court agreed, accepted that a business *may* be found to have been carried on fraudulently notwithstanding that there was only one fraudulent transaction; but, he added, this did not mean that, whenever a fraud is perpetrated in the course of carrying on business, the business is being carried on with intent to defraud.[34] The distinction is a fine one. Suppose a creditor is defrauded in a transaction involving agricultural produce, by a company which usually trades only in aluminium. Does the fraud fall outside the fraudulent trading provisions because the company's aluminium-trading business is not fraudulent?

[29] April 6, 1977; see *In Re Gerald Cooper Chemicals Ltd* [1978] 1 Ch. 262 at 267.
[30] [1978] 1 Ch. 262 at 268.
[31] *Re Sarflax Ltd* [1979] Ch. 592 at 598.
[32] *Lockwood* [1986] Crim. L.R. 244.
[33] [2003] EWCA Civ 289; [2003] Ch. 552.
[34] [2003] EWCA Civ 289; [2003] Ch. 552 at [46].

In practice, proceedings for fraudulent trading tend to involve a substantial number of transactions. This is because, where many transactions are involved, it has in the past been common to charge fraudulent trading in preference to the now-abolished deception offences under the Theft Act 1968, thus avoiding the need for a separate count for each transaction. This has been approved by the Court of Appeal as "clearly a much less cumbersome procedure and much easier for the jury".[35] Fraudulent trading arguably has a similar advantage over fraud by false representation, which is committed every time a dishonest false representation is made; but a series of false representations may constitute a "course of conduct" within the meaning of r.14.2(2) of the Criminal Procedure Rules 2005, in which case they can be charged in a single count.[36] **8–020**

A "business" includes activities necessary or incidental to the carrying on of the business. In *Philippou*[37] the company was a tour operator. It was an integral part of the company's business to provide air travel for its customers, and it could not do so without a licence. It was held to be part of the company's business to apply for the licence. Fraud in the application for the licence could therefore be fraudulent trading. **8–021**

"Business" has also been held to include the collection and distribution of a company's assets after it has ceased trading. In *Re Sarflax Ltd*,[38] Oliver J. rejected an argument that the collection and distribution of assets was the very negation of carrying on business, and held that carrying on business was not synonymous with actively carrying on trade. He concluded that the collection of assets acquired in the course of business, and the distribution of the proceeds in payment of debts, could constitute the carrying on business within the meaning of the section. He contrasted the "passive suffering of undischarged liabilities" (which, in his view, could not be classified as the carrying on of any business of the company) with "a continuous course of active conduct in the collection and distribution of business assets" (which could).[39] **8–022**

Whether a particular activity does amount to the carrying on of a business is a question of fact. In *Burgess*[40] it was alleged that the defendants had fraudulently disposed of vehicles leased to their haulage company. The jury were directed that the company's business was haulage and included the obtaining and disposal of vehicles. On appeal it was conceded that the point should have been left to the jury. If the jury had found only one disposal proved, it would have been open to them to conclude that that disposal was not in the course of the company's business. **8–023**

[35] *Kemp* [1988] 1 Q.B. 645 at 653.
[36] See below, paras 25–003 *et seq.*
[37] (1989) 5 B.C.C. 665.
[38] [1979] Ch. 592.
[39] [1979] Ch. 592 at 599.
[40] July 28, 1994.

THE FRAUDULENT CHARACTER OF THE BUSINESS

8–024 An offence of fraudulent trading is committed if the business in question is carried on either "with intent to defraud creditors" or "for any [other][41] fraudulent purpose". It has therefore been said that the section creates two different kinds of offence: fraudulent trading with intent to defraud creditors, and fraudulent trading with the purpose of achieving certain objectives.[42] The second limb is clearly wider than the first; but it is worth examining the scope of the first, because it may affect the construction of the second.

INTENT TO DEFRAUD CREDITORS

8–025 We have already examined what it means to "defraud" someone.[43] It has been said that the authorities on the scope of that concept are equally applicable to the words "intent to defraud" in the fraudulent trading provisions.[44] It would seem to follow that a trader intends to defraud a creditor where he intends[45] to do something which, if he agreed with another to do it, would render them guilty of conspiracy to defraud. But, in view of the legislative context, this may be an over-simplification. Although it is not easy to describe comprehensively all the different types of activity that will constitute the carrying on of business with intent to defraud creditors, three categories emerge from the authorities:

- putting the trader's existing creditors at risk of not being paid;
- causing people who are not his existing creditors to become his creditors at a time when he is, or is likely to become, insolvent; and
- doing things which give rise to causes of action sounding in damages against him in favour of people who are not his existing creditors.

[41] The word "other" appears only in FA 2006.

[42] *Inman* [1967] 1 Q.B. 140 at 148.

[43] Above, paras 7–005 *et seq.*

[44] *Grantham* [1984] 1 Q.B. 675 at 683; *Terry* [1984] A.C. 374 at 380–381, *per* Lord Fraser of Tullybelton.

[45] In *Re Gerald Cooper Chemicals Ltd* [1978] 1 Ch. 262 at 267, Templeman J. said in this context that a person that a man must be taken to intend the natural or foreseen consequences of his act; but, as a proposition of criminal law, that would be inconsistent with the Criminal Justice Act 1967, s.8. For the purposes of the criminal offences the test is plainly subjective. In *Re Leyland DAF Ltd* [1995] 2 A.C. 394 at 408, Lightman J. said (citing *Lockwood* [1986] Crim. L.R. 244) that it is necessary to show either an intent to defraud or a reckless indifference whether or not creditors were defrauded; but it is clear that nothing less than intent will suffice. The dictum is explicable on the basis that a dishonest intention to expose a person to a risk of loss *is* an intent to defraud him: above, para.7–008.

Putting existing creditors at risk of not being paid

A trader intends to defraud creditors if he does things which he knows will result in his existing creditors not being paid.[46] A director is guilty of fraudulent trading if he deliberately trades in such a way as to dissipate the company's assets for inadequate consideration, so that the company's creditors cannot be paid. Moreover, since one can defraud a person by exposing him to a risk of loss,[47] a trader can intend to defraud creditors if he dishonestly carries on business in a way which entails a *risk* that his existing creditors will not be paid. Whether this is dishonest will depend largely on the magnitude of the risk. **8–026**

Although the bare fact of preferring one creditor to another may prejudice the economic interests of the other, it is established that such a preference is not an intent to defraud creditors. Subject to the insolvency legislation, a debtor may pay his creditors in any order he likes.[48] In *Re Sarflax Ltd*[49] a company was faced with a claim for damages by an Italian company. It passed a resolution to cease trading and applied its assets to the payment of its other creditors, chief among them being its parent company. This left virtually nothing with which to meet the Italian company's claim. The liquidator sought a declaration that the company's business had been carried on with intent to defraud the Italian company. Oliver J. struck out the summons as disclosing no reasonable cause of action. He held that it made no difference that one of the creditors who were paid in full was the parent company, in which the directors of the insolvent company held the majority shareholding. They were under no duty to put the other creditors first, or even to treat them equally. **8–027**

It is clear from the authorities on conspiracy to defraud, which are said to be equally applicable to the words "intent to defraud creditors" in the fraudulent trading provisions, that a person can defraud another by deceiving him into doing something that he would not otherwise have done.[50] If this principle were applied mechanically to the fraudulent trading provisions, it would follow that a trader can intend to defraud creditors if his intention is to induce existing creditors to adopt economically neutral (or perhaps even beneficial) courses of action—for example, by misleading them into entering into a debt-for-equity swap or some form of derivatives contract, which would not necessarily be disadvantageous. This conclusion might not be appropriate in every case: the historical association of the fraudulent trading offence with the Insolvency Act 1986, s.213 and its precursors makes it clear that the possibility of economic loss has always been at the heart of the offence. But it is also clear that a person can be "defrauded" by being misled into taking a financial risk which he would not **8–028**

[46] *In Re Gerald Cooper Chemicals Ltd* [1978] 1 Ch. 262 at 267, *per* Templeman J.

[47] *Allsop* (1976) 64 Cr.App.R. 29, followed in the context of fraudulent trading in *Grantham* [1984] Q.B. 675; *Wai Yu-Tsang* [1992] 1 A.C. 269; above, para.7–008.

[48] *Glegg v Bromley* [1912] 3 K.B. 474 at 485, *per* Fletcher Moulton L.J.

[49] [1979] Ch. 592.

[50] Above, paras 7–019 *et seq.*

otherwise have taken; and it is difficult to see how, in practice, inducing a commercial creditor to do *x* rather than *y* might *not* involve risks which are inherent in *x* but not in *y*.

Causing persons to become creditors

8–029 The courts have tended to assume that a trader can defraud creditors by inducing people who are not already his creditors to become his creditors, at a time when he is or is likely to become insolvent—for example by purchasing goods on credit from suppliers who are unaware of the true state of his finances. In *Re William C. Leitch Brothers Ltd* Maugham J. said:

> "[I]f a company continues to carry on business and to incur debts at a time when there is to the knowledge of the directors no reasonable prospect of the creditors ever receiving payment of those debts, it is, in general, a proper inference that the company is carrying on business with intent to defraud."[51]

8–030 This dictum has often been applied. In *Re Gerald Cooper Chemicals Ltd*, companies were carrying on the business of selling indigo. Templeman J. said that

> "they carried on that business with intent to defraud creditors if they accepted deposits knowing that they could not supply the indigo and were insolvent. They were carrying on business with intent to defraud creditors as soon as they accepted one deposit knowing that they could not supply the indigo and would not repay the deposit."[52]

In *Grantham*[53] a director was held to have participated in the carrying on of business with the intent to defraud a creditor when he allowed a supplier to continue supplying potatoes although there was no hope of the supplier's being paid. In *Lockwood*[54] the defendant was similarly held to have intended to defraud creditors by ordering supplies for which he knew his company could not pay.

8–031 This tendency to equate fraudulent trading with insolvent trading has been extended so as to include creditors who have not even been deceived into becoming creditors.

> "The intent to defraud is to be judged by its effect on the person who is the object of the conduct in question . . . There appears to me to be two types, relevantly, of such object-persons. There are those who choose to make the company their debtor, as ordinary trade suppliers, and those in whose favour liability from the company arises by the choice of the company, not their own, e.g. the Inland Revenue as to PAYE and national insurance contributions and the Customs and Excise as to value added tax. As to trade creditors . . . [t]here is intent to defraud within the meaning of the section if the person responsible

[51] [1932] 2 Ch. 71 at 77.
[52] [1978] Ch. 262 at 267–268.
[53] [1984] 1 Q.B. 675.
[54] [1986] Crim. L.R. 244.

> was intending to deceive or actually deceiving a supplier that he would be paid at the stipulated time or shortly thereafter when the person so intending or deceiving knew perfectly well that there was no hope of that coming about.
>
> As to 'non-choice' creditors, there is no question of deceit. The intent to defraud in my view lies in continuing to incur the liability for tax or national insurance contributions or value added tax when there is no honest belief that those liabilities will be discharged when they become due or shortly thereafter."[55]

The assumption that insolvent trading can constitute trading "with intent to defraud creditors" is questionable. In cases of insolvent trading, the people at whom the fraudulent intent is aimed will not necessarily be existing creditors. In some cases they will not become creditors unless and until the intended fraud takes place. As a matter of ordinary English, this cannot be described as the defrauding *of creditors*. A possible counter-argument is that the defrauding of non-creditors prejudices existing creditors too, by increasing the trader's liabilities and worsening his insolvency. Looked at in this way, insolvent trading is relevant only because it is a fraud on *existing* creditors. **8–032**

Even if insolvent trading *can* be fraudulent, it is not *in fact* fraudulent unless it is dishonest. Maugham J.'s dictum,[56] which implies that fraudulent intent can be readily inferred from the fact of insolvent trading, has for this reason been described as "not a very helpful generalisation".[57] Whether insolvent trading is dishonest is a question of fact in each case. Everything depends on the degree of genuine optimism of those running the business. In *Re White and Osmond (Parkstone) Ltd*, Buckley J. said: **8–033**

> "In my judgment, there is nothing wrong in the fact that directors incur credit at a time when, to their knowledge, the company is not able to meet all its liabilities as they fall due. What is manifestly wrong is if directors allow a company to incur credit at a time when the business is being carried on in such circumstances that it is clear that the company will never be able to satisfy its creditors. However, there is nothing to say that directors who genuinely believe that the clouds will roll away and the sunshine of prosperity will shine upon them again and disperse the fog of their depression are not entitled to incur credit to help them to get over the bad time."[58]

Acting in such a way as to give rise to damages claims

The third type of activity to emerge from the authorities involves doing things which give rise to causes of action sounding in damages against the trader in favour of people who are not existing creditors—for example, the obtaining of customers' money by deception. There is some confusion over whether this can be described as trading "with intent to defraud creditors". **8–034**

[55] *Re a Company (No.001418 of 1988)* [1991] B.C.L.C. 197 at 199, *per* Judge Bromley Q.C.
[56] Above, para.8–029.
[57] *Aktieselskabet Dansk Skibsfinansiering v Brothers* [2001] 2 B.C.L.C. 324 at 332, *per* Lord Hoffmann.
[58] June 30, 1960.

8–035 The older authorities suggest that neither ordinary customers nor defrauded customers can be described as "creditors", and that a claimant in an action to recover unliquidated damages is not a "creditor" until recovery of judgment.[59] In *Re Gerald Cooper Chemicals Ltd* Templeman J. held that defrauding a customer is not the same as defrauding a creditor. He used an example of a dishonest car dealer[60] to illustrate the point.

> "He did not carry on that business with intent to defraud creditors if he told lies every time he sold a motor car to a customer or only told one lie when he sold one motor car to one single customer. When the dealer told a lie, he perpetrated a fraud on a customer, but he did not intend to defraud a creditor. It is true that the defrauded customer had a right to sue the dealer for damages, and to the extent of the damages was a contingent creditor, but the dealer did nothing to make it impossible for the customer, once he had become a creditor, to recover the sum due to him as a creditor."[61]

8–036 On the other hand, it has been argued that the word "creditors" in the fraudulent trading provisions should be interpreted flexibly so as to include *potential* creditors, such as defrauded customers and other people with causes of action against the trader. A case often cited in support of this argument is *Seillon*.[62] The offence charged in that case was not fraudulent trading but conspiracy to defraud. The intended victims of the conspiracy were alleged to have been the defendant's creditors. It was therefore necessary to consider what constituted an intent to defraud creditors, not because the offence required such intent but by way of construction of the particulars. A submission of no case was rejected, and the jury were directed that "creditors" was to be interpreted in a subjective sense as being persons who the defendant feared would pursue him with legal claims in court. The defendant appealed on the ground that potential claimants for unliquidated damages were not "creditors". It was held that the term "creditor" admitted of some flexibility, and was capable of meaning "potential creditor".

8–037 It has been argued, on the strength of *Seillon*, that the word "creditors" in the fraudulent trading provisions must be construed to include potential creditors such as defrauded customers. In *Smith (Wallace Duncan)*,[63] for example, the Court of Appeal held that "creditors" included persons to whom money would be owed at a future date. Whether the debt could presently be sued for was immaterial. On this view, virtually any fraud is a fraud on creditors, because the victim will always be at least a *potential* creditor.

8–038 A close reading of *Seillon* reveals that it does not support this view. The word "creditor" was held to be capable of meaning "potential creditor"

[59] *Hopkins* [1896] 1 Q.B. 652; *Garlick* (1958) 42 Cr.App.R. 141.
[60] An example posed by Oliver J. in *Re Murray-Watson Ltd*, April 6, 1977.
[61] [1978] 1 Ch. 262 at 267.
[62] [1982] Crim. L.R. 676.
[63] [1996] 2 Cr.App.R. 1.

only because the alleged intent related to a time in the future. The defendant, who expected to have creditors in the future, intended to defraud his creditors as and when they came into existence. It was therefore irrelevant that he did not yet have any creditors. *Seillon* is not authority for the proposition that the defrauding of customers is in itself the carrying on of business "with intent to defraud creditors". It is consistent with the view that the defrauding of customers does not amount to the defrauding of creditors unless the business is carried on in such a way as to make it impossible for the defrauded customers to enforce judgment against the trader.

"ANY [OTHER] FRAUDULENT PURPOSE"

In any event the fraudulent trading offences are not limited to cases involving an "intent to defraud creditors". It is sufficient under CA 2006, s.993 that a business of a company has been carried on for "any fraudulent purpose", and under FA 2006, s.9 that any other business has been carried on "for any other fraudulent purpose". It was formerly thought that "any fraudulent purpose" added little to "intent to defraud creditors", and that they should be construed *ejusdem generis*. A car dealer who fraudulently misdescribed a vehicle, for example, was not carrying on business for a fraudulent purpose. In *Re Murray-Watson Ltd*, Oliver J. said: **8–039**

> "The director of a company dealing in second-hand motor cars who wilfully misrepresents the age and capabilities of a vehicle is, no doubt, a fraudulent rascal, but I do not think that he can be said to be carrying on the company's business for a fraudulent purpose, although no doubt he carries out a particular business transaction in a fraudulent manner."[64]

But in *Kemp*[65] the Court of Appeal took a less restrictive view. The defendant carried out carbon paper frauds through the medium of limited companies. He was charged with knowingly being a party to the carrying on of the business of a company for a fraudulent purpose, namely the obtaining of property by deception. The indictment did not refer to the defrauding of *creditors* at all. It was argued that the phrase "fraudulent purpose" should be construed *ejusdem generis* with the alternative of an intent to defraud creditors, and that the company's business had not been carried on for a "fraudulent purpose" in that more restricted sense. The submission was rejected. **8–040**

> "The difficulty with that submission is this, that the genus there is creditors. The category of creditors listed exhaust [*sic*] the genus and leaves no room for any others. Even if the category of creditors listed did not exhaust the genus, the argument could not prevail, first, because if it did not exhaust the genus,

[64] April 6, 1977.
[65] [1988] Q.B. 645.

> that genus would certainly include potential creditors, for the reasons set out in *Seillon*,[66] and secondly, on any construction one could only exclude potential creditors by simply ignoring the additional words to be found in the statute which is impermissible. If words [*sic*] add anything to the section, they must apply to potential creditors as being the nearest thing to creditors and therefore they must apply to customers."[67]

The decision in *Kemp* was thus based in part on *Seillon*. But, as explained above,[68] the decision in *Seillon* was that an "intent to defraud creditors" existed because the defendant expected to have creditors in the future, and intended to defraud them as and when they came into existence. In *Kemp* the court appears to have thought that Seillon intended to defraud creditors because he intended to turn his victims into creditors by defrauding them.

8–041 The limits of the first limb of the fraudulent trading provisions may or may not affect the scope of the second limb. This depends on the application of the *ejusdem generis* rule. Under that rule, a provision in the form "*x*, *y* or other *z*" can be read narrowly so as to include only those examples of *z* that belong to the same genus as *x* and *y*. Does the rule cut down the scope of the words "any fraudulent purpose" in CA 2006, s.993 and the words "any other fraudulent purpose" in FA 2006, s.9?

8–042 One difficulty in applying the *ejusdem generis* rule in this context is that CA 2006, s.993 does not use the word "other". Applying the rule would mean reading the word "other" into the section *and* construing it to mean "similar". Before the enactment of FA 2006 this would have been difficult. But FA 2006, s.9 does say "any other fraudulent purpose", presumably on the basis that an intent to defraud creditors is one kind of fraudulent purpose. While FA 2006 does not directly affect the offence under CA 2006, s.993,[69] it is plain that the elements of the new offence are intended (with the exception of the kind of business organisation affected) to be the same as those of the older one. This is confirmed by FA 2006, s.9(5), which provides that "fraudulent purpose" in s.9 has the same meaning as in the older offence. If the words "for any other fraudulent purpose" in FA 2006, s.9 fall to be construed in accordance with the *ejusdem generis* rule, the same must be true of the words "for any fraudulent purpose" in CA 2006, s.993.

8–043 So does the *ejusdem generis* rule apply to the words "any other fraudulent purpose" in FA 2006, s.9? This time there is a difficulty in the preceding words. The *ejusdem generis* rule normally applies where the general expression is preceded by two or more expressions, and can therefore be construed as including only things which have characteristics *shared* by the things expressly mentioned. In FA 2006, s.9 this is not the case: the *only* alternative to "any other fraudulent purpose" is "intent to defraud creditors of any person". CA 2006, s.993, on the other hand, does provide for two

[66] [1982] Crim. L.R. 676.
[67] [1988] Q.B. 645 at 654–655.
[68] Para.8–038.
[69] Except by increasing the maximum sentence.

specific alternatives: intent to defraud creditors of the company, and intent to defraud creditors of some other person. It could be argued that these more specific expressions share the common characteristic of involving an intent to defraud people who can be classed as creditors. If "any fraudulent purpose" in CA 2006, s.993 is read as *ejusdem generis* with these two specific expressions, "any other fraudulent purpose" in FA 2006, s.9 must equally be read as *ejusdem generis* with "intent to defraud creditors of any person".

The Court of Appeal held in *Kemp*,[70] however, that the two specific expressions in s.993's predecessor exhaust the genus by including every person who possesses the essential characteristics of the genus. This leaves no room for the application of the *ejusdem generis* rule. If this is right, the words "any [other] fraudulent purpose" must be given a very wide meaning. They presumably include any purpose which involves "defrauding" someone as that expression is understood in other contexts, such as that of conspiracy to defraud.[71] 8–044

In practice, the courts have had difficulty in knowing where to draw the line. In *Kemp*, the Court of Appeal suggested that fraudulent trading was not just an offence against creditors (actual or potential) but a general fraud offence, whose only real limitation was that it required the fraud to be perpetrated through the medium of a company—a limitation now removed by FA 2006. In *Burgess*, on the other hand, where the essence of the prosecution's case was the simple theft of vehicles leased to the company, the Court of Appeal said: 8–045

> "[W]e seriously question the propriety or wisdom of laying a compendious fraudulent trading charge in relation to transactions of the kind which were at issue in the present case, which seem a very far cry from the original purpose of [the section]".[72]

In *Goldman*[73] and *Williams (Roy)*[74] convictions of fraudulent trading were upheld where the fraudulent purpose alleged was the obtaining of money by simple deceptions about the value of (respectively) goods sold and services provided. But in neither case does it appear to have been questioned whether fraudulent trading was an appropriate charge.

A serious objection to the *Kemp* construction is that it makes the offence just as vague as conspiracy to defraud, without even the requirement of conspiracy. It virtually amounts to saying that the offence is committed if a business is carried on in a way which a jury consider to be dishonest in some respect. This is not only unsatisfactory but arguably unlawful. It is arguable that conspiracy to defraud does not comply with the minimum standard of legal certainty required by the European Convention on 8–046

[70] [1988] Q.B. 645.
[71] See above, Ch.7.
[72] July 28, 1994.
[73] [1997] Crim. L.R. 894.
[74] [2001] 1 Cr.App.R. 23 (p.362).

Human Rights.[75] If that is so, the same must be true of fraudulent trading as interpreted in *Kemp*. And in that case the Human Rights Act 1998 would require a court to adopt an alternative construction which does not define the scope of the offence entirely in terms of dishonesty. *Kemp* was decided before the Human Rights Act, and it cannot be assumed that it would survive challenge in the House of Lords.

PARTY TO THE CARRYING ON OF THE BUSINESS

8–047 Where a business has been carried on with intent to defraud creditors or for another fraudulent purpose, an offence of fraudulent trading is committed by everyone who is knowingly a party to the carrying on of business in the relevant manner. The offence is no longer confined to directors.[76] The defendant must however be *a party* to the carrying on of the fraudulent business. It is not clear how much of a restriction this is. In *Re Maidstone Buildings Provisions Ltd*, Pennycuick V.C. said:

> "The expression 'party to the carrying on of a business' is not, I think, a very familiar one but, so far as I can see, the expression 'party to' must on its natural meaning indicate no more than 'participates in,' 'takes part in,' or 'concurs in'."[77]

It was sufficient that the person in question was "taking some positive steps in the carrying on of the company's business in a fraudulent manner".

8–048 In *Miles*,[78] however, it was said that the section was designed to include only those who exercise a controlling or managerial function, or who are "running" the business. A person is not a party to the carrying on of a business merely because he is involved in the activities of the business. At first sight this is a significant narrowing of the offence. But the prosecution presented its case on the basis that Miles did have a managerial role. He claimed that he was only a salesman, acting under orders. The jury were directed that the offence could be committed by "concurring in the trade which is involved in the business of the company". The Court of Appeal seems to have concluded that this was a misdirection in view of the issue raised. "Concurring in the trade which is involved in the business of the company" is not the same thing as participating in a fraud. It does not follow that *only* a person "running" the business is a party to the carrying on of the business.

8–049 Indeed, it is now clear that that test is too narrow in at least one respect, because it would exclude altogether persons who deal with the organisation carrying on the fraudulent business but are not its employees or agents. *Re Bank of Credit and Commerce International SA*[79] concerned a claim against

[75] See above, paras 2–099 *et seq.*
[76] See above, para.8–003.
[77] [1971] 1 W.L.R. 1085 at 1092.
[78] [1992] Crim. L.R. 657.
[79] [2001] 1 B.C.L.C. 263.

Banque Arabe under the Insolvency Act 1986, s.213(2) on the ground that Banque Arabe had been party to the fraudulent carrying on of business by BCCI. Banque Arabe sought to raise as a preliminary issue the question whether it could be liable under s.213(2) if it had not exercised a controlling or managerial function within BCCI. Neuberger J. held that it could, and that the contrary view was not arguable. Indeed the words "any persons who were knowingly parties to the carrying on of the business in the manner above mentioned" referred more naturally to third parties than to persons employed by the company conducting the fraudulent business. He concluded that

> "a company or other entity which carries on (so far as it is concerned) a bona fide business with the company, does not fall within s.213(2), but a company which is involved in, and assists and benefits from, the offending business, or the business carried on in an offending way, and does so knowingly and, therefore, dishonestly does fall or at least can fall within s.213(2)."[80]

Miles was relevant only by analogy, because it was concerned with the position of an employee or agent of the fraudulent company; but it showed that 8–050

> "an employee of the company who was merely carrying out orders does not fall within [the section] whereas somebody who orchestrates, organises or can seize[81] of the business concerned does fall within the section".[82]

On the other hand, Neuberger J. pointed out that *Re Maidstone Buildings Provisions Ltd* was cited "with apparent approval" in *Miles*.

Even if *Miles* is authority for the proposition that an employee is not "a party to" the carrying on of the fraudulent business merely because he plays a minor part in it, it may still be arguable that he commits the offence because he aids and abets those who *are* parties to it. Indeed the Crown argued in *Miles* that the conviction could be sustained on this ground. The court did not expressly decide the point. It may be arguable that, by quashing the conviction, it implicitly rejected the argument. If so, this could only be on the basis that the fraudulent trading provisions by implication exclude the ordinary principles of secondary liability. But it is more likely that the court was simply unwilling to uphold the conviction on a basis other than that on which the jury had been directed. 8–051

Assuming that it is possible to commit the offence as a secondary party, this opens up the possibility of committing it by acquiescence or omission. The expression "a party to" does not cover everyone who has noticed that the business of the company is being carried out fraudulently. A company secretary's failure to give appropriate advice to the directors cannot in itself make him a party to the carrying on of the business in a fraudulent 8–052

[80] [2001] 1 B.C.L.C. 263 at 273.
[81] A word such as "control" seems to be missing.
[82] [2001] 1 B.C.L.C. 263 at 273.

manner.[83] Acquiescence on the part of a director, however, might be a different matter: the directors, unlike the secretary, are responsible for the management of the company. A person can aid and abet an offence by failing to prevent it, if he has the authority to do so.[84] A director who turns a blind eye to his colleagues' fraudulent running of the business might therefore be guilty of aiding and abetting their offences even if he is not "a party to" the fraud.

8–053 A lender who presses for payment is not a party to a fraud merely because he knows that the debtor cannot pay him without resorting to dishonesty. But it is sufficient if a creditor accepts money which he knows has been procured by carrying on the business fraudulently for the purpose of paying him.[85]

THE MENTAL ELEMENT

8–054 The requirement that the business be carried on with intent to defraud creditors, or for a fraudulent purpose, relates to the state of mind of those carrying on the business. We are here concerned with the required mental element in relation to the person charged with the offence, who may or may not have been carrying on the fraudulent business himself.

KNOWLEDGE

8–055 The defendant must be proved to have *knowingly* been a party to the carrying on of the fraudulent business. Obviously this adds nothing if he was himself carrying on the business with intent to defraud or for a fraudulent purpose. Where he was not, "knowingly" probably includes "wilful blindness". In relation to the Insolvency Act 1986, s.213 it is sometimes said that "reckless indifference" will suffice, but in relation to the criminal offences this cannot be so. An express requirement of knowledge cannot be satisfied by proof of recklessness in the criminal sense.

DISHONESTY

8–056 The business must be carried on with intent to defraud creditors or for a fraudulent purpose. *That* intent or purpose must by definition be dishonest, because dishonesty is an element of fraud. It is not expressly provided that *the person charged* must have acted dishonestly—only that he must have knowingly been party to the carrying on of the business in a fraudulent manner. In practice, however, it seems to be assumed that dishonesty is

[83] *In Re Gerald Cooper Chemicals Ltd* [1978] 1 Ch. 262 at 268, *per* Templeman J.
[84] *Tuck v Robson* [1970] 1 W.L.R. 741.
[85] *Re Maidstone Buildings Provisions Ltd* [1971] 1 W.L.R. 1085.

essential. In *Cox*,[86] for example, the trial judge directed the jury that dishonesty was not an ingredient of the offence, and this was held to be a serious misdirection because dishonesty is an ingredient of fraud. The fact that the section does not require intent to defraud on the part of the defendant, but only on the part of those actually carrying on the business, seems to have been ignored.

Dishonesty means the same thing in this context as in other offences. In **8–057** *Lockwood*[87] the judge directed the jury as to dishonesty in accordance with the decision in *Ghosh*.[88] The defendant appealed on the ground that the *Ghosh* direction was inappropriate in the context of a commercial case. The appeal was dismissed.

86 (1982) 75 Cr.App.R. 291.
87 [1986] Crim. L.R. 244.
88 [1982] Q.B. 1053; above, para.2–013.

CHAPTER 9

THEFT

Section 1(1) of the Theft Act 1968 ("TA 1968") provides: **9–001**

> "A person is guilty of theft if he dishonestly appropriates property belonging to another with the intention of permanently depriving the other of it; and 'thief' and 'steal' shall be construed accordingly."

Theft is triable either way,[1] and is punishable on conviction on indictment with seven years' imprisonment.[2] The requirement of dishonesty is discussed in Ch.2; in this chapter we consider the other elements of the

[1] Magistrates' Courts Act 1980, s.17(1), Sch.1.
[2] TA 1968, s.7.

offence. Although we are concerned only with those issues likely to arise in a fraud case, this is still a long and complicated chapter. Prosecutors will probably prefer to charge fraud rather than theft whenever possible.

PROPERTY

9–002 The aim of fraud is nearly always to obtain some valuable thing. TA 1968 distinguishes between things that qualify as "property" and things that do not. Under the law in force before January 15, 2007, two questions turned on this distinction: (a) *which* offence was committed when something was obtained *by deception*,[3] and (b) whether the obtaining of a thing *without* deception was any offence at all. The offence of obtaining property by deception was complemented by offences of obtaining by deception things other than property; but theft was not complemented by offences of dishonestly appropriating things other than property.

9–003 Until recently the concept of property was therefore a crucial one. The Fraud Act 2006 makes it less so, for two reasons.

- The dishonest making of false representations is now fraud irrespective of the thing thereby obtained, and indeed irrespective of whether anything is obtained at all.[4] A person who lies to obtain a service is guilty of the *same* offence as a person who lies to obtain property.
- The dishonest obtaining of services is now an offence whether or not the services are obtained by deception.[5] But it is not *theft*. The choice between a charge of theft and one of obtaining services depends whether the thing appropriated or obtained was property or services.

9–004 For the purposes of theft, and the old offence of obtaining property by deception, "property" is defined by TA 1968, s.4(1):

> "'Property' includes money and all other property, real or personal, including things in action and other intangible property."

The effect of this definition is to import the ordinary legal concept of property. Anything that can belong to a person is property for the purposes of TA 1968. Indeed, the definition of theft requires not only that the thing obtained should be *capable* of belonging to a person—that is, that it should be property—but that it should *in fact* belong to a person other than the defendant. In a sense, therefore, the concept of property can be regarded as one aspect of the more specific requirement that what the defendant

[3] See above, paras 4–094 *et seq*.
[4] See above, Ch.4.
[5] See below, Ch.10.

appropriates should be something "belonging to another".[6] For that requirement to be satisfied, it is necessary (though not sufficient) that the thing appropriated should be property.

There are two kinds of property to which special considerations apply. 9–005

CORPOREAL LAND

Real property is expressly included in the term "property". Land can 9–006
therefore be stolen (or, under the old law, obtained by deception). TA 1968, s.4(2), however, provides that a person can steal land only in certain circumstances. Of these, only the first is of importance for the law of fraud:

> ". . . when he is a trustee or personal representative, or is authorised by power of attorney, or as liquidator of a company, or otherwise, to sell or dispose of land belonging to another, and he appropriates the land or anything forming part of it by dealing with it in breach of the confidence reposed in him . . ."

So a person authorised to sell land for a stipulated minimum price can be guilty of stealing it if he dishonestly sells it to an associate for less than that price. Indeed he can be guilty of stealing it even if no minimum price has been specified, since the fact that his act is within his authority does not prevent it from being an appropriation.[7]

It would appear that anyone guilty of theft by virtue of s.4(2) will 9–007
necessarily be guilty of fraud by abuse of position.[8] But an agent could commit fraud by making arrangements for the sale of his principal's land by the principal or a third party, whereas he would not be *stealing* the land unless he sold it himself.

INTANGIBLE PROPERTY

"Property" includes "things in action and other intangible property". 9–008
This expression includes debts, shares, intellectual property and, it seems, any valuable entitlement that can be bought and sold.[9] All these things can therefore be stolen. This does not mean that any dishonest infringement of another's rights is theft. For a theft charge to succeed, there must have been some *property* which belonged to someone other than the defendant and which the defendant appropriated. In some cases it might appear that money has changed hands, but on closer inspection it transpires that there never was any property to be appropriated. If a person dishonestly induces a bank to open a credit in his favour, for example, all that has happened is that a new item of property has been created (namely the customer's right to the sum credited). The bank has not (yet) lost any property at all.[10]

[6] Below, paras 9–027 *et seq.*
[7] *Gomez* [1993] A.C. 442.
[8] Above, Ch.6.
[9] *Att-Gen of Hong Kong v Chan Nai-Keung* [1987] 1 W.L.R. 1339 (export quotas).
[10] *Caresana* [1996] Crim. L.R. 667.

9–009 Even where intangible property can be shown to have existed, it raises particular difficulties for the law of theft because it consists only of legal rights. Legal rights are usually unaffected by unlawful interference. It may therefore be arguable either that the defendant's conduct does not amount to an appropriation of the property, or that he has no intention of permanently depriving its owner of it.[11]

CREDIT BALANCES

9–010 The form of intangible property that most commonly presents difficulty in a fraud case is the thing in action owned by the holder of an account with a bank or other financial institution.[12] The holder does not own any of the assets held by the bank: he is merely its creditor.[13] But the debt owed to him by the bank—the credit balance of the account—is intangible property which belongs to him, and can therefore be stolen by someone else. There are several ways in which this can be done.

Authorised withdrawals

9–011 The defendant may have a general authority to draw on the account, in which case any drawings by him will diminish the amount owed by the bank to the account-holder. Any dishonest exercise of that authority is theft of the amount withdrawn. In *Kohn*[14] a company director fraudulently drew cheques on the company's account. The cheques were honoured because he had authority to draw them, and the credit balance was thus reduced. So the company was in fact deprived of its property, and there was no defence to a charge of theft.

9–012 In *Preddy*[15] the House of Lords held that procuring a transfer of funds between bank accounts by deception was not an obtaining of property belonging to another for the purposes of the old offence of obtaining property by deception, contrary to TA 1968, s.15. In *Graham* the Court of Appeal had to consider what alternative offences might be substituted where defendants guilty of such conduct had been wrongly convicted of that offence. With reference to the possibility of substituting a conviction for theft, the court said:

> "If in any case the reasoning in *Preddy* is fatal to a conviction under section 15, it is likely to be fatal to a conviction under section 1 also unless, in the case of a chose in action, it can be shown that the chose in action appropriated was at the time of appropriation the property of another. For reasons given in *Preddy*, this will not ordinarily be so where the result of the defendant's dishonesty is

[11] See below, paras 9–096 *et seq.* (appropriation), 9–145 (intention permanently to deprive).
[12] See Edward Griew, "Stealing and Obtaining Bank Credits" [1986] Crim. L.R. 356.
[13] *Foley v Hill* (1848) 2 H.L. Cas. 28; *Davenport* [1954] 1 W.L.R. 569 at 571.
[14] (1979) 69 Cr.App.R. 395.
[15] [1996] A.C. 815.

the creation of a new chose in action which the victim did not at the time of appropriation own and had never owned."[16]

9–013 This is mystifying. The decision in *Preddy* turned on the fact that TA 1968, s.15 required an *obtaining* of property belonging to another. TA 1968, s.1, by contrast, requires only an *appropriation* of such property. On the assumption that the defendant could be shown to have appropriated the victim's chose in action by destroying it, it is not clear what aspect of the reasoning in *Preddy* the court thought would ordinarily be fatal to a charge of theft. When the court reconvened to consider certain matters arising out of its decision, it indicated that its earlier judgment had not been intended to cast doubt on *Kohn*,[17] or on the principle that a chose in action can be stolen by destroying it. The court sadly did not explain what its earlier statement *had* meant, but in the light of this disclaimer it can presumably be disregarded. In *Hilton*[18] it was confirmed that any dishonest transfer of funds by an authorised signatory can be theft, whether the funds are transferred electronically or by cheque.[19]

9–014 The same applies to a person who has authority to withdraw funds from another's bank account because he holds a valid cheque drawn on the account. It was confirmed in *Williams (Roy)*[20] that the presenting of a cheque is an appropriation of the funds that are debited to the drawer's account as a result. It is therefore theft of those funds if it is done dishonestly, for example because the cheque was obtained by deception.

Deception of the bank

9–015 Alternatively, a person who in fact has no authority to draw on the account may succeed in securing a transfer of funds by presenting a forged cheque or otherwise deceiving the bank, or by gaining access to its computer system. In this case his conduct will probably not reduce the amount owed by the bank to the account-holder, who will be entitled to insist that the missing funds should be re-credited to the account if and when he discovers what has happened. It is therefore debatable, first, whether the fraudster's conduct can fairly be described as an appropriation of those funds,[21] and secondly whether he intends permanently to deprive

[16] [1997] 1 Cr.App.R. 302 at 313.

[17] (1979) 69 Cr.App.R. 395; above, para.9–011.

[18] [1997] 2 Cr.App.R. 445.

[19] The court thought that Sir John Smith had proposed a distinction between these forms of transfer, but did not understand why. Sir John explained in his note on *Hilton* at [1997] Crim. L.R. 761 that the distinction he had intended to draw was a completely different one—viz. between (a) the defendant who is able to withdraw the funds *himself*, either because he has general authority to draw on the account (as in *Kohn* and *Hilton*) or because he holds a cheque drawn on it (as in *Williams (Roy)* [2001] 1 Cr.App.R. 23 (p.362)), and (b) one who *deceives the account-holder* into transferring the funds without using a cheque. For the latter situation, see below, para.9–114.

[20] [2001] 1 Cr.App.R. 23 (p.362).

[21] Below, paras 9–091 *et seq*.

the account-holder of them.[22] But it seems that this too can be theft of the funds debited to the account.[23]

Deception of the account-holder

9–016 Yet another possibility is that the defendant may deceive the account-holder into instructing the bank to transfer the funds. The House of Lords held in *Preddy*[24] that in this case the deceiver was not guilty of obtaining the credit balance by deception contrary to TA 1968, s.15, because the credit balance that appears in the second account is a different chose in action from the one originally owned by the victim. Nor, in these circumstances, is the defendant guilty of *stealing* the funds by securing their transfer. The reason for this is not, as the court suggested in *Graham* before correcting itself, that the reasoning in *Preddy* applies to theft as well as to obtaining by deception. It is because deceiving someone into parting with their property is not, in itself, an appropriation of the property.[25]

The need to identify a credit balance

9–017 This discussion presupposes that there is a credit balance to be appropriated. But the prosecution must identify that credit balance and adduce evidence of its existence prior to the appropriation. In *Ali* (one of the appeals heard with *Graham*) the defendant presented for payment four bankers' drafts for a total of £1m, bearing forged signatures. He was convicted of attempting to steal a credit of £1m belonging to the bank on which the drafts were drawn. It was held that the conviction could not stand in the light of *Preddy,* since the indictment did not identify any property belonging to another.[26] The court later explained in *Hilton* that this was because the instruments were bankers' drafts rather than cheques.

> "If the forged signatures had been genuine, each draft was an undertaking by the bank itself to pay the stated sum to the payee. The payment, which normally would be made between banks either by electronic means or through the CHAPS settlements system, would be made out of what can loosely be described as the bank's own funds. No doubt, in the ordinary course of business, and if the draft had been genuine, then the bank would have obtained or secured the funds for itself by debiting its customer's account, and it might be possible in such a case to say that the draft was used as a means of obtaining funds from that account, which was the property of the customer. But that consideration did not arise in Ali's case, where the drafts were forged. Therefore, *Preddy* having underlined the need to identify 'property' in terms of

[22] Below, paras 9–132 *et seq*.

[23] *Chan Man-Sin v Att-Gen of Hong Kong* [1988] 1 W.L.R. 196; below, paras 9–098 and 9–145. See also *Burke* [2000] Crim. L.R. 413, where the defendant presented a forged cheque and was arrested. A conviction of attempting to obtain property by deception was quashed on *Preddy* grounds (above, para.4–104), and a conviction of attempting to steal a credit balance was substituted.

[24] [1996] A.C. 815.

[25] See below, paras 9–113 *et seq.*

[26] [1997] 1 Cr.App.R. 302 at 327–328.

> a legal chose in action, it followed that no such property had been identified by the evidence in Ali's case."[27]

While this analysis is correct, it is not *Preddy* that makes it so. The need to prove the *existence* of property allegedly stolen is quite distinct from the need, on a charge of obtaining property by deception, to prove that the defendant *obtained* the property in question. The former requirement was well established before *Preddy*.

OVERDRAFTS

The position may be different if the victim's account is overdrawn. In that case the debt is owed by the account-holder to the bank, and is therefore the property of the bank, not the account-holder. Further drawings on the account will not deprive the bank of that property, but on the contrary will increase the size of the debt. It may therefore be crucial whether, at the moment of the alleged appropriation, the account is in credit.[28] **9–018**

It was recognised in *Kohn*,[29] however, that if the bank has agreed to allow the account-holder to overdraw up to a certain amount he has a contractual right to have his cheques honoured until the agreed limit is reached. This right is itself a form of intangible property, and can therefore be stolen. Suppose A has an account with an overdraft facility of £300. It is already overdrawn by £100. The overdraft facility currently represents a right to withdraw a further £200, and is a thing in action belonging to A. If B dishonestly draws £200 from the account, he has stolen that thing in action. But if A has no overdraft facility, or has already used it up, he has nothing left to steal. Whether the bank exercises its discretion to allow further drawings is immaterial. Nor, it would seem, is there anything to steal if, although the account in question is in credit, the account-holder nevertheless owes money to the bank (and has no right to overdraw further) because of the state of his *other* accounts with the bank.[30] **9–019**

CHOSES IN ACTION AND CHEQUES

A cheque is tangible property which represents a chose in action, namely the payee's right to payment as against the drawer. In certain circumstances it may be possible to treat an appropriation of a cheque as theft of the **9–020**

[27] [1997] 2 Cr.App.R. 445 at 451.

[28] In *Forsyth* [1997] 2 Cr.App.R. 299, £400,000 was dishonestly withdrawn from an account. The account had been £7m overdrawn at the start of business on that day, but £11m was credited during the day. The evidence as to the state of the account at the time of the transfer was "inconclusive". But it now seems that the moment of appropriation of a credit balance is the time when the bank is instructed to make the transfer, not the time when it actually makes it: see below, paras 9–101 *et seq.*

[29] (1979) 69 Cr.App.R. 395.

[30] Edward Griew, [1986] Crim. L.R. 356 at 360.

chose in action it represents—for example, where X has drawn a cheque in favour of V, and D appropriates the cheque with the intention that V shall not get the sum due. But the chose in action represented by the cheque cannot be stolen *from X*, because it does not belong to him: it belongs to V. It makes no difference to this that D intends X to pay D instead. If D uses the cheque to withdraw funds from X's account, he may have stolen X's credit balance; but that is a chose in action owned by X, consisting in X's rights against his bank. It is distinct from the chose in action represented by the cheque. That belongs to V alone, and consists in V's rights against X.

9–021 Moreover, a chose in action, like any other property, cannot be stolen (or, under the old law, obtained by deception) if it does not exist until the moment of appropriation (or obtaining), because in that case the defendant does not appropriate (or obtain) property belonging to another. This presents a difficulty where the defendant has dishonestly obtained a cheque from the drawer. He cannot be charged with obtaining or stealing the chose in action conferred on him by the cheque, because that chose in action belongs to him. It did not even exist, let alone belong to anyone else, before he got it. This was eventually confirmed by the House of Lords in *Preddy*.[31] But Lord Goff went further, saying that it is also impossible to charge an obtaining (or, by implication, a theft) of the cheque itself. This is because there is no intention to deprive the drawer of his cheque: he can have it back once it has been presented. The Court of Appeal has applied this dictum several times, though not always with enthusiasm.[32] It is examined below, in the context of the requirement of intention permanently to deprive.[33]

TRUSTS OF INTANGIBLE PROPERTY

9–022 An owner of property can steal it from someone else who also has a proprietary interest in it, for example under a trust. Where the funds in an account represent the proceeds of fraud (for example because they were dishonestly transferred out of another account), those funds belong at law to the account-holder, but in equity to the victim of the fraud. The account-holder can therefore steal them from their beneficial owner.

9–023 This offers a possible solution where the defendant has by deception procured a transfer of funds from another's account to his own. According to *Preddy*[34] he has not obtained property belonging to another, because the chose in action he obtains is not the one that the victim loses. But the victim arguably has an equitable interest in the chose in action that the fraudster obtains, because it is the *proceeds* of the one that the victim has

[31] [1996] A.C. 815.

[32] *Graham* [1997] 1 Cr.App.R. 302; *Horsman* [1997] 2 Cr.App.R. 418; *Clark* [2001] EWCA Crim 884; [2002] 1 Cr.App.R. 14 (p.141).

[33] Paras 9–151 *et seq*.

[34] [1996] A.C. 815; above, para.4–104.

lost.[35] In that case, any subsequent use of the funds can be theft. TA 1968, s.3(1) provides that appropriation can include

> "where [a person] has come by the property (innocently or not) without stealing it, any later assumption of a right to it by keeping or dealing with it as owner".

In *Nathan*[36] a solicitor obtained by deception a bank loan which was paid into his client account. His conviction of obtaining property by deception was quashed because of *Preddy.*[37] But it was argued that he could properly have been convicted of *stealing* the credit balance from the client account, by dishonestly distributing the funds in breach of his undertaking to the bank to use them only for the purpose for which they were advanced. **9–024**

> "Counsel accepts that once the transfer was made by [the bank] to the appellant's client account, the appellant became the owner of the chose in action constituted by the debt of his bank to him. But counsel suggests—rightly as we conceive—that that was a chose in action which the appellant held as a trustee. The beneficial owner of that chose in action was [the bank] since the appellant was under a fiduciary obligation to apply the money in accordance with the terms of the trust on which he held it. Accordingly, counsel submits, there was a criminal misappropriation when the appellant dishonestly applied the money otherwise than in accordance with the terms of that trust."

The court regarded this analysis as "in principle sound".

Hallam[38] is a more dubious application of a similar idea. Investment advisers were charged with stealing funds which their clients had paid by cheque. The appropriation alleged in each case was the defendant's payment of the cheque into his account. It was argued that at that time the cheque did not belong to the drawer but to the defendant. The court took a robust view of this argument. **9–025**

> "The appellants had been entrusted with their clients' funds to invest on their behalf. The clients had and retained an equitable interest in any cheque which they drew . . . in favour of the appellants. . . That equitable interest attached not only to the cheque but to its proceeds and to the balance in any account operated by the appellants . . . to which the payment could be traced . . . In our opinion the argument that the property stolen (whether it was correctly or incorrectly described or identified in the indictment) was not the property of the clients is untenable."

[35] "Although it is difficult to find clear authority for the proposition, when property is obtained by fraud equity imposes a constructive trust on the fraudulent recipient": *Westdeutsche Landesbank Girozentrale v Islington L.B.C.* [1996] A.C. 669 at 716, *per* Lord Browne-Wilkinson; *R. v Governor of Brixton Prison, ex p. Levin* [1997] Q.B. 65 at 82–83.

[36] [1997] Crim. L.R. 835.

[37] [1996] A.C. 815; above, para.4–104.

[38] (1994) 158 J.P. 427.

9–026 Clearly the *proceeds* of the cheques belonged to the clients. The court thought that, if the defendants had dishonestly appropriated those proceeds, it made no difference that the appropriation alleged was at the earlier time when the cheques were presented. But the court seems to have gone further, by saying that the clients' equitable interest attached not just to the proceeds but to the cheques themselves. The intangible property represented by each cheque consisted in the rights against the client which the cheque conferred on the defendant. It belonged, in law, to the defendant. The proposition that the client had an equitable interest in the cheque appears to mean that the defendant held his rights against the client on trust for the client. It may be only logical that if the proceeds of the cheques were held on trust for the clients then the cheques themselves must also have been so held. But the notion of a trust of a chose in action, whose beneficiary is the very person against whom the chose in action exists, is a curious one which merited closer examination than it received. A more convincing analysis is that by presenting the cheque the defendant stole neither the cheque itself nor the intangible property it represented, but the funds debited to the client's account as a result.[39]

BELONGING TO ANOTHER

9–027 Property cannot be stolen unless it "belongs" to someone other than the thief at the moment of appropriation. This excludes not only property which has never belonged to anyone other than the defendant (such as the rights conferred on him by a cheque drawn in his favour),[40] but also property which has ceased to belong to another before the defendant appropriates it.[41] Identifying the person or persons to whom property "belongs" can involve fine points of civil law. Judges sometimes suggest that the simplicity of the criminal law should not be sullied with the complications of civil law, or that the law of theft should be reformed so that such complications are no longer necessary.[42] But the function of the law of theft is to provide criminal sanctions for certain infringements of rights conferred by the law of property. It cannot ignore what that law says about the scope of those rights.[43] The criminal courts have no option but to examine and apply the law of property whenever it is relevant.

9–028 A random example is *Tillings*.[44] The defendants were alleged to have unlawfully induced an old lady to alter her will in their favour, and were

[39] *Williams (Roy)* [2001] 1 Cr.App.R. 23 (p.362).
[40] See above, para.9–021.
[41] Russell Heaton, "Deceiving without Thieving?" [2001] Crim. L.R. 712.
[42] e.g. *Hallam* [1995] Crim. L.R. 323.
[43] See *Dobson v General Accident Fire and Life Assurance Co plc* [1990] 1 Q.B. 274 at 289, *per* Bingham L.J.; *Gomez* [1993] A.C. 442 at 491, *per* Lord Lowry (dissenting); *Hinks* [2001] 2 A.C. 241 at [65], *per* Lord Hobhouse (dissenting).
[44] [1985] Crim. L.R. 393.

charged with attempting to steal the residuary estate from the personal representatives appointed under the original will. A submission of no case succeeded because the personal representatives never had any interest in the estate: the first will was revoked by the second, and never took effect.[45] The case could not have been decided without reference to the civil law of succession. That is what it was about.

PROPERTY IN WHICH ANOTHER HAS A PROPRIETARY INTEREST

TA 1968, s.5(1) provides: **9–029**

> "Property shall be regarded as belonging to any person having possession or control of it, or having in it any proprietary right or interest (not being an equitable interest arising only from an agreement to transfer or grant an interest)."

Since there is no requirement that the property should *not* belong to the defendant, but only that it *should* belong to someone else, it follows that property in which more than one person has an interest can be stolen by any of those persons from any of the others.[46] In *Clowes (No.2)*[47] it was held sufficient that one of the defendants had dishonestly withdrawn funds from a bank account into which funds contributed by investors had been paid, because the investors had a proprietary interest in the entire credit balance of the account. It was immaterial that part of the balance had not been contributed by them.

The victim's interest in the property may be equitable rather than legal **9–030** (unless it arises only from an agreement to transfer or grant an interest). So a trustee, although the sole owner at law, can steal the trust property, because the beneficiaries have an equitable interest in it. It belongs to them as well as to him. Whether this principle extends to *constructive* trustees is doubtful.[48]

In *Sullivan*[49] the defendants were charged with stealing money which a **9–031** drug-dealer had brought to their home before dying there. He had obtained the money on behalf of some local dealers, and the trial judge (Aikens J.) ruled that there could be no theft from those dealers because their title was unenforceable on grounds of illegality. It is submitted that the ruling was wrong. The civil law does sometimes prevent a party to proceedings from relying on his own illegal act to *establish* his title to property,[50] but it does

[45] *Quaere* whether the defendants' conduct was in any event an appropriation: see below, paras 9–113 *et seq.* The commentary at [1985] Crim. L.R. 393 suggests that conspiracy to defraud would have been a more appropriate charge, but the defendants were spouses: cf. *Mawji* [1957] A.C. 526.

[46] *Bonner* [1970] 1 W.L.R. 838.

[47] [1994] 2 All E.R. 316.

[48] Below, paras 9–078 *et seq*.

[49] [2002] Crim. L.R. 758.

[50] *Tinsley v Milligan* [1994] 1 A.C. 340.

not say that his illegal act prevents him from acquiring title at all.[51] And the existence of a proprietary interest is sufficient even if its owner cannot enforce it.[52]

COMPANY PROPERTY

9–032 The literal application of TA 1968, s.5(1) produces a curious result where the property appropriated belongs to a company owned by the defendant. The company is a legal person in its own right, distinct from the shareholders. But in substance its property belongs to the shareholders, and it is arguable that the criminal law should look to the substance rather than the form. In *Squire*[53] it was conceded at the trial that it would not be theft for the shareholders to siphon off the company's funds. In *Arthur*[54] most of the shares were held by the fraudulent directors but a few were held by their wives. An appeal against conviction of fraudulent conversion was dismissed on the ground that the company was a separate entity, consisting of more shareholders than the parties to the fraud. This implies that if there had not been other shareholders the company would not have been defrauded.

9–033 In *Attorney-General's Reference (No.2 of 1982)*,[55] however, where the directors and sole shareholders of a company were alleged to have drawn company cheques for their own purposes, the argument was confined to the issue of dishonesty: it was apparently assumed that the funds belonged to another. And in *Gomez*[56] it was confirmed by the House of Lords (including Lord Lowry, who dissented on the main issue) that, if dishonesty is proved, there is no obstacle to a conviction of theft in such a case. Sir John Smith pointed out that

> "[I]f all the shareholders are the alleged thieves, we are left with a strange sort of stealing. The company cannot go hungry, or feel the cold, or feel deprived. It does not seem to merit the protection of the law of theft against the entire body of shareholders for whose benefit it exists. The invocation of the law of theft must be for the protection of the company's creditors. But if the only directors and shareholders had formed a partnership instead of a company and otherwise behaved in exactly the same way, a charge of theft could never have got off the ground. There seems to be no difference in substance. The case is more properly one for the company law concerned with the protection of the company's creditors than for the law of theft."[57]

A charge of fraud by abuse of position would be open to the same objection (assuming that the defendant is not in the kind of position required by the

[51] *Bowmakers Ltd v Barnet Instruments Ltd* [1945] K.B. 65; *Belvoir Finance Co v Stapleton* [1971] 1 Q.B. 210.

[52] cf. *Meech* [1974] Q.B. 549; below, para.9–064.

[53] [1963] Crim. L.R. 700.

[54] (1967) 111 S.J. 435.

[55] [1984] Q.B. 624.

[56] [1993] A.C. 442; see also *Philippou* (1989) 89 Cr.App.R. 290.

[57] [1989] Crim. L.R. 589 (commentary on *Philippou* (1989) 89 Cr.App.R. 290).

Fraud Act 2006, s.4(1)(a) in relation to the *creditors* as distinct from the company).[58] If the gravamen of the defendant's conduct is the defrauding of creditors, it would be more appropriate to charge an offence under the Insolvency Act 1986.[59]

An unincorporated body is not a legal person, and a person beneficially entitled to the property of such a body can no more steal it than he could his own.[60] The prosecution may therefore need to show either that he was not beneficially entitled to the property or that he was not the *only* person so entitled.[61] **9–034**

PROPERTY HELD IN A FIDUCIARY CAPACITY

Property may "belong to another" even where the defendant is the only person beneficially entitled to it, if he holds it in a fiduciary capacity. Most if not all cases of this kind can now be charged as fraud by abuse of position instead,[62] thus avoiding the need to show that the property belonged to another at all. If the defendant's conduct in relation to the property is not a breach of any legal duty in relation to the property it is doubtful whether it can properly be regarded either as an abuse of position or as dishonest, but the intention seems to be that fraud by abuse of position should not require any such breach. **9–035**

Trustees

Misappropriation of trust property by a trustee can be theft even if there is no identifiable beneficiary. TA 1968, s.5(2) provides: **9–036**

> "Where property is subject to a trust, the persons to whom it belongs shall be regarded as including any person having a right to enforce the trust, and an intention to defeat the trust shall be regarded accordingly as an intention to deprive of the property any person having that right."

There is rarely any need to invoke this provision because the beneficiaries of a trust usually have an equitable interest in the property, so the property normally belongs to them by virtue of TA 1968, s.5(1). Charitable trusts do not have identifiable beneficiaries, but can be enforced by the Attorney-General or the Charity Commissioners. By virtue of TA 1968, s.5(2), property subject to such a trust is deemed to belong to another, and an intention to defeat the objects of the trust is deemed to be an intention **9–037**

[58] cf. the argument that dishonesty in theft must relate to the person to whom the property belongs, and in the case of fraud by abuse of position to the person whose financial interests the defendant is expected to safeguard: above, para.2–096.

[59] Below, Ch.15.

[60] *Boakye*, March 12, 1992.

[61] As in *Clowes (No.2)* [1994] 2 All E.R. 316.

[62] Above, Ch.6.

permanently to deprive that other of the property. It can therefore be stolen by a sole trustee, although no-one else has a proprietary interest in it or possession or control of it.

9–038 This appears to have been overlooked by the prosecution in *Dyke*.[63] Trustees of a charity were alleged to have stolen money collected from the public. The prosecution were "concerned at the concept of the appellants stealing from themselves, as trustees", and instead chose to allege theft of money belonging to persons unknown (namely the members of the public who had donated it). The jury were directed that "If the property did not belong to the person who is said to have taken it that is really sufficient. You need not trouble yourself too much about worrying to whom it belonged." The convictions were quashed because the money could not have been stolen from the public: it belonged to the charity as soon as it was collected. A charge of theft from the charity would have been good.[64]

Property Entrusted to the Defendant

9–039 Property entrusted to the defendant will usually belong to another within the meaning of TA 1968, s.5(1); but the prosecution has an alternative route to the same conclusion. TA 1968, s.5(3) provides:

> "Where a person receives property from or on account of another, and is under an obligation to the other to retain and deal with that property or its proceeds in a particular way, the property or proceeds shall be regarded (as against him) as belonging to the other."

9–040 The effect of this provision is that property entrusted to a person in such circumstances that he is not entitled to use it as his own is regarded as "belonging to another". So too are the proceeds of the property if he converts it into some other form. A person holding property subject to an obligation of this kind will almost invariably be a trustee.

> "It is clear that if the terms upon which the person receives the money are that he is bound to keep it separate, either in a bank or elsewhere, and to hand that money so kept as a separate fund to the person entitled to it, then he is a trustee of that money and must hand it over to the person who is his cestui que trust.
>
> If on the other hand he is not bound to keep the money separate, but is entitled to mix it with his own money and deal with it as he pleases, and when called upon to hand over an equivalent sum of money, then, in my opinion, he is not a trustee of the money, but merely a debtor."[65]

In *Clowes (No.2)* these propositions were said to have "stood the test of time". The court went on:

[63] [2001] EWCA Crim 2184; [2002] 1 Cr.App.R. 30 (p.404).

[64] It was said that "any theft would have been from the beneficiaries of the charity", but strictly speaking it would have been from the Attorney-General, by virtue of TA 1968, s.5(2).

[65] *Henry v Hammond* [1913] 2 K.B. 515 at 521, *per* Channell J.

> "As to segregation of funds, the effect of the authorities seems to be that a requirement to keep moneys separate is normally an indicator that they are impressed with a trust, and that the absence of such a requirement, *if there are no other indicators of a trust,* normally negatives it."[66]

If the defendant is a trustee, the property will belong to another by virtue of TA 1968, s.5(1), and it will be strictly unnecessary to resort to s.5(3). In most cases, and arguably all,[67] s.5(3) adds nothing of substance. Its significance is that, even where a proprietary interest could if necessary be shown to exist, the requirements of s.5(3) may in practice be easier to satisfy. If the defendant is under an obligation to keep the property separate, it does not matter whether that obligation makes him a trustee: s.5(3) applies anyway. The subsection is therefore useful where a trader or professional person is paid money for one purpose and dishonestly uses it for another, knowing that he has little or no prospect of providing the consideration for which the money was paid. If it cannot be proved that he intended to misapply the money at the time when he received it, a charge of fraud by false representation will fail. If the money became his to use as he liked, a charge of theft will also fail.[68] But if he is under an obligation to deal with the money in a particular way, his use of it in another way can be theft. It is immaterial whether the client retains a proprietary interest. **9–041**

In some cases it may be possible to satisfy s.5(3), but only by showing that the alleged victim had a proprietary interest—in which case there is no need to invoke s.5(3) anyway. In *Floyd v DPP*[69] the defendant was charged with stealing cash which she had collected from colleagues on the understanding that she would give it to a company. It was held that the cash belonged to the company by virtue of s.5(3), since she had received it on the company's account and was under an obligation to the company to hand it over. It was immaterial whether the company had any proprietary interest in it. But it is not clear what sort of obligation the defendant owed to the company. There was no contract between them, and the company was not a party to any contracts she may have made with her colleagues.[70] It is hard to see how she could be under a legal obligation to the company unless she held the cash on trust for it. But if the prosecution has to establish a trust in order to establish the obligation required by s.5(3), it might as well rely on s.5(1). **9–042**

66 [1994] 2 All E.R. 316 at 325 (italics in original).

67 In *Klineberg* [1999] 1 Cr.App.R. 427 it was said that TA 1968, s.5(3) is "essentially a deeming provision by which property or its proceeds 'shall be regarded' as belonging to another, even though, on a strict civil law analysis, it did not". The court thought that *Smith (Adrian)* (May 14, 1997) was an example of a case which fell within s.5(3) although the victims had no proprietary interest in the funds in question; but Sir John Smith pointed out at [1999] Crim. L.R. 417 that s.5(3) had made it unnecessary to decide whether they had such an interest.

68 *Hall* [1973] Q.B. 126.

69 [2000] Crim. L.R. 411.

70 But see now the Contracts (Rights against Third Parties) Act 1999.

9–043 In *Arnold*[71] s.5(3) was applied in a novel way. As part of an agreement under which they acquired franchises in the defendant's business, agents signed bills of exchange provided by him. The bills were valid for 180 days. It was understood that they were intended as security for the agents' obligations under the agreement. When the defendant presented them after 180 days he would transfer the proceeds to the agents, who would provide further bills, and so on. In breach of that understanding, he discounted the bills to a third party, who presented them without having to reimburse the agents, who thus lost their money. The defendant was convicted of stealing the bills. The prosecution successfully argued that, even if the agents had no proprietary interest in them, the bills were deemed to belong to the agents under s.5(3) because of the defendant's contractual obligation to keep them and use them only as security.

> "[P]rovided the obligation is one which clearly requires the recipient of the property to retain and deal with that property or its proceeds in a particular way for the benefit of the transferor, we see no good reason to introduce words of limitation in relation to the interest of the transferor, save that at the time of handing over the property to the recipient he should lawfully be in possession of it in circumstances which give him a legal right vis-à-vis the recipient to require that the property be retained or dealt with in a particular way for the benefit of the transferor.
>
> Nor do we consider that the position must be different where the recipient is throughout the 'true owner' if by agreement (whether made earlier or at the time) he recognises a legal obligation to retain or deal with the property in the interest and/or for the benefit of the transferor, but subsequently, in knowing breach of that obligation, misappropriates it to his own unfettered use."[72]

9–044 One objection to this conclusion is that s.5(1) expressly excludes an equitable interest arising only from an agreement to transfer or grant an interest. Clearly it cannot have been intended that such an interest should fall within s.5(3), or it would have been pointless to exclude it from s.5(1). This suggests that s.5(3) was not intended to apply where the victim's rights over the property are purely contractual. Another objection is that s.5(3) clearly could not have applied if the agents had never had possession of the bill forms, but had merely signed them in the defendant's presence. In that case, the bills would not have been property that he *received from* the agents. It is not obvious why the circumstances in which the bills were signed should be crucial to his liability for misusing them.

9–045 Even if the court was right in holding that the bills belonged to the agents by virtue of s.5(3), there was a further difficulty. The defendant could not be guilty of stealing them unless it was proved that he had intended permanently to deprive the agents of them. It was argued on his behalf that he had no such intention, because when the bills were presented they would be returned to the agents' bank. But it was held that the

[71] [1997] 4 All E.R. 1.
[72] [1997] 4 All E.R. 1 at 9–10.

necessary intention could be deemed to exist by virtue of TA 1968, s.6(1):[73] he had intended to treat the bills as his own, or to dispose of them regardless of the agents' rights.

> "It seems to us that, in a case where a defendant has appropriated a valuable security handed over on the basis of an obligation that he will retain or deal with it for the benefit or to the account of the transferor, there is good reason for the application of section 6(1) if the intention of the transferee at the time of the appropriation is that the document should find its way back to the transferor only after all benefit to the transferor has been lost or removed as a result of its use in breach of such obligation."

This underestimates the difficulties in applying TA 1968, s.6 to property whose existence is potentially detrimental to the person to whom it "belongs". The bills could never have conferred any "benefit" on the agents. They were, in effect, a key to the agents' bank accounts, which the agents had allowed the defendant to hold. The notion that, by using them, he had deprived the agents of their value is bizarre. Moreover it is hard to reconcile with recent authorities holding that a cheque cannot be stolen from its drawer.[74]

Before the property appropriated can be deemed to belong to another person by virtue of TA 1968, s.5(3), two requirements must be satisfied: **9–046**

(1) That property must
    (a) have itself been received by the defendant from that person, or
    (b) have been received by him on that person's account, or
    (c) be the proceeds of other property so received.
(2) He must be under an obligation to that person to retain and deal with the property[75] in a particular way.

Property received from another

To say that a person has "received" property seems to imply that the property existed before it came into his hands. If it does, the drafter overlooked in TA 1968, s.5(3) the same point that he overlooked in s.15. Where funds are (loosely speaking) transferred from one bank account to another, the credit balances in both accounts are property; but they are not the *same* property. According to *Preddy*,[76] therefore, procuring such a transfer by deception was not an offence under s.15. The property obtained by the transferee was not property that had ever belonged to another. Arguably there is a similar difficulty in applying s.5(3) to the chose in action **9–047**

[73] Below, para.9–136.
[74] Below, paras 9–151 *et seq*.
[75] i.e. the property originally received or its proceeds, as the case may be.
[76] [1996] A.C. 815; above, para.4–104.

that is created. The transferee has become the owner of that chose in action, but has he *received* it? It was his as soon as it came into existence.

9–048 This argument, if accepted, would render s.5(3) largely nugatory. A similar point in the law of handling was anticipated by the Theft (Amendment) Act 1996, but this point seems to have been overlooked. It may not matter much, since s.5(3) hardly extends the substantive scope of theft at all. If the defendant has a legal obligation to another person to deal with the property in a particular way, that other person will almost inevitably have a proprietary interest in the property and it will "belong to another" by virtue of s.5(1). If, but for the *Preddy* point, a chose in action would have been deemed to belong to another by virtue of s.5(3), it will nearly always be possible to fall back on s.5(1) by arguing that the chose in action is subject to a trust in favour of the person to whom the s.5(3) obligation is owed.

Property received on another's account

9–049 Where D receives property from X on account of Y—that is, as Y's agent—it may be deemed to belong to Y if D is under the necessary obligation to Y. But D does not receive the property on Y's account merely because he is obliged to account to Y for it, for example because it is obtained by a breach of his fiduciary duty to Y.[77] This is so even if X *thinks* that D is receiving it on Y's account. In *Attorney-General's Reference (No.1 of 1985)* the manager of a tied public house sold his own beer instead of his employers'. The court rejected the argument that the proceeds of the sales could be deemed to belong to the employers by virtue of s.5(3).

> "Whether that argument is correct or not depends on whether [the manager] can properly be said to have received property (i.e., the payment over the counter for the beer he has sold to the customer) 'on account of' the employers. We do not think he can. He received the money on his own account as a result of his private venture. No doubt he is in breach of his contract with the employers; no doubt he is under an obligation to account to the employers at least for the profit he has made out of his venture, but that is a different matter. The fact that A may have to account to B for money he has received from X does not mean necessarily that he received the money on account of B."[78]

Even if the manager *had* received the money on his employers' account, s.5(3) would still not have applied because the court went on to hold that his obligation to account for the money was a purely personal one: he did not hold the money as trustee or otherwise in a fiduciary capacity.[79]

9–050 In *Lamb*,[80] by contrast, a solicitor arranged a remortgage of a client's property and kept part of the advance for himself instead of paying it to a

[77] *Powell v McRae* [1977] Crim. L.R. 571; cf. *Cullum* (1873) L.R. 2 C.C.R. 28.
[78] [1986] Q.B. 491 at 501.
[79] Below, para.9–079.
[80] [1995] Crim. L.R. 77.

bank which held a prior mortgage. It was held that the advance belonged to the bank under s.5(3) even though the solicitor held it on trust for the client. This is a surprising decision. While he may have been obliged to account to the bank for the money,[81] it is questionable whether he received it on the bank's account. Surely he received it on the *client's* account.

Proceeds of property received

"Proceeds" is not defined. The word also appears in TA 1968, s.24(2), which extends references to "stolen goods" so as to include not only the goods originally stolen but also **9–051**

> "(a) any other goods which directly or indirectly represent or have at any time represented the stolen goods in the hands of the thief as being the proceeds of any disposal or realisation of the whole or part of the goods stolen or of goods so representing the stolen goods; and
>
> (b) any other goods which directly or indirectly represent or have at any time represented the stolen goods in the hands of a handler of the stolen goods or any part of them as being the proceeds of any disposal or realisation of the whole or part of the stolen goods handled by him or of goods so representing them."

Section 24(2) has caused difficulty where stolen and non-stolen funds are mixed together in a bank account. In *Attorney-General's Reference (No.4 of 1979)*[82] it was held that funds withdrawn from such an account could be deemed stolen only if it were proved that they represented the stolen goods, and that this could not be proved solely by reference to the intentions of the person receiving them. The court left open the possibility that it might be proved by reference to the intentions of the account-holder in paying the money out of the account. But, since the account-holder seems to have no power to decide which parts of the fund are to be regarded as coming from which source, it is not clear how proof of his intentions might help.

TA 1968, s.24(3) further provides that **9–052**

> "no goods shall be regarded as having continued to be stolen goods after . . . the person from whom they were stolen . . . and any other person claiming through him have . . . ceased as regards those goods to have any right to restitution in respect of the theft".

It seems to follow that the balance of a bank account cannot be regarded as stolen goods by virtue of s.24(2) unless the owner of the goods originally stolen can trace his proprietary interest into the funds in the account. The civil law is not entirely clear as to the circumstances in which he can do this. Section 5(3), however, is subject to no such proviso. Property can therefore

[81] But it is not clear that his undertaking to pay the advance to the bank was legally binding: cf. below, para.9–062.
[82] (1981) 71 Cr.App.R. 341.

be the "proceeds" of the property originally received, within the meaning of s.5(3), even though the owner of the property originally received could not trace his proprietary interest into the new property.

9–053 In *R. v Governor of Brixton Prison, ex p. Levin*[83] the applicant secured the transfer of funds from certain banks' accounts with Citibank by sending unauthorised instructions to Citibank's computer. The funds were transferred to accounts with the Bank of America which had been set up by the applicant's accomplice. It was held that, had these events occurred in England, the applicant would have committed theft when the funds were withdrawn from the Bank of America accounts. The funds in those accounts belonged to the banks whose accounts with Citibank had been wrongly debited, by virtue of s.5(3), even if those banks could not trace the proceeds into the mixed fund. In *Klineberg*[84] it was said to be neither necessary nor desirable to construe "proceeds" in a way that necessitated consideration of "complicated civil concepts such as tracing".

9–054 Provided that some property was "received" from someone,[85] *Preddy*[86] does not present any further difficulty in regarding a chose in action as the proceeds of that property. Funds credited to an account can be the proceeds of funds debited to another account even if they are not the *same* funds.

Obligation to deal with the property in a particular way

9–055 The second requirement for the application of TA 1968, s.5(3) is that the defendant must be under an obligation to retain and deal with the property in a particular way. We consider below

- what it is that the defendant must be obliged to do;
- to whom he must owe this obligation;
- what sort of obligation it must be; and
- the factors that will determine whether it exists.

Obligation to do what?

9–056 The obligation that must exist, before s.5(3) can come into play, is an obligation to retain and deal with the property received, or with its proceeds, in a particular way. It is not sufficient that the defendant has an obligation to provide an agreed consideration for the property he receives, or to account for its value or, where the property is money, for an equivalent sum. There must be an obligation to preserve the property as a separate fund.[87] If the defendant is not obliged to deal with any particular

[83] [1997] Q.B. 65; affirmed at [1997] A.C. 741, but without considering this point.
[84] [1999] 1 Cr.App.R. 427.
[85] i.e. provided the difficulty identified above at para.9–047 does not arise.
[86] [1996] A.C. 815; above, para.4–104.
[87] *Robertson* [1977] Crim. L.R. 629.

property in any particular way, it cannot be unlawful for him to deal with any particular property in some other way. Thus in *Hall*[88] s.5(3) was held not to apply to a travel agent who accepted payment for flights but failed to provide the tickets or refund the money. He was obliged to provide the tickets, but not to keep the money separate for that purpose. Subject to the law of insolvency,[89] he was entitled to use the money in any way he chose. Similarly a fiduciary who misuses his position to make a secret profit does not steal the profit from his principal merely because he is obliged to account for it, but only if he is obliged to keep it separate from his own money in the meantime.[90]

On the other hand the defendant need not be obliged to preserve the property in its original form. An obligation to retain and deal with the *proceeds* of that property is enough. In *Rader*[91] it was regarded as sufficient that the defendant had accepted money on the basis that it would be "put to good use" and returned on a fixed date with "some sort of profit". The jury must have been satisfied that he had been obliged to invest it in the form of an identifiable fund rather than mixing it with his own money. Similarly, s.5(3) may apply to a sum of money even though the recipient is expected to put it in a bank account. **9–057**

Nor is it fatal to an argument based on s.5(3) that the recipient of the money is entitled to put it in his own account rather than a separate one, such as a client account.[92] In *Davidge v Bunnett*[93] the defendant stole money entrusted to her by her flat-mates to pay the gas bill. The money belonged to the others by virtue of s.5(3), even though the defendant would have been entitled to pay it into her own bank account (had she had one) and to pay the bill with her own cheque. Her obligation in that event would presumably have been to pay the bill within a reasonable time and in the meantime to keep the account in credit at least to the extent of the others' contributions, thus keeping the fund in existence (albeit as an unidentifiable part of the larger fund represented by the credit balance). Had she been entitled to draw on the account for her own purposes so as to reduce the balance below the sum contributed by the others (or to pay that sum into an account that was already overdrawn, so that the fund would be automatically depleted), it would seem that s.5(3) could not have applied. **9–058**

In *Re Kumar*[94] the applicant was the proprietor of a travel agency business, ARG. By agreement with IATA, ARG was permitted to sell flight tickets on behalf of IATA members. Money received from the sale of such tickets was to be held on trust and transferred to IATA by direct debit from ARG's account on the 15th of each month. The account became overdrawn **9–059**

[88] [1973] Q.B. 126.
[89] Below, Ch.15.
[90] *Att-Gen's Reference (No.1 of 1985)* [1986] Q.B. 491; below, para.9–079.
[91] [1992] Crim. L.R. 663.
[92] cf. *Banyard* [1958] Crim. L.R. 49 (stockbroker); *Yule* [1964] 1 Q.B. 5 (solicitor).
[93] [1984] Crim. L.R. 297.
[94] [2000] Crim. L.R. 504.

and, because ARG had no credit facility, the bank refused to make the direct debits. Turner J. held that it could safely be inferred that the applicant had committed theft. Presumably the obligation owed to IATA was to deal with the receipts from each transaction in such a way as to ensure that they were transferred to IATA on the 15th of the following month. As long as the account was in credit, all ARG had to do was pay the money into the account. But once the account became overdrawn, the effect of paying the money into the account would be to diminish ARG's indebtedness to the bank rather than getting the money to IATA. So any such payment would itself have been a breach of trust and, if dishonest, theft. In these circumstances the applicant's obligation to IATA was either to hand the money over to IATA immediately or to find some other home for it until the 15th of the next month. Since he had done neither of these things, it could be assumed that he had stolen the money.

Obligation owed to whom?

9–060 It is not enough that the defendant is under an obligation to deal with the property or its proceeds in a particular way. That obligation must be owed to the person from whom or on whose account he receives the property, and to whom it is sought to establish that the property belongs. If a professional association requires its members to keep client accounts separate from their general trading accounts, this does not in itself give the clients any right to have their money segregated. The obligation owed by the members may be owed only to the association, or to each other. But if it is the usual practice in a particular trade or profession to keep client accounts, a contract with a particular client may be construed as including an implied term that that practice is to be followed; and in that case s.5(3) will apply. Similarly, professional people who are required by statute to keep client accounts are probably under an implied contractual obligation to their clients to comply with the legislation.

9–061 The corollary of this is that s.5(3) operates only against the person who receives the property and incurs the obligation to deal with it in a particular way, not against a third party. If A pays money to B in such circumstances that B owns it beneficially but is obliged to A to use it for a particular purpose, B can steal the money by virtue of s.5(3). If *C* is charged with stealing the money, s.5(3) does not apply; but it does not need to, because the money does in fact belong to a person other than C, namely B.

Legal and unenforceable obligations

9–062 The "obligation" referred to in TA 1968, s.5(3) must in general be a legally enforceable obligation. It is not sufficient that the defendant does in practice keep certain funds separate, nor even that the person from whom he receives them requests or expects him to do so:[95] if he is not legally

[95] cf. *Cuffin* (1922) 127 L.T. 564.

obliged to do so, s.5(3) does not apply.[96] It may therefore be necessary to determine the position in civil law.[97]

It was at one time thought that it is for the jury to decide what amounts to an obligation for this purpose,[98] but the correct procedure was laid down in *Mainwaring*: 9–063

> "Whether or not an obligation arises is a matter of law, because an obligation must be a legal obligation. But a legal obligation arises only in certain circumstances, and in many cases the circumstances cannot be known until the facts have been established. It is for the jury, not the judge, to establish the facts, if they are in dispute.
>
> What, in our judgment, a judge ought to do is this: if the facts relied upon by the prosecution are in dispute he should direct the jury to make their findings on the facts, and then say to them: 'If you find the facts to be such-and-such, then I direct you as a matter of law that a legal obligation arose to which section 5(3) applies.'"[99]

The requirement that the obligation be a legally enforceable one must be qualified in one respect. In *Meech*[100] the defendant was charged with stealing the proceeds of a cheque which had been entrusted to him by one McCord. McCord had obtained the cheque by means of a forged instrument, but Meech did not know this when he accepted the cheque. He was held to have been under an obligation to McCord to deal with the proceeds as requested. It was immaterial that any attempt by McCord to enforce that obligation could have been met with a plea of illegality. While the reasoning is obscure, the court seems to have accepted that an obligation tainted by illegality would not normally suffice. The crucial point was that Meech did not at first *know* that the obligation he was undertaking was tainted by illegality. This cannot be right. Either an obligation tainted by illegality is the kind of obligation contemplated by s.5(3) or it is not. If it is not, it cannot make any difference that the defendant thinks he is under the kind of obligation that is. 9–064

Discharged obligations

Even if Meech was properly regarded as having initially been under an "obligation" on the ground that he did not then know how the cheque had been obtained, this would not justify the decision, since he had discovered the truth before he appropriated the proceeds. But this was held to be irrelevant. In the court's view, 9–065

[96] *Cullen* (1974), cited in J.C. Smith, *The Law of Theft*, 8th edn (1997), para.2–76, was probably wrong in holding that a man's mistress was under a legal obligation to use a housekeeping allowance for the purpose for which it was given to her: cf. *Balfour v Balfour* [1919] 2 K.B. 571. In *Davidge v Bunnett* [1984] Crim. L.R. 297, by contrast, the parties were not cohabitants but only flat-mates, and a legal obligation probably did exist.

[97] See *Breaks* [1998] Crim. L.R. 349, where the trial judge wrongly ruled that s.5(3) made it unnecessary to examine the civil law.

[98] *Hall* [1973] Q.B. 126; *Hayes* (1977) 64 Cr.App.R. 82.

[99] (1981) 74 Cr.App.R. 99 at 107. In *Dubar* [1994] 1 W.L.R. 1484 it was confirmed that the *Mainwaring* direction is correct.

[100] [1974] Q.B. 549.

> "The opening words of section 5(3) clearly look to the time of the creation of or the acceptance of the obligation by the bailee and not to the time of performance by him of the obligation so created and accepted by him."[101]

This seems to mean that, once the necessary obligation comes into existence, s.5(3) continues to apply even if the obligation is discharged before the property is appropriated. This too cannot be right. Section 5(3) requires the defendant to be under the obligation at the time when the property is alleged to belong to another (i.e. the time of the dishonest appropriation).

9–066 In *Brewster*[102] the defendant received money on his clients' account, but it appeared that the clients might have subsequently agreed that he could treat the money as his own. The fiduciary relationship would in that case have been converted by agreement into one of debtor and creditor.[103] The reasoning in *Meech* would imply that Brewster could steal the money anyway, because, having once "belonged" to his clients by virtue of s.5(3), it continued to do so even after the relevant obligation had ceased to exist. But it was held to be a question for the jury whether the clients had in fact agreed to abandon their rights in this respect. It was apparently assumed that, if they had, the conviction of theft could not be supported. It is submitted that this must be right.

Determining whether the obligation exists

9–067 Whether the required obligation exists in particular circumstances is a question of law.[104] It may involve the construction of legislation.[105] More often, the property will have been received by the defendant in pursuance of a written or oral agreement between himself and the person from whom (or on whose account)[106] he receives it. The extent of his obligations will then depend on the terms of that agreement. If the agreement expressly deals with the point, the question is one of construction. If not, the question is whether it deals with the point by implication, and if so to what effect. The law of contract recognises three main grounds for incorporating into an agreement a term on which the parties have not expressly agreed:

[101] [1974] Q.B. 549 at 555.

[102] (1979) 69 Cr.App.R. 375.

[103] cf. *Wilsons and Furness-Leyland Line Ltd v British and Continental Shipping Co Ltd* (1907) 23 T.L.R. 397; *Neste Oy v Lloyds Bank plc (The "Tiiskeri", "Nestegas" and "Enskeri")* [1983] 2 Lloyd's Rep. 658.

[104] *Clowes (No.2)* [1994] 2 All E.R. 316.

[105] e.g. *DPP v Huskinson* [1988] Crim. L.R. 620, where it was argued (unsuccessfully) that a recipient of housing benefit was legally obliged to use it directly for the payment of rent.

[106] Or both, in which case the necessary obligation may be imposed by either. The point seems to have been overlooked in *Lewis v Lethbridge* [1987] Crim. L.R. 59, where money collected for charity was held not to have been stolen because the charity's rules did not require collectors to hand over the actual notes and coins collected. This decision was overruled in *Wain* [1995] 2 Cr.App.R. 660 on the basis that those giving the money could be taken to have intended to make the collector a trustee. See also H.H. Judge Wiggs, "Theft from Charity Collections" [1999] 8 Archbold News 5.

- that the agreement is of such a kind that the term is implied as a matter of law (such as the terms implied in a contract for the sale of goods);
- that the term is implied by the custom of the trade or market in which the agreement is made; or
- that the parties can be presumed to have intended to include the term, because without it the agreement would lack business efficacy.

Terms implied by law

If the transaction is of such a kind that a particular obligation is implied as a matter of law, there can be no doubt that that obligation existed in the case in question. But it may be less clear whether the defendant *knew* that it existed, and how much difference it makes if he did not.[107] 9–068

Terms implied by custom

The extent of the defendant's obligations may also be affected by the established practices of the particular trade or market in which he operates. 9–069

> "A person who deals in a particular market must be taken to deal according to the custom of that market, and he who directs another to make a contract at a particular place, must be taken as intending, that the contract may be made according to the usage of that place."[108]

Subject to an important qualification referred to below, this is so whether or not both parties are aware of the custom in question.[109] The term is implied not on the basis that the parties know of the custom, but because they are presumed to intend to comply with whatever the prevailing custom may be.

It would seem to follow that a client who engages an intermediary to act for him, expecting the intermediary to act as his agent and to be subject to the fiduciary obligations inherent in that position, may find this expectation defeated by an accepted practice which allows intermediaries of that class to deal with their clients as principals and at arm's length. In *Limako BY v H. Hentz & Co Inc*[110] such a practice was found to exist in relation to commodity brokers, and was held to preclude a relationship of agent and principal between broker and client. Earlier authority to the contrary[111] was 9–070

[107] See above, para.2–076.

[108] *Bayliffe v Butterworth* (1847) 1 Ex. 425 at 429, *per* Alderson B.

[109] *Sutton v Tatham* (1839) 10 Ad. & El. 27; *Pollock v Stables* (1848) 12 Q.B. 765. *Bartlett v Pentland* (1830) 10 B. & C. 760 appears to be authority to the contrary, but can be explained on the ground that the custom was unreasonable: cf. *Sweeting v Pearce* (1861) 9 C.B.(N.S.) 534.

[110] [1979] 2 Lloyd's Rep. 23.

[111] *Woodward v Wolfe* [1936] 3 All E.R. 529; *E. Bailey & Co Ltd v Balholm Securities Ltd* [1973] 2 Lloyd's Rep. 404.

not referred to. In the light of this decision a prosecution of commodity brokers for deception and conspiracy to defraud was halted on the ground that they had owed their clients no duty of disclosure.[112] It seems to follow that client money in the hands of such a broker will not normally "belong to another".[113]

9–071 However, a contracting party is not bound by a custom of which he is unaware unless it is reasonable;[114] and there is high authority for the proposition that a custom which allows a broker to act as a principal vis-à-vis his client is not a reasonable one. In *Robinson v Mollett*[115] brokers were engaged to purchase tallow, but, in accordance with the usual practice of the London market, bought in their own names and offered the client the required quantity out of their own purchases. The client lived in Liverpool and knew nothing of this practice. The House of Lords held that he was under no obligation to accept the tallow, because the custom was inconsistent with the relationship of broker and client. It was therefore unreasonable, and was not binding on a party without notice of it.

9–072 *Limako v Hentz* is not inconsistent with this decision, since the client in that case was a dealer with experience of the market and was assumed to have known of the practice in question. Moreover it was not the broker who was relying on the practice but the client. But in the light of *Robinson v Mollett* it seems that the relationship between broker and client is one of agency unless there is an established usage to the contrary *and* the client can be taken to know of that usage, whether through previous dealings on the market in question or from information provided by the broker. In the absence of such experience or information, a small investor on the commodity markets may be able to argue that his broker is in a fiduciary position, and a broker who misappropriates funds received from such a client may be guilty of theft.

Terms presumably intended by the parties

9–073 If the term in question cannot be implied by reference either to law or to custom, its inclusion can be justified only on the basis that the parties must have thought it so obvious that there was no need to make express provision for it. The classic formulation of the test is that of MacKinnon L.J.:

> "Prima facie that which in any contract is left to be implied and need not be expressed is something so obvious that it goes without saying; so that, if while the parties were making their bargain an officious bystander were to suggest some express provision for it in their agreement, they would testily suppress him with a common 'Oh, of course'."[116]

[112] Trial of Sir Bruce Tuck and others, *The Times*, January 15, 1983.

[113] Unless, perhaps, he belongs to a professional association which requires client accounts to be kept: above, para.9–060.

[114] *Sweeting v Pearce* (1861) 9 C.B.(N.S.) 534; *Pearson v Scott* (1878) 9 Ch. D. 198.

[115] (1874) L.R. 7 H.L. 802.

[116] *Shirlaw v Southern Foundries (1926) Ltd* [1939] 2 K.B. 206 at 227.

9–074 In *McHugh (Christopher)*[117] a financial consultant and intermediary was charged with stealing funds paid to him by his clients. The question was whether he was obliged to deal with the funds in a particular way, or was entitled to use them for his own purposes and obliged only to account for them at a later date. The former obligation could only be based on the presumed intentions of the parties. The judge therefore explained the "officious bystander" test in terms that were unusually lucid and accurate.[118] The Court of Appeal thought that the direction "could well be criticised as an exposition of the civil law of contract" (though without saying what was wrong with it) and suggested a simpler test.

> "In our judgment, it would have been better if, instead of referring to the 'officious bystander', the learned judge had simply told the jury that section 5(3) would only apply if they were sure that the appellant and his client both clearly understood that the latter's investment or its proceeds were to be kept separate from the appellant's own money and that of his business."[119]

This test may be easier to explain than that of the officious bystander, but the court does not appear to have realised that it is harder to satisfy. A term can be implied under the officious bystander test where it has not in fact occurred to the parties that the term is necessary, but, if asked, they would readily agree that it goes without saying. There is no need to show that they "clearly understood" what was implicitly agreed. But, according to *McHugh*, this is necessary for the purposes of s.5(3).

9–075 In *Wills* it was said that "Whether a person is under an obligation to deal with property in a particular way can only be established by proving that he had knowledge of that obligation".[120] This confuses the question of whether the defendant *is* under an obligation with that of whether he *knows* he is: clearly he may be subject to an obligation of which he knows nothing, for example because the obligation is imposed by law or by custom, or (as in *Wills*) because it was undertaken by an agent on his behalf. Admittedly it would be contrary to principle to hold him criminally responsible for breach of such an obligation, because, even if the actus reus were proved, he would lack mens rea. But this does not explain why it should be necessary to prove that the other party understood the position too.

9–076 Often the relationship between the parties will give rise to a rebuttable presumption one way or the other. Property transferred between parties dealing at arm's length, for example as an advance payment for goods or services, will normally become the property of the transferee to treat as his own, even if it is given to him for a specific purpose such as the purchase of necessary equipment.[121] But this is subject to any agreement to the contrary,

[117] (1993) 97 Cr.App.R. 335.

[118] The test is commonly supposed to be concerned with what the hypothetical officious bystander would have thought, rather than how the parties would have answered his question. The judge in *McHugh* avoided this mistake.

[119] (1993) 97 Cr.App.R. 335 at 339–340.

[120] (1991) 92 Cr.App.R. 297 at 301.

[121] *Jones* (1948) 33 Cr.App.R. 11; cf. *Hughes* [1956] Crim. L.R. 835.

for example where goods are delivered on a "sale or return" basis[122] or subject to a *Romalpa* clause.[123] If, on the other hand, the defendant receives the property by virtue of an existing fiduciary relationship, such as one of agency, he will normally be a fiduciary (if not a trustee or bailee) of property received from his principal for the purpose of dealings with third parties, and of property received from third parties in the course of such dealings.[124] But if the relationship is a continuing one and the agent is expected merely to keep a running account, remitting the balance due at periodic intervals, this principle may be overridden by commercial convenience[125] and the agent treated as a debtor and not a trustee.[126] It is ultimately a matter of the construction of the contract.

9–077 These considerations may in turn raise the question of whether the parties *were* dealing as fiduciary and principal or at arm's length; but again this is essentially a matter of construction. The fact that an intermediary is described as an agent is not conclusive, since that term is commonly applied to a number of relationships which do not amount to agency in the strict sense. More important are the terms of the contract, such as those that determine the mode of accounting required. If, for example, the intermediary accounts to his client only for goods *delivered* to him, he is probably a purchaser in his own right.[127] If he accounts for the goods as sold, he is probably an agent—even if his commission depends on the price he obtains.[128] The characteristics of fiduciary relationships are examined further in Ch.6.

SECRET PROFITS

9–078 Where property is acquired in such circumstances that it would be inequitable for the legal owner to retain it beneficially, a constructive trust may be imposed, with the effect that in equity the property belongs to someone else. For present purposes this doctrine is most likely to arise in the context of fiduciaries who use their position to make a profit at the expense of those to whom their duty is owed. Such conduct would probably be charged today as fraud by abuse of position.[129] But is it theft? It is sometimes said that anyone who misuses property (or even information) entrusted to him, in such circumstances that he holds it in a fiduciary capacity, is a constructive trustee of any resulting profit. If this were so, the

[122] *John Towle & Co v White* (1873) 29 L.T. 78.

[123] i.e. one which prevents the buyer from acquiring title until the price is paid: *Aluminium Industrie Vaassen BV v Romalpa Aluminium Ltd* [1976] 1 W.L.R. 676.

[124] *Burdick v Garrick* (1870) L.R. 5 Ch. App. 233; *Re Strachan, ex p. Cooke* (1876) 4 Ch. D. 123; *Re Cotton, ex p. Cooke* (1913) 108 L.T. 310.

[125] *New Zealand & Australian Land Co v Watson* (1881) 7 Q.B.D. 374 at 382, *per* Bramwell L.J.

[126] *Kirkham v Peel* (1880) 43 L.T. 171; *King v Hutton* [1900] 2 Q.B. 504; cf. *Robertson* [1977] Crim. L.R. 629.

[127] *John Towle & Co v White* (1873) 29 L.T. 78 at 79, *per* Lord Selborne L.C.

[128] *Re Smith, ex p. Bright* (1879) 10 Ch. D. 566.

[129] Above, Ch.6.

person thus defrauded would have an equitable interest in the proceeds, and on a literal reading of TA 1968, s.5(1) they would belong to him. It would follow that subsequent dealings with them might amount to theft, even if the making of the profit were not in itself an offence. However, the authorities for this theory consist largely of dicta in cases where the issue was not whether the fiduciary was a *trustee* of the profit but whether he was liable to account for it at all.[130]

As far as the law of theft is concerned, the theory was rejected in *Attorney-General's Reference (No.1 of 1985)*.[131] The manager of a public house, employed by the brewery to sell only their beer, fraudulently sold his own beer and kept the proceeds. It was held that he had not stolen the proceeds because they did not belong to the brewery. He was liable to account for his profit, but he was not a trustee of it. There were two grounds for this conclusion. **9–079**

The first ground was that the making of a secret profit does not give rise to a constructive trust at all. On this point the court followed *Lister & Co v Stubbs*,[132] where it was held that a fiduciary who accepts a bribe does not hold it on trust but is merely liable to account for it.[133] **9–080**

> "It seems to us that the draftsmen of the Act of 1968 must have had that decision in mind when considering the wording of section 5. Had they intended to bring within the ambit of the Theft Act 1968 a whole new area of behaviour which had previously not been considered to be criminal, they would, in our judgment, have used much more explicit words than those which are to be found in section 5. Nor do we think it permissible to distinguish that decision by saying that bribes are in a different category from such transactions as those in the instant case. There is, in our view, no distinction in principle between the two."[134]

Lister & Co v Stubbs had been widely criticised, and was not followed by the Privy Council in *Attorney-General of Hong Kong v Reid*.[135] While *Lister* has not yet been overruled, *Reid* now seems to be accepted as representing English law.[136] If bribes *are* held on trust, it arguably follows that bribes and other secret profits "belong to another" within the meaning of TA 1968 **9–081**

130 e.g. *Parker v McKenna* (1874) L.R. 10 Ch. App. 96; *Cook v Deeks* [1916] 1 A.C. 554; *Phipps v Boardman* [1967] 2 A.C. 46.
131 [1986] Q.B. 491.
132 (1890) 45 Ch. D. 1.
133 And therefore does not steal it: *Powell v MacRae* [1977] Crim. L.R. 571.
134 [1986] Q.B. 491 at 505.
135 [1994] 1 A.C. 324.
136 *Ocular Sciences Ltd v Aspect Vision Care Ltd* [1997] R.P.C. 289, 412–413; *Fyffes Group Ltd v Templeman* [2000] 2 Lloyd's Rep 643; *Daraydan Holdings Ltd v Solland International Ltd* [2004] EWHC 622; [2005] Ch. 119; *Ultraframe Ltd v Fielding* [2005] EWHC 1638 at [1490]. The Criminal Division of the Court of Appeal would probably follow *Reid* too: cf. *James* [2006] EWCA Crim 14; [2006] Cr.App.R. 29 (p.440), following the Privy Council's decision in *Att-Gen for Jersey v Holley* [2005] UKPC 23; [2005] 2 A.C. 580 rather than the House of Lords' decision in *DPP v Morgan Smith* [2001] 1 A.C. 146. On the application of the doctrine of precedent in such circumstances, see *Re Spectrum Plus Ltd* [2005] UKHL 41; [2005] 2 A.C. 680 at [163], *per* Baroness Hale.

after all. But in the *Attorney-General's Reference* the court thought that those who framed TA 1968 must have intended to exclude bribes, and therefore other secret profits, because the law was then thought to be as stated in *Lister*. If that was the intention, it seems immaterial that it was based on a mistaken view of the civil law. If, on the other hand, Parliament intended only to incorporate the relevant rules of the law of property, *whatever they might be*, the demise of *Lister* invalidates the first ground of the decision.

9–082 The second ground was that, even if a secret profit *could* be subject to a constructive trust and therefore property "belonging to another" (which in the light of *Reid* it probably can), this was not so on the facts.

> "A [the manager] used the employers' property and his own money to make a private profit in breach of contract. He received from customers sums of money which represented in part the cost of the beer he had bought and in part possible profit for which he was accountable to the employers. This profit element, assuming it existed, never became a separate piece of property of which A could be trustee. It remained part of a mixed fund. Therefore there never was a moment at which A was trustee of a definite fund. It follows that there never was a moment when the employers had any proprietary interest in any of the money. The money did not belong to another. There was therefore no theft."[137]

9–083 This reasoning underestimates the flexibility of equity, which can accommodate a trust of an unidentifiable part of a fund.[138] But the decision was approved by the House of Lords in *Cooke*[139] (before *Reid*), and probably owes less to the subtleties of the civil law than to the court's instinctive reluctance to categorise the defendant's conduct as theft.

> "No less difficulty would arise in the proof of dishonesty and guilty intent. A might very well say, and say truthfully, that he knew that he was breaking the terms of his contract, but the idea that he might be stealing from his employers the profit element in this transaction had never occurred to him. There are topics of conversation more popular in public houses than the finer points of the equitable doctrine of the constructive trust.
>
> It is said in answer to that objection that the employers could, by giving in advance the necessary warnings, instruct their servants what the true meaning of the Theft Act 1968 is. That seems to us to be a good illustration of the objectionability of the whole proposition. If something is so abstruse and so far from the understanding of ordinary people as to what constitutes stealing, it should not amount to stealing."[140]

9–084 It has been objected that the difficulty of proving dishonesty was apparently no obstacle in *Cooke*,[141] where convictions of conspiracy to defraud were upheld on facts essentially similar to those of the *Attorney-*

[137] [1986] Q.B. 491 at 506.
[138] Jill Martin [1987] Conv. 209 at 211.
[139] [1986] A.C. 909.
[140] [1986] Q.B. 491 at 506–507.
[141] [1986] A.C. 909.

General's Reference.[142] However, theft requires an intention permanently to deprive of the property the person to whom it belongs. There can be no such intention if the defendant does not realise that the property may belong to another at all. Conspiracy to defraud, by contrast, requires only an intent to deprive another "of something to which he is or would or might but for the perpetration of the fraud be entitled".[143] It need not involve an intention to deprive another of property belonging to him.

It is true that English law, unlike American, regards the constructive trust as a substantive proprietary concept and not merely a remedial device. Property subject to such a trust is, literally, property "belonging to another". There is nevertheless a real distinction between a fiduciary who misappropriates property entrusted to him and one who merely obtains a profit which, as a matter of law, is deemed to belong to his principal. In the civil law there may be good reasons to treat both cases alike. In particular, the imposition of a trust will give the principal preferential status in the event of the fiduciary's insolvency. But such considerations have little relevance to the purposes served by the criminal law. **9–085**

Attorney-General's Reference (No.1 of 1985) does not rule out the possibility of a theft charge based on a constructive trust of the property appropriated. The case was concerned only with the defendant's making of a secret profit by misusing property entrusted to him. It would be otherwise if the monies in question represented the *proceeds* of the property entrusted to him. **9–086**

> "There is a clear and important difference between on the one hand a person misappropriating specific property with which he has been entrusted, and on the other hand a person in a fiduciary position who uses that position to make a secret profit for which he will be held accountable. Whether the former is within section 5, we do not have to decide."[144]

The former case clearly can be within TA 1968, s.5(1), s.5(3) or both. In *Daraydan Holdings Ltd v Solland International Ltd*[145] Lawrence Collins J. distinguished *Lister & Co v Stubbs* and held that a bribe was held on trust for the claimants because it was reflected in the price paid by them under a contract: it had in effect been paid by them. Presumably it would also be property belonging to them for the purposes of a theft charge.

THE NEED FOR DISHONESTY

By proving that property held in a fiduciary capacity belongs to another, either in equity or by virtue of TA 1968, s.5(3), the prosecution establishes only one element of the offence. It must also prove that the defendant's **9–087**

[142] J.C. Smith, *The Law of Theft*, 8th edn (1997), para.2–79.
[143] *Scott v Metropolitan Police Commissioner* [1975] A.C. 819 at 839, *per* Viscount Dilhorne.
[144] [1986] Q.B. 491 at 503.
[145] [2004] EWHC 62; [2005] Ch. 119.

appropriation of the property was dishonest. The fact that he subsequently decided not to replace the property, or found himself unable to do so, is not sufficient.

> "[I]t is . . . essential . . . that dishonesty should be present at the time of appropriation. We are alive to the fact that to establish this could present great (and maybe insuperable) difficulties when sums are on different dates drawn from a general account. Nevertheless, they must be overcome if the Crown is to succeed."[146]

9–088 It is apparently unnecessary to prove that the defendant knew the property belonged to another;[147] but it must be proved that he did not believe he was entitled to appropriate the property, and that he intended permanently to deprive of the property the person to whom it belonged. Arguably this is a distinction without a difference.

PROPERTY GOT BY ANOTHER'S MISTAKE

9–089 TA 1968, s.5(4) provides:

> "Where a person gets property by another's mistake, and is under an obligation to make restoration (in whole or in part) of the property or its proceeds or of the value thereof, then to the extent of that obligation the property or proceeds shall be regarded (as against him) as belonging to the person entitled to restoration, and an intention not to make restoration shall be regarded accordingly as an intention to deprive that person of the property or proceeds."

This provision is directed at the person who obtains property as a result of someone else's mistake (such as an employee who is overpaid due to a clerical error) and keeps it. Like s.5(3), it adds little to s.5(1), because where its requirements are satisfied the original owner of the property will almost inevitably retain at least an equitable interest anyway.[148] Its relevance to fraud is limited. If the property is obtained dishonestly, the obtaining will be theft; there is no need to treat subsequent dealings with the property as theft too.

9–090 In *R. v Governor of Brixton Prison, ex p. Levin*[149] s.5(4) was held to apply to funds which had been obtained as a result of the applicant making unauthorised transfers from other people's accounts with Citibank. It was said that the funds were obtained by Citibank's mistaken belief that the account-holders had authorised the transfers, and the applicant was under an obligation to restore the funds or their proceeds or value. So s.5(4) applied, and the applicant committed theft when the funds were withdrawn.

146 *Hall* [1973] Q.B. 126 at 131; applied in *Hayes* (1977) 64 Cr.App.R. 82.
147 Above, paras 2–075 *et seq.*
148 *Shadrokh-Cigari* [1988] Crim. L.R. 465; *Webster* [2006] All E.R. (D) 150.
149 [1997] Q.B. 65; affirmed at [1997] A.C. 741, but without considering this point.

But this conclusion was unnecessary to the decision, since it was held that s.5(3) also applied. It was also a dubious conclusion on the facts, since the applicant had merely sent unauthorised instructions to Citibank's computer. Citibank was not *mistaken* at all.

APPROPRIATION

The defendant must have "appropriated" the property in question. The Oxford English Dictionary defines "appropriate" as "to take possession of for one's own, to take to oneself". An appropriation of property in the ordinary sense would involve taking possession of it, or obtaining ownership of it, or otherwise dealing with it in such a way as to deprive its owner of it and to make it effectively one's own. But TA 1968, s.3(1) begins by giving the word an extended meaning: **9–091**

> "Any assumption by a person of the rights of an owner amounts to an appropriation . . .."

This seems wide enough to cover any act falling within the word's ordinary meaning. Its importance lies in the fact that it includes others too. There are at least two kinds of conduct which, while arguably not amounting to appropriation in the ordinary sense, appear to be caught by TA 1968, s.3(1): **9–092**

- an act which infringes the owner's rights over his property without itself depriving him of it, and
- an act which does not infringe the owner's rights at all.

ACTS NOT DEPRIVING THE OWNER OF THE PROPERTY

The "rights of an owner" are the rights that an owner has by virtue of his ownership—the right to possess the property, to use it, to dispose of it, to destroy it and so on. One cannot do all these things at once. What then is an assumption of the rights of an owner? Arguably this means an assumption of *all* the rights of an owner—an act which in itself deprives the owner of the property and makes it de facto the defendant's. This would fit the ordinary meaning of the word "appropriate". But it seems that the expression is much wider than that. In *Morris*[150] the House of Lords conceded that the narrower construction might have some force if the phrase were read literally and out of context, but held it to be inconsistent with expressions used elsewhere in TA 1968.[151] The prosecution could show **9–093**

[150] [1984] A.C. 320.

[151] viz. "any later assumption of a right" later in s.3(1); "no later assumption by him of rights" in s.3(2); and s.2(1)(a), which provides that an appropriation of property belonging to another is not dishonest if done in the belief that the defendant has in law the right to deprive the other of it. The relevance of this last provision is not apparent.

an appropriation by showing that the defendant had assumed *any* of the rights of an owner.[152] In *Gomez*[153] Lord Keith, with whom the majority agreed, said that this was "undoubtedly right". So an appropriation need not itself deprive the property's owner of the property—though it is not theft unless done with the *intention* of depriving him of the property, either immediately or at some later stage.

9–094 This interpretation is hard to reconcile with the Court of Appeal's decision in *Gallasso*,[154] an appeal heard on the day that judgment was given in *Gomez*. The defendant was responsible for the care of mentally handicapped adults, and used cheques payable to one of them to open building society trust accounts of which the patient was the named beneficiary. She was convicted of stealing one of the cheques, on the basis that her intention had been to withdraw at least some of the balance for her own benefit. On her application for leave to appeal it was successfully argued that this conduct could not amount to an appropriation, even after *Gomez*. *Gomez* had established that the patient's consent would not in itself prevent the defendant's conduct from being an appropriation.[155] But there still had to be an assumption of the rights of an owner. The defendant had not assumed the rights of an owner because, by paying the cheque into a trust account in the patient's favour, she was not assuming the owner's rights but affirming them. The court seems to have thought that she could appropriate the cheque by paying it into an account in her own name (even with the owner's consent), but not by paying it into an account in the owner's name. There is force in this distinction. But it resembles the theory that an appropriation must be an assumption of *all* the rights of the owner, an assertion of dominion over the property; and that theory was rejected in *Morris* and *Gomez*.

9–095 An alternative explanation of *Gallasso* is that the defendant's conduct did not affect the owner's rights at all, since he was still entitled to the sum for which the cheque was drawn. But, even if it were correct that an act which leaves intangible property unaffected cannot be an appropriation of that property,[156] the owner's rights were not unaffected by the applicant's conduct: his legal chose in action against the drawer of the cheque was extinguished. It was replaced by an equitable interest in a chose in action for the same sum against the building society, but that was a different item of property and (because of the risk of a breach of trust) not necessarily worth as much. It is submitted that *Gallasso* cannot stand with *Gomez* and must be regarded as wrongly decided.

[152] [1984] A.C. 320 at 332, *per* Lord Roskill, with whom the other members of the House agreed. Lord Roskill actually referred to an assumption of any of the rights of *the* owner (sc. of the particular property in question); but TA 1968, s.3(1) refers to the rights of *an* owner (sc. in general). The slip was corrected by Lord Keith in *Gomez* [1993] A.C. 442.

[153] [1993] A.C. 442.

[154] [1993] Crim. L.R. 459.

[155] Below, para.9–123.

[156] Which it is not: below, paras 9–096 *et seq.*

ACTS NOT AFFECTING THE PROPERTY

9–096 A further question is whether an act can be an appropriation if, though in one sense an assumption of the rights of an owner, it does not *infringe* the owner's rights because it does not affect the property in any way. It seems that intangible property, at least, can be appropriated in such a way. This view was at first rejected in *Kohn*, where a company director was held to have stolen the company's bank balance by drawing cheques for his own purposes. The court said:

> "The cheque is the means by which the theft of this property is achieved. The completion of the theft does not take place until the transaction has gone through to completion."[157]

In other words the mere drawing of the cheque was not enough. This passage was applied in *Doole*,[158] where the defendant gave instructions for the transfer of funds from a security deposit account (intended for eventual payment to a creditor) to another account held by him. It was held that there was no appropriation of the debt because there was no evidence that the account was actually debited. It had not been argued that the instruction to transfer the funds was itself an appropriation.[159]

9–097 In *Navvabi* it was pointed out that the dictum in *Kohn* was obiter,[160] and in *Wille*[161] that it had been criticised as being inconsistent with the wording of TA 1968, s.3(1). The point was left open "as there appears to be force in the criticism",[162] and it was held that a credit balance could be stolen by means of a cheque which the bank had no mandate to honour. The jury had been directed that

> "it matters not that the bank were acting contrary to the mandate, that is wholly irrelevant for this purpose, it is the drawing and the issuing of the cheque without authority which constitutes the appropriation."

The Court of Appeal said that it was not possible to improve on this direction.

9–098 Similarly, in *Chan Man-Sin v Attorney-General of Hong Kong*[163] the Privy Council held that the defendant had stolen a company's credit balance by forging cheques which were honoured by the bank. In this case, unlike *Kohn*, the unauthorised cheques were not binding on the company and did not affect its rights against the bank.[164] Therefore, it was argued, the

[157] (1979) 69 Cr.App.R. 395 at 407.

[158] [1985] Crim. L.R. 450.

[159] *R. v Governor of Pentonville Prison, ex p. Osman* (1990) 90 Cr.App.R. 281 at 296.

[160] (1986) 83 Cr.App.R. 271 at 275; see also *R. v Governor of Pentonville Prison, ex p. Osman* (1990) 90 Cr.App.R. 281 at 295.

[161] (1987) 86 Cr.App.R. 296.

[162] (1987) 86 Cr.App.R. 296 at 301.

[163] [1988] 1 W.L.R. 196.

[164] *Tai Hing Cotton Mill Ltd v Liu Chong Hing Bank Ltd* [1986] A.C. 80.

defendant had neither appropriated the company's property nor had any intention of depriving the company of it.[165] It was held that this was an appropriation within the extended meaning given to that term by the Hong Kong counterpart of TA 1968, s.3(1), because it was an "assumption . . . of the rights of an owner".

> "The owner of the chose in action consisting of a credit with his bank or a contractual right to draw on an account has, clearly, the right as owner to draw by means of a properly completed negotiable instrument or order to pay and it is, in their Lordships' view, beyond argument that one who draws, presents and negotiates a cheque on a particular bank account is assuming the rights of the owner of the credit in the account or (as the case may be) of the pre-negotiated right to draw on the account up to the agreed figure. . .
>
> It is, in their Lordships' view, entirely immaterial that the end result of the transaction may be a legal nullity for it is not possible to read into [section 3(1)] any requirement that the assumption of rights there envisaged should have a legally efficacious result."[166]

9–099 In *Hilton*[167] a conviction of stealing a credit balance was similarly upheld although the instructions to transfer the funds had been signed by only one of the two signatories required by the bank's mandate. It was said that, in so far as there was a conflict between *Doole* on the one hand and *Wille* and *Chan Man-Sin* on the other, the latter authorities were to be preferred.

> "In our judgment, . . . the offence of theft is committed when there is a dishonest appropriation of the property in question (section 1(1)), and when the property consists of a credit balance, in the accepted meaning of that term, then the defendant appropriates it by assuming the rights of the owner of the balance and so causing the transfer to be made out of the account. His instructions to the bank to make the transfer, whether given by cheque or otherwise, are the key which sets the relevant inter-bank (or inter-account) machinery in motion. The fact that a transfer is made is enough to complete the offence, even if there remains an obligation on the bank (as debtor to its customer) to replenish the account. . .
>
> We can see that it might be argued that the decision in *Preddy* makes it necessary to concentrate exclusively on the legal obligation owed by the bank to its customer, and that if this remains unaffected, because the cheque was forged or the instructions were not within the bank's mandate, then the transfer in fact made by the bank has to be ignored. We are not prepared to hold, however, that the reasoning in *Preddy* should be taken this far. It would not be right, in our view, to ignore the reality of the situation to this extent."[168]

9–100 The court did not explain why (*Preddy* aside) "the reality of the situation" dictated that the lack of authority for the transfer should be disregarded. The property alleged to have been stolen consists entirely of legal rights. If, despite the transfer, the bank owes the account-holder the

[165] On the latter point see below, para.9–145.
[166] [1988] 1 W.L.R. 196 at 199–200.
[167] [1997] 2 Cr.App.R. 445.
[168] [1997] 2 Cr.App.R. 445 at 456.

same sum as before, the reality of the situation is that the account-holder has lost nothing. The true victim is the bank, which, because of its failure to detect the lack of authority, has made a transfer of funds which it cannot set against its indebtedness to the account-holder. A theft charge should relate to the funds lost by the bank, not the funds owned (but not lost) by the account-holder. To make out a charge of stealing the bank's funds, the prosecution would have to show that the transaction resulted in the loss of property owned by the bank—a chose in action consisting in a credit balance with another bank, perhaps—and this might be hard to do.[169] But the prosecution should not be allowed to circumvent the problem by alleging a theft of property which, though easier to identify, has not been lost.

If a credit balance could not be appropriated without actually diminishing the owner's entitlement against the bank, it would follow that the act of appropriation could not occur until the account was debited. But it now seems that a credit balance can be stolen by procuring a transfer of funds out of the account, even if the transfer is unauthorised and therefore does not affect the owner's right to the original balance. This conclusion reopens the possibility (dismissed in *Kohn*) that the appropriation may occur *before* the funds are transferred. In *Chan Man-Sin* it was thought unnecessary to decide whether the appropriation occurred when the cheques were presented, or when the transactions were completed by the making of consequential entries in the relevant accounts. It was apparently not suggested that the appropriation might have consisted in the *drawing* of the cheques. **9–101**

In *Stringer* it was said that in both *Wille* and *Chan Man-Sin* **9–102**

> "it must have been not the drawing of the cheques which results in the appropriation of the chose or thing in action at the bank, but the innocent activities of those clearing the cheques."[170]

The defendant was held to have stolen funds from his company's bank account by signing false invoices which junior staff passed for payment by cheque. The court apparently thought that the appropriation was complete only when the cheques were cleared, presumably because the drawing and presentation of the cheques would not in themselves affect the account-holder's chose in action.

In *Tomsett*[171] one of the defendants sent a telex from London purporting to instruct a bank in New York to transfer funds to another bank, also in New York, for an account held by the other defendant at a branch in Geneva. It was argued that the alleged conspiracy was not indictable in England and Wales because the contemplated theft would have occurred in **9–103**

[169] cf. *Ali*, one of the appeals heard with *Graham* [1997] 1 Cr.App.R. 302.
[170] (1992) 94 Cr.App.R. 13 at 17.
[171] [1985] Crim. L.R. 369.

New York or Geneva.[172] The court invited counsel for the Crown to argue that the theft had occurred in London because that was where the telex was sent. Counsel declined the invitation, and argued only that the theft must have occurred in London because the funds to be stolen belonged to a bank situated there. This argument was rejected.

> "Prima facie a theft takes place where the property is appropriated; prima facie appropriation takes place where the property is situated. The subject matter of the theft in the present case was either a debt or alternatively cash over the counter. If it was a debt then the debt was unquestionably situated in New York. If it was cash over the counter, the cash was unquestionably situated in Geneva."[173]

9–104 In *R. v Governor of Pentonville Prison, ex p. Osman*,[174] on essentially similar facts, the Divisional Court accepted the argument that counsel in *Tomsett* had declined to advance, namely that the appropriation was complete when the telex was sent.[175] That act was itself an assumption of the rights of the person entitled to the funds. Therefore the theft was committed in the country from which the telex was sent (though the court left open the possibility that it might also be committed where the telex was received).

> "So far as the customer is concerned, he has a right as against the bank to have his cheques met. It is that right which the defendant assumes by presenting a cheque, or by sending a telex instruction without authority. The act of sending the telex is therefore the act of theft itself, and not a mere attempt. It is the last act which the defendant has to perform and not a preparatory act. It would matter not if the account were never in fact debited. We can find no way of excluding the sending of the telex in such circumstances from the definition of appropriation contained in section 3(1) of the Act."[176]

9–105 In *R. v Governor of Brixton Prison, ex p. Levin*[177] the applicant withdrew funds from an account held with a bank in America by accessing the bank's computer from a computer in Russia. The Divisional Court thought it artificial to regard the act of appropriation as having occurred in one place or the other, and would have preferred to hold that it occurred in both. But, if it were necessary to choose, the court preferred to regard it as having occurred in America. *Ex p. Osman* was distinguished on the ground that in that case a person with control of the account had simply given instructions to the bank. In *Ex p. Levin*, by contrast, no instructions could be given without first gaining entry to the bank's computer.

172 See below, Ch.22.
173 The quotation is taken from the judgment in *R. v Governor of Pentonville Prison, ex p. Osman* (1988) 90 Cr.App.R. 281.
174 (1988) 90 Cr.App.R. 281.
175 The court consisted of two of the members of the court that had decided *Tomsett*.
176 (1988) 90 Cr.App.R. 281 at 296.
177 [1997] Q.B. 65.

In *Ngan*,[178] however, it was confirmed that the position was as stated in *Ex p. Osman*. Funds had been mistakenly credited to the defendant's account with a London bank, and therefore belonged to another by virtue of TA 1968, s.5(4).[179] The defendant drew cheques on the account with knowledge of the mistake. It was held that the funds were appropriated when the cheques were presented by the defendant's sister in Scotland, not when the account in London was debited. There was therefore no theft within the jurisdiction.[180] *Ex p. Levin* was not referred to. **9–106**

The *Osman* rule creates a practical problem. If the appropriation occurs when the cheque is presented or the bank is otherwise instructed to debit the account, it may be necessary to prove that the account was in credit (or within an agreed overdraft facility) at that time, rather than when it was debited. This may be difficult or impossible. It may however be possible to argue that the appropriation is a continuing act, so that it is sufficient if the account is in credit by the time it is debited if not before.[181] **9–107**

SUCCESSIVE APPROPRIATIONS

The same property may be the subject of successive appropriations. After defining appropriation in general terms, TA 1968, s.3(1) goes on: **9–108**

> ". . . and this includes, where [a person] has come by the property (innocently or not) without stealing it, any later assumption of a right to it by keeping or dealing with it as owner."

The words "without stealing it" imply that a person who does steal the property when he first comes by it cannot steal it again by dealing with it as owner. If he first acquires the property and then disposes of it, the disposal may be an appropriation and therefore a theft, but only if the acquisition was not a theft.

Thus in *Meech*[182] one of the defendants had withdrawn money from a bank on behalf of another man, whereupon the others pretended (with his connivance) to rob him of it. It was argued that the money was stolen when it was withdrawn from the bank with the intention of defrauding its owner, and therefore could not be stolen again at the time of the bogus robbery. It was held that the money was not stolen when it was withdrawn,[183] but the **9–109**

[178] [1998] 1 Cr.App.R. 331.

[179] Above, para.9–089.

[180] But a conviction was upheld in the case of one cheque which had been presented in England. Cf. *Burke* [2000] Crim. L.R. 413, where the appellant presented a forged cheque. The court quashed a conviction for attempting to obtain property by deception and substituted one of attempting to steal the credit balance in the account. It was apparently not suggested that by presenting the cheque he might already have stolen the credit balance.

[181] Edward Griew, *The Theft Acts*, 7th edn (1995), para.2–153.

[182] [1974] Q.B. 549.

[183] But in the light of *Gomez* [1993] A.C. 442 it presumably was: below, para.9–123.

court accepted that only if it were not stolen at that stage could it be stolen later.

9–110 Similarly it was held in *Atakpu* that a person who steals property abroad cannot steal it again by appropriating it within the jurisdiction:

> "If [the defendant] has come by the property by stealing it then his later dealing with the property is by implication not included among the assumptions of the right of an owner which amount to an appropriation within the meaning of section 3(1)."[184]

The court's application of this principle to the facts was questionable,[185] but this does not affect the principle.

9–111 The principle might create difficulties where funds in one country are transferred on the instructions of the defendant in another. According to *R. v Governor of Pentonville Prison, ex p. Osman*[186] and *Ngan*[187] the defendant appropriates the funds in the country from which he sends the instructions; according to *Tomsett*[188] he does so in the country from which the funds are transferred. It seems that he does so twice, once when he sends the instructions and again when the funds are transferred. If the funds are in England and he is in France, the first appropriation is in France. But that is not theft because it occurs outside the jurisdiction; and, according to *Atakpu*, the second appropriation is not theft either, because the defendant has already "stolen" the funds once and cannot steal them again. This conclusion would be absurd. In the case of events occurring on or after June 1, 1999 it may be possible to avoid it by treating the first appropriation as occurring in England by virtue of the Criminal Justice Act 1993, s.4(b).[189]

9–112 If the property first stolen is converted into other property, it seems that the thief can steal that other property. In *R. v Governor of Brixton Prison, ex p. Levin*[190] the applicant dishonestly secured the transfer of funds into accounts controlled by his accomplice. It was argued that he had stolen the funds not only by securing their transfer, but also by withdrawing them from the accounts to which they were transferred. He argued that he had appropriated them by securing the transfer, and could not steal them again by withdrawing them. The argument was rejected on the ground that the funds he withdrew were not the same funds that had been transferred. This is a rare example of *Preddy*[191] assisting the prosecution rather than the defence.

[184] [1994] Q.B. 69 at 79.
[185] See below, para.22–013.
[186] [1990] 1 W.L.R. 277.
[187] [1998] 1 Cr.App.R. 331.
[188] [1985] Crim. L.R. 369.
[189] Below, para.22–039.
[190] [1997] Q.B. 65.
[191] [1996] A.C. 815; above, para.4–104.

APPROPRIATION BY PROXY

DECEIVING ANOTHER INTO DISPOSING OF PROPERTY

A person can in effect be deemed to have appropriated property belonging to another when he has actually induced an innocent party to do so for him. In *Stringer*[192] the defendant signed false invoices which junior staff then submitted for payment, assuming from the fact that he had signed them that they must be properly payable. He was held to have stolen the funds debited to the company's account when the cheques issued in payment were presented. The junior staff who passed the invoices, and the accounts staff who issued the cheques, were acting as his innocent agents. It was as if he had issued the cheques himself. A similar conclusion was reached in *Shuck*.[193] The crucial feature of both cases is that the junior staff simply did what they were told. In *Stringer* it was said that the situation might be different if the other staff exercised an independent judgment as to whether to pass the invoice for payment.[194] 9–113

It is similarly doubtful whether one can appropriate property by deceiving its owner into parting with it, for example by transferring funds out of a bank account. In *Naviede*[195] the court said: 9–114

> "We are not satisfied that a misrepresentation which persuades the account holder to direct payment out of his account is an assumption of the rights of the account holder as owner such as to amount to an appropriation of his rights within section 3(1) of the 1968 Act."

Similar doubts were expressed in *Hilton*.[196]

In *Briggs*[197] the defendant arranged the sale of a house owned by her elderly relatives, and the purchase of another house with the proceeds. It was argued that she had appropriated the proceeds by forwarding to the conveyancers handling the sale a letter from her relatives instructing them to transfer the proceeds to the solicitors for the vendor of the house they were purchasing. That appropriation was alleged to be dishonest because her intention was to register the title in her own name.[198] It was held that the giving of the instructions was not an appropriation of the money, because the defendant did not help herself to the money but only deceived the conveyancers into transferring it. But the conveyancers were not the owners of the sale proceeds. It was not for them to decide whether to obey the relatives' instructions. Their duty was to remit the proceeds according 9–115

192 (1992) 94 Cr.App.R. 13.
193 [1992] Crim. L.R. 209.
194 (1992) 94 Cr.App.R. 13 at 17.
195 [1997] Crim. L.R. 662.
196 [1997] 2 Cr.App.R. 445 at 453.
197 [2003] EWCA Crim 3662; [2004] Crim. L.R. 495.
198 The fact that the defendant was doing what the relatives had authorised her to do was no defence: *Gomez* [1993] A.C. 442.

to those instructions. Their position was analogous to that of the junior staff in *Stringer* and *Shuck*, who simply did what they were told. In effect, Briggs did help herself to the proceeds.

9–116 Where the defendant deceives another into transferring funds from the other's own account, Sir John Smith suggested that the question is essentially one of causation.[199] The account-holder decides for himself whether to make the transfer, and his decision to do so therefore breaks the chain of causation. The fact that he does so under a misapprehension induced by the defendant does not mean that the *transfer* is brought about by the defendant—just as it would not be murder to induce a person to commit suicide by falsely telling him he is about to be arrested for a crime. The chain of causation is broken only if the deception relates to the nature of the victim's act, rather than the reasons for doing it—for example, where the victim is an actor playing a character who shoots himself, and the defendant substitutes a loaded gun for the stage prop. Similarly, it is submitted, inducing a person to transfer funds is not an appropriation of the funds unless the victim does not realise that he is transferring funds at all, for example because he is induced to sign instructions which he does not understand.

9–117 This discussion relates only to the question whether the transfer of the funds by the victim is itself an appropriation by the defendant. If the funds, once transferred, continue to belong to the victim, the defendant may steal them by appropriating them at a later stage. And, if the victim does not himself transfer the funds but draws a cheque in the defendant's favour, the defendant may appropriate the funds by presenting the cheque.[200] The cheque enables him to withdraw the funds himself, rather than relying on the account-holder to do it for him.

Compelling Another to Dispose of Property

9–118 In *Navvabi*[201] the defendant drew cheques in favour of a casino, guaranteeing them with a cheque card and thus ensuring that the bank had to honour them. He had neither funds nor an overdraft facility, and was therefore not authorised to use the cheque card. He was convicted of stealing the bank's funds by delivering the cheques and tendering the cheque card. The conviction was quashed on the ground that those acts merely gave the payee a contractual right to the specified sum. The bank lost no identifiable property until the cheques were presented and honoured. It was conceded that the defendant could properly have been convicted of stealing the funds lost if the prosecution had relied upon an appropriation at the time when the cheques were honoured, rather than when they were drawn. The court doubted whether this concession was

[199] Commentary on *Williams (Roy)* [2001] 1 Cr.App.R. 23 (p.362) at [2001] Crim. L.R. 253.
[200] *Williams (Roy)* [2001] 1 Cr.App.R. 23 (p.362).
[201] [1986] 1 W.L.R. 1311.

correct. Arguably it was not, because the honouring of the cheques would not involve the bank in transferring any particular property to the payee's bank: the value of the cheques would merely figure in the cheque clearing, the banks' daily accounting exercise.[202]

If the bank was deprived of an item of property, did Navvabi appropriate that property? In principle this ought to depend on whether the honouring of the cheques was the bank's voluntary act, or something that he had forced the bank to do. In the latter case it might perhaps be said that the bank did act as his innocent agent—not blindly doing his bidding like the junior employees in *Stringer* and *Shuck* and the conveyancers in *Briggs,* but reluctantly doing what he had forced it to do. It had no choice.[203] In *Bevan,* however, a defendant who misused a cheque card in essentially the same way as Navvabi was held to have obtained a pecuniary advantage (namely being allowed to borrow by way of overdraft) by deception, contrary to TA 1968, s.16(2)(b) (now repealed). The fact that the bank could not realistically have refused to honour the cheques, and thus to let him overdraw, did not mean that it had not "allowed" him to do so. **9–119**

> "When the appellant's bank received a request by the paying bank for reimbursement in respect of a cheque drawn by the appellant, it of course readily complied. The bank's motive was no doubt the protection of its own reputation, as well as its contractual obligation owed directly to the paying bank. . . But reimbursement by the appellant's bank was nevertheless an act of will; when it took place the appellant was allowed by the bank to borrow money on overdraft; and the overdraft was consensual, since the appellant had impliedly requested it and the bank had, albeit reluctantly, agreed."[204]

If this is right, it follows that Navvabi's bank *voluntarily* paid the funds to his order, in which case (even after *Gomez*)[205] the payment cannot be described as an appropriation by him through the agency of the bank. Indeed it was said in *Bevan*, on the authority of *Navvabi,* that the defendant was clearly not guilty of theft from the bank.[206]

[202] Edward Griew, *The Theft Acts*, 7th edn (1995), para.2–26. This difficulty may not be insuperable. The end result of the clearing exercise is that the necessary adjustments are made between the clearing banks' own accounts at the Bank of England. If it could be proved that on the day in question the paying bank's own account was debited, would this not be in part the result of having to honour the defendant's cheques? The fact that it is impossible to identify *which* funds have been lost from the account at the Bank of England is surely immaterial: it is not a defence to a charge of stealing part of a private individual's credit balance that on the day in question there were credits as well as debits, so that it is impossible to identify the particular funds lost.

[203] *First Sport Ltd v Barclays Bank plc* [1993] 1 W.L.R. 1229; cf. *Beck* [1985] 1 W.L.R. 22.

[204] (1987) 84 Cr.App.R. 143 at 148.

[205] [1993] A.C. 442; below, para.9–123.

[206] (1987) 84 Cr.App.R. 143 at 146.

APPROPRIATION, CONSENT AND OWNERSHIP

9–120 The most controversial question in the history of theft has been whether the owner's consent to an act can prevent it from being an appropriation. For the old offence of larceny, the taking of the property had to be "without the consent of the owner". But larceny was construed as including a fraudulent obtaining of possession (as distinct from ownership). The Criminal Law Revision Committee intended that the new concept of appropriation should achieve the same result in the case of theft.

9–121 Some of the earlier cases on TA 1968 suggested that the requirement of appropriation excluded not only the obtaining of ownership but also the dishonest obtaining of possession with the owner's consent. In *Skipp*[207] the defendant collected goods for delivery elsewhere, intending to steal them instead. It was held that he did not steal them when he collected them with dishonest intent, but only when he diverged from the route to their authorised destination. In *Fritschy*[208] the defendant was held not to have stolen Krugerrands by taking them to Switzerland with the intention of keeping them, because the owner had asked him to take them to Switzerland. The most authoritative statement of this view was a dictum of Lord Roskill's in *Morris* that

> "the concept of appropriation involves not an act expressly or impliedly authorised by the owner but an act by way of adverse interference with or usurpation of [his] rights".[209]

But in *Gomez*[210] the House of Lords held that a dishonest obtaining of possession can be theft even if it is done with the owner's consent. *Skipp* and *Fritschy* were overruled, and Lord Roskill's dictum was disapproved.

9–122 Where a person by deception induces another to transfer the *ownership* of property, he would before TA 1968 have been guilty of obtaining by false pretences but not of larceny. The Criminal Law Revision Committee's intention was that he should not be guilty of theft either.

> "Obtaining by false pretences is ordinarily thought of as different from theft, because in the former the owner in fact consents to part with his ownership; a bogus beggar is regarded as a rogue but not as a thief, and so are his less petty counterparts. To create a new offence of theft to include conduct which ordinary people would find difficult to regard as theft would be a mistake."[211]

9–123 But the drafting of TA 1968 failed to make the Committee's intention clear. In *Lawrence v Metropolitan Police Commissioner*[212] the House of

[207] [1975] Crim. L.R. 114.
[208] [1985] Crim. L.R. 745.
[209] [1984] A.C. 320 at 332.
[210] [1993] A.C. 442.
[211] *Eighth Report: Theft and Related Offences*, Cmnd.2977 (1966), para.38. See also Sir John Smith, "The Sad Fate of the Theft Act 1968" in W. Swadling and G. Jones (eds) *The Search for Principle: Essays in Honour of Lord Goff of Chieveley*.
[212] [1972] A.C. 626.

Lords held that a taxi-driver committed theft by taking from a foreign passenger's wallet a sum far in excess of the correct fare, even though the passenger assumed that the sum taken was correct and was content to let the driver take it. The driver clearly obtained ownership of the money by deception. In *Dobson v General Accident Fire and Life Assurance Corp plc*[213] the Court of Appeal followed *Lawrence* by holding that goods paid for with a worthless cheque had been lost through "theft" for the purposes of an insurance policy, but had difficulty in reconciling this conclusion with Lord Roskill's dictum in *Morris*. In *Gomez*[214] the House of Lords held that that dictum was wrong. This meant that theft could be committed by obtaining either possession *or* ownership. Gomez was an assistant manager in a retail store. He falsely assured the manager that a bank had confirmed the validity of instruments tendered by his accomplice as payment for goods, and the manager allowed the accomplice to take the goods. It was held, on the basis of *Lawrence*, that this was theft.

The title acquired by Gomez's accomplice was clearly voidable for fraud. **9–124**
Although their Lordships' reasoning did not expressly attach any importance to this fact, for a time it remained arguable that *Gomez* did not apply where the title acquired was indefeasible. In *Mazo*[215] it was conceded by the prosecution, and accepted by the Court of Appeal, that it cannot be theft to accept a gift if the donor is of full capacity and the gift is not vitiated by deception, undue influence or any other factor. The court cited the assertion of Viscount Dilhorne in *Lawrence* that

> "a person is not to be regarded as acting dishonestly if he appropriates another's property believing that, with full knowledge of the circumstances, that other person has in fact agreed to the appropriation",[216]

and went on: "It is implicit in that statement that if in all the circumstances there is held to be a valid gift there can be no theft."[217] The court did not say whether this was because the acceptance of a valid gift cannot be an appropriation, or because it cannot be dishonest. Viscount Dilhorne's dictum would suggest the latter.

The proposition that the obtaining of an indefeasible title is not an **9–125**
appropriation was doubted by the Court of Appeal in *Kendrick*,[218] and rejected by the House of Lords (Lord Hobhouse dissenting) in *Hinks*.[219] Both cases, like *Mazo,* involved the allegedly dishonest acceptance of "gifts" from vulnerable donors. The view accepted in *Mazo* was regarded as inconsistent with *Lawrence* and *Gomez*, although both those cases were concerned with the obtaining of ownership by deception.

[213] [1990] 1 Q.B. 274.
[214] [1993] A.C. 442.
[215] [1997] 2 Cr.App.R. 518.
[216] [1972] A.C. 626 at 632.
[217] [1997] 2 Cr.App.R. 518 at 521.
[218] [1997] 2 Cr.App.R. 524.
[219] [2001] 2 A.C. 241.

> "It is true of course that the certified question in *Gomez* referred to the situation where consent had been obtained by fraud. But the majority judgments do not differentiate between cases of consent induced by fraud and consent given in any other circumstances. The ratio involves a proposition of general application. *Gomez* therefore gives effect to section 3(1) of the Act by treating 'appropriation' as a neutral word comprehending 'any assumption by a person of the rights of an owner'. If the law is as held in *Gomez*, it destroys the argument advanced on the present appeal, namely that an indefeasible gift of property cannot amount to an appropriation."[220]

Mazo is not mentioned in the majority speeches, despite being endorsed in the dissenting speeches of Lords Hutton[221] and Hobhouse. *Hinks* thus settles the question of whether it is possible to "appropriate" property to which one acquires an indefeasible title: it is. But *Hinks* does not necessarily settle the separate question of whether such an appropriation can be *dishonest*, because the majority declined to discuss that question. It is examined in Ch.2.[222]

DISPOSALS BY AGENTS

9–126 An agent may commit theft by fraudulently disposing of his principal's property, for example to an accomplice at an undervalue. According to *Gomez*,[223] the fact that he has the principal's authority to dispose of the property does not prevent the disposal from being an appropriation. There is no longer any need to draw a distinction between disposals which are authorised but fraudulent and those that are not authorised at all.

9–127 Where the fraudulent agent acts on behalf of a company, however, there is a complication. We have seen that, even where the defendant is the beneficial owner of all the shares in a company, the law takes the (arguably artificial) view that the company's property is, as against him, property "belonging to another".[224] But, if his position within the company is such that he can be identified with it, it may be arguable that his disposal of its property cannot be an "appropriation" because it is not just authorised by the company but is, in law, company's own act. The law on this point has developed through two lines of authority which have not always taken account of one another.

9–128 In *Tarling (No.1) v Government of the Republic of Singapore*[225] a company chairman was alleged to have purchased certain shares from his company at an undervalue. Three members of the House of Lords thought that on those facts a charge of theft would not have been made out. Lord Wilberforce said:

220 [2001] 2 A.C. 241 at 251, *per* Lord Steyn.
221 Lord Hutton agreed with the majority on the issue of appropriation, but dissented from the decision.
222 See paras 2–032 *et seq.*
223 [1993] A.C. 442.
224 Above, para.9–032.
225 (1978) 70 Cr.App.R. 77.

"[T]here was no evidence of any appropriation of property belonging to another so as to satisfy the Theft Act 1968, section 1. There were, putting it briefly, transfers of property, passing the property, possibly for inadequate consideration, but nothing approaching theft."[226]

Lord Salmon said:

"If a vendor transfers shares to a purchaser under a contract of sale and is paid the agreed price for them, I do not understand how the purchaser can be said to be appropriating the property belonging to another within the meaning of the word 'appropriate' in section 1 of the Theft Act 1968."[227]

Lord Keith agreed.[228] These statements suggest that an extraction of company property by the company's *alter ego* is not an appropriation.

In *McHugh (Eileen)* a company director drew cheques on the company's **9–129** account to meet the liabilities of other companies in the same group. It was argued that there was insufficient evidence either of appropriation or of dishonesty. The Court of Appeal deduced the following propositions from the earlier authorities, and in particular from *Lawrence, Morris* and *Tarling*:

"(1) The word 'appropriation' connotes a misappropriation. (2) It is immaterial whether the act was ultra vires the company, or was otherwise ineffectual in law. (3) The question whether the company or its creditors or its liquidator has a civil remedy against the actor, or against those who derived benefit from the transaction is immaterial. (4) An act done with the authority of the company cannot in general amount to an appropriation. Such authority may be—(a) express, or (b) implied. (5) Where the actor is beneficially entitled to the entire issued share capital (or at least the entire voting share capital) of the company it may be that his act is not an appropriation because—(a) his act is equivalent to an act of the company, and his intent is the intent of the company, so that there can be no circumstance in which any of his acts is unauthorised; and/or (b) since he has the irresistible power to determine what policies the company shall pursue, there is nothing which he himself may do in the company's name which could in practice be unauthorised."[229]

Unfortunately the authorities referred to did not include *Attorney-* **9–130** *General's Reference (No.2 of 1982)*,[230] where a proposition resembling no.(5) in this passage had been rejected. The argument was there directed at the issue of dishonesty rather than that of appropriation, but it was held that the actions of a company's controllers cannot be attributed to the company if they are a fraud on the company; and this must logically apply to the issue of appropriation as well as that of dishonesty. In *Attorney-General of Hong Kong v Chan Nai-Keung*[231] the defendant had general authority to sell property belonging to a company of which he was a director, but sold it at a

[226] (1978) 70 Cr.App.R. 77 at 110.
[227] (1978) 70 Cr.App.R. 77 at 131.
[228] (1978) 70 Cr.App.R. 77 at 137.
[229] (1989) 88 Cr.App.R. 385 at 393.
[230] [1984] Q.B. 624; above, para.2–087.
[231] [1987] 1 W.L.R. 1339.

gross undervalue. The Court of Appeal of Hong Kong quashed his conviction of theft on the ground that he was the *alter ego* of the company, which had therefore sold the property itself. The Privy Council found the Court of Appeal's reasoning "difficult to understand" and restored the conviction. In *Philippou*[232] it was held that the sole shareholders and directors of a company had stolen the company's funds. The court that decided *Attorney-General's Reference (No.2 of 1982)* had been right to assume that the requirement of an appropriation was satisfied. But *McHugh*, which had been decided shortly beforehand and without reference to *Attorney-General's Reference (No.2 of 1982)*, was in turn not referred to. It was not clear which of these various decisions, reached in apparent ignorance of one another, was *per incuriam*.

9–131 In *Gomez*[233] the House of Lords approved the line of authority culminating in *Philippou*. Lord Browne-Wilkinson thought that, for the reasons given in *Attorney-General's Reference (No.2 of 1982)*, the approach adopted in *McHugh* would be wrong even if Lord Roskill were right in saying that an appropriation must be unauthorised. But the majority's preference for *Lawrence* over Lord Roskill's dictum rendered the question irrelevant. Lord Browne-Wilkinson said:

> "Whether or not those controlling the company consented or purported to consent to the abstraction of the company's property by the accused, he will have appropriated the property of the company. The question will be whether the other necessary elements are present, viz. was such appropriation dishonest and was it done with the intention of permanently depriving the company of such property? In my judgment . . . the statements of principle in *McHugh* are not correct in law and should not be followed. As for *Att-Gen's Reference (No.2 of 1982)*, in my judgment both the concession made by counsel (that there had been an appropriation) and the decision in that case were correct, as was the decision in *Philippou*.
>
> I am glad to be able to reach this conclusion. The pillaging of companies by those who control them is now all too common. It would offend both common sense and justice to hold that the very control which enables such people to extract the company's assets constitutes a defence to a charge of theft from the company. The question in each case must be whether the extraction of the property from the company was dishonest, not whether the alleged thief has consented to his own wrongdoing."[234]

The rest of the majority agreed. Even Lord Lowry, who thought that the consent of the owner did preclude an appropriation, agreed that this principle did not extend to a consent which is attributed to the owner only because the defendant is the owner's *alter ego*. The dicta in *Tarling* were not referred to.

[232] (1989) 89 Cr.App.R. 290.
[233] [1993] A.C. 442.
[234] [1993] A.C. 442 at 496–497.

INTENTION PERMANENTLY TO DEPRIVE

The final element of theft is that the defendant must appropriate the property with the intention of permanently depriving of it the person to whom it belongs. This was also an element of the offence of obtaining property by deception contrary to TA 1968, s.15 (now repealed). 9–132

ACTUAL INTENTION

In a fraud case it will often be undeniable that the defendant intended to deprive the other permanently of the particular property appropriated (or, under the old law, obtained by deception). It is immaterial for this purpose that the defendant intends to (or does) replace that property with other property of equivalent value, even if the two are for practical purposes interchangeable. Thus a person who "borrows" cash without authority intends to deprive the owner permanently even if he intends to repay the same amount, because he does not intend to return the actual cash he appropriates.[235] His intention to repay an equivalent sum goes only to dishonesty. Dishonesty is distinct from intention permanently to deprive, and must be left to the jury even if the latter is admitted.[236] 9–133

An owner of tangible property is deprived of it if he loses possession of it. But intangible property consists solely of legal rights. Since it cannot be possessed, its owner cannot be deprived of it by being dispossessed. He is not *in fact* deprived of it unless he loses his rights. This may happen if another person has authority to dispose of the property. In *Kohn*[237] a director who fraudulently drew cheques on his company's bank account was held to have stolen the debt owed to the company by the bank and represented by the credit balance in the account. The company was not entitled to have the funds restored to the account when the fraud was discovered, and was therefore literally deprived of them. 9–134

Often, however, the owner of the intangible property will continue to own it despite the defendant's appropriation of it. A person who without authority secures the transfer of funds from other people's bank accounts to his own, for example, is likely to be charged with stealing those funds. But he has not affected the account-holders' *property* (their rights against the bank) at all. They are still entitled to payment of the sums originally due. The defendant may hope that they will not notice the discrepancy and will not assert their right to have the funds re-credited. More likely, he will not care whether they notice it or not, because even if the bank has to restore the funds it will not be able to recover them from him. In either case, if he 9–135

[235] *Halstead v Patel* [1972] 1 W.L.R. 661; *Velumyl* [1989] Crim. L.R. 299.

[236] *O'Connell* [1991] Crim. L.R. 771. In *Velumyl* [1989] Crim. L.R. 299 the court said that "dishonesty was not in issue"; but this was presumably because the defendant had changed his plea to guilty when the judge ruled that he had intended permanently to deprive.

[237] (1979) 69 Cr.App.R. 395.

knows the legal position he does not literally intend to deprive the account-holders of their rights.

CONSTRUCTIVE INTENTION

9–136 In such a case the defendant may nevertheless be deemed to have the necessary intention. TA 1968, s.6(1) provides:

> "A person appropriating property belonging to another without meaning the other permanently to lose the thing itself is nevertheless to be regarded as having the intention of permanently depriving the other of it if his intention is to treat the thing as his own to dispose of regardless of the other's rights; and a borrowing or lending of it may amount to so treating it if, but only if, the borrowing or lending is for a period and in circumstances making it equivalent to an outright taking or disposal."

9–137 It has been said that s.6 merely gives "illustrations" of what can amount to an intention permanently to deprive, that it is a misconception to interpret it as "watering down" the definition of theft in TA 1968, s.1(1),[238] and that it does not enlarge the scope of that definition but is purely expository.[239] But if anything is clear about s.6 it is that in certain circumstances a person who does not literally intend permanently to deprive can be deemed so to intend. The Court of Appeal has confirmed that this is so.[240] The section did not appear in the Criminal Law Revision Committee's draft Bill, and was inserted during the Bill's passage to ensure that the requirement of intention permanently to deprive would be interpreted in the same way for the purposes of theft as it had been in the law of larceny.[241] The Court of Appeal has indicated that it should if possible be interpreted as doing no more than that, and that in the vast majority of cases it need not be referred to at all.[242]

9–138 The drafting of s.6(1) is incomprehensible. It begins with the cryptic proposition that it is sufficient if the defendant intends to treat "the thing itself" as his own to dispose of, regardless of the rights of the person to whom the property belongs. It then qualifies this proposition (confusingly prefacing the qualification with "and" instead of "but") by saying, in effect, that if the defendant's intention is to "borrow" or "lend" the "thing" then the criterion is *not* whether his intention is to treat it as his own to dispose of regardless of the other's rights, but whether the borrowing or lending is for a period and in circumstances making it equivalent to an outright taking or disposal. On a literal reading, the questions to be asked are therefore:

(1) Did the defendant intend to borrow or lend the thing?

[238] *Warner* (1970) 55 Cr.App.R. 93 at 97.
[239] *Coffey* [1987] Crim. L.R. 498.
[240] *Lloyd* [1985] Q.B. 829 at 834.
[241] See J.R. Spencer, "The Metamorphosis of Section 6 of the Theft Act" [1977] Crim. L.R. 653.
[242] *Lloyd* [1985] Q.B. 829 at 835.

(2) If so, was the intended borrowing for a period and in circumstances making it equivalent to an outright taking or disposal?

(3) If (but only if) the answer to question 1 is "no", did he intend to treat the thing as his own to dispose of regardless of the other's rights?

In other words it must first be determined whether the *second* limb of s.6(1) applies: only if the second limb does not apply can the first limb be invoked. We shall therefore examine the two limbs in reverse order. But the courts have tended to ignore what s.6(1) actually says about the relationship between the two limbs.

BORROWING AND LENDING: OUTRIGHT TAKING AND DISPOSAL

To "borrow" or "lend" a thing is to take or part with possession of it, **9–139** with or without the permission of the person to whom it belongs, but with the intention that he shall get it back later. Where a person appropriates property belonging to another with the intention of borrowing or lending it, the second limb of s.6(1) may deem him to intend permanently to deprive the other person of it (because it deems him to intend to treat the thing as his own to dispose of regardless of the other's rights, which the first limb deems to be an intention permanently to deprive) if, but only if, the intended borrowing or lending would be for a period and in circumstances making it equivalent to an outright taking or disposal.

In *Lloyd* the Court of Appeal tried to explain when this requirement **9–140** would be satisfied.

> "This [second] half of the subsection, we believe, is intended to make it clear that a mere borrowing is never enough to constitute the necessary guilty mind unless the intention is to return the 'thing' in such a changed state that it can truly be said that all its goodness or virtue has gone . . ."[243]

This requirement was not satisfied in *Lloyd* itself, where the defendants borrowed feature films from a cinema for the purpose of making unauthorised copies before returning the originals. It could not be said that all the value had been taken from the films before they were returned, and indeed the court thought that the films themselves (as distinct from the wider commercial interests of the owners of the distribution rights) had not diminished in value at all.

This interpretation may be unduly restrictive. In *Coffey*[244] the defendant **9–141** obtained certain machinery by deception with the intention of exerting pressure on its owner, with whom he had been in dispute, by keeping the machinery until he got what he wanted. It was not clear exactly what he

[243] [1985] Q.B. 829 at 836.
[244] [1987] Crim. L.R. 498.

wanted, nor what he proposed to do with the machinery if he did not get what he wanted. His conviction of obtaining property by deception was quashed on other grounds, but the court thought he could properly have been convicted had the jury taken the view that the intended detention of the machinery was "equivalent to an outright taking". Apparently this was a possible conclusion although there was no question of the machinery being drained of its "goodness" before it was returned.

9–142 The court thought there were two views of the facts that might justify such a conclusion. If the jury had thought that the defendant might have intended to return the machinery eventually even if he did not get what he wanted, they would still have been entitled to convict if they were sure that he intended to keep it for such a long time as to make the detention equivalent to an outright taking. Alternatively, they would have been entitled to convict on the basis that his intention was to keep the machinery *for good* unless he got what he wanted—but only if they thought he regarded this outcome as sufficiently likely to make his intended conduct equivalent to an outright taking. This last qualification is surprising. It is surely reasonable to say that a person is effectively taking property outright if his intention is to keep it permanently unless its owner complies with certain conditions, even if he thinks that the owner probably will comply. In *Barnett*[245] it was said that the taking of property by way of security would normally amount to an intention permanently to deprive, though there might be rare circumstances in which it would not.

Treating a Thing as One's Own to Dispose of Regardless of the Other's Rights

9–143 If (but, on a literal reading of the section, *only* if) the defendant does not intend to "borrow" or "lend" the thing, he may be deemed to intend permanently to deprive under the first limb of s.6(1) if his intention is to treat the thing as his own to dispose of regardless of the owner's rights. In *Lloyd* this provision was explained as follows:

> "[T]he first part of section 6(1) seems to us to be aimed at the sort of case where a defendant takes things and then offers them back to the owner for the owner to buy if he wishes. If the taker intends to return them to the owner only upon such payment, then, on the wording of section 6(1), that is deemed to amount to the necessary intention permanently to deprive . . . There are other cases of similar intent: for instance, 'I have taken your valuable painting. You can have it back on payment to me of £X,000. If you are not prepared to make that payment, then you are not going to get your painting back.'"[246]

The only real difference between these examples is that in the former the owner is apparently not intended to realise that he is buying his own

[245] July 21, 1987.
[246] [1985] Q.B. 829 at 836.

property back, whereas in the latter he is. This distinction cannot be crucial to the defendant's liability for appropriating the property in the first place, though it will determine whether his subsequent attempt to obtain the money is an offence of deception or of blackmail.

Subsequent cases have blurred the distinction drawn in *Lloyd* between the two limbs. In *Coffey*[247] the retention of another's property with a view to inducing him to comply with the appellant's demands was regarded as a case where the first limb might usefully have been "illustrated" by the second. And in *Fernandes*[248] it was said: **9–144**

> "In our view, section 6(1), which is expressed in general terms, is not limited in its application to the illustrations given by Lord Lane C.J. in *Lloyd.* Nor, in saying that in most cases it would be unnecessary to refer to the provision, did Lord Lane suggest that it should be so limited. The critical notion, stated expressly in the first limb and incorporated by reference in the second, is whether a defendant intended 'to treat the thing as his own to dispose of regardless of the other's rights'. The second limb of subsection (1), and also subsection (2),[249] are merely specific illustrations of the application of that notion."[250]

This ignores the words "a borrowing or lending of it may amount to so treating it if, but only if, . . .". The second limb does not "illustrate" the first at all: it lays down a different requirement which, in cases of borrowing and lending, must be satisfied *instead* of that laid down by the first. In neither *Coffey* nor *Fernandes* does the court appear to have considered whether the appellant intended to "borrow" the property. Yet, on the wording of the section, it is this that determines which limb applies.

Intangible property

Where the property appropriated is intangible—which in a fraud case it usually is—it is likely to be the first limb of s.6(1) that is invoked in any event,[251] since the concepts of "borrowing" and "lending" are of doubtful relevance. In *Doole*[252] the Court of Appeal was disinclined to accept the argument that an owner of intangible property is not deprived of it unless he loses his legal rights, and in *Chan Man-Sin v Attorney-General of Hong Kong*[253] this argument was rejected by the Privy Council. The defendant was held to have stolen the credit balances of the accounts of certain companies by drawing forged cheques which were honoured by the companies' bank. He had not only appropriated the companies' property but had done so with the intention of permanently depriving them of it. The Privy Council **9–145**

[247] [1987] Crim. L.R. 498.
[248] [1996] 1 Cr.App.R. 175.
[249] Below, para.9–148 (footnote supplied).
[250] [1996] 1 Cr.App.R. 175 at 188.
[251] It seems to be assumed that there is a "thing itself" even if the property is intangible.
[252] [1985] Crim. L.R. 450.
[253] [1988] 1 W.L.R. 196.

thought that this would be so whether or not he intended the forgery of the cheques to remain undetected. In either case the companies would continue to be entitled to the sums in question, and if they discovered the fraud they would doubtless require the bank to account for them; but the defendant would be caught by the Hong Kong counterpart of s.6(1).

> "Quite clearly here the defendant was purporting to deal with the companies' property without regard to their rights."[254]

9–146 But this is not clear at all. The defendant was certainly not "purporting" to deal with the companies' property without regard to their rights: he was *purporting* (falsely) to act honestly and with due regard to their rights. In any event, his conduct did not in fact affect their rights. If he was disregarding anyone's rights it was the bank's, and he should have been charged with stealing the bank's property rather than that of the companies. Moreover, the first limb of s.6(1) does not come into play in every case where a person deals with another's property without regard to the other's rights, but only where he intends to treat the thing as his own *to dispose of* regardless of those rights. The Court of Appeal has said that those words are to be given their dictionary definition—"to deal with definitely: to get rid of; to get done with, finish. To make over by way of sale or bargain, sell"—and that their omission is a misdirection.[255] Chan Man-Sin made no attempt to dispose of the companies' property at all. If the requirement of intention permanently to deprive was satisfied in this case then, in the context of intangible property, it adds little or nothing.

Owner put at risk of permanent loss

9–147 The first limb of s.6(1) appears to catch a defendant whose intention is to dispose of the property appropriated in such a way that the owner may or may not get it back. In *Fernandes* a solicitor transferred client money to a money-lender. It was held that, even if he hoped to get it back, he could be regarded as having intended to treat it as his own to dispose of regardless of the owner's rights.

> "We consider that section 6 may apply to a person in possession or control of another's property who, dishonestly and for his own purpose, deals with that property in such a manner that he knows he is risking its loss.
>
> In the circumstances alleged here, an alleged dishonest disposal of someone else's money on an obviously insecure investment, we consider that the judge was justified in referring to section 6. His direction, looked at as a whole, did not water down the requirement that the jury should be sure of an intention permanently to deprive as illustrated by that provision."[256]

[254] [1988] 1 W.L.R. 196 at 199.
[255] *Cahill* [1993] Crim. L.R. 141; but cf. *DPP v Lavender*, *The Times*, June 2, 1993, where the words appear to have been overlooked again.
[256] [1996] 1 Cr.App.R. 175 at 188.

The effect of this construction is to "water down" the requirement of an *intention* to bring about permanent deprivation. Recklessness appears to be sufficient.

There is at least one case in which s.6(1) is clearly meant to apply even though the owner is merely put at risk of losing the property for good. TA 1968, s.6(2) provides: **9–148**

> "Without prejudice to the generality of subsection (1) above, where a person, having possession or control (lawfully or not) of property belonging to another, parts with the property under a condition as to its return which he may not be able to perform, this (if done for purposes of his own and without the other's authority) amounts to treating the property as his own to dispose of regardless of the other's rights."

This is primarily aimed at the person who has possession of another's property and pledges it without authority. The "condition as to its return" is the redemption of the pledge. But s.6(2) does not say that a person who parts with property in the circumstances described is deemed to have the intention permanently to deprive the other of it. It says that he is thereby treating the property[257] as his own to dispose of regardless of the other's rights—which in turn means that an *intention* to act in such a way is deemed to be an intention permanently to deprive, by virtue of the first limb of s.6(1). Therefore a person who pledges another's property, certain that he will be able to redeem it, is not caught by s.6(2). He does not *intend* to part with the property under a condition as to its return which he may not be able to perform, because he thinks he will be able to perform it. Section 6(2) does not therefore deem him to intend to treat the property as his own to dispose of regardless of the other's rights.

But s.6(2) is without prejudice to the generality of s.6(1). Such a person might be regarded as intending to treat the property as his own to dispose of, regardless of the other's rights, without reference to s.6(2). It would follow that s.6(2) is redundant; and in *Fernandes*[258] it was said to be only a "specific illustration" of the first limb of s.6(1). It might be argued that "lending" in the second limb of s.6(1) *includes* a pledge, in which case the only question would be whether the pledge was intended to be for a period or in circumstances making it equivalent to an outright disposal. That would in turn depend on whether, and if so how soon, the defendant expected to be able to redeem the pledge.[259] If he thought he could do so without difficulty then the pledge could not be equivalent to an outright disposal. **9–149**

[257] Not, as s.6(1) would have it, the "thing".

[258] [1996] 1 Cr.App.R. 175.

[259] cf. *Coffey* [1987] Crim. L.R. 498; above, para.9–141.

INSTRUMENTS RETURNABLE TO THEIR OWNER

9–150 The requirement of intention permanently to deprive has caused particular difficulty in the case of defendants who appropriate (or, under the old law, obtain by deception) instruments conferring some kind of entitlement as against their owner. It is in the nature of such instruments that, once used to secure the entitlement they confer, they may find their way back to their owner. In these circumstances, it is questionable whether an intention permanently to deprive can properly be found, even with the help of TA 1968, s.6.

Cheques

9–151 It appears that no such intention can be established in the case of a defendant who dishonestly induces another to draw a cheque in his favour.[260] As a preliminary point, the defendant in these circumstances cannot be charged with stealing (or, under the old law, obtaining by deception) the *chose in action* thereby conferred on him. This is because that chose in action did not belong to anyone else, and indeed did not exist, until he obtained it.[261] A charge of theft (or, under the old law, obtaining property by deception) must therefore relate to the cheque itself, rather than the chose in action that it represents. The cheque itself is tangible property, and belongs to the drawer until he hands it over. But this approach has difficulties of its own. One (relatively minor) objection is that it is absurd to charge a theft (or an obtaining) of a piece of paper which has no value beyond that of the intangible property it represents. A more serious difficulty is that, once the cheque is presented and returned to the drawer's bank, he can if he wishes get it back. So there is arguably no intention to deprive him of it permanently.

9–152 In *Duru* this objection was overcome by fudging the distinction between the tangible cheque and the intangible property it represents.

> "So far as the cheque itself is concerned, true it is a piece of paper. But it is a piece of paper which changes its character completely once it is paid, because then it receives a rubber stamp on it stating that it has been paid and it ceases to be a thing in action, or at any rate it ceases to be, in its substance, the same thing as it was before: that is, an instrument on which payment falls to be made. It was the intention of the defendants, dishonestly and by deception, not only that the cheques should be made out and handed over, but also that they should be presented and paid, thereby depriving the [drawer] of the cheques in their substance as things in action."[262]

9–153 *Duru* was followed in *Mitchell*,[263] where it was said that by the time the cheque was returned to the drawer "its character would have been changed,

[260] It is different if he appropriates or obtains a cheque previously drawn in favour of a third party, because he may be stealing or obtaining the chose in action belonging to the third party: above, para.9–020.

[261] See above, para.9–020.

[262] [1974] 1 W.L.R. 2 at 8.

[263] [1993] Crim. L.R. 788.

its virtue lost and its force spent". In *Preddy*, however, Lord Goff (with whose speech the other members of the House agreed) said that it was impossible to charge a theft of the cheque *form* because it "would on presentation of the cheque for payment be returned to the drawer via his bank".[264] The implication is that the prosecution cannot have it both ways. If it wishes to treat the cheque as tangible property, it cannot establish an intention permanently to deprive by arguing that the cheque has the character of intangible property. The point did not arise for decision in *Preddy*, but Lord Goff's view was treated as effectively conclusive in *Graham*,[265] *Horsman*[266] and *Clark*.[267] The decision in *Clark* was reached with reluctance, but the court felt unable to depart from Lord Goff's conclusion, particularly since it had been followed by the Lord Chief Justice's court in *Graham*.

Had the matter been free from authority, the court in *Clark* would have **9–154** found "highly persuasive" an article in which Sir John Smith argued that obtaining a cheque from the drawer can indeed be charged as theft of the cheque (or, under the old law, obtaining it by deception).[268] Smith's argument was that the cheque is not *just* a piece of paper: it is a particular kind of tangible property with a special character, namely a valuable security. A person who obtains it from its owner can therefore be regarded as intending to deprive the owner of it if his intention is that the owner shall get it back only when it has ceased to have that special character. This is essentially the same reasoning as in *Duru*, minus the red herring about things in action.

Smith's argument is not without difficulty. It is true that when the cheque **9–155** is returned to the drawer it is a different kind of thing; but it is not *less valuable* to the drawer. On the contrary, before it is presented its existence is a potential detriment to him, because it can be used to diminish his bank balance. Its "value" to him is negative. He would be better off if it did not exist. If he gets it back from the bank after it has been cleared, on the other hand, its value to him at that stage is neither negative nor positive. Its potential for damaging his financial position is spent. It is hard to see how the elimination of that potential can be regarded as "depriving" him of anything. Indeed, Smith acknowledged that the obtaining of the cheque could not be charged as theft (or, under the old law, obtaining by

[264] [1996] A.C. 815 at 836–837.
[265] [1997] 1 Cr.App.R. 302.
[266] [1997] 2 Cr.App.R. 418.
[267] [2001] EWCA Crim 884; [2002] 1 Cr.App.R. 14 (p.141).
[268] "Obtaining Cheques by Deception or Theft" [1997] Crim. L.R. 396. Smith demonstrated that the old case of *Danger* (1857) Dears. & B. 307, which was cited by Lord Goff in support of his conclusion in *Preddy*, did not support that conclusion. It was held in *Danger* that deceiving a person into signing a bill by way of acceptance did not amount to the obtaining of a valuable security by false pretences. But, as Smith demonstrates by reference to subsequent authorities, the real basis of the decision seems to have been that the bill never belonged to the victim at all—all the defendant obtained was the victim's signature on the *defendant's* bill. So *Danger* has no relevance to the case where the victim creates a cheque by filling in his own cheque form.

deception) if the defendant for some reason intended not to present the cheque but to destroy it. This demonstrates the weakness of the argument. It cannot be right that the defendant deprives the drawer of the cheque if he returns it, thereby depriving it of its character as a valuable security (a character which the drawer would prefer it not to have), but not if he destroys it.

9–156 Moreover, having said that it found Smith's reasoning persuasive, the court in *Clark* went on to advance a completely different reason:

> "It seems to us that a cheque form has a value, however modest, and is property capable of appropriation."

This is true, but does not meet the difficulty of establishing an intention permanently to deprive. Smith did not attempt to meet that difficulty by arguing that a cheque *form* has a "modest" value. Even if true, this would not help. It cannot seriously be argued that the drawer has lost the benefit of a piece of paper that was useful for drawing cheques on. Smith was arguing that the form has substantial value *once converted into a cheque*.

9–157 The strongest argument against Lord Goff's conclusion is that, as Smith demonstrates, until the passing of TA 1968 the obtaining of a cheque by deception could be charged as obtaining by false pretences. It is clear that the Criminal Law Revision Committee intended the offence of obtaining property by deception to catch all conduct which could formerly have been charged as obtaining by false pretences, and it seems most unlikely that Parliament intended otherwise. However, the pre-1968 rule depended on the theory that when the defendant returns the cheque to the drawer he is returning something essentially different from, though no less valuable to the owner than, what he obtained. It is not clear that that position can be preserved without the help of TA 1968, s.6; and it is not clear that s.6 preserves it either. The section was not mentioned by Lord Goff in *Preddy*. It was relied upon in *Clark*, but without success:

> "[T]here are, as it seems to us, three difficulties. First, as is apparent from the Report of the argument in *Preddy* at 825g, section 6 was relied on by the Crown in that case, so it cannot be said that the House of Lords was unaware of its possible significance. Secondly, although section 6 is relevant to intention, it does not, in our judgment, assist in identifying the nature of the property being appropriated: it may be for this reason that no reference is made to it in Lord Goff's speech. Thirdly, the appellant was not treating this cheque 'as his own to dispose of regardless of the other's rights'. He was, as [the company on whose account it was drawn] anticipated, paying it into his own account."[269]

9–158 The first of these reasons is relevant in as much as the decision in *Clark* was based on the court's view that Lord Goff's words could not properly be disregarded as mere *obiter dicta*. The second reason is irrelevant, since there is no difficulty in identifying an appropriation. *Gomez*[270] clearly

[269] [2001] EWCA Crim 884; [2002] 1 Cr.App.R. 14 (p.141) at [11].
[270] [1993] A.C. 442.

enables the payee's receipt of the cheque to be treated as an appropriation of it, despite the drawer's consent to that act. Following *Gomez*, the only obstacle to a charge of stealing the cheque is the need to prove an intention permanently to deprive—which is precisely where s.6 may assist.

The third reason is not fully explained, but seems to be hinting at the fact that the defrauded company *had* no rights over the cheque once it was given to the payee; so the payee could not act "regardless of" those rights. If that is a difficulty, the prosecution might consider relying on the second limb of s.6(1) instead. The obtaining of a cheque which will eventually be returned could perhaps be regarded as a "borrowing" of the cheque (though again this carries the dubious implication that the cheque has value to the drawer). If so, the question is not whether the defendant intends to treat the cheque as his own to dispose of regardless of the drawer's rights, but whether the "borrowing" is "equivalent to an outright taking". *Lloyd*[271] suggests that this will be so if the defendant intends to return the cheque only when it has lost all its value. And in a sense that is true. But it cannot have been envisaged that the second limb would apply where the property was never of any value to the person deprived of it. **9–159**

If s.6 is to help in this situation, it would be better to rely on the first limb—which may be justifiable (despite the words "if, but only if" in the second limb) on the basis that obtaining a cheque is not "borrowing" it. According to *Lloyd*, the first limb applies "where a defendant takes things and then offers them back to the owner for the owner to buy if he wishes". In a sense the payee of a cheque is selling it back to the drawer, because the drawer only gets it back once his account has been debited. But the words "if he wishes" point to the difficulty. The drawer does not *want* the cheque back. He does not even want to be in a position in which he could get it back if he wanted to. He would prefer it not to be presented, because his account will be debited if it is. That is why it makes no sense to treat him as being "deprived" of it. **9–160**

It is therefore submitted that, despite the court's misgivings in *Clark*, the law is as stated in that case and in *Preddy*. Obtaining a cheque from the drawer cannot be charged as theft (or, under the old law, obtaining) of a chose in action, because there is no chose in action before the cheque is obtained. And it cannot be charged as theft (or, under the old law, obtaining) of the cheque itself, because there is no intention permanently to deprive. **9–161**

This reasoning seems equally valid where the defendant has extracted funds from the victim's account by *himself* drawing cheques on it. In such a case the prosecution might be tempted to avoid the technicalities of choses in action by charging a theft of the cheques rather than the funds. But it is submitted that, for the reasons above, this would be wrong. The account-holder can get the cheques back. It is the funds that he has lost. **9–162**

[271] [1985] Q.B. 829.

Other instruments

9–163 In the case of instruments other than cheques, the courts have not yet adopted the *Preddy* approach. In *Downes*[272] the defendant sold to a third party sub-contractors' vouchers issued to him by the Inland Revenue, which entitled him to be paid by head contractors without deduction of tax. He knew that the buyer of the vouchers would improperly use them for that purpose. Once used, the vouchers would be returned to the Revenue, to show that the head contractor had acted properly in not deducting the tax. It was held that the defendant had nevertheless intended permanently to deprive the Revenue of the vouchers, because, once sold,

> "the documents cease to be in substance the same thing as they were before. They are no longer part of the statutory machinery for the collection of tax, but have deliberately been made available to be used as forgeries by dishonest subcontractors and contractors to evade tax."[273]

9–164 The facts of *Downes* are not precisely analogous to those of the cases on the obtaining of a cheque from the drawer. It was not alleged that the defendant had stolen the vouchers by obtaining them from the Revenue, but by dishonestly allowing a third party to have them. However, much the same difficulty arises. It is true that, when the vouchers get back to the Revenue, they have lost their special character: they no longer confer a right to payment without deduction of tax. They are records rather than instruments. But, as in the case of a cheque and its drawer, the vouchers have no value *to the Revenue* in the first place. On the contrary, they have potential for misuse which would deprive the Revenue of tax. It therefore makes no sense to say that, from the Revenue's point of view, they have lost their value when they are returned.

9–165 Arguably this was not the basis of the decision anyway. In the passage quoted the court seems to have been saying, not that the vouchers would lose their special character when they were returned to the Revenue after their fraudulent use, but that they lost it as soon as they left the possession of the person by whom the Revenue intended them to be used. This cannot be right. The vouchers retained their character until they were used. They did not become a different kind of property merely because they had fallen into the wrong hands. If this is what the court meant, it amounts to saying that the defendant's sale of the vouchers was theft because it was dishonest, and the requirement of intention permanently to deprive adds nothing. However, the court did rely on *Duru*. This suggests that the real basis of the decision is the change in the character of the vouchers when they are *used*, rather than when they are dishonestly sold to another potential user. And, since *Duru* was effectively overruled in *Preddy*, the basis for the decision has gone. It is submitted that *Downes* too should now be regarded as wrongly decided.

[272] (1983) 77 Cr.App.R. 260; see also *Mulligan* [1990] Crim. L.R. 427.

[273] (1983) 77 Cr.App.R. 260 at 266. The court thought it unnecessary to invoke TA 1968, s.6 but added that the case would also be covered by that section.

In *Arnold*[274] the defendant fraudulently discounted bills of exchange which franchising agents had lodged with him by way of security. He was convicted of stealing the bills from the agents, who lost their money as a result. It was argued on the basis of *Preddy* that, while the bills would have lost their character as valuable securities by the time the agents got them back, that character related to their value as choses in action; and they had that value for the defendant, not the agents. They were, in effect, a key to the agents' bank accounts, which the agents had entrusted to the defendant. It made no sense to regard him as stealing the key by using it. The argument was rejected on the ground that the bills could be regarded as belonging to the agents by virtue of TA 1968, s.5(3).[275] That being so, the court saw no difficulty in regarding the defendant's discounting of the bills as an act done with the intention of permanently depriving the agents of the benefit of the bills. **9–166**

> "It seems to us that, in a case where a defendant has appropriated a valuable security handed over on the basis of an obligation that he will retain or deal with it for the benefit or to the account of the transferor, there is good reason for the application of s.6(1) if the intention of the transferee at the time of the appropriation is that the document should find its way back to the transferor only after all benefit to the transferor has been lost or removed as a result of its use in breach of such obligation."[276]

But, as in the case of a cheque, it is hard to see how the bills could be said to have had any "benefit" for the agents at all. It is submitted that the reasoning in *Arnold* is inconsistent with that in *Preddy*.

Lord Goff's analysis in *Preddy* was again distinguished in *Marshall*.[277] The defendants were charged with stealing London Underground tickets, which they had acquired from paying passengers, by reselling them to other passengers. On the assumption that the tickets would get back to London Underground when they were unlawfully used,[278] it was argued that the defendants could no more steal the tickets from London Underground than they could steal a cheque from its drawer. The court found this submission "attractive . . . at first blush", but rejected it and applied s.6(1), following *Fernandes*.[279] **9–167**

> "On the issuing of an underground ticket a contract is created between London Underground Limited and the purchaser. Under that contract each party has rights and obligations. Theoretically those rights are enforceable by action. Therefore, it is arguable, we suppose, that by the transaction each party has acquired a chose in action. On the side of the purchaser it is represented

[274] [1997] 4 All E.R. 1.

[275] Above, para.9–043.

[276] [1997] 4 All E.R. 1 at 15.

[277] [1998] 2 Cr.App.R. 282; discussed in J.C. Smith, "Stealing Tickets" [1998] Crim. L.R. 723.

[278] It is unlikely that this was the case, for the same reason that explains why the original passengers still had them at the end of their journey. The tickets probably allowed unlimited use on that day, but only by one person.

[279] [1996] 1 Cr.App.R. 175.

> by a right to use the ticket to the extent which it allows travel on the underground system. On the side of London Underground Limited it encompasses the right to insist that the ticket is used by no one other than the purchaser. It is that right which is disregarded when the ticket is acquired by the appellant and sold on. But here the charges were in relation to the tickets and travel cards themselves and a ticket form or travel card and, dare we say, a cheque form is not a chose in action. The fact that the ticket form or travel card may find its way back into the possession of London Underground Limited, albeit with its usefulness or 'virtue' exhausted, is nothing to the point."

9–168 As the court acknowledged, both a ticket and a cheque are instruments, conferring on their holder rights against their owner. The question is why a person who appropriates one kind of instrument should be regarded as intending permanently to deprive its owner of it, whereas a person who appropriates a different kind is not. The only distinction offered by the court is that the ticket is non-transferable. That explains why the sale of the ticket is not just an appropriation but a *mis*appropriation. It does not explain why the reseller is regarded as intending to deprive the issuer of the ticket. The decision appears to be based on the same notion as *Downes*—namely that, where an instrument is passed on to someone who intends to use it to defraud its issuer, the act of passing it on is deemed to be done with the intention of permanently depriving the issuer of it. It is submitted that, like *Downes* and *Arnold*, *Marshall* cannot stand alongside the cheque cases and is wrongly decided.

Chapter 10

OBTAINING SERVICES DISHONESTLY

Section 11 of the Fraud Act 2006 ("FA 2006") provides: **10–001**

> "(1) A person is guilty of an offence under this section if he obtains services for himself or another—
>
> (a) by a dishonest[1] act, and
>
> (b) in breach of subsection (2).
>
> (2) A person obtains services in breach of this subsection if—
>
> (a) they are made available on the basis that payment has been, is being or will be made for or in respect of them,
>
> (b) he obtains them without any payment having been made for or in respect of them or without payment having been made in full, and
>
> (c) when he obtains them, he knows—
>
> (i) that they are being made available on the basis described in paragraph (a), or
>
> (ii) that they might be,
>
> but intends that payment will not be made, or will not be made in full."

The offence is triable either way, and is punishable on conviction on indictment with five years' imprisonment.[2]

This offence is essentially an expanded[3] version of the old offence of obtaining services by deception, contrary to s.1 of the Theft Act 1978 ("TA 1978").[4] It is wider in that it does not require deception, but only the dishonest obtaining of services for which payment is required. The old **10–002**

[1] For the element of dishonesty, see above, Ch.2.
[2] FA 2006, s.11(3).
[3] But it is narrower in one respect: below, para.10–011.
[4] Above, para.4–121.

offence was drafted on the assumption that the only way in which it is possible to obtain a service is by inducing another person to provide it, and that (apart from threats, which are the province of blackmail) the only dishonest way of doing this is by deceiving the other person. Now that services are increasingly provided by automated systems, this assumption is no longer true. Where a service is provided automatically it cannot be obtained by deception, because only human beings can be deceived.[5] This is not a problem if the thing obtained is *property*, because in that case a charge of theft will lie. Where the thing obtained is not property but a service, however, under the old law there may be no offence at all.

10–003 The Law Commission rejected the option of simply extending the concept of deception so as to include what may loosely be called the deception of a machine.

> "Rather than requiring deception but diluting its meaning, we need to accept that deception should not be essential at all. This is because, where a person dishonestly obtains a service by giving false information to a machine, the gravamen of that person's conduct is not the provision of the false information but the taking of a valuable benefit without paying for it.
>
> Suppose, for example, that an internet website offers valuable information to subscribers, who are supposed to gain access to the information by giving their password. If a non-subscriber dishonestly downloads the information, it hardly matters whether she does so by giving the password of a genuine subscriber (and thus impliedly representing herself to be that subscriber) or by somehow bypassing the password screen altogether. To distinguish between these two situations would be like distinguishing between the person who puts a foreign coin into a vending machine and the one who gets at the contents by opening up the machine with a screwdriver, on the basis that the former makes a 'misrepresentation' to the machine (that the coin is legal tender) whereas the latter does not. This would be absurd. Both are guilty of stealing the contents. Equally, in our view, a person who 'steals' a service should be guilty of an offence, whether it is obtained by providing false information or in any other way."[6]

The Commission's approach was therefore to reserve the new fraud offence for the more traditional kinds of fraud, and deal separately with the problem of automated services. On this view, obtaining services from a machine is more like theft than fraud. The obtainer does not "deceive" the machine: he simply helps himself to the service that the machine provides, just as he might appropriate property dispensed by a machine. The offence under FA 2006, s.11 is essentially one of *stealing* a service.

10–004 The Government preferred a belt-and-braces approach. FA 2006 includes the Law Commission's offence of obtaining services (with or without making a false representation), but also provides in s.2(5) that fraud by false representation can be committed by a representation made to a machine. Thus, if a person obtains services by making a false representation to a machine, he may commit both the s.11 offence *and* the fraud

[5] Above, para.4–072.

[6] Law Com. No.276, *Fraud*, Cm.5560, paras 8.4–8.5.

offence. It is argued above that s.2(5) is misconceived because the idea of an implied representation to a machine is nonsensical.[7] Where the defendant has obtained property from a machine, theft is a more suitable charge than fraud. Where he has obtained services from a machine, a charge under s.11 is more suitable.

SERVICES

The Law Commission explained that 10–005

> "a service need not be provided by one person directly to another. It may be provided through the medium of a machine. Obviously this can be done by directly causing the machine to behave in the manner required—for example, by switching it on—but it can also be done indirectly. Where a machine is designed or programmed to perform a task automatically whenever certain criteria are satisfied at any future date, a person who causes the machine to perform that task on a particular occasion is obtaining a service, even though those responsible for designing or programming the machine may not be personally aware that the necessary criteria have been satisfied on that occasion."[8]

Where financial information is provided electronically to subscribers, for example, that is clearly the provision of a service. It does not matter whether the information is provided by a person through an electronic medium or automatically without human input. In either case the recipient is obtaining a service. If he is not a subscriber, obtains the information by a dishonest act (such as using a subscriber's password) and intends not to pay, he commits the offence.

Once we move away from the idea that a service is something done by a 10–006
person, however, it is not clear where the line is to be drawn. Some services are such that, having once acquired the power to help oneself to the service, one can go on helping oneself indefinitely. For example, a person who attends a concert is presumably obtaining the services of the performers.[9] If he has gained entry without paying, he commits the offence. The same must be true of someone who watches a live broadcast of the concert on television or the internet, if the broadcast is intended for subscribers only. And it cannot make a difference whether the broadcast is live or recorded, since its content is identical in either case. This suggests that, if subscribers

[7] Paras 4–077 *et seq.*

[8] Law Com. No.276, para.8.9.

[9] Sir John Smith argued that the service is merely admission to the premises, but the Law Commission rejected this view: Law Com. No.276, para.8.6, fn.7. In Committee, David Heath MP asked whether the offence would be committed by someone who finds a vantage point from which he can see a rugby match without having to pay for admission to the ground. The Solicitor General replied that it would not, because such a person would not be dishonest: *Hansard*, SC Deb.B, col.55 (June 20, 2006). If he were not obtaining the services of the players, the question of dishonesty would not arise.

can watch the broadcast repeatedly, a non-subscriber who watches it repeatedly is committing the offence every time he does so.[10]

10–007 It seems to be necessary at least that something should be *done*, either by another person or by a machine (in the widest sense of that word), as a result of the defendant's dishonest act.[11] Where a fee is charged for admission to premises, but nothing is done on the premises for the benefit of those who pay to enter—for example where the only reason for entering is to admire the view—it is submitted that a person does not obtain services merely by gaining entry.

SERVICES TO BE PAID FOR

GRATUITOUS SERVICES

10–008 FA 2006, s.11(2)(a) requires that the services obtained be made available on the basis that payment in respect of them has been, is being or will be made. This reflects the wording of TA 1978, s.1. A person who obtained a service by deception did not commit an offence under TA 1978, s.1 if it was understood that the service was provided gratuitously—even if payment *would* have been required but for the deception. This was a curious anomaly, and in 1999 the Law Commission proposed to rectify it by extending the definition of "services" to include such a case. FA 2006, s.11 does not incorporate this proposal, because nearly every such case would be fraud by false representation anyway.[12] So, for example, it is not an offence under s.11 to obtain a service free by falsely pretending to have no money.

SERVICES PROVIDED ON SUBSCRIPTION

10–009 FA 2006, s.11 applies not only where payment is expected for the particular services obtained, but also where payment is expected *in respect of* those services. The Law Commission explained:

> "This wording is intended to meet the case where services are provided to those within a limited class of people who pay for the privilege of belonging to that class, rather than paying directly for the services themselves."[13]

[10] A further possibility is that he makes his own recording. Perhaps he obtains a service every time he watches the recording. But, even if he does, the service he obtains is not one for which payment is expected, because it is not intended to be provided at all.

[11] This might be relevant in a case where it is clear that the defendant obtained services but it is not clear whether he did so within the jurisdiction: below, para.22–051.

[12] The Commission accepted that there might be some cases which arguably fall outside the fraud offence (see above, para.3–14), but thought that such cases were of insufficient importance to justify making special provision for them: Law Com. No.276, para.8.15.

[13] Law Com. No.276, para.8.12, fn.13.

A subscriber to an information service is not expected to pay separately for every piece of information he receives, because he has already paid for the *right* to obtain the information. If a non-subscriber obtains information, he is arguably not obtaining a service for which payment is required, but he is clearly obtaining a service in respect of which payment is required.

DISHONEST ACT

The defendant must obtain the services by a dishonest *act*: an omission, however dishonest, is not enough. **10–010**

> "This offence would not, for example, be committed by a person who innocently happened to be on a boat and, despite hearing an announcement that anyone who had not paid for the next trip should disembark, remained on the boat and thus received a free ride."[14]

INTENT TO AVOID PAYMENT

The broad effect of FA 2006, s.11(2)(b) and (c) is that the offence requires an intent to avoid payment. Payment in full must not have been made, whether by the defendant or anyone else on his behalf; he must know that the services are not intended to be gratuitous, or at least be aware of the possibility that payment may be expected; and he must intend that payment in full will never be made.[15] In this respect the offence is narrower than that under TA 1978, s.1. Under the old offence, the crucial question was whether the services were intended to be paid for. If they were, and the defendant obtained them dishonestly and by deception, it was no defence that he intended to pay as required. The Law Commission gave the example of a parent who lies about a child's religious upbringing in order to obtain a place at a fee-paying school, with every intention of paying the fees.[16] Such a person would (if dishonest) be guilty of the old offence, but is not guilty of the offence under FA 2006, s.11. **10–011**

Unlike fraud, the offence does not require an intent to make a gain or cause a loss or a risk of loss. Such a requirement might be hard to satisfy where the cost of providing the service is independent of the number of people to whom it is provided, and the defendant would not pay for it if he could not get it for nothing. **10–012**

[14] Law Com. No.276, para.8.11.

[15] So it is not enough that he intends to pay later, whereas the provider of the service thinks he has already paid; or that he intends to pay at a time later than the time at which he is expected to pay.

[16] Law Com. No.276, para.8.12.

CHAPTER 11

FORGERY AND RELATED OFFENCES

FORGERY

The offence of forgery is created by s.1 of the Forgery and Counterfeiting Act 1981 ("FCA 1981"), which provides: **11–001**

> "A person is guilty of forgery if he makes a false instrument, with the intention that he or another shall use it to induce somebody to accept it as genuine, and by reason of so accepting it to do or not to do some act to his own or any other person's prejudice."

The offence is triable either way and is punishable on conviction on indictment with 10 years' imprisonment.[1]

INSTRUMENTS

FCA 1981, s.8(1) provides: **11–002**

> "[I]n this Part of this Act 'instrument' means—

[1] FCA 1981, s.6(2).

(a) any document, whether of a formal or informal character;[2]

(b) any stamp issued or sold by a postal operator;[3]

(c) any Inland Revenue stamp;[4] and

(d) any disc, tape, sound track or other device on or in which information is recorded or stored by mechanical, electronic or other means."

11–003 The background to this definition is curious. The old offence of forgery was one of making a false *document*.[5] The Law Commission, on whose recommendations the new offence was based, thought that there was no need to include every kind of document:

> "In the straightforward case a document usually contains messages of two distinct kinds—first a message about the document itself (such as the message that the document is a cheque or a will) and secondly a message to be found in the words of the document that is to be accepted and acted upon (such as the message that a banker is to pay a specified sum or that property is to be distributed in a particular way). In our view it is only documents which convey not only the first type of message but also the second type that need to be protected by the law of forgery."[6]

11–004 The word "instrument" was intended to denote a document conveying both types of message. There is some authority for confining the term to documents of this kind. In *Attorney-General of Hong Kong v Pat Chiuk-Wah* the Privy Council said that it includes "any document intended to have some effect, as evidence of, or in connection with, a transaction which is capable of giving rise to legal rights or obligations."[7] But in the context of earlier forgery legislation it was sometimes more widely construed. In *Riley*[8] the defendant placed a bet by means of a telegram which falsely purported to have been sent before the race took place. His conviction of obtaining money by means of a forged instrument was upheld. Hawkins J. thought the word "instrument" wide enough to cover "an infinite variety of writings, whether penned for the purposes of creating binding obligations or as records of business or other transactions".[9] Wills J. thought the word was meant to include "writings of every description if false and known to be false".[10] This was followed in *Howse*[11] on essentially similar facts. But neither decision is inconsistent with the *Pat Chiuk-Wah* definition, because

[2] But not a currency note within the meaning of FCA 1981, Part II: FCA 1981, s.8(2).

[3] Including a mark denoting payment of postage which a postal operator authorises to be used instead of an adhesive stamp: FCA 1981, s.8(3). "Postal operator" has the same meaning as in the Postal Services Act 2000: FCA 1981, s.8(3A).

[4] As defined by the Stamp Duties Management Act 1891, s.27: FCA 1981, s.8(4).

[5] Forgery Act 1913, s.1(1).

[6] Law Com. No.55, *Criminal Law: Report on Forgery and Counterfeit Currency*, HC 320, para.22.

[7] [1971] A.C. 835 at 840.

[8] [1896] 1 Q.B. 309.

[9] [1896] 1 Q.B. 309 at 314.

[10] [1896] 1 Q.B. 309 at 321.

[11] (1912) 107 L.T. 239.

in each case the communication effected a legal transaction (albeit one invalidated by the Gaming Act 1845, s.18). Hawkins J. described the telegram in *Riley* as an "instrument of contract".[12] Wills J., though preferring a broad construction, went on:

> "I think further that, even if the true construction of the word 'instrument' required a more restricted meaning, the telegram in the present case would fall within it. It was a writing which, if accepted and acted upon, would establish a business relation and lead directly to business dealings with another person . . ."[13]

In *Cade*[14] the document in question was a letter purporting to be signed by the victim's employee and requesting money for the hire of equipment. A conviction under the Forgery Act 1913, s.7 (the successor to the offence charged in *Riley*) was upheld on the grounds that the letter was a "business document" and fell within Wills J.'s alternative, narrower interpretation. **11–005**

The Law Commission's intention was that the term "instrument" should include *only* documents conveying "a message . . . that is to be accepted and acted upon". This intention seems to have been thwarted by the definition of "instrument" as including "any document". A document may be an "instrument" within the meaning of FCA 1981 even if it is not an instrument in the narrow sense. This is clear not only from s.8(1)(a) but also from s.8(1)(d). A device on or in which information is recorded or stored is not necessarily an instrument in the narrow sense. **11–006**

It does not follow that the use of the word "instrument" has no significance. The word "document" itself gave rise to problems of interpretation under the old law, particularly in relation to objects which, though bearing written or printed information, are primarily designed for some purpose other than the communication of that information. A signed painting, for example, was held not to be a document, although it conveyed information about the identity of the artist[15] and was arguably indistinguishable from a certificate purporting to be signed by him.[16] If it is not clear whether an article is a "document" within the meaning of FCA 1981, s.8(1)(a), it may be arguable that that word is coloured by the fact that it appears in a definition of the word "instrument", and therefore includes only those articles whose *primary* function lies in the writing they bear. So a signed painting is arguably not an "instrument" even if it is, in one sense, a document. **11–007**

[12] [1896] 1 Q.B. 309 at 315.
[13] [1896] 1 Q.B. 309 at 322.
[14] [1914] 2 K.B. 209.
[15] *Closs* (1858) Dears. & B. 460. Caroline Fry, "Forgery and signatures on paintings" (1993) 143 N.L.J. 1233, points out that *Closs* was effectively reversed by the Fine Arts (Copyright) Act 1862, s.7, which made it an offence to "fraudulently affix upon any painting, drawing or photograph . . . any names, initials or monograms". This provision was repealed by the Copyright Act 1956, s.50. The Law Commission appears to have been unaware of it.
[16] cf. *Douce* [1972] Crim. L.R. 105.

FALSE INSTRUMENTS

11–008 At common law it was necessary to prove that the document was not merely misleading but "false", in the sense that it purported to be something it was not.[17] It must not only tell a lie, but tell a lie about itself. The Law Commission's intention was that this requirement of "automendacity"[18] should be retained in the new legislation.

> "[T]he primary reason for retaining a law of forgery is to penalise the making of documents which, because of the spurious air of authenticity given to them, are likely to lead to their acceptance as true statements of the facts related in them. We do not think that there is any need for the extension of forgery to cover falsehoods that are reduced to writing, and we do not propose any change in the law in this regard."[19]

11–009 The actus reus of forgery is the making of a false instrument. FCA 1981, s.9(1) provides:

> "An instrument is false for the purposes of this Part of this Act—
>
> (a) if it purports to have been made in the form in which it is made by a person who did not in fact make it in that form; or
>
> (b) if it purports to have been made in the form in which it is made on the authority of a person who did not in fact authorise its making in that form; or
>
> (c) if it purports to have been made in the terms in which it is made by a person who did not in fact make it in those terms; or
>
> (d) if it purports to have been made in the terms in which it is made on the authority of a person who did not in fact authorise its making in those terms; or
>
> (e) if it purports to have been altered in any respect by a person who did not in fact alter it in that respect; or
>
> (f) if it purports to have been altered in any respect on the authority of a person who did not in fact authorise the alteration in that respect; or
>
> (g) if it purports to have been made or altered on a date on which, or at a place at which, or otherwise in circumstances in which, it was not in fact made or altered; or
>
> (h) if it purports to have been made or altered by an existing person but he did not in fact exist."

This definition appears to be exhaustive.[20]

[17] *Re Windsor* (1865) 10 Cox C.C. 118 at 123, *per* Blackburn J.
[18] A term coined by Edward Griew, [1970] Crim. L.R. 548.
[19] Law Com. No.55, para.42.
[20] Criminal Justice Act 1925, s.35, which provided in effect that the statutory definition of falsity was merely illustrative, is repealed by FCA 1981.

"PURPORTS"

11–010 In each of the cases set out in FCA 1981, s.9(1), the instrument purports to have been made or altered by (or on the authority of) a certain person, or in certain circumstances. The word "purports" is not defined. The Oxford English Dictionary definition is: "(of a picture, statue, document, book, or the like . . .): To profess or claim by its tenor . . .". This implies that the purport of an instrument is something narrower than the impression that it tends to convey. In *Gilchrist* Buller J. said that "the purport of an instrument . . . is that alone which appears on the face of it".[21] In *Keith*, Coleridge J. said that "an instrument purports to be that which on the face of the instrument it more or less accurately resembles".[22] On this view, a document could purport to be written by a person if it resembles his handwriting, even if it does not mention him. But the offence under discussion in *Keith* was that of engraving a promissory note purporting to be that of a banking company,[23] and Crompton J. pointed out that "one must give the word 'purporting' a larger meaning than it ordinarily bears, or the statute would be ineffectual in many cases".[24]

11–011 In *More*[25] the defendant acquired a cheque intended for one Michael Richard Jessel and payable to "M.R. Jessell". He opened a building society account in the name "Mark Richard Jessell" and paid the cheque into it. A few days later he completed a withdrawal form in the name "M.R. Jessell" and was given a cheque. The House of Lords held that the withdrawal form was not a false instrument by virtue of FCA 1981, s.9(1)(a) or (c).[26] Since it made no mention of the cheque that had been paid into the account, it did not purport to have been made by the real Mr Jessel: it purported to have been made by the person who had opened the account. And this was true.

11–012 It does not follow that, in determining how or when or by whom the instrument purports to have been made, it is permissible to look *only* at the instrument itself. There must be some basis in the instrument itself for the "purport" that the prosecution seeks to establish. But, if there is such a basis, the *content* of that purport probably depends to some extent on the surrounding circumstances.[27] Suppose a document is signed "John Smith". Clearly it purports to have been signed by one of the many men of that name; but which? If it carries information relating to a particular John Smith, such as his address or (as in *More*) the number of his bank account, there is no difficulty. But what if it carries no such information? Buller J.'s definition ("that alone which appears on the face of it") would imply that the document could not then purport to have been made by any particular

[21] (1795) 2 Leach 657 at 662.
[22] (1855) 24 U.M.C. 110 at 112.
[23] Forgery Act 1830, s.18.
[24] (1855) 24 U.M.C. 110 at 112.
[25] [1987] 1 W.L.R. 1578.
[26] On the question whether it was false within FCA 1981, s.9(1)(h), see below, para.11–018.
[27] Roger Leng, "Falsity in Forgery" [1989] Crim. L.R. 687.

John Smith, even if its intended recipient would be likely to assume that it had (for example because he only knows one). But this seems too restrictive: once it is established that the document purports to be signed by *a* John Smith, it must surely be legitimate to look at all the circumstances in order to establish *which* John Smith the document purports to be signed by.

11–013 It would follow that if a man called John Smith signs a document "John Smith", in such circumstances that its recipient is likely to think it is signed by some other John Smith, the document purports to be signed by the other John Smith. This was so under the old law.[28] The rule was enacted as the Forgery Act 1913, s.1(2)(c), which provided that a document was false if it was made in the name of its maker but with the intention that it should pass as having been made by some other person. FCA 1981 contains no corresponding provision, but the situation probably falls within s.9(1) anyway.[29]

11–014 In *Brittain v Bank of London* the drawer of a cheque disguised his handwriting when the cheque was returned to him by the bank, and claimed that the payee had forged it. According to Cockburn C.J. he was not guilty of forgery.[30] Similarly in *Macer*[31] the defendant did not commit forgery by drawing a cheque in his own name but with an unusual signature. The cheque did not purport to be signed by anyone other than the defendant. Had it been proved that he intended the signature to be taken as that of some other person, s.1(2)(c) of the 1913 Act would presumably have applied. Since FCA 1981 contains no corresponding provision, he would probably not be guilty of forgery today even if such an intention could be proved. In the absence of any reference to another person on the face of the cheque, it would still purport (truthfully) to have been drawn by him. The fact that he intended it to *look* as if it were drawn by someone else would be irrelevant.

MATTERS ON WHICH AN INSTRUMENT MAY "TELL A LIE ABOUT ITSELF"

11–015 FCA 1981, s.9 sets out various matters on which an instrument may "tell a lie about itself". Broadly speaking these matters may be grouped into four categories:

- the identity of the person making the instrument;

[28] *Mead v Young* (1790) 4 T.R. 28, approved by Parke B., Patteson J. and Pollock C.B. *arguendo* in *White* (1847) 2 Cox C.C. 210 at 215; *Hudson* [1943] 1 All E.R. 642; *Abdullah* [1982] Crim. L.R. 122; cf. *Mitchell* (1844) 1 Den. 282; *Nisbett* (1853) 6 Cox C.C. 320; *Mahony* (1854) 6 Cox C.C. 487.

[29] The fact that s.1(2)(c) of the 1913 Act was thought necessary arguably suggests that this situation would not otherwise have been covered, and therefore that the document would not "purport" to have been made by a person by whom it was not in fact made. But s.1(2)(c) apparently applied even where the document was intended to pass as the work of someone who did *not* have a similar name to the one it bore, and therefore did not "purport" to be his.

[30] (1863) 3 F. & F. 465 at 473.

[31] [1979] Crim. L.R. 659.

- the identity of the person authorising its making;
- the date, place or circumstances of its making; and
- the circumstances of any alteration to it.

Identity of maker

Where an instrument purports to have been made in its present form and terms by a particular person, it will be false within FCA 1981, s.9(1)(a) or (c) if that person did not make it at all. It will also be false if he did make it, but it has since been altered so that its present form or terms are not those in which he made it. **11–016**

The corresponding provision in the 1913 Act[32] was construed so as not to apply where a document was made with the authority of the person in question, even if it purported to have been made by him in person.[33] Such a document would clearly fall within FCA 1981, s.9(1). An instrument is also false under s.9(1)(a) if it purports to have been made by a company before it went into liquidation, but was in fact made afterwards.[34] Where the purported maker of the instrument did make it, but did so under some misapprehension (perhaps fraudulently induced) as to its nature or contents, it seems that forgery would not have been committed under the old law,[35] and it would be difficult to bring such a case within s.9(1). The maker of an instrument is still its maker even if he does not know what it is, and would not be bound by it under the doctrine of *non est factum*. **11–017**

Instrument purporting to be made by a non-existent person

FCA 1981, s.9(1)(h) provides for a specific example of an instrument which purports to have been made by a person who did not in fact make it—namely one which purports to have been made by a person who could not make it because he did not exist. At common law it was sufficient not only if the document purported to have been made by a person who did not exist,[36] but also if the person who made it (and by whom it truthfully purported to have been made) was pretending to be another person who did not exist.[37] FCA 1981, s.9(1)(h) includes the former case (which is surely covered by s.9(1)(a) and (c) in any event) but not the latter. In *More*[38] the allegedly false instrument was a withdrawal form in the name "M.R. Jessell". The defendant had previously opened an account in the name "Mark Richard Jessell" with a cheque intended for one Michael Richard Jessel and payable to "M.R. Jessell". The Court of Appeal held **11–018**

[32] s.1(2).
[33] *Vincent* (1972) 56 Cr.App.R. 281; cf. *Potter* [1958] 1 W.L.R. 638, where the difficulty was evaded by invoking the Criminal Justice Act 1925, s.35.
[34] *Lack* (1986) 84 Cr.App.R. 342.
[35] *Collins* (1843) 2 M. & Rob. 461; *Chadwick* (1844) 2 M. & Rob. 545.
[36] *Lewis* (1754) Fost. 116.
[37] *Dunn* (1765) 1 Leach 57; cf. *Hassard* [1970] 2 All E.R. 647; *Gambling* [1975] Q.B. 207.
[38] [1987] 1 W.L.R. 1578.

that the withdrawal form did not fall within s.9(1)(a) or (c)[39] but did fall within s.9(1)(h), because it purported to have been made by a person (Mark Richard Jessell) who did not exist. The House of Lords held that it was not a false instrument at all, because it did not purport to have been made by anyone other than the defendant (real or otherwise). He was merely using a name that was not his own.[40] He was guilty of deception but not of forgery. In the light of this decision it is hard to see what, if anything, s.9(1)(h) adds to s.9(1)(a) and (c). It clearly does *not* qualify the principle that an instrument is only false if it tells a lie about itself.

Identity of person authorising making

11–019 Under FCA 1981, s.9(1)(b) and (d), an instrument is false if it purports to have been made in its present form and terms on the authority of a particular person, and that person either did not authorise its making at all or did not authorise its making in that form or in those terms. There is arguably a lacuna where the instrument purports to have been made on the authority of a person who did not in fact exist—for example, the holder of some impressive-sounding but non-existent post in an organisation. It could be argued that this case falls within s.9(1)(b) or (d), or both: the instrument purports to have been made on the authority of a person who did not authorise its making (and indeed did not exist). This argument would have more force if s.9(1)(h) had been omitted. Its inclusion arguably suggests that a fictitious person is not "a person" within the meaning of s.9(1)(a) and (c), and presumably therefore not within the meaning of s.9(1)(b) and (d) either. But the effect of *More*[41] is that s.9(1)(h) is redundant, since it applies only when the instrument purports to have been made by someone who did not make it (and incidentally does not exist)—in which case s.9(1)(a) or (c) applies anyway. If s.9(1)(h) is redundant, it probably throws no light on the rest of s.9(1).

Date, place or circumstances of making

11–020 Under FCA 1981, s.9(1)(g) an instrument is false if it falsely purports to have been made on a certain date, or at a certain place, or otherwise in certain circumstances. Thus it would be forgery to make out a bill of lading with a date earlier or later than that on which the goods were in fact shipped, or to ante-date a deed with a view to tax evasion.[42] Misdating a *cheque* might not suffice: since cheques are commonly post-dated, a cheque probably does not purport to have been drawn on the date that it bears.

11–021 The wording of s.9(1)(g) makes it clear that the "circumstances" in which the instrument purports to have been made may include matters other than the date and place of its making. Read literally, this means that a document

[39] Above, para.11–011.
[40] Glanville Williams, "Forgery and Falsity" [1974] Crim. L.R. 71.
[41] [1987] 1 W.L.R. 1578; above, para.11–018.
[42] cf. *Wells* [1939] 2 All E.R. 169.

can be false even if it does not tell a lie *about itself*. In *Donnelly*[43] the manager of a jeweller's shop, for the purpose of an insurance fraud, made out a valuation certificate describing six items of jewellery which did not exist. It was conceded that this document would not have been a forgery either at common law or under the Forgery Act 1913,[44] but it was held to fall within FCA 1981, s.9(1)(g).

> "There can be no doubt that in 1981 Parliament intended to make new law. . . . In our judgment the words coming at the end of paragraph (g) 'otherwise in circumstances . . .' expand its ambit beyond dates and places to *any* case in which an instrument purports to be made when it was not in fact made. This valuation purported to be made after the appellant had examined the items of jewellery set out in the schedule. He did not make it after examining these items because they did not exist. That which purported to be a valuation after examination of items was nothing of the kind: it was a worthless piece of paper."[45]

This was followed in *Jeraj*,[46] where a bank manager signed a document purporting to verify the endorsement of a letter of credit which did not exist.[47] In *Warneford*,[48] however, an employment reference was held not to be "false" although the person it described had never been employed by the person who wrote it. The lie did not relate to the circumstances of the document's making, but was extraneous to the document itself. The same was true of the valuation in *Donnelly*, and that decision could not stand with the House of Lords' confirmation in *More* that the document must tell a lie about itself.[49]

In *Attorney-General's Reference (No.1 of 2000)*[50] the distinction drawn in *Warneford* was broadly accepted, but put in a slightly different way. **11–022**

> "Both *Donnelly* and *Jeraj* should . . . be restricted in their application so that they apply only where circumstances need to exist before the document can be properly made or altered. If those circumstances do not exist there will then be a false instrument for the purposes of section 9(1)(g). If the circumstances do not exist the document is telling a lie about itself because it is saying it was made in circumstances which do not exist."[51]

[43] [1984] 1 W.L.R. 1017.
[44] In *Dodge* [1972] 1 Q.B. 416, for example, bonds were executed in respect of a non-existent debt for the purpose of inducing a third party to believe that the debt was in fact owed. The bonds were held not to be forgeries because they were what they purported to be, viz. bonds executed by the person named in them: they did not tell a lie about themselves, but only about the existence of the debt.
[45] [1984] 1 W.L.R. 1017 at 1018–1019.
[46] [1994] Crim. L.R. 595.
[47] The court also thought that the document purported to be part of "a kind of articulated document", consisting of itself and the letter of credit to which it referred, and was not in fact part of any such document. For this argument s.9(l)(g) was not required.
[48] [1994] Crim. L.R. 753.
[49] *Jeraj* had not been reported and was not cited.
[50] [2001] 1 Cr.App.R. 15 (p.218).
[51] [2001] 1 Cr.App.R. 15 (p.218) at [24].

Even on this "restricted" basis, however, *Donnelly* was rightly decided.

> "It is of the essence of a valuation that the articles, the subject of the valuation, have been examined. This is because a bona fide valuation requires some examination of what is the subject of the valuation. The lie in *Donnelly* therefore related to an event which must have occurred before a genuine valuation could be made."[52]

Warneford was therefore wrong in disapproving *Donnelly*. And the reference in *Warneford* was indistinguishable from the valuation in *Donnelly*, so *Warneford* itself was wrongly decided.

> "In each case where we would hold the instrument to be false it could not have been made honestly if the circumstances which we have identified did not exist. Thus in *Donnelly* you could not make a valuation without having seen the jewellery which you purport to have valued. In *Jeraj* there had to be a letter of credit which could be endorsed. In *Warneford and Gibbs* there had to have been the relationship of master and servant before you could make a reference as an employer relating to an employee. The need for the existence of these circumstances prior to the making of the instrument explains why if the circumstances do not exist the document is telling a lie about itself."[53]

11–023 The *Attorney-General's Reference* concerned the tachograph record sheet of a passenger coach. The driver falsified the sheet so as to show that at a certain time he was not driving, whereas in fact he was. It was held that the circumstances in which the sheet purported to have been made were circumstances that had to exist before it could properly be made, and that it therefore fell within s.9(1)(g).

> "The tachograph record is produced continuously over the period indicated by the record. It is being made throughout this time. In so far as the record was being produced in this case while the first driver was shown as driving there was no falsity in relation to its making. It was, however, capable of being a false instrument during the period when it showed that the first driver was not driving and that a second driver must therefore have been driving. To make that part of the instrument, it was essential for there to be a second driver during the period the tachograph was operated in the second driver position. There was no second driver and therefore the instrument was false. The circumstance which was false was that the record was being made during a period when there wrongly purported to be a second driver who was driving."[54]

11–024 The distinction drawn in the *Attorney-General's Reference* is unlikely to prove workable. Certain circumstances need to exist before *any* statement can be properly made. Those circumstances are that the statement should, to the best of the maker's belief, be true. Indeed the court accepted that if the driver had filled out a form instead of operating a tachograph, the form

[52] [2001] 1 Cr.App.R. 15 (p.218) at [15]. The court adopted the argument of Roger Leng in "Falsity in Forgery" [1989] Crim. L.R. 687.
[53] [2001] 1 Cr.App.R. 15 (p.218) at [24].
[54] [2001] 1 Cr.App.R. 15 (p.218) at [25].

would not have been a false instrument. But the driver could not properly produce a form stating that he was not driving unless certain circumstances existed, namely that he was not driving. The court's own distinction fails to explain why the two cases are different. It is submitted that the criterion proposed in *Warneford* (whether the document tells a lie about the circumstances *of its making*) is to be preferred to that in the *Attorney-General's Reference*. That is so even if the *Attorney-General's Reference* was right in holding that the actual decision in *Warneford* should have gone the other way. Arguably the employment reference *was* a document that told a lie about its own making, because it was not merely untruthful but purported to be written by the person's employer.

Circumstances of alteration

Under FCA 1981, s.9(1)(e) to (h), an instrument which was originally made in the circumstances in which it purports to have been made may nevertheless be false if it "tells a lie" about a subsequent alteration, real or fictitious. The requirements are parallel to those relating to the making of the instrument. The instrument must *purport* to have been altered in some respect. This excludes an instrument which has been altered in such a way as to give the impression that it has *not* been altered; but such an instrument would purport to have been originally made in its present form and terms, and would therefore be false under s.9(1)(a) or (c). The alteration must purport to have been made **11–025**

- by a person who did not in fact make it[55] (for example because he did not exist);[56] or
- on the authority of a person who did not in fact authorise it[57] (for example, it is submitted, where that person did not exist);[58] or
- on a certain date, at a certain place or in certain circumstances, where that is not in fact the case.[59]

MAKING A FALSE INSTRUMENT

The actus reus of forgery is the *making* of a false instrument. FCA 1981, s.9(2) provides: **11–026**

> "A person is to be treated for the purposes of this Part of this Act as making a false instrument if he alters an instrument so as to make it false in any respect (whether or not it is false in some other respect apart from that alteration)."

[55] FCA 1981, s.9(1)(e).
[56] FCA 1981, s.9(1)(h).
[57] FCA 1981, s.9(1)(f).
[58] cf. above, para.11–019.
[59] FCA 1981, s.9(1)(g).

"Making a false instrument" thus includes

- making an instrument which is false as soon as it is made,
- altering a genuine instrument so as to make it false, and
- altering an instrument which is already false so as to make it false in some other way.

11–027 Where the defendant does not physically produce or alter the instrument himself, but deceives another person into producing or altering it, it might be argued that he has "made" the instrument through an innocent agent. But this is probably so only if the victim does not realise that he is making an instrument at all.[60] If he knows that that is what he is doing, it is he who "makes" it within the meaning of FCA 1981. The defendant is guilty of fraud by false representation (or, under the old law, procuring the execution of a valuable security by deception)[61] but not forgery.

MENS REA

11–028 The mens rea of forgery is threefold.[62] The maker of the false instrument must intend

- that he or another shall use it to induce somebody to accept it as genuine,
- that the person accepting it as genuine shall, by reason of so accepting it, do (or not do) some act, and
- that that act or omission shall be to his own or someone else's prejudice.

The jury must be directed separately on these elements.[63] They are elements of the mens rea, not the actus reus. It is neither necessary nor sufficient that someone should in fact accept the instrument as genuine or

[60] cf. above, para.9–116.

[61] Theft Act 1968, s.20(2); above, para.4–151. But not all instruments are valuable securities: see paras 4–154 *et seq.*

[62] *Winston* [1999] 1 Cr.App.R. 337 at 343. There is arguably a further requirement, too obvious to require express provision: viz. that the maker of the false instrument must realise that it is false. Admittedly FCA 1981, s.2, which creates the offence of *copying* a false instrument, expressly requires not only an intention that the copy be accepted as genuine (i.e. as a copy of a genuine instrument) but also knowledge or belief that the original is false; and this arguably implies that the latter requirement is not implicit in the former. But it is submitted that s.2 merely makes express what would otherwise be implied. Dishonesty is not required: *Campbell* (1985) 80 Cr.App.R. 47.

[63] *Tobierre* [1986] Crim. L.R. 243; *Garcia* (1988) 87 Cr.App.R. 175; *Att-Gen's Reference (No.1 of 2001)* [2002] EWCA Crim 1768; [2003] 1 W.L.R. 395. These cases refer to a requirement of "double intention", meaning that the intention to induce another to accept the instrument as genuine must be distinguished from the intention that that other shall do some act to someone's prejudice. *Winston* [1999] 1 Cr.App.R. 337 demonstrates the importance of drawing a further distinction between the act to be induced and the prejudicial character of that act.

act upon it. Like fraud by false representation (but unlike the old deception offences), forgery is inchoate in character. If the required act is done with the required intention to bring about certain consequences, it is immaterial whether those consequences actually occur.[64]

ACCEPTANCE OF THE INSTRUMENT AS GENUINE

The defendant must intend that he or another shall use[65] the false instrument to induce somebody to accept it as genuine. The word "accept" does not imply that anyone else must be intended to take possession of the instrument, or even see it. In *Ondhia*[66] the defendant sent a fax of a false instrument. He did not intend the recipient to see the original, but only a copy generated by the recipient's fax machine. It was argued that he should have been charged with making a *copy* of a false instrument contrary to FCA 1981, s.2,[67] or with using a copy of a false instrument contrary to s.4.[68] The argument was rejected. 11–029

> "The ways in which the document may be used, whether by the maker himself or someone else, with his knowledge, or as his agent, to 'induce somebody to accept it as genuine' are not defined or limited, and the maker of the false document does not avoid prosecution under section 1 of the 1981 Act merely because at the time when he is creating the document he has not made up his mind about the method of despatch or intends that it should be transmitted by fax rather than delivered through the ordinary postal system, or by hand, direct to the intended ultimate recipient. . . . In the present case, . . . at the time when the appellant made the false document he intended that it should be used to induce [the recipient] to accept, without ever seeing it, that the original false document of which they had received a duplicate was genuine."[69]

This is clearly right. But it appears to treat "accepting an instrument as genuine" as a synonym for assuming that the instrument is genuine. Arguably there is a difference, in that acceptance implies not just a state of mind but an act or omission resulting from that state of mind. But this cannot be what is meant, because FCA 1981 refers both to acceptance *and* to an act or omission by reason of the acceptance. It is therefore not clear whether the word "accept" is intended to have any special significance. Presumably it is immaterial that the victim is unlikely to care whether the instrument is genuine or not—which will often be so in the case of stolen credit cards and similar instruments[70]—provided that he is intended to "accept" that it is. This situation creates less difficulty here than in the law 11–030

[64] *Ondhia* [1998] 2 Cr.App.R. 150.
[65] It is not clear how one might induce someone to accept an instrument as genuine without using it, and it may be that this requirement is redundant.
[66] [1998] 2 Cr.App.R. 150.
[67] See below, para.11–044.
[68] See below, para.11–048.
[69] [1998] 2 Cr.App.R. 150 at 156.
[70] See above, paras 4–055 *et seq*.

of deception and fraud by false representation: it is more natural to say that the apathetic victim "accepts" the instrument as genuine than that he is "deceived" as to the holder's right to use it, or that the holder intends to make a gain *by* representing that he is entitled to do so.[71] But it would be equally natural to say that the victim assumes the instrument to be genuine.

11–031 FCA 1981, s.10(3) provides:

> "In this Part of this Act references to inducing somebody to accept a false instrument as genuine . . . include references to inducing a machine to respond to the instrument . . . as if it were a genuine instrument . . ."

The Act thus avoids the difficulties involved in the notion of deceiving a machine.[72] The false instrument need not be intended to come to the attention of a human being at all. It must be established that what the defendant made was an "instrument"; but that term is defined so as to include discs, tapes and other devices for the storage of information,[73] so the input of data into a computer must by definition involve the making of an instrument. Even the computer's short-term memory is a device for the (temporary) storage of information.[74] But the drafting is obscure. To speak of a machine responding to an instrument "as if it were a genuine instrument" implies that the machine is supposed to respond in one way if the instrument appears to be genuine and another way if it does not. If the machine is programmed to respond in the same way whatever the instrument says, these words appear to be meaningless. What seems to be meant is that it is sufficient if the machine responds *in the usual way*.

ACT OR OMISSION

11–032 The defendant must intend that the person accepting the instrument as genuine shall, by reason of so accepting it, do (or not do) some act. Under the old law there might be an intent to defraud even if the defendant's intention was to obtain by deception something to which he was legally entitled, such as the payment of a debt.[75] The Law Commission thought that "it should not be forgery to make a false instrument to induce another to do what he is obliged to do or refrain from doing what he is not entitled to do".[76] FCA 1981, s.10(2) therefore provides:

[71] See above, para.3–004.

[72] Above, para.4–072.

[73] FCA 1981, s.8(1)(d).

[74] In *Gold* [1988] A.C. 1063 it was held that the defendants had not made a false instrument by sending false identification to a computer; but in that case the identification details were held in the computer's memory for only a tiny fraction of a second while they were checked. The input of false data or instructions, to be held in the computer's memory until saved to a magnetic disk, can clearly amount to the making of a false instrument. So, *a fortiori*, can the saving of data or instructions to such a disk: *R. v Governor of Brixton Prison, ex p. Levin* [1997] Q.B. 65.

[75] *Parker* (1910) 74 J.P. 208; *Smith* (1919) 14 Cr.App.R. 101.

[76] Law Com. No.55, para.34.

"An act which a person has an enforceable duty to do and an omission to do an act which a person is not entitled to do shall be disregarded for the purposes of this Part of this Act."

So it is not forgery if the defendant intends only to induce another person to do what he is legally obliged to do. In that case, the effect of s.10(2) is that the defendant is deemed not to intend that the other shall do anything at all. So the question of whether the other's act would be prejudicial does not arise.

However, this defence is available only if the other person is *already* under an obligation to do what the defendant intends him to do (or, presumably, the defendant thinks he is). It is not enough that the other person would come under such an obligation if the defendant made a genuine instrument instead of a false one. In *Winston*[77] the defendant submitted forged documents in support of his claim for housing benefit. His defence was that his circumstances were in fact as the documents stated them to be. Since he was entitled to the benefit he claimed, the effect of s.10(2) was that he did not intend the local authority to act to its prejudice. This argument was rejected. Under the terms of the relevant legislation, the local authority was not liable to pay the benefit unless and until the defendant provided the documents required by the regulations. The forged documents he provided did not comply with the regulations. So he never became entitled to the benefit, and s.10(2) did not apply. **11–033**

This was not in fact the argument advanced by the Crown. The Crown had argued instead that, even if the local authority was legally obliged to pay the benefit, the defendant's conduct still fell within the section because he intended the local authority's *officials* to act on the documents by examining and verifying his claim. This would be an act to the officials' prejudice by virtue of s.10(1)(c), because it would result from their acceptance of the documents in connection with their performance of their duty.[78] In the court's view this argument did not get round s.10(2), because if the local authority was under a duty to pay the benefit then the officials must equally have been under a duty to approve the application. If the duty relied upon for the purposes of s.10(1)(c) is a duty to do the very act that the defendant intends to secure, that act must be disregarded under s.10(2), and there is no "act" to which s.10(1)(c) can apply. **11–034**

"[W]hen one analyses the proposition advanced by [Counsel for the Crown], one is driven, as was he, to draw a distinction between a situation where the document is presented direct to the employer or individual under the enforceable obligation and where it is presented to a person who is his employee. Thus, [Counsel] argued that whenever the person under an enforceable obligation was a corporate entity there would be an offence under section 1 unless the employee or officer to whom the document was presented could be categorised as the alter ego of the corporate entity. This would produce

[77] [1999] 1 Cr.App.R. 337.
[78] See below, para.11–038.

> arbitrary results. It would also involve artificially distinguishing between the employee or agent and the principal on whose behalf he was, in all material respects, acting."[79]

The court accepted that there might be situations in which such a distinction could properly be drawn, but *Winston* was not such a case.

11–035 *Winston* was followed in *Attorney-General's Reference (No.1 of 2001).*[80] The defendants submitted a false invoice to the trustees of a trust fund set up for their support in connection with their daughter's prosecution for a crime. It was argued that there was no intention to induce the trustees to do an act to anyone's prejudice, because the trust fund belonged to the defendants anyway. The argument was rejected on the ground that the act which they intended to secure (namely the payment of a cheque for the sum stated in the invoice) was not an act that the trustees were obliged to do. It was immaterial that the defendants might lawfully have secured payment of the money by other means.

PREJUDICE

11–036 The defendant must intend that the act or omission he intends to induce by using the false instrument shall be to someone's prejudice—either that of the person who is induced to act or not to act, or that of some third person. "Prejudice" is defined by FCA 1981, s.10(1):

> "Subject to subsections (2) and (4) below, for the purposes of this Part of this Act an act or omission intended to be induced is to a person's prejudice if, and only if, it is one which, if it occurs—
>
> (a) will result—
>
> (i) in his temporary or permanent loss[81] of property; or
>
> (ii) in his being deprived of an opportunity to earn remuneration or greater remuneration; or
>
> (iii) in his being deprived of an opportunity to gain a financial advantage otherwise than by way of remuneration; or
>
> (b) will result in somebody being given an opportunity—
>
> (i) to earn remuneration or greater remuneration from him; or
>
> (ii) to gain a financial advantage from him otherwise than by way of remuneration; or
>
> (c) will be the result of his having accepted a false instrument as genuine . . . in connection with his performance of any duty."

[79] [1999] 1 Cr.App.R. 337 at 342.
[80] [2002] EWCA Crim 1768; [2003] 1 W.L.R. 395.
[81] "Loss" includes not getting what one might get as well as parting with what one has: FCA 1981, s.10(5). Cf. above, Ch.3.

The concept of an intent to cause prejudice is thus very similar to that of intent to defraud in the old law of forgery and in conspiracy to defraud.[82] It is enough if the maker of the instrument intends some other person to suffer financial loss, or intends a third party to gain a financial advantage at that person's expense. It is enough if the intention is to induce the victim to part with money or other property, even if the defendant intends to provide the expected consideration.[83] **11–037**

It is also sufficient if the defendant intends someone to do an act as a result of his having accepted a false instrument as genuine in connection with his performance of any duty. This seems to have broadly the same effect as the *Welham* principle in relation to common law fraud.[84] In these circumstances it is the person intended to act who is deemed to be prejudiced, rather than a third party.[85] **11–038**

FCA 1981, s.10(4) adds that, where s.10(3) applies—that is, where it is a machine that is intended to "accept" the instrument as genuine— **11–039**

> "the act or omission intended to be induced by the machine responding to the instrument . . . shall be treated as an act or omission to a person's prejudice."

The defendant's intention need not be to induce the victim to take any positive action. It may be to induce him "*not* to do some act to his own or any other person's prejudice".[86] In this expression, the words "to his own or any other person's prejudice" qualify the whole phrase "not to do some act", not just the words "some act". It is the victim's intended *omission* to act that must be to his or another's prejudice—not the act that he is intended to omit to do. This might seem obvious, but in *Utting*[87] the prosecution managed to get it wrong. The defendant, a solicitor, appropriated money belonging to a client, and produced a photocopy of a document purporting to be an agreement by the client to lend him the money. It was argued that he intended to induce the police to refrain from doing an act which, if done, would be to *his* prejudice—namely prosecuting him. It should have been argued that *not* prosecuting him would have been an *omission* to *the police's* prejudice, because it would be the result of their accepting the document as genuine in connection with their performance of their duty.[88] **11–040**

[82] See above, paras 7–005 *et seq.*
[83] *Dzirvinski*, August 18, 1992.
[84] *Welham v DPP* [1961] A.C. 103; above, para.7–020.
[85] In *Winston* [1999] 1 Cr.App.R. 337 the court appears to have regarded this as throwing light on the effect of s.10(2), but it is probably no more than a drafting device. The drafter might equally have said that, where the intention is that a person shall act or not act as a result of his having accepted the false instrument as genuine in connection with his performance of a duty, the act or omission need not be to anyone's "prejudice" at all.
[86] Italics supplied.
[87] [1987] Crim. L.R. 636.
[88] Above, para.11–038.

CAUSATION

11–041 The maker of the false instrument must not only intend that another person shall be induced to accept the instrument as genuine, and to do (or not do) some act to someone's prejudice: he must also intend that the other person shall do the latter "by reason of" doing the former. He need not intend that the other's acceptance of the instrument should be the *only* reason for the other's act or omission, but he must intend that it should be *a* reason for it. This is analogous to the requirement in the new fraud offence that the defendant must intend to make a gain or cause a loss or a risk of loss *by* making the false representation, failing to disclose the information or abusing his position (as the case may be).[89]

11–042 It is not clear whether this requirement is as generous to the defendant as the old rule that the document must be false in a material particular. Suppose he intends another person to accept the instrument as genuine, and to act accordingly, and he knows that if the instrument were false in certain respects the other person would not knowingly accept it. But he believes that the particular respect in which the instrument is in fact false is one that would be of no concern to the other person even if he knew that the instrument is false in that respect. On a literal interpretation he would seem to fall within FCA 1981, s.1. It is submitted, however, that what is implicitly required is an intention that the person accepting the instrument as genuine should act in a way in which he would not have acted had he known that the instrument was false *in the respect in which it is false*. In other words, the defendant must know or believe that the instrument is false in a material particular.

REFUGEES

11–043 Under the Immigration and Asylum Act 1999, s.31, a refugee[90] charged with forgery or one of the other offences discussed in this chapter[91] (or an attempt[92] to commit any such offence) has a defence if he shows that, having come to the United Kingdom directly from a country where his life or freedom was threatened, he presented himself to the authorities without delay, showed good cause for his illegal entry or presence, and made a claim for asylum as soon as was reasonably practicable after his arrival. But if he stopped in another country before reaching the United Kingdom, the

[89] Above, para.3–004.

[90] i.e. a person who "owing to well-founded fear of being persecuted for reasons of race, religion, nationality, membership of a particular social group or political opinion, is outside the country of his nationality and is unable or, owing to such fear, is unwilling to avail himself of the protection of that country; or who, not having a nationality and being outside the country of his former habitual residence, is unable or, owing to such fear, is unwilling to return to it": Immigration and Asylum Act 1999, s.31(6); Convention Relating to the Status of Refugees, art.1.

[91] Except the one under the Theft Act 1968, s.20(1).

[92] But not conspiracy.

defence is available only if he shows that he could not reasonably have expected to be given protection under the Convention in that other country.[93] It is not available in relation to any offence committed by him after making a claim for asylum.[94] The burden of showing that he is a refugee is an evidential one, but he must prove the other conditions on a balance of probabilities.[95]

MAKING A COPY OF A FALSE INSTRUMENT

The act of making a copy of a false instrument is unlikely to constitute forgery, because the copy will not normally "tell a lie" about its own making but only about that of the original.[96] It would only be forgery if the person making it intended to pass it off as the original. But FCA 1981, s.2 provides: **11–044**

> "It is an offence for a person to make a copy of an instrument which is, and which he knows or believes to be, a false instrument, with the intention that he or another shall use it to induce somebody to accept it as a copy of a genuine instrument, and by reason of so accepting it to do or not to do some act to his own or any other person's prejudice."

The offence carries the same penalties as forgery.[97]

Most of the elements of the offence are, *mutatis mutandis*, the same as those of forgery. The main difference is the express requirement that the maker of the copy must know or believe the original to be false.[98] Since the original must in fact be false, it is not clear how the maker of the copy might believe it to be false without knowing it to be false. By analogy with the authorities on handling stolen goods,[99] where the same difficulty arises, the courts would presumably hold that the maker of a copy does not believe the original to be false merely because he suspects it may be. It is necessary that in the light of the circumstances known to him there can be no other reasonable conclusion, and he must realise that that is so. **11–045**

USING A FALSE INSTRUMENT

The old offence of uttering a forged document is replaced by FCA 1981, s.3, which provides: **11–046**

93 Immigration and Asylum Act 1999, s.31(2).
94 Immigration and Asylum Act 1999, s.31(5).
95 *Makuwa* [2006] EWCA Crim 175; [2006] 1 W.L.R. 2755.
96 Another point overlooked by the prosecution in *Utting* [1987] Crim. L.R. 636.
97 FCA 1981, s.6(1), (2).
98 But it is suggested above, para.11–028, fn.62, that a similar requirement is implicit in s.1.
99 Theft Act 1968, s.22(1); see *Hall* [1985] Crim. L.R. 377; *Forsyth* [1997] Crim. L.R. 589.

> "It is an offence for a person to use an instrument which is, and which he knows or believes to be, false, with the intention of inducing somebody to accept it as genuine, and by reason of so accepting it to do or not to do some act to his own or any other person's prejudice."

The offence carries the same penalties as forgery.[100] Where the instrument is made by one person and used by another, the maker will normally be guilty of forgery and the user will commit the offence under s.3. But there is no need for the instrument to be *forged,* in the sense that its maker is guilty of forgery. It is enough that the instrument is in fact false and the user knows or believes[101] that it is. Thus a person who deceives another into making a false instrument, and then uses it himself, would be guilty under s.3 even if the maker were innocent.

11–047 The *use* of an instrument appears to involve some direct nexus, though not necessarily physical contact, between the user and the instrument. A person who acts in a way that he knows is likely to result in a request for, and the supply of, a false instrument—for example, by applying for a mortgage in the expectation that the reference supplied will be false—does not thereby "use" that instrument.[102]

USING A COPY OF A FALSE INSTRUMENT

11–048 It seems to follow that a person who uses a copy of an instrument does not thereby "use" the original within the meaning of FCA 1981, s.3. FCA 1981, s.4 therefore provides:

> "It is an offence for a person to use a copy of an instrument which is, and which he knows or believes to be, a false instrument, with the intention of inducing somebody to accept it as a copy of a genuine instrument, and by reason of so accepting it to do or not to do some act to his own or any other person's prejudice."

The offence carries the same penalties as forgery.[103]

11–049 Read literally, s.4 would appear not to apply if, by the time the copy is used, the original is no longer in existence or no longer false, nor even if the user of the copy wrongly believes that either of these is the case. Such an interpretation would defeat the object of the section. It must be sufficient that the instrument was false when the copy was made, and that the defendant knows or believes that it was.

[100] FCA 1981, s.6(1), (2).
[101] See above, para.11–045.
[102] *Warneford* [1994] Crim. L.R. 753.
[103] FCA 1981, s.6(1), (2).

POSSESSION OF SPECIFIED FALSE INSTRUMENTS

The Law Commission was of the opinion that the mere possession of certain types of false instruments should constitute an offence, because of the ease with which they may pass from hand to hand and be accepted as genuine.[104] The instruments in question are listed in FCA 1981, s.5(5): 11–050

> "(a) money orders;
> (b) postal orders;
> (c) United Kingdom postage stamps;
> (d) Inland Revenue stamps;
> (e) share certificates;[105]
> (g) cheques and other bills of exchange;
> (h) travellers' cheques;
> (ha) bankers' drafts;
> (hb) promissory notes;
> (j) cheque cards;
> (ja) debit cards;
> (k) credit cards;
> (l) certified copies relating to an entry in a register of births, adoptions, marriages, civil partnerships or deaths and issued by the Registrar General, the Registrar General for Northern Ireland, a registration officer or a person lawfully authorised to issue certified copies relating to such entries; and
> (m) certificates relating to entries in such registers."

There are two offences of possessing a false instrument in this list—one requiring the usual mens rea (namely intent to pass the instrument off as genuine and thereby cause prejudice) and one of mere possession without lawful excuse. FCA 1981, s.5(1) provides: 11–051

> "It is an offence for a person to have in his custody or under his control an instrument to which this section applies which is, and which he knows or believes to be, false, with the intention that he or another shall use it to induce somebody to accept it as genuine, and by reason of so accepting it to do or not to do some act to his own or any other person's prejudice."

[104] Law Com. No.55, para.63.

[105] Defined as instruments entitling or evidencing the title of a person to a share or interest (a) in any public stock, annuity, fund or debt of any government or state, including a state which forms part of another state; or (b) in any stock, fund or debt of a body (whether corporate or unincorporated) established in the United Kingdom or elsewhere: FCA 1981, s.5(6).

This offence carries the same penalties as forgery.[106]

11–052 FCA 1981, s.5(2) provides:

> "It is an offence for a person to have in his custody or under his control, without lawful authority or excuse, an instrument to which this section applies which is, and which he knows or believes to be, false."

This offence is triable either way and is punishable on conviction on indictment with two years' imprisonment.[107] There is no requirement that the defendant should be aware that he has custody or control of the instrument, but this is presumably implied.[108] He will not have a lawful excuse for the possession merely because he has no intention to defraud or to cause "prejudice".[109] Indeed it is hard to imagine what would constitute such an excuse, short of an intention to hand the instrument to the police.[110]

MAKING AND POSSESSION OF MATERIALS FOR THE MAKING OF SPECIFIED INSTRUMENTS

11–053 The Law Commission pointed out that forgery itself is essentially a preparatory offence, and thought it unnecessary to go a step further by punishing acts preparatory to forgery.[111] However, FCA 1981 includes two such offences relating to the making of the instruments listed in s.5(5).[112] Section 5(3) provides:

> "It is an offence for a person to make or to have in his custody or under his control a machine or implement, or paper or any other material, which to his knowledge is or has been specially designed or adapted for the making of an instrument to which this section applies, with the intention that he or another shall make an instrument to which this section applies which is false and that he or another shall use the instrument to induce somebody to accept it as genuine, and by reason of so accepting it to do or not to do some act to his own or any other person's prejudice."

This offence carries the same penalties as forgery.[113]

11–054 The defendant must know that the materials in question are designed or adapted for the making of specified instruments. Belief is not enough. There is no requirement that the materials be designed or adapted for the production of *false* instruments, but the defendant must have intended them to be used for that purpose.

[106] FCA 1981, s.6(1), (2).
[107] FCA 1981, s.6(4).
[108] cf. *Harran* [1969] Crim. L.R. 662.
[109] cf. *Dickins v Gill* [1896] 2 Q.B. 310.
[110] *Wuyts* [1969] 2 Q.B. 476.
[111] Law Com. No.55, para.64.
[112] Above, para.11–050.
[113] FCA 1981, s.6(1), (2).

FCA 1981, s.5(4) provides: 11–055

> "It is an offence for a person to make or to have in his custody or under his control any such machine, implement, paper or material, without lawful authority or excuse."

This offence carries the same penalties as that under s.5(2). The reference to "any such . . . material" appears to mean not just material designed or adapted for the making of the specified instruments, but material that the defendant *knows* to have been so designed or adapted. Since there is no requirement that he should intend to use the material to make false instruments, the words "without lawful authority or excuse" need more generous interpretation than in s.5(2).

SUPPRESSION OF DOCUMENTS

The law of forgery is supplemented by s.20(1) of the Theft Act 1968, 11–056
which provides:

> "A person who dishonestly, with a view to gain for himself or another or with intent to cause loss to another, destroys, defaces or conceals any valuable security, any will or other testamentary document or any original document of or belonging to, or filed or deposited in, any court of justice or any government department shall on conviction on indictment be liable to imprisonment for a term not exceeding seven years."

The offence is triable either way. The expressions "dishonestly", "view to gain . . . or . . . intent to cause loss" and "valuable security" have already been discussed.[114]

The offence is primarily one of *suppressing* documents. The valuable 11–057
security or other document must be destroyed, defaced or concealed. This may be done either because the fraud requires the absence of the document in question (for example where a testator's relative destroys a will which disinherits him) or because the document is to be replaced with a forged substitute. The making of the substitute itself would not fall within s.20(1), but would be forgery.

Forgery committed by *altering* a document might perhaps be "deface- 11–058
ment" of the document within the meaning of s.20(1). Indeed this might be a useful alternative if there were any doubt whether the alteration rendered the document "false" within the meaning of FCA 1981. "Deface" is defined by the Oxford English Dictionary as "to mar the face, features or appearance of; . . . to disfigure". It is arguable that a document is defaced if it is altered in any way. It is submitted, however, that the word should be construed *ejusdem generis* with "destroys" and "conceals", and that an

[114] Ch.2 (dishonesty), Ch.3 (gain and loss), para.4–154 (valuable security).

alteration therefore does not amount to defacement for this purpose unless it renders some of the document illegible. So a person who adds letters and numbers to a cheque so as to increase the amount payable, without altering or erasing any of the writing already there, is guilty of forgery but not under s.20(1).

Chapter 12

FALSE ACCOUNTING AND FALSE STATEMENTS

FALSE ACCOUNTING

Under s.17(1) of the Theft Act 1968 ("TA 1968") a person commits an offence if he **12–001**

> "dishonestly, with a view to gain for himself or another or with intent to cause loss to another—
>
> (a) destroys, defaces, conceals or falsifies any account or any record or document made or required for any accounting purpose; or
>
> (b) in furnishing information for any purpose produces or makes use of any account, or any such record or document as aforesaid, which to his knowledge is or may be misleading, false or deceptive in a material particular".

The offence is triable either way, and is punishable on conviction on indictment with seven years' imprisonment.[1]

ACCOUNTS AND ACCOUNTING PURPOSES

The article suppressed, falsified, produced or made use of must be either an account or a record or document which, though not itself an account, is made or required for an accounting purpose.[2] The indictment should expressly refer to at least one of these alternatives.[3] **12–002**

[1] TA 1968, s.17(1).

[2] Clearly an *account* need not be "made or required for an accounting purpose": *Scot-Simmonds* [1994] Crim. L.R. 933.

[3] *Hawkins* [1997] 1 Cr.App.R. 234.

12–003 "Account" is not defined, and bears its ordinary meaning.[4] It presumably includes accounts held in electronic form. It also includes a wholly fictitious document purporting to be an account.[5]

12–004 "Accounting purpose" should also be given its ordinary and natural meaning. It is not confined to the sort of purposes for which a record or document may be required by an accountant or auditor.[6] But the obtaining of money is not in itself an accounting purpose.[7]

12–005 A record or document[8] falls within the section if it is made or required for an accounting purpose. Whether it is *made* for such a purpose depends on the intentions of the person who makes it. Whether it is *required* for such a purpose depends on the intentions of any other person who may have required it to be made, or who may require it once it is made.[9] In *Mallett*[10] it was conceded that a hire-purchase application form was required for an accounting purpose, and the concession appears to have been correct. In *Attorney-General's Reference (No.1 of 1980)*[11] it was held that personal loan proposal forms, though not made for an accounting purpose, were required for one because they would be used in compiling the finance company's accounts if the proposals were accepted. It was immaterial that they would not be used in this way if the proposals were declined.

> "[I]t is to be observed that section 17(1)(a) in using the words 'made or required' indicates that there is a distinction to be drawn between a document made specifically for the purpose of accounting and one made for some other purpose but which is required for an accounting purpose. Thus it is apparent that a document may fall within the ambit of the section if it is made for some purpose other than an accounting purpose but is required for an accounting purpose as a subsidiary consideration. In the present circumstances the borrower would be making the document for the purpose of his loan proposal to be considered, whereas, at the same time, the document might be 'required' by the finance company for an accounting purpose."[12]

12–006 The reference to a document required for an accounting purpose "as a subsidiary consideration" is confusing. If a document is required for an accounting purpose, it is within the section, even if the person requiring it requires it primarily for some other purpose. A subsidiary purpose is still a purpose. But a document is also within the section if it is made partly for an

[4] *Hawkins* [1997] 1 Cr.App.R. 234.
[5] *Scot-Simmonds* [1994] Crim. L.R. 933.
[6] *Re Baxter* [2002] EWHC 300 at [21], *per* Auld L.J.
[7] This was assumed in *Att-Gen's Reference (No.1 of 1980)* [1981] 1 W.L.R. 34. See also *Okanta* [1997] Crim. L.R. 451; *Sundhers* [1998] Crim. L.R. 497.
[8] It is clear from the words "record or document" that a record need not be a document. So a turnstile is a record made for an accounting purpose if it records the number of people passing through: *Edwards v Toombs* [1983] Crim. L.R. 43.
[9] It seems from *Shama* [1990] 1 W.L.R. 661 that a document is also required for an accounting purpose if the defendant does not make it at all, but ought to: below, para.12–019.
[10] [1978] 1 W.L.R. 820.
[11] [1981] 1 W.L.R. 34.
[12] [1981] 1 W.L.R. 34 at 38.

accounting purpose, even if it is made primarily for some other purpose and is not *required* for an accounting purpose at all. The *Attorney-General's Reference* was applied in *Osinuga v DPP*,[13] where a housing benefit claim form was held to be required for an accounting purpose because the information in it would be used not only to determine whether any benefit was payable (which was not an accounting purpose) but also to calculate the amount payable.

The courts have not been entirely consistent in their willingness to treat a document as being required for an accounting purpose in the absence of evidence as to how it would be used. In *Okanta*[14] the document in question was a letter sent to a building society in support of a mortgage application, falsely stating the applicant's salary. The court was not prepared to assume that the building society would use the information in compiling its internal accounting records, or that the auditors would use it in preparing or checking the accounts—especially since the calculation of instalments and interest rates would probably be unaffected by the applicant's salary. But in *Cummings-John*[15] this assumption was made in the case of a report on title. This was partly because the point had not been taken at the trial, but in any event the court thought it "wholly unreal" to suggest otherwise. In *Sundhers*[16] the convictions were again quashed. This time the document was an insurance claim form. The inference that the form would be kept for inspection by the auditors might seem obvious to lawyers, and very little evidence would be needed, if it were unchallenged. But it was not an inference that a jury could be allowed to draw without any evidence at all. **12–007**

Sundhers was distinguished in *Manning*,[17] where the documents in question were maritime insurance cover notes issued by the defendant to his clients. They set out the insured and the insurer, the period and the interest covered, the rate to be paid and the dates at which premiums had to be paid. The court had no doubt that the cover notes would play a role in the clients' accounting processes, and concluded that the jury was entitled to make the same assumption even in the absence of any evidence on the point. **12–008**

> "The cover note is a different sort of document from a claim form. . . . [I]t clearly sets out what the client has to pay and how he has to pay it. Although we have not found this issue an easy one, and regard it as being close to the borderline, we think on balance that it would be open in this case to a reasonable juror to conclude, simply by looking at the document, that it was required for an accounting purpose, in that it sets out what the client owes. It differs from the claim form in *Reg. v Sundhers*, from which any such conclusion could not be drawn without knowledge of audit practice, which the jury cannot be assumed to possess without evidence to that effect."[18]

[13] [1998] Crim. L.R. 216.
[14] [1997] Crim. L.R. 451.
[15] [1997] Crim. L.R. 660.
[16] [1998] Crim. L.R. 497.
[17] [1999] Q.B. 980.
[18] [1999] Q.B. 980 at 986.

But the court expressed the hope that in future prosecutors would call brief evidence (which would probably be unchallenged) as to the purposes for which the document was required.

12–009 Private individuals can have accounting purposes too. In *Re Baxter*[19] an "application package" setting out the terms of an investment solicited from individuals, and purporting to record for their benefit the nature and status of any investment they might make, was held to be capable of being a document required by them for potential use as an accounting document—the sort of document that the recipient "might wish to put in his wall safe rather than the wastepaper basket". It was immaterial whether he did in fact use it for an accounting purpose. But a general solicitation to invest, with a description of the mechanism of the proposed investment, was held to be insufficient.

SUPPRESSING OR FALSIFYING AN ACCOUNT, ETC.

12–010 For the form of the offence described in TA 1968, s.17(1)(a), the account, record or document must be destroyed, defaced, concealed or falsified. The first three verbs are the same as those used in TA 1968, s.20(1) with reference to the suppression of valuable securities and other documents.[20] However, the question whether a document is "defaced" by being altered is academic in this case, since the offence is committed if the account, record or document is *falsified*. TA 1968, s.17(2) provides:

> "For purposes of this section a person who makes or concurs in making in an account or other document an entry which is or may be misleading, false or deceptive in a material particular, or who omits or concurs in omitting a material particular from an account or other document, is to be treated as falsifying the account or document."

It seems that this is not an exhaustive definition.[21] If what is done is falsification in the ordinary sense, it is immaterial that it does not fall within the terms of s.17(2). The word's ordinary meaning clearly includes any case where the account, record or document is deliberately rendered inaccurate, even if it is not rendered "false" within the meaning of the Forgery and Counterfeiting Act 1981.[22]

12–011 In so far as s.17(2) extends the meaning of "falsify" beyond its ordinary meaning, it applies only to accounts and other documents. Unlike s.17(1), it does not extend to records which are neither accounts nor documents. In the case of such records, "falsify" can only have its ordinary meaning. This may have been overlooked in *R. v Governor of Brixton Prison, ex p. Levin*.[23]

[19] [2002] EWHC 300.
[20] Above, para.11–056.
[21] *Edwards v Toombs* [1983] Crim. L.R. 43.
[22] Above, paras 11–008 *et seq*.
[23] [1997] Q.B. 65.

Section 17(2) was held to apply to the transmission of unauthorised instructions to a bank's computer, although the court seems to have accepted that the disk to which the instructions were written was a record made or required for an accounting purpose rather than itself being an account.[24] But the disk may have been regarded as a *document* made or required for an accounting purpose, in which case s.17(2) would apply.

MISLEADING, FALSE OR DECEPTIVE

The words "misleading, false or deceptive" are used both in s.17(2), which defines "falsifying" for the purposes of s.17(1)(a), and in s.17(1)(b). They are something of a statutory formula, appearing in a number of offence-creating provisions. This is unfortunate, because the formula is a confusing one. A statement is false if it asserts a proposition which is not true. It is misleading if, while not actually asserting a proposition which is not true, it is likely to induce people to infer the truth of such a proposition. It is deceptive if the person making it intends thereby to deceive others (that is, induce them to believe that a false proposition is true) or is aware that it may have that effect.[25] The alternative "or deceptive" adds nothing, because a statement cannot be deceptive without being false or misleading. **12–012**

The reference in s.17(2) to an entry which is *or may be* misleading, false or deceptive is curious. In what circumstances can it be said that an entry *may* be misleading, false or deceptive but not that it *is*? It is presumably not sufficient that it is unclear whether the impression conveyed is true or false, even if the defendant knows that that is unclear. It is submitted that the alternative "or may be" should be construed as applying only to "misleading"[26] and not to "false"—the object being to rule out any argument that the entry must be *certain* to mislead, and not merely *capable* of doing so. **12–013**

Whether accounts are misleading may be a difficult question. In the case of company accounts, the overriding principle is that they should present a "true and fair view" of the company's financial position; but this requirement is notoriously imprecise. The process of valuing a company's assets is bound to involve an element of subjectivity. There is, moreover, a twilight zone between those accounting practices that are clearly acceptable and those that clearly are not. One such dubious practice is that of "window-dressing" (borrowing for a short period over the end of the financial year so **12–014**

[24] The court concluded that the applicant "must be treated as having falsified the account", but it had previously said that the question was "Did the applicant falsify a record made or required for an accounting purpose?" The reference to "the account" may therefore have been shorthand for "record made or required for an accounting purpose".

[25] Some offences require the defendant to make the statement knowingly or recklessly, and in these cases it may still be arguable that he can be reckless without actually being aware that the statement may be false or misleading: see below, para.13–013. But the idea of making a *deceptive* statement without realising that it may be deceptive is a contradiction in terms.

[26] And "deceptive", though that adds nothing.

as to create a false impression of liquidity). The accountancy profession is not united in condemning this device, because a balance-sheet does not purport to show the company's normal position, but only its position on a particular date.

12–015 If a substantial body of expert opinion believes a given practice to be legitimate it may be difficult to establish that a particular instance of that practice was dishonest. The defence can argue either that what was done was not dishonest according to ordinary standards or that, even if it was, the defendant did not realise that it was.[27] But the issue of dishonesty is distinct from that of whether the accounts are in fact misleading, false or deceptive. For this purpose, it is submitted, it is sufficient if the accounts are likely to cause at least some readers to believe something which is not true. A valuation of an asset suggests that the valuer believes the valuation to be fair; if he does not, it is deceptive about his state of mind.[28] Window-dressing gives the impression that the company has a level of liquidity which it does not have. Accounts which resort to window-dressing are therefore deceptive.

12–016 It is essential to distinguish between expert evidence as to the legitimacy of a particular accounting practice and evidence as to the impression that that practice is likely to create. If a balance-sheet is not in fact expected to reflect the company's normal position but only the position at the year-end, window-dressing involves no deception, however abnormal and artificial the year-end position may be. In *Williams*[29] the defendant entered a sum in his accounts as "balance in hand". That sum was correct in the sense that it represented the difference between receipts and expenditure, but he could not produce it. He was held not to have falsified the accounts. Had "balance in hand" meant that the sum in question could be immediately produced, the accounts would have been false. A more appropriate charge would be theft.[30]

FALSITY IN A MATERIAL PARTICULAR

12–017 In *Mallett*[31] a hire-purchase application falsely stated that the hirer had for eight years been a director of a certain company. This statement was held to be false "in a material particular" despite being unconnected with the accounting purpose for which the form was required. This is surprising. Accounting purposes are what the section is about. Preserving the integrity of accounting processes is its *raison dêtre*. A statement which has no bearing on the accounting purpose for which the document is made or required is outside the mischief at which the offence is aimed. But *Mallett* is effectively

[27] See above, Ch.2.
[28] See above, para.4–024.
[29] (1899) 19 Cox C.C. 239.
[30] *Eden* (1971) 55 Cr.App.R. 193 at 198–199.
[31] [1978] 1 W.L.R. 820.

confirmed by *Attorney-General's Reference (No.1 of 1980)*,[32] where it was held sufficient if the document *as a whole* is required for an accounting purpose, even if the part that is falsified is not. Perhaps the explanation is that a document may be required for an accounting purpose even if it is primarily required for some other purpose. A statement in such a document is therefore "material" not only if it is material to the accounting purpose but also if it is material to the primary purpose (or, presumably, some third purpose).

OMISSION

Where TA 1968, s.17(2) applies, it is sufficient not only if a false entry is **12–018**
made but also if a material particular is omitted. Clearly this does not mean that the account or document is deemed to have been falsified unless it includes everything that might conceivably be relevant to any of the purposes for which it is made or required. The phrase "material particular" must be read in a narrower sense in this context than in that of a false entry. An omission is not "material" for this purpose merely because the item omitted would have been relevant had it been included, but only if in all the circumstances it results in the account or document giving a false impression. A half-truth may be as deceptive as a downright lie.[33] Whether an omission has this effect will depend on the nature both of the account or document and of the omission. In *Keatley*[34] an employee made unauthorised purchases and sales without including them in his accounts. A submission of no case was accepted because he had no duty to include them. Presumably the accounts were not regarded as a *complete* statement of his sales and purchases. Had they been so regarded, the omission would have been falsification.

The idea of false accounting by omission was generously interpreted in **12–019**
Shama.[35] An international telephone operator was held to have committed the offence by connecting a call without filling in a "charge ticket" as he was required to do, with the result that the subscriber was not charged for that call. The court pointed out that he would be guilty if, instead of filling in a separate form for each call, he were required to fill in a new *line* on a single sheet, and he omitted a line. Clearly it would be anomalous if it made a difference which method was used.

> "We are of opinion that as soon as the operator's duty [to fill in a ticket] arose, one of the standard printed forms became a document 'required' for an accounting purpose . . . The fact that he may have had more than one of the standard forms in front of him at the material time does not prevent there being an identifiable document for the purposes of the section. A supply of

[32] [1981] 1 W.L.R. 34.
[33] Above, para.4–029.
[34] [1980] Crim. L.R. 505.
[35] [1990] 1 W.L.R. 661.

> forms, one to be used for each call, was to be expected. The fact that the operator might choose to pick up the second form before him rather than the first, the two forms being identical, does not mean that no document is in existence."[36]

This is hard to follow. The offence is one of falsifying a document by omitting a material particular from it. The judgment accepts that there must be an "identifiable document", and asserts that there was. But it is impossible to say which of the blank forms on the operator's desk he was falsifying by not filling it in. Surely he was not falsifying any single form at all, but only the collection of completed forms that he handed in at the end of his shift. Perhaps the explanation is that the completed forms were a kind of composite document, which was misleading because it was one form short.

CONCURRING

12–020 It is sufficient for s.17(2) that, though not himself making a false entry or omitting a material particular, the defendant "concurs in" the making of such an entry or the omission of such a particular by someone else. In *Attorney-General's Reference (No.1 of 1980)*[37] the offending forms had been filled in by the defendant's customers at his instigation. On those facts the defendant would in any event have been guilty as a secondary party; but the expression "or concurs in" might extend to acquiescence falling short of encouragement and therefore not amounting to secondary participation. It does not seem natural to say that one person concurs in the falsification of an account by a second, if the former provides the false information and the latter innocently incorporates it in the account; but in that case the former is regarded as making the entry himself.[38]

MENS REA

12–021 False accounting requires dishonesty and either a view to gain or an intent to cause loss. These requirements are discussed in Chs 2 and 3 respectively.

12–022 It is not clear what mens rea is required, on a charge of *falsifying* an account, record or document, as regards the fact that the entry in question is or may be misleading, false or deceptive in a material particular, or that a material particular is omitted. If the defendant has no idea that this may be so, he is clearly not dishonest; but the Act does not say whether he must *know* that it is so, or whether it is sufficient that he is aware that it *may* be so (that is, he is reckless).[39] TA 1968, s.17(1)(b) provides for this point

[36] [1990] 1 W.L.R. 661 at 665.

[37] [1981] 1 W.L.R. 34.

[38] *Butt* (1884) 15 Cox C.C. 564; *Oliphant* [1905] 2 K.B. 67.

[39] A person who is aware that an entry may be false is not necessarily reckless whether it is false, because it may be reasonable in the circumstances to take that risk; but in that case it could scarcely be dishonest to take it.

(albeit ambiguously) in relation to the *using* of a false account, etc.[40] but s.17(1)(a) does not.

The point was discussed in *Atkinson*,[41] but no clear conclusion emerged. A pharmacist submitted for payment a number of prescription forms containing false statements about the patients for whom the prescriptions were issued. In some cases the effect was that she was overpaid. Her defence was that she had innocently made errors through paying insufficient attention while completing large numbers of forms. The jury were directed that they would be entitled to convict if they were sure that she had known that some of the forms were *likely* to be inaccurate. On appeal this was said to be wrong. 12–023

> "The mental state has to be dishonest with a view to gain or with intent to cause loss. But that is a composite mental state which only lawyers would think of breaking into component parts. Dishonesty in this context connotes deliberately and intentionally making a false accounting statement knowing it to be false. The purpose or intention of making the false statement has to be established."

The court seems to have taken the view that, while it was not a separate element of the offence that the defendant should know that some of the forms were false, she could not properly be found to have acted dishonestly unless she knew this.[42] The mental state described by the judge, it was said, "sits uncomfortably on the border line between deliberate dishonesty and carelessness" (though the court rejected the suggestion that it was simply recklessness, which it clearly was). This view seems surprisingly lenient. The general principle is that, in the absence of express provision, an offence requires *either* knowledge that the relevant circumstances exist *or* awareness that they may exist (commonly described as recklessness). If the defendant knew that, because she had not been paying attention, some of the forms were likely to contain errors, her conduct might or might not be dishonest. It is not clear why such conduct should be *incapable* of being dishonest. But the court did not actually apply this rule anyway. The appeal was dismissed on the ground that the summing-up as a whole had made clear the facts of which the jury had to be satisfied. This conclusion is hard to reconcile with the court's disapproval of the judge's clear and uncorrected statements that (in effect) recklessness was enough. 12–024

In *Graham*[43] the court said it was not persuaded that the mens rea of the offence includes knowledge that a record or document is required for an accounting purpose. This does seem to be the natural reading; but on 12–025

[40] Below, para.12–026.

[41] [2004] EWCA Crim 3031; [2004] Crim. L.R. 226.

[42] The court may have been influenced by the requirement of a view to gain or intent to cause loss. But the defendant would have had a view to gain even if she had been sure that all the forms were accurate, because her purpose in submitting them was to obtain payment. See above, para.3–009.

[43] [1997] 1 Cr.App.R. 302 at 314.

principle the mens rea ought to include awareness of the circumstances that bring the particular record or document within the ambit of the section.

PRODUCING OR USING A FALSE ACCOUNT

12–026 Under TA 1968, s.17(1)(b) it is also an offence to *produce or make use of* an account, or a record or document made or required for an accounting purpose, which is or may be misleading, false or deceptive. In this case the mens rea includes not only dishonesty and a view to gain or intent to cause loss, but also knowledge that the account (etc.) is or may be misleading (etc.) It is arguable that the phrase "which to his knowledge . . . may be misleading" includes a person who is not sure whether the account is misleading but realises that it may be—that is, a person who is reckless as to that possibility. But it is submitted that the words "or may be" refer to an account which is capable of misleading but is not certain to do so, and that the express requirement of knowledge should be read as excluding recklessness.[44] In other words, the prosecution must prove that the account was in fact capable of misleading and that the defendant knew it was, but need not prove that he *intended* anyone to be misled.

LIABILITY OF COMPANY OFFICERS

12–027 TA 1968, s.18(1) provides:

> "Where an offence committed by a body corporate[45] under section 17 of this Act is proved to have been committed with the consent or connivance of any director, manager, secretary or other similar officer of the body corporate, or any person who was purporting to act in any such capacity, he as well as the body corporate shall be guilty of that offence, and shall be liable to be proceeded against and punished accordingly."

12–028 An offence can only be committed by a corporation where an officer of the corporation commits the actus reus of the offence with the necessary mens rea (if any), *and* his position in the corporation is such that his acts and state of mind can be attributed to the corporation for the purposes of the particular provision creating the offence.[46] Where these conditions are satisfied in relation to an offence of false accounting, TA 1968, s.18 imposes liability for that offence on other officers of the company who have allowed the offence to be committed. The fact that the company cannot be

[44] It might further be argued that the wider interpretation would give rise to an anomaly, since it was said in *Atkinson* that recklessness was not sufficient under TA 1968, s.17(1)(a). But it is submitted that that was wrong (above, para.12–024), and that the narrower interpretation of s.17(1)(b) is justified solely by the wording of that paragraph.

[45] This presumably has the same meaning as in the Companies Acts. If so, it includes a foreign corporation: below, para.14–006.

[46] *Meridian Global Funds Management Asia Ltd v Securities Commission* [1995] 2 A.C. 500.

prosecuted (for example because it has gone into liquidation) is not a defence.[47]

The section adds little to the position at common law. An officer who positively encourages or assists in the commission of the offence will in any event be guilty as an accessory. It is arguable that the same would apply to a director (at least) who simply acquiesces in the fraud, on the ground that a person who has the authority to prevent an offence being committed may be implicated by the failure to exercise that authority.[48] But s.18 makes it unnecessary to rely on the common law of secondary liability. Neglect of duty is not enough:[49] one cannot consent to something, or connive at it, without knowing about it. But once knowledge is established, passive acquiescence seems to be all that is required. **12–029**

FALSE STATEMENTS BY COMPANY DIRECTORS, ETC.

Under TA 1968, s.19(1) an offence is committed where **12–030**

> "an officer of a body corporate or unincorporated association (or person purporting to act as such), with intent to deceive members or creditors of the body corporate or association about its affairs, publishes or concurs in publishing a written statement or account which to his knowledge is or may be misleading, false or deceptive in a material particular . . ."

The offence is triable either way, and is punishable on conviction on indictment with seven years' imprisonment. Since it will often be committed where a company's annual accounts are misleading, it may be regarded as an alternative to false accounting.

The actus reus of the offence is the publication of a written statement or account which is or may be misleading, false or deceptive in a material particular. As in the case of TA 1968, s.17, it is submitted that this means the statement or account must either be false or at least be capable of giving a false impression. The requirement of falsehood "in a material particular", in the light of the required mental element, presumably means only that the falsehood must relate to the affairs of the corporation or association. **12–031**

It is also sufficient if the defendant does not publish the statement or account himself but concurs in its publication by someone else. Although oral statements are not caught, it is arguable that a director who makes an oral statement to the press is concurring in the subsequent publication of a written statement. **12–032**

[47] *Dickson*, April 16, 1991.
[48] *Tuck v Robson* [1970] 1 W.L.R. 741.
[49] cf. Companies Act 1985, s.733: below, para.14–083.

12–033 The mens rea of the offence does not include dishonesty. Two elements are required: knowledge that the statement or account is or may be misleading, false or deceptive, and intent to deceive members or creditors[50] of the corporation or association about its affairs. But the second of these is unlikely to exist without the first. A person intends to deceive members or creditors if he intends to induce them to believe in the truth of a proposition which is false. An intent to deceive *prospective* members or creditors does not appear to be sufficient.[51]

FALSE STATEMENTS IN DOCUMENTS REQUIRED BY STATUTE

12–034 A further offence that may be committed by the submission of false accounts, tax returns, etc. is that created by the Perjury Act 1911, s.5. A person commits this offence if he

> "knowingly and wilfully makes (otherwise than on oath) a statement false in a material particular, and the statement is made—
>
> (a) in a statutory declaration;[52] or
>
> (b) in an abstract, account, balance sheet, book, certificate, declaration, entry, estimate, inventory, notice, report, return, or other document which he is authorised or required to make, attest, or verify, by any public general Act of Parliament for the time being in force; or
>
> (c) in any oral declaration or oral answer which he is required to make by, under, or in pursuance of any public general Act of Parliament for the time being in force".

The offence is triable either way,[53] and is punishable on conviction on indictment with two years' imprisonment.

12–035 Section 5(b) would seem to cover the accounting records, annual accounts, annual returns, etc. required by the Companies Acts 1985 and 2006. But the document must be authorised or required by the primary legislation itself. For s.5(c), by contrast, it is sufficient if the defendant is required to make the declaration or answer "in pursuance of" the primary legislation.

12–036 The statement must be false in a material particular, and by virtue of s.13 of the Act there must be corroboration as to its falsity.[54] The statement must be *known* to be false: recklessness is not enough. The requirement of wilfulness appears to add little, apart from leaving open the defence of lawful excuse.

[50] Including persons who have entered into a security for the benefit of the corporation or association: TA 1968, s.19(2).

[51] But this might amount to one of the offences discussed in Ch.13 below.

[52] See the Statutory Declarations Act 1835.

[53] Magistrates' Courts Act 1980, s.17, Sch.1.

[54] *Hamid* (1979) 69 Cr.App.R. 324.

FALSE STATEMENTS TO OR BY AGENTS

12–037 The Prevention of Corruption Act 1906, s.1(1) not only creates offences of corruption but also provides that an offence is committed

> "if any person knowingly gives to any agent, or if any agent knowingly uses with intent to deceive his principal, any receipt, account, or other document in respect of which the principal is interested, and which contains any statement which is false or erroneous or defective in any material particular, and which to his knowledge is intended to mislead the principal".

The offence is triable either way,[55] and is punishable on conviction on indictment with seven years' imprisonment.

12–038 "Agent" and "principal" have the same meanings in this context as for the purposes of the 1906 Act generally.[56] But, unlike the two corruption offences created by s.1(1), this offence's territorial ambit is not extended by the Anti-terrorism, Crime and Security Act 2001, s.109.[57]

12–039 Not only is there no requirement that the agent be bribed, but, for the form of the offence that consists in giving a false document to an agent, it is not even necessary that the agent should be a party to the fraud. In *Sage v Eicholz*[58] it was held that the offence was committed where the defendant gave a document containing a false statement to an agent of the Metropolitan Water Board with the intention of deceiving the agent's superiors, even though the agent was unaware that the statement was false. In the expression "which to his knowledge is intended to mislead the principal" the word "his" was held to refer to the defendant, not necessarily the agent. The court pointed out that this paragraph of s.1(1), unlike the preceding paragraphs, does not include the word "corruptly". But the explanation for this is probably that, as the Attorney-General explained to the Royal Commission on Standards of Conduct in Public Life, "it may sometimes be easier to prove the intention to mislead than to demonstrate any associated bribery".[59] In other words the offence appears to be aimed at cases in which an agent may well have been bribed but this cannot be proved. It is not aimed at cases in which the prosecution accepts that the agent was deceived. The appropriate charge today would be one of fraud by false representation.

12–040 In *Tweedie*[60] the defendant submitted to his employer's accounting staff details of transactions which he had not in fact made. It was argued that he had knowingly used a document containing a false statement with intent to deceive his principal. The argument was rejected. The third paragraph of s.1(1) was not intended to catch every false document given by an employee

[55] Magistrates' Courts Act 1980, s.17, Sch.1.
[56] See below, para.19–027.
[57] Anti-terrorism, Crime and Security Act 2001, s.109(3)(c).
[58] [1919] 2 K.B. 171.
[59] Cmnd.6524 (1976), para.78.
[60] [1994] Q.B. 729.

to his employer: the document must be one given to the employee by a third party, someone outside the employer's organisation. This reasoning does not sit happily with the interpretation of the "gives to any agent" limb in *Sage v Eicholz*. It seems that a person outside the organisation commits the offence if he gives a false document to an agent within it, even if the agent is innocent; but a person within the organisation who gives an internal document to a fellow employee does not commit the offence even if the recipient is a party to the fraud. It is submitted that *Sage v Eicholz* is wrongly decided, and the offence is committed in neither case.

Chapter 13

INVESTMENT FRAUD

The process of investment by its nature involves a risk of fraud. The investor usually has to hand over his money before seeing any tangible return on it, and may end up with neither money nor return. This may be because he was deceived into investing, or because his money has been applied to some unauthorised purpose. In either case, at least one of the offences already considered will probably have been committed. If the investor is deceived, there will be a fraud by false representation.[1] The deception may involve offences of false accounting or of publishing misleading statements about a company's affairs.[2] Misapplication of the money invested will probably be theft if the investor is legally entitled that **13–001**

[1] Above, Ch.4.
[2] Above, Ch.12.

the money should be applied in the way he intended,[3] and will arguably be fraud by abuse of position[4] even if he is not. In addition, there are several offences aimed specifically at investment fraud. The Financial Services and Markets Act 2000 ("FSMA 2000") creates offences of misleading prospective investors and of market manipulation, replacing similar offences under the Financial Services Act 1986 ("FSA 1986") with effect from December 1, 2001. The Criminal Justice Act 1993 ("CJA 1993") creates a further offence of insider dealing.

MISLEADING STATEMENTS AND CONCEALMENT

13–002 FSMA 2000, s.397 provides, in part:

> "(1) This subsection applies to a person who—
>
> (a) makes a statement, promise or forecast which he knows to be misleading, false or deceptive in a material particular;
>
> (b) dishonestly conceals any material facts whether in connection with a statement, promise or forecast made by him or otherwise; or
>
> (c) recklessly makes (dishonestly or otherwise) a statement, promise or forecast which is misleading, false or deceptive in a material particular.
>
> (2) A person to whom subsection (1) applies is guilty of an offence if he makes the statement, promise or forecast or conceals the facts for the purpose of inducing, or is reckless as to whether it may induce, another person (whether or not the person to whom the statement, promise or forecast is made)—
>
> (a) to enter or offer to enter into, or to refrain from entering or offering to enter into, a relevant agreement; or
>
> (b) to exercise, or refrain from exercising, any rights conferred by a relevant investment."

13–003 The offence is triable either way, and is punishable on conviction on indictment with seven years' imprisonment.[5] It is based on FSA 1986, s.47(1), which was in turn based on s.13 of the Prevention of Fraud (Investments) Act 1958 ("PFIA 1958").

ACTUS REUS

13–004 The offence may be committed by

[3] Above, paras 9–039 *et seq*.
[4] Above, Ch.6.
[5] FSMA 2000, s.397(8).

- making a statement, promise or forecast which is misleading, false or deceptive in a material particular, or
- concealing any material facts.

MISLEADING STATEMENTS, ETC.

The words "misleading, false or deceptive" are discussed at para. 12–00, where it is argued that the "deceptive" limb adds nothing. A statement is false if it asserts a proposition which is not true. Whether it is misleading depends who it is made to (or is likely to be communicated to), because different people may draw different inferences from the same statement. Some statements might be misleading for private investors, but not for market professionals. **13–005**

Promises and forecasts cannot be *false*, because they do not assert a proposition of existing fact. They are misleading if they are likely to lead people to infer the truth of a proposition of existing fact which is not true—for example that the maker of a promise intends to keep it, or that there are reasonable grounds for believing that a forecast will prove correct.[6] **13–006**

The statement, promise or forecast must be false or misleading *in a material particular*. In other words, the false proposition asserted, or which people are likely to infer, must be material. This requirement did not appear in FSA 1986, s.47(1). A proposition cannot be material or immaterial in the abstract: it depends on the purposes for which it is asserted, or for which a person is led to infer it. The requirement must therefore be applied in relation to the investment purpose for which s.397(2) requires the statement (etc.) to be made. For example, if a statement is made for the purpose of inducing people to buy a certain investment, it is not sufficient that the statement is false or misleading. The false proposition that it asserts, or which it is likely to lead prospective investors to believe, must be one which is material to the decision whether to buy that investment. **13–007**

A single count may allege several false or misleading statements, promises or forecasts,[7] and it is sufficient if any of them is proved; but at least one of them must be proved to the satisfaction of the jury. It is not sufficient that different members of the jury are satisfied as to different statements.[8] **13–008**

CONCEALMENT

Concealment of material facts is also sufficient, provided it is dishonest. Concealment in this context seems to include not only the taking of positive steps to ensure that facts are not disclosed, but also a mere failure to **13–009**

[6] See above, paras 4–016 *et seq.*
[7] *Linnell* [1969] 1 W.L.R. 1514.
[8] *Brown (Kevin)* (1983) 79 Cr.App.R. 115.

disclose them when they ought to be disclosed.[9] Concealment may therefore occur where a statement, promise or forecast is made, and facts which should have been included in it are not included. This may or may not make the statement (etc.) misleading. In *Mackinnon* Salmon J. said:

> "If any fact that is omitted from a statement, promise or forecast is material, it can only be material in that its omission makes what has been said misleading, false or deceptive."[10]

But this confuses two questions: whether a statement (etc.) is misleading at all, and (if so) whether the respect in which it is misleading is a material respect. A fact is material to a prospective investor if it is relevant to his decision whether to invest. There may be many such facts. A statement of one of them is not misleading merely because it does not include all the others. A statement of part of the truth may be misleading,[11] but it is not misleading per se. So an omission from a statement may be a concealment of material facts even if what *is* stated is not itself misleading.

13–010 Moreover, s.397(1)(b) makes it clear that there may be concealment of material facts even if no statement, promise or forecast is made in which those facts should have been disclosed. The concealment may consist in the failure to make a statement (etc.) which should have been made. FSA 1986, s.47(1) was less clear on this point.

13–011 Just as a promise or forecast may be misleading if it gives a false impression about the maker's state of mind, so the defendant's state of mind may be a "material fact" within the meaning of s.397(1)(b). So the offence can be committed by "concealing" (that is, failing to disclose) one's own state of mind.[12]

MENS REA

KNOWLEDGE OR RECKLESSNESS

13–012 Where a person is charged with making a false or misleading statement, promise or forecast, it must be proved either that he knew it was false or misleading or that he was reckless as to whether it was. It is generally thought that the House of Lords' decision in *G.*[13] put an end to the

[9] This interpretation is supported by the fact that concealment, unlike the making of a false or misleading statement (etc.) must be dishonest. It would be odd to draw this distinction between the making of a false or misleading statement and the taking of positive steps to conceal the truth. As between positive conduct and mere omission, it is a natural distinction to draw.

[10] [1959] 1 Q.B. 150 at 154.

[11] e.g. *Linnell* [1969] 1 W.L.R. 1514. In *Delmayne* [1970] 2 Q.B. 170 the failure to disclose a material fact was treated as a dishonest concealment, but it probably amounted to a positive misrepresentation.

[12] *R. (Young) v Central Criminal Court* [2002] EWHC 548; [2002] 2 Cr.App.R. 12 (p.178).

[13] [2003] UKHL 50; [2004] 1 A.C. 1034.

uncertainty which had surrounded the concept of recklessness since *Caldwell v Metropolitan Police Commissioner*.[14] In *Caldwell* the House had held that a person acts recklessly with a regard to a risk not only where he is aware of the risk and acts unreasonably in the light of it, but also where the risk is obvious and he has given no thought to the possibility that it might exist. According to *G.*, only the first of these is sufficient.

It may be that *G.* does settle the meaning of recklessness throughout the criminal law.[15] But *G.* was concerned only with the offence of criminal damage. *Caldwell* was overruled on the question of what Parliament meant by the word "reckless" in the Criminal Damage Act 1971, and this was largely on the ground that the *Caldwell* interpretation involved a departure from the mens rea that had previously been required. In the context of the precursors of FSMA 2000, s.397, by contrast, it had long been held that recklessness required only a high degree of negligence.[16] This probably accords with its ordinary meaning,[17] which is the meaning that the House tried to give it in *Caldwell*. Indeed the words "dishonestly or otherwise" were inserted into PFIA 1958, s.13 by the Protection of Depositors Act 1963 in order to reverse a ruling[18] that a statement is reckless only if made without any genuine belief in its truth.[19] It is therefore arguable that, despite *G.*, recklessness in FSMA 2000, s.397 still has an objective meaning. On the other hand the drafting of s.397(1) differs slightly from that of its predecessors, with a view to clarifying certain points. It is not *simply* a re-enactment of a provision drafted before the word "reckless" acquired its modern, subjective interpretation. In using the word "reckless" in a modern statute, Parliament can probably be taken to have intended it in its modern, subjective sense. In effect this means it must be proved that the statement (etc.) was not merely false or misleading, but "deceptive". **13–013**

In *Page*[20] (a case decided on FSA 1986, s.47) the jury were directed that the statement must be "a rash statement made by the defendant with no real basis of fact to support it and not caring whether it was true or false". **13–014**

[14] [1982] A.C. 341.

[15] See *Att-Gen's Reference (No.3 of 2003)* [2004] EWCA Crim 868; [2005] Q.B. 73.

[16] *Bates* [1952] 2 All E.R. 842, Donovan J. The Court of Criminal Appeal agreed, *obiter*, sub nom. *Russell* [1953] 1 W.L.R. 77. In *Grunwald* [1963] 1 Q.B. 935 Paull J. said that a statement was reckless if it was "a rash statement to make" and the defendant had no real basis of facts on which he could support it.

[17] "The ordinary meaning of the word 'reckless' in the English language is 'careless', 'heedless', 'inattentive to duty'. Literally, of course, it means 'without reck'. 'Reck' is simply an old English word, now, perhaps, obsolete, meaning 'heed', 'concern', or 'care'": *Bates* [1952] 2 All E.R. 842 at 845, *per* Donovan J.

[18] *Mackinnon* [1959] 1 Q.B. 150, Salmon J.

[19] To modern eyes this was a clumsy way of clarifying the point, because even a person who *knows* he is making a false representation (let alone a person who is merely reckless) does not necessarily act dishonestly in making it: see (e.g.) Fraud Act 2006, s.2(1)(a). But in 1963 this proposition would have seemed very strange. Donovan J.'s "objective" ruling in *Bates* [1952] 2 All E.R. 842 was given on a submission that a count alleging recklessness was bad because it did not allege dishonesty. It was assumed that *subjective* recklessness would necessarily be dishonest. For the accidental invention of the modern concept of dishonesty, see above, Ch.2.

[20] [1996] Crim. L.R. 821.

On appeal it was conceded that this was correct. But, if the defendant knows that the statement (etc.) may be false, it is plainly immaterial that he would much prefer it to be true. A more accurate way of putting it would be that he must be aware that the statement (etc.) may be false or misleading, and it must be objectively unreasonable for him to make it in the light of that possibility.

Dishonesty

13–015 Where the defendant does not make a false or misleading statement (etc.) but only conceals material facts, he must do so dishonestly. The concept of dishonesty is examined in Ch.2. It is there suggested that it cannot properly be regarded as dishonest for a person to do what the law gives him a right to do. Concealment has been defined as "non-disclosure of a fact which it is a man's duty to disclose".[21] Even if that is too narrow, and it is possible to "conceal" facts which one has no duty to disclose, it may be arguable that such concealment cannot be dishonest.

Investment Purpose

13–016 The offence is committed only if the defendant makes the statement, promise or forecast, or conceals the facts,

(1) for the purpose of inducing another person

  (a) to enter into a relevant agreement, or offer to do so,

  (b) to exercise any rights conferred by a relevant investment, or

  (c) to refrain from doing (a) or (b); or

(2) being reckless as to whether it may induce another person to do any of those things.

The other person need not be a person to whom the statement, promise or forecast is made, or from whom the facts are concealed.[22]

[21] *London Assurance v Mansel* (1879) 11 Ch. D. 363 at 370, *per* Sir George Jessel M.R.

[22] The words "or from whom the facts are concealed" appeared in FSA 1986, s.47(1) but are omitted from FSMA 2000, s.397(2). The reason for the omission is not clear. It is true that facts may be concealed by ensuring that they are revealed to no-one, without there being an identifiable person *from whom* they are concealed; but it is equally possible to make a statement (etc.) without making it to anyone in particular, e.g. by publishing it to the world at large. Moreover, the words "whether or not the person to whom the statement, promise or forecast is made" are not, as one might expect, qualified so that they apply only where a statement (etc.) *is* made. This suggests that the omission may be an oversight.

Relevant investments

"Investment" includes any asset, right or interest.[23] A relevant investment is an investment of a kind specified in an order made by the Treasury,[24] or falling within a class of investment prescribed in regulations made by the Treasury.[25] The kinds of investment falling within Pt 2 of Sch.1 to the Financial Services and Markets Act 2000 (Financial Promotion) Order 2005[26] are specified for the purposes of FSMA 2000, s.397.[27] 13–017

Relevant agreements

A relevant agreement is an agreement 13–018

(a) the entering into or performance of which by either party constitutes an activity of a kind specified in an order made by the Treasury, or one which falls within a class of activity so specified, and

(b) which relates to a relevant investment.[28]

The kinds of activity falling within Pt 1 of Sch.1 to the Financial Services and Markets Act 2000 (Financial Promotion) Order 2005,[29] together with certain activities falling within Pt 2 of the Financial Services and Markets Act 2000 (Regulated Activities) Order 2001,[30] are specified for the purposes of FSMA 2000, s.397.[31]

Purpose or recklessness

It is debatable whether it is the defendant's *purpose* to induce another person to invest in securities if he does not want to bring about that result for its own sake, but only as a means of achieving some other purpose, such as supporting the market price.[32] But the point is now somewhat academic. Under FSMA 2000, s.397(2) (unlike PFIA 1958, s.13(1)) it is sufficient that the defendant is *reckless* as to whether the statement, promise, forecast or concealment may induce another person to invest (etc.). 13–019

[23] FSMA 2000, s.397(13).
[24] FSMA 2000, s.397(10), (14).
[25] FSMA 2000, ss.397(10), 417(1). No classes of investment have been prescribed.
[26] SI 2005/1529.
[27] Financial Services and Markets Act 2000 (Misleading Statements and Practices) Order 2001 (SI 2001/3645), arts 2 and 4. This Order actually refers to the Financial Promotion Order of 2001 (SI 2001/1335), but this can be construed as a reference to the 2005 Order by virtue of the Interpretation Act 1978, s.17(2)(a) (which applies to subordinate legislation by virtue of s.23(1) of that Act).
[28] FSMA 2000, s.397(9), (14).
[29] SI 2005/1529.
[30] SI 2001/544.
[31] Financial Services and Markets Act 2000 (Misleading Statements and Practices) Order 2001 (SI 2001/3645), art. 3.
[32] *Tarling (No.1) v Government of the Republic of Singapore* (1978) 70 Cr.App.R. 77 suggests not.

DEFENCES

13–020 While dishonesty is not required in the case of false or misleading statements, promises or forecasts, there are limited circumstances in which it is permissible to make a statement, promise or forecast in the knowledge that it is false or misleading.[33] Where a defendant is charged with the offence on this basis, FSMA 2000, s.397(4) provides that it is a defence for him to show that the statement, promise or forecast was made in conformity with

- price stabilising rules,
- control of information rules, or
- the relevant provisions of the Buy-back and Stabilisation Regulation.[34]

STABILISATION

13–021 Price stabilising is a process designed to assist in the orderly distribution of a new issue. It is

> "a complex transactional process, but broadly speaking it consists of the buying and selling of securities by the lead manager in the open market, as well as overallotment or underallotment of securities in order to provide a price support mechanism for the securities and thereby preventing any downward slide of the price of the securities during the issue period".[35]

Since the whole object of stabilising is to keep the price of the securities higher than it might otherwise be, it might infringe FSMA 2000, s.397(2) but for the defence in s.397(4)(a). FSMA 2000, s.144(1) enables the Financial Services Authority ("FSA") to make rules as to the circumstances and manner in which, the conditions subject to which, and the time when or the period during which, action may be taken for the purpose of stabilising

[33] But, oddly, not if the statement (etc.) is made recklessly. While it may be true that a person acting in conformity with the price stabilising rules (etc.) would normally know exactly how and why the statement (etc.) was false or misleading, there might be exceptions. If the inclusion of information in a statement would infringe a Chinese wall, for example, the person making the statement is (or should be) entitled to omit the information even if he is not sure whether the omission makes the statement misleading.

[34] Commission Regulation (EC) No.2273/2003 of December 22, 2003. This Regulation implements the Market Abuse Directive of the European Parliament and of the Council (2003/6/EC, January 28, 2003) as regards exemptions for buy-back programmes and stabilisation of financial instruments. Buy-back programmes involve a company trading in its own shares in accordance with Arts 19–24 of the plc Safeguards Directive (the Second Council Directive of December 13, 1976 on coordination of safeguards for the protection of the interests of members and others in respect of the formation of public limited liability companies and the maintenance and alteration of their capital, with a view to making such safeguards equivalent, No.77/91/EEC).

[35] Ravi Tennekoon, "Stabilisation of Securities after the Financial Securities Act 1986" [1989] J.I.B.L. 304.

the price of investments of specified kinds. These rules are to be found in section MAR 2 of the FSA Handbook.[36]

CONTROL OF INFORMATION RULES

Control of information rules are intended to prevent information in the hands of one part of a company, or group of companies, from flowing to another part of that company or group. FSMA 2000, s.147 enables the FSA to make rules which **13–022**

> "(a) require the withholding of information which A would otherwise have to disclose to a person ('B') for or with whom A does business in the course of carrying on any regulated or other activity;
>
> (b) specify circumstances in which A may withhold information which he would otherwise have to disclose to B;
>
> (c) require A not to use for the benefit of B information A holds which A would otherwise have to use in that way; [or]
>
> (d) specify circumstances in which A may decide not to use for the benefit of B information A holds which A would otherwise have to use in that way."

A person who makes a statement, promise or forecast "in conformity with" such rules has a defence to a charge under FSMA 2000, s.397(2) even if he knows the statement (etc.) to be false or misleading. However, the only such rule so far made by the FSA is rule COB 2.4.4 r.(1), which provides: **13–023**

> "When a firm establishes and maintains a Chinese wall (that is, an arrangement that requires information held by a person in the course of carrying on one part of its business to be withheld from, or not to be used for, persons with or for whom it acts in the course of carrying on another part of its business), it may:
>
> (a) withhold or not use the information held; and
>
> (b) for that purpose, permit persons employed in the first part of its business to withhold the information held from those employed in that other part of the business;
>
> but only to the extent that the business of one of those parts involves the carrying on of designated investment business or related ancillary activities."

Where a Chinese wall requires or permits a person to withhold information, a statement, promise or forecast made by that person is presumably "made in conformity with control of information rules" if it is misleading by virtue only of omitting that information.

[36] Available at *http://fsahandbook.info/FSA/html/handbook/MAR/2.*

TERRITORIAL SCOPE

13–024 FSMA 2000, s.397(6) relaxes the usual rule that an offence under English law can only be committed in England and Wales.[37] It provides:

> "Subsections (1) and (2) do not apply unless—
>
> (a) the statement, promise or forecast is made in or from, or the facts are concealed in or from, the United Kingdom or arrangements are made in or from the United Kingdom for the statement, promise or forecast to be made or the facts to be concealed;
>
> (b) the person on whom the inducement is intended to or may have effect is in the United Kingdom; or
>
> (c) the agreement is or would be entered into or the rights are or would be exercised in the United Kingdom."

Although drafted as if it were a restriction on the scope of s.397(1) and (2), this gives the offence an extra-territorial effect which it would not otherwise have. For example, it is sufficient if a false statement is made in Scotland, or if it is made in France for the purpose of inducing people in England to invest.

PROCEEDINGS

13–025 Proceedings for an offence under FSMA 2000 may be instituted only by the FSA or the Secretary of State, by or with the consent of the DPP,[38] or by the Director of the SFO.[39]

LIABILITY OF COMPANY OFFICERS, ETC.

13–026 FSMA 2000, s.400 provides for the personal liability of officers of a corporation, and members of a partnership or other unincorporated association, which commits an offence under the Act. Section 400(1) provides:

> "If an offence under this Act committed by a body corporate is shown—
>
> (a) to have been committed with the consent or connivance of an officer,[40] or
>
> (b) to be attributable to any neglect on his part,

[37] See below, Ch.22.
[38] FSMA 2000, s.401(2).
[39] Criminal Justice Act 1987, Sch.1 para.4(1).
[40] i.e. (a) a director, member of the committee of management, chief executive, manager, secretary or other similar officer of the body, or a person purporting to act in any such capacity, or (b) an individual who is a controller of the body: FSMA 2000, s.400(5). Where the affairs of a body corporate are managed by its members, s.400(1) applies in relation to the acts and defaults of a member in connection with his functions of management as if he were a director: s.400(2).

the officer as well as the body corporate is guilty of the offence and liable to be proceeded against and punished accordingly."

Where an offence under FSMA 2000 is committed by a partnership, s.400(3) similarly makes the partners liable; and, where it is committed by an unincorporated association other than a partnership, s.400(6) imposes liability on officers of the association or members of its governing body. In these cases FSA 1986, s.202(3) and (4) formerly imposed liability unless the partner, officer, etc. were "proved to have been ignorant of or to have attempted to prevent the commission of the offence"; but this was probably inconsistent with the presumption of innocence under Art.6(2) of the European Convention on Human Rights, and FSMA 2000 now requires proof that the partner, officer, etc. consented to or connived at the offence, or that it was attributable to neglect on his part. **13–027**

MARKET MANIPULATION

FSMA 2000, s.397(3) creates a further offence which catches more sophisticated frauds than s.397(1) and (2). It provides: **13–028**

> "Any person who does any act or engages in any course of conduct which creates a false or misleading impression as to the market in or the price or value of any relevant investments is guilty of an offence if he does so for the purpose of creating that impression and of thereby inducing another person to acquire, dispose of, subscribe for or underwrite those investments or to refrain from doing so or to exercise, or refrain from exercising, any rights conferred by those investments."

The offence is triable either way, and is punishable on conviction on indictment with seven years' imprisonment.[41]

It has been suggested that any of the following situations may be covered by this offence: **13–029**

"(1) a company supports its shares on its own account;

(2) an offeree arranges for a third party to buy shares in it to raise the market price beyond the bidder's resources;

(3) one bidder undersells shares of a rival bidder to depress the latter's market price;

(4) dealing to create an impression of market interest;

(5) buying shares at an inflated price to create the impression of a rising market;

(6) purchasing an offeror's shares to maintain their price;

(7) a bidder makes an announcement of his intention which is not fully candid about his long term intentions;

[41] FSMA 2000, s.397(8).

(8) an offeror says he does not intend to increase his bid when he is aware of circumstances when he may do so;

(9) an offeree announces a bid is inadequate unless it has been properly advised that the bid actually is financially inadequate."[42]

ACTUS REUS

13–030 The actus reus of the offence is the doing of an act, or engaging in a course of conduct, which creates a false or misleading impression as to the market in, or the price or value of, any relevant investments.[43]

MARKET, PRICE OR VALUE

Market

13–031 The market in an investment is made up of all those buyers and sellers who can influence its price. A false impression as to the market in an investment would be an impression that the supply of, or the demand for, the investment is greater or smaller than it actually is.

Price

13–032 The "price" of an investment in this context must mean, not the price at which the investment is in fact changing hands in the market (which would normally be common knowledge), but the price at which it *would* change hands in a bargain between parties who are fully informed and acting at arm's length. If it is in fact changing hands at some other price, that other price is not the true price, and the impression that it is the true price would be a false impression.

Value

13–033 In economic terms, the "value" of a thing is the rate at which it can be exchanged for other things: in this sense its "price" is merely its value measured in monetary terms, and there is no practical difference between the two. But "value" also has a less technical meaning, in which it refers to a thing's objective worth, which may bear no relation to its price.[44] It is presumably this sense that is intended. It must be sufficient that a false impression is given as to a company's profit-making potential, or its cash-flow, or its attractiveness as a target for a takeover, or any other factor not necessarily reflected in its market price.

[42] Simon Morris, *Financial Services: Regulating Investment Business*, 2nd edn (1995) at 207–208.

[43] For the definition of relevant investments see above, para.13–017.

[44] cf. Oscar Wilde's definition of a cynic as "a man who knows the price of everything, and the value of nothing". Similarly the investment strategy known as "value investment" involves finding investments whose objective value exceeds their market price.

FALSE OR MISLEADING IMPRESSION

13–034 A false or misleading impression must actually be created. It is not sufficient under s.397(3) that the defendant's act or conduct is likely to create such an impression, or even that it is intended to do so (though in this case there may be an attempt).

13–035 A false impression is created as to the market in, or the price or value of, an investment if a person is led to believe any proposition with respect to any of those matters which is in fact false. It may also be that one can create an "impression" that a proposition is true without anyone being wholly convinced that it is true: a vague feeling that it is probably true may suffice.

13–036 It is not clear how an impression might be misleading without being false. A statement or act is misleading if it tends to lead others to believe that a false proposition is true—in other words, if it tends to create an impression which is false. To mislead *is* to create a false impression. So an impression, though not itself false, might be misleading if it tends to create *another* impression which is false. In the context of s.397(3) this might mean that it is sufficient if an impression is created as to primary facts and is correct as regards those facts, but incorrect inferences are likely to be drawn from those facts. For example, the buying of securities is likely to create the impression that there is a buyer for those securities at that price, which is true. But someone learning of the trade may draw inferences as to *why* there is a buyer at that price (for example, that a takeover bid is imminent), and those inferences may be false. The impression that the trade has taken place is not false, but it is arguably misleading. If someone does in fact draw false inferences, a false impression has been created about the *reasons* for the trade, so there is no need to rely on a misleading (but true) impression about the *making* of the trade. But the actus reus is arguably complete if it is made known (truthfully) that the trade has occurred, without the need to prove that investors were in fact led to draw false inferences from that fact: it is sufficient that they were likely to do so. The impression about the making of the trade is misleading, though true.

13–037 If a false or misleading impression is created, it is not a defence that no reasonable person would have formed that impression. The defendant must have acted for the purpose of creating the impression. If that is his purpose, he cannot be heard to say that he would never have succeeded if his victims had had their wits about them.[45]

ACT OR COURSE OF CONDUCT

13–038 The creation of the false or misleading impression must be the result of an act done by the defendant or a course of conduct engaged in by him. An act might be the purchase or sale of securities, or the making of a statement

[45] cf. above, para.4–036.

(whether oral or in writing). A course of conduct might consist simply of a series of acts. It is less clear whether it might consist in a continuing omission. If in a particular market the usual practice is to make disclosure, a continuing failure to do so might perhaps be regarded as a course of conduct.

MENS REA

13–039 The defendant must do the act that creates the false or misleading impression, or engage in the course of conduct that creates it, for two purposes:

(1) to create that impression, and

(2) thereby to induce another person

(a) to acquire, dispose of, subscribe for or underwrite the relevant investments in question,

(b) to exercise any rights conferred by those investments, or

(c) to refrain from doing (a) or (b).

It need not be his purpose to create a *false or misleading* impression, but only to create the particular impression that is in fact created. That impression must in fact *be* false or misleading, but it need not be part of the defendant's purpose that it should be. Indeed, he need not even know that it will be. This is clear from s.397(5)(a), which gives him a defence if he can show that he reasonably believed that his act or conduct would not create an impression that was false or misleading.[46] This would be otiose if the prosecution had to prove that the creation of a false or misleading impression was part of his purpose.

DEFENCES

13–040 FSMA 2000, s.397(5) provides four defences to the offence under s.397(3). Three of them are effectively the same as the defences to the offence under s.397(2), namely that the defendant's act or conduct was in conformity with the FSA's price stabilising or control of information rules or with the Buy-back and Stabilisation Regulation.[47] In addition, s.397(5) provides:

> "In proceedings brought against any person for an offence under subsection (3) it is a defence for him to show—

[46] Below, para.13–040.
[47] Above, fn.34.

(a) that he reasonably believed that his act or conduct would not create an impression that was false or misleading as to the matters mentioned in that subsection . . ."

The prosecution must prove that the defendant's purpose was (in part) to create the impression that he did create, and that that impression was false or misleading. It need not prove that it was his purpose to create an impression that was false or misleading, or that he knew that the impression he was seeking to create was false or misleading, or that he was even aware that it might be. But he has a defence if he can show **13–041**

(1) that he believed that no impression which his act or conduct would create—that is, neither the impression that it was his purpose to create nor any other impression that he thought might incidentally be created—would be false or misleading; and

(2) that he had reasonable grounds for that belief.

It is not enough that he was unaware that any impression which he expected to create might be false or misleading as to the matters in question: he must have positively believed that no such impression would be false or misleading as to those matters. So the defence is not available if he did not consider the possibility that he might be creating a false or misleading impression—even if, had he considered that possibility, he would have rejected it.

However, by requiring the defendant to "show" that he had the belief specified and that he had reasonable grounds for it, s.397(5)(a) appears to reverse the burden of proof as regards an essential element of the offence. This would infringe the presumption of innocence under Art.6(2) of the European Convention on Human Rights. It is difficult to see why the prosecution should not be required to prove that the defendant had no such belief, or that he had no reasonable grounds for it, once he has adduced evidence that he did or had. In all probability, therefore, s.397(5)(a) would be read down under the Human Rights Act 1998, s.3 so as to impose on the defendant an evidential burden only.[48] **13–042**

TERRITORIAL SCOPE

FSMA 2000, s.397(7) provides: **13–043**

"Subsection (3) does not apply unless—

(a) the act is done, or the course of conduct is engaged in, in the United Kingdom; or

(b) the false or misleading impression is created there."

[48] See *Lambert* [2001] UKHL 37; [2002] 2 A.C. 545; *Johnstone* [2003] UKHL 28; [2003] 1 W.L.R. 1736; *Sheldrake v DPP* [2004] UKHL 43; [2005] 1 A.C. 264.

Again the effect is to extend the territorial ambit of the offence rather than restrict it. By contrast with the general rule, it is sufficient if the act is done (or the impression created) in Scotland; or if the act is done overseas, provided that the impression is created in the United Kingdom. An impression is presumably created in the United Kingdom if any person to whom it is given is in the United Kingdom when he is given it.

PROCEEDINGS

13–044 Proceedings for an offence under FSMA 2000 may be instituted only by the FSA or the Secretary of State, by or with the consent of the DPP,[49] or by the Director of the SFO.[50]

LIABILITY OF COMPANY OFFICERS, ETC.

13–045 FSMA 2000, s.400, which is discussed at para.13–00, applies equally to the offence under s.397(3).

INSIDER DEALING

13–046 Investment fraud need not involve the making of false statements or the creation of misleading impressions: it may consist in the exploitation of an unfair imbalance of information. Where one party to a transaction is in possession of material facts of which the other is unaware, it is conceivable that the former might be guilty of dishonest concealment contrary to FSMA 2000, s.397(2), or even of fraud by false representation[51] or failing to disclose information.[52] But Pt V of CJA 1993 creates a further offence designed to implement the EC Directive on the Co-ordination of Laws on Insider Dealing. It replaces the Company Securities (Insider Dealing) Act 1985, which itself replaced provisions of the Companies Act 1980. It differs substantially from the earlier legislation, and authorities decided under the earlier legislation are likely to be of limited value in construing it.[53]

[49] FSMA 2000, s.401(2).
[50] Criminal Justice Act 1987, Sch.1 para.4(1).
[51] Above, Ch.4.
[52] Above, Ch.5.
[53] e.g. *Att-Gen's Reference (No.1 of 1988)* [1989] A.C. 971, on the construction of the requirement that the defendant must have "obtained" the inside information—a requirement which does not appear in CJA 1993.

Under CJA 1993, s.52, subject to certain defences,[54] the offence of insider dealing[55] is committed by an individual[56] who "has information as an insider" and, in specified circumstances,[57] 13–047

- deals in securities[58] that are price-affected securities in relation to the information,
- encourages another person to do so, or
- discloses the information to another person.

The offence is triable either way, and is punishable on conviction on indictment with seven years' imprisonment.[59]

HAVING INFORMATION AS AN INSIDER

CJA 1993, s.57(1) provides that, for the purposes of Pt V of the Act, 13–048

> "a person has information as an insider if and only if—
>
> (a) it is, and he knows that it is, inside information, and
>
> (b) he has it, and knows that he has it, from an inside source."

INFORMATION

In *Gray* the trial judge ruled in the context of the 1985 Act that "information" means *correct* information.[60] This is arguably too restrictive. The mischief at which the offence is aimed is the exploitation of information not generally available. Whether the information in question is correct would seem to be immaterial. In any event, a person who acts on incorrect information which he believes to be correct, and which would be inside information if it were correct, is presumably guilty of an attempt.[61] 13–049

[54] See below, paras 13–066 *et seq*.

[55] *Archbold* regards s.52 as creating three offences (para.30–250), but the drafting suggests that there is one offence which can be committed in several ways. The section is headed "The offence" and comes under the cross-heading "The offence of insider dealing". Section 53, which deals with defences, provides that in specified circumstances an individual is not guilty of insider dealing *by virtue of* dealing, encouraging another to deal or disclosing information. Even if two forms of the offence can theoretically be charged in the same count without duplicity, however, it is difficult to imagine circumstances in which it might be justifiable to do so.

[56] i.e. not a corporation; but there seems no reason in principle why a corporation should not be guilty of aiding and abetting the commission of the offences by an individual, or of conspiracy with an individual to commit them.

[57] See below, para.13–062.

[58] The securities to which CJA 1993, Pt V applies are those listed in Sch.2 (set out in *Archbold*, para.30–247), subject to the conditions in the Insider Dealing (Securities and Regulated Markets) Order 1994 (SI 1994/187) arts 4–8.

[59] CJA 1993, s.61(1).

[60] See [1995] 2 Cr.App.R. 100 at 118. The trial judge was Judge Bruce Laughland Q.C.

[61] Criminal Attempts Act 1981, s.1(2) and (3).

INSIDE INFORMATION

13–050 CJA 1993, s.56(1) defines "inside information" as information which

"(a) relates to particular securities or to a particular issuer of securities or to particular issuers of securities and not to securities generally or to issuers of securities generally;

(b) is specific or precise;[62]

(c) has not been made public; and

(d) if it were made public would be likely to have a significant effect on the price of any securities."

13–051 Information may thus be inside information if it relates to a number of different securities (such as those in a particular market sector) but not if it is information about a likely movement in the market as a whole. An issuer of securities is any company,[63] public sector body[64] or individual by which or by whom the securities have been or are to be issued.[65] Information relates to a company not only where it is about the company itself but also where it may affect the company's business prospects, for example because it relates to one of the company's suppliers, customers or competitors.[66]

Information not made public

13–052 Information cannot be "inside information" once it has been made public. CJA 1993, s.58(2) provides for four cases in which information is made public, but it is not exhaustive.[67] Section 58(3) sets out five factors which (contrary to what might otherwise be assumed) do not in themselves mean that the information has *not* been made public. So information *is* made public (and therefore is no longer inside information) if it falls within s.58(2); if it does not fall within s.58(2), it *may* have been made public, even if it falls within s.58(3). It is a question of fact.[68]

[62] It is clear that information may be specific without being precise: for example, the fact that a company's profits are substantially greater than last year's is specific information, whereas the fact that they are 50% greater is precise. But it is hard to see how information could be precise without being specific.

[63] i.e. any body (whether or not incorporated, and wherever incorporated or constituted) which is not a public sector body: CJA 1993, s.60(3)(a).

[64] i.e. (i) the government of the United Kingdom, of Northern Ireland or of any country or territory outside the United Kingdom; (ii) a local authority in the United Kingdom or elsewhere; (iii) any international organisation the members of which include the United Kingdom or another member State; (iv) the Bank of England; or (v) the central bank of any sovereign State: CJA 1993, s.60(3)(b).

[65] CJA 1993, s.60(2).

[66] CJA 1993, s.60(4).

[67] CJA 1993, s.58(1).

[68] *Archbold* 30–254 suggests that, even if the information has not been made public within the ordinary meaning of those words, it may be treated as having been made public under the "deeming provisions" in s.58(3). But s.58(3) does not deem any information to have been made public when in fact it has not. It merely ensures that the circumstances specified do not preclude the conclusion that the information has in fact been made public.

CJA 1993, s.58(2) provides: 13–053

> "Information is made public if—
>
> (a) it is published in accordance with the rules of a regulated market for the purpose of informing investors and their professional advisers;
>
> (b) it is contained in records which by virtue of any enactment are open to inspection by the public;
>
> (c) it can be readily acquired by those likely to deal in any securities—
>
> (i) to which the information relates; or
>
> (ii) of an issuer to which the information relates; or
>
> (d) it is derived from information which has been made public."

Under earlier legislation,[69] information could be "unpublished price sensitive information" if it was not *generally known* to those persons who were accustomed or would be likely to deal in the securities in question. This probably meant that a person who had advance knowledge of the information could not deal as soon as it was made public, but had to wait while the rest of the market absorbed it. Under CJA 1993, by contrast, information ceases to be inside information as soon as it is published in accordance with the rules of the market in question. 13–054

CJA 1993, s.58(3) provides: 13–055

> "Information may be treated as made public even though—
>
> (a) it can be acquired only by persons exercising diligence or expertise;
>
> (b) it is communicated to a section of the public and not to the public at large;
>
> (c) it can be acquired only by observation;
>
> (d) it is communicated only on payment of a fee; or
>
> (e) it is published only outside the United Kingdom."

In each of these cases it is a question of degree whether the general public would have such difficulty in acquiring the information that it cannot be said to have been made public at all.

In determining whether information has been made public, it will be necessary to identify the precise nature of the information. In *Gray*[70] (a case decided under the 1985 Act) an item of information relied upon by the Crown was the fact that a company was about to announce a takeover. The defence relied on a report in the *Financial Times*, two weeks before the alleged offence, attributing to the chairman a statement that the company had recently started discussions which might lead to one or more purchases 13–056

[69] Company Securities (Insider Dealing) Act 1985, s.10(b).

[70] [1995] 2 Cr.App.R. 100.

being made in the near future. There was held to be ample evidence on which the jury could conclude that it was not generally known that the announcement of an acquisition was imminent.

> "There is, in common sense, a great deal of difference between a company indicating in general terms that it is interested in acquisitions, or is in discussions that might lead to a specific acquisition, and the news that an acquisition is in fact shortly to be announced."[71]

Moreover the fact that the defendant took a close interest in the timing of the announcement was evidence that the subject matter of the announcement was not already public knowledge, and that it was likely to affect the price of the company's securities when it became public.

INSIDE SOURCE

13–057 CJA 1993, s.57(2) provides that, for the purposes of s.57(1),[72]

> "a person has information from an inside source if and only if—
>
> (a) he has it through—
>
> (i) being a director, employee or shareholder of an issuer of securities; or
>
> (ii) having access to the information by virtue of his employment, office or profession; or
>
> (b) the direct or indirect source of his information is a person within paragraph (a)."

So, as long as he has got the information (directly or indirectly) from a person within paragraph (a), and knows that he has, it is immaterial that he is not himself such a person.

FORMS OF THE OFFENCE

13–058 The offence takes three forms: dealing, encouraging another to deal, and disclosure.

DEALING

13–059 CJA 1993, s.52(1) provides:

> "An individual who has information as an insider is guilty of insider dealing if, in the circumstances mentioned in subsection (3), he deals in securities that are price-affected securities in relation to the information."

[71] [1995] 2 Cr.App.R. 100 at 117.
[72] For s.57(1) see above, para.13–048.

Securities are price-affected in relation to information (and the information is "price-sensitive" in relation to them) if, and only if, the information would, if made public, be likely to have a significant effect on their price.[73] The price-affected securities need not be the ones to which the information "relates" within the meaning of s.56(1)(a). But information "relates" to a company in such a wide range of circumstances[74] that, if particular information does not relate to a particular company or its securities, it is hard to see how its release might have a significant effect on the price of that company's securities. 13–060

A person "deals" in securities if 13–061

- he acquires[75] or disposes of[76] the securities (whether as principal or agent); or
- he procures, directly or indirectly, their acquisition or disposal by any other person.[77]

This form of the offence is committed only if the defendant deals in the securities in the circumstances mentioned in s.52(3). Those circumstances are: 13–062

(a) that the acquisition or disposal in question occurs on a regulated market,[78] or

(b) that the person dealing relies on, or is himself acting as, a professional intermediary.

A professional intermediary is a person who

(1) carries on a business consisting of

(a) acquiring or disposing of securities (whether as principal or agent), or

(b) acting as an intermediary between persons taking part in any dealings in securities,[79]

[73] CJA 1993, s.56(2). "Price" includes value: s.56(3).

[74] CJA 1993, s.60(4); above, para.13–051.

[75] "Acquiring" a security includes agreeing to acquire it and entering into a contract which creates it: CJA 1993, s.55(2). So it is immaterial that the information has been made public by the time the defendant actually acquires the securities if it was not public when he agreed to acquire them.

[76] "Disposing" of a security includes agreeing to dispose of it and bringing to an end a contract which created it: CJA 1993, s.55(3).

[77] CJA 1993, s.55(1). A person procures an acquisition or disposal of a security if (inter alia: s.55(5)) the security is acquired or disposed of by a person who is his agent, his nominee or a person acting at his direction, in relation to the acquisition or disposal: s.55(4).

[78] i.e. one established under the rules of one of the investment exchanges listed in the Schedule to the Insider Dealing (Securities and Regulated Markets) Order 1994 (SI 1994/187) or OFEX: see art.9 of that Order.

[79] But a person is not to be treated as carrying on a business consisting of such an activity if the activity in question is merely incidental to some other activity, or merely because he occasionally conducts such an activity: CJA 1993, s.59(3).

and holds himself out to the public or any section of the public (including a section of the public constituted by persons such as himself) as willing to engage in any such business, or

(2) is employed by such a person to carry out any such activity;

and a person dealing in securities relies on a professional intermediary, within the meaning of s.52(3), if and only if a person who is acting as a professional intermediary carries out such an activity in relation to that dealing.[80]

ENCOURAGING ANOTHER TO DEAL

13–063 Under CJA 1993, s.52(2)(a), an individual who has information as an insider is also guilty of insider dealing if

> "he encourages another person to deal in securities that are (whether or not that other knows it) price-affected securities in relation to the information, knowing or having reasonable cause to believe that the dealing would take place in the circumstances mentioned in subsection (3)".[81]

13–064 The offence is complete when the encouragement is given, whether or not the other person acts upon it. If he does act upon it, he may himself be guilty of the dealing form of the offence—but only if the encouragement is sufficiently "specific" to be inside information (not just unexplained advice to buy or sell) and he knows that it is inside information and that he has it from an inside source.

DISCLOSURE

13–065 Under CJA 1993, s.52(2)(b), an individual who has information as an insider is also guilty of insider dealing if

> "he discloses the information, otherwise than in the proper performance of the functions of his employment, office or profession, to another person."

DEFENCES

13–066 CJA 1993 provides for a number of defences to a charge of insider dealing. Some apply to the dealing and encouraging forms of the offence, others to the disclosure form. One (pursuit of monetary policy, etc.) applies to all three.

[80] CJA 1993, s.59(4).

[81] For the circumstances mentioned in s.52(3) see above, para.13–062.

Most of the defences apply only if the defendant "shows" specified facts. 13–067
The intention appears to be that the defendant should have the burden of proving the facts in question on the balance of probabilities.[82] But it may be arguable, in each case, that this construction would infringe the presumption of innocence under Art.6(2) of the European Convention on Human Rights, and that the provision in question must therefore be read down under the Human Rights Act 1998, s.3 so as to impose on the defendant an evidential burden only.[83]

DEALING AND ENCOURAGING

In relation to the dealing and encouraging forms of the offence, three 13–068
general defences appear in CJA 1993, s.53(1). Four more defences, aimed at market professionals, appear in Sch.1.

General defences

No expectation of profit

Under CJA 1993, s.53(1)(a) and (2)(a), an individual is not guilty of 13–069
insider dealing by virtue of dealing in securities or encouraging another person to do so if he shows

> "that he did not at the time expect the dealing to result in a profit[84] attributable to the fact that the information in question was price-sensitive information in relation to the securities".[85]

This defence would be available in the unlikely event of a person selling shares when in possession of inside information which he expected, when it became public, to result in a *rise* in the price. A more likely case is that of a person who deals in securities in ignorance of the fact that the information he has is price-sensitive. But such a person would not need to invoke this defence, because he would not know that the information was inside information and therefore would not have it "as an insider".

Belief that information sufficiently disclosed

Under CJA 1993, s.53(1)(b), an individual is not guilty of the dealing 13–070
form of the offence if he shows

> "that at the time he believed on reasonable grounds that the information had been disclosed widely enough to ensure that none of those taking part in the dealing would be prejudiced by not having the information".

[82] cf. *Cross* (1990) 91 Cr.App.R. 115.
[83] See *Lambert* [2001] UKHL 37; [2002] 2 A.C. 545; *Johnstone* [2003] UKHL 28; [2003] 1 W.L.R. 1736; *Sheldrake v DPP* [2004] UKHL 43; [2005] 1 A.C. 264.
[84] "Profit" includes the avoidance of a loss: CJA 1993, s.53(6).
[85] Information is price-sensitive information in relation to securities if the securities are price-affected in relation to the information: see above, para.13–060.

This would apply, for example, where both (or all) the parties to the transaction are in possession of the same information.

13–071 In the case of the encouraging form of the offence, under s.53(2)(b) it is a defence that the defendant reasonably believed either that the information had already been disclosed widely enough to ensure that no-one would be prejudiced by not having it, or that it would have been disclosed widely enough to ensure this by the time the dealing took place.

Defendant would have done the same anyway

13–072 Under CJA 1993, s.53(1)(c) and (2)(c), an individual is not guilty of the dealing or the encouraging form of the offence if he shows "that he would have done what he did even if he had not had the information". A defendant might be able to rely on this defence if, for example, he could show that he would in any case have had to sell the securities that he sold, because he needed the money; or if he were a trustee and had been advised, in that capacity, to buy securities in respect of which he happened to have inside information.

Market professionals

13–073 In addition to the general defences provided by CJA 1993, s.53(1), four further defences appear in Sch.l to the Act.[86] These defences are intended to protect market professionals against the risk of incurring liability for insider dealing when they have acted in good faith and in accordance with market practice.

Market makers

13–074 Under CJA 1993, Sch.1 para.1(1), an individual is not guilty of the dealing or the encouraging form of the offence if he shows that he acted in good faith in the course of his business as, or his employment in the business of, a market maker. A market maker is a person who holds himself out at all normal times in compliance with the rules of a regulated market or an approved organisation[87] as willing to acquire or dispose of securities, and is recognised as doing so under those rules.[88]

Market information

13–075 Under CJA 1993, Sch.1 para.2(1), an individual is not guilty of the dealing or the encouraging form of the offence if he shows that the information which he had as an insider was market information, and that it was reasonable for an individual in his position to have acted as he did despite having that information as an insider at the time. Market information is information consisting of one or more of the following facts:

[86] CJA 1993, s.53(4).

[87] i.e. an international securities self-regulating organisation approved by the Treasury under any relevant order under FSMA 2000, s.22: CJA 1993, Sch.1 para.1(3).

[88] CJA 1993, Sch.1 para.1(2).

"(a) that securities of a particular kind have been or are to be acquired or disposed of, or that their acquisition or disposal is under consideration or the subject of negotiation;

(b) that securities of a particular kind have not been or are not to be acquired or disposed of;

(c) the number of securities acquired or disposed of or to be acquired or disposed of or whose acquisition or disposal is under consideration or the subject of negotiation;

(d) the price (or range of prices) at which securities have been or are to be acquired or disposed of or the price (or range of prices) at which securities whose acquisition or disposal is under consideration or the subject of negotiation may be acquired or disposed of;

(e) the identity of the persons involved or likely to be involved in any capacity in an acquisition or disposal."[89]

In determining whether it is reasonable for an individual to do an act despite having market information at the time, relevant factors include **13–076**

"(a) the content of the information;

(b) the circumstances in which he first had the information and in what capacity; and

(c) the capacity in which he now acts."[90]

Acquisitions and disposals

Under CJA 1993, Sch.1 para.3, an individual is not guilty of the dealing or the encouraging form of the offence if he shows **13–077**

"(a) that he acted—

(i) in connection with an acquisition or disposal which was under consideration or the subject of negotiation, or in the course of a series of such acquisitions or disposals; and

(ii) with a view to facilitating the accomplishment of the acquisition or disposal or the series of acquisitions or disposals; and

(b) that the information which he had as an insider was market information[91] arising directly out of his involvement in the acquisition or disposal or series of acquisitions or disposals."

Stabilisation

Under CJA 1993, Sch.1 para.5(1), an individual is not guilty of the dealing or the encouraging form of the offence if he shows that he acted in conformity with the price stabilisation rules or the Buy-back and Stabilisation Regulation.[92] **13–078**

[89] CJA 1993, Sch.1 para.1(4).
[90] CJA 1993, Sch.1 para.2(2).
[91] For the definition of "market information" see above, para.13–075.
[92] See above, fn.34.

DISCLOSURE

13–079 The disclosure form of the offence is not committed by an individual who discloses information in the proper performance of the functions of his employment, office or profession.[93] CJA 1993, s.53(3) provides two further defences. An individual is not guilty of insider dealing by virtue of a disclosure of information if he shows

(a) that he did not at the time expect any person, because of the disclosure, to deal in securities in the circumstances mentioned in s.52(3);[94] or

(b) that, although he had such an expectation at the time, he did not expect the dealing to result in a profit attributable to the fact that the information was price-sensitive information in relation to the securities.

PURSUIT OF MONETARY POLICY, ETC.

13–080 CJA 1993, s.63(1) provides that s.52 does not apply to anything done by an individual acting on behalf of a public sector body[95] in pursuit of monetary policies or policies with respect to exchange rates or the management of public debt or foreign exchange reserves.

TERRITORIAL SCOPE

DEALING

13–081 Under CJA 1993, s.62(1), an individual is not guilty of the dealing form of the offence unless

(a) he is in the United Kingdom when he does any act constituting or forming part of the dealing,

(b) the regulated market on which the dealing occurs is one of those regulated in the United Kingdom for the purposes of CJA 1993, Pt V,[96] or

(c) the professional intermediary is in the United Kingdom when he does anything by means of which the offence is committed.

[93] CJA 1993, s.52(2)(b).

[94] For the circumstances mentioned in CJA 1993, s.52(3) see above, para.13–062.

[95] See above, fn.64.

[96] viz. the markets established under the rules of the London Stock Exchange Ltd, LIFFE Administration and Management, OMLX, the London Securities and Derivatives Exchange Ltd, virt-x Exchange Ltd or COREDEALMTS, plus OFEX: Insider Dealing (Securities and Regulated Markets) Order 1994 (SI 1994/187, art.10).

ENCOURAGING AND DISCLOSURE

Under CJA 1993, s.62(2), an individual is not guilty of the encouraging or the disclosure form of the offence unless **13–082**

(a) he is in the United Kingdom when he encourages the dealing or discloses the information, or

(b) the recipient of the encouragement or information is in the United Kingdom when he receives it.

PROCEEDINGS

Proceedings for an offence of insider dealing may be commenced only by or with the consent of the Secretary of State or the DPP,[97] or by the FSA[98] or the Director of the SFO.[99] **13–083**

[97] CJA 1993, s.61(2).
[98] FSMA 2000, s.402(1)(a).
[99] Criminal Justice Act 1987, Sch.1 para.4(1).

CHAPTER 14

COMPANY FRAUD

There are various ways in which a company may be a vehicle for fraud. They include the abuse of company officers' position to enter into transactions in their own interests rather than those of the company, the wrongful depletion of the company's capital, and the use of the company as a means of defrauding third parties (for example by inducing them to extend credit to the company), which will often involve the production of misleading accounts. The Companies Act 1985 ("CA 1985") creates a large number of offences, most of which are summary only. This chapter examines only a selection of the offences most likely to be charged in a fraud case. **14–001**

CA 1985 is largely repealed and replaced by the Companies Act 2006 ("CA 2006"). CA 2006 is not expected to be fully in force until October 2008. Even then, offences committed before the relevant offence-creating **14–002** provision came into force will have to be charged under the corresponding provision of CA 1985. This chapter therefore refers to the relevant provisions of both CA 1985 and CA 2006. In most cases there is little substantive difference.[1]

PRELIMINARIES

"COMPANY", "BODY CORPORATE" AND "CORPORATION"

"COMPANY"

14–003 CA 1985, s.735(1) defines the word "company" to mean a company formed and registered under CA 1985 or earlier Companies Acts, unless the contrary intention appears.[2] CA 1985 extends to England and Wales and Scotland but not Northern Ireland,[3] and, except where otherwise expressly provided, does not apply to companies registered or incorporated in Northern Ireland or outside the United Kingdom.[4] So the definition in CA 1985, s.735(1) includes only companies registered in Great Britain. CA 2006, by contrast, extends to the whole of the United Kingdom.[5] CA 2006, s.1(1) accordingly defines "company" so as to mean a company formed and registered under CA 2006, earlier Companies Acts or earlier Northern Ireland legislation, unless the context otherwise requires.

14–004 In neither CA 1985 nor CA 2006 does the definition of a company include a company incorporated outside the United Kingdom. However, the definition in CA 1985, s.735(1) applies "unless the contrary intention appears",[6] and that in CA 2006, s.1(1) applies "unless the context otherwise requires". In *Re International Bulk Commodities Ltd*[7] Mummery J. held that a "contrary intention" need not be express, but could be inferred from the subject and purpose of the Act in question. On this basis, whenever an offence-creating provision refers to a "company", it would be necessary to ask whether the statutory purpose would be achieved or thwarted by a construction which excluded companies incorporated outside the United Kingdom. But Mummery J. was concerned with provisions of the Insolvency Act 1986. CA 1985, s.735 was relevant only because s.251 of the 1986

[1] Part X of CA 1985 contains highly complex provisions prohibiting a company from entering into loan or credit transactions with its directors or persons connected with them, and s.342 makes this an offence punishable with two years' imprisonment. CA 2006, ss.197–214 make corresponding provision, but there is no criminal sanction for breach. The offence under CA 1985, s.342 is accordingly not considered in this chapter: see paras 6–011 *et seq*. of the second edition of this book.

[2] CA 1985, s.735(4).

[3] CA 1985, s.745(2).

[4] CA 1985, s.745(1).

[5] CA 2006, s.1299.

[6] CA 1985, s.735(4).

[7] [1992] B.C.L.C. 1074.

Act applies the definitions in Pt XXVI of CA 1985 (which include s.735). CA 1985, s.745(1), under which nothing in CA 1985 applies to companies registered or incorporated outside Great Britain unless the Act *expressly* so provides, was not in point; and, in the case of offences under CA 1985, it would appear to preclude Mummery J.'s approach. That approach was in any event doubted in *Re Devon & Somerset Farmers Ltd*.[8]

The qualifying words "unless the context otherwise requires" in CA 2006, s.1(1) arguably amount to legislative endorsement of Mummery J.'s approach, by acknowledging the relevance of the statutory context. On the other hand it seems equally arguable that the context does not "require" an alternative construction merely because that construction seems more appropriate to the context, but only if the definition would, in that context, be unworkable or absurd. It is hard to imagine how, in this sense, the context of an offence-creating provision could ever *require* the provision to apply to a foreign company. In the interests of certainty it is submitted that, in both CA 1985 and CA 2006, offence-creating provisions which refer to a "company" should not be construed as applying to companies incorporated outside the United Kingdom unless it is expressly so provided. **14–005**

"BODY CORPORATE" AND "CORPORATION"

This view is supported by the fact that some offence-creating provisions in CA 1985 and CA 2006 refer to a "body corporate" or a "corporation" rather than a company. These terms are defined by CA 1985, s.740 to include "a company incorporated elsewhere than in Great Britain", and by CA 2006, s.1173(1) to include "a body incorporated outside the United Kingdom". They are thus wider than "company" in that they include foreign companies and other juristic persons and associations existing under foreign laws, as well as bodies corporate which exist under the law of a part of the United Kingdom but are not companies (such as limited liability partnerships).[9] They do not include "a partnership that, whether or not a legal person, is not regarded as a body corporate under the law by which it is governed".[10] Nor do they include a corporation sole.[11] **14–006**

UNREGISTERED COMPANIES

Certain provisions of CA 1985 are applied by CA 1985, s.718, or regulations made thereunder,[12] to a body corporate incorporated in and having a principal place of business in Great Britain which is not a company within the meaning of the Act, unless it is **14–007**

[8] [1994] 1 B.C.L.C. 99.
[9] Limited Liability Partnerships Act 2000, s.1(2).
[10] CA 2006, s.1173(1). There is no corresponding provision in CA 1985, but it seems implicit.
[11] CA 1985, s.740; CA 2006, s.1173(1).
[12] Companies (Unregistered Companies) Regulations 1985 (SI 1985/680).

(a) a body incorporated by, or registered under, a public general Act;

(b) a body not formed for the purpose of carrying on a business which has for its object the acquisition of gain by the body or its individual members;

(c) a body for the time being exempted by direction of the Secretary of State; or

(d) an open-ended investment company.[13]

This would include, for example, a company formed by letters patent or by private Act. Subject to the same exceptions, CA 2006, s.1043 enables the Secretary of State to make provision by regulations applying specified provisions to bodies corporate incorporated in and having a principal place of business in the United Kingdom.

"DIRECTOR" AND "SHADOW DIRECTOR"

DE JURE DIRECTORS AND DE FACTO DIRECTORS

14–008 The term "director" is defined to include "any person occupying the position of director, by whatever name called".[14] It thus includes not only de jure directors, who have been validly appointed as such, but also de facto directors, who act as directors without having been formally appointed.[15] In *Re Hydrodam (Corby) Ltd* Millett J. said:

> "A de facto director is a person who assumes to act as a director. He is held out as a director by the company, and claims and purports to be a director, although never actually or validly appointed as such. To establish that a person was a de facto director of a company it is necessary to plead and prove that he undertook functions in relation to the company which could properly be discharged only by a director. It is not sufficient to show that he was concerned in the management of the company's affairs or undertook tasks in relation to its business which can properly be performed by a manager below board level."[16]

14–009 In *Secretary of State for Trade and Industry v Tjolle*, Jacob J. said:

> "It may be difficult to postulate any one decisive test. I think what is involved is very much a question of degree. The court takes into account all the relevant factors. Those factors include at least whether or not there was a holding out by the company of the individual as a director, whether the individual used the

[13] See the Open-Ended Investment Companies Regulations 2001 (SI 2001/1228).

[14] CA 1985, s.741(1); CA 2006, s.250.

[15] *Re Canadian Land Reclaiming and Colonising Co, Coventry and Dixon's Case* (1880) 14 Ch. D. 660 at 664–665, *per* Sir George Jessel M.R.; *Re Lo-Line Electric Motors Ltd* [1988] Ch. 477 at 490, *per* Sir Nicolas Browne-Wilkinson V.C.

[16] [1994] 2 B.C.L.C. 180 at 183.

title, whether the individual had proper information (e.g. management accounts) on which to base decisions, and whether the individual had to make major decisions and so on. Taking all these factors into account, one asks, 'Was this individual part of the corporate governing structure?' "[17]

In *Re Kaytech International plc*, Robert Walker L.J. pointed out that the factors mentioned by Jacob J. were not conditions which must all be satisfied before de facto directorship can be established. The crucial question is whether the individual assumed the status and functions of a director, so as to make himself responsible as if he were a de jure director.[18]

SHADOW DIRECTORS

Some provisions of the legislation, such as those of CA 2006 which define the general duties of a director, apply also (though not necessarily to the same extent or in the same way) to a "shadow director". This is defined to mean "a person in accordance with whose directions or instructions the directors of the company are accustomed to act".[19] But a person is not regarded as a shadow director by reason only of the fact that the directors act on advice given by him in a professional capacity.[20] **14–010**

In *Secretary of State for Trade and Industry v Deverell*,[21] Morritt L.J. said that shadow directors are those (other than professional advisers) with real influence in the corporate affairs of the company, though not necessarily over the whole field of its corporate activities.[22] Whether communications from the alleged shadow director amount to "directions or instructions" is a question of fact. If they do, and the directors are accustomed to act in accordance with them, it is not necessary to show that the directors cast themselves in a subservient role or surrendered their discretion. **14–011**

"OFFICER WHO IS IN DEFAULT"

Some of the offences under CA 1985 and CA 2006 can be committed by any "officer who is in default". This expression is wider in CA 2006 than in CA 1985. **14–012**

"OFFICER"

In both CA 1985 and CA 2006, "officer" includes a "director, manager or secretary".[23] It has been held that "manager" is not confined to a managing or other director or general manager, but includes any person who in the **14–013**

[17] [1998] 1 B.C.L.C. 333 at 343.
[18] [1999] 2 B.C.L.C. 351 at 423.
[19] CA 1985, s.741(2); CA 2006, s.251(1).
[20] CA 1985, s.741(2); CA 2006, s.251(2).
[21] [2001] Ch. 340.
[22] See also *Australian Securities Commission v AS Nominees Ltd* (1995) 133 A.L.R. 1 at 52–53, *per* Finn J.; *Re Kaytech International plc* [1999] 2 B.C.L.C. 351 at 424, *per* Robert Walker L.J.
[23] CA 1985, s.744; CA 2006, s.1121(2)(a).

affairs of the company exercises a supervisory control which reflects the general policy of the company for the time being, or which is related to the general administration of the company.[24] CA 2006 adds that "officer" also includes "any person who is to be treated as an officer of the company for the purposes of the provision in question".[25] This appears to be implicit in CA 1985.

"IN DEFAULT"

Companies Act 1985

14–014 For the purpose of any provision imposing criminal liability on an "officer who is in default", CA 1985, s.730(5) defines that expression to mean "any officer of the company or other body who knowingly and wilfully authorises or permits the default, refusal or contravention mentioned in the enactment."

14–015 In *Saunders*[26] the chairman and chief executive of Guinness plc was charged with a breach of CA 1985, s.151 (which prohibits a company from giving financial assistance for the acquisition of its shares)[27] in connection with Guinness's takeover bid for Distillers plc. It was contended by the defence that, as s.730(5) required a knowing and wilful breach of s.151, the prosecution had to prove that the defendant had known of the effect of the prohibition and had deliberately authorised or permitted Guinness to contravene it. In relation to the word "knowingly", the defence relied upon a number of authorities indicating that the prosecution had to establish knowledge of the prohibition;[28] the prosecution contended that the term required only an awareness of the facts that constituted the offence, not awareness that those facts did constitute an offence.[29] In relation to the word "wilfully", the defence contended that a high degree of deliberate intention was required;[30] the prosecution argued that the term meant only that "the act is done deliberately and intentionally, not by accident or inadvertence, but so that the mind of the person who does the act goes with it".[31]

14–016 Henry J. rejected the defence's arguments. After a detailed review of the authorities he said:

[24] *Re a Company (No.00996 of 1979)* [1980] Ch. 138 at 144, *per* Shaw J.
[25] CA 2006, s.1121(2)(b).
[26] November 6, 1989.
[27] Below, paras 14–049 *et seq.*
[28] *Frailey v Charlton* [1920] 1 K.B. 147; *Ocean Accident & Guarantee Corp v Cole* [1932] 2 K.B. 100; *Hussein* [1969] 2 Q.B. 567.
[29] *Browne v Speak* [1903] 1 Ch. 586; *Watts v Bucknall* [1903] 1 Ch. 766; *Manning v Cory* [1974] W.A.R. 60; *McPherson v Gerke* [1978] 3 A.C.L.R. 631; *Mudge v Wolstenholme* [1965] V.R. 707; *Steen v Law* [1964] A.C. 287.
[30] *Sheppard v Midland Railway* (1915) 85 L.J. K.B. 283.
[31] *Senior* [1899] 1 Q.B. 283, *per* Lord Russell of Killowen C.J.

"I recognize the difficulty in applying the words 'knowingly and wilfully . . . authorises or permits an offence' to a case in which the offence is one of omission—a failure to do something which the law requires to be done. I would have thought, however, that those words require that the prosecution, to establish a case to answer, must lead evidence upon which, if accepted, it could be held that the accused knew that the thing not done was not done and in the free exercise of his will authorised or permitted the non-doing of it. But I cannot accept the view that in addition the prosecution must call evidence upon which it could be found that the accused knew that there was a law in force which made the failure to do the act unlawful . . ."

He distinguished the authorities suggesting otherwise on the basis that **14–017** they turned on the statutory wording used in each case.

"It is quite clear that in those statutory formulations the intent to evade the actual prohibition was an ingredient of the offence. Examination of the Companies Act shows that where the draftsman wished a director only to be liable if he knew or had reasonable cause to believe that the transaction in question constituted a breach of the Act, then in those circumstances the matter is not dealt with under the officer in default formulation of section 730(5), but is expressly spelled out. By way of example, section 330 lists prohibitions on loans to directors . . . Section 342 deals with criminal penalties in relation to breaches of the section and provides in subsection (1): 'A director of a relevant company who authorises or permits the company to enter into a transaction or arrangement knowing or having reasonable cause to believe that the company was thereby contravening section 330 is guilty of an offence.' There clearly the prosecution must prove (1) that the director authorized or permitted the acts constituting the offence and (2) that the director knew or had reasonable cause to believe that the company was thereby contravening section 330 . . . That formula must be contrasted with the 'officer in default' provisions, where the officer in default is liable if he knowingly or wilfully authorizes or permits the contravention and the contravention is established by the proof of the section 151 offence and not by proof of the fact that the officer knew the law making that an offence."

Companies Act 2006

CA 2006, s.1121(3) provides that, for the purposes of a provision to the **14–018** effect that, in the event of contravention of an enactment in relation to a company, an offence is committed by every officer of the company who is in default, an officer is "in default" if he "authorises or permits, participates in, or fails to take all reasonable steps to prevent, the contravention". The words "knowingly and wilfully" do not appear. In response to an amendment which would have inserted them, the Minister[32] explained that their inclusion might risk excluding from the definition officers who are reckless, who deliberately close their eyes to their responsibilities, or who claim that they did not know that their act or omission constituted an offence (though Henry J.'s ruling in *Saunders* would have avoided that). He said:

[32] Lord Sainsbury, Parliamentary Under-Secretary of State for the Department of Trade and Industry.

> "I understand the concern underlying the amendment; namely, that an innocent officer could in theory permit a contravention by being ignorant of its commission. But I would emphasise that an officer would be liable under this provision only if his ignorance constituted a tacit authorisation, permission or failure to take reasonable steps. I would say that any officer who is so deliberately or recklessly ignorant of his responsibilities as to be liable in this way cannot be described as 'innocent' and it is right that he should be liable under this clause."[33]

OTHER DEFINITIONS

14–019 The terms "subsidiary", "holding company" and "wholly owned subsidiary" are defined by CA 1985, ss.736 and 736A and CA 2006, s.1159(1) and (2). "Public company" is defined by CA 1985, s.1(3) and CA 2006, s.4(2); a "private company" is a company that is not a public company.[34] Various other definitions are contained in CA 1985, s.744 and CA 2006, s.1173(1). CA 1985, s.744A and CA 2006, Sch.8 contain indexes of provisions defined or explained.

ACTS OF THE COMPANY

14–020 Some of the statutory provisions apply only when a specified thing is done by the company. To decide whether such a condition is satisfied, it may be necessary to consider the company's constitution, and to ascertain who has been entrusted with the exercise of its powers and who represents its directing mind and will.[35] The question is whether the human beings who do the acts in question have sufficient status and authority to make their acts those of the company, for the purposes of the provision in question. This ultimately turns on the construction of that provision.[36]

14–021 Often, however, the thing allegedly done by the company will have been done by its officers in order to defraud the company. In these circumstances it may be odd to attribute their fraudulent acts to the company which is the victim of the fraud, and there is some authority suggesting that this cannot be done.[37] But, where the question is whether a company has done a particular thing within the meaning of a statutory provision,[38] it must in principle be a question of construction whether an act which would otherwise have been attributed to the company for the purposes of that

[33] *Hansard*, HL Vol.680, col.GC368 (March 30, 2006).

[34] CA 1985, s.1(3); CA 2006, s.4(1).

[35] *Tesco Supermarkets Ltd v Nattrass* [1972] A.C. 153; *Att-Gen's Reference (No.2 of 1982)* [1984] Q.B. 624 at 640.

[36] *Meridian Global Funds Management Asia Ltd v Securities Commission* [1995] 2 A.C. 500.

[37] *Belmont Finance Corp Ltd v Williams Furniture Ltd* [1979] Ch. 250; *Att-Gen's Reference (No.2 of 1982)* [1984] Q.B. 624.

[38] This was not the case in *Belmont Finance Corp Ltd v Williams Furniture Ltd* [1979] Ch. 250, where the question was whether the company was a party to a conspiracy at common law. It was the case in *Att-Gen's Reference (No.2 of 1982)* [1984] Q.B. 624, and it is submitted that that decision is questionable: see above, para.2–089.

provision is not to be so attributed if it is a fraud on the company.[39] Where the provision is intended to protect the company's shareholders and creditors against fraud, and a construction which excluded acts done in fraud of the company would tend to defeat that purpose, an alternative construction is likely to be adopted. There is certainly no rule that an act intended to defraud a company *cannot* be treated as the company's own act.[40]

DECLARATION OF INTEREST

Both CA 1985 and CA 2006 make it an offence, in certain circumstances, for a director to fail to disclose to his fellow directors a personal interest in transactions entered into by the company. These provisions are intended to prevent the situation in which (for example) a director causes his company to enter into a contract with another company, on terms favourable to that other company, without disclosing that he is himself a director or shareholder of that other company. The offences are triable either way but are punishable only with a fine. They are mentioned here not because they are likely to be regarded as appropriate charges in a fraud case but because they may be relevant to a charge of fraud by abuse of position[41] or by failing to disclose information.[42] **14–022**

COMPANIES ACT 1985

CA 1985, s.317(1) provides: **14–023**

> "It is the duty of a director of a company who is in any way, whether directly or indirectly, interested in a contract[43] or proposed contract with the company to declare the nature of his interest at a meeting of the directors of the company."

A director who fails to comply with this requirement commits an offence under s.317(7), triable either way but punishable only with a fine.[44] Shadow directors[45] are subject to a similar requirement, except that they must declare their interest by a notice in writing to the directors.[46]

[39] cf. *Meridian Global Funds Management Asia Ltd v Securities Commission* [1995] 2 A.C. 500.
[40] *Moore v I. Bresler Ltd* [1944] 2 All E.R. 515.
[41] See above, Ch.6.
[42] See above, Ch.5.
[43] Including any transaction or arrangement: CA 1985, s.317(5).
[44] CA 1985, Sch.24.
[45] Above, para.14–010.
[46] CA 1985, s.317(8).

14–024 The legislation gives no assistance as to the circumstances in which a director is "interested in" a transaction.[47] The section is presumably to be construed in the light of the equitable principles governing a director's fiduciary duties towards the company.[48]

14–025 The director is required to disclose the nature of his interest. The disclosure must be full and frank, so as to show the true nature *and extent* of his interest.[49] It must be made at a meeting of the full board of directors, duly convened.[50]

COMPANIES ACT 2006

14–026 Chapter 2 of Pt 10 of CA 2006 replaces the fiduciary duties imposed on a director[51] by equity with express statutory duties, such as the duty to avoid conflicts of interest (s.175), the duty not to accept benefits from third parties (s.176) and the duty to declare any interest in a proposed transaction or arrangement (s.177). Breaches of these express statutory duties result in civil liability under s.178, and (if dishonest) may amount to fraud by abuse of position or by failing to disclose information; but they do not in themselves give rise to any criminal liability.

14–027 CA 2006, s.182 corresponds to CA 1985, s.317; but, unlike that provision, it applies only to a director (or, with modifications, a shadow director)[52] who is interested in a transaction or arrangement that has *already* been entered into by the company. Failure to declare an interest in a *proposed* transaction (as required by CA 2006, s.177) is not an offence in itself; but s.182 requires the director or shadow director to disclose his interest once the transaction has been entered into, unless he has already done so under s.177. It is an offence under CA 2006, s.183(1) to fail to comply with the requirements of s.182. The offence is triable either way but is punishable only with a fine.

14–028 Like s.317 of CA 1985, CA 2006, s.182 does not define what constitutes being "interested in" a transaction. But a director need not declare an interest if it cannot reasonably be regarded as likely to give rise to a conflict of interest;[53] and the duty imposed by s.177 (though not necessarily the one

[47] Except that a transaction or arrangement of a kind described in CA 1985, s.330 (prohibition of loans, quasi-loans, etc. to directors) made by a company for a director of the company or a person connected with such a director is treated as a transaction or arrangement in which the director is interested, whether or not it is prohibited by s.330: CA 1985, s.317(6). See paras 6–011 *et seq*. of the second edition of this book.

[48] See above, paras 6–011 *et seq*.

[49] *Imperial Mercantile Credit Association v Coleman* (1873) L.R. 6 H.L. 189 at 205, *per* Lord Cairns; *Movitex Ltd v Bulfield* [1988] B.C.L.C. 104 at 121.

[50] *Guinness plc v Saunders* [1988] 1 W.L.R. 863.

[51] Or a shadow director, but only to the extent that the corresponding equitable duties apply to him: CA 2006, s.170(5).

[52] CA 2006, s.187.

[53] CA 2006, s.182(6)(a).

imposed by s.182) is to be interpreted and applied in the same way as the equitable principles on which it is based.[54] According to the explanatory notes on the Act,

> "The director does not need to be a party to the transaction with the company in order for a declaration to be required under this section. For example, where the director's spouse enters into a transaction with the company that may (but need not necessarily) give rise to an indirect interest on the part of the director in that transaction."

MAINTENANCE OF CAPITAL

A company's capital, contributed by its shareholders in exchange for shares, is its lifeblood. Of course, the capital may be diminished by expenditure on the company's objects, or some of it may be lost in carrying on the company's business operations. Creditors and potential creditors are aware of these possibilities, and take the risk that unsecured debts owed to them by the company will go unpaid in the event of the company's insolvency. But such persons have a right to rely on the capital remaining undiminished by any expenditure outside these limits, or by the return of any part of it to the shareholders. CA 1985 and CA 2006 therefore contain various provisions designed to ensure that a company's capital is not wrongfully diminished. They fall into two categories: **14–029**

- provisions relating to the allotment of shares, designed to ensure that shares are not allotted for a consideration below the nominal value of the shares; and
- provisions relating to the reduction of capital, designed to ensure that directors do not diminish the company's capital in a manner prejudicial to the interests of the company's shareholders or creditors.

ALLOTMENT OF SHARES

The rules relating to payment for shares are contained in Pt IV of CA 1985 and Ch.5 of Pt 17 of CA 2006. If a company contravenes these provisions, an offence under CA 1985, s.114 or CA 2006, s.590(1) is committed by every officer of the company who is in default.[55] These offences are punishable only with a fine. But any non-cash consideration for an allotment of shares in a *public* company must be independently valued, and there is a more serious offence of misleading the valuer. **14–030**

[54] CA 2006, s.170(4). For these principles, see above, paras 6–011 *et seq.*
[55] See above, paras 14–012 *et seq.*

ALLOTMENT OF SHARES AT A DISCOUNT

14–031 Shares in a company may not be allotted at a discount[56]—that is, for a consideration worth less than their nominal value. There is no rule that the consideration may not be less than their *market* value, though this would no doubt be a breach of duty on the part of the directors[57] (and, if dishonest, fraud by abuse of position).[58]

14–032 Subject to the special rules for public companies, the consideration payable for an allotment of shares may take the form of either money or money's worth (including goodwill and know-how).[59] Although valuation of an asset is not an exact science,[60] there might be an offence under CA 1985, s.114 or CA 2006, s.590(1) if it is clear that non-cash assets provided as consideration for shares are insufficiently valuable.[61]

ADDITIONAL RULES FOR PUBLIC COMPANIES

14–033 Shares allotted by a public company must be paid up as to at least a quarter of the nominal value, plus the whole of any premium.[62] The required proportion need not be paid up in cash, but there are several situations in which an allotment of shares for a consideration other than cash[63] may be an offence.

- A subscriber to the memorandum of a public company who undertakes in the memorandum to take shares in the company must pay for the shares (including any premium) in cash.[64]
- A public company must not accept, by way of payment for shares,
  - an undertaking to do work or perform services;[65]
  - an undertaking of any kind which may be performed more than five years after the date of the allotment;[66] or

[56] CA 1985, s.100(1); CA 2006, s.580(1).
[57] *Shaw v Holland* [1900] 2 Ch. 305.
[58] Above, Ch.6.
[59] CA 1985, s.99(1); CA 2006, s.582(1).
[60] *Re Bradford Investments plc (No.2)* [1991] B.C.L.C. 688.
[61] cf. *Ooregum Gold Mining Co of India v Roper* [1892] A.C. 125 at 137; *Re Wragg* [1897] 1 Ch. 796; *Re Innes & Co Ltd* [1903] 2 Ch. 254 at 262; *Park Business Interiors Ltd v Park* [1992] B.C.L.C. 1034 at 1040.
[62] CA 1985, s.101(1); CA 2006, s.586(1). There is an exception for shares allotted in pursuance of an employees' share scheme: CA 1985, s.101(2); CA 2006, s.586(2).
[63] Payment in cash includes, for this purpose, payment by cheque received by the company in good faith which the directors have no reason for suspecting will not be paid, the release of a liability of the company for a liquidated sum, and an undertaking to pay cash to the company at a future date, but not the payment of cash to a third party: CA 1985, s.738; CA 2006, s.583. See also *Systems Control plc v Munro Corporate plc* [1990] B.C.L.C. 659.
[64] CA 1985, s.106; CA 2006, s.584.
[65] CA 1985, s.99(2); CA 2006, s.585.
[66] CA 1985, s.102(1); CA 2006, s.587.

- any other non-cash consideration which has not been independently valued under CA 1985, s.103 or CA 2006, s.593.[67]

This last rule is given teeth by CA 1985, s.110(1) and CA 2006, s.1153(1), under which the independent valuer is entitled to require, from the officers of a company proposing to accept or give the consideration, such information and explanation as he thinks necessary to enable him to carry out the valuation. A person commits an offence under CA 1985, s.110(2) or CA 2006, s.1153(2) if he knowingly or recklessly makes an oral or written statement to a valuer which conveys or purports to convey any information or explanation which the valuer requires, or is entitled to require, under CA 1985, s.110(1) or CA 2006, s.1153(1), and which is misleading, false or deceptive[68] in a material particular. These offences are triable either way, and are punishable on conviction on indictment with two years' imprisonment.[69] **14–034**

This offence is one of several considered in this chapter which are defined in terms of knowledge or recklessness. Most of these offences are of long standing. Until recently the element of recklessness would probably have been construed in an objective sense, denoting "a high degree of negligence without dishonesty".[70] This interpretation has arguably been ruled out by the House of Lords' "subjective" approach in *G.*,[71] overruling its earlier decision in *Caldwell v Metropolitan Police Commissioner*.[72] On this view, a person makes a false or misleading statement recklessly—and it is therefore a "deceptive" statement—if he is aware that it may be false or misleading and, in the light of that awareness, he takes an unreasonable **14–035**

[67] CA 1985, s.103; CA 2006, s.593. A valuation report under CA 1985, s.103 must state the nominal value of the shares to be wholly or partly paid for by the consideration in question, the amount of any premium payable, the description of the consideration, and the extent to which the nominal value of the shares and any premium are to be treated as paid up (i) by the consideration, and (ii) in cash: CA 1985, s.108(4). A report under CA 2006, s.593 must state all these matters and also the method and date of valuation: CA 2006, s.596(2). In addition, a note to the valuer's report must state: (a) in the case of a valuation made by a person other than himself, that it appeared reasonable to arrange for it to be so made or to accept a valuation so made; (b) that the method of valuation was reasonable in all the circumstances; (c) that it appears to the valuer that there has been no material change in the value of the consideration in question since the valuation; and (d) that, on the basis of the valuation, the value of the consideration, together with any cash by which the nominal value of the shares or any premium payable on them is to be paid up, is not less than so much of the aggregate of the nominal value and the whole of any such premium as is treated as paid up by the consideration and any such cash: CA 1985, s.108(6); CA 2006, s.596(3). The valuation procedure is not required in two cases: (a) where a takeover bid involves the offer of shares in the offeror company in exchange for shares in the target company, provided that the offer is open to all the shareholders of the target company (or, where it relates only to shares of a particular class, to all the holders of shares of that class): CA 1985, s.103(3); CA 2006, s.594; (b) where the shares are allotted in connection with a proposed merger of the company with another company: CA 1985, s.103(4), (5); CA 2006, s.595.

[68] See above, para.12–012.

[69] CA 1985, s.110(2), Sch.24; CA 2006, s.1153(4).

[70] *Bates* [1952] 2 All E.R. 842, *per* Donovan J.

[71] [2003] UKHL 50; [2004] 1 A.C. 1034.

[72] [1982] A.C. 341.

risk by making it. But it may also be arguable that, where an offence has long been defined in terms of recklessness, the meaning of that expression is what Parliament intended it to be when the offence was first introduced—before recklessness acquired its modern, subjective sense. *Caldwell* was wrong about Parliament's intention in enacting the Criminal Damage Act 1971, but would arguably be right about Parliament's intention in enacting CA 2006 and its predecessors.[73]

REDUCTION OF CAPITAL

14–036 In certain circumstances, the directors of a company may legitimately form the view that the company's capital exceeds its reasonable requirements and that it is desirable to repay a portion of the capital to the shareholders.[74] In other cases, the directors may take the view that there has been a loss of capital, for example through unprofitable trading, and that it is necessary to reduce the company's capital in order to restore reality to the company's accounts.[75]

14–037 A company can reduce its capital by special resolution, but this is subject to confirmation by the court.[76] CA 2006 introduces another option. Under CA 2006, s.641(1)(a) a private company can reduce its capital by following the procedure under ss.642–644, which involves the passing of a special resolution supported by a solvency statement. A solvency statement is

> "a statement that each of the directors—
>
> (a) has formed the opinion, as regards the company's situation at the date of the statement, that there is no ground on which the company could then be found to be unable to pay (or otherwise discharge) its debts; and
>
> (b) has also formed the opinion—
>
> (i) if it is intended to commence the winding up of the company within twelve months of that date, that the company will be able to pay (or otherwise discharge) its debts in full within twelve months of the commencement of the winding up; or
>
> (ii) in any other case, that the company will be able to pay (or otherwise discharge) its debts as they fall due during the year immediately following that date."[77]

[73] cf. above, para.13–013, on "recklessly" in the Financial Services and Markets Act 2000, s.397.

[74] *British and American Trustee and Finance Corp v Couper* [1894] A.C. 399 at 413; *Ex p. Westburn Sugar Refineries Ltd* [1951] A.C. 625.

[75] *Re Jupiter House Investments (Cambridge) Ltd* [1985] 1 W.L.R. 975; *Re Grosvenor Press plc* [1985] 1 W.L.R. 980.

[76] CA 1985, s.135; CA 2006, s.645. A private company can also finance a redemption or purchase of its shares out of capital by following the procedure under CA 1985, ss.171–177 or Ch.5 of Pt 18 of CA 2006: below, paras 14–045 *et seq.*

[77] CA 2006, s.643(1).

This procedure does not require an application to the court, and the lack of judicial scrutiny means that the solvency statement is crucial. It is the means by which the process is commenced, and the primary material on which the shareholders will form a view as to whether the reduction is viable. CA 2006, s.643(4) therefore provides that, if the directors make a solvency statement without having reasonable grounds for the opinions expressed in it, and it is delivered to the registrar of companies, an offence is committed by every director who is in default.[78] The offence is triable either way and is punishable on conviction on indictment with two years' imprisonment.[79] **14–038**

ACQUISITION BY A COMPANY OF ITS OWN SHARES

The general rule is that a company may not purchase its own shares.[80] The main reason for this is the need to avoid the unauthorised return of capital to the shareholders. If a company purports to act in contravention of the rule, an offence under CA 1985, s.143(2) or CA 2006, s.658(2) is committed by the company and every officer of the company who is in default.[81] The offence is triable either way, and is punishable on conviction on indictment with two years' imprisonment.[82] **14–039**

The general rule is subject to a number of exceptions. **14–040**

- A limited company may acquire any of its own fully paid shares otherwise than for valuable consideration, for example by way of gift.[83] Such an acquisition is outside the primary mischief because it does not deplete the company's assets.
- A company may acquire its own shares in a reduction of capital duly made.[84]
- A company may acquire its own shares in pursuance of an order of the court, under various provisions which enable this to be used as a means of remedying some other default.[85]
- A company may forfeit shares (or accept shares surrendered in lieu) for failure to pay any sum payable in respect of the shares, if its articles so permit.[86]

[78] See above, para.14–018.
[79] CA 2006, s.643(5). It is also an offence, punishable with a fine, to deliver to the registrar a solvency statement that has not been provided to the shareholders in accordance with the statutory procedure: CA 2006, s.644(7).
[80] *Trevor v Whitworth* (1887) 12 App. Cas. 409.
[81] See above, paras 14–012 *et seq.*
[82] CA 1985, s.143(2), Sch.24; CA 2006, s.658(3).
[83] CA 1985, s.143(3); CA 2006, s.659(1). See also *Kirby v Wilkins* [1929] 2 Ch. 444; *Re Castiglione's Will Trusts* [1958] Ch. 549.
[84] CA 1985, s.143(3)(b); CA 2006, s.659(2)(a). See above, paras 14–036 *et seq.*
[85] CA 1985, s.143(3)(c); CA 2006, s.659(2)(b).
[86] CA 1985, s.143(3)(d); CA 2006, s.659(2)(c).

- A company is not precluded from acquiring the shares of another company in circumstances in which the sole asset of the acquired company is shares in the acquiring company.[87]
- A company may purchase its own shares in accordance with the procedure under Ch. VII of Pt V of CA 1985 or Ch.4 of Pt 18 of CA 2006. This is a major exception to the general rule and we consider it below.

THE STATUTORY PROCEDURE

14–041 Chapter VII of Pt V of CA 1985 and Ch.4 of Pt 18 of CA 2006 permit a company to purchase its own shares, provided that its articles authorise it to do so, and subject to certain safeguards. These safeguards are concerned partly with the funds that must be available to finance the transaction, and partly with the procedure that must be followed. The two aspects interrelate in that additional procedural steps are required when the transaction is to be financed out of capital. Compliance, in both respects, will prevent the transaction from being an offence under CA 1985, s.143(2) or CA 2006, s.658(2).[88] Failure to comply, in either respect, will render the transaction unlawful,[89] and an offence under CA 1985, s.143(2) or CA 2006, s.658(2) will be committed.

14–042 The rules as to the funds that must be available for the redemption or purchase are stricter in the case of public companies. A private company may, subject to additional procedural requirements, finance the transaction out of capital.[90] A public company (and a private company which does not follow the stipulated procedure) must ensure that its capital is preserved. Consequently, the price must come out of either distributable profits[91] or the proceeds of a fresh issue made for the purpose.[92] Insofar as the lost share capital is not replaced by a fresh issue, it must be "topped up" by a transfer of an equivalent sum to the capital redemption reserve.[93] Certain payments other than the purchase price itself must be made out of distributable profits in any event, whether the company is a public or a private one. Such payments include the consideration for a contingent purchase contract (such as an option) and the consideration for the variation of such a contract or of a contract for an "off-market" purchase.[94]

[87] *Acatos & Hutcheson plc v Watson* [1995] 1 B.C.L.C. 218. But, if the directors of the acquiring company do not act solely in the interests of that company, they might be guilty of fraud by abuse of position: above, Ch.6.

[88] CA 1985, s.143(3)(a); CA 2006, s.658(1).

[89] *Re R.W. Peak (Kings Lynn) Ltd* [1998] 1 B.C.L.C. 193.

[90] See below, paras 14–045 *et seq*.

[91] i.e. in relation to the making of a payment, those profits out of which a distribution equal in value to the payment could lawfully be made: CA 1985, s.181(a); CA 2006, s.736.

[92] CA 1985, s.160(1)(a); CA 2006, s.687(2).

[93] CA 1985, s.170; CA 2006, s.733.

[94] CA 1985, s.168; CA 2006, s.705.

If these payments are made otherwise than out of distributable profits, the purchase of the shares under the contract in question will not be lawful[95] and an offence under CA 1985, s.143(2) or CA 2006, s.658(2) will be committed.

If a company were permitted to purchase its own shares on the basis that some or all of the consideration is to be paid at a later date, difficulties would arise in the event of the company having insufficient profits to complete the contract when the time comes.[96] The company must therefore hand over the consideration simultaneously with the transfer of the shares.[97] **14–043**

The purchase by a company of its own shares requires prior authorisation, by ordinary resolution in the case of a market purchase[98] and by special resolution in the case of an off-market purchase[99] or a contingent purchase contract.[100] A special resolution is ineffective if it is only passed through the exercise of the voting rights carried by any of the shares in question.[101] **14–044**

PURCHASE OUT OF CAPITAL BY PRIVATE COMPANY

By way of exception to the rule that a company's purchase of its own shares must be financed out of distributable profits or the proceeds of a fresh issue, CA 1985, ss.171–177 and Ch.5 of Pt 18 of CA 2006 permit a private company to make payments for this purpose out of capital if certain additional steps are taken.[102] The directors must first make a statement in the prescribed form[103] and supported by an auditors' report,[104] that, having made full inquiry into the affairs and prospects of the company, they have formed the opinion **14–045**

(a) as regards its initial situation immediately following the date on which the payment out of capital is proposed to be made, that there will be no grounds on which the company could then be found unable to pay its debts,[105] and

95 CA 1985, s.168(2)(a); CA 2006, s.705(2).

96 See the Department of Trade's consultative document *The Purchase by a Company of its Own Shares*, Cmnd.7944, para.38.

97 CA 1985, ss.159(3), 162(2); CA 2006, s.691(2).

98 CA 1985, s.166; CA 2006, s.701.

99 CA 1985, s.164; CA 2006, s.694(1), (2).

100 CA 1985, s.165; CA 2006, s.694(3).

101 CA 1985, s.164(5); CA 2006, s.695(3).

102 Under CA 1985, but not CA 2006, this is permissible only if authorised by the articles.

103 CA 1985, s.173(5); CA 2006, s.714(5). Under CA 1985, but not CA 2006, this must be a statutory declaration.

104 CA 1985, s.173(5); CA 2006, s.714(6).

105 Under CA 2006, s.714(4) the directors must take into account all of the company's liabilities, including any contingent or prospective liabilities. Under CA 1985, s.173(4) they need only take into account those liabilities that would be relevant under the Insolvency Act 1986, s.122 (winding up by the court) to the question whether the company is unable to pay its debts.

(b) as regards its prospects for the year immediately following that date, that, having regard to

(i) their intentions with respect to the management of the company's business during that year, and

(ii) the amount and character of the financial resources that will in their view be available to the company during that year,

the company will be able to continue to carry on business as a going concern (and will accordingly be able to pay its debts as they fall due) throughout that year.[106]

14–046 A director who makes such a statement under CA 1985 without having reasonable grounds for the opinion expressed commits an offence under CA 1985, s.173(6). If the statement is made under CA 2006 without reasonable grounds for the opinion expressed, an offence under CA 2006, s.715(1) is committed by every director who is in default. In each case the offence is triable either way and is punishable on conviction on indictment with two years' imprisonment.[107]

14–047 Within a week of the directors' statement,[108] the company must pass a special resolution approving the payment out of capital.[109] The resolution is ineffective if it is passed as a result of the exercise of voting rights carried by the shares in question.[110] The directors' statement and auditors' report must then be made available for inspection.[111] A creditor, or a member who did not consent to the resolution or vote in favour of it, may apply to the court to have it cancelled.[112] If no such application is made, or the court confirms the resolution, the payment out of capital must be made between five and seven weeks after the date of the resolution[113] unless the court orders otherwise.[114]

14–048 Subject to any order of the court on an application for cancellation of the resolution, a payment out of capital is not lawful unless these requirements are satisfied.[115] The exception for transactions in accordance with Ch.VII of Pt V of CA 1985 or Pt 18 of CA 2006 will not apply, and the offence under CA 1985, s.143(2) or CA 2006, s.658(2) will be committed.

[106] CA 1985, s.173(3); CA 2006, s.714.
[107] CA 1985, s.173(6), Sch.24; CA 2006, s.715(2).
[108] CA 1985, s.174(1); CA 2006, s.716.
[109] CA 1985, s.173(2); CA 2006, s.716(1).
[110] CA 1985, s.174(2); CA 2006, s.717(3).
[111] CA 1985, s.175(6); CA 2006, s.720.
[112] CA 1985, s.176; CA 2006, s.721.
[113] CA 1985, s.174(1); CA 2006, s.723.
[114] CA 1985, s.177(2); CA 2006, s.721(5).
[115] CA 1985, s.173(1); CA 2006, s.713(1).

FINANCIAL ASSISTANCE FOR ACQUISITION OF SHARES

The giving by a company of assistance in the acquisition of the company's own shares has been prohibited since the Companies Act 1929. It is currently an offence under CA 1985, s.151. There is a corresponding offence under CA 2006, s.680, but this is narrower in that it applies only to public companies.[116] CA 1985, ss.155–158 provide a "whitewash" procedure by which a private company may obtain exemption from the prohibition, but this procedure is not required under CA 2006 and is not discussed here.[117] **14–049**

CA 1985, s.151 provides that **14–050**

- where a person is acquiring or is proposing to acquire shares in a company, it is not lawful for the company or any of its subsidiaries to give financial assistance directly or indirectly for the purpose of that acquisition before or at the same time as the acquisition takes place;[118] and
- where a person has acquired shares in a company and any liability has been incurred (by that or any other person)[119] for the purpose of that acquisition, it is not lawful for the company or any of its subsidiaries to give financial assistance directly or indirectly for the purpose of reducing or discharging the liability so incurred.[120]

If a company contravenes either rule, an offence under CA 1985, s.151(3) is committed by the company and every officer who is in default.[121] The offence is triable either way, and is punishable on conviction on indictment with two years' imprisonment.[122]

CA 2006, ss.678 and 679 provide that **14–051**

- where a person is proposing to acquire shares in a public company, it is not lawful for that company, or a company that is a subsidiary of that company, to give financial assistance directly or indirectly for the purpose of the acquisition before or at the same time as the acquisition takes place;[123]
- where a person has acquired shares in a company and a liability has been incurred (by that or another person) for the purpose of

[116] The offence was thought to be unnecessary in the case of private companies, as the mischief in question can be controlled through the provisions on directors' duties, wrongful trading and market abuse: *Company Law Reform*, White Paper, Cm.6456, p.41.

[117] See the second edition of this book, paras 6–080 *et seq*.

[118] CA 1985, s.151(1).

[119] This plainly means "by that person or any person other than that person": it does not exclude the company itself. See *Chaston v SWP Group plc* [2002] EWCA Civ 1999; [2003] 1 B.C.L.C. 675 at [14].

[120] CA 1985, s.151(2).

[121] For "officer who is in default", see above, paras 14–012 *et seq.*

[122] CA 1985, s.151(3), Sch.24.

[123] CA 2006, s.678(1).

the acquisition, it is not lawful for that company, or a company that is a subsidiary of that company, to give financial assistance directly or indirectly for the purpose of reducing or discharging the liability if, at the time the assistance is given,[124] the company in which the shares were acquired is a public company;[125]

- where a person is acquiring or proposing to acquire shares in a private company, it is not lawful for a public company that is a subsidiary of that company to give financial assistance directly or indirectly for the purpose of the acquisition before or at the same time as the acquisition takes place;[126] and
- where a person has acquired shares in a private company and a liability has been incurred by that or another person for the purpose of the acquisition, it is not lawful for a public company that is a subsidiary of that company to give financial assistance directly or indirectly for the purpose of reducing or discharging the liability.[127]

If a company contravenes any of these rules, an offence under CA 2006, s.680(1) is committed by the company and every officer who is in default.[128] The offence is triable either way, and is punishable on conviction on indictment with two years' imprisonment.[129]

14–052 Under both CA 1985, s.151 and CA 2006, s.680 it is sufficient that the financial assistance is given by a subsidiary of the company whose shares are being or have been acquired. In *Arab Bank plc v Mercantile Holdings Ltd*[130] Millett J. held that the phrase "any of its subsidiaries" in CA 1985, s.151 refers to subsidiaries which are companies within the meaning of CA 1985, and that a foreign subsidiary was therefore not prohibited from giving financial assistance for the purpose of the acquisition of shares in its English parent company. This interpretation is confirmed by CA 2006: ss.678 and 679 refer to "a [public] company that is a subsidiary" of the company whose shares are or have been acquired. A foreign subsidiary does not count because it is not a "company" within the meaning of the Act.[131]

14–053 In *Charterhouse Investment Trust Ltd v Tempest Diesels Ltd*,[132] Hoffmann J. said that the offence has two elements: the giving of financial assistance,

[124] So the prohibition does not apply if the company was a public company when the shares were acquired but has re-registered as a private company by the time the assistance is given. Conversely, it does apply if the company is a public company when the assistance is given, even if it was a private company when the shares were acquired.
[125] CA 2006, s.678(3).
[126] CA 2006, s.679(1).
[127] CA 2006, s.679(3).
[128] For "officer who is in default", see above, paras 14–012 *et seq.*
[129] CA 2006, s.680(2).
[130] [1994] Ch. 71.
[131] Above, para.14–003.
[132] [1986] B.C.L.C. 1 at 10.

and the prohibited purpose. While this is true, the two are not entirely distinct. To speak of one person assisting another is meaningless without reference to the thing that the other is assisted to do. In the present context, this means that the company whose shares are acquired must assist the acquirer to acquire them, or to reduce or discharge a liability incurred for the purpose of acquiring them. There is then a further requirement as to the company's *purpose* in giving that assistance.

THE ASSISTANCE

"Financial assistance" is defined as **14–054**

(a) financial assistance given by way of gift;

(b) financial assistance given

- by way of guarantee, security or indemnity (other than an indemnity in respect of the indemnifier's own neglect or default), or
- by way of release or waiver;

(c) financial assistance given

- by way of a loan or any other agreement under which any of the obligations of the person giving the assistance are to be fulfilled at a time when in accordance with the agreement any obligation of another party to the agreement remains unfulfilled, or
- by way of the novation of, or the assignment of rights arising under, a loan or such other agreement; or

(d) any other financial assistance given by a company where

- the net assets of the company are reduced to a material extent by the giving of the assistance, or
- the company has no net assets.[133]

The definition is circular, since each of the four paragraphs refers to "financial assistance". In *Chaston v SWP Group plc*, Ward L.J. described it as "singularly unhelpful". **14–055**

> "I can understand [a] to [c] and they seem all to be related to direct or indirect assistance given for the actual acquisition of the shares, that is to say help in meeting the consideration for the transaction. But [d] tells one nothing about what comprises financial assistance. The words are as wide as they can be—

[133] CA 1985, s.152(1)(a); CA 2006, s.677(1).

'any other financial assistance'. Rather it tells you when financial assistance is not financial assistance, namely when it is *de minimis*."[134]

14–056 With the exception of "financial assistance" itself, the expressions used in paras (a) to (c) of the definition have recognised legal meanings. "Financial assistance", by contrast, has no technical meaning, and its frame of reference is the language of ordinary commerce.[135] The question whether financial assistance has been given therefore involves an examination of the commercial substance of the transaction.[136] Subject to this, Ward L.J. suggested in *Chaston v SWP Group plc* that "A jury would not need an over-elaborate direction of any further meaning to be given to 'financial assistance' than the words literally bear." The language of the statute must not be strained so as to include transactions not fairly within it; but the question is whether, from a commercial point of view, the transaction amounts to financial assistance. If it does, the statutory language is not strained.[137] Each case turns on its own facts.[138]

14–057 The most obvious way in which a company can assist in the acquisition of its shares, and the one at which the prohibition is primarily aimed,[139] is by using its assets to fund the purchase price. Lord Greene M.R. said in *Re V.G.M. Holdings Ltd*:

> "Those whose memories enable them to recall what had been happening after the last war for several years will remember that a very common form of transaction in connection with companies was one by which persons—call them financiers, speculators, or what you will—finding a company with a substantial cash balance or easily realisable assets such as war loan, bought up the whole or the greater part of the shares of the company for cash and so arranged matters that the purchase money which they then became bound to provide was advanced to them by the company whose shares they were acquiring, either out of its cash balance or by realisation of its liquid investments. That type of transaction was a common one, and it gave rise to great dissatisfaction and, in some cases, great scandals."[140]

In *Wallersteiner v Moir*, Lord Denning M.R. added:

> "Since that time financiers have used more sophisticated methods . . . Circular cheques come in very handy. So do puppet companies. The transactions are

[134] [2002] EWCA Civ 1999; [2003] 1 B.C.L.C. 675 at [57]–[58]. But paras (a) to (c) are not redundant because, when one of them applies, it is immaterial whether the company has net assets or its net assets are materially reduced: ibid. at [37], *per* Arden L.J.

[135] *Charterhouse Investment Trust Ltd v Tempest Diesels Ltd* [1986] B.C.L.C. 1; approved in *Barclays Bank plc v British & Commonwealth Holdings plc* [1996] 1 W.L.R. 1.

[136] *Chaston v SWP Group plc* [2002] EWCA Civ 1999; [2003] 1 B.C.L.C. 675 at [32], *per* Arden L.J.

[137] *Chaston v SWP Group plc* [2002] EWCA Civ 1999; [2003] 1 B.C.L.C. 675 at [39], *per* Arden L.J.

[138] *M.T. Realisations Ltd v Digital Equipment Co Ltd* [2003] EWCA Civ 494; [2003] 2 B.C.L.C. 117 at [35], *per* Mummery L.J.

[139] *Brady v Brady* [1989] A.C. 755 at 780, *per* Lord Oliver.

[140] [1942] Ch. 235 at 239; see also *Selangor United Rubber Estates Ltd v Cradock (No.3)* [1968] 1 W.L.R. 1555.

extremely complicated, but the end result is clear. You look to the company's money and see what has become of it. You look to the company's shares and see into whose hands they have got. You will then soon see if the company's money has been used to finance the purchase."[141]

In *Chaston v SWP Group plc*, Ward L.J. suggested that paras (a) to (c) of the definition at para.14–054 are concerned *only* with "help in meeting the consideration for the transaction".[142] That construction may be unduly narrow, but the point is academic since it is clear from the decision in *Chaston* that para.(d) of the definition is not so limited. SWP wished to acquire shares in a company, and to carry out a "due diligence" exercise in connection with the acquisition. The target company paid for a firm of accountants to do some of the necessary work. It was found by the trial judge that this was done "to facilitate the progress of the negotiations and to enable SWP to conclude its due diligence exercise: and, having done so, then to enable it to make up its mind as to whether or not to acquire the shares". **14–058**

The Court of Appeal held that the payment assisted SWP in the acquisition, because it relieved SWP of the need to pay its own accountants to do the work: it reduced the overall cost of the acquisition. As a matter of commercial reality, the payment "smoothed the path" to the acquisition of the shares.[143] It was immaterial that it was made in good faith and in the interests of the company, that it was in fact beneficial to the company,[144] or (provided it was made "for the purpose of" the acquisition) that it did not affect the purchase price or go towards it. These facts did not take it outside the mischief at which the prohibition was aimed, namely that **14–059**

> "the resources of the target company and its subsidiaries should not be used directly or indirectly to assist the purchaser financially to make the acquisition. This may prejudice the interests of the creditors of the target or its group, and the interests of any shareholders who do not accept the offer to acquire their shares or to whom the offer is not made."[145]

It was also immaterial that the assistance was given in advance of the acquisition rather than in the course of it. The legislation provides that the assistance may be given "directly or indirectly", and also that it may be

[141] [1974] 1 W.L.R. 991 at 1014.
[142] [2002] EWCA Civ 1999; [2003] 1 B.C.L.C. 675 at [58].
[143] [2002] EWCA Civ 1999; [2003] 1 B.C.L.C. 675 at [38], *per* Arden L.J. But this expression should not be read as a gloss on the statutory wording: *TFB (Mortgages) Ltd v Anglo Petroleum Ltd* [2006] EWHC 258 at [134], *per* Peter Smith J.
[144] This is subject to the proviso that, if the assistance does not fall within any of paras (a) to (c) of the definition at para.14–054 above and the company has net assets, those assets must be materially reduced. In *Saunders* (below, para.14–060) Henry J. similarly rejected a submission that there could be no financial assistance where the company obtained a net financial advantage from the transaction (as, it was argued, Guinness had), ruling that this "balance sheet approach" applied only to financial assistance within para.(d) of the definition above.
[145] [2002] EWCA Civ 1999; [2003] 1 B.C.L.C. 675 at [31], *per* Arden L.J.

given not only where the other person is already acquiring the shares but also where he is "proposing" to do so.[146]

14–060 *Chaston v SWP Group plc* is consistent with a ruling given by Henry J. in the first Guinness trial.[147] Guinness plc had made a takeover bid for Distillers plc. Argyll plc made a rival bid. The terms of Guinness's bid offered Distillers' shareholders the choice of either cash or a combination of cash and Guinness shares. The value of the Guinness bid therefore depended on the price of Guinness shares. The prosecution alleged that Guinness artificially inflated that price by agreeing to indemnify certain purchasers of its shares against any losses they might sustain on the resale of the shares, and to pay them "success fees" if Guinness succeeded in its bid. The defence argued that it was not enough for the prosecution to show that the alleged assistance had persuaded or encouraged the purchaser of shares to purchase them: it had to be shown that the company had provided him with the funds needed to pay for the shares, or had in some other way *enabled* him to buy them.[148]

14–061 Henry J. rejected this argument.

> "It seems to me perfectly clear that those who render assistance often enable those who they assist to do that which they could not otherwise have done. It does not follow from that that that which does not enable is not assistance—assistance is a much wider concept than enablement. Junior counsel hope to assist leading counsel, they do not usually expect to 'enable' their leader to present the case, and would be surprised to hear that only such enablement constituted assistance . . .
>
> As a matter of language . . . the meaning of the words seem equally clear to me in the context of giving financial assistance for the purpose of the acquisition of the shares. It seems to me that you give financial assistance for that purpose when, to induce the purchaser to acquire them, you make the financial terms on which those shares are offered to him more attractive to him than they would be in the open market—whether by giving him a special price, loaning him the price on favourable interest terms, guaranteeing his overdraft at the bank, indemnifying original price plus cost, or by simply saying that on a certain contingency he will be paid a reward not available to other purchasers. Some of these financial inducements might be necessary to *enable* some purchasers to purchase, others might be necessary to *persuade* others to purchase, but it seems to me that as a matter of language all are financial assistance given for the purpose of the purchase.
>
> On this basis the clear 'purpose' of the agreement or promise is that someone who might not otherwise acquire the shares would decide to do so. Both elimination of the downside risk and promise of a success fee improve the financial terms on which the shares are sold and therefore in my judgment are or can be financial assistance in ordinary parlance."

[146] [2002] EWCA Civ 1999; [2003] 1 B.C.L.C. 675 at [42], *per* Arden L.J.

[147] *Saunders*, November 6, 1989.

[148] Hoffmann J. had said in *Charterhouse Investment Trust Ltd v Tempest Diesels Ltd* [1986] B.C.L.C. 1 at 10: "[It] can properly be described as giving financial assistance if the effect is to provide the purchaser of its shares with the cash needed to pay for them . . . It follows that if the only or main purpose of such a transaction is to enable the purchaser to buy the shares, the section is contravened."

Henry J. went on to consider whether there was any reason to construe the words differently in the context of the Act, and concluded that there was not. 14–062

> "First, to assist and to enable are two quite different concepts, and in ordinary parlance assistance can be both given and accepted by those who have no need of it. To read assistance as meaning necessary assistance is to add a gloss to the statute. If Parliament meant to limit financial assistance to necessary financial assistance, it would have done so.
>
> Further, there is no reason to see why they should have wished to do so . . . The mischief was the plunder of companies by financiers, and not merely the plunder of companies by impoverished or illiquid financiers."

Chaston v SWP Group plc makes it clear that financial assistance is not limited to the provision by the target company of the purchase price. But the court also emphasised the importance of examining the "commercial substance" of the transaction. This process led to a different conclusion in *M.T. Realisations Ltd v Digital Equipment Co Ltd*,[149] where the arrangement relied upon as constituting financial assistance was made after the acquisition of the shares. In effect it enabled the purchaser to receive sums to which it was already entitled by virtue of the acquisition agreement, but to do so by a less circuitous route than would otherwise have been required. As a matter of commercial reality, the company did not give the purchaser any financial assistance at all. 14–063

In *Corporate Development Partners LLC v E-Relationship Marketing Ltd*[150] a management consultancy firm (CDP) introduced a client (E-RM) to another company (Red Eye) with a view to a possible takeover. E-RM later agreed to pay CDP a transaction fee in the event of its being taken over by Red Eye. Rimer J. held that this was not assistance in Red Eye's acquisition of shares in E-RM, because it could not affect the outcome. 14–064

> "Since CDP was playing no role in the negotiation of the acquisition—and was neither intended nor required to—the commitment to pay it the transaction fee was not going to, was not intended to and did not in fact assist or advance the acquisition at all. The payment commitment was not a condition of the takeover; it would not serve to reduce Red Eye's acquisition obligations by a single penny; and it was neither intended to, nor did it, smooth the path towards any ultimate acquisition. No doubt the reason for the commitment was because CDP had earlier introduced a party who might thereafter acquire E-RM; and it was intended to be by way of a financial reward to CDP for that introduction. But, for reasons given, the commitment was not entered into 'for the purpose' of such an acquisition."

Aldous L.J. pointed out in *Barclays Bank plc v British & Commonwealth Holdings plc*[151] that it is not enough that assistance is given: the assistance must be financial. Assistance which involves the payment of money is 14–065

149 [2003] EWCA Civ 494; [2003] 2 B.C.L.C. 117.
150 [2007] EWHC 436.
151 [1996] 1 W.L.R. 1 at 15.

financial by definition. Even if it takes some other form, such as the provision of services, it might arguably be financial if it is worth money to the person to whom it is provided.

THE PURPOSE OF THE ASSISTANCE

14–066 The assistance must be given for the purpose of the acquisition, or for the purpose of reducing or discharging a liability incurred for that purpose (as the case may be). Moreover there is no offence if the acquisition, or the reduction or discharge of the liability,

- is not the company's *principal* purpose in giving the assistance; or
- although the principal purpose, is only "an incidental part of some larger purpose"—

provided, in either case, that the assistance is given in good faith in the interests of the company.[152]

14–067 These provisions are extremely obscure. In *Brady v Brady* Lord Oliver drew a distinction between the purpose for which assistance is given and the reason for forming that purpose.

> "The ultimate reason for forming the purpose of financing an acquisition may, and in most cases probably will, be more important to those making the decision than the immediate transaction itself. But 'larger' is not the same thing as 'more important' nor is 'reason' the same as 'purpose'. If one postulates the case of a bidder for control of a public company financing his bid from the company's own funds—the obvious mischief at which the section is aimed—the immediate purpose which it is sought to achieve is that of completing the purchase and vesting control of the company in the bidder. The reasons why that course is considered desirable may be many and varied. The company may have fallen on hard times so that a change of management is considered necessary to avert disaster. It may merely be thought, and no doubt would be thought by the purchaser and the directors whom he nominates once he has control, that the business of the company will be more profitable under his management than it was heretofore. These may be excellent reasons but they cannot, in my judgment, constitute a 'larger purpose' of which the provision of assistance is merely an incident. The purpose and the only purpose of the financial assistance is and remains that of enabling the shares to be acquired and the financial or commercial advantages flowing from the acquisition, whilst they may form the reason for forming the purpose of providing assistance, are a by-product of it rather than an independent purpose of which the assistance can properly be considered to be an incident."[153]

Where the company's principal purpose is the acquisition, therefore, that will be "an incidental part of some larger purpose" only if the larger purpose is some additional objective which exists *alongside* the acquisition. The benefits expected to flow *from* the acquisition are not a larger purpose, but are merely reasons or motives for forming the principal purpose.

[152] CA 1985, s.153(1), (2); CA 2006, ss.678(2), (4) and 679(2), (4).
[153] [1989] A.C. 755 at 799–780.

In *Chaston v SWP Group plc*[154] Ward L.J. observed with studied understatement that in a criminal case he "probably would not direct the jury to the subtleties of distinction between 'purpose' and 'reason', helpful though Lord Oliver's words always are". Fortunately the issue is unlikely to be crucial in a fraud case, because the prosecution will in any event be alleging that the assistance was not given in good faith in the interests of the company. But in the first Guinness trial[155] Henry J. accepted a defence submission that the onus was on the prosecution to prove that the conditions at para.14–066 above were not satisfied. He pointed out that CA 1985, s.151 "does not prohibit" transactions satisfying those conditions,[156] and contrasted these words with other provisions to the effect that an accused person has a defence if he *proves* specified facts. **14–068**

> "Such a formula could have been followed in this Chapter and it seems to me significant that it was not . . . Here the question is whether the financial assistance in question was given in prohibited circumstances. That does not seem to me to be a matter of exception or statutory defence, but something that is not even prima facie unlawful. If you apply the words of section 101 of the Magistrates' Courts Act, the defendant does not have to rely for his defence on any exception—his defence is simply that the ingredients of the offence have not been made out."

EXEMPTIONS

The following transactions are permissible as a matter of general company law and are expressly excluded from the prohibition by CA 1985, s.153(3) and CA 2006, s.681: **14–069**

- a distribution of a company's assets by way of dividend lawfully made, or a distribution made in the course of the company's winding up;
- the allotment of bonus shares;
- a reduction of capital confirmed by order of the court under CA 1985, s.137, or made under Ch.10 of Pt 17 of CA 2006;
- a redemption or purchase of shares made in accordance with Ch.VII of Pt V of CA 1985 or under Ch.3 of Pt 18 of CA 2006, or a purchase of shares under Ch.4 of Pt 18 of CA 2006;[157]
- anything done in pursuance of an order of the court under CA 1985, s.425 or Pt 26 of CA 2006 (compromises and arrangements with creditors and members);

[154] [2002] EWCA Civ 1999; [2003] 1 B.C.L.C. 675 at [65].
[155] See above, para.14–060.
[156] CA 1985, s.153(1), (2). The words "does not prohibit" are retained in CA 2006, ss.678(2), (4) and 679(2), (4).
[157] See above, para.14–041.

- anything done under an arrangement made in pursuance of the Insolvency Act 1986, s.110 (acceptance of shares by liquidator in winding up as consideration for sale of property); and
- anything done under an arrangement made between a company and its creditors which is binding on the creditors by virtue of Pt 1 of the Insolvency Act 1986.

14–070 CA 1985, s.153(4) and CA 2006, s.682 provide for limited exceptions in cases involving money-lending companies, employees' share schemes, acquisition of shares by employees and the relatives of employees, and the making of loans to employees for the purpose of share acquisitions. These exceptions do not apply to financial assistance by a public company unless the company has net assets which are not thereby reduced, or, to the extent that they are so reduced, the assistance is provided out of distributable profits.[158]

DISAPPLICATION OF PRE-EMPTION RIGHTS

14–071 CA 1985, s.89 and CA 2006, s.561 require an issue of new shares to be offered first to existing shareholders in proportion to their holdings, so as to ensure that their holdings are not diluted without their consent. The members of a company can disapply these pre-emption rights in certain circumstances. In relation to a particular allotment of shares, this may be done by special resolution,[159] but only if such a resolution has been recommended by the directors.[160] The directors must have made, and circulated to the shareholders, a written statement setting out

- their reasons for making the recommendation,
- the amount to be paid to the company in respect of the shares to be allotted, and
- the directors' justification of that amount.[161]

A person who knowingly or recklessly[162] authorises or permits the inclusion in such a statement of any matter that is misleading, false or deceptive[163] in a material particular commits an offence under CA 1985, s.95(6) or CA 2006, s.572(2). The offence is triable either way, and is punishable on conviction on indictment with two years' imprisonment.[164]

REGISTRATION OF COMPANY CHARGES

14–072 A floating charge is a charge over a fluctuating fund. For example, a charge over a trading company's stock covers the company's stock at any one time, but does not prohibit the company from selling such stock in the

[158] CA 1985, s.154(1); CA 2006, s.682(1).
[159] CA 1985, s.95(2); CA 2006, s.571(1).
[160] CA 1985, s.95(5); CA 2006, s.571(5)(a).
[161] CA 1985, s.95(5); CA 2006, s.571(5)(b), (6), (7).
[162] See above, para.14–035.
[163] See above, para.12–012.
[164] CA 1985, s.95(6), Sch.24; CA 2006, s.572(3).

ordinary course of business.[165] The benefit of a floating charge is that it gives the creditor an effective security over the debtor company's assets, while leaving the company free to deal with its assets and pay its trade creditors in the ordinary course of business without reference to the holder of the charge. But the floating charge is potentially a vehicle for fraud. A company director could formerly advance money to his own company by way of loans rather than by way of capital, grant himself a floating charge over the company's undertaking in respect of the sums owed to him by the company, allow the company to incur credit to third parties despite the existence of the charge, and yet step in at any time, confident of taking priority over the ordinary trade creditors.

The remedy adopted by Parliament was to require floating charges to be **14–073** registered, so that those proposing to extend credit to a company could discover their existence. The requirements are now contained in Pt XII of CA 1985[166] and Pt 25 of CA 2006, s.860. If the company fails to register a registrable charge, an offence is committed by the company and every officer who is in default.[167] In addition, a company must keep its own register of charges available for inspection. An officer of the company commits an offence if he knowingly and wilfully authorises or permits the omission of an entry required to be made in the company's register.[168] Both offences are triable either way, and are punishable on conviction on indictment with a fine.[169]

ACCOUNTS AND RECORDS

In this section we consider a number of offences relating to a company's **14–074** annual accounts, its accounting records, and other documents relating to the company's affairs. All the offences under CA 1985 discussed in this section apply in relation to certain bodies corporate which are not companies within the meaning of the Act.[170] Where CA 2006 contains corresponding provisions, they may be applied to such bodies by regulations under CA 2006, s.1043.

[165] For the history of the floating charge, see *Agnew v Commissioners of Inland Revenue* [2001] UKPC 28; [2001] 2 A.C. 710.

[166] These provisions were repealed by the Companies Act 1989, but the repeal was never brought into force.

[167] CA 1985, s.399(3); CA 2006, s.860(4). For "officer who is in default", see above, paras 14–012 *et seq.*

[168] CA 1985, s.407(3); CA 2006, s.876(3).

[169] CA 1985, ss.399(3) and 407(3), and Sch.24; CA 2006, ss.860(5) and 876(4).

[170] CA 1985, s.718, Sch.22; Companies (Unregistered Companies) Regulations 1985 (SI 1985/680).

ANNUAL ACCOUNTS

FALSE OR MISLEADING STATEMENT TO AUDITOR

14–075 The directors of a company must prepare accounts for each financial year, and a directors' report. In most cases, Pt VII of CA 1985 and Pt 16 of CA 2006 require the accounts to be audited. CA 1985, s.389A(1)(b) and CA 2006, s.499(1)(b) empower the auditor to require various persons, including any officer or employee of the company, to provide him with such information and explanations as he thinks necessary for the performance of his duties. Under CA 1985, s.389B(1)[171] and CA 2006, s.501(1), a person commits an offence if he knowingly or recklessly[172] makes to an auditor a statement (oral or written) that

- conveys or purports to convey any information or explanations which the auditor requires, or is entitled to require, under CA 1985, s.389A(1)(b) or CA 2006, s.499, and
- is misleading, false or deceptive[173] in a material particular.

The offence is triable either way, and is punishable on conviction on indictment with two years' imprisonment.[174]

STATEMENT IN DIRECTORS' REPORT AS TO DISCLOSURE TO AUDITOR

14–076 Unless the directors take advantage of a statutory exemption from this requirement, their report must contain a statement that, in the case of each director who is in post when the report is approved,

- so far as he is aware, there is no information needed by the auditor of which the auditor is unaware, and
- he has taken all the steps that he ought to have taken to make himself aware of any information needed by the auditor and to establish that the auditor is aware of it. It is sufficient for this purpose that he has made such enquiries of his fellow directors and of the auditors, and taken such other steps (if any), as are required by his duty to exercise reasonable care, skill and diligence.[175]

Where a directors' report containing such a statement is approved and the statement is false, an offence under CA 1985, s.234ZA(6)[176] or CA 2006,

[171] Inserted by the Companies (Audit, Investigations and Community Enterprise) Act 2004 with effect from April 6, 2005.
[172] See above, para.14–035.
[173] See above, para.12–012.
[174] CA 1985, s.389B(1), Sch.24; CA 2006, s.501(2).
[175] CA 1985, s.234ZA(4); CA 2006, s.418(4).
[176] Inserted by the Companies (Audit, Investigations and Community Enterprise) Act 2004 with effect from April 6, 2005.

s.418(5) is committed by every director who knew that the statement was false or was reckless[177] as to whether it was false, and failed to take reasonable steps to prevent the report from being approved. The offence is triable either way, and is punishable on conviction on indictment with two years' imprisonment.[178]

ACCOUNTING RECORDS

DUTY TO KEEP ACCOUNTING RECORDS

Every company is required to keep accounting records. They must **14–077**

- be sufficient to show and explain the company's transactions,
- be such as to disclose with reasonable accuracy, at any time, the company's financial position at that time, and
- be such as to enable the directors to ensure that the accounts comply with the statutory requirements.[179]

CA 1985, s.221 and CA 2006, s.386 set out in more detail the information that the accounting records must contain. If a company fails to comply with these requirements, every officer of the company who is in default commits an offence under CA 1985, s.221(5) or CA 2006, s.387(1). The offence is triable either way, and is punishable on conviction on indictment with two years' imprisonment.[180]

It is a defence for the defendant to show that he acted honestly, and that **14–078** in the circumstances in which the company's business was carried on the default was excusable.[181] Since he will not be prima facie guilty unless the records are inadequate *and* he is "in default", the courts are likely to accept that Art.6(2) of the European Convention on Human Rights is not infringed by reading this literally as imposing on the defence a legal burden of proof as distinct from an evidential burden. But the point may be less clear under CA 2006, since the definition of "in default" is wider.[182]

DUTY TO KEEP ACCOUNTING RECORDS OPEN FOR INSPECTION

A company's accounting records must be kept open for inspection by the **14–079** company's officers.[183] If they are kept at a place outside Great Britain, CA 1985, s.222(2) requires accounts and returns with respect to the business

177 See above, para.14–035.
178 CA 1985, s.234ZA(6), Sch.24; CA 2006, s.418(6).
179 CA 1985, s.221(1); CA 2006, s.386(2).
180 CA 1985, s.221(6), Sch.24; CA 2006, s.387(3).
181 CA 1985, s.221(5); CA 2006, s.387(2).
182 See above, para.14–018.
183 CA 1985, s.222(1); CA 2006, s.388(1).

dealt with in the accounting records to be sent to a place in Great Britain and kept open for inspection there. CA 2006, s.388(2) replaces this with a requirement for accounts and returns relating to accounting records kept outside the United Kingdom to be sent to, and kept at, a place in the United Kingdom. Under both Acts the accounts and returns must be such as to disclose with reasonable accuracy the financial position of the business in question at intervals of not more than six months, and enable the directors to ensure that the accounts comply with the statutory requirements.[184]

14–080 If a company fails to comply with any of these requirements, an offence under CA 1985, s.222(4) or CA 2006, s.389(1) is committed by every officer who is in default. The offence is triable either way, and is punishable on conviction on indictment with two years' imprisonment.[185] It is a defence for a person charged with the offence to show that he acted honestly, and that in the circumstances in which the company's business was carried on the default was excusable.[186] Again this can probably be construed as imposing a legal burden without infringing Art.6(2) of the European Convention on Human Rights, but again this is less clearly so under CA 2006 because the definition of "in default" is wider.[187]

DUTY TO PRESERVE ACCOUNTING RECORDS

14–081 Except where a direction as to the disposal of its records has been made under winding-up rules, a private company must preserve its accounting records for three years from the date on which they are made, and a public company for six years.[188] An officer of a company commits an offence under CA 1985, s.222(6) or CA 2006, s.389(3) if he fails to take all reasonable steps for securing the company's compliance with this requirement, or intentionally causes any default by the company in so complying. The offence is triable either way, and is punishable on conviction on indictment with two years' imprisonment.[189]

FALSIFICATION AND SUPPRESSION OF RECORDS

14–082 CA 1985, s.450 creates offences of falsifying or suppressing company records. It is not replaced by CA 2006. An officer of a company[190] commits an offence under s.450(1) if he

[184] CA 1985, s.222(3); CA 2006, s.388(3).
[185] CA 1985, s.222(4), Sch.24; CA 2006, s.389(4).
[186] CA 1985, s.222(4); CA 2006, s.389(2).
[187] See above, para.14–018.
[188] CA 1985, s.222(5); CA 2006, s.388(4).
[189] CA 1985, s.222(6), Sch.24; CA 2006, s.389(4).
[190] Or a limited liability partnership or a European Economic Interest Grouping: Limited Liability Partnership Regulations 2001 (SI 2001/1090) reg.4(1), Sch.2; European Economic Interest Grouping Regulations 1989 (SI 1989/638) reg.18, Sch.4.

"(a) destroys, mutilates or falsifies, or is privy to the destruction, mutilation or falsification of a document affecting or relating to the company's property or affairs, or

(b) makes, or is privy to the making of, a false entry in such a document, . . .

unless he proves that he had no intention to conceal the state of affairs of the company or to defeat the law."

And he commits an offence under s.450(2) if he

- fraudulently parts with, alters or makes an omission in any such document, or
- is privy to any such fraudulent conduct.

Both offences are triable either way, and are punishable on conviction on indictment with seven years' imprisonment.[191] Proceedings require the consent of the Secretary of State or the DPP,[192] unless brought by the SFO.[193]

Where an officer committing an offence under s.450 is of such status as **14–083**
to render the *company* guilty of the offence,[194] and it is proved that the offence

- occurred with the consent or connivance of, or
- was attributable to any neglect on the part of,

any director,[195] manager, secretary "or other similar officer" of the company, or any person purporting to act in any such capacity, he too is guilty of the offence under s.450.[196] It seems clear from the reference to "neglect" that in this case the absence of any fraudulent intention is not a defence.

These offences appear in Pt XIV of CA 1985, which is primarily **14–084**
concerned with the inspection and investigation of companies by DTI inspectors. They are not expressly confined to companies which are the subject of such inspection, but it is arguable that in view of the context a qualification to that effect must be implied.[197] There are similar provisions dealing with the falsification of records where the company in question is being wound up, and these are discussed in the context of insolvency fraud.[198]

[191] CA 1985, s.450(3), Sch.24.
[192] CA 1985, ss.450(4), 732; CA 2006, s.1126.
[193] Criminal Justice Act 1987, Sch.1 para.4.
[194] See above, para.14–020.
[195] This includes a shadow director: CA 1985, s.733(4). For shadow directors, see above, para.14–010.
[196] CA 1985, s.733.
[197] cf. *DPP v Schildkamp* [1971] A.C. 1. The section was originally introduced into the Companies Act 1967. The Jenkins Committee had noted instances of directors destroying or fabricating evidence in the course of inspections by the Board of Trade, and accordingly recommended that the preservation of documents should be required by statute from the moment the Board of Trade appointed an inspector or informed a company that it proposed to make a preliminary investigation.
[198] See below, paras 15–016 *et seq*.

14–085 The type of documents covered by CA 1985, s.450 was considered in *Saunders*.[199] The defendant was charged with destroying a jottings book, some correspondence, some pages from an address book and a 1986 diary. The defence argued that, in its statutory context, the section must be read as being confined to primary and formal documents which the legislation requires a company to maintain and keep. After considering the legislative history of the section, Henry J. rejected the submission as being inconsistent with the use of the words "affecting or relating to the company's property or affairs".

> "Those words show that the embargo against destruction goes beyond the formal documents that are the company's documents, to the officer's private documents, provided they affect or relate to the company's property or affairs . . . In my judgment, the ordinary, literal construction of the word 'document' is the correct one, it being the intention of the legislature to forbid all unjustifiable destruction of documents relating to or affecting the affairs of the company, whether formal documents or other less formal documents, whether the company's documents or not, and whether in the company's possession or not."

14–086 If this is right, the words "unless he proves that he had no intention to conceal the state of affairs of the company or to defeat the law" in CA 1985, s.450(1) must be read down under the Human Rights Act 1998, s.3 so as to impose on the defendant a merely evidential burden. It cannot be consistent with Art.6(2) of the European Convention on Human Rights that, merely because a defendant is proved to have destroyed private documents which had some bearing on company matters, he must prove on the balance of probabilities that his intentions were honest. If the submission made by the defence in *Saunders* were correct, on the other hand, the imposition of a legal burden would be easier to justify. The problem does not arise under s.450(2), because in that case the prosecution must prove fraud.

FALSE STATEMENTS TO REGISTRAR

14–087 CA 2006, s.1112(1) creates an offence which has no direct counterpart in CA 1985. A person commits this offence if, for any purpose of the Companies Acts,[200] he knowingly or recklessly[201]

- delivers or causes to be delivered to the registrar of companies a document, or
- makes to the registrar a statement,

[199] Revised Ruling No.1, December 20, 1989.
[200] Defined by CA 2006, s.2.
[201] See above, para.14–00.

that is misleading, false or deceptive[202] in a material particular. The offence is triable either way, and is punishable on conviction on indictment with two years' imprisonment.[203]

[202] See above, para.12–012.
[203] CA 2006, s.1112(2).

CHAPTER 15

INSOLVENCY FRAUD

Frauds on creditors may be divided into three basic types. The first consists in incurring debts which the debtor has no intention of paying or does not expect to be able to pay. This often involves the use of a company. Sometimes this is an existing company whose suppliers are unaware of a change of ownership. In other cases, a subsidiary is created and allowed to run up debts with the intention of the parent company ultimately escaping liability.[1] **15–001**

The second type of insolvency fraud consists in the evasion of debts already incurred, innocently or otherwise. This may be done by deceiving creditors, absconding, or concealing or disposing of property out of which the debts might have been paid. Where a company is or is likely to become insolvent, the siphoning off of the company's assets by its directors will be a fraud on its creditors rather than (or as well as) its shareholders. **15–002**

The third type involves dishonesty and concealment in connection with insolvency proceedings. In such cases, the debtor may try to conceal the true state of his finances (for example by destroying accounts) or act in collusion with some creditors to the detriment of others. This type of fraud also includes the so-called "phoenix company" fraud,[2] in which the directors of an insolvent company set up a new company which buys the stock and plant of the insolvent company at an undervalue. **15–003**

[1] *Re Southard & Co Ltd* [1979] 1 W.L.R. 1198 at 1208, *per* Templeman L.J.
[2] e.g. *Re Centrebind Ltd* [1967] 1 W.L.R. 377.

15–004 Insolvency frauds will usually amount to one or more of the offences of general application discussed in previous chapters. Frauds of the first type may involve fraud by false representation,[3] on the basis that the incurring of the debt carries an implied representation as to the debtor's solvency, his intention to pay, or both. The creditor will presumably have made assumptions as to both, but it may be easier to establish a representation as to the latter, since the mere fact of trading does not in itself imply that the trader is solvent.[4] But if there *is* a representation of solvency it will be comparatively easy to prove that that representation was false, whereas it may be harder to establish that the defendant never intended to pay. Dishonesty can often be disguised as misplaced optimism.

15–005 Where there is deception in respect of an existing debt, a charge of fraud by false representation may again be appropriate. The misapplication of company assets, or of funds to which a creditor is specifically entitled, may constitute theft.[5] A scheme to defraud creditors may be a conspiracy to defraud at common law,[6] even if the debtor is not yet insolvent[7] and even if no creditor yet has more than an unliquidated claim.[8] It is unlikely that it could be charged as fraud by abuse of position,[9] since a debtor is probably not "expected to safeguard . . . the financial interests" of his creditor for the purposes of that offence.

15–006 There are also a number of statutory offences specifically aimed at frauds on creditors. One of them, fraudulent trading,[10] has been enlarged by judicial interpretation so that it now extends to trading for *any* fraudulent purpose, whether or not the intended victims are creditors.[11] This offence is considered in Ch.8. In this chapter we examine a number of offences which are confined to the context of insolvency and are now to be found in the Insolvency Act 1986 ("IA 1986"). They fall into two categories: those relating to corporate insolvency (winding up), and those relating to individual insolvency (bankruptcy).

OFFENCES IN WINDING UP

FALSE DECLARATION OF SOLVENCY

15–007 Under IA 1986, s.89(1), where it is proposed to wind up a company voluntarily, a majority of the directors may make a statutory declaration of solvency,[12] stating that they have made a full inquiry into the company's

[3] Above, Ch.4.
[4] *Parker* (1916) 25 Cox C.C. 145 at 149, *per* Avory J.
[5] Above, Ch.9.
[6] Above, Ch.7.
[7] *Hall* (1858) 1 F. & F. 33; *Heymann* (1873) L.R. 8 Q.B. 102 at 105, *per* Blackburn J.
[8] *Seillon* [1982] Crim. L.R. 676; above, para.8–036.
[9] Above, Ch.6.
[10] Companies Act 1985, s.458; Companies Act 2006, s.993; Fraud Act 2006, s.9.
[11] *Kemp* [1988] Q.B. 645.
[12] cf. the solvency statement on the basis of which a private company may resolve to reduce its capital: Companies Act 2006, ss.641–644; above, para.14–037.

affairs and have formed the opinion that the company will be able to pay its debts in full within such period (not exceeding 12 months from the commencement of the winding up) as may be specified in the declaration. The significance of the declaration is that, if it is made, the winding up will be a members' (i.e. solvent) voluntary winding up; otherwise it will be a creditors' (i.e. insolvent) voluntary winding up.[13] Under IA 1986, s.89(4) it is an offence, triable either way and punishable on conviction on indictment with two years' imprisonment,[14] for a director to make such a declaration without having reasonable grounds for the opinion stated. There is no requirement that he should know the true position: negligence is sufficient. If the company is wound up in pursuance of a resolution passed within five weeks after the making of the declaration, and its debts are not paid or provided for within the period specified in the declaration, it is presumed that the director did not have reasonable grounds for his opinion unless the contrary is shown.[15]

CONCEALMENT OR DISPOSAL OF PROPERTY

IA 1986, ss. 206 and 207 create offences which may be committed when a **15–008** company is ordered to be wound up by the court or passes a resolution for voluntary winding up. Section 206(1) provides, in part, that in these circumstances a past or present officer[16] of the company is deemed to have committed an offence if, within the 12 months immediately preceding the commencement of the winding up, he has

> "(a) concealed any part of the company's property to the value of £500[17] or more, or concealed any debt due to or from the company, or
>
> (b) fraudulently removed any part of the company's property to the value of £500[18] or more, . . . or
>
> (f) pawned, pledged or disposed of any property of the company which has been obtained on credit and has not been paid for (unless the pawning, pledging or disposal was in the ordinary way of the company's business)."[19]

If such a person does any of these things *after* the commencement of the winding up, he commits an offence under IA 1986, s.206(2). These offences

[13] IA 1986, s.90.
[14] IA 1986, Sch.10.
[15] IA 1986, s.89(5).
[16] Including a shadow director: IA 1986, s.206(3). A shadow director is a person in accordance with whose directions or instructions the directors of the company are accustomed to act, unless they act merely on advice given by him in a professional capacity: IA 1986, s.251. See above, para.14–010.
[17] This sum may be altered by order under IA 1986, s.416: s.206(7).
[18] This sum may be altered by order under IA 1986, s.416: s.206(7).
[19] Where a person is guilty of this offence, an offence (similarly punishable) is committed by any person who takes the property in pawn or pledge, or otherwise receives it, knowing it to be pawned, pledged or disposed of in circumstances constituting the offence: IA 1986, s.206(5).

are triable either way, and are punishable on conviction on indictment with seven years' imprisonment.[20]

15–009 Under IA 1986, s.207, where a company is ordered to be wound up by the court or passes a resolution for voluntary winding up, an offence is also deemed to have been committed if a person who was at the time an officer of the company has

(a) not more than five years before the commencement of the winding up, made (or caused to be made) any gift or transfer[21] of, or charge on, the company's property, or caused or connived at the levying of any execution against such property, or

(b) concealed or removed any part of such property since, or within two months before, the date of any unsatisfied judgment or order for the payment of money obtained against the company.

These offences are triable either way, and are punishable on conviction on indictment with two years' imprisonment.[22]

NO INTENT TO DEFRAUD

15–010 In the case of the offence under IA 1986, s.206(1)(b) and the corresponding offence under s.206(2), fraud must be proved by the prosecution.[23] In the case of the other offences above, the prosecution need not prove fraud, but it is a defence for the defendant to prove

- in the case of a charge under s.206(1) or (2) of doing the things mentioned in s.206(1)(a) or (f), that he had no intent to defraud;[24] and
- in the case of a charge under s.207, that he had no intent to defraud the company's creditors.[25]

15–011 What constitutes defrauding has already been considered in the context of conspiracy to defraud.[26] An intent to defraud might consist in an intent to cause loss to another (such as a creditor[27] or shareholder), or to cause the liquidator (or any person concerned in the resolution of the company's affairs) to act in a way in which he would not act if he knew the true position.[28]

15–012 The defence under IA 1986, s.207, however, is not that the defendant did not intend to defraud, but that he did not intend to defraud *creditors*. A

[20] IA 1986, s.206(6), Sch.10.

[21] The cancellation of a debt owed to the company is not a transfer of its property: *Davies* [1955] 1 Q.B. 71.

[22] IA 1986, s.207(3), Sch.10.

[23] cf. *Lusty* [1964] 1 W.L.R. 606.

[24] IA 1986, s.206(4)(a).

[25] IA 1986, s.207(2)(b).

[26] Above, paras 7–005 *et seq*.

[27] But not, it seems, simply by paying another creditor: above, para.8–027.

[28] *Welham v DPP* [1961] A.C. 103; above, para.7–020.

person with an unliquidated claim against the company is not an *existing* creditor, and it has therefore been held that an intent to defeat such a claim is not an intent to defraud a creditor.[29] But intent necessarily relates to the future. In principle it is immaterial whether any creditors are yet in existence: it should be sufficient if there is a present intention to defraud, at some future date, persons who will by that time be creditors.[30]

In *Carass*[31] the Court of Appeal thought that, although the absence of intent to defraud purports to be a defence, it was "unrealistic" to argue that the existence of such an intent was not an important element of the offence under IA 1986, s.206(1)(a). Applying the House of Lords' reasoning in *Lambert,*[32] the court concluded that requiring the defendant to disprove that element would infringe the presumption of innocence under Art.6(2) of the European Convention on Human Rights, and that the requirement should therefore be read down under the Human Rights Act 1998, s.3 as imposing an evidential rather than a legal burden. **15–013**

In *Attorney-General's Reference (No.1 of 2004)*,[33] however, it was held that *Carass* had been impliedly overruled by the more tolerant approach to reverse burdens adopted by the House of Lords in *Johnstone*.[34] **15–014**

> "The law gives those involved in the affairs of a company the benefit of its corporate personality and in the case of most companies the additional very great benefit of limited liability. In the case of individual insolvency, the law relieves the bankrupt of personal liability for his debts, which are met out of his estate. These benefits drastically affect the rights and remedies of creditors. The proper working of our insolvency law depends on the inclusion in the assets of an insolvent company and in the estate of a bankrupt of all the assets that should be comprised in them. It can be tempting for those involved in the management of a company or a bankrupt to conceal or to dispose of such assets to the disadvantage of creditors. Furthermore, such concealment or disposals may be done by a person alone and in private: a failure to record or to disclose an asset, or a disposal of stock at an undervalue or the making of a disposal for nil consideration, may be known only to those involved in the transaction. There may well be no independent witnesses to the act in question. Whether there has been fraud will often be known only to the individual or individuals who are alleged to have committed the fraud.
>
> In our judgment, these considerations will normally justify the imposition on a defendant, who is proved to have deliberately acted in a manner that gives rise to an inference that he sought to defraud his creditors, of the burden of proving, on a balance of probabilities, that he did not intend to do so. In such cases, we bear in mind that Parliament might have created an offence to which fraud was irrelevant. It will be less easy to justify a reverse burden of proof in other cases: such offences must be considered individually."[35]

In *Sheldrake v DPP*[36] the House of Lords confirmed that *Carass* was wrongly decided.

[29] *Hopkins* [1896] 1 Q.B. 652.
[30] cf. *Seillon* [1982] Crim. L.R. 676; above, para.8–036.
[31] [2001] EWCA Crim 2845; [2002] 1 W.L.R. 1714.
[32] [2001] UKHL 37; [2002] 2 A.C. 545.
[33] [2004] EWCA Crim 1025; [2004] 1 W.L.R. 2111.
[34] [2003] UKHL 28; [2003] 1 W.L.R. 1736.
[35] [2004] EWCA Crim 1025; [2004] 1 W.L.R. 2111 at [81]–[82].
[36] [2004] UKHL 43; [2005] 1 A.C. 264 at [32], *per* Lord Bingham.

15–015 There are a number of offence-creating provisions in IA 1986 which similarly impose reverse burdens. The reasoning in *Attorney-General's Reference (No.1 of 2004)* is potentially relevant to all of them, though the court recognised that a legal burden may not be justified in every case. But in *Sheldrake* the House of Lords disagreed with the Court of Appeal's view that decisions of the House prior to *Johnstone* (such as *Lambert*) should no longer be cited on this issue,[37] or that Parliament should be assumed to have had good reason for imposing a reverse burden.[38]

FALSIFICATION OF DOCUMENTS

15–016 The various general offences relating to the falsification of documents[39] are supplemented by specific offences which apply only in the context of winding up. IA 1986, s.209 provides:

> "When a company is being wound up, an officer or contributory of the company commits an offence if he destroys, mutilates, alters or falsifies any books, papers or securities, or makes or is privy to the making of any false or fraudulent entry in any register, book of account or document belonging to the company with intent to defraud or deceive any person."

The offence is triable either way, and is punishable on conviction on indictment with seven years' imprisonment.[40]

15–017 Section 209 is highly ambiguous. The punctuation (especially the absence of commas before or after the words "belonging to the company") suggests that the provision has two separate limbs, namely:

- destroying, mutilating, altering or falsifying any books, papers or securities; and
- making (or being privy to the making of) any false or fraudulent entry in any register, book of account or document[41] belonging to the company, with intent to defraud or deceive.

In other words the expressions "belonging to the company" and "with intent to defraud or deceive" appear at first sight to qualify the second limb but not the first. It would follow that an officer or contributory of a company being wound up would be committing an offence under the first

[37] [2004] UKHL 43; [2005] 1 A.C. 264 at [32], *per* Lord Bingham.
[38] [2004] UKHL 43; [2005] 1 A.C. 264 at [31], *per* Lord Bingham.
[39] Above, Chs 11 and 12; paras 14–082 *et seq*.
[40] IA 1986, s.209(2), Sch.10.
[41] "Document" is not defined by IA 1986, but s.251 adopts the definition in what is now the Companies Act 2006, s.1114, under which "document" means "any information recorded in any form". This appears to be sufficiently wide to cover computer records. See also *Derby & Co Ltd v Weldon (No.9)* [1991] 1 W.L.R. 652; *Alliance & Leicester Building Society v Ghahremani* (1992) 32 R.V.R. 198; *Rollo v H.M. Advocate* (1997) S.L.T. 958; *Victor Chandler International Ltd v Customs and Excise Commissioners* [2000] 1 W.L.R. 1296. But cf. IA 1986, s.436, which defines "records" as including "computer records and other non-documentary records", thus implying that a computer record is not a "document".

limb if he innocently altered a document of his own which had nothing to do with the company at all. This cannot be right.

An alternative construction is that the words "with intent to defraud or deceive" must be read into the first limb too. On this view the suppression or falsification of books, papers or securities, whether or not belonging to the company, would be sufficient if (but only if) done with an intent to defraud or deceive. **15–018**

A third possibility is that the first limb is qualified not only by the words "with intent to defraud or deceive" but also by the words "belonging to the company". This would exclude the suppression or falsification of documents not *belonging* to the company even if they *affect* the company, which would arguably make the offence too narrow. On the other hand, the absence of punctuation between the two phrases makes it hard to justify extending one of them to the first limb and not the other. It is therefore submitted that the expressions "belonging to the company" and "with intent to defraud or deceive" qualify both limbs. If that is right, the offence can be committed by **15–019**

- destroying, mutilating, altering or falsifying any books, papers or securities belonging to the company, with intent to defraud or deceive; or
- making (or being privy to the making of) any false or fraudulent entry in any register, book of account or document belonging to the company, with intent to defraud or deceive.

An intent to deceive is sufficient but not essential: an intent to defraud will suffice. If the defendant destroys records in order to suppress evidence of dishonest transactions, it might be difficult to argue that he intends to deceive others, who have never suspected that such transactions might have taken place, into believing that they have not.[42] But it is possible to defraud without deceiving,[43] and a dishonest intention to avoid the consequences of his misconduct would presumably suffice. **15–020**

Under IA 1986, s.206(1), an offence is deemed to have been committed if a company is ordered to be wound up by the court, or passes a resolution for voluntary winding up, and, within the 12 months immediately preceding the commencement of the winding up, a past or present officer of the company (including a shadow director, past or present)[44] has **15–021**

> "(c) concealed, destroyed, mutilated or falsified any book or paper affecting or relating to the company's property or affairs, or
>
> (d) made any false entry in any book or paper affecting or relating to the company's property or affairs, or
>
> (e) fraudulently parted with, altered or made any omission in any document[45] affecting or relating to the company's property or affairs".

[42] cf. above, para.4–009.

[43] Above, paras 7–011 *et seq*.

[44] IA 1986, s.206(3).

[45] "Document" means information recorded in any form: Companies Act 2006, s.1114, which applies by virtue of IA 1986, s.251. See above, fn.41.

15–022 IA 1986, s.206(2) goes on to provide (in part) that such a person

- is also deemed to have committed an offence if, within that period, he has been privy to the doing by others[46] of any of the things mentioned in s.206(1)(c)–(e); and
- commits an offence if, at any time after the commencement of the winding up, he does, or is privy to the doing by others of, any of those things.

The offences under s.206(1) and (2) are triable either way, and are punishable on conviction on indictment with seven years' imprisonment.[47]

15–023 IA 1986, s.206(1)(e), and s.206(2) to the extent that it refers to things done contrary to s.206(1)(e), require proof of fraud. Section 206(1)(c) and (d), and s.206(2) to the extent that it refers to them, do not require proof of fraud; but under s.206(4)(b) it is a defence for the defendant to prove that he had no intent to conceal the state of affairs of the company or to defeat the law. This last phrase is somewhat obscure and it may be doubted whether it is a true alternative: if a defendant has done one of the things mentioned in s.206(1)(c) or (d), but proves that he did not intend to conceal the state of the company's affairs, it is hard to see how he could be convicted on the ground that he has failed to prove that he did not intend to defeat the law.

15–024 In view of the reasoning in *Attorney-General's Reference (No.1 of 2004)*,[48] an argument that s.206(4)(b) must be read down so as to impose only an evidential burden would be unlikely to succeed.

DECEPTION OF CREDITORS

15–025 IA 1986, s.211(1) provides that, where a company is being wound up (whether by the court or voluntarily), a past or present officer[49] of the company

> "(a) commits an offence if he makes any false representation or commits any other fraud for the purpose of obtaining the consent of the company's creditors or any of them to an agreement with reference to the company's affairs or to the winding up, and
>
> (b) is deemed to have committed that offence if, prior to the winding up, he has made any false representation, or committed any other fraud, for that purpose."

The offence is triable either way, and is punishable on conviction on indictment with seven years' imprisonment.[50]

[46] The others need not be past or present officers of the company, and need not be guilty of an offence.
[47] IA 1986, s.206(6), Sch.10.
[48] [2004] EWCA Crim 1025; [2004] 1 W.L.R. 2111; above, para.15–014.
[49] Including a shadow director: IA 1986, s.211(2). For shadow directors, see above, para.14–010.
[50] IA 1986, s.211(3), Sch.10.

"False representation" in this context seems to mean much the same as in the Fraud Act 2006, s.2—that is, a representation which is not only objectively false but which the person making it *knows* is or might be false.[51] In the case of a false representation, dishonesty[52] appears not to be required. In the context of the precursor of the corresponding provision relating to bankruptcy,[53] it was held that "false" means "fraudulent",[54] and the word "fraudulent" in other contexts has since been construed as importing a requirement of dishonesty;[55] but a representation can probably be "false" without being dishonest. **15–026**

The offence can consist in a fraud other than a false representation. This might include, for example, non-disclosure as distinct from positive misrepresentation. But in this case dishonesty would appear to be necessary, because it is an essential element of fraud. **15–027**

A similar offence is created by IA 1986, s.6A(1), under which an officer[56] of a company commits an offence if, for the purpose of obtaining the approval of the company's members or creditors to a proposal for a voluntary arrangement, he (a) makes any false representation, or (b) fraudulently does, or omits to do, anything. This applies even if the proposal is not approved.[57] The offence is triable either way, and is punishable on conviction on indictment with seven years' imprisonment.[58] **15–028**

MATERIAL OMISSIONS IN STATEMENTS

Under IA 1986, s.210(1), a past or present officer[59] of a company commits an offence if the company is being wound up (whether by the court or voluntarily) and he makes any material omission in any statement relating to its affairs. Under s.210(2), such a person is deemed to have committed the offence under s.210(1) if the company is ordered to be wound up by the court, or passes a resolution for voluntary winding up, and he has previously made any material omission in any such statement. The offence is triable either way, and is punishable on conviction on indictment with seven years' imprisonment.[60] **15–029**

On a literal reading the offence would be remarkably wide. It is not confined to written statements, and it applies to omissions rather than positive misstatements. One would expect an omission to be material if the **15–030**

[51] See above, para.4–084.
[52] See above, Ch.2.
[53] IA 1986, s.356.
[54] *Cherry* (1871) 12 Cox C.C. 32.
[55] See above, para.7–02.
[56] Including a shadow director: IA 1986, s.6A(3). For shadow directors, see above, para.14–010.
[57] IA 1986, s.6A(2).
[58] IA 1986, s.6A(4), Sch.10.
[59] Including a shadow director: IA 1986, s.210(3). For shadow directors, see above, para.14–010.
[60] IA 1986, s.210(5), Sch.10.

fact omitted is material. But it can hardly be the law that an officer of a company which is being wound up must not make any statement about the company's affairs which does not include everything that his hearers would regard as material. Still less can it be the law that he must *never* make such a statement, in case the company is *subsequently* wound up. Perhaps, therefore, an omission is "material" only if it renders misleading what *is* said. Such a construction would not be strictly logical,[61] but it would keep the offence within reasonable bounds.

15–031 It is not necessary to prove that the omission was fraudulent, or even deliberate; but it is a defence for the defendant to prove that he had no intent to defraud.[62] Whether this infringes Art.6(2) of the European Convention on Human Rights, and must therefore be read down under the Human Rights Act so as to impose only an evidential burden, would seem to depend largely on the interpretation of "material omission". If that expression is read literally, as including any omission from a statement of any fact material to the subject matter, it would include most if not all statements about company affairs; and it would clearly be unjustifiable to require the maker of such a statement to prove that the omission was not fraudulent merely because the company is being wound up or is subsequently wound up. If, however, an omission from a statement is "material" *only* where it makes the statement positively misleading, it might arguably be justifiable for the law to say that a person who is proved to have made a material omission in this sense must prove that it was not fraudulent.[63]

OTHER MISCONDUCT

15–032 Under IA 1986, s.208(1) an offence is committed if a company is being wound up (whether by the court or voluntarily), and a past or present officer[64] of the company

> "(a) does not to the best of his knowledge and belief fully and truly discover to the liquidator all the company's property, and how and to whom and for what consideration and when the company disposed of any part of that property (except such part as has been disposed of in the ordinary way of the company's business), or
>
> (b) does not deliver up to the liquidator (or as he directs) all such part of the company's property as is in his custody or under his control, and which he is required by law to deliver up, or
>
> (c) does not deliver up to the liquidator (or as he directs) all books and papers in his custody or under his control belonging to the company and which he is required by law to deliver up, or

[61] cf. above, para.13–009.

[62] IA 1986, s.210(4). For the meaning of "defraud", see above, paras 7–005 *et seq*.

[63] cf. *Att-Gen's Reference (No.1 of 2004)* [2004] EWCA Crim 1025; [2004] 1 W.L.R. 2111; above, para.15–014.

[64] Including a shadow director: IA 1986, s.208(3). For shadow directors, see above, para.14–010.

(d) knowing or believing that a false debt has been proved by any person in the winding up, fails to inform the liquidator as soon as practicable, or

(e) after the commencement of the winding up, prevents the production of any book or paper affecting or relating to the company's property or affairs."

These offences are triable either way, and are punishable on conviction on indictment with seven years' imprisonment.[65] None of them requires proof of fraud; but s.208(4) provides that it is a defence for the defendant to prove, in the case of paras (a) to (c) that he had no intent to defraud, and in the case of para.(e) that he had no intent to conceal the state of affairs of the company or to defeat the law.[66] The effect of *Attorney-General's Reference (No.1 of 2004)*[67] is that the reverse burden does not infringe Art.6(2) of the European Convention on Human Rights in relation to para.(a),[68] and almost certainly not in relation to paras (b), (c) and (e) either.

IA 1986, s.208(2) provides that a past or present officer of the company **15–033**

- commits an offence if, after the commencement of the winding up, he attempts to account for any part of the company's property by fictitious losses or expenses; and
- is deemed to have committed that offence if he has so attempted at any meeting of the company's creditors within the 12 months immediately preceding the commencement of the winding up.

This offence too is triable either way and is punishable on conviction on indictment with seven years' imprisonment.

OFFENCES IN BANKRUPTCY

Fraudulent conduct on the part of an individual insolvent may constitute **15–034** one or more of a variety of offences which are now contained almost exclusively in Ch.VI of Pt IX of IA 1986. Most of these offences correspond closely to those under the provisions on corporate insolvency that we have already considered, but some of them have no counterpart in those provisions. Proceedings relating to bankruptcy offences may not be instituted except by the Secretary of State or by or with the consent of the DPP,[69] or by the Director of the SFO.[70] The individual insolvent is referred to throughout the Act as "the bankrupt", which means an individual who has been adjudged bankrupt.[71]

[65] IA 1986, s.208(5), Sch.10.
[66] On intent to defeat the law, see above, para.15–023.
[67] [2004] EWCA Crim 1025; [2004] 1 W.L.R. 2111; above, para.15–014.
[68] It was held that the reverse burden imposed by IA 1986, s.352 in relation to the offence under s.353 did not infringe Art.6. Section 353 is the bankruptcy counterpart of s.208(1)(a): see below, para.15–048.
[69] IA 1986, s.350(5).
[70] Criminal Justice Act 1987, Sch.1 para.4.
[71] IA 1986, s.381(1).

15–035 Most of the offences considered here are subject to IA 1986, s.352. Where that section applies to an offence, a person is not guilty of the offence if he proves that, at the time of the conduct constituting the offence, he had no intent to defraud[72] or to conceal the state of his affairs (including his business, if any).[73] *Attorney-General's Reference (No.1 of 2004)*[74] suggests that Art.6(2) of the European Convention on Human Rights will not normally be infringed by reading IA 1986, s.352 as imposing a legal burden of proof on the defence. But it can be read down so as to impose only an evidential burden if the offence is so widely defined that a legal burden would be unjustified.

CONCEALMENT OR DISPOSAL OF PROPERTY

15–036 Under IA 1986, s.357(1) a bankrupt commits an offence if he makes or causes to be made, or has in the period of five years ending with the commencement of the bankruptcy made or caused to be made, any gift or transfer of, or any charge on, his property.[75] Under s.357(3) he commits an offence if he conceals or removes, or has at any time before the commencement of the bankruptcy concealed or removed, any part of his property after, or within two months before, the date on which a judgment or order for the payment of money (other than one satisfied before the commencement of the bankruptcy) has been obtained against him. These offences are triable either way, and are punishable on conviction on indictment with two years' imprisonment.[76]

15–037 IA 1986, s.352[77] applies to both offences. As regards s.357(1), however, it was held in *Attorney-General's Reference (No.1 of 2004)*[78] that s.352 must be read down under the Human Rights Act 1998, s.3 so as to impose on the defence an evidential burden only, leaving the onus on the prosecution to prove fraud if the defence raises the issue.[79] The court thought it clear that fraud is an integral constituent of the offence, since Parliament cannot have intended that an innocent disposition should be retrospectively made punishable with two years' imprisonment. Fraud aside, the ambit of the offence is very wide indeed.

> "It applies to disposals of property made long before the commencement of bankruptcy, and possibly at a time when there was no indication of insolvency. The prosecution does not have to prove that the bankrupt was aware of the

[72] For "defrauding", see above, paras 7–005 *et seq.*
[73] IA 1986, s.385(2).
[74] [2004] EWCA Crim 1025; [2004] 1 W.L.R. 2111; above, para.15–014.
[75] This includes causing or conniving at the levying of any execution against the property: s.357(2).
[76] IA 1986, s.350(6), Sch.10.
[77] Above, para.15–035.
[78] [2004] EWCA Crim 1025; [2004] 1 W.L.R. 2111; above, para.15–014.
[79] The court rejected the view expressed in *Daniel* [2002] EWCA Crim 959; [2003] 1 Cr.App.R. 6 (p.99) that the wording of s.352 is not capable of being read down in this way.

possibility of his insolvency when he made the gift or disposal. There is no time limit on prosecutions. They cannot be brought until the insolvent has been made bankrupt, and are unlikely to be brought until a significant time afterwards. There is no minimum value of the gift or transfer for which the bankrupt may be called to account. The prosecution does not have to establish anything unusual or irregular in relation to the gift or disposition."[80]

The court saw no evidence that Parliament had addressed these characteristics of the offence when it decided to require the defendant to disprove fraud. However, these considerations would have less force if the defendant made the disposition *after* being made bankrupt, and it may be arguable that the decision does not apply to such a case.

Similarly, the decision may not apply to the offence under IA 1986, s.357(3) where the defendant conceals or removes the property after being made bankrupt. Even where he has done so before being made bankrupt, the requirement that he must have done so after or shortly before the obtaining of judgment against him makes this offence considerably narrower than the one under s.357(1). It may therefore be arguable that a legal burden is justified in this case too. **15–038**

An offence in similar terms remains in force in s.13 of the Debtors Act 1869, which provides that a person commits an offence **15–039**

- if he has with intent to defraud his creditors, or any of them, made or caused to be made any gift, delivery, or transfer of or any charge on his property; or
- if he has, with intent to defraud his creditors, concealed or removed any part of his property since or within two months before the date of any unsatisfied judgment or order for payment of money obtained against him.

This offence is triable either way,[81] and is punishable on conviction on indictment with one year's imprisonment. Unlike the offences under IA 1986, s.357, it can be committed whether or not the defendant has been adjudged bankrupt.[82] Intent to defraud creditors is an element of the offence; but, to the extent that the burden imposed on the defence by IA 1986, s.352 in relation to the offences under s.357 is evidential only, there is little practical difference.

A bankrupt is also guilty of an offence **15–040**

- under IA 1986, s.354(1)(b) if he conceals any debt due to or from him or conceals any property the value of which is not less than the prescribed amount[83] and possession of which he is required to deliver up to the official receiver or trustee;[84]

[80] [2004] EWCA Crim 1025; [2004] 1 W.L.R. 2111 at [87].
[81] Magistrates' Courts Act 1980, Sch.1 para.7.
[82] *Rowlands* (1882) 8 Q.B.D. 530.
[83] Currently £1,000: Insolvency Proceedings (Monetary Limits) Order 1986 (SI 1986/1996) as amended by SI 2004/547.
[84] In relation to a bankruptcy, "trustee" means the trustee of the bankrupt's estate: IA 1986, s.385.

- under IA 1986, s.354(1)(c) if, in the 12 months before petition[85] or in the initial period,[86] he did anything which would have been an offence under s.354(1)(b) if the bankruptcy order had been made immediately before he did it;
- under IA 1986, s.354(2) if he removes, or in the initial period removed, any property the value of which was not less than the prescribed amount[87] and possession of which he has or would have been required to deliver up to the official receiver or the trustee; and
- under IA 1986, s.359(1) if, in the 12 months before petition or in the initial period, and otherwise than in the ordinary course of a business carried on by him at the time,[88] he disposed of[89] any property which he had obtained on credit and had not paid for.[90]

These offences are all triable either way, and are punishable on conviction on indictment with seven years' imprisonment.[91] IA 1986, s.352 applies, so it is a defence for the defendant to prove that he had no intent to defraud or to conceal the state of his affairs. *Attorney-General's Reference (No.1 of 2004)*[92] suggests that this is to be read literally as imposing a legal burden in each case, though the point may still be arguable in the case of acts done before the presentation of the petition.[93]

ABSCONDING WITH PROPERTY

15–041 Under IA 1986, s.358 an offence is committed by a bankrupt who

(a) leaves, or attempts or makes preparations to leave, England and Wales with any property the value of which is not less than the prescribed amount[94] and possession of which he is required to deliver up to the official receiver or the trustee; or

(b) in the six months before petition, or in the initial period, did anything which would have been an offence under (a) if the bankruptcy order had been made immediately before he did it.

[85] A reference to a number of months or years before petition is to that period ending with the presentation of a bankruptcy petition: IA 1986, s.351(c).

[86] The period between the presentation of a bankruptcy petition and the commencement of bankruptcy: IA 1986, s.351(b).

[87] Currently £1,000: Insolvency Proceedings (Monetary Limits) Order 1986 (SI 1986/1996) as amended by SI 2004/547.

[88] IA 1986, s.359(4). For the purposes of determining whether property is disposed of in the ordinary course of business, regard may be had, in particular, to the price paid for the property.

[89] This includes pawning or pledging: IA 1986, s.359(5).

[90] A person who acquires or receives the property commits an offence if he knows or believes that the bankrupt owes money in respect of it and does not intend to pay or is unlikely to be able to do so: IA 1986, s.359(2).

[91] IA 1986, s.350(6), Sch.10.

[92] [2004] EWCA Crim 1025; [2004] 1 W.L.R. 2111; above, para.15–014.

[93] cf. above, para.15–037.

[94] Currently £1,000: Insolvency Proceedings (Monetary Limits) Order 1986 (SI 1986/1996) as amended by SI 2004/547.

The offence is triable either way, and is punishable on conviction on indictment with two years' imprisonment.[95] IA 1986, s.352 applies, so it is a defence for the defendant to prove that he had no intent to defraud or to conceal the state of his affairs. *Attorney-General's Reference (No.1 of 2004)*[96] suggests that this is to be read literally as imposing a legal burden, though the point may be arguable in the case of acts done before the presentation of the petition.[97]

FALSIFICATION OF DOCUMENTS

A bankrupt is guilty of an offence under IA 1986, s.355(2) if **15–042**

> "(a) he prevents, or in the initial period prevented, the production of any books, papers or records relating to his estate or affairs;
>
> (b) he conceals, destroys, mutilates or falsifies, or causes or permits the concealment, destruction, mutilation or falsification of, any books, papers or other records relating to his estate or affairs;
>
> (c) he makes, or causes or permits the making of, any false entries in any book, document or record relating to his estate or affairs; or
>
> (d) in the 12 months before petition, or in the initial period, he did anything which would have been an offence under paragraph (b) or (c) above if the bankruptcy order had been made before he did it."

And he is guilty of an offence under IA 1986, s.355(3) if

> "(a) he disposes of, or alters or makes any omission in, or causes or permits the disposal, altering or making of any omission in, any book, document or record relating to his estate or affairs, or
>
> (b) in the 12 months before petition, or in the initial period, he did anything which would have been an offence under paragraph (a) if the bankruptcy order had been made before he did it."

In the case of trading records, the period of 12 months before petition is **15–043** extended to two years for the purposes of s.355(2)(d) and (3)(b).[98] A trading record is

> "a book, document or record which shows or explains the transactions or financial position of a person's business, including—
>
> (a) a periodic record of cash paid and received,
>
> (b) a statement of periodic stock-taking, and
>
> (c) except in the case of goods sold by way of retail trade, a record of goods sold and purchased which identifies the buyer and seller or enables them to be identified."[99]

[95] IA 1986, s.350(6), Sch.10.
[96] [2004] EWCA Crim 1025; [2004] 1 W.L.R. 2111; above, para.15–014.
[97] cf. above, para.15–037.
[98] IA 1986, s.355(4).
[99] IA 1986, s.355(5).

All the offences under IA 1986, s.355 are triable either way and are punishable on conviction on indictment with seven years' imprisonment.[100] IA 1986, s.352 applies, so it is a defence for the defendant to prove that he had no intent to defraud or to conceal the state of his affairs. *Attorney-General's Reference (No.1 of 2004)*[101] suggests that this is to be read literally as imposing a legal burden in each case. Given the nature of the acts prohibited, it seems unlikely that it would be read down as imposing only an evidential burden, even in the case of acts done before the presentation of the petition.[102] This is particularly so in the case of trading records, in view of the importance of such records being properly kept.[103]

FALSE STATEMENTS

15–044 A bankrupt is guilty of an offence under IA 1986, s.356(2) if

> "(a) knowing or believing that a false debt has been proved by any person under the bankruptcy, he fails to inform the trustee as soon as practicable; or
>
> (b) he attempts to account for any part of his property by fictitious losses or expenses; or
>
> (c) at any meeting of his creditors in the 12 months before petition or (whether or not at such a meeting) at any time in the initial period, he did anything which would have been an offence under paragraph (b) if the bankruptcy order had been made before he did it; or
>
> (d) he is, or at any time has been, guilty of any false representation or other fraud for the purpose of obtaining the consent of his creditors, or any of them, to an agreement with reference to his affairs or to his bankruptcy."

The offence is triable either way, and is punishable on conviction on indictment with seven years' imprisonment.[104]

15–045 IA 1986, s.352 does not apply. So, where the defendant is charged under s.356(2)(d) with making a false representation (as distinct from fraud), it is not a defence for him to prove that he had no intent to defraud or to conceal the state of his affairs. This suggests that a representation is not "false" within the meaning of the section unless the maker knows that it is or may be false—though, if he does know this, there is no need to prove that he made it dishonestly.[105]

15–046 A bankrupt commits an offence under IA 1986, s.262A if, for the purpose of obtaining his creditors' approval to a proposal for a voluntary arrangement, he (a) makes any false representation, or (b) fraudulently does, or

[100] IA 1986, s.350(6), Sch.10.
[101] [2004] EWCA Crim 1025; [2004] 1 W.L.R. 2111; above, para.15–014.
[102] cf. above, para.15–037.
[103] Failure to keep proper records was formerly an offence under IA 1986, s.361 if the trader became insolvent. Sir Baliol Brett M.R. thought it was "one of the greatest offences which can be committed by a trader": *Re Wallace, ex p. Campbell* (1885) 15 Q.B.D. 213 at 217.
[104] IA 1986, s.350(6), Sch.10.
[105] cf. above, para.15–026.

omits to do, anything. This applies even if the proposal is not approved.[106] This offence corresponds to the one under IA 1986, s.6A in relation to winding up. It is triable either way, and is punishable on conviction on indictment with seven years' imprisonment.[107] Again IA 1986, s.352 does not apply, so a false representation is sufficient even if there is no intent to defraud.

MATERIAL OMISSIONS IN STATEMENTS

A bankrupt is guilty of an offence under IA 1986, s.356(1) if he makes or has made any material omission in any statement made under any provision in Pts VIII to XI of IA 1986 relating to his affairs (including his business, if any).[108] The offence is triable either way, and is punishable on conviction on indictment with seven years' imprisonment.[109] IA 1986, s.352 applies, so it is again a defence for the defendant to prove that he had no intent to defraud or to conceal the state of his affairs. The question of what constitutes a material omission, and the related question of whether s.352 should be read down so as to impose an evidential burden only, is considered above in relation to the corresponding winding up offence under IA 1986, s.210.[110] **15–047**

OTHER MISCONDUCT IN RELATION TO BANKRUPTCY PROCEEDINGS

A bankrupt is guilty of an offence **15–048**

- under IA 1986, s.353(1) if he
  - does not to the best of his knowledge and belief disclose all the property comprised in his estate to the official receiver or the trustee, or
  - does not inform the official receiver or trustee of any disposal (other than a disposal in the ordinary course of business, or a payment of his or his family's ordinary expenses)[111] of any property which, but for the disposal, would be so comprised, stating how, when, to whom and for what consideration the property was disposed of;
- under IA 1986, s.354(1)(a) if he does not deliver up possession to the official receiver or trustee (or as he directs) of such part of the property comprised in his estate as is in his possession or under

[106] IA 1986, s.262A(2).
[107] IA 1986, s.262A(3), Sch.10.
[108] IA 1986, s.385(2).
[109] IA 1986, s.350(6), Sch.10.
[110] Above, para.15–030.
[111] IA 1986, s.353(2).

his control, and possession of which he is required by law so to deliver up; and

- under IA 1986, s.355(1) if he does not deliver up possession to the official receiver or trustee (or as he directs) of all books, papers and other records of which he has possession or control and which relate to his estate or affairs.

All these offences are triable either way, and are punishable on conviction on indictment with seven years' imprisonment.[112] IA 1986, s.352 applies in each case, so it is a defence for the defendant to prove that he had no intent to defraud or to conceal the state of his affairs. It was held in *Attorney-General's Reference (No.1 of 2004)*[113] that this does not infringe Art.6(2) of the European Convention on Human Rights in the case of the offence under s.353(1)(b), and a similar conclusion would probably be reached in respect of the others.

ENGAGING IN TRADE OR BUSINESS

15–049 Undischarged bankrupts are automatically subject to certain disabilities in respect of their business activities. Bankrupts are also now subject to a regime of bankruptcy restrictions orders and undertakings,[114] similar in nature to that for the disqualification of errant company directors.[115] Under the Company Directors Disqualification Act 1986, s.11, an undischarged bankrupt, or a person in respect of whom a bankruptcy restrictions order is in force, commits an offence if, without the leave of the court by which he was adjudged bankrupt, he acts as director of a company or directly or indirectly takes part in or is concerned in its promotion, formation or management. The offence is triable either way, and is punishable on conviction on indictment with two years' imprisonment.[116] It would seem to cover a bankrupt who plays any part in a company's management, even if he is neither a director nor an employee but (for example) a management consultant.[117]

15–050 It is also an offence under IA 1986, s.360(1)(b) for an undischarged bankrupt to engage (directly or indirectly)[118] in any business under a name other than that under which he was adjudged bankrupt, without disclosing the latter name (though not necessarily the fact of his bankruptcy) to all

[112] IA 1986, s.350(6), Sch.10.

[113] [2004] EWCA Crim 1025; [2004] 1 W.L.R. 2111; above, para.15–014.

[114] IA 1986, Sch.4A, inserted by the Enterprise Act 2002.

[115] The Company Directors Disqualification Act 1986, s.6 requires the court to make a disqualification order against any person who is or has been a director of a company which has at any time become insolvent and whose conduct as a director makes him unfit to be concerned in the management of a company. Sch.1 to that Act provides guidance on the determination of unfitness.

[116] Company Directors Disqualification Act 1986, s.13.

[117] cf. *Campbell* (1984) 78 Cr.App.R. 95.

[118] cf. *Doubleday* (1964) 49 Cr.App.R. 62.

persons with whom he enters into any business transaction. The offence is triable either way, and is punishable on conviction on indictment with two years' imprisonment.[119]

OBTAINING CREDIT

Under IA 1986, s.360(1)(a) an offence is committed by an undischarged bankrupt, or a person in respect of whom a bankruptcy restrictions order is in force,[120] if, either alone or jointly with any other person, he obtains credit to the extent of the prescribed amount[121] or more without informing the person from whom he obtains it that he is an undischarged bankrupt or is subject to a bankruptcy restrictions order[122] (as the case may be). The offence is triable either way, and is punishable on conviction on indictment with two years' imprisonment.[123] **15–051**

Unlike most of the other bankruptcy offences, s.360(1)(a) is concerned not with the evasion of existing debts but with the incurring of fresh ones. The Cork Committee regarded it as essentially an offence of deception. **15–052**

> "Logically, in our view, the wrong consists, not in the failure to pay the debt (which is a civil wrong), but in the deception practised on the creditor by obtaining credit from him knowing that he would not extend it if he knew the circumstances. Even where the bill is paid at once, the creditor was still put unjustifiably at risk."[124]

This reflects the fact that deceiving another into taking a financial risk is one of the established forms of criminal fraud.[125]

CREDIT

A person obtains credit if he obtains a benefit from another without immediately giving the consideration in return for which the benefit is conferred.[126] A loan is clearly a form of credit.[127] The fact that the bankrupt provides security for the loan does not necessarily make any difference, though it may do so if the security is obviously worth more than the amount lent.[128] Another clear case is the purchase of goods or the obtaining of services on the basis that payment is deferred until later, even if the delay is **15–053**

[119] IA 1986, s.350(6), Sch.10.
[120] IA 1986, s.360(5).
[121] The figure from April 1, 2004 is £500: Insolvency Proceedings (Monetary Limits) Order 1986 (SI 1986/1996) as amended by SI 2004/547.
[122] IA 1986, s.360(6).
[123] IA 1986, s.350(6), Sch.10.
[124] *Report of the Review Committee on Insolvency Law and Practice*, Cmnd.8558, para.1844.
[125] *Allsop* (1976) 64 Cr.App.R. 29; above, para.7–008.
[126] *Miller* [1977] 1 W.L.R. 1129 at 1134. The decision has been reversed by IA 1986, s.360(2), but this statement of principle is unaffected.
[127] *Pryce* (1949) 34 Cr.App.R. 21.
[128] *Fryer* (1912) 7 Cr.App.R. 183.

to be very short (as where a meal is provided in a restaurant and the customer is expected to pay after eating but before leaving).[129] IA 1986, s.360(2) provides that a bankrupt also obtains credit where

(a) goods are bailed to him under a hire-purchase agreement, or agreed to be sold to him under a conditional sale agreement, or

(b) he is paid in advance (whether in money or otherwise) for the supply of goods or services.

15–054 Other types of transaction present more difficulty. In *Smith*[130] it was treated as self-evident that an agreement for the letting of a house at a monthly rent involved the obtaining of credit by the lessee. But this is not necessarily so. It is not sufficient that the bankrupt incurs an obligation to pay money at some future date: the essence of credit is that payment is not to be made until after receipt of the benefit in question. In principle, therefore, it should be crucial whether the rent is payable in advance or in arrears.[131] Only in the latter case is credit obtained. The case of hire-purchase agreements and conditional sale agreements, on the other hand, has been put beyond doubt by s.360(2)(a), and in the case of such agreements it seems to be irrelevant whether payment is made in advance or in arrears.

15–055 The question has arisen whether a person obtains credit whenever he does in fact obtain a benefit before paying for it, or whether the creditor must agree to his doing so. This issue may be subdivided into two. First, is it necessary that the defendant be legally entitled to defer payment? If not, is it at least necessary that the creditor should consent to the delay?

Right to defer payment

15–056 A leading authority on the former question is *Peters*, where the defendant, an undischarged bankrupt living in Newcastle, bought a horse on f.o.b. terms from a man living in County Antrim, and having taken delivery of the horse failed to pay the price. His conviction of an offence under a precursor of s.360(1)(a) was upheld. Lord Coleridge C.J., speaking for the majority, said:

> "The words of the section are 'obtains credit'. Did the prisoner obtain credit? It is said that he did not because he did not stipulate for it; but the Act does not say that there must be a stipulation for credit, or that it must be obtained on a specific contract to give credit. In such a case as the present, where a man

[129] *Jones* [1898] 1 Q.B. 119. In other words, credit may be obtained even if payment "on the spot" is required for the purposes of the offence of making off without payment (Theft Act 1978, s.3).

[130] (1915) 11 Cr.App.R. 81.

[131] cf. *Miller* [1977] 1 W.L.R. 1129 at 1132, where Roskill L.J. explained the decision in *Hartley* [1972] 2 Q.B. 1 (that the defendant obtained credit by falling behind with the rent) on the basis that "the rent in question was rent in arrears and not in advance". This was not in fact the ground of the decision (see below), but logically the distinction ought to be crucial.

> obtains goods and does not pay for them for a substantial period of time, I am not prepared to say that we ought to limit the plain meaning of the words in the Act of Parliament. The prisoner has obtained credit and has had it, whether or no he stipulated for it at the time of purchase."[132]

This would seem to imply that under the terms of the contract the defendant had no *right* to defer payment until after taking delivery of the horse—indeed, that was the ground of Manisty J.'s dissenting judgment—but that the absence of such a right was immaterial.

In *Miller*,[133] however, the Court of Appeal explained the decision as resting on the fact that there *was* such a right, because in the absence of an express term as to payment it was implied that Peters was not obliged to pay the price as soon as the horse was put on board ship (and title therefore passed) but only within a reasonable time.[134] The court expressed its agreement with this reasoning, and went on to say that credit is obtained only if the creditor does not acquire an immediate cause of action for the money due. The acquisition of such a cause of action was described as "the antithesis of giving credit". It follows that the defendant does not obtain credit unless he is entitled to defer payment; and it was accordingly held that the mere failure to pay a debt when it falls due does not constitute an obtaining of credit. **15–057**

However, the court also suggested that the position might be otherwise if, instead of simply defaulting, the defendant persuaded the creditor to give him more time to pay. But this is hard to reconcile with the court's earlier reasoning, since even if the creditor agreed not to press for payment he would still have a cause of action when the debt became due. In *Hartley*[135] it was held that the defendant had obtained credit by writing cheques which were honoured by the bank despite his account being overdrawn. Yet he was not entitled to an overdraft facility under the terms of his contract with the bank, and it seems clear that on honouring each cheque the bank acquired an immediate cause of action against him for reimbursement of the amount paid out. **15–058**

Creditor's consent to the delay in payment

Whether or not *Miller* is correct in suggesting that credit necessarily involves a *right* to defer payment, it does at least appear to require some degree of consent on the part of the creditor. The decision is that a person does not obtain credit merely by failing to pay a debt when it falls due, though it may be otherwise if the creditor agrees to wait. This less radical interpretation is easily reconciled with *Peters*, since the vendor in that case, **15–059**

[132] (1885) 16 Q.B.D. 636 at 640–641.

[133] [1977] 1 W.L.R. 1129.

[134] This interpretation is open to question. In a contract of sale, payment and delivery are concurrent conditions unless otherwise agreed: Sale of Goods Act 1979, s.28. In the absence of any stipulation to the contrary, the vendor would therefore be entitled to payment against the shipping documents.

[135] [1972] 2 Q.B. 1.

by not insisting on payment against documents, did by implication allow the defendant to have credit. *Hartley*, however, is still an obstacle. The defendant in that case was held to have obtained credit not only by overdrawing on his bank account (with the bank's consent) but also by falling into arrears with his rent (without his landlord's consent). On the latter point the decision seems flatly inconsistent with *Miller*. The only ground of distinction suggested in *Miller* is that in *Hartley* the rent was payable in arrears, not in advance. This might have been crucial if the defendant had been charged with obtaining credit by entering into the rental agreement in the first place, but that was not how the case was presented.

15–060 The credit obtained by the defendant must amount to at least £500, but there is no requirement that this sum be attributable to any one transaction: it is the aggregate amount that is crucial.[136] However, it is clear from the wording of IA 1986, s.360(1)(a) ("obtains credit . . . to the extent of the prescribed amount or more without giving the person from whom he obtains it . . .") that the £500 must all be owed to the same creditor.

OBTAINS

15–061 It is not sufficient that the defendant is given credit: he must *obtain* credit. In *Hayat*[137] the defendant's bank account became overdrawn when one of his customers stopped two cheques. The Crown conceded that he could not be said to have obtained credit unless his own conduct had that effect,[138] but argued that it had, because he was in the habit of accepting post-dated cheques and drawing on the account in such circumstances that it would become overdrawn if the cheques were not paid. The Court of Appeal did not deny that this might be sufficient, but held that the jury should have been directed to consider whether the defendant's conduct amounted to an obtaining of credit.

CREDIT FOR WHOM?

15–062 Another question which must be left to the jury is that of whether the credit is given to the defendant himself or to some other person, such as a relative or a company with which the defendant is associated.[139] In *Godwin* it was said that

[136] *Juby* (1886) 16 Cox C.C. 160; *Hartley* [1972] 2 Q.B. 1.

[137] (1976) 63 Cr.App.R. 181.

[138] In *Att-Gen's Reference (No.1 of 1988)* [1989] A.C. 971 counsel sought to draw an analogy between IA 1986, s.360(1)(a) and the Company Securities (Insider Dealing) Act 1985, s.1(3), under which it was an offence in certain circumstances for an individual to deal in securities of a company on the basis of information which he had "knowingly obtained (directly or indirectly) from another individual". (See now Pt V of the Criminal Justice Act 1993, above, paras 13–046 *et seq.*) The House of Lords held that a person could obtain information within the meaning of the 1985 Act by coming into possession of it, with or without effort on his own part, but did not dispute the assumption that IA 1986, s.360(1)(a) does require conduct: [1989] A.C. 971 at 993, *per* Lord Lowry.

[139] *Goodall* (1959) 43 Cr.App.R 24.

> "The critical question always is whether on the evidence the bankrupt holds himself out as the person for whom credit is sought, or whether it is for a genuine and separate business and not a charade to disguise the fact that he is the person seeking credit."[140]

The reference to a "charade" is potentially misleading. In principle the crucial question is simply whether the person who incurs the obligation to pay is the defendant or someone else, a question which falls to be answered in accordance with the law of contract and agency. If it is someone other than the bankrupt who undertakes the liability, the case falls outside the mischief at which the offence is aimed, because the credit is not given to someone who is (unknown to the creditor) already insolvent; and this is so even if that person's sole objective is to assist the bankrupt. But if he is in fact the bankrupt's agent, it will be the bankrupt himself who is obtaining credit. If the bankrupt is running a business there may in addition be an offence under IA 1986, s.360(1)(b).[141]

DISCLOSURE

The offence under IA 1986, s.360(1)(a) is not committed if the defendant informs the creditor that he is an undischarged bankrupt or that a bankruptcy restrictions order is in force in respect of him (as the case may be). He need not disclose this fact at the moment of obtaining the credit—it is sufficient if he does so at about that time[142]—but the creditor must be told *before* the transaction is effected. The offence does not require an intent to defraud,[143] and it is no defence that the defendant reasonably believed that the creditor had been told.[144] **15–063**

TERRITORIAL SCOPE

IA 1986, s.350(4) provides that it is not a defence in proceedings for an offence under Ch.VI of Pt IX of the Act (ss.350–360) that anything relied on, in whole or in part, as constituting that offence was done outside England and Wales. Since English criminal law generally prohibits only conduct in England and Wales, *not* conduct elsewhere in the United Kingdom,[145] the natural meaning of this provision is that conduct anywhere in the world will suffice. **15–064**

140 (1980) 71 Cr.App.R. 97 at 99.
141 Above, para.15–050.
142 *Zeitlin* (1932) 23 Cr.App.R. 163.
143 *Dyson* [1894] 2 Q.B. 176.
144 *Duke of Leinster* [1924] 1 K.B. 311.
145 See below, Ch.22.

Chapter 16

TAX FRAUD

Tax fraud usually involves either positive deception of the tax authorities or breach of duties of disclosure imposed by the tax legislation. It will usually, therefore, involve the commission of fraud by false representation,[1] fraud by failing to disclose information[2] or both. Often the particular form of deception adopted will give rise to liability for false accounting,[3] forgery[4] or the making of false statements contrary to the Perjury Act 1911, s.5(b).[5] Sometimes a tax fraud is essentially no more than an insolvency fraud in which the defrauded creditor is Her Majesty's Revenue and Customs; in that case some of the offences considered in Ch.15 may be relevant (and possibly theft,[6] if the insolvent debtor is a company looted by its controllers). Fraudulent trading may be a useful charge, especially now that the defaulting business need no longer be a company.[7] In this chapter we consider some further offences specifically aimed at tax fraud. **16–001**

VAT FRAUD

Serious tax frauds often involve abuse of the VAT system. A trader must account for the "output tax" charged by him to his customers, minus any deduction for the "input tax" paid by him to his suppliers. It is possible to **16–002**

[1] Above, Ch.4.
[2] Above, Ch.5. This assumes that fraud by failing to disclose information is not confined to non-disclosure which induces the victim to enter into a transaction with the defendant: see paras 5–004 *et seq*.
[3] Above, paras 12–001 *et seq*.
[4] Above, Ch.11.
[5] Above, para.12–034.
[6] Above, Ch.9.
[7] Above, Ch.8.

exaggerate the input tax paid (an "input fraud"), to understate the output tax collected, or fail to account for it at all (an "output fraud"), or both. A trader who fails to account for all the output tax he has collected is not guilty of stealing it, because it does not "belong to another". He is not a trustee for HMRC, nor is he obliged to keep the tax separate from the rest of his assets so as to bring the Theft Act 1968, s.5(3) into play:[8] his obligation is merely to account for an equivalent sum at the appropriate time. He might now be guilty of fraud on the basis that he falsely represents to his customers that he intends to account for the tax; but this would require proof that he intended to make a gain *by* making that false representation, and therefore that he thought the customers would not pay the tax if they knew that he did not intend to account for it.[9]

FRAUDULENT EVASION

16–003 A person commits an offence under s.72(1) of the Value Added Tax Act 1994 ("VATA 1994") if he

> "is knowingly concerned in, or in the taking of steps with a view to, the fraudulent evasion[10] of VAT by him or any other person".

The offence is triable either way, and is punishable on conviction on indictment with seven years' imprisonment.

16–004 There is an evasion of tax if the tax is not paid when it should be, even if it is paid eventually. A person may be knowingly concerned in fraudulent evasion if he is not himself liable for the tax but knowingly co-operates with the person who is, for example by supplying false invoices. Suspicion is not enough, though "wilful blindness" may perhaps be equated with knowledge.

16–005 An evasion of tax may be fraudulent even if there is no deception of HMRC officers.[11] In *Fairclough*[12] it was held that the defendant had been guilty of fraudulent evasion by failing to register, using invoices bearing a cancelled registration number and charging VAT for which he failed to account. Evasion may be fraudulent even if there is no intent to make permanent default.[13]

16–006 A person may be knowingly concerned in the taking of steps with a view to fraudulent evasion even if no evasion actually occurs, for example because the fraud is detected before the false return is due to be submitted.

[8] Above, paras 9–039 *et seq*.

[9] See above, para.3–004.

[10] "Evasion" includes the obtaining of (a) the payment of a VAT credit, (b) a refund under VATA 1994, s.35, 36 or 40 or the Value Added Tax Act 1983, s.22, (c) a refund under any regulations made under VATA 1994, s.13(5), or (d) a repayment under VATA 1994, s.39: VATA 1994, s.72(2).

[11] *Att-Gen's Reference (No.1 of 1981)* [1982] Q.B. 848.

[12] October 25, 1982.

[13] *Dealy* [1995] 2 Cr.App.R. 398.

It is a kind of inchoate offence.[14] But it is submitted that a person is not concerned in the taking of steps with a view to fraudulent evasion unless fraudulent evasion is the *purpose* of the steps in which he is concerned.[15]

16–007 In *McCarthy*[16] the defendant carried on business without registering for VAT, although his turnover exceeded the threshold. He was charged with taking steps with a view to the evasion of tax. He argued that a failure to register was not the taking of steps, but a failure to take steps. It was held that, even if this was correct, carrying on business without registering *was* the taking of steps. It would seem that there was in any event an actual evasion.

FURNISHING FALSE INFORMATION

16–008 A person commits an offence under VATA 1994, s.72(3) if he

> "(a) with intent to deceive produces, furnishes or sends[17] for the purposes of this Act or otherwise makes use for those purposes of any document which is false in a material particular, or
>
> (b) in furnishing any information for the purposes of this Act makes any statement which he knows to be false in a material particular or recklessly makes a statement which is false in a material particular".

The offence is triable either way, and is punishable on conviction on indictment with seven years' imprisonment.

16–009 The requirement in s.72(3)(a) of an intent to deceive originally caused difficulty because VAT returns are processed by computer, and a false return is therefore not intended to deceive. VATA 1994, s.72(6) accordingly provides:

> "The reference in subsection (3)(a) above to furnishing, sending or otherwise making use of a document which is false in a material particular, with intent to deceive, includes a reference to furnishing, sending or otherwise making use of such a document, with intent to secure that a machine will respond to the document as if it were a true document."

The effect is comparable to that of the Forgery and Counterfeiting Act 1981, s.10(3)[18] and the Fraud Act 2006, s.2(5).[19] Like those provisions, s.72(6) sits uneasily in the context of provisions aimed primarily at the deception of humans. The machine is not induced to respond "as if" the document were true: it responds in the same way whether the document is true or false. It would have been better simply to omit the requirement of intent to deceive.

[14] *Robertson v Rosenberg* [1951] 1 T.L.R. 417.
[15] cf. above, paras 3–021 *et seq.*
[16] [1981] S.T.C. 298.
[17] This includes causing a document to be produced, furnished or sent: VATA 1994, s.72(7).
[18] Above, para.11–031.
[19] Above, para.4–071.

EVASION OVER A PERIOD

16–010 VATA 1994, s.72(8) provides:

> "Where a person's conduct during any specified period must have involved the commission by him of one or more offences under the preceding provisions of this section, then, whether or not the particulars of that offence or those offences are known, he shall, by virtue of this subsection, be guilty of an offence . . ."

The offence is triable either way, and is punishable on conviction on indictment with seven years' imprisonment. It was intended that the offence should not be charged in cases of minor evasion by small taxpayers but only as an alternative to conspiracy charges in cases of serious fraud, and undertakings were given in Parliament to that effect.

16–011 Section 72(8) enables allegations of multiple offences under s.72(1) or (3), or both, to be wrapped up in a single charge.[20] In *Asif*[21] it was used in this way although particulars of the individual offences were available and were indeed included in the indictment. An argument that the charge was bad for duplicity was rejected. The court thought it was clearly the intention of Parliament to create one offence embracing the commission of numerous offences. The words "whether or not the particulars of that offence or those offences are known" confirmed that this was so even if the individual offences could have been separately charged.

16–012 In *Choudhury*[22] the defendants systematically suppressed bills rendered to customers in the running of three restaurants. They were convicted on three counts under the precursor of VATA 1994, s.72(8). Each count alleged that they had so conducted themselves in relation to a particular restaurant that their conduct must have involved the commission by them of one or more offences under the precursors of VATA 1994, s.72(1) and (3). The particulars recited the statutory wording but gave no details of the facts alleged. On appeal it was argued that the jury could not properly convict unless unanimous that the defendants must have been knowingly concerned in the fraudulent evasion of VAT, or that they must been knowingly concerned in the taking of steps with a view to the fraudulent evasion of VAT, or that they must have furnished false VAT returns with intent to deceive.[23] The Crown argued that what is now s.72(8) came into being precisely because there may be a "general deficiency" which is so striking that a fraud must have been perpetrated, but it is impossible to give particulars as to how that was done; and the defence's submission would therefore defeat the object of the provision.

16–013 The court did not express a view on this point. The convictions were affirmed on the ground that, on the facts, it would be unrealistic to suppose

[20] cf. below, Ch.25.
[21] (1986) 82 Cr.App.R. 123.
[22] [1996] 2 Cr.App.R. 484.
[23] cf. *Brown (Kevin)* (1984) 79 Cr.App.R. 115; above, para.4–196.

that a defendant might have been involved in one aspect of the fraud but not in others. But the court added that, if the necessary information is available, it is desirable to give factual particulars of the conduct alleged (as was done in *Asif*). The conduct thus particularised will necessarily constitute offences under s.72(1) or (3) or both, and it may therefore be unnecessary to resort to s.72(8) (though *Asif* makes it clear that s.72(8) may still be invoked in such a case). The particulars should also spell out the mens rea required by s.72(1) or (3), as the case may be.[24] Even where the only offence charged is that under s.72(8), if the prosecution alleges more than one kind of conduct (such as understatement of output tax *and* false claims for input tax) there should be separate counts for each of them.[25]

In *Martin*[26] it was said that multiple transactions can be charged under VATA 1994, s.72(1) even without resort to s.72(8). This dictum would be open to question if it meant that s.72(8) was redundant. But, even if it is correct, s.72(8) may still be needed where it is clear that the defendant must have committed an offence under s.72(1) or (3), but it is not clear which. **16–014**

EVASION OF DUTY

The Customs and Excise Management Act 1979 ("CEMA 1979"), s.170 creates two offences of fraudulently evading duty payable on goods (including VAT chargeable on their importation).[27] A person commits an offence under s.170(1) if, inter alia, he **16–015**

> "(a) knowingly acquires possession of any of the following goods, that is to say—
>
> (i) goods which have been unlawfully removed from a warehouse or Queen's warehouse;
>
> (ii) goods which are chargeable with a duty which has not been paid;
>
> (iii) goods with respect to the importation or exportation of which any prohibition or restriction is for the time being in force under or by virtue of any enactment; or
>
> (b) is in any way knowingly concerned in carrying, removing, depositing, harbouring, keeping or concealing or in any manner dealing with any such goods,
>
> and does so with intent to defraud Her Majesty of any duty payable on the goods . . .".

And a person commits an offence under s.170(2) if, inter alia, he

> "is, in relation to any goods, in any way knowingly concerned in any fraudulent evasion or attempt at evasion—

[24] *Ike* [1996] Crim. L.R. 515.
[25] *Stanley*, *The Times*, December 8, 1998.
[26] [1998] 2 Cr.App.R. 385.
[27] VATA 1994, s.16(1).

(a) of any duty chargeable on the goods . . .".

Both offences are triable either way, and are punishable on conviction on indictment with seven years' imprisonment.

16–016 As in the case of VATA 1994, s.72(1), it is sufficient that the defendant is "knowingly concerned in" fraudulent activities by others. This phrase is sufficiently vague to cover not only acts done before the goods are imported (and outside the jurisdiction)[28] but also dealings with them at any time after the importation.[29] The prosecution must, however, establish a "link or nexus" between the defendant's act and the importation[30] (though he need not be "connected with the original smuggling team"),[31] and it must be proved that at the time of his contribution[32] he intended to defraud the Crown of the duty payable,[33] or, in the case of s.170(2), that another party intended to do so and the defendant knew of that intention. He need not know the exact nature of the goods in question, but he must know that a fraudulent evasion of duty is taking place.[34] As in the case of VATA 1994, s.72(1), it is sufficient (under both s.170(1) and (2)) that an evasion of duty is intended, even if it does not actually occur because the plan is thwarted before the duty becomes payable.

16–017 In *Martin* the defendants were convicted on two counts under CEMA 1979, s.170(2) alleging that they had been knowingly concerned in the fraudulent evasion of duty chargeable on beer and wine. Each count related to a different method of evasion. The two methods had been used during different but overlapping periods. The first method was used for 27 loads, the second for 227. It was held on appeal that neither count was bad for duplicity.

> "In the judgment of this Court, . . . the offence created by section 170(2) . . . is an 'activity' offence to be defined by the nature of the evasion and of the 'knowing concern'. In some cases, the evasion and the knowing concern will arise in relation to only one transaction; in other cases there will be many giving rise to continuing activity: but in both types of case, the language of the section is such as properly to permit charging the offence in one count."[35]

The court found support for this view in *Asif*,[36] where a similar conclusion was reached in relation to what is now VATA 1994, s.72(8). The fact that that was a decision on s.72(8) rather than s.72(1), and that CEMA 1979, s.170 contains no provision corresponding to VATA 1994, s.72(8), made no

[28] *Wall* [1974] 1 W.L.R. 930.
[29] *Ardalan* [1972] 1 W.L.R. 463.
[30] *Watts* (1979) 70 Cr.App.R. 187 at 192.
[31] *Neal* [1984] 3 All E.R. 156; *Latif* [1996] 2 Cr.App.R. 92.
[32] Not necessarily at the time of importation: *Jakeman* (1982) 76 Cr.App.R. 223.
[33] Not necessarily by deception of customs officers: *Att-Gen's Reference (No.l of 1981)* [1982] Q.B. 848.
[34] *Hussain* [1969] 2 Q.B. 567; *Forbes* [2001] UKHL 40; [2002] 2 A.C. 512.
[35] [1998] 2 Cr.App.R. 385 at 393.
[36] (1986) 82 Cr.App.R. 123; above, para.16–011.

difference. In the court's view VATA 1994, s.72(1) was *itself* capable of embracing multiple transactions, even without the help of s.72(8); and CEMA 1979, s.170(2) was indistinguishable from VATA 1994, s.72(1) in this respect.

The indictment in *Martin* had originally included a single count under s.170(2) in respect of both methods of evasion: this count was split into two in the course of the defence case. The Court of Appeal expressed the view that the original count had been duplicitous because it related to two different activities. **16–018**

> "The wide scope given by section 170(2) does not obviate the need to draft indictments so as to avoid duplicity and to achieve, so far as the facts allow, counts that are substantive and specific. More than one count may be necessary to identify differing aspects of the prosecution case and to avoid overlap."[37]

EVASION OF INCOME TAX

Section 144(1) of the Finance Act 2000 provides: **16–019**

> "A person commits an offence if he is knowingly concerned in the fraudulent evasion of income tax by him or any other person."

The offence is triable either way,[38] and is punishable on conviction on indictment with seven years' imprisonment.[39] It applies only to acts and omissions on or after January 1, 2001.[40] The fact that it was not introduced until recently reflects the preference of what was formerly the Inland Revenue for settlements and civil proceedings rather than criminal proceedings. Its introduction was recommended by Lord Grabiner in his report *The Informal Economy*,[41] to facilitate prosecutions in the magistrates' court for minor and straightforward tax evasion. This may explain why it applies only to evasion of income tax, and not capital gains tax or corporation tax. However, the maximum of seven years' imprisonment on conviction on indictment suggests that it is intended to be used in more complex cases too. In this context, the courts are likely to have difficulty in distinguishing between avoidance and evasion.[42]

The statutory language bears a close resemblance to VATA 1994, s.72(1),[43] and the authorities on that provision are likely to be relevant. In particular, the requirement of fraud implies that dishonesty must be **16–020**

[37] [1998] 2 Cr.App.R. 385 at 394.

[38] It is not clear whether Lord Grabiner, in recommending the offence, intended it to be summary. At para.7.13 of his report it is said that the offence "could be tried in a magistrates' court rather than the Crown Court", but in the summary of Part 7 it is said that the offence "would be tried in the magistrates' court".

[39] Finance Act 2000, s.144(2).

[40] Finance Act 2000, s.144(3).

[41] Available from *www.hm-treasury.gov.uk*.

[42] See below, paras 16–045 *et seq.*; David Ormerod, "Summary Evasion of Income Tax" [2002] Crim. L.R. 3.

[43] Above, para.16–003.

proved—which, in the context of minor tax evasion, could result in surprising acquittals.[44] But the offence is narrower than that under VATA 1994, s.72(1) in that it is committed only where tax is actually evaded, not where steps are taken with a view to evading it. This seems to mean that the tax must remain unpaid after it falls due. If that outcome is intended but does not occur, there is presumably an attempt.

FALSE DOCUMENTS AND STATEMENTS

16–021 The tax legislation creates several offences of creating or providing false documents or information, in addition to the offence under VATA 1994, s.72(3).[45]

UNTRUE DECLARATIONS, ETC.

16–022 CEMA 1979, s.167(1) provides:

> "If any person either knowingly or recklessly—
>
> (a) makes or signs, or causes to be made or signed, or delivers or causes to be delivered to the Commissioners[46] or an officer, any declaration, notice, certificate or other document whatsoever; or
>
> (b) makes any statement in answer to any question put to him by an officer which he is required by or under any enactment to answer,
>
> being a document or statement produced or made for any purpose of any assigned matter, which is untrue in any material particular, he shall be guilty of an offence under this subsection . . ."

The offence is triable either way, and is punishable on conviction on indictment with two years' imprisonment.[47]

16–023 The document or statement must be produced or made for the purpose of an assigned matter. Since the merger of H.M. Customs and Excise with the Inland Revenue, "assigned matter" is now defined to include any matter in relation to which H.M. Commissioners for Revenue and Customs, or officers of Revenue and Customs, have a power or duty.[48] But the Commissioners for Revenue and Customs Act 2005, Sch.2 para.6 provides that CEMA 1979, s.167 shall not apply in relation to a declaration, document or statement in respect of a function relating to a matter to which s.7 of the 2005 Act applies. Section 7 of the 2005 Act applies to the

[44] See above, para.2–019.
[45] Above, para.16–008.
[46] i.e. the Commissioners for H.M. Revenue and Customs: CEMA 1979, s.1(1).
[47] CEMA 1979, s.167(2). There is a corresponding summary offence under s.167(3) which does not require proof of mens rea.
[48] CEMA 1979, s.1(1).

matters listed in Sch.1 to that Act, which are the matters for which the Inland Revenue was formerly responsible. The effect is that CEMA 1979, s.167 continues to apply only in relation to matters that were formerly the responsibility of H.M. Customs and Excise. False declarations in relation to the matters listed in Sch.1 to the 2005 Act should be charged as fraud by false representation[49] or false accounting,[50] or under the Perjury Act 1911, s.5[51] or the Taxes Management Act 1970, s.20BB.[52]

The document or statement must in fact be untrue in a material particular. Deciding whether it is untrue may involve deciding what it means; if so, that is a question for the judge.[53] The possibility that the defendant may have intended the document to be understood in a sense in which it was untrue would appear to be immaterial, if the document is objectively true;[54] but if he thought it was objectively untrue, he may be guilty of an attempt. It is presumably sufficient if the document or statement is literally true but conveys a false impression by virtue of what is left unsaid. **16–024**

The defendant must either know that the document or statement is untrue in a material particular or be reckless as to whether it is. It seems likely that the test of recklessness will now be construed as a subjective one:[55] the defendant must be aware that the document or statement may be untrue in a material particular and it must be unreasonable for him to make or sign it (etc.) in view of that possibility. But it may be arguable that a high degree of negligence will suffice.[56] **16–025**

COUNTERFEITING AND FALSIFICATION OF DOCUMENTS

CEMA 1979, s.168(1) provides: **16–026**

> "If any person—
>
> (a) counterfeits or falsifies any document which is required by or under any enactment relating to an assigned matter or which is used in the transaction of any business relating to an assigned matter; or
>
> (b) knowingly accepts, receives or uses any such document so counterfeited or falsified; or
>
> (c) alters any such document after it is officially issued; or
>
> (d) counterfeits any seal, signature, initials or other mark of, or used by, any officer for the verification of such a document or for the security of goods or for any other purpose relating to an assigned matter,

[49] Above, Ch.4.
[50] Above, paras 12–001 *et seq*.
[51] Above, para.12–034.
[52] Below, para.16–029.
[53] *Cross* [1987] Crim. L.R. 43.
[54] cf. above, para.4–036.
[55] cf. *G.* [2003] UKHL 50; [2004] 1 A.C. 1034.
[56] cf. above, para.13–013.

he shall be guilty of an offence under this section . . .”

The offence is triable either way, and is punishable on conviction on indictment with two years’ imprisonment.[57]

16–027 Again the wide definition of an “assigned matter”[58] is subject to the exclusion by the Commissioners for Revenue and Customs Act 2005, Sch.2 para.6 of matters listed in Sch.1 to that Act, for which the Inland Revenue was formerly responsible.

16–028 The offence has an affinity with that of forgery,[59] but is probably wider in scope. A “counterfeit” document would presumably be “false” for the purposes of the Forgery and Counterfeiting Act 1981,[60] but a “falsified” document would not be “false” in that sense if it did not “tell a lie about itself” but was merely inaccurate.[61] Certainly in the context of false accounting a document can be falsified without being forged, and this would probably be so even if the Theft Act 1968, s.17(2) did not expressly so provide.[62]

FALSIFICATION, ETC. OF DOCUMENTS REQUIRED UNDER THE TAXES MANAGEMENT ACT

16–029 The Taxes Management Act 1970, ss.20 and 20A, in combination with the Commissioners for Revenue and Customs Act 2005, ss.5 and 7, confer on the Commissioners and officers of Revenue and Customs various powers to give notices requiring a person (inter alia) to deliver documents or make them available for inspection. Section 20B(1) of the 1970 Act requires that a person be given a reasonable opportunity to do so before being given a notice requiring him to do so. Section 20BA further enables a judicial authority to make an order requiring a person to deliver documents if satisfied that there is reasonable ground for suspecting an offence involving serious fraud in relation to tax. Section 20BB(1) provides that, with certain exceptions, a person commits an offence if he intentionally falsifies, conceals, destroys or otherwise disposes of (or causes or permits the falsification, concealment, destruction or disposal of) a document which he has been required under s.20, 20A or 20BA, or given an opportunity under s.20B(1), to deliver or make available for inspection. The offence is triable either way, and is punishable on conviction on indictment with two years’ imprisonment.[63]

16–030 The wording of s.20BB(1) implies that there must be an existing document which the defendant is required or given an opportunity to

[57] CEMA 1979, s.168(2).
[58] See above, para.16–023.
[59] Above, Ch.11.
[60] cf. Forgery and Counterfeiting Act 1981, s.28(1), which defines a “counterfeit” of a currency note or protected coin as a thing which resembles such a note or coin to such an extent that it is reasonably capable of passing for such a note or coin.
[61] Above, paras 11–008 *et seq*.
[62] cf. *Edwards v Toombs* [1983] Crim. L.R. 43; above, para.12–010.
[63] Taxes Management Act 1970, s.20BB(5).

deliver or make available for inspection, and which he then falsifies (etc.). It appears to be insufficient that he falsifies (etc.) a document in anticipation of being required or given an opportunity to deliver it or make it available, or that, having been required or given an opportunity to do so, he creates a false document for the purpose.

FRAUDS ON THE EUROPEAN UNION

Section 71 of the Criminal Justice Act 1993 ("CJA 1993") creates what is in effect an offence of aiding and abetting frauds on the European Union committed outside the United Kingdom. It has been little used.[64] **16–031**

CJA 1993, s.71(1) provides: **16–032**

> "A person who, in the United Kingdom, assists in or induces any conduct outside the United Kingdom which involves the commission of a serious offence against the law of another member State[65] is guilty of an offence under this section if—
>
> (a) the offence involved is one consisting in or including the contravention[66] of provisions of the law of that member State which relate to any of the matters specified in subsection (2);
>
> (b) the offence involved is one consisting in or including the contravention of other provisions of that law so far as they have effect in relation to any of those matters; or
>
> (c) the conduct is such as to be calculated[67] to have an effect in that member State in relation to any of those matters."

The matters specified in s.71(2) are **16–033**

> "(a) the determination, discharge or enforcement of any liability for a Community duty or tax;[68]

[64] See the Ninth Report of the House of Lords Select Committee on European Communities (*http://www.publications.parliament.uk/pa/ld199899/ldselect/ldeucom/62/6202.htm*), para.30. The Revenue and Customs Prosecutions Office has not used the provision since its creation in April 2005. A rare example is *Ghiselli*, prosecuted by H.M. Customs and Excise at Southwark Crown Court in 1996. The case concerned the diversion of tobacco products on to the European market without the appropriate payment of duty, by way of falsified export documentation. The case was dismissed because of technical discrepancies in a certificate issued by the Ministry of Justice in Spain and relied upon by the prosecution to prove that the alleged conduct was a serious offence under Spanish law. A summary of the allegations and the legal argument can be found in the evidence of the Freight Transport Association given to the European Parliament Committee of Inquiry into the Community Transit System (Hearing XV Pt III, November 27, 1996).

[65] i.e. a member State other than the United Kingdom: CJA 1993, s.71(9).

[66] Including a failure to comply: CJA 1993, s.71(9).

[67] It seems clear from CJA 1993, s.71(5)(f) (below, para.16–036) that "calculated" is used in its legal sense (meaning "objectively likely") rather than its ordinary sense (meaning "intended").

[68] i.e. any Community customs duty; an agricultural levy of the Economic Community; VAT under the law of another member State; any duty or tax on tobacco products, alcoholic liquors or hydrocarbon oils which, in another member State, corresponds to any excise duty; or any other duty, tax or charge imposed by or in pursuance of any Community instrument on the movement of goods into or out of any member State: CJA 1993, s.71(9).

(b) the operation of arrangements under which reliefs or exemptions from any such duty or tax are provided or sums in respect of any such duty or tax are repaid or refunded;

(c) the making of payments in pursuance of Community arrangements made in connection with the regulation of the market for agricultural products and the enforcement of the conditions of any such payments;

(d) the movement into or out of any member State of anything in relation to the movement of which any Community instrument imposes, or requires the imposition of, any prohibition or restriction;[69] and

(e) such other matters in relation to which provision is made by any Community instrument as the Secretary of State may by order specify."[70]

The offence is triable either way, and is punishable on conviction on indictment with seven years' imprisonment.[71]

16–034 The offence has two elements:

- conduct outside the United Kingdom which involves the commission of a serious offence against the law of another member State, of a kind specified in CJA 1993, s.71(1)(a)–(c) and (2); and
- assistance in or inducement[72] of that conduct within the United Kingdom.

The serious offence outside the United Kingdom must actually be committed: it is not sufficient that the defendant intends or expects it to be committed. This is clear from the reference to conduct which *involves* (not "would involve") the commission of a serious offence. The conduct outside the United Kingdom may consist of acts, omissions or statements.[73]

16–035 The offence under the law of another member State must be "serious". An offence is serious if it is punishable with 12 months' imprisonment.[74] The question whether the conduct involves the commission of a serious offence is to be determined according to the law in force in the member State in question at the time of the assistance or inducement (*not* the time when the conduct occurs).[75]

16–036 Proof of the position under the law of the member State in question is assisted by CJA 1993, s.71(5), which provides:

"For the purposes of any proceedings for an offence under this section, a certificate purporting to be issued by or on behalf of the government of

[69] Including the movement of anything between member States, and the doing of anything which falls to be treated for the purposes of the Community instrument in question as involving the entry into, or departure from, the territory of the Community of any goods (within the meaning of CEMA 1979): CJA 1993, s.71(10).

[70] No such order has been made.

[71] CJA 1993, s.71(6). CEMA 1979, ss.145–152 and 154, which contain general provisions as to legal proceedings, apply as if CJA 1993, s.71 were contained in CEMA 1979: CJA 1993, s.71(7).

[72] "Induces" appears to be synonymous with "procures". A person induces conduct by another if, by persuasion or otherwise, he brings it about.

[73] CJA 1993, s.71(9).

[74] CJA 1993, s.71(3)(a).

[75] CJA 1993, s.71(3)(b).

another member State which contains a statement, in relation to such times as may be specified in the certificate—

(a) that a specified offence existed against the law of that member State,

(b) that an offence against the law of that member State was a serious offence within the meaning of this section,

(c) that such an offence consists in or includes the contravention of particular provisions of the law of that member State,

(d) that specified provisions of the law of that member State relate to, or are capable of having an effect in relation to, particular matters,

(e) that specified conduct involved the commission of a particular offence against the law of that member State, or

(f) that a particular effect in that member State in relation to any matter would result from specified conduct,

shall, in the case of a statement falling within paragraphs (a) to (d), be conclusive of the matters stated and, in the other cases, be evidence . . . of the matters stated."

Statements falling within CJA 1993, s.71(5)(a)–(d) are statements as to **16–037** the law of the member State in question, and are conclusive. A statement falling within s.71(5)(f) is a statement of fact, and can be countered by other evidence. Section 71(5)(e) is ambiguous. One reading is that it refers to a statement that specified conduct did in fact occur, and that it involved the commission of a particular offence. On that reading, the statement would be hearsay on the former point, but admissible by virtue of s.71(5).[76] An alternative reading is that s.71(5)(e) refers only to a statement that specified conduct *would* involve the commission of a particular offence *if* it occurred. The latter reading seems marginally more natural,[77] but the fact that the statement is not conclusive points strongly towards the former.

The offence does not expressly require mens rea. But CJA 1993, s.71(4) **16–038** provides a limited defence:

"In any proceedings against any person for an offence under this section it shall be a defence for that person to show—

(a) that the conduct in question would not have involved the commission of an offence against the law of the member State in question but for circumstances of which he had no knowledge; and

(b) that he did not suspect or anticipate the existence of those circumstances and did not have reasonable grounds for doing so."

[76] The Criminal Justice Act 2003, s.114(1)(a) preserves existing statutory exceptions to the rule against hearsay.

[77] The past tense "involved" is arguably attributable to the qualification "in relation to such times as may be specified in the certificate". The past tense is also used in s.71(5)(a) and (b), but oddly not in s.71(5)(c) or (d).

16–039 The circumstances referred to must be such that, had they not existed, the conduct in question would not have involved the commission of *any* offence under the law of the member State in question,[78] let alone a serious offence. The words "or anticipate" seem to imply that the material time for this purpose is the time at which the defendant assists in or induces the conduct outside the United Kingdom. At that time, he must *neither* suspect that the circumstances already exist[79] *nor* anticipate that they will exist at the time when the conduct outside the United kingdom occurs; *and* he must not have reasonable grounds for suspecting the former or anticipating the latter. Read literally, s.71(4) would require the defence to prove these facts on the balance of probabilities; but it seems likely that this construction would infringe Art.6(2) of the European Convention on Human Rights, and that the subsection would therefore be read down under the Human Rights Act 1998, s.3 so as to impose only an evidential burden.[80]

CHEATING THE PUBLIC REVENUE

16–040 It is an offence at common law to defraud or "cheat" the general public. In modern times the application of the offence has been largely confined to frauds on the public revenue, but its continuing existence in that context was confirmed by *Hudson*.[81] The defendant was charged with submitting false accounts to an inspector of taxes with intent to defraud. The Court of Criminal Appeal held, approving a ruling by Bray J.,[82] that the indictment disclosed an offence. The Theft Act 1968 abolishes the offence of cheating in general, but expressly preserves "offences relating to the public revenue".[83] In *Less*[84] the Court of Appeal upheld a direction in the following terms:

> "The common law offence of cheating the public Revenue does not necessarily require a false representation either by words or conduct. Cheating can include any form of fraudulent conduct which results in diverting money from the Revenue and in depriving the Revenue of the money to which it is entitled. It has, of course, to be fraudulent conduct. That is to say, deliberate conduct by the defendant to prejudice, or take the risk of prejudicing, the Revenue's right to the tax in question, knowing that he has no right to do so."

It should have been added that the conduct must be dishonest,[85] since dishonesty is an element of fraud.[86]

[78] It is immaterial that it would have involved the commission of an offence under the law of some *other* member State.

[79] The defence appears to be unavailable if he suspects that the circumstances already exist, even if he believes that they will no longer exist at the time of the conduct outside the UK.

[80] *Lambert* [2001] UKHL 37; [2002] 2 A.C. 545; *Johnstone* [2003] UKHL 28; [2003] 1 W.L.R. 1736; *Sheldrake v DPP* [2004] UKHL 43; [2005] 1 A.C. 264.

[81] [1956] 2 Q.B. 252.

[82] *Bradbury* [1956] 2 Q.B. 262n.

[83] Theft Act 1968, s.32(1)(a).

[84] March 12, 1993. *Less* was cited with approval in *Hunt* [1994] S.T.C. 819 and *Stannard* [2005] EWCA Crim 2717.

[85] See above, Ch.2.

[86] See above, para.7–002.

The offence is distinct from that of conspiracy to defraud.[87] It is narrower in that it is confined to frauds on the public at large, but wider in that it can be committed by one person acting alone. Unlike conspiracy to defraud, it is punishable at large. A conspiracy to cheat the revenue is a statutory conspiracy contrary to the Criminal Law Act 1977, s.1.[88] **16–041**

Although the offence was traditionally used by the Inland Revenue, the expression "the public revenue" appears to embrace all the taxes and duties now levied by HMRC,[89] including those formerly administered by the Board of Customs and Excise such as VAT.[90] In the absence of statutory extension, the offence presumably does not apply to frauds on the European Union.[91] **16–042**

The offence is a continuing one. A single count can cover a number of false tax returns,[92] and probably also the evasion of more than one tax (for example where income is diverted from a company and paid covertly to a director, thus evading both corporation tax and income tax). Like conspiracy to defraud and fraudulent trading, the offence thus offers the prosecution a convenient way of encapsulating a large-scale fraud in a single count.[93] It has been held that the offence is available even if a statutory offence is available on the facts.[94] This will nearly always be the case, especially now that there is a statutory offence of fraudulently evading income tax[95] as well as the offence under s.1 of the Fraud Act 2006. But it may be arguable that a charge at common law is inappropriate where the alleged conduct falls clearly within a statutory offence and the maximum punishment for that offence would be adequate.[96] **16–043**

The offence is one of conduct intended to *defraud* the revenue in the common law sense. It follows that deception is not required.[97] It is sufficient that the defendant fails to pay sums lawfully due to the Crown, for example by failing to register for VAT[98] or to notify HMRC of profits from overseas companies.[99] Nor (*pace* the *Less* direction) is it necessary that money should actually be diverted from the revenue: conduct intended to have that effect is enough.[100] **16–044**

As in the case of other offences defined in terms of fraudulent conduct or intent, therefore, the ambit of the offence is dictated largely by the concept of fraud. The taking of steps designed to minimise one's tax liability is, in **16–045**

[87] *Fountain* [1965] 2 All E.R. 671n.
[88] *Mulligan* [1990] Crim. L.R. 427.
[89] But not by local government: *Lush v Coles* [1967] 1 W.L.R. 685.
[90] e.g. *Tonner* [1985] 1 W.L.R. 344.
[91] But see above, paras 16–031 *et seq*.
[92] *Hunt* [1994] S.T.C. 819.
[93] See below, Ch.25.
[94] *Redford* (1989) 89 Cr.App.R. 1.
[95] Finance Act 2000, s.144: above, para.16–019.
[96] See the remarks of Lord Bingham in *Rimmington* [2005] UKHL 63; [2006] 1 A.C. 459 at [30], quoted above, para.7–034.
[97] cf. *Scott v Metropolitan Police Commissioner* [1975] A.C. 819; above, para.7–012.
[98] *Mavji* [1986] 1 W.L.R. 1388; *Redford* (1989) 89 Cr.App.R. 1.
[99] *Charlton* [1996] S.T.C. 1418; *Dimsey* [2000] Q.B. 744.
[100] *Hunt* [1994] S.T.C. 819.

itself, entirely lawful. The courts are often called upon to distinguish between tax avoidance and tax evasion. It has been said that "Tax saving crosses the border from lawful to criminal when it involves the deliberate and dishonest making of false statements to the Revenue,"[101] but this understates the width of the offence. False statements are not necessary: a dishonest failure to pay tax is enough. The problem is to distinguish an intention not to pay tax from a *dishonest* intention not to pay tax. For this purpose, it is submitted, the crucial questions are: did the defendant intend to avoid paying tax for which he was or expected to be liable? And, if so, was that a dishonest intention?

16–046 Tax avoidance often involves the setting up of structures and procedures which have no purpose other than the saving of tax. Where such a scheme is effective as a matter of tax law, it cannot be fraudulent as a matter of criminal law.[102] Whether a jury might regard it as dishonest is immaterial, because it does not involve depriving the revenue of any tax to which the revenue is entitled: it merely reduces the amount of tax to which the revenue is entitled. If (dishonesty aside) the facts are agreed, the judge should in principle rule on whether the scheme was effective, and, if it was, withdraw the case from the jury. If the facts are in dispute, the judge should in principle explain to the jury the relevant principles of tax law and direct the jury to acquit unless, applying those principles, they are satisfied that the scheme was ineffective. But this approach is unlikely to be practicable. The jury will probably be allowed to convict if, tax law aside, they think the scheme was a sham.[103] Their judgment of what constitutes a sham may be less well informed than that of leading tax counsel; but an appeal against conviction should in principle succeed if the Court of Appeal concludes that, on a view of the facts which the jury may have taken, the scheme would have been effective in law.

16–047 Where the scheme is ineffective as a matter of tax law, it is intended to avoid paying tax which *is in fact* payable. Whether it is criminal should in principle depend on whether the defendant *knows* that that will be the effect if the scheme works as intended. If he knows that the scheme is ineffective but seeks to exploit it anyway, there is no obstacle to a finding of dishonesty. If he mistakenly believes that the scheme is effective, on the other hand, it is submitted that he cannot properly be found to have acted dishonestly, because his intention is merely to exercise his legal right to minimise his liability.[104] A jury should therefore be directed to acquit a person charged with cheating the revenue if they are not satisfied that he knew he was evading tax rather than avoiding it. In practice, however, the position may not become clear until the point has been determined by the courts. The defendant may have been advised that the scheme might be

[101] *R. (Inland Revenue Commissioners) v Kingston Crown Court* [2001] EWHC 581; [2001] 4 All E.R. 721 at [2], *per* Stanley Burnton J.

[102] *Dimsey* [2001] UKHL 46; [2002] 1 A.C. 509 at [21]–[22], *per* Lord Scott of Foscote.

[103] e.g. *Charlton* [1996] S.T.C. 1418.

[104] cf. above, paras 2–063 *et seq*.

effective in law, but that it could be challenged by HMRC, and that the challenge might succeed. If the scheme turns out to be ineffective and a charge of cheating the revenue is brought, it would seem to be a matter for the jury whether it was dishonest of the defendant to make the attempt.

In view of the dominant role of dishonesty in the definition of the offence, it has been questioned whether the offence satisfies the requirement of legal certainty imposed by Art.7 of the European Convention on Human Rights.[105] It is submitted that this depends on whether a defendant can be convicted solely on the ground that it was dishonest (in the *Ghosh* sense)[106] to avoid paying tax in the way he did. If he can, it is impossible to be sure that a particular avoidance scheme will not be regarded as dishonest, and the offence is as objectionable as conspiracy to defraud (which the Joint Committee on Human Rights has said is incompatible with the Convention), fraudulent trading or (as interpreted in *Hinks*)[107] theft. If the reasoning above is accepted, however, a defendant cannot be convicted unless his intention was to *evade* tax (and, incidentally, to do so dishonestly). That would reduce the element of dishonesty to a relatively minor role. The offence would be essentially one of dishonestly evading the payment of a particular kind of debt; and that would seem sufficiently narrow to satisfy the requirements of Art.7. **16–048**

In *Pattni*[108] H.H. Judge Mercer rejected an argument that cheating the public revenue (as well as the offence under VATA 1994, s.72(8))[109] was too uncertain to satisfy Art.7. **16–049**

> "[P]rior, at any rate, to the passing of the Human Rights Act 1998 the common law offence of cheating the Revenue was alive and well and in appropriate cases provided a relevant charge . . . . In my view the common law offence of cheating the Revenue as interpreted by recent judicial decisions, and if properly understood and adequately particularised, is clear and ascertainable as well as readily understood by a jury."

The proviso that the offence must be adequately particularised is important. Moreover, the defendants' position in *Pattni* was not that they had acted in good faith but that they had not done the acts alleged. The Art.7 point may still be arguable in relation to a case of "avoidance gone wrong".[110]

In debate on the Bill that became the Fraud Act 2006, Lord Kingsland tabled an amendment which would have abolished the offence of cheating the revenue on the ground that it is just as ill-defined as conspiracy to defraud. The Attorney General pointed out that it was one of the "specialist" fraud offences that the Law Commission had excluded from **16–050**

[105] David Ormerod, "Cheating the Public Revenue" [1998] Crim. L.R. 627.
[106] [1982] Q.B. 1053; above, paras 2–013 *et seq*.
[107] [2000] UKHL 53; [2001] 2 A.C. 241; above, paras 9–125 *et seq*.
[108] [2001] Crim. L.R. 570.
[109] Above, para.16–010.
[110] David Ormerod, [2001] Crim. L.R. 570 at 571–572.

consideration, and that if there were a problem it would require a separate review. He cited *Pattni* on the issue of legal certainty, and said:

> "If anyone thought that [cheating the revenue] was analogous to conspiracy to defraud, contrary to what the noble Lord has said, the criticism cannot be made of cheating the public revenue that it creates an offence which is not an offence for one person to do, but is for two to do."[111]

This stands the argument on its head. Conspiracy to defraud makes it an offence for two people to do something which is not otherwise an offence, on the basis that it is dishonest. Cheating the revenue arguably makes it an offence for *one* person to do something which is not otherwise an offence, on the basis that it is dishonest and the victim is HMRC. If that is correct, the position can hardly be defended on the ground that the offence does not even require two people to be involved.

[111] *Hansard*, HL Vol.673, cols 1457–1458 (July 19, 2005).

CHAPTER 17

SOCIAL SECURITY FRAUD

The fraudulent obtaining of social security benefits almost inevitably involves fraud by false representation,[1] fraud by failing to disclose information[2] or both. But offences specifically aimed at such frauds are contained in s.111A of the Social Security Administration Act 1992 ("SSAA 1992"), which was inserted by the Social Security Administration (Fraud) Act 1997 and amended by the Social Security Fraud Act 2001. **17–001**

Prior to the 1997 legislation, the only offence dealing specifically with benefit fraud was a summary offence contained in SSAA 1992, s.112 and punishable with three months' imprisonment. This was used frequently for small-scale fraud, but was obviously inappropriate for more sophisticated frauds. Such cases were usually charged as obtaining (or attempting or conspiring to obtain) property by deception under the Theft Act 1968, s.15,[3] or as conspiracy to defraud.[4] **17–002**

This approach involved significant problems. First, certain social security benefits (such as income support) required a claimant to sign a declaration every two weeks before the fortnightly girocheque was provided. Since a prosecution under s.15 of the 1968 Act required proof that the girocheque was obtained by deception, it was the deception contained in the fortnightly declaration (rather than in the initial application) that had to be relied upon in relation to each obtaining. Moreover, where multiple false claims had been made, it was not possible to specify a handful of payments as specimen counts and, in the event of conviction, ask the court to pass a sentence reflecting the totality of benefits paid.[5] **17–003**

[1] Above, Ch.4.
[2] Above, Ch.5.
[3] Above, para.4–095.
[4] Above, Ch.7.
[5] See below, para.25–017.

17–004 The 1997 Act was intended to overcome these problems. Introducing the Bill, the Minister explained:

> "We . . . need an offence—as serious as those under the Theft Act 1968—for those cases in which dishonest obtaining of benefit over a period is a direct consequence of a single false statement or failure to notify change of circumstances, so that we can avoid having to charge for each girocheque obtained. This is intended to relate the entire dishonest overpayment to the person's initial false statement."[6]

Unlike the old offence under s.15 of the Theft Act 1968, the fraud offence created by s.1 of the Fraud Act 2006 does not require an obtaining of property at all, so the need for a separate offence is alleviated to some extent. However, since the false representation must be made with a view to making a gain *by* making the false representation,[7] it may still be easier to rely on the offences introduced by the 1997 Act.

FALSE STATEMENTS, ETC.

17–005 SSAA 1992, s.111A(1) provides:

> "If a person dishonestly—
>
> (a) makes a false statement or representation; or
>
> (b) produces or furnishes, or causes or allows to be produced or furnished, any document or information which is false in a material particular;
>
> with a view to obtaining any benefit or other payment or advantage under the relevant social security legislation (whether for himself or for some other person), he shall be guilty of an offence."

This offence is triable either way, and is punishable on conviction on indictment with seven years' imprisonment.[8]

17–006 SSAA 1992, s.112(1) remains in force, and provides:

> "If a person for the purpose of obtaining any benefit or other payment under the relevant social security legislation, whether for himself or some other person, or for any other purpose connected with that legislation—
>
> (a) makes a statement or representation which he knows to be false; or
>
> (b) produces or furnishes, or knowingly causes or knowingly allows to be produced or furnished, any document or information which he knows to be false in a material particular,
>
> he shall be guilty of an offence."

[6] *Hansard*, HC Vol.289, col.818 (February 4, 1997): Oliver Heald MP, Under-Secretary of State for Social Security.

[7] See above, para.3–004.

[8] SSAA 1992, s.111A(3).

This offence is summary only.

ACTUS REUS

Both offences can be committed in three ways—by 17–007

- making a false statement or representation,
- producing or furnishing any document or information which is false in a material particular, or
- causing or allowing any document or information which is false in a material particular to be produced or furnished.

The fact that "statement" and "representation" are alternatives suggests 17–008
that "representation" has its technical meaning, in which a statement in the ordinary sense is not strictly required.[9] If that is right, a person could make a false representation by deliberately conveying a false impression without actually making a false statement. But, since benefits are only paid upon the making of express statements, such a case is more likely to be charged as one of the "change of circumstances" offences.[10]

The statement, representation, document or information must in fact be 17–009
false (not merely misleading). If it is ambiguous, and would be true if read in one sense but false if read in another, its meaning is a question of law. It seems to be immaterial that the defendant hoped it would be understood in a sense in which it would be false, if it was objectively true.[11]

Statements and representations need only be false, but documents and 17–010
information must be false in a material particular. This presumably means that they must be material to the purpose for which they are produced or furnished, namely the obtaining of benefit (etc.) In *Talbott*[12] a claimant for housing benefit gave a false name for her landlord, so that her real landlord would not find out that she was claiming benefit. If she were now charged under ss.111A or 112 with producing or furnishing a false document or false information, it would be necessary to show that the identity of her landlord was material to her claim. If she were charged with making a false statement or representation, it would not.

KNOWLEDGE AND DISHONESTY

THE SUMMARY OFFENCE

For the summary offence under SSAA 1992, s.112(1), the defendant 17–011
must *know* that the statement or representation is false, or that the document or information is false in a material particular. It is not sufficient

[9] See above, para.4–008.
[10] See below, paras 17–022 *et seq*.
[11] cf. above, para.4–036.
[12] [1995] Crim. L.R. 396.

that he signs a document containing a statement or representation which is false: he must be aware of the contents, and must know that they are false. Constructive knowledge is not enough.[13] Even recklessness is not enough, though "wilful blindness" probably counts as knowledge.

17–012 Where the charge is one of producing or furnishing a false document or false information, or causing or allowing a false document or false information to be produced or furnished, the defendant must know not only that the document or information is false but also that it is false in a material particular. If Talbott[14] were charged on this basis, it would be a defence *either* that the identity of her landlord was not in fact material to her claim *or* that, though it was material, she did not know that it was. On this point too, actual knowledge is required. It would not be sufficient that Talbott strongly suspected that the identity of her landlord might be material.

17–013 Where the charge is one of causing or allowing a false document or false information to be produced or furnished, the defendant must also know that he is causing or allowing the document or information to be produced or furnished. It is not sufficient that he knows it is false, if he does not expect it to be used in support of the claim.

THE INDICTABLE OFFENCE

17–014 By contrast, SSAA 1992, s.111A(1) makes no reference to knowledge at all: it requires dishonesty instead.[15] On a literal reading this means that, provided he acts dishonestly, a person can commit the indictable offence by

- making a false statement or representation, being reckless whether it is false;
- producing or furnishing (or causing or allowing to be produced or furnished) a document or information which is false in a material particular, being reckless whether it is false *and* whether the falsity is material; or
- causing or allowing a false document or false information to be produced or furnished, without knowing that he is doing so—

even though he would not be guilty of the summary offence in any of these cases. It seems unlikely that Parliament intended this result.[16] In its context, it is submitted that s.111A(1) must be read as requiring all the elements of the offence under s.112(1), *plus* dishonesty. If this is right, the offence of fraud by false representation under the Fraud Act 2006 is substantially

[13] *Flintshire County Council v Reynolds* [2006] EWHC 195.
[14] See above, para.17–010.
[15] See above, Ch.2.
[16] It may be relevant that SSAA 1992, s.111A(1A), (1B), (1D) and (1E) all require actual knowledge that a change of circumstances affects an entitlement to benefit, etc.: below, paras 17–022 *et seq*.

wider than that under SSAA 1992, s.111A(1), because it can be committed recklessly as well as knowingly.

It is of course unlikely that a defendant who satisfies all the requirements of s.112(1) would be found not to have acted dishonestly, but on a charge under s.111A(1) he is entitled to raise the issue. It may therefore be prudent to charge the summary offence unless the prosecution wishes to seek trial on indictment. **17–015**

VIEW TO OBTAINING BENEFIT

Under SSAA 1992, s.111A(1) the defendant must act with a view to obtaining any benefit or other payment or advantage under the relevant social security legislation, whether for himself or for some other person. Under s.112(1) he must act for the purpose of obtaining any benefit or other payment under the relevant social security legislation, whether for himself or some other person, or for any other purpose connected with that legislation. **17–016**

In both cases, the relevant social security legislation consists of the following except in so far as they relate to contributions, statutory sick pay or statutory maternity pay: **17–017**

- the Social Security Contributions and Benefits Act 1992;
- the Social Security Administration Act 1992;
- the Pension Schemes Act 1993, except Pt III;
- the Social Security (Incapacity for Work) Act 1994, s.4;
- the Jobseekers Act 1995;
- the Social Security (Recovery of Benefits) Act 1997;
- the Social Security Act 1998, Pts I and IV;
- the Welfare Reform and Pensions Act 1999, Pt V;
- the State Pension Credit Act 2002;
- the Social Security Pensions Act 1975;
- the Social Security Act 1973; and
- any subordinate legislation made, or having effect as if made, under any of the above.[17]

It is not clear whether there is intended to be any difference between making a false statement, etc. "with a view to" obtaining a benefit, etc. (as required by s.111A(1)) and doing so "for the purpose of" obtaining a benefit, etc. (as required by s.112(1)). It was suggested in the first **17–018**

[17] SSAA 1992, ss.121DA(1), 191.

supplement to the second edition of this book that the wording of s.111A(1) was an attempt to make it easier to prosecute multiple offending without resorting to specimen counts, on the basis that a person may make a false statement "with a view to" obtaining benefits in the longer term, whereas his "purpose" must be the immediate purpose of obtaining benefit as a direct result of the statement. That may or may not have been the intention,[18] but it is hard to see how the wording of s.111A(1) might be thought to achieve it if that of s.112(1) does not. It is submitted that both do.[19] The ordinary meaning of the two expressions is exactly the same.[20] A person acts with a view to obtaining benefit, it is submitted, if the hope of obtaining benefit is his reason (or at least one of his reasons) for acting as he does.

17–019 There is, however, a potentially important difference between the wording of both offences and that of the offence of fraud by false representation contrary to the Fraud Act 2006, ss.1 and 2. Under the Fraud Act the defendant must intend to make a gain (etc.) *by* making the false representation. In other words he must think that, if he makes the gain he intends to make, it will be as a result of making the representation.[21] Under SSAA 1992, ss.111A(1) and 112(1) there is no such requirement: it is sufficient that the defendant makes the statement (etc.) because he hopes to obtain benefit. In *Talbott*,[22] for example, the defendant may have thought that the false statement about her landlord's identity would not be a *cause* of her obtaining benefit; but she certainly made the statement with a view to (that is, for the purpose of) obtaining benefit. Had she not wanted to obtain benefit, she would have had no reason to make the statement. This may be a good reason for charging the offence under s.111A(1) in preference to the fraud offence, provided that knowledge (as against recklessness) can be proved.

17–020 It is sufficient for both offences that the defendant acts with a view to (that is, for the purpose of) obtaining benefit (etc.) for another person. But in neither case is there a provision corresponding to the now-repealed s.15(2) of the Theft Act 1968, under which, for the purpose of the old offence of obtaining property by deception, a person was treated as "obtaining" property not only if he obtained it for another but also if he enabled another to obtain it. If D makes a false statement so that E can obtain benefit, D commits no offence under SSAA 1992, ss.111A(1) or

[18] It seems more likely that the drafter first decided to refer to the obtaining of an "advantage" under the legislation rather than a "purpose connected with" the legislation (below, para.17–021), and then concluded that this made it unnecessary to use the word "purpose" in relation to the obtaining of benefits or payments either.

[19] cf. *Abdullahi* [2006] EWCA Crim 2060; [2007] 1 Cr.App.R. 14 (p.206), where it was held that a person causes a child to look at an image of sexual activity "for the purpose of obtaining sexual gratification" within the meaning of the Sexual Offences Act 2003, s.12(1) if his purpose is to put the child in the mood for sexual activity later.

[20] cf. above, paras 3–021 *et seq*.

[21] Above, para.3–004.

[22] [1995] Crim. L.R. 396; above, para.17–010.

112(1) unless the obtaining by E could fairly be said to be an obtaining by D for E. Arguably it could; but in that case the reference in s.15(2) of the 1968 Act to enabling another to obtain was redundant.

Under neither offence is it necessary that the defendant act with a view to (or for the purpose of) obtaining a *benefit or payment* under the relevant social security legislation. Under s.112(1) it is sufficient that he acts for some other purpose "connected with" that legislation, and under s.111A(1) that he acts with a view to obtaining some other "advantage" under that legislation. It may be arguable that a purpose might be "connected with" the legislation even though its achievement would not constitute the obtaining of an "advantage" for the defendant or anyone else. **17–021**

FAILING TO NOTIFY OF CHANGE OF CIRCUMSTANCES

SSAA 1992, ss.111A and 112 make it an offence not only to provide false information but also to fail to notify the authorities of changes of circumstances which affect the entitlement to benefit. Where the benefit in question is paid by automated credit transfer rather than girocheque or order book, the claimant is not required to confirm before each payment that his circumstances are unchanged. If his circumstances have changed but he fails to say so, it may be difficult to establish that his conduct amounts to an implied positive representation that his circumstances have *not* changed.[23] The non-notification offences make it unnecessary to establish this. Failure to notify is an offence in itself. **17–022**

As originally enacted, the provisions required a failure to give notification of a change of circumstances where such notification was required by regulations; but the challenge of drafting regulations specifying every change of circumstances that ought to be notified proved insuperable.[24] SSAA 1992, ss.111A and 112 were therefore amended by the Social Security Fraud Act 2001 so as to apply to *any* change of circumstances which affects an entitlement and is not *excluded* by regulations. No such changes have so far been excluded. **17–023**

As amended, SSAA 1992, ss.111A and 112 each create four further offences. Those under s.111A are triable either way and are punishable on conviction on indictment with seven years' imprisonment. Those under s.112 are summary. **17–024**

FAILURE BY CLAIMANT

The first offence (under each section) is aimed at the simplest case, where the claimant himself fails to give notification of a change of circumstances. SSAA 1992, s.111A(1A) provides: **17–025**

[23] But cf. *Rai* [2000] 1 Cr.App.R. 242; above, para.4–054.

[24] Explanatory notes to the Social Security Fraud Act 2001, para.176.

"A person shall be guilty of an offence if—

(a) there has been a change of circumstances affecting any entitlement of his to any benefit or other payment or advantage under any provision of the relevant social security legislation;[25]

(b) the change is not a change that is excluded by regulations from the changes that are required to be notified;

(c) he knows that the change affects an entitlement of his to such a benefit or other payment or advantage; and

(d) he dishonestly fails to give a prompt notification of that change in the prescribed manner to the prescribed person."[26]

17–026 The defendant must know (not merely suspect) that the change affects his entitlement, and must dishonestly fail to give a prompt notification of the change. A notification is prompt if, and only if, it is given as soon as reasonably practicable after the change occurs.[27] SSAA 1992, s.112(1A) creates a summary offence which is identical except that the failure to give prompt notification need not be dishonest: forgetfulness, or not getting round to it, would appear to be enough.

17–027 These provisions came into force on October 18, 2001. In *Parry v Halton Magistrates' Court*[28] the defendant was in receipt of incapacity benefit from 1999 to 2003. He was charged under SSAA 1992, s.111A(1) with failing, between December 8, 2001[29] and November 5, 2003, to notify the Department of Work and Pensions that he had been in paid employment from August 2000 to January 2001. It was argued that he had not failed to give prompt notification once s.111A(1) was in force, because even if he had done so on October 18, 2001 he would not have done so as soon as reasonably practicable after the change of circumstances in August 2000; and he could not lawfully be required to give notification in October 2001 of a change that had occurred in August 2000, because compliance with that requirement would involve incriminating himself of an offence he had already committed under the provision replaced by s.111A(1A) (SSAA 1992, s.111(1)(c)).[30] The court thought the submission "misconceived". When s.111A(1A) came into force, the defendant came under a fresh obligation to give prompt notification of the change. Had he done so, such

[25] For the relevant social security legislation, see above, para.17–017. Where two kinds of benefit are claimed under the same procedure (e.g. housing benefit and council tax benefit), a charge of failing to give notification of a change of circumstances affecting both benefits is not duplicitous: *Gateshead Metropolitan Borough Council v Rankin* [2006] EWHC 957.

[26] The persons to whom, and the manner in which, a change of circumstances must be notified are prescribed by the Social Security (Notification of Change of Circumstances) Regulations 2001 (SI 2001/3252) and the Child Benefit and Guardian's Allowance (Administration) Regulations 2003 (SI 2003/492), reg.4.

[27] SSAA 1992, s.111A(1G).

[28] [2005] EWHC 1486.

[29] This date appears to have been chosen under the impression that SSAA 1992, s.111A(1A) came into force on December 1, 2001.

[30] The transcript refers to s.111(1C), but this appears to be an error.

notification would not have been self-incriminatory because it would preclude a charge under s.111A(1A), and he could not have been charged under the old s.111(1)(c) because it had been repealed.[31]

The court's view that s.111A(1A) created a fresh obligation to notify (presumably as soon as reasonably practicable after s.111A(1A) came into force) is not easy to reconcile with the definition of a "prompt" notification as one given as soon as reasonably practicable *after the change occurs*. The decision may be explicable on the basis that the offence is a continuing one. Failure to give prompt notification *commences* once the period within which it was reasonably practicable to give notification has expired, but it *continues* as long as notification is not given. If this is right, it may affect the time limit for proceedings for the summary offence under s.112(1A). SSAA 1992, s.116(2) enables proceedings to be commenced within 12 months of the commission of the offence (or within three months of evidence of the offence coming to light, if later). If the offence is a continuing one, the 12 months presumably run from the date when the defendant ceases to commit it. If he never gives notification at all, the offence appears to continue for as long as benefit continues to be paid. **17–028**

In any event the court's answer to the self-incrimination point is plainly wrong, since proceedings for an offence can of course be brought after the provision creating the offence has been repealed.[32] The defendant could certainly have been charged under s.111(1)(c), after it was repealed, on the basis that he had failed to give prompt notification when he started work in August 2000. If the offences under ss.111A(1A) and 112(1A) are treated as continuing offences, they do in effect involve liability for failing, once a reasonable opportunity for notification has expired, to confess that one has already committed an offence by failing to give notification as soon as reasonably practicable. The self-incrimination point needs a better answer than the one given by the court. **17–029**

CAUSING OR ALLOWING FAILURE BY CLAIMANT

SSAA 1992, ss.111A(1B) and 112(1B) create further offences which are identical to those under ss.111A(1A) and 112(1A) except that the defendant must be a person other than the claimant and, knowing that the change of circumstances affects the claimant's entitlement, must cause or allow the claimant to fail to give prompt notification of the change. The explanatory notes to the 2001 Act give the example of a woman whose husband is claiming income support, and whose part-time earnings increase. If she knows that this change affects her husband's entitlement but does not inform him of it, thus causing him to fail to give notification of it, she commits the summary offence under s.112(1B) and, if her conduct is dishonest, the indictable offence under s.111A(1B). **17–030**

[31] [2005] EWHC 1486 at [12]–[13], *per* Field J. Rose L.J. agreed.
[32] Interpretation Act 1978, s.16(1).

PERSONS RECEIVING BENEFIT ON CLAIMANT'S BEHALF

17–031 Further offences under SSAA 1992, s.111A(1D) and (1E), and s.112(1C) and (1D), are aimed at the situation in which a third party is entitled to receive payments on behalf of the claimant. The explanatory notes to the 2001 Act give as an example the case where a claimant is unable to act for himself and a person is therefore appointed to exercise rights on his behalf, including the right to receive benefit payable to him. If the person so appointed knows that a change of circumstances affects the claimant's entitlement, but fails to give a prompt notification of it, he commits a summary offence under s.112(1C) and, if his conduct is dishonest, an indictable offence under s.111A(1D). If a *third* party knows that a change in circumstances affects the claimant's entitlement, and causes or allows the person entitled to receive payments to fail to give prompt notification of the change, the third party commits a summary offence under s.112(1D) and, if his conduct is dishonest, an indictable offence under s.111A(1E).

17–032 These provisions are qualified by ss.111A(1F) and 112(1E) where a landlord is entitled to payment of housing benefit on his tenant's behalf. In this case the landlord cannot commit the offence under ss.111A(1D) or 112(1C), and a third party cannot commit the offence under ss.111A(1E) or 112(1D), unless the change of circumstances relates to the claimant's occupation of the dwelling or to his liability to pay rent. On the other hand, in this case it is not necessary that the defendant should *know* that the change of circumstance affects the claimant's entitlement: it is sufficient that he could reasonably be expected to know.[33] In the case of the indictable offences, however, this is subject to the requirement of dishonesty. A landlord might act dishonestly by failing to give notification that he *suspects* his tenant may have moved out, but it could not be dishonest to fail to do so where he had no such suspicion and was merely remiss in failing to notice.

FRAUDULENT OBTAINING OF TAX CREDITS

17–033 The Tax Credits Act 2002 is not part of the "relevant social security legislation" for the purposes of SSAA 1992, ss.111A and 112. Instead, s.35(1) of the 2002 Act provides:

> "A person commits an offence if he is knowingly concerned in any fraudulent activity undertaken with a view to obtaining payments of a tax credit by him or any other person."

The offence is triable either way, and is punishable on conviction on indictment with seven years' imprisonment.

[33] SSAA 1992, s.111A(1F)(b).

The wording resembles that of s.72(1) of the Value Added Tax Act 1994[34] and s.170(2) of the Customs and Excise Management Act 1979.[35] It is sufficient not only if the defendant engages in fraudulent activity himself, but also if he is knowingly concerned in fraudulent activity by others. By contrast with SSAA 1992, ss.111A(1) and 112(1),[36] it is sufficient that the object of the activity is to enable a person other than the defendant to obtain payments (as distinct from the defendant's obtaining them *for* another person). **17–034**

The *activity* must be fraudulent, and therefore dishonest.[37] Where the activity is not the defendant's, there is technically no requirement that the defendant's involvement should itself be dishonest; but in practice dishonesty is likely to be required.[38] **17–035**

EVASION OF CONTRIBUTIONS

SSAA 1992, s.114(1) similarly provides: **17–036**

> "Any person who is knowingly concerned in the fraudulent evasion of any contributions which he or any other person is liable to pay shall be guilty of an offence."

The offence is triable either way, and is punishable on conviction on indictment with seven years' imprisonment. "Contributions" means contributions under Pt I of the Social Security Contributions and Benefits Act 1992. Again it is sufficient if the defendant is knowingly concerned in activity by another which is fraudulent (and therefore dishonest).

[34] Above, para.16–003.
[35] Above, para.16–015.
[36] Above, para.17–020.
[37] See above, para.7–002.
[38] cf. above, para.8–056.

Chapter 18

GAMBLING FRAUD

Some frauds involving gambling fall within an offence created by the Gaming Act 1845, s.17. That offence is repealed and replaced by s.42 of the Gambling Act 2005 ("GA 2005") with effect from September 1, 2007.[1] Frauds committed before that date will have to be charged under the 1845 Act or as some other offence (such as fraud by false representation,[2] or conspiracy to defraud).[3] **18–001**

GAMING ACT 1845, SECTION 17

The Gaming Act 1845, s.17 provides that an offence is committed by **18–002**

> "[e]very person who shall, by any fraud or unlawful device or ill practice in playing at or with cards, dice, tables, or other game, or in bearing a part in the stakes, wagers, or adventures, or in betting on the sides or hands of them that do play, or in wagering on the event of any game, sport, pastime, or exercise, win from any other person to himself, or any other or others, any sum of money or valuable thing . . ."

The offence is triable either way, and is punishable on conviction on indictment with two years' imprisonment.

FORMS OF FRAUD

The offence takes two main forms. The "fraud or unlawful device or ill practice" may be **18–003**

[1] SI 2006/3272, art.2(4).
[2] Above, Ch.4.
[3] Above, Ch.7.

- in playing at, betting on or accepting bets on "cards, dice, tables, or other game", or
- in wagering on "any game, sport, pastime, or exercise".

"Game, sport, pastime, or exercise" in the second limb is wider than "cards, dice, tables, or other game" in the first. This is partly because it includes sports, pastimes and exercises which are not games, and partly because "other game" in the first limb is probably to be read *ejusdem generis* with "cards, dice, tables"[4] and thus as referring only to games of chance (including those that have an element of skill). So the section covers frauds in *wagering* on sports and games, but not cheating at a sport or (probably) a game of pure skill. It does not catch a professional footballer who wins a crucial penalty by pretending to have been fouled, or (probably) a chess player who wins a tournament by secretly consulting a computer.[5]

18–004 The offence appears not to catch frauds which involve betting on one side and ensuring that the other side loses, for example by doping a horse or bribing the players. In such a case the fraud probably lies in the rigging of the result, not the wagering on it.[6] At present such a case can be charged as conspiracy to defraud, assuming that more than one person is involved.[7] Where players, stable hands, etc. are bribed, offences of corruption can be charged, or, in the case of conduct on or after January 15, 2007, fraud by abuse of position on the part of those bribed. The section also does not extend to frauds which involve betting on events other than games, sports, pastimes and exercises (such as the movements of a financial index), or on existing but disputed facts (such as the results of past sporting events).

18–005 Deceiving a person into playing a card game for money, for example by staging a game which an accomplice appears to win, is not a fraud in playing the game *or* in wagering on it.[8] It has been said that sleight of hand in playing the game is not a fraud, unlawful device or ill practice;[9] but there is presumably fraud if the effect is to give a false impression, for example that one of three cards is a queen when in fact none of them is.

WINNING

18–006 The defendant must win money or a valuable thing. He does not "win" it unless he obtains it. If he wins the bet but does not get the money, he is guilty only of an attempt.[10] Moreover, he must win the money or valuable

[4] "Tables" is an old name for the game now known as backgammon.

[5] Such conduct may amount to a deception offence under the law in force up to January 14, 2007: above, paras 4–093 *et seq*. Since January 15, 2007 it is probably fraud by false representation, though it is questionable whether there is any representation in the ordinary sense: see above, para.4–014.

[6] Law Commission Working Paper No.104, *Criminal Law: Conspiracy to Defraud*, Appendix B, para.2; A.T.H. Smith, *Property Offences* (1994) para.26–14. Examples of fraud in wagering include placing bets on credit, with the intention of defaulting on the stake if the bet is unsuccessful (*Leon* [1945] K.B. 136; *Clucas* [1959] 1 W.L.R. 244), and submitting fabricated evidence that a bet was placed (*Butler* (1954) 38 Cr.App.R. 57).

[7] *Fountain* [1966] 1 W.L.R. 212.

[8] *R. v Governor of Brixton Prison, ex p. Sjoland* [1912] 3 K.B. 568.

[9] *R. v Governor of Brixton Prison, ex p. Sjoland* [1912] 3 K.B. 568.

[10] *Harris* [1963] 2 Q.B. 442.

thing *by* the fraud, unlawful device or ill practice. Provided that he does win, it is sufficient that the fraud (etc.) improves his chances of winning.[11] But in *Clucas*[12] a person who deceived a bookmaker into accepting bets was held to have won the money not by the fraud but by backing the right horse.[13] Section 16(2)(c) of the Theft Act 1968 plugged the lacuna until it was repealed by the Fraud Act 2006.[14] The false representation would now be fraud in itself, even if the defendant did not win at all.

GAMBLING ACT 2005, SECTION 42

GA 2005, s.42(1) provides: **18–007**

> "A person commits an offence if he—
>
> (a) cheats at gambling, or
>
> (b) does anything for the purpose of enabling or assisting another person to cheat at gambling."

The offence is triable either way, and is punishable on conviction on indictment with two years' imprisonment.[15]

"GAMBLING"

GA 2005, s.3 defines "gambling" to mean gaming, betting or participating in a lottery. For the purposes of the offence under s.42 it does not matter which form of gambling is involved. **18–008**

Gaming

"Gaming" is defined by GA 2005, s.6(1) as playing a game of chance for a prize. **18–009**

Game of chance

GA 2005, s.6(2)(a) defines "game of chance" as including **18–010**

> "(i) a game that involves both an element of chance and an element of skill,

[11] *Button* [1900] 2 Q.B. 597.
[12] [1949] 2 K.B. 226.
[13] In *Clucas* [1959] 1 W.L.R. 244 (which concerned a similar fraud by the same defendant) the court reached the opposite conclusion, referring to the earlier case but apparently unaware that the earlier case had decided the point.
[14] See above, para.4–146.
[15] GA 2005, s.42(4).

(ii) a game that involves an element of chance that can be eliminated by superlative skill, and

(iii) a game that is presented as involving an element of chance".

18–011 Section 6(2)(a)(i) appears to mean that any game involving any element of chance is a game of chance, even if the element of chance is far outweighed by the element of skill. This does not appear to have been the intention. In debate on the Bill the Minister said that a pub quiz is not a game of chance because answering the questions requires an element of skill.[16] When it was pointed out that there is also an element of chance—for example, in the questions that individual competitors or teams are asked—the Minister appeared not to understand the point.[17] On the other hand he confirmed that poker is a game of chance even though consistent success requires a high degree of skill.[18] This seems to accord with the old law, under which a game was not a "game of mere skill" within the meaning of the Gaming Act 1845 merely because the element of skill was the dominant or governing factor in the game, but only if the element of chance (if any) was so slight as to render the game one which could properly be said to be one of mere skill.[19]

18–012 Indeed the effect of GA 2005, s.6(2)(a)(ii) is that a game may be a game of chance even if a very skilful player will always win. Blackjack, for example, is a game of chance even though a player skilled in "card counting" has a small advantage over the house and, if allowed to keep playing, would in the long run come out ahead.[20] *A fortiori*, if a game does have an element of chance it does not cease to be a game of chance merely because some players use a strategy which they *think* guarantees success.

18–013 GA 2005, s.6(2)(a)(iii) includes a game which appears to be a game of chance but in fact is not, for example because the cards are marked.

18–014 Regulations may provide that a specified activity, or an activity carried on in specified circumstances, is or is not to be treated as a game of chance.[21]

18–015 An activity cannot be a game of chance (even if it has an element of chance) unless it is a *game*. GA 2005 does not define a game,[22] so the word presumably has its ordinary meaning. It was held under the old law that a

[16] He later said that it is not a game at all, but a competition: below, para.18–015.

[17] *Hansard*, SC Deb.B, col.082 (November 11, 2004). On the other hand the Minister appeared at col.087 to envisage that a virtual golf game, requiring skill and luck in the same proportions as real golf, might be the subject of regulations under s.6(6) deeming it to be a game of chance.

[18] *Hansard*, SC Deb.B, col.087 (November 11, 2004).

[19] *Tompson* [1943] K.B. 650. On January 16, 2007, Derek Kelly was convicted at Snaresbrook Crown Court of organising poker without a licence, the jury rejecting expert evidence that poker is a game of skill.

[20] But card-counting is probably not cheating: below, para.18–027.

[21] GA 2005, s.6(6).

[22] Regulations under s.6(6) may provide that a specified activity (or an activity carried on in specified circumstances) is or is not to be treated as a game. If the regulations provide that an activity is to be treated as a game, without saying whether it is to be treated as a game of chance, it will have to be determined whether the activity involves an element of chance (etc.) and therefore falls within s.6(2)(a).

game necessarily involves active participation by the players, such as the exercise of skill or choice;[23] and this seems to accord with the word's ordinary meaning.[24] It has been suggested that there must be "some element of pastime or entertainment": for example, the process of tendering for a government contract is not a game even though there is a prize (the contract) at stake.[25] This is probably true, though an activity which would be a pastime or entertainment at lower levels is still a game when played by professionals for whom it is hard work. In debate on the Bill, the Minister said that a pub quiz is not a game but a competition.[26] This seems unconvincing, in view of the similarity between a pub quiz and certain board games involving the answering of questions.

A sport, even if it is a "game"[27] and has an element of chance, is not a game of chance within the meaning of the Act.[28] So cricket is not a game of chance, even though the result may hinge on who wins the toss. **18–016**

Playing a game of chance

A person *plays* a game of chance if he participates in such a game, even if he is the only participant (for example, he plays against a machine)[29] and even if the actions of other participants are simulated by computer.[30] "Participant" includes a person who discharges an administrative or other function in relation to the game.[31] **18–017**

Playing for a prize

A person plays a game of chance *for a prize* if by playing the game he acquires a chance of winning a prize, whether or not he risks losing anything.[32] "Prize" means money or money's worth. It includes both a prize provided by the organiser and winnings of money staked.[33] **18–018**

[23] *DPP v Regional Pool Promotions* [1964] 2 Q.B. 244; *Armstrong v DPP* [1965] A.C. 1262.

[24] But passive participation may be either betting or participation in a lottery, and therefore gambling.

[25] C. Rohsler in *Current Law Statutes Annotated*.

[26] *Hansard*, SC Deb.B, col.088 (November 11, 2004).

[27] The Licensing Act 2003, Sch.1 para.16, defines "sport" for the purposes of that paragraph as including any game in which physical skill is the predominant factor, and any form of physical recreation which is also engaged in for purposes of competition or display.

[28] GA 2005, s.6(2)(b). Regulations under s.6(6) may provide that a specified activity, or an activity carried on in specified circumstances, is to be treated as a sport (and is therefore not a game of chance even if it has an element of chance) or is not to be so treated (and is therefore a game of chance if it is a game *and* has an element of chance).

[29] Playing a gaming machine is gaming, not betting: *Seay v Eastwood* [1976] 3 All E.R. 153.

[30] GA 2005, s.6(3).

[31] GA 2005, s.353(1).

[32] GA 2005, s.6(4).

[33] GA 2005, s.6(5). But, in the case of a gaming machine, "prize" does not include the opportunity to play another game: s.239. For "prize" in the context of a lottery, see s.14.

BETTING

18–019 GA 2005, s.9(1) defines "betting" to mean making or accepting[34] a bet on

"(a) the outcome of a race, competition or other event or process,
(b) the likelihood of anything occurring or not occurring,[35] or
(c) whether anything is or is not true".

It includes betting on something that has already happened (or *not* happened), even if one party knows that it has[36]—for example where A and B bet at 2pm on the result of a football match which A thinks is due to start at 3pm, whereas B knows that the match started at noon and is already over. But it is not clear whether this would be "cheating" by A.[37]

Spread bets

18–020 GA 2005, s.10(1) excludes the making or acceptance of financial spread bets and similar investments, by providing that "betting" does not include a regulated activity within the meaning of the Financial Services and Markets Act 2000, s.22. Regulated activities include investments in rights under contracts for differences, or under any other contract the purpose or pretended purpose of which is to secure a profit or avoid a loss by reference to fluctuations in the price or value of property, or fluctuations in an index or other factor specified in the contract.[38]

Prize competitions

18–021 GA 2005, s.11 ensures that prize competitions involving guesswork (such as "fantasy football") count as betting even if the participants do not put up a stake in the ordinary way. Section 11(1) provides that a person makes a bet if

"(a) he participates in an arrangement in the course of which participants are required to guess any of the matters specified in section 9(1)(a) to (c),
(b) he is required to pay to participate, and
(c) if his guess is accurate, or more accurate than other guesses, he is to—
  (i) win a prize,[39] or

[34] This includes negotiating a bet: GA 2005, s.353(2)(a).
[35] This presumably means "whether anything will or will not occur". A bet on the *likelihood* of its occurring would be within s.9(1)(c)—for example, a bet on whether it is true that, once red has come up several times in succession, the probability of black's coming up next is greater than 0.5.
[36] GA 2005, s.9(2), (3).
[37] It is arguably "deception . . . in connection with [an] event to which gambling relates": GA 2005, s.42(3). But, even if it is, it is not necessarily cheating: see below, para.18–027.
[38] Financial Services and Markets Act 2000 (Regulated Activities) Order 2001 (SI 2001/544) art.85.
[39] "Prize" includes any money, articles or services, whether or not described as a prize, and whether or not consisting wholly or partly of money paid, or articles or services provided, by the members of the class among whom the prizes are allocated: GA 2005, s.11(4).

(ii) enter a class among whom one or more prizes are to be allocated (whether or not wholly by chance)."

Section 11 is not intended to catch competitions which require skill rather than guesswork.[40] GA 2005, s.339 provides that participating in a competition or other arrangement under which a person may win a prize is not gambling for the purposes of the Act *unless* it is gaming, participating in a lottery or betting.[41] But "guess" includes predicting and using skill or judgment.[42] The distinction between pure skill and informed guesswork is a fine one. **18–022**

Payment to participate

A person's participation in a prize competition counts as betting only if he is required to pay to participate. He pays to participate if he pays money or transfers money's worth for the opportunity to do so, or pays for goods or services at a premium price or rate,[43] but not if he merely incurs the expense of sending a letter by ordinary post,[44] making a telephone call (unless at a premium rate) or using any other method of communication.[45] It is immaterial to whom the payment is made, and who receives benefit from it,[46] and whether the person making it knows that he is participating in a competition.[47] A person is treated as being required to pay to participate if he has to pay to find out whether he has won,[48] or to collect a prize.[49] He is not required to pay if he has a choice whether to enter by paying or by sending a communication (such as a letter or email),[50] even if in practice most entrants will do so by paying. **18–023**

[40] Explanatory notes to GA 2005, para.64. The words "participants are required to guess" in s.11(1)(a) were substituted for "he guesses" so as to make it clear that a competition requiring knowledge does not become a prize competition merely because some participants guess the answers: *Hansard*, SC Deb.B, col.104 (November 11, 2004).

[41] Since those are the only activities that qualify as gambling under s.6, this seems redundant.

[42] GA 2005, s.11(2).

[43] GA 2005, Sch.1 para.2.

[44] i.e. ordinary first-class or second-class post (without special arrangements for delivery). Fax does not count as post: GA 2005, s.353(2)(f).

[45] GA 2005, Sch.1 para.5.

[46] GA 2005, Sch.1 para.3.

[47] GA 2005, Sch.1 para.4.

[48] GA 2005, Sch.1 para.6.

[49] GA 2005, Sch.1 para.7. This applies only if he is *required* to pay. It is not sufficient that in practice it might cost him money to collect the prize, e.g. because he has to travel.

[50] GA 2005, Sch.1 para.8. The alternative mode of entry (if not a letter sent by ordinary post) must be neither more expensive nor less convenient than paying, the choice must be publicised in such a way as to be likely to come to the attention of all entrants, and the system for allocating prizes must not differentiate between those who pay and those who do not.

PARTICIPATING IN A LOTTERY

18–024 GA 2005, s.14 defines a lottery as an arrangement under which persons are required to pay in order to participate,[51] and prizes[52] are allocated to one or more members of a class either by a process which relies wholly on chance or by a series of processes, the first of which relies wholly on chance. In the latter case it is immaterial that processes subsequent to the first (such as tie-breakers) require skill or judgment.

18–025 To prevent lottery organisers from escaping regulation by dressing the lottery up as a competition requiring skill, GA 2005, s.14(5) provides that a process is to be treated as relying wholly on chance if, while it requires the exercise of skill or judgment or the display of knowledge, that requirement cannot reasonably be expected to prevent a significant proportion of entrants from winning, or a significant proportion of persons wishing to enter from doing so. According to the explanatory notes, this test

> "is intended to be a practical one. So, for example, the level of skill or judgement required to win or go forward to the next round in a children's competition should be set at an appropriate level for the age of the children at which the competition is aimed. Equally, a competition in a specialist magazine needs to be suitably challenging for the specialists likely to read the magazine and enter the competition."

But a requirement would have to be very easy indeed before the proportion of entrants or potential entrants unable to satisfy it became insignificant.[53]

18–026 Entering the National Lottery[54] is gambling for the purposes of GA 2005, s.42,[55] but buying premium bonds is not.[56]

[51] In *Readers Digest Association Ltd v Williams* [1976] 1 W.L.R. 1109 at 1113 Lord Widgery C.J. pointed out the reason for this requirement: "[T]he evil which the lottery law has sought to prevent was the evil which existed where poor people with only a few pence to feed their children would go and put these few pence into a lottery and lose them, and this sociologically was a bad thing." An arrangement is therefore not a lottery if it can be entered for nothing, even if the organisers hope that most entrants will make a purchase or will otherwise pay. Under the old law it was sufficient that the arrangement could not be entered without making a purchase, even if the purchase price did not reflect the value of the chance to win a prize: *Imperial Tobacco v Att-Gen* [1981] A.C. 718. GA 2005, Sch.2 makes provision similar to that of Sch.1 (above, para.18–023) about what counts as a requirement of payment to participate. The rule in *Imperial Tobacco* is effectively reversed, since a requirement to pay for goods or services is sufficient only if the price or rate reflects the opportunity to participate.

[52] i.e. any money, articles or services, whether or not described as a prize, and whether or not contributed wholly or partly by the class of prize-winners: GA 2005, s.14(4).

[53] "[I]n a survey of 2000 UK citizens conducted in 2004, 53% of those questioned believed that Lord Nelson had commanded the British troops at the battle of Waterloo, and more than 25% could not name the century in which the Great War took place": C. Rohsler, *Current Law Statutes Annotated.*

[54] See the National Lottery etc. Act 1993.

[55] GA 2005, s.15(2)(a).

[56] Finance Act 1956, s.43.

CHEATING

"Cheating" is not defined; but GA 2005, s.42(3) provides that it may, in particular, consist of actual or attempted deception or interference in connection with the process by which gambling is conducted, or a real or virtual[57] game, race or other event or process to which gambling relates. Such deception or interference is not cheating per se: whether it constitutes cheating in a particular case is a jury question. The Minister was asked whether the use of electronic equipment to narrow the odds in casino games (for example by predicting the likely path of a roulette ball) would be cheating. He answered, somewhat evasively, that the clause covered everything that the Government would want to stop. Increasing one's chances of winning by "underhand or unfair" methods is cheating; doing so by a proper use of skill is not.[58] Card-counting at blackjack is probably a proper use of skill although casino operators discourage it, and although a card-counter arguably deceives the croupier by appearing to be using more conventional methods. The secret use of an electronic device is probably deception too, and would probably be regarded by most people as unfair. Arguably it is the use of a device, as distinct from one's own brain, that makes the difference. But if the casino displays rules which prohibit conduct of a particular kind, and to which all players may be taken to agree, it would be difficult to argue that conduct of that kind was not cheating. **18–027**

Conversely, the section leaves open the possibility of cheating *without* deception or interference in connection with the gambling process or a process to which gambling relates. If A induces B to play poker by pretending to be a novice, this is not deception in connection with the game or the betting process: it is deception in connection with A's skill at the game. Arguably it is cheating, of a kind; but the offence consists of cheating *at gambling* (or enabling or assisting another person to do so). If A is cheating at all, he is cheating at the process of setting up a game, not at the game itself. His conduct might be fraud by false representation, but only if he is regarded as *representing* that he is a novice.[59] Failing to disclose that he is an expert would not suffice, even for a charge of fraud by failing to disclose information, because he is under no legal duty to disclose that.[60] **18–028**

[57] A game, race, event or process is "virtual" if it consists of computer-generated images resembling a game (etc.) of a kind played by or involving actual people, animals or things, or representing an imaginary game (etc.), or if the result is determined by computer: GA 2005, s.353(3). A game, event or process (and presumably a race) is "real" if it is not virtual: s.353(1).

[58] *Hansard*, SC Deb.B, cols 229–230 (November 30, 2004).

[59] By referring to deception rather than false representation, GA 2005 avoids this difficulty.

[60] See above, para.5–003.

18–029 By contrast with the offence under the 1845 Act, it is immaterial whether the defendant wins anything or even improves his chances of winning anything.[61] But he presumably does not cheat unless he *intends* to improve his chances, or at least to damage someone else's.

[61] GA 2005, s.42(2).

CHAPTER 19

CORRUPTION

Many frauds require some degree of co-operation from those in the employment of the victim, and such co-operation will usually be procured by bribery or other forms of corruption. This will normally involve one or more offences under the interlocking provisions of the Public Bodies Corrupt Practices Act 1889 ("PBCPA 1889"), the Prevention of Corruption Act 1906 ("PCA 1906") and the Prevention of Corruption Act 1916 ("PCA 1916")—known collectively as the Prevention of Corruption Acts. Corruption in public bodies is dealt with by PBCPA 1889, and corruption of agents in general by PCA 1906. The provisions of PCA 1916 are purely ancillary. These Acts are supplemented by legislation on the procuring of honours by corruption, and by the common law. Some of these offences are given extra-territorial effect by the Anti-terrorism, Crime and Security Act 2001 ("ACSA 2001"). **19–001**

In 1998 the Law Commission made recommendations for the reform of the Prevention of Corruption Acts, including a draft Bill.[1] In 2000 the Government published a White Paper broadly accepting the recommendations,[2] and in 2003 a draft Bill based on the Law Commission's draft;[3] but **19–002**

[1] Law Com. No.248, *Legislating the Criminal Code: Corruption*, HC 524. See G.R. Sullivan, "Proscribing Corruption: Some Comments on the Law Commission's Report" [1998] Crim. L.R. 547.

[2] *Raising Standards and Upholding Integrity: the Prevention of Corruption*, Cm.4759.

[3] *Corruption: Draft Legislation*, Cm.5777.

the draft was heavily criticised on pre-legislative scrutiny[4] and the Bill was not introduced. In December 2005 the Home Office published a consultation paper with a view to finding a way forward,[5] and in March 2007 asked the Law Commission to reconsider the matter. At the time of writing the Law Commission planned to publish another consultation paper in November 2007, and a final report with another draft Bill in the autumn of 2008.

19–003 It is questionable whether the law of corruption has much of an independent role in English law, since those guilty of it will usually be guilty of other serious offences (such as theft,[6] false accounting,[7] conspiracy to defraud[8] or even blackmail). This is especially so now that both dishonest misrepresentation and dishonest abuse of a fiduciary position constitute the statutory offence of fraud.[9] A person who receives or solicits a bribe will nearly always be guilty of fraud. A person who pays a bribe will nearly always be aiding and abetting fraud by the recipient; a person who offers a bribe will nearly always be inciting the offeree to commit fraud by accepting it. The Law Commission, in its report on fraud, did not explain how the new fraud offence was intended to relate to the existing corruption offences or to the Commission's own draft Bill.

19–004 According to the Home Office consultation paper there are only about 25 prosecutions a year for offences under the Prevention of Corruption Acts, but the CPS considers that there might be three times as many "if the law were clarified". Unfortunately the challenge of devising rules which are both clear and simple has so far proved insuperable.[10] Even if the law is changed, it is unlikely to become much clearer as regards the central issue, namely the circumstances in which conduct can properly be described as corrupt. Since the uncertainty on this issue is one of the main reasons for prosecutors' reluctance to bring corruption charges, it seems more likely that the sort of case which has hitherto been charged as corruption will in future be charged as fraud—thus requiring a decision on whether the defendant's conduct was dishonest (as to which the law is relatively clear)[11] rather than whether it was corrupt.

[4] *Draft Corruption Bill: Report and Evidence*, HL Paper 157, HC 705. See also *Draft Corruption Bill: the Government Reply to the Joint Committee*, Cm.6068.
[5] *Bribery: Reform of the Prevention of Corruption Acts and SFO Powers in Cases of Bribery of Foreign Officials*.
[6] Above, Ch.9.
[7] Above, Ch.12.
[8] Above, Ch.7.
[9] Above, Chs 4 and 6.
[10] The Government's draft Bill was reasonably clear, but was widely regarded as excessively complicated (though the Criminal Bar Association thought that the "apparent intricacy" of the definition of corruption "should evaporate as soon as the abstract definition is translated onto the facts of a specific case": evidence to the Joint Committee, Ev.155). The Joint Committee's preferred approach was that a person should be guilty of corruption if he gives an improper advantage (defined as an advantage to which the recipient is not legally entitled) with the intention of influencing the recipient in the performance of his duties, or receives an improper advantage with the intention that it will influence him in the performance of his duties. This is simple enough but, as the Home Office demonstrated at para.21 of its consultation paper, hopelessly unclear.
[11] See above, Ch.2.

CORRUPTION IN PUBLIC BODIES

PBCPA 1889, s.1 provides: 19–005

> "Every person who shall by himself or by or in conjunction with any other person, corruptly solicit or receive, or agree to receive, for himself, or for any other person, any gift, loan, fee, reward, or advantage whatever as an inducement to, or reward for, or otherwise on account of any member, officer, or servant of a public body as in this Act defined, doing or forbearing to do anything in respect of any matter or transaction whatsoever, actual or proposed, in which the said public body is concerned, shall be guilty of an offence.
>
> Every person who shall by himself or by or in conjunction with any other person corruptly give, promise, or offer any gift, loan, fee, reward, or advantage whatsoever to any person, whether for the benefit of that person or of another person, as an inducement to or reward for or otherwise on account of any member, officer, or servant of any public body as in this Act defined, doing or forbearing to do anything in respect of any matter or transaction whatsoever, actual or proposed, in which such public body as aforesaid is concerned, shall be guilty of an offence."

These offences are triable either way, and are punishable on conviction on indictment with seven years' imprisonment and a range of other sanctions such as disqualification from public office and loss of pension.[12] A prosecution requires the consent of the Attorney-General.[13]

PUBLIC BODIES

The main limitation on the scope of the offences under PBCPA 1889 is 19–006 the requirement that the person for whose favour the bribe is given (or solicited, offered, etc.) must be a member, officer or servant of a "public body".[14] This phrase is defined in part by PBCPA 1889, s.7:

> "The expression 'public body' means any council of a county or county[15] of a city or town, any council of a municipal borough, also any board, commissioners, select vestry, or other body which has power to act under and for the purposes of any Act relating to local government, or the public health, or to poor law or otherwise to administer money raised by rates in pursuance of any public general Act . . ."

PBCPA 1889, s.7 applies only to local authorities.[16] But it is extended by 19–007 PCA 1916, s.4(2), which provides:

> "In this Act and in the Public Bodies Corrupt Practices Act 1889, the expression 'public body' includes in addition to the bodies mentioned in the last-mentioned Act, local and public authorities of all descriptions . . ."

[12] PBCPA 1889, s.2.

[13] PBCPA 1889, s.4.

[14] It is not a defence that his appointment or election is invalid: PBCPA 1889, s.3(2).

[15] *Sic* presumably an error for "council".

[16] *Joy* (1976) 60 Cr.App.R. 132 at 133, H.H. Judge Rigg. See also *Natji* [2002] EWCA Crim 271; [2002] 1 W.L.R. 2337 at [25].

It has been said that this includes any authority which is either local *or* public.[17] A public authority, for this purpose, is a body which has public or statutory duties to perform and which performs those duties and carries out its transactions for the benefit of the public and not for private profit,[18] whether or not it is expressly described as a public authority in the legislation creating it (if any).[19] This includes a corporation administering a nationalised industry,[20] but presumably not a company which is only partly in public ownership.

19–008 It is expressly provided that "public body" includes the Scottish Parliament,[21] the National Assembly for Wales and the Assembly Commission,[22] the Civil Aviation Authority,[23] the Housing Corporation[24] and the Port of London Authority.[25] It is arguable that it includes the House of Commons.[26]

19–009 In *Natji*[27] it was held that a Government department is not a public body by virtue of PCA 1916, and that corruption of a Crown servant therefore could not be charged under PBCPA 1889 but only under PCA 1906. The crucial question, in the court's view, was what Parliament had meant when it extended the definition in 1916. It was irrelevant that a Government department was a public authority for the purposes of the Human Rights Act 1998. Since Parliament had expressly provided for Crown servants in PCA 1906,[28] there was no reason why it should have intended to extend PBCPA 1889 to them as well. Moreover PCA 1916, s.2 referred to "a person in the employment of [Her] Majesty or any government department or a public body". This formulation would have been unnecessary if it had been intended that a person in the employment of Her Majesty or a government department should count as a person in the employment of a public body.

PUBLIC BODIES OUTSIDE THE UNITED KINGDOM

19–010 PBCPA 1889, s.7 formerly provided that the expression "public body" did not include any public body existing elsewhere than in the United Kingdom. ACSA 2001, s.108(3) amends PBCPA 1889, s.7 so as to provide that the expression "includes any body which exists in a country or territory outside the United Kingdom and is equivalent to any body described

[17] *Hirst* (1975) 64 Cr.App.R. 151 at 152, H.H. Judge Buzzard.
[18] *The Johannesburg* [1907] P. 65, decided under the Public Authorities Protection Act 1893 but equally applicable to the Prevention of Corruption Acts: *DPP v Holly* [1978] A.C. 43.
[19] *DPP v Holly* [1978] A.C. 43.
[20] *DPP v Holly* [1978] A.C. 43.
[21] Scotland Act 1998, s.43.
[22] Government of Wales Act 2006, s.44.
[23] Civil Aviation Act 1982, s.19(1).
[24] Housing Associations Act 1985, s.74, Sch.6 para.1(2).
[25] Port of London Act 1968, s.204.
[26] G. Zellick, "Bribery of Members of Parliament and the Criminal Law" [1979] P.L. 31.
[27] [2002] EWCA Crim 271; [2002] 1 W.L.R. 2337.
[28] PCA 1906, s.1(3); below, para.19–027.

above". ACSA 2001, s.108(4) similarly amends PCA 1916, s.4(2) so as to bring within the expression "public body" (in both PBCPA 1889 and PCA 1916) local and public authorities existing in a country or territory outside the United Kingdom.[29] These amendments came into force on February 14, 2002,[30] and apply only in relation to things done on or after that date. Moreover the offences can be committed outside the United Kingdom only by a UK national or a body incorporated in the United Kingdom.[31]

INDUCEMENTS AND REWARDS

The offences under PBCPA 1889, s.1 require the giving (or offering, solicitation, etc.) of a "gift, loan, fee, reward, or advantage". The last and apparently widest of these terms is defined by PBCPA 1889, s.7: **19–011**

> "The expression 'advantage' includes any office or dignity, and any forbearance to demand money or money's worth or valuable thing, and includes any aid, vote, consent, or influence, or pretended aid, vote, consent, or influence, and also includes any promise or procurement of or agreement or endeavour to procure, or the holding out of any expectation of any gift, loan, fee, reward, or advantage, as before defined."

The advantage must be given (or offered, solicited, etc.) **19–012**

- as an *inducement* to a member, officer or servant of a public body to do or forbear to do something in respect of a matter or transaction, actual or proposed, in which the public body is concerned;
- as a *reward* for such a person's doing or forbearing to do such a thing; or
- otherwise *on account of* such a person's doing or forbearing to do such a thing.

It is not clear what, if anything, the third alternative adds to the first two. A bribe may be both a reward for past favours and an inducement to repeat them;[32] but a reward for past favours is sufficient even if there is no element of inducement for the future, and even if there was no agreement in advance that the favours would be rewarded.[33]

In *Richards*[34] the indictment alleged the corrupt acceptance of certain sums "as an inducement or reward", and it was argued that each count was bad for duplicity because accepting money as an inducement is different from accepting it as a reward. The argument was rejected. **19–013**

[29] But the expression "public authorities" must be construed in the light of *Natji* [2002] EWCA Crim 271; [2002] 1 W.L.R. 2337; above, para.19–009. Presumably PBCPA 1889 would not extend to an employee of the government of a republic.

[30] SI 2002/228 (c.4).

[31] See below, para.19–044.

[32] cf. *Morgan v DPP* [1970] 3 All E.R. 1053.

[33] *Andrews-Weatherfoil Ltd* [1972] 1 W.L.R. 118; *Parker* (1986) 82 Cr.App.R. 69.

[34] October 6, 1994.

"The offence is the corrupt acceptance of the money. It is that act which constitutes the offence and the reference to 'inducement or reward' is simply a description of the criminality of the act and the character of the corrupt element."[35]

19–014 The conduct in respect of which the inducement or reward is given (or offered, solicited, etc.) may consist of any action in respect of any of the public body's affairs, or even a forbearance from such action. The reference to "any matter or transaction" suggests that the bribe must relate to some specific matter, and that it is not sufficient if the intention is merely to render the recipient generally well-disposed towards the giver in case a favour should be required. PCA 1906, by contrast, refers to "showing or forbearing to show favour or disfavour to any person".[36] But in *Grierson*[37] it was held that it is an offence under PBCPA 1889 to bribe an officer of a public body to "show favour": one cannot show favour without either doing something or forbearing from doing something. PCA 1906 had merely made express what in PBCPA 1889 was implicit.

"CORRUPTLY"

19–015 The offences under PBCPA 1889 (as well as the corresponding offences under PCA 1906) are not committed unless the bribe is given (or offered, solicited, etc.) "corruptly". This term is not defined. It has been stated that it implies an element of dishonesty[38] and that mere sharp practice is not enough,[39] but more recent authorities have rejected this view.[40] It is now clear that dishonesty is not required, under either Act.[41] A person acts corruptly, it is said, if he purposely does an act which the law forbids as tending to corrupt. This vacuous formula has been repeatedly endorsed.[42] As became apparent from the variety of interpretations offered in responses to the Law Commission's consultation paper, there is no consensus as to the word's ordinary meaning.[43] This makes borderline cases something of a lottery.

19–016 In *Smith*[44] the offer of a bribe was held sufficient even if the intention was to expose the recipient for accepting it. If this is right it is hard to see

[35] It was pointed out that PCA 1916, s.2, which in certain circumstances creates a presumption that a payment is made as an inducement or reward (see below, para.19–018), would be useless if it were necessary to prove *which*.

[36] Below, para.19–026.

[37] [1960] Crim. L.R. 773.

[38] *Lindley* [1957] Crim. L.R. 321. For dishonesty see above, Ch.2.

[39] *Calland* [1967] Crim. L.R. 236.

[40] *Wellburn* (1979) 69 Cr.App.R. 254; *Parker* (1985) 82 Cr.App.R. 69; *Harvey* [1999] Crim. L.R. 70.

[41] *Godden-Wood* [2001] EWCA Crim 1586; [2001] Crim. L.R. 810. But corrupt conduct may be dishonest even if the principal suffers no loss: *Wheatley v Commissioner of Police of the British Virgin Islands* [2006] UKPC 24; [2006] 1 W.L.R. 1683.

[42] *Wellburn* (1979) 69 Cr.App.R. 254; *Parker* (1985) 82 Cr.App.R. 69; *Harvey* [1999] Crim. L.R. 70; *Godden-Wood* [2001] EWCA Crim 1586; [2001] Crim. L.R. 810.

[43] See Law Com. No.248, para.5.65.

[44] [1960] 2 Q.B. 423.

what the word "corruptly" adds. It was suggested that it may add something in the case of a reward for past favours, even if it is redundant in the case of an inducement for the future.[45] On this view, the offer or acceptance of an inducement to show favour in the future may be corrupt by definition, but, where a reward is offered or accepted for favour already shown, something more may be required. But the circumstances in which such a reward would *not* be corrupt were not explained, and it seems doubtful whether any such circumstances exist. In *Parker* the defendant was the chairman of a district council's planning committee, and accepted money from a building firm to which the committee had granted planning permission. It was argued that the judge had been wrong to give the jury the impression that this conduct was corrupt per se. On appeal it was held that he had not done so; but the court added:

> "During the course of argument all three members of the court invited assistance from the Bar for the description of some act by a councillor in these circumstances in receiving a reward in the context of the execution, albeit in the past, of a public duty, which would not be corrupt. But we cannot say that any cogent example emerged."[46]

It is submitted that the distinction drawn in *Smith* between inducements and rewards is at best a partial explanation of the mental element required. There are at least five different situations in which it might be argued that a suspect transaction is not corrupt. 19–017

(1) Neither party to the transaction intends it to be corrupt. For example, a payment is made which is understood by both parties to be gratuitous or to be in respect of some innocent consideration. Obviously the payment is not made corruptly; but in any event the payment is not made as an inducement to show favour or as a reward for doing so.

(2) One party intends the transaction to be corrupt but the other does not. For example, a payment is made which is intended by the donor to be an inducement to show favour, but is understood by the recipient to be gratuitous or to be in respect of an innocent consideration. The donor is acting corruptly; the recipient (even if he can be said to receive the payment as an inducement) is not.[47]

(3) One party intends the transaction to be corrupt; the other knows that that is the intention, but in his own mind justifies his participation on the basis of some non-corrupt consideration which he has provided or intends to provide. For example, a payment is made which is intended by the donor to be a reward

[45] [1960] 2 Q.B. 423 at 428–429.

[46] (1986) 82 Cr.App.R. 69 at 73.

[47] *Millray Window Cleaning Co Ltd* [1962] Crim. L.R. 99; *Andrews-Weatherfoil Ltd* [1972] 1 W.L.R. 118; *Richards*, October 6, 1994.

for past favours, and which is understood by the recipient to be so intended, but to which the recipient believes he is legally or morally entitled by virtue of services innocently rendered by him. His conduct is arguably not dishonest, but is nevertheless corrupt.[48]

(4) One party intends the transaction to be corrupt; the other knows that that is the intention, but has no intention of performing his side of the bargain. This situation by its nature can only arise in the case of inducements rather than rewards. There may in addition be the element of supposed justification ((3) above) for accepting the bribe without showing favour in return (or vice versa). With or without that element, the transaction is still corrupt on both sides.[49]

(5) One party intends the transaction to be corrupt; the other knows that that is the intention, and co-operates only for the purpose of subsequently exposing the first party. The Court of Appeal has said that such conduct "would plainly not be corrupt".[50] But in the case of a person *offering* a bribe, the intention to expose the recipient is not a defence,[51] and it is not clear why the two situations are distinguishable. Possibly it is corrupt to instigate the transaction, irrespective of one's motives for so doing, but it is not corrupt merely to accept another's proposal with a view to securing evidence against him.

PRESUMPTION OF CORRUPT INDUCEMENT OR REWARD

19–018 The task of proving that a transaction was made by way of an inducement to show favour or a reward for past favours, and (in so far as it is a separate requirement) that it was made corruptly, may be eased for the prosecution by PCA 1916, s.2:

> "Where in any proceedings against a person for an offence under the Prevention of Corruption Act 1906, or the Public Bodies Corrupt Practices Act 1889, it is proved that any money, gift, or other consideration has been paid or given to or received by a person in the employment of [Her] Majesty or any Government Department or a public body or from a person, or agent of a person, holding or seeking to obtain a contract from [Her] Majesty or any Government Department or public body, the money, gift, or consideration shall be deemed to have been paid or given and received corruptly as such inducement or reward as is mentioned in such Act unless the contrary is proved."

[48] *Mills* (1978) 68 Cr.App.R. 154.
[49] *Carr* [1957] 1 W.L.R. 165; *Mills* (1978) 68 Cr.App.R. 154.
[50] *Mills* (1978) 68 Cr.App.R. 154 at 159; cf. *Carr* [1957] 1 W.L.R. 165.
[51] *Smith* [1960] 2 Q.B. 423.

THE EFFECT OF THE PRESUMPTION

The effect of PCA 1916, s.2 was explained in *Braithwaite*. **19–019**

> "The effect of [section 2] is that when the matters in that section have been fulfilled, the burden of proof is lifted from the shoulders of the prosecution and descends on the shoulders of the defence. It then becomes necessary for the defendant to show, on a balance of probabilities, that what was going on was not reception corruptly as inducement or reward. In an appropriate case it is the judge's duty to direct the jury first of all that they must decide whether they are satisfied so as to feel sure that the defendant received money or gift or consideration, and then to go on to direct them that if they are so satisfied, then under section 2 of the 1916 Act the burden of proof shifts."[52]

Thus in *Evans-Jones*[53] it was held that, where the presumption is raised, the jury may properly be directed to convict if they are left in any doubt whether the payment was corrupt. It is for the defence to satisfy them, on the balance of probabilities, that it was not. For this reason it would only be in "wholly exceptional" circumstances that the judge could properly withdraw the case from the jury and direct an acquittal.[54] The presumption can be rebutted only by evidence of an innocent explanation, not merely by the defendant's unsupported assertion that such an explanation existed.[55]

While clearly correct as regards Parliament's intention in 1916, this **19–020** approach is, on the face of it, inconsistent with the presumption of innocence. Whether it infringes Art.6(2) of the European Convention on Human Rights depends whether it goes further than is reasonably necessary.[56] In 1916 it may have been necessary to impose on the defendant a burden of proof, because otherwise he could remain silent and claim that the prosecution had not proved that there was no innocent explanation. But, as the Law Commission pointed out in its report,[57] the position is now transformed by the Criminal Justice and Public Order Act 1994, ss.34 and 35. Now that adverse inferences may be drawn from a defendant's failure to offer an explanation when questioned or to give evidence at trial, it is arguably unnecessary to impose an additional burden on the defence in a corruption case. The Law Commission felt unable to state with certainty that the presumption did not comply with Art.6, but did conclude that it was unnecessary to include a corresponding provision in the new legislation.

If the literal application of PCA 1916, s.2 would infringe Art.6, under the **19–021** Human Rights Act 1998, s.3 a court must, if possible, apply the section in a way that would comply with Art.6. This could be done by construing the section as imposing an evidential rather than a legal burden. On this

[52] [1983] 1 W.L.R. 385 at 389.
[53] (1923) 17 Cr.App.R. 121.
[54] *Richards*, October 6, 1994.
[55] *Mills* (1978) 68 Cr.App.R. 154.
[56] *Lambert* [2001] UKHL 37; [2002] 2 A.C. 545; *Johnstone* [2003] UKHL 28; [2003] 1 W.L.R. 1736; *Sheldrake v DPP* [2004] UKHL 43; [2005] 1 A.C. 264.
[57] Law Com. No.248, paras 4.31 *et seq*.

reading, once PCA 1916, s.2 is triggered it would be incumbent on the defence to adduce sufficient evidence to raise the issue of whether the alleged conduct was corrupt; but, if such evidence were adduced, it would be for the prosecution to prove corruption beyond reasonable doubt. Such a construction would in practice deprive the section of any real effect, since a defendant who offers no explanation of suspicious circumstances is now likely to be convicted anyway. According to the Home Office consultation paper, "the CPS have concluded that the risk of ECHR challenge is so great that they do not in practice rely on the presumption", and the presumption is "therefore a dead letter in any case".

THE OFFENCES TO WHICH THE PRESUMPTION APPLIES

19–022 The presumption under PCA 1916, s.2 applies only to proceedings for an offence under PBCPA 1889 or PCA 1906. By virtue of the Accessories and Abettors Act 1861, s.8, this includes proceedings for aiding and abetting such an offence. It does not include proceedings for conspiracy, attempt or incitement to commit such an offence.[58]

THE CIRCUMSTANCES IN WHICH THE PRESUMPTION APPLIES

19–023 PCA 1916, s.2 applies to payments made to employees of public bodies as defined by PBCPA 1889, s.7 and PCA 1916, s.4(2), except where the recipient's employer is a public body outside the United Kingdom and is therefore brought within those provisions by virtue only of the amendments made to them by ACSA 2001, s.108.[59] Similarly, it does not apply where the payment is made outside the jurisdiction and is therefore alleged to be an offence by virtue only of ACSA 2001, s.109.[60] Where the payment is made in England and Wales to an employee of a UK public body, it applies even if the charge is brought under PCA 1906 and therefore does not require proof that the payment was made to such an employee. But it applies only to employees, not members (such as councillors), and only where a contract is involved rather than an exercise of discretion (such as a grant of planning permission).[61]

19–024 If the prosecution can establish that some "money, gift, or other consideration" was received by such an employee, it remains only to show that the person providing the consideration (or the person for whom he was acting) was holding or seeking to obtain a contract from Her Majesty or a Government department or public body. In *Braithwaite* the defendants admitted receiving goods and services respectively, but claimed that they had paid for them in full and that it was for the prosecution to prove that

[58] *R v Att-Gen, ex p. Rockall* [2000] 1 W.L.R. 882.
[59] ACSA 2001, s.110.
[60] ACSA 2001, s.110.
[61] cf. *Dickinson* (1948) 33 Cr.App.R. 5.

they had not. It was held to be for the defendants to prove that they had, because the receipt of the goods or services was either a gift or a consideration and therefore brought PCA 1916, s.2 into play.

> "In our judgment the word 'consideration' connotes the existence of something in the shape of a contract or a bargain between the parties. In the context of the present case, take E as the employee of the public body and A as the agent of the contractor. E, the employee, promises to pay A, the agent of the contractor, £x. The consideration for that promise is that the contractor will supply tyres for E's car, or will do work on E's car, as the case may be. That is the consideration, namely the work done on the car or the supplying of the tyres for the car. If that is correct, then on proof of the receipt of the tyres or the doing of the work, the defendant is called upon for an explanation. In our view the word 'gift', according to the Crown's argument, is not otiose. The word 'gift' is the other side of the coin, that is to say it comes into play where there is no consideration and no bargain. Consideration deals with the situation where there is a contract or a bargain and something moving the other way."[62]

It follows that any benefit received in the circumstances set out in PCA **19–025** 1916, s.2 will give rise to the presumption: either there is consideration for the benefit, in which case the benefit is itself a "consideration" within the meaning of s.2, or there is not, in which case the benefit is a "gift". In either case the receipt of the benefit may or may not be corrupt: the existence of a bargain between the parties is neither necessary nor sufficient. But it will be for the defence to prove, or at least adduce evidence, that the benefit was conferred either in exchange for an innocent consideration or out of pure philanthropy.

CORRUPTION OF AGENTS

PCA 1906, s.1(1) provides, in part:[63] **19–026**

> "If any agent corruptly accepts or obtains, or agrees to accept or attempts to obtain, from any person, for himself or for any other person, any gift or consideration as an inducement or reward for doing or forbearing to do, or for having after the passing of this Act done or forborne to do, any act in relation to his principal's affairs or business, or for showing or forbearing to show favour or disfavour to any person in relation to his principal's affairs or business; or
>
> if any person corruptly gives or agrees to give or offers any gift or consideration to any agent as an inducement or reward for doing or forbearing to do, or for having after the passing of this Act done or forborne to do, any act in relation to his principal's affairs or business, or for showing or forbearing to show favour or disfavour to any person in relation to his principal's affairs or business; . . .
>
> he shall be guilty of an offence . . .".

[62] [1983] 1 W.L.R. 385 at 391.

[63] For a further offence created by PCA 1906, s.1(1), see above, para.12–037.

These offences are triable either way, and are punishable on conviction on indictment with seven years' imprisonment.[64] A prosecution requires the consent of the Attorney-General or the Solicitor General.[65]

AGENTS

19–027 Whereas PBCPA 1889 is concerned only with corruption in public bodies, the offences under PCA 1906 extend to all "agents". PCA 1906, s.1 further provides:

> "(2) For the purposes of this Act . . . the expression "agent" includes any person employed by or acting for another; and the expression "principal" includes an employer.
>
> (3) A person serving under the Crown or under any corporation or any borough, county, or district council, or any board of guardians, is an agent within the meaning of this Act."

19–028 PCA 1916, s.4(3) provides:

> "A person serving under any such public body is an agent within the meaning of the Prevention of Corruption Act 1906 . . ."

The words "any such public body" refer back to PCA 1916, s.4(2), which extends the definition of a public body in PBCPA 1889 so as to include "local and public authorities of all descriptions".[66] This seems to mean simply that a person serving under *any* public body is an agent within the meaning of PCA 1906.[67]

19–029 The expression "acting for another" in PCA 1906, s.1(2) is somewhat vague. Arguably it includes any person who provides another with his services, even if he is neither an employee nor an agent in the strict sense but an independent contractor acting as a principal in his own right; but it is equally arguable that a person does not act *for* another unless he acts *on his behalf*—that is, as his agent in the strict sense. In that case PCA 1906 would apply to employees (whether or not they are strictly agents), agents in the strict sense (whether employees or independent contractors) and persons serving under the Crown, public bodies, etc. (whether or not they are employees or agents in the strict sense).[68]

[64] PCA 1906, s.1(1).

[65] PCA 1906, s.2(1); Law Officers Act 1997, s.1(1).

[66] See above, para.19–007.

[67] It might perhaps be arguable that the word "such" in PCA 1916, s.4(3) must be given some meaning, and that "any such public body" must therefore mean *only* the bodies which PCA 1916, s.4(2) *adds* to the category of public bodies (viz. "local and public authorities of all descriptions"), not those mentioned in PBCPA 1889 itself. This would mean that agents of the public bodies covered by PBCPA 1889 without the help of PCA 1916 would be covered by PBCPA 1889 but not PCA 1906—which seems unlikely to have been the intention.

[68] *Barrett* [1976] 1 W.L.R. 946.

AGENTS OF FOREIGN PRINCIPALS

19–030 PCA 1906 does not expressly extend to agents of principals in other countries. According to the Home Office consultation paper there is case law to the effect that it does by implication extend to them; but the only authority cited is *Raud*,[69] where the point appears not to have arisen for decision.[70] ACSA 2001, s.108(2) puts the point beyond doubt by inserting PCA 1906, s.1(4), which provides:

> "For the purposes of this Act it is immaterial if—
>
> (a) the principal's affairs or business have no connection with the United Kingdom and are conducted in a country or territory outside the United Kingdom;
>
> (b) the agent's functions have no connection with the United Kingdom and are carried out in a country or territory outside the United Kingdom."

19–031 Also, because the definition of a public body was enlarged by ACSA 2001 to include public bodies outside the United Kingdom, a person serving under a public body outside the United Kingdom is an "agent" for the purposes of PCA 1906 by virtue of PCA 1916, s.4(3).[71] The amendments made by ACSA 2001 came into force on February 14, 2002,[72] and apply only to things done on or after that date.

INDUCEMENTS AND REWARDS

19–032 With one exception which is not an offence of corruption and is considered elsewhere,[73] the offences created by PCA 1906 broadly resemble those under PBCPA 1889. Again the corrupt[74] payment of an inducement or reward is an offence on the part of both the donor and the recipient. There are certain differences which are probably more apparent than real. Whereas PBCPA 1889 expressly prohibits the *soliciting* of an inducement or reward, PCA 1906 refers instead to an attempt to obtain it. It is doubtful whether the mere solicitation of a bribe is (in the terminology of the Criminal Attempts Act 1981) "more than merely preparatory"[75] to the

[69] [1989] Crim. L.R. 809. The main issue seems to have been whether a conspiracy entered into in a foreign embassy in England would be indictable under English law, but the court found it unnecessary to decide even that.

[70] According to a discussion paper for The Corner House by S. Hawley (*Enforcing the Law on Overseas Corruption Offences: Towards a Model for Excellence*, para.1.5), the SFO remains unconvinced that the Home Office view would prevail if the point were tested.

[71] Above, para.19–028.

[72] SI 2002/228 (c.4).

[73] Above, para.12–037.

[74] For the element of corruption see above, paras 19–015 *et seq*. "Corruptly" means the same in PCA 1906 as in PBCPA 1889: *Godden-Wood* [2001] EWCA Crim 1586; [2001] Crim. L.R. 810. The presumption created by PCA 1916, s.2 (above, para.19–018) applies.

[75] The statutory formula appears not to be applicable by virtue of the Criminal Attempts Act 1981, s.3(3), since that provision applies only to an offence which "is expressed as an offence of attempting to commit another offence": s.3(2)(b). In this case there would seem to be one offence, which can be committed either by obtaining the bribe or by attempting to do so.

obtaining of the bribe; but it is hard to imagine what else might amount to an attempt to obtain without amounting to an agreement to receive.

19–033 PBCPA 1889 also appears to be somewhat wider in terms of the parties involved. PCA 1906 does not expressly prohibit a person other than the agent himself from accepting a bribe on his behalf, nor a third party from offering a bribe to such a person. But the intermediary will commit an offence when he passes the bribe on to the agent, or offers to do so; and both he and the original briber are presumably guilty of a conspiracy to commit that offence.

19–034 The inducement or reward itself must be a "gift, loan, fee, reward, or advantage" under PBCPA 1889, but a "gift or consideration"[76] under PCA 1906. If the agent innocently provides some service (or property) for which he receives fair but not excessive payment, he does no doubt accept a consideration,[77] whether or not it is a "reward" or "advantage"; but obviously the consideration cannot be regarded either as corrupt or as an inducement to show favour or a reward for doing so.[78]

19–035 Under PCA 1906 the gift or consideration must be an inducement or reward either for doing (or forbearing to do) any act in relation to the agent's principal's affairs or business, or for showing (or forbearing to show) favour or disfavour to any person in relation to those affairs or business. Clearly the bribe need not relate to any particular transaction: general "sweeteners" are sufficient. Moreover the expression "in relation to his principal's affairs or business" is "designedly very wide".[79] The corrupt payment need not relate to work with which the agent's duties bring him into direct contact,[80] nor even to matters in respect of which he owes his principal any duty at all. So a trade union official commits the offence if he accepts a bribe in respect of the union's affairs.[81]

19–036 *A fortiori* it would seem that an employee who accepts a payment in return for accepting another job is being induced to do an act in relation to his employer's affairs, namely to hand in his notice; yet such a payment appears not to be illegal.[82] Perhaps the explanation is simply that it is not "corrupt". The employer has no legally protected interest in retaining the employee's services beyond the required period of notice. Indeed the situation is scarcely distinguishable from the mere offer of a higher salary.

CORRUPTION IN CONNECTION WITH THE GRANTING OF HONOURS

19–037 The Honours (Prevention of Abuses) Act 1925, s.1 provides:

[76] "Consideration" includes valuable consideration of any kind: PCA 1906, s.1(2).
[77] cf. *Braithwaite* [1983] 1 W.L.R. 385; above, para.19–024.
[78] *Bateman* [1955] Crim. L.R. 108.
[79] *Dickinson* (1948) 33 Cr.App.R. 5 at 9.
[80] *Dickinson* (1948) 33 Cr.App.R. 5.
[81] *Morgan v DPP* [1970] 3 All E.R. 1053.
[82] *Huessener* (1911) 6 Cr.App.R. 173.

"(1) If any person accepts or obtains or agrees to accept or attempt to obtain from any person, for himself or for any other person, or for any purpose, any gift, money or valuable consideration as an inducement or reward for procuring or assisting or endeavouring to procure the grant of a dignity or title of honour to any person, or otherwise in connection with such a grant, he shall be guilty of an offence.

(2) If any person gives, or agrees or proposes to give, or offers to any person any gift, money or valuable consideration as an inducement or reward for procuring or assisting or endeavouring to procure the grant of a dignity or title of honour to any person, or otherwise in connection with such a grant, he shall be guilty of an offence."

These offences are triable either way, and are punishable on conviction on indictment with two years' imprisonment.[83]

There is a substantial overlap between these offences and those created by the Prevention of Corruption Acts. The main advantage of a charge under the 1925 Act, for prosecutors, is that it avoids the need to establish that the recipient or proposed recipient was a member, officer or servant of a "public body" or an "agent", or that the transaction was "corrupt". **19–038**

BRIBERY OF PUBLIC OFFICERS

Bribery of a public officer is a common law offence, for which the punishment on conviction on indictment is at large. The acceptance of a bribe by a public officer will also amount to the more general offence of misconduct in public office.[84] This offence is committed (inter alia) by any public officer who abuses his position for private gain, whether or not through bribery.[85] However, the bribery offence seems to include the offering of a bribe which is not accepted.[86] In this case there is no actual misuse of public office, but only an incitement to such misuse. **19–039**

PUBLIC OFFICER

It has been said that a public officer is an officer who discharges any duty in the discharge of which the public are interested.[87] This includes **19–040**

[83] Honours (Prevention of Abuses) Act 1925, s.1(3).

[84] *Bembridge* (1783) 3 Doug. 327; *Llewellyn-Jones* [1968] 1 Q.B. 429; *Att-Gen's Reference (No.3 of 2003)* [2004] EWCA Crim 868; [2005] Q.B. 73; C. Nicholls, T. Daniel, M. Polaine and J. Hatchard, *Corruption and Misuse of Public Office* (Oxford, 2006), Ch.3. The Law Commission's draft Bill, and the Government draft Bill based on it, provided for the abolition of common law bribery but did not deal with misuse of public office, which was the subject of separate advice given to the Home Office by the then Law Commissioner for criminal law (now Silber J.): see the Commission's 33rd Annual Report (Law Com. No.258) at para.4.3.

[85] e.g. *Bowden* [1996] 1 W.L.R. 98.

[86] *Russell on Crime,* 12th edn (1964) at 381.

[87] *Whitaker* [1914] 3 K.B. 1283 at 1296, *per* Lawrence J.

judges,[88] ministers,[89] (probably) Members of Parliament,[90] and local government officials,[91] as well as unpaid officers such as lay justices[92] and jurors.[93] Moreover it now includes officers of other countries. ACSA 2001, s.108(1) provides:

> "For the purposes of any common law offence of bribery it is immaterial if the functions of the person who receives or is offered a reward have no connection with the United Kingdom and are carried out in a country or territory outside the United Kingdom."

This provision came into force on February 14, 2002,[94] and applies only to bribery committed on or after that date.

BRIBERY

19–041 The bribe must be intended to influence the officer's discharge of his public duties, by inducing him either to act otherwise than in accordance with his duty or to do what his duty requires anyway. It is not sufficient that the bribe is intended to induce him to exercise influence on the briber's behalf,[95] or to refrain from doing something which he could do even if he were not a public officer.[96]

OFFENCES COMMITTED OUTSIDE THE JURISDICTION

19–042 ACSA 2001, s.109 provides:

> "(1) This section applies if—
>
> (a) a national of the United Kingdom or a body incorporated under the law of any part of the United Kingdom does anything in a country or territory outside the United Kingdom, and
>
> (b) the act would, if done in the United Kingdom, constitute a corruption offence (as defined below).
>
> (2) In such a case—
>
> (a) the act constitutes the offence concerned, and

[88] e.g. *Bacon* (1620) 2 State Tr. 1087.
[89] *Vaughan* (1769) 4 Burr. 2494.
[90] Ruling of Buckley J. in *Currie* (1992), cited in C. Nicholls et al., *Corruption and Misuse of Public Office* at para.3.36; G. Zellick, "Bribery of Members of Parliament and the Criminal Law" [1979] P.L. 31. But a prosecution of an MP would be difficult in view of the privilege conferred by the Bill of Rights 1688.
[91] *Bowden* [1996] 1 W.L.R. 98 (not a bribery case).
[92] *Gurney* (1867) 10 Cox C.C. 550.
[93] *Young* (1801) 2 East 14. Bribery of jurors is also the common law offence of embracery.
[94] SI 2002/228 (c.4).
[95] cf. *H.M. Advocate v Dick* 1901 3F (Ct of Sess.) 59.
[96] *Att-Gen for Hong Kong v Ip Chiu* [1980] A.C. 663.

(b) proceedings for the offence may be taken in the United Kingdom."

It is immaterial whether the act in question is an offence under the law of the country or territory where it takes place.

THE OFFENCES

The offences that are "corruption offences" for the purposes of ACSA 2001, s.109 are defined by s.109(3) as **19–043**

(a) any common law offence of bribery;

(b) the offences under PBCPA 1889, s.1; and

(c) the first two offences under PCA 1906, s.1.

They do not include—

- misconduct in a public office (even, it seems, if the misconduct involves bribery);
- conspiracy, attempt or incitement to commit a "corruption offence";[97]
- the third offence under PCA 1906, s.1, which is one of false documentation rather than corruption;[98] or
- offences under the Honours (Prevention of Abuses) Act 1925.

UK NATIONALS AND BODIES

The offences can be committed outside the United Kingdom only by UK nationals and bodies incorporated under the law of any part of the United Kingdom. "UK national" means **19–044**

- a British citizen, a British Dependent Territories citizen, a British National (Overseas) or a British Overseas citizen,
- a person who under the British Nationality Act 1981 is a British subject, or
- a British protected person within the meaning of that Act.[99]

The offences can be committed outside the United Kingdom by any body incorporated under the law of England and Wales, Scotland or Northern Ireland. Under the law of England and Wales, for example, this might include not only a company but also a limited liability partnership. But the offences cannot be committed outside the United Kingdom by a foreign subsidiary of a body incorporated in the United Kingdom. **19–045**

[97] For extra-territorial inchoate offences generally, see below, paras 22–065 *et seq*.
[98] See above, para.12–037.
[99] ACSA 2001, s.109(4).

OFFENCES IN SCOTLAND OR NORTHERN IRELAND

19–046 ACSA 2001, s.109 applies only to things done in a country or territory outside the United Kingdom. Under the principles examined in Ch.22, something done in Scotland or Northern Ireland is not in general an offence under English law; and s.109 does not make it so.

CROSS-BORDER OFFENCES

19–047 ACSA 2001 does not attempt to clarify the position in relation to corruption committed across state borders, for example where a person in England offers a bribe to a person in France.[100] The Criminal Justice Act 1993, s.4(b), which in some cases enables a cross-frontier communication to be treated as made in either jurisdiction, does not apply to the corruption offences because they are not Group A offences within the meaning of that Act. The position therefore falls to be determined under the default principles examined in Ch.22.

[100] See Michael Hirst, *Jurisdiction and the Ambit of the Criminal Law* (2003) at 275.

CHAPTER 20

CARTELS

Anti-competitive practices were until recently the exclusive province of the civil law, except in so far as they amount to conspiracy to defraud; but they are now the subject of a statutory offence created by s.188 of the Enterprise Act 2002 ("EA 2002"). **20–001**

BACKGROUND

Anti-competitive agreements are regulated by Art.81 of the EC Treaty[1] and Pt I of the Competition Act 1998,[2] which impose civil sanctions for breach of the regime. These provisions prohibit agreements, decisions or concerted practices which have the object or effect of preventing, restricting or distorting competition in the Common Market[3] and the United Kingdom[4] respectively. They apply only to commercial entities or undertakings, not to individuals, and do not extend to criminal sanctions. **20–002**

Before EA 2002, the only criminal offence that might arguably be committed by entering into a cartel agreement, without more, was **20–003**

[1] Ex Art.85.

[2] Part I of the Competition Act 1998 was introduced to align domestic competition law with European law.

[3] The EC Treaty, Art.81(3) exempts certain agreements that are held to restrict competition if they are found to contribute to the improvement of the production or distribution of goods or to promoting technical or economic progress, while allowing consumers a fair share of the resulting benefit, and do not (a) impose on the undertakings concerned restrictions which are not indispensable to the attainment of these objectives; (b) afford such undertakings the possibility of eliminating competition in respect of a substantial part of the products in question.

[4] Council Regulation 1/2003 rendered Art.81 directly applicable with direct effect. The entire article, including the exemption under Art.81(3), may be relied on before national courts.

conspiracy to defraud.[5] In *Norris v Government of the USA*[6] it was held by the Divisional Court that a price-fixing agreement could be a conspiracy to defraud,[7] though leave to appeal is being sought at the time of writing. Senior executives of several British drug companies are currently facing charges of conspiracy to defraud, brought by the SFO, in relation to (inter alia) alleged price-fixing in the supply of generic drugs to the NHS.

20–004 The statutory criminalisation of cartels thus marks a departure from the civil European regulatory tradition. It is to some extent informed by s.1 of the USA's Sherman Act 1890, which makes it a criminal offence for corporations or individuals to engage in cartel activity. The Sherman Act simply provides that

> "Every contract, combination in the form of trust or otherwise, or conspiracy, in restraint of trade or commerce among the several States, or with foreign nations, is declared to be illegal."[8]

20–005 The new and more severe approach to cartel conduct was recommended by the Organisation for Economic Co-operation and Development in 1998. It called for effective sanctions, of a kind and at a level to deter firms and individuals from participating in "hard-core" cartels. A hard-core cartel was defined as

> "an anti-competitive agreement, anti-competitive practice or anti-competitive arrangement by competitors to fix prices, make rigged bids (collusive tenders), establish output restrictions or quotas, or share or divide markets by allocating customers, suppliers, territories, or lines of commerce."[9]

This definition was adopted in the 2001 White Paper *Productivity and Enterprise: A World Class Competition Regime*, which announced the Government's intention of introducing criminal sanctions against individuals who engage in hard-core cartels.

20–006 The Office of Fair Trading ("OFT") commissioned Sir Anthony Hammond and Roy Penrose to review the options for introducing such sanctions. The Penrose report recommended that the definition of a criminal cartel offence should not be directly linked to Art.81 of the EC Treaty or to Pt 1 of the Competition Act 1998. It advised that the offence should include a requirement of dishonesty, and should cover "hard-core"

[5] Auld L.J.'s reasoning in *Norris v Government of the USA* [2007] EWHC 71 suggests that a price-fixing agreement may be a conspiracy to defraud because it involves deception: see above, para.4–048. On that basis it might perhaps have been arguable that such an agreement amounted to a deception offence such as obtaining property by deception (Theft Act 1968, s.15, now repealed). But it is scarcely arguable that undertakings operating a secret cartel are making implied false representations to those with whom they deal, for the purpose of the new fraud offence.

[6] [2007] EWHC 71.

[7] See above, Ch.7.

[8] 15 U.S.C. 1.

[9] Recommendation of the Council Concerning Effective Action Against Hard Core Cartels, March 25, 1998 [C/M(98)7/PROV].

cartels engaged in price-fixing, market-sharing, bid-rigging or agreements to restrict production or supply. A restrictive approach which targeted individuals, rather than undertakings, was recommended in order to exclude "cartels which might attract exemption under either domestic or EC law".[10]

THE STATUTORY OFFENCE

EA 2002, s.188(1) provides: **20–007**

> "An individual is guilty of an offence if he dishonestly agrees with one or more other persons to make or implement, or to cause to be made or implemented, arrangements of the following kind relating to at least two undertakings (A and B)."

Section 188 came into force on June 20, 2003,[11] and does not apply to any conduct before that date. The offence is triable either way, and is punishable on conviction on indictment with five years' imprisonment.[12] Proceedings may be instituted only by the Director of the SFO, or by or with the consent of the OFT.[13]

THE PROHIBITED ARRANGEMENTS

The arrangements agreed upon must relate to at least two undertakings. **20–008** "Undertaking" has the same meaning as in Pt 1 of the Competition Act 1998,[14] but is not defined in that Act. It derives from Arts 81 and 82 of the EC Treaty, and has been defined by case law to include "every entity engaged in commercial activity regardless of the legal status of the entity, and the way in which it is financed".[15]

The kinds of arrangements prohibited are set out in s.188(2), which **20–009** provides:

> "The arrangements must be ones which, if operating as the parties to the agreement intend, would—
>
> (a) directly or indirectly fix a price for the supply by A in the United Kingdom (otherwise than to B) of a product or service,
>
> (b) limit or prevent supply by A in the United Kingdom of a product or service,
>
> (c) limit or prevent production by A in the United Kingdom of a product,
>
> (d) divide between A and B the supply in the United Kingdom of a product or service to a customer or customers,

[10] *Proposed Criminalisation of Cartels in the UK*, OFT 365, [2002] U.K.C.L.R. 97 at para.2.4.
[11] SI 2003/1397.
[12] EA 2002, s.190(1).
[13] EA 2002, s.190(2).
[14] EA 2002, s.188(7).
[15] Case C–41/90, *Höfner and Elser v Macroton GmbH* [1991] E.C.R. 1–1979, para.21.

(e) divide between A and B customers for the supply in the United Kingdom of a product or service, or

(f) be bid-rigging arrangements."[16]

20–010 Where the arrangements fall *only* within s.188(2)(a)–(c),[17] s.188(3) provides that they must *also* be ones which, if operating as the parties to the agreement intend, would

"(a) directly or indirectly fix a price for the supply by B in the United Kingdom (otherwise than to A) of a product or service,

(b) limit or prevent supply by B in the United Kingdom of a product or service, or

(c) limit or prevent production by B in the United Kingdom of a product."[18]

So the offence does not catch an agreement under which only *one* of the undertakings involved is to fix its prices or limit its supply or production. But the arrangements need not be symmetrical: it would be sufficient, for example, if the agreement fixed a price for supply by A but limited supply by B.

20–011 Section 188(2)(a)–(d) and (3)(a)–(c) are subject to s.189, which broadly restricts them to agreements for "horizontal" arrangements: the undertakings involved must be operating at the same level in the chain of supply or production. Arrangements involving undertakings at different levels (such as producer and distributor, or distributor and retailer) are caught only if they fall within s.188(2)(e) or (f).

AGREEMENT

20–012 The offence consists in *agreeing* on the making or implementation of arrangements of the prohibited kinds. It is immaterial whether the arrangements are in fact made or implemented, or even whether those making the

[16] "Bid-rigging arrangements" are arrangements under which, in response to a request for bids for the supply of a product or service in the United Kingdom, or for the production of a product in the United Kingdom, (a) A but not B may make a bid, or (b) A and B may each make a bid but, in one case or both, only a bid arrived at in accordance with the arrangements: EA 2002, s.188(5). Arrangements are not bid-rigging arrangements if, under them, the person requesting bids would be informed of them at or before the time when a bid is made: s.188(6).

[17] This further requirement is unnecessary in the case of market-sharing and bid-rigging because these activities are by nature reciprocal.

[18] According to the explanatory notes on the Act, s.188(3) "requires, in the case of price-fixing or limitation of production or supply, that for the offence to be committed the other party must reciprocally have intended that the agreement, if implemented according to the intentions of the parties, should result in one of these activities." This is wrong. An arrangement does not fall within s.188(2) unless both or all the parties to the agreement intend the arrangements agreed upon to operate in one of the ways specified in s.188(2). The additional requirement imposed by s.188(3) relates to the ways in which the agreed arrangements must be intended (by both or all the parties to the agreement) to operate. It is about the nature of the arrangements that the parties must intend, not about who must intend what.

agreement have any power to make or implement them. The offence is, in effect, a special kind of conspiracy. But, like conspiracy to defraud, it is a conspiracy to do something which is not itself an offence.

The offence is defined in terms of an agreement by an *individual* with one or more other persons. If D and E dishonestly agree that their respective employers, X Ltd and Y plc, will operate prohibited arrangements, D and E are guilty of the offence. X Ltd and Y plc cannot commit the offences as principal offenders, even if D and E hold such positions that their acts and intentions can be attributed to the companies;[19] but it may be arguable that they can, on that basis, be convicted of aiding and abetting the offences committed by D and E. This would depend whether, by providing that the offence can only be committed by an individual, Parliament is to be taken as having intended that a company should not be liable even as an accessory. **20–013**

DISHONESTY

An individual commits the offence only if he makes the agreement dishonestly. This requirement seems to have been included to make it clear that the offence is aimed at only the most reprehensible conduct. But juries will presumably be directed simply in accordance with *Ghosh*.[20] In the absence of the clearest deception, even the first limb of the *Ghosh* test (that is, whether the defendant's conduct is dishonest according to ordinary standards) is likely to be problematic. **20–014**

> "Is it certain that 'ordinary and honest people' would consider the planning of a prohibited cartel as 'dishonest' behaviour, rather than, for instance, crafty but tolerable business tactics? What (it may be asked) is wrong with maximising your profits and making the customer pay more, if you are in business and that is your commercial role? (Imagine the jury room banter regarding expected standards of business behaviour.) Agreed, the law prohibits the conduct, but does that render its planning a 'dishonest' act? Given that the degree of moral censure directed at cartel participation has hitherto been muted in Britain and most of Europe, is the 'ordinary and honest person' likely to suddenly consider this kind of behaviour 'dishonest'?"[21]

In the case of bid-rigging, the explanatory notes to EA 2002 state that "for all practical purposes the carrying out of the activity . . . will in itself invariably indicate a dishonest intention and amount to the commission of the offence". This is an extraordinary assertion. Having chosen to include a requirement of dishonesty in the definition of the offence, the Department of Trade and Industry cannot prejudge the way in which juries will apply that requirement. Ordinary people might consider that bid-rigging is not **20–015**

[19] See above, para.14–020.

[20] [1982] Q.B. 1053; above, paras 2–013 *et seq*.

[21] Christopher Harding and Julian Joshua, "Breaking Up the Hard Core: the Prospects for the Proposed Cartel Offence" [2002] Crim. L.R. 933 at 938.

inherently dishonest because it is up to the person inviting bids to decide whether to accept the bids he does receive, and if he chooses to accept one he presumably thinks it is worth accepting.

20–016 Given these doubts about the first limb of the *Ghosh* test, moreover, the second limb (that is, whether the defendant *knew* that his conduct was dishonest according to ordinary standards) may well prove an insuperable obstacle. The same difficulties would of course arise on a charge of conspiracy to defraud; but it is questionable whether that is an appropriate charge either. The concept of dishonesty was invented in the context of offences against property and offences of deception. It implies that the offence in question has an identifiable victim whose rights are infringed.[22] It cannot sensibly be used in relation to conduct which is anti-social in less direct ways, with the effect that such conduct is criminal only if it is *very* anti-social.[23]

EXTRA-TERRITORIALITY

20–017 EA 2002, s.190(3) provides:

> "No proceedings may be brought for an offence under section 188 in respect of an agreement outside the United Kingdom, unless it has been implemented in whole or in part in the United Kingdom."

Recent developments in the law relating to extra-territorial offences suggest that, as a matter of substantive English law, an agreement made anywhere in the world may be an offence if it is intended to be implemented in England and Wales.[24] But s.190(3) prevents such an offence from being *prosecuted* unless it is in fact implemented in England and Wales or elsewhere in the United Kingdom.

20–018 If the agreement is made outside the United Kingdom but is intended to be implemented in Scotland or Northern Ireland, principle would suggest that it is not an offence under English law at all. But s.190(3) might arguably be read as making such an agreement an offence, *as well as* permitting it to be prosecuted if it has been implemented in the United Kingdom.

20–019 If the agreement is made in England and Wales, it seems to be immaterial whether it has been, or was intended to be, implemented in the United Kingdom or abroad. If it is made in Scotland or Northern Ireland,

[22] See above, paras 2–096 *et seq*.

[23] Harding and Joshua, [2002] Crim. L.R. 933 at 939, fn.1, refer to the Law Commission's provisional conclusion (Consultation Paper No.155, *Legislating the Criminal Code: Fraud and Deception*, paras 3.12–3.17) that dishonesty is an unnecessary complication in a properly defined offence. But the Law Commission had already performed a volte-face in its final report (Law Com. No.276, *Fraud*, Cm.5560), recommending an offence which is not properly defined and therefore has to be propped up with a requirement of dishonesty: see above, Ch.6.

[24] See below, paras 22–085 *et seq*.

the position is more doubtful. Conduct outside England and Wales is not normally an offence under English law unless the legislation so provides. But s.190(3), by barring proceedings in respect of certain agreements outside the United Kingdom, could arguably be read as implying that there is no bar to proceedings for an agreement made *in* the United Kingdom, and therefore that an agreement made anywhere in the United Kingdom may be an offence under English law.

COMPETING REGIMES

It remains an immutable principle that in the event of any conflict between domestic and EC law the latter takes precedence.[25] The Penrose report recognised that "the EC, with its wider public interest responsibility to the citizens of all EC member states, would be unlikely to stay its own civil proceedings pending the completion in the UK of any related criminal proceedings against individuals".[26] This may prove particularly problematic given the recommendation that, wherever possible, criminal proceedings against individuals should precede any related civil proceedings against undertakings. This was intended to ensure that defendants in criminal proceedings could not claim that their case had been prejudiced. The OFT has indicated that it will discuss with the Commission on a case by case basis the handling of individual EC cartel cases where the United Kingdom wishes to initiate criminal proceedings.[27] **20–020**

INVESTIGATIVE POWERS

EA 2002 gives the OFT extensive powers to conduct an investigation where there are reasonable grounds for suspecting that the offence under s.188 has been committed.[28] These include powers to require any person (including the person under investigation) to answer questions, provide information or produce documents.[29] These powers are similar to those of the SFO[30] and carry similar criminal sanctions for non-compliance or obstructive behaviour. The OFT has further powers to obtain warrants to enter and search premises and confiscate relevant documents,[31] and also to conduct intrusive surveillance operations.[32] **20–021**

[25] *Costa v ENEL* case 6/64 [1964] C.M.L.R.

[26] *Proposed Criminalisation of Cartels in the UK*, para.6.10.

[27] M. Bloom, "Key Challenges in Public Enforcement: A Speech to the British Institute of International and Comparative Law", May 17, 2002; cited in M. Furse and S. Nash, *The Cartel Offence* (2004) at 19.

[28] EA 2002, s.192(1).

[29] EA 2002, s.193.

[30] See below, Ch.23.

[31] EA 2002, s.194.

[32] EA 2002 amends the Regulation of Investigatory Powers Act 2000 by adding the OFT to the list of agencies eligible for authorisation to conduct intrusive surveillance operations in the United Kingdom. EA 2002, s.200 authorises the OFT to interfere with private property in order to install surveillance devices, amending ss.93 and 94 of the Police Act 1997. For intrusive surveillance to be used, the OFT must establish that it is necessary to prevent or detect the cartel offence and that surveillance is proportionate to what is to be achieved.

POWER TO GRANT IMMUNITY

20–022 EA 2002, s.190(4) enables the OFT to give a person a written notice (commonly known as a "no-action letter"), the effect of which is that no proceedings for an offence under s.188 falling within a description specified in the notice may be brought against that person except in circumstances specified in the notice. The objective is to encourage informants to come forward. According to the OFT's guidance, a no-action letter will not be issued to an individual unless he

- admits participation in the offence;
- provides the OFT with all information available to him regarding the existence and activities of the cartel;
- maintains continuous and complete co-operation throughout the investigation and until the conclusion of any criminal proceedings arising as a result;
- has not taken steps to coerce another undertaking to take part in the cartel, and
- refrains from further participation in the cartel from the time of its disclosure to the OFT (except as may be directed by the investigating authority).

20–023 Even if these conditions are satisfied, the OFT will not issue a no-action letter if it believes that it already has, or is in the course of gathering, sufficient information to secure a conviction against the individual (presumably without the help of his admission of guilt). If the letter is issued, its terms will ensure that the exception for "circumstances specified in the notice" will apply if the recipient ceases to satisfy any of the conditions above, or has knowingly or recklessly provided information that is false or misleading in a material particular.

CHAPTER 21

INCHOATE FRAUD

The substantive law of fraud, in itself now very wide, is extended still **21–001**
further by the law of inchoate liability. This chapter does not attempt to provide a complete account of that law, but examines some issues which may arise, under the old law or the new (or both), in relation to attempt and conspiracy. We also discuss the offence of unauthorised access to a computer with intent to commit an offence, which is in effect a statutory inchoate offence of general application. Finally we deal with inchoate offences aimed at conduct preparatory to fraud in particular.

SOME ISSUES IN ATTEMPT AND CONSPIRACY

IDENTIFYING THE OFFENCE INTENDED

ATTEMPT

The offence of attempt requires an intent to commit a single offence. An **21–002**
intent to commit one of two or more offences will not suffice. A charge of attempt must therefore specify the offence attempted, and it must be proved that the defendant intended to commit that offence. More fully, it must be proved that he would have committed that offence if he had done

any further acts that he may have intended to do,[1] and any further events that he may have intended to occur had occurred. Where the commission of the full offence would require the occurrence of a particular event, the prosecution must adduce evidence that he intended that event.

21–003 This requirement was a source of difficulty under the old law of deception. Where the deception was successful, the particular offence committed would depend on the kind of event that was secured by the deception.[2] Where it was unsuccessful, the particular offence attempted would similarly depend on the kind of event that the defendant intended to secure. If he intended to obtain a money transfer, for example, he could not be convicted of attempting to obtain property, or services, or to procure the execution of a valuable security.[3] The crucial question was not what would in fact have happened if the plan had succeeded, but what the defendant intended to happen.

21–004 So, where a mortgage fraud was charged as an attempt to procure the execution of a valuable security by deception, the prosecution had to prove that the defendant either wanted or expected the advance to be paid in a form that would qualify as the execution of a valuable security, or that he expected it to be paid in one of two or more different ways, any of which would qualify. Proof that he thought a valuable security *might* be used was not enough. That would be recklessness, not intention. Conversely, under the Criminal Attempts Act 1981, s.1(2), a person who intends to commit an offence can be guilty of attempting to do so even though the facts are such that the commission of the offence is impossible. If, in a case of mortgage fraud under the old law, it could be proved that the defendant thought the advance would be paid by cheque, he could be charged with attempting to procure the execution of a valuable security by deception. It was immaterial that the lender had in fact given up mortgage cheques in favour of telegraphic transfers.

21–005 Under the Fraud Act 2006 ("FA 2006"), these issues cannot arise in the same form. The fraud offence does not require that the events intended by the defendant should occur at all, but only that he should act (or omit to act) in one of certain dishonest ways. A person who makes a false representation to get money is guilty of the full offence even if the plan fails, so it is immaterial *how* the money would be paid (if it were) or how he thinks it would be paid. Indeed, for this reason it will be rare for someone to commit attempted fraud without committing the full offence.[4] The same is true of other "conduct crimes"[5] such as theft, forgery and false accounting.

[1] But, if further acts on his part were required, this may mean that the act done was "merely preparatory" and therefore not an attempt.

[2] Above, paras 4–094 *et seq.*

[3] *Mensah-Lartey* [1996] 1 Cr.App.R. 143.

[4] If a person sends a false representation which does not arrive, he is probably guilty only of an attempt: above, paras 4–080 *et seq*. There is an attempt if a person dishonestly makes a representation which is true but which he believes to be false: below, para.21–014.

[5] See below, para.22–058.

Conspiracy

21–006 Similar issues could arise under the old law in relation to conspiracy to commit a specific deception offence.[6]

> "[W]here the charge is conspiracy, the question is what crime did the parties intend to commit? The crime actually committed may provide very good evidence of the crime they intended; but that is all. If the parties conspired to commit crime X and their efforts to do so resulted in crime Y (or the *actus reus* of crime Y), they are guilty of conspiracy to commit crime X but (unless X includes Y) not of conspiracy to commit crime Y."[7]

21–007 But it seems that in the context of conspiracy the problem may be avoidable (where it still arises). A conspiracy, unlike an attempt, may relate to more than one intended offence. But a count of conspiracy to commit both or all of those offences probably requires proof that each defendant agreed to the commission of each offence,[8] and this may not be possible. The problem was particularly acute in cases where, prior to the commencement of Pt 7 of the Proceeds of Crime Act 2002, persons were engaged in money-laundering but it was not clear whether the money was the proceeds of drug trafficking or of other criminal activity. In the former case they would be guilty of an offence under the Drug Trafficking Act 1994, s.49(2); in the latter, the Criminal Justice Act 1988, s.93C(2). In *Hussain*[9] a count of conspiracy to commit *one or other* of these offences was held to be good. This was confirmed in *Suchedina (Attorney-General's Reference (No.4 of 2003))*, where the court accepted the Crown's submission that

> "The offence of conspiracy itself is completed by the agreement and not by the way in which the agreement is to be implemented. Thus an agreement to commit a number of different offences remains an offence under s.1 of the 1977 Act even if only one, or even none, of those offences is in fact committed. It is the agreement which constitutes the offence. Equally, if the agreement is to commit either of two offences, that is also an indictable conspiracy. For example, if conspirators agree that they will steal a particular item and that they will, if necessary, either commit burglary or commit robbery in order to obtain that item, that will amount to an agreement to commit the offences of theft, burglary and robbery . . . The fact that the agreement to burgle or rob is contingent on the particular circumstances, does not affect the nature of the conspiracy."[10]

21–008 The natural meaning of s.1(1) of the Criminal Law Act 1977 ("CLA 1977") is that a person is guilty of conspiracy to commit two or more offences only if the course of conduct on which he agrees would necessarily

[6] *Dhillon* [1992] Crim. L.R. 889; *Mensah-Lartey* [1996] 1 Cr.App.R. 143; *Bolton* (1992) 94 Cr.App.R. 74.

[7] J.C. Smith, commentary on *El-Kurd* [2001] Crim. L.R. 234.

[8] *Roberts* [1998] 1 Cr.App.R. 441 at 449. A similar rule applies to conspiracy to defraud: *Bennett* May 6, 1999.

[9] [2002] EWCA Crim 6; [2002] 2 Cr.App.R. 26 (p.363), following dicta in *El-Kurd* [2001] Crim. L.R. 234.

[10] [2004] EWCA Crim 1944; [2005] 1 W.L.R. 1574 at [14].

amount to or involve the commission of *both or all* those offences. But the reasoning accepted in *Suchedina* seems to be that the conspirators do in fact agree to commit both of the alternative offences, even though their agreement to commit each offence is conditional on factors as yet unknown, and even though they do not envisage any scenario in which they would actually commit both. In *Hussain* the court warned that this solution would not necessarily be available outside the context of money laundering, but the reasoning in *Suchedina* seems to be of general application. For example, a mortgage fraud committed before January 15, 2007 could presumably be charged as a conspiracy to obtain a money transfer *or* to procure the execution of a valuable security by deception. Which offence would actually be committed depends how the money would be paid; but that seems to be immaterial to the conspiracy, provided that the parties knew that the money might be paid in either way.

INTENTION THAT REQUIRED CIRCUMSTANCES SHOULD EXIST

21–009 There may be further difficulties in identifying the mental element of an inchoate offence in a case where the full offence would require the existence of specified circumstances. This problem does not arise on a charge of attempt: the requirement of intention to commit the full offence can be satisfied by recklessness whether a circumstance exists, if recklessness in relation to that circumstance is sufficient for the full offence.[11] But in the case of conspiracy it raises difficult issues of interpretation. CLA 1977, s.1(2) provides:

> "Where liability for any offence may be incurred without knowledge on the part of the person committing it of any particular fact or circumstances necessary for the commission of the offence, a person shall nevertheless not be guilty of conspiracy to commit that offence . . . unless he and at least one other party to the agreement intend or know that that fact or circumstance shall or will exist at the time when the conduct constituting the offence is to take place."

21–010 "Fact or circumstance" in this context means an element of the actus reus of the full offence.[12] Where the definition of an offence is such that a person cannot commit it unless a specified circumstance exists, but, if it does exist, he can commit the offence without knowing that it exists, he

[11] *Khan* [1990] 1 W.L.R. 813, followed in *Att-Gen's Reference (No.3 of 1992)* (1994) 98 Cr.App.R. 383. *Khan* was actually distinguishable in the latter case, which was concerned with recklessness in relation to a *consequence* (viz. the endangering of life, on a charge under the Criminal Damage Act 1971, s.1(2)). But the requirement of intention to commit the full offence is more clearly satisfied by recklessness in relation to a circumstance than by recklessness in relation to a consequence.

[12] In *Sakavickas* [2004] EWCA Crim 2686; [2005] 1 W.L.R. 857 at [17] it was suggested that the existence of the mens rea required for the full offence is itself a "fact or circumstance" within the meaning of CLA 1977, s.1(2), but this was disapproved in *Saik* [2006] UKHL 18; [2006] 2 W.L.R. 993.

cannot be guilty of conspiracy to commit the offence unless he either intends that the circumstance shall exist or knows that it will. This provision too has been subjected to close analysis in recent decisions on conspiracy to commit offences of money laundering. These offences (now repealed) required proof that the property in question was in fact the proceeds of criminal activity,[13] but did not require *knowledge* that it was: suspicion, if based on reasonable grounds, was enough. In *Saik*,[14] however, the House of Lords held that on a charge of conspiracy to commit these offences, suspicion was not enough. CLA 1977, s.1(2) requires intention or knowledge. The majority rejected the argument that a party to an agreement "intends" a fact or circumstance to exist, within the meaning of s.1(2), if he intends the agreement to be carried out *whether or not* the fact exists.

The relevance of this decision for present purposes is that in some **21–011** offences of dishonesty the actus reus includes the existence of a circumstance, but the mens rea may be something less than knowledge in relation to that circumstance. Fraud by false representation is an example. It is part of the actus reus of the offence that the representation made should be untrue or misleading. It is part of the mens rea that the person making the representation should know *either* that it is untrue or misleading *or* that it might be. Knowledge that it *is* untrue or misleading is "knowledge . . . of [a] particular fact or circumstances necessary for the commission of the offence". Knowledge that it *might* be untrue or misleading clearly is not: it is closer to recklessness (but without the need for the defendant's conduct to be unreasonable in view of the risk as he perceives it). So liability for the offence "may be incurred without knowledge on the part of the person committing it of any particular fact or circumstances necessary for the commission of the offence".[15] So CLA 1977, s.1(2) applies to a conspiracy to commit the offence. According to *Saik*, on a charge of such a conspiracy, the prosecution must prove that the defendant intended or knew that the representation would be untrue or misleading at the time when it was to be made. Proof that he knew that it *might* be untrue or misleading is insufficient.[16]

[13] *Montila* [2004] UKHL 50; [2004] 1 W.L.R. 3141.

[14] [2006] UKHL 18; [2006] 2 W.L.R. 993.

[15] In *Saik* [2006] UKHL 18; [2006] 2 W.L.R. 993 at [21] Lord Nicholls of Birkenhead concluded that CLA 1977, s.1(2) applies to any conspiracy to commit an offence where an ingredient of the offence is the existence of a particular fact or circumstance, even if the offence does require knowledge of that ingredient. But this was *obiter*, since the offences under consideration did not require knowledge but only suspicion.

[16] In *Saik* [2006] UKHL 18; [2006] 2 W.L.R. 993 at [79] Lord Hope of Craighead suggested that intention might in some circumstances be inferred from suspicion: if a person agrees to convert cash, and knows that the purpose of doing so is to assist someone to avoid prosecution, it might be inferred that he intended the cash to be the proceeds of criminal activity, "because he knew that that was the only purpose of the transaction". This was *obiter*, and it is submitted with respect that it cannot be right: intention and suspicion are distinct states of mind. In any event the dictum would be difficult to apply in the context of a conspiracy to commit fraud. The "purpose of the transaction" will usually be to obtain property or services. That purpose can be achieved whether the representation actually made is true or false.

IS A CONSPIRACY COUNT BAD IF IT ALLEGES A MENTAL ELEMENT LESS THAN INTENTION OR KNOWLEDGE?

21–012 If, on a charge of conspiracy to make a false representation, it is insufficient to prove that the defendant knew that the representation *might* be untrue or misleading, it is arguable that a count alleging this would be bad. In *Singh*[17] the Court of Appeal rejected an analogous suggestion (in the context of conspiracy to convert or transfer the proceeds of criminal activity) on the ground that an allegation of a lesser mental element than was actually required would be an immaterial averment. This suggestion was made at a time when it was thought that it was not an element of the offences in question that the property should actually *be* the proceeds of criminal activity. In *Ali*[18] it was said that the suggestion was inconsistent with the House of Lords' subsequent decision[19] that this *was* an element of the offences.

21–013 In *Saik* Lord Hope of Craighead agreed,[20] and also said:

> "I find it hard to accept that an averment taken from the substantive offences is an immaterial averment where the defendant is charged with conspiracy to commit those offences when it would be an essential averment if the substantive offences themselves were the subject of the charge."[21]

Lord Nicholls of Birkenhead, however (with whom Lord Steyn agreed), said:

> "In respect of a material fact or circumstance conspiracy has its own mental element. In conspiracy this mental element is set as high as 'intend or know'. This subsumes any lesser mental element, such as suspicion, required by the substantive offence in respect of a material fact or circumstances. In this respect the mental element of conspiracy is distinct from and supersedes the mental element in the substantive offence. When this is so, the lesser mental element in the substantive offence becomes otiose on a charge of conspiracy. It is an immaterial averment. To include it in the particulars of the offence of conspiracy is potentially confusing and should be avoided."[22]

The statement that including the lesser mental element makes the charge "potentially confusing" implies that it does not make the charge bad in law.

EXISTENCE OF REQUIRED CIRCUMSTANCES

21–014 Where an offence requires the existence of a circumstance, the question may also arise whether the actual existence of that circumstance is equally essential to an inchoate offence. In the case of attempt this is clearly not so.

17 [2003] EWCA Crim 3712.
18 [2005] EWCA Crim 87; [2006] Q.B. 322.
19 *Montila* [2004] UKHL 50; [2004] 1 W.L.R. 3141.
20 [2006] UKHL 18; [2006] 2 W.L.R. 993 at [72].
21 [2006] UKHL 18; [2006] 2 W.L.R. 993 at [67].
22 [2006] UKHL 18; [2006] 2 W.L.R. 993 at [8].

The Criminal Attempts Act 1981, s.1(2) provides that a person may be guilty of an attempt even though the facts are such that the commission of the offence is impossible; and s.1(3) adds that a person intends to commit an offence if that would have been his intention had the facts been as he believes them to be. So a person who dishonestly makes a true statement, believing it to be false,[23] is guilty of attempted fraud by false representation.

Again, however, the position in conspiracy is less clear. On a charge of conspiracy to commit fraud by false representation, must the prosecution prove that the representation actually *was* false? Under CLA 1977, s.1(2), the conspirators must intend or know it to be false. Obviously they cannot know it to be false if it is true; but what if they *intend* it to be false? Where two or more persons agree to make a representation at some future time, and intend that it shall be false when it is made, the principles of inchoate liability would suggest that they are guilty of conspiracy to commit fraud by false representation—irrespective of whether they ever make the representation at all, let alone whether (if they do) it is in fact false. What matters is their intention, not whether that intention was fulfilled.[24] **21–015**

In the case of conspiracy, however, the position is complicated by two factors. One is the obscure drafting of CLA 1977. The other is the fact that, for tactical reasons,[25] prosecutors tend to bring conspiracy charges not only where the agreement remained inchoate but also where the full offence was committed and can be proved. Yet again it is the recent case law on money laundering that has revealed the difficulties inherent in this approach. Lord Hope of Craighead explained in *Saik*: **21–016**

> "Dealing with a series of completed criminal acts by charging the defendant with conspiracy is a device. Its aim is to ensure that the entire course of conduct is brought under scrutiny in one count and that, when it comes to sentence, the defendant is punished for the totality of his criminal activity. This is as it should be, of course. But the statutory offence of conspiracy was not designed for use in this way. The prosecutor is trying to fit a square peg into a round hole. That is not always possible. . . .
>
> Concepts which were designed to fit with the idea that conspiracy is an inchoate offence are being applied to cases where the only proof that there was a conspiracy is provided by evidence of the course of conduct, from which inferences as to the state of mind of the participants are then drawn. . . .
>
> It seems to me that the best way to discover the meaning of the words used in s.1 to define the statutory offence of conspiracy is to assume that one is dealing, as the Law Commission intended, with an allegation of an inchoate crime. A conspiracy is complete when the agreement to enter into it is formed, even if nothing is done to implement it. Implementation gives effect to the conspiracy, but it does not alter its essential elements. The statutory language adopts this approach. It assumes that implementation of the agreement lies in

[23] e.g. *Deller* (1952) 36 Cr.App.R. 184; cf. *Patel* [2006] EWCA Crim 2689; [2007] 1 Cr.App.R. 12 (p.191), above, para.4–085.

[24] But at common law this principle is subverted by the rule that there cannot be a conspiracy to do the impossible: *DPP v Nock* [1978] A.C. 979. This rule presumably still applies to conspiracy to defraud.

[25] See below, Ch.28.

> the future. The question whether its requirements are fulfilled is directed to the stage when the agreement is formed, not to the stage when it is implemented."[26]

21–017 The House of Lords held in *Montila*[27] that a person could not commit an offence of converting or transferring property "having reasonable grounds to suspect" that it is the proceeds of crime unless it actually *is* the proceeds of crime. In *Harmer*[28] the Court of Appeal interpreted this as meaning that a *conspiracy* to commit such an offence must similarly be an agreement to convert or transfer property which is in fact the proceeds of crime, because an agreement to convert or transfer property which was not the proceeds of crime would fall outside CLA 1977, s.1(1)(a). Even if carried out in accordance with the parties' intentions, the agreed course of conduct would not amount to the full offence.

21–018 The conventional view is that this was essentially the point at which CLA 1977, s.1(1)(b) is aimed. Section 1(1)(b) catches an agreement that a course of conduct shall be pursued which, if the agreement is carried out in accordance with the parties' intentions, would necessarily amount to or involve the commission of an offence "but for the existence of facts which render the commission of the offence impossible". The effect is to bring within the offence of conspiracy an agreement to do something which, if done, would not in fact be an offence, but which *would* have been an offence if the circumstances had been as the parties believe them to be. But in *Harmer* it was held that s.1(1)(b) did not meet the point, because *Harmer* was

> "not a case where the prosecution could prove the agreement alone, apart from what they could show might be the substantive offence. They had to ask the jury to infer the agreement from the subsequent putting of it into operation. Although the offence of conspiracy comprises an agreement to commit an offence (not the subsequent committing of the agreed offence), the agreement has to have a material object. In the present case, the appellant was not alleged to have been party to an abstract agreement to convert or transfer theoretical property which might turn out opportunistically to be the proceeds of crime. The alleged agreement concerned the particular money to which the Crown's evidence related and was, on the Crown's case, to be inferred from that evidence."[29]

[26] [2006] UKHL 18; [2006] 2 W.L.R. 993 at [41], [63] and [75].

[27] [2004] UKHL 50; [2004] 1 W.L.R. 3141.

[28] [2005] EWCA Crim 1; [2005] 2 Cr.App.R. 2 (p.23).

[29] [2005] EWCA Crim 1; [2005] 2 Cr.App.R. 2 (p.23) at [24]. At [25] the court referred to a further objection, raised by Sir John Smith at [2002] Crim. L.R. 407 and based on CLA 1977, s.1(2): if the parties do not know whether the property is the proceeds of drug trafficking or of other criminal conduct, they cannot *intend* to convert property which is the proceeds of drug trafficking, and they cannot *intend* to convert property which is the proceeds of other criminal conduct. In *Ali* [2005] EWCA Crim 87; [2006] Q.B. 322 it was conceded that this passage in *Harmer* was *obiter*; but this is questionable, since the court in *Harmer* had said that the objection was "fatal" to the argument based on CLA 1977, s.1(1)(b). In any event the problem arises only where circumstances unknown to the conspirators determine which of two offences they will be committing if they carry out the agreement. This situation is less likely to arise in the context of fraud.

The real objection to the convictions, therefore, was not (as the court said) that the prosecution could not prove that the property *was* the proceeds of crime.[30] It was that the agreement could only be inferred from what was done; and, since the prosecution could not prove that what was done was an offence, they were similarly unable to prove that what the defendants *agreed* to do was an offence. This suggests that the problem arose only because, as Lord Hope put it in *Saik*, the prosecution were "trying to fit a square peg into a round hole". Had it been clear that the defendants agreed to convert or transfer property which they *believed* to be the proceeds of crime, the correctness of that belief would have been crucial on a charge of the full offence but immaterial on a charge of conspiracy (or attempt) to commit that offence. **21–019**

However, Lord Nicholls of Birkenhead seems to have thought in *Saik* that this was not so. He argued that, if the property to which the conspiracy relates is specifically identified at the time of the agreement, CLA 1977, s.1(2) requires the prosecution to prove that each defendant *knew* the property was the proceeds of crime.[31] The alternative of intention was, in his Lordship's view, irrelevant to this situation; and the requirement of knowledge must be strictly construed. **21–020**

> "The phrase under consideration ('intend or know') in s.1(2) is a provision of general application to all conspiracies. In this context the word 'know' should be interpreted strictly and not watered down. In this context knowledge means true belief. . . . As applied to s.93C(2) [of the Criminal Justice Act 1988] it means that, in the case of identified property, a conspirator must be aware the property was in fact the proceeds of crime. The prosecution must prove the conspirator knew the property was the proceeds of criminal conduct."[32]

This suggests that, on a charge of conspiracy to make a false representation which is formulated at the time of the agreement, it must be proved that the representation was in fact false. Otherwise it cannot be said that any of the parties knew it to be false, which (if intention is irrelevant) is what CLA 1977, s.1(2) requires.

This conclusion was unnecessary to the decision in *Saik* (where it was not disputed that the property actually was the proceeds of crime) and it is submitted with respect that it cannot be right. If the allegation is that the parties agreed to make a representation which they intended to be false at the time when they intended that it should be made, on a conspiracy charge it is clearly immaterial whether any representation was in fact made. *A fortiori* it must be immaterial whether any representation that may have been made was in fact false. It makes no difference whether the agreement was to make a particular representation which the parties believed to be false, or to formulate the representation later but to do so in such a way that it would be false. The latter case is clearly within CLA 1977, s.1(1)(a), **21–021**

[30] In *Ali* [2005] EWCA Crim 87; [2006] Q.B. 322 at [110], *Harmer* was doubted on this point.
[31] [2006] UKHL 18; [2006] 2 W.L.R. 993 at [25].
[32] [2006] UKHL 18; [2006] 2 W.L.R. 993 at [26].

because the agreement is to do something which, if done, would be fraud. The former case arguably falls outside s.1(1)(a), but, if it does, s.1(1)(b) applies instead. The agreement is an agreement to do something which would be fraud but for the fact that the representation is not false—a fact which makes it impossible to commit the offence as intended.

INTENTION TO ENCOURAGE OR ASSIST IN FRAUD BY A THIRD PARTY

21–022 The law on the relationship between inchoate offences and secondary liability is currently in a confused and unsatisfactory state. There cannot be an attempt to aid, abet, counsel or procure an offence by another,[33] but it is not clear whether there can be a conspiracy to do so.

21–023 In *Hollinshead*[34] the defendants agreed to make and sell "black boxes" designed to make the unit counter on an electricity meter run backwards, thus understating the amount of electricity used. If they were so used, the defendants would be guilty of aiding and abetting the offences committed by the users. But the Court of Appeal held that they were not guilty of conspiracy to commit those offences, because the course of conduct agreed upon would not involve the commission of an offence *by one or more of them* as CLA 1977 requires.[35] The House of Lords thought it unnecessary to decide whether this was correct,[36] and it seems that the Court of Appeal's decision therefore stands.[37] However, the House held that the agreement was a conspiracy to defraud at common law. On this point the decision confirms *Attorney-General's Reference (No.1 of 1982)*,[38] where the defendants agreed to produce, label and distribute bottles of whisky in such a way that at the point of sale they could be passed off as a well-known brand. The court thought this was clearly a conspiracy to defraud potential purchasers, although that fraud would ultimately have been committed by

[33] Criminal Attempts Act 1981, s.1(4)(b).

[34] [1985] A.C. 975.

[35] [1985] 1 All E.R. 850.

[36] Lord Roskill said that he could see "no evidence whatever" that the defendants agreed to aid and abet the commission of offences by the ultimate users of the black boxes: [1985] A.C. 975 at 998. In view of the decision that it was the defendants' purpose that those offences should be committed with equipment which the defendants were to supply for that purpose, this is puzzling. In any event the House's decision to restore convictions of conspiracy to defraud necessarily implied that there was no statutory conspiracy, because of the rule in *Ayres* [1984] A.C. 447: see above, para.7–001.

[37] Lord Roskill suggested that "in any future case in which that question does arise it should be treated as open for consideration de novo, as much may depend on the particular facts of the case in question": [1985] A.C. 975 at 998. But the answer to the question "Is it an offence under CLA 1977, s.1(1) to agree to aid and abet an offence by a third party?" cannot depend on the facts of any particular case. Nor is it clear that the House of Lords can deprive a Court of Appeal decision of its binding force by saying that the point is still open without actually reversing or overruling the decision.

[38] [1983] Q.B. 751. The case was not cited in the Court of Appeal in *Hollinshead.*

persons who were not party to the agreement.[39] In *James*[40] the facts were similar to those of *Hollinshead*, and it was said that a count of conspiracy to defraud would "without question" have been appropriate.

Part 2 of the Serious Crime Bill, if enacted, will dispense with the need to charge conspiracy to defraud in such a case. It is based on the Law Commission's report *Inchoate Liability for Assisting and Encouraging Crime*.[41] Under what is at the time of writing cl.39, a person would commit an offence if he does an act capable of encouraging or assisting the commission of an offence, and he intends to encourage or assist its commission. Under cl.40, a person would commit an offence if he does an act capable of encouraging or assisting the commission of an offence, and he believes that the offence will be committed and that his act will encourage or assist its commission. Under cl.41, a person would commit an offence if he does an act capable of encouraging or assisting the commission of one or more of a number of offences, and he believes that one or more of those offences will be committed (but has no belief as to which), and that his act will encourage or assist the commission of one or more of them. The defendants in *Hollinshead* would be guilty of at least the offence under cl.41, and possibly the one under cl.40. **21–024**

UNAUTHORISED ACCESS TO A COMPUTER WITH INTENT TO COMMIT AN OFFENCE

Acts preparatory to fraud may in some circumstances be an offence under s.2 of the Computer Misuse Act 1990 ("CMA 1990"). The offence under s.2 is an aggravated form of the offence of unauthorised access to a computer, created by s.1.[42] The offence under s.1 is extended by the Police and Justice Act 2006 ("PJA 2006"), and the offence under s.2 is thus automatically extended too, but at the time of writing these amendments have not been brought into force. **21–025**

CMA 1990, s.1(1) currently provides that a person is guilty of an offence if **21–026**

> "(a) he causes a computer to perform any function with intent to secure access to any program or data held in any computer;
>
> (b) the access he intends to secure is unauthorised; and
>
> (c) he knows at the time when he causes the computer to perform the function that that is the case."

[39] The prosecution had been unable to frame the charge in that way because the whisky was to be sold abroad. See below, para.22–079.

[40] (1986) 82 Cr.App.R. 226.

[41] Law Com. No.300, Cm.6878.

[42] Except that the defendant need not actually be guilty of the offence under CMA 1990, s.1, if the only reason he is not guilty of it is that he is abroad when he does the act in question: CMA 1990, s.4(3); below, para.22–090.

PJA 2006 amends CMA 1990, s.1(1)(a) and (b) so as to refer not only to an intent to secure unauthorised access but also to an intent to enable such access to be secured. This will catch a person whose intention is to enable access to be secured by another person. According to the explanatory notes on PJA 2006 it will also catch a person whose intention is to enable *himself* to secure access at some later time; but such a person is caught already. Where a person does *x* so that he will be able to do *y* later, he plainly does *x* with intent to do *y*.

21–027 The offence under CMA 1990, s.1 is currently summary. PJA 2006 makes it indictable, and punishable on conviction on indictment with two years' imprisonment, but only in the case of offences committed after the amendment comes into force.[43]

21–028 CMA 1990, s.2(1) provides:

> "A person is guilty of an offence under this section if he commits an offence under section 1 above . . . with intent—
> (a) to commit an offence to which this section applies; or
> (b) to facilitate the commission of such an offence (whether by himself or by any other person) . . ."

21–029 The offence under CMA 1990, s.2 is triable either way, and is punishable on conviction on indictment with five years' imprisonment.[44] The section applies to all offences for which the sentence is fixed by law or which carry five years' imprisonment on a first conviction.[45] It is immaterial whether the further offence is to be committed on the same occasion as the offence under s.1 or on some future occasion.[46] So a person who accesses a program or data without authority, intending to commit or facilitate an offence of dishonesty, will usually be guilty of the offence. It is analogous to attempt in that it requires an intent in respect of a further offence. Like attempt, it can be committed even if the facts are such that the commission of the further offence is impossible.[47] But, unlike attempt, it extends to conduct which is "merely preparatory" to the offence intended,[48] and an intention to facilitate the commission of the further offence by another person is enough.[49]

CAUSING A COMPUTER TO PERFORM A FUNCTION

21–030 The actus reus of the offence under CMA 1990, s.1, and therefore also of the offence under s.2, is simply causing a computer[50] to "perform a function". This seems to mean that the defendant must cause the computer

[43] PJA 2006, s.38(2).
[44] CMA 1990, s.2(5).
[45] CMA 1990, s.2(2).
[46] CMA 1990, s.2(3).
[47] CMA 1990, s.2(4).
[48] cf. Criminal Attempts Act 1981, s.1(1).
[49] There is no offence of attempting to aid and abet an offence: Criminal Attempts Act 1981, s.1(4)(b).
[50] "Computer" is not defined.

to do something, as distinct from merely observing the screen display, reading a printout or moving the computer elsewhere.

MENS REA

The mens rea of the offence under CMA 1990, s.2 is 21–031

- an intent to secure (or, when the amendment made by PJA 2006 is brought into force, to enable to be secured) access to any program[51] or data held in any computer, which the defendant knows would be unauthorised; and
- an intent to commit, or facilitate the commission of, an offence punishable with at least five years' imprisonment.

The defendant need not intend to secure access to any particular program or data, or a program or data of any particular kind or held in any particular computer.[52] But he must *intend* to secure access (or enable access to be secured), as against being aware that his activities may have that effect; and he must *know* that the access he intends to secure (or enable to be secured) would be unauthorised, as against being aware that it might be.

Although the offences under CMA 1990, ss.1 and 2 are primarily aimed 21–032
at the practice of "hacking" from one computer into another, there is no requirement that two or more computers be involved. It is sufficient if the defendant causes a computer to perform a function with intent to secure (or enable to be secured) unauthorised access to programs or data held in the *same* computer.[53]

SECURING ACCESS TO PROGRAMS OR DATA

Where a program or data is "held in a computer",[54] CMA 1990, s.17(2) 21–033
provides that a person "secures access" to it if

> "by causing a computer to perform any function he—
>
> (a) alters or erases the program or data;
>
> (b) copies or moves it to any storage medium other than that in which it is held or to a different location in the storage medium in which it is held;[55]

[51] Including part of a program: CMA 1990, s.17(10).

[52] CMA 1990, s.1(2).

[53] *Att-Gen's Reference (No.1 of 1991)* [1993] Q.B. 94.

[54] A program or data is "held in a computer" if it is held in any removable storage medium which is for the time being "in the computer": CMA 1990, s.17(6). This expression is presumably intended to include an external storage medium used by the computer, whether or not physically connected to the computer.

[55] This presumably includes the "moving" of a file to a different folder, even if the file physically remains in the same place on the disk and the only change is to the index in the file allocation table.

(c) uses it;[56] or

(d) has it output from the computer in which it is held (whether by having it displayed or in any other manner)[57] . . ."

UNAUTHORISED ACCESS

21–034 Under CMA 1990, s.17(5), a person's access to any program or data held in a computer is unauthorised if

"(a) he is not himself entitled to control access of the kind in question to the program or data; and

(b) he does not have consent to access by him of the kind in question to the program or data from any person who is so entitled."

21–035 The words "access of the kind in question" refer to the various forms of "access" listed in CMA 1990, s.17(2).[58] In relation to each program or data, there will be one or more persons who are "entitled to control" each form of access. Once it is established that the defendant intended to secure his own access to a program or data, the first question is whether he was himself entitled to control access, of the kind that he intended to secure, to that program or data. If he was, the kind of access that he intended to secure would not be unauthorised. Even if he was not, the kind of access that he intended to secure would still not be unauthorised if a person who *was* entitled to control access of that kind, to that program or data, consented to his securing that kind of access to that program or data. Since the offence requires an *intent* to secure unauthorised access, the offence is not committed if, at the time when the defendant causes the computer to perform the function, he expects to have got the necessary consent by the time he secures access.

21–036 When the PJA 2006 amendments come into force, it will be sufficient that the defendant intends to enable access to be secured by another person, and that access would be unauthorised, and the defendant knows that it would be unauthorised. So, if D causes a computer to perform a function with intent to enable E to secure access, it must be proved that E was not himself entitled to control access of the kind that D intended to enable E to secure; that, if E did secure access of that kind, E would not have the consent of a person who was entitled to control such access; and that D knew, when he caused the computer to perform the function, that E was not entitled to control such access *and* would not have the consent of a person who was.

[56] A person "uses" a program if the function he causes the computer to perform causes the program to be executed, or is itself a function of the program: CMA 1990, s.17(3).

[57] A program is output if the instructions of which it consists are output; and the form in which any such instructions or any other data is output is immaterial: CMA 1990, s.17(4).

[58] *R. v Bow Street Metropolitan Stipendiary Magistrate, ex p. Government of USA* [2000] 2 A.C. 216 at 224, *per* Lord Hobhouse of Woodborough.

The word "control" in CMA 1990, s.17(5) does not signify physical control. It has been said that in this context it "clearly means authorise and forbid",[59] but this cannot be strictly correct: to say that a person is entitled to *forbid* access would imply that he is entitled to override an authority granted by another. If access can be authorised by either of two persons without the agreement of the other, neither is entitled to forbid access. The drafter would not have used the word "control" if it were intended to mean "authorise" and nothing more, but it is hard to see what else it might mean. **21–037**

CMA 1990, s.17(5) seems to have been aimed only at the person who is not authorised to access the program or data at all, and not at the person who is authorised to do so but is abusing that authority. The Law Commission said: **21–038**

> "Where the offence is allegedly committed by an employee, we think that an employer should only have the support of the hacking offence if he has clearly defined the limits of authorisation applicable to each employee, and if he is able to prove that the employee has knowingly and intentionally exceeded that level of authority . . .
>
> There was strong support on consultation for the view . . . that an authorised user should not commit a hacking offence merely because he uses the computer for an unauthorised purpose, and we so recommend . . . Generally, . . ., our view remains that there is nothing to distinguish the misuse of an employer's computer from the misuse of the office photocopier or typewriter . . ."[60]

It was accordingly held in *DPP v Bignell*[61] that a police officer who is authorised to extract details of vehicles from the Police National Computer does not secure unauthorised access within the meaning of CMA 1990, even if his access is for an unauthorised purpose. In *R. v Bow Street Metropolitan Stipendiary Magistrate, ex p. Government of USA*,[62] by contrast, the House of Lords held that, where an employee was authorised to access only those customer accounts that were assigned to her, her access to similar data in accounts not assigned to her was unauthorised. It was immaterial that the data she accessed was of the same kind as the data she was authorised to access: the words "of the kind in question" in s.17(5) qualify "access", not "program or data". The decision in *Bignell* was said to be "probably right", though Astill J.'s judgment included certain glosses on the statutory wording which were unnecessary and misleading. **21–039**

The question, therefore, is not whether the defendant (or, under the PJA 2006 amendments, the person whom the defendant intended to enable to secure access) was an insider or an outsider, but whether the intended **21–040**

[59] *R. v Bow Street Metropolitan Stipendiary Magistrate, ex p. Government of USA* [2000] 2 A.C. 216 at 224, *per* Lord Hobhouse of Woodborough. This dictum was applied in *Stanford* [2006] EWCA Crim 258; [2006] 1 W.L.R. 1554 in the context of the Regulation of Investigatory Powers Act 2000.

[60] Law Com. No.186, *Criminal Law: Computer Misuse*, Cm.819, paras 3.37–3.38.

[61] [1998] 1 Cr.App.R. 1.

[62] [2000] 2 A.C. 216.

access would in fact be unauthorised and whether the defendant knew that it would. *Bignell* was correctly decided on the assumption that the defendant police officers were authorised to obtain from the computer the details of *any* motor vehicle, though it would be a disciplinary offence (and an offence under the Data Protection Act) to do so otherwise than for police purposes. But there is a fine line between doing an authorised act for an unauthorised purpose and doing an unauthorised act. If the rules governing the use of the Police National Computer stated that the *only* authorised access is access for police purposes—which is surely implicit—the user's purpose in accessing the computer would itself determine whether his access was unauthorised. And it may be arguable that an intent to commit a serious offence (which is essential to the offence under CMA 1990, s.2) is in itself sufficient to make the access unauthorised.

MAKING, SUPPLYING OR OBTAINING ARTICLES FOR USE IN COMPUTER MISUSE OFFENCES

21–041 When the PJA 2006 amendments come into force, inchoate liability for computer misuse will be extended even further by CMA 1990, s.3A. This will create three new offences, of

- making, adapting, supplying or offering to supply an article intending it to be used to commit, or to assist in the commission of, an offence under CMA 1990, s.1 or 3;[63]
- supplying or offering to supply an article believing that it is likely to be used in this way;[64] and
- obtaining an article with a view to its being supplied for use in this way.[65]

"Article" includes any program or data held in electronic form,[66] such as a password. These offences will be triable either way, and punishable on conviction on indictment with two years' imprisonment.

POSSESSION, ETC. OF ARTICLES FOR USE IN FRAUDS

21–042 FA 2006, s.6(1) provides:

> "A person is guilty of an offence if he has in his possession or under his control any article[67] for use in the course of or in connection with any fraud."

[63] CMA 1990, s.3A(1). CMA 1990, s.3, as substituted by PJA 2006, creates an offence of impairing the operation of a computer as distinct from using it for criminal purposes.
[64] CMA 1990, s.3A(2).
[65] CMA 1990, s.3A(3).
[66] CMA 1990, s.3A(4).
[67] "Article" includes any program or data held in electronic form: FA 2006, s.8(1).

The offence is triable either way, and is punishable on conviction on indictment with five years' imprisonment. Examples given by the Attorney-General in debate on the Bill include the dishonest possession of a credit card reader, or of goods with the intention of using false representations to sell them.[68] There is no requirement that the article should be made or adapted for use in the commission of fraud.

The offence is in effect an extension of the offence of going equipped, contrary to s.25(1) of the Theft Act 1968 ("TA 1968"). Before it was amended by FA 2006, TA 1968, s.25(1) provided: 21–043

> "A person shall be guilty of an offence if, when not at his place of abode, he has with him any article for use in the course of or in connection with any burglary, theft or cheat."

"Cheat" for this purpose meant the offence of obtaining property by deception.[69] FA 2006 abolishes that offence, and repeals the reference to it in TA 1968, s.25. FA 2006, s.6 is wider than TA 1968, s.25 in two respects. First, it applies to articles intended for use in "any fraud", and the offence of fraud is much wider than that of obtaining property by deception. Secondly, it applies to articles which a person has in his possession or under his control at his place of abode. TA 1968, s.25 continues to apply to burglary and theft; but the two offences overlap where the article is intended for use in a theft which would also be fraud. In such a case, the fact that the article is at the defendant's place of abode is a defence under TA 1968, s.25, but not under FA 2006, s.6.

The explanatory notes to FA 2006 state: 21–044

> "Section 6 makes it an offence for a person to possess or have under his control any article for use in the course of or in connection with any fraud. This wording draws on that of the existing law in section 25 of the Theft Act 1968 . . . The intention is to attract the case law on section 25, which has established that proof is required that the defendant had the article for the purpose or with the intention that it be used in the course of or in connection with the offence, and that a general intention to commit fraud will suffice."

As authority for this proposition the notes cite *Ellames*,[70] where the court said:

> "In our view, to establish an offence under s.25(1) the prosecution must prove that the defendant was in possession of the article, and intended the article to be used in the course of or in connection with some future burglary, theft or cheat. But it is not necessary to prove that he intended it to be used in the course of or in connection with any specific burglary, theft or cheat; it is enough to prove a general intention to use it for some burglary, theft or cheat; we think that this view is supported by the use of the word 'any' in s.25(1). Nor,

[68] *Hansard*, HL Vol.673, col.1451 (July 19, 2005).
[69] TA 1968, s.25(5).
[70] (1974) 60 Cr.App.R. 7.

in our view, is it necessary to prove that the defendant intended to use it himself; it will be enough to prove that he had it with him with the intention that it should be used by someone else."

The Attorney-General confirmed (resisting an amendment which would have expressly required intention) that the drafting of s.6 was intended to attract the case law on TA 1968, s.25.[71] Thus it will be necessary, on a charge under FA 2006, s.6, to prove that the defendant intended the article to be used by someone (not necessarily him) in the course of, or in connection with, an offence of fraud contrary to FA 2006, s.1.

21–045 It has been held that the offence under TA 1968, s.25 was committed where the defendant kept counterfeit goods in a warehouse, with a view to selling them to agents who he knew would sell them on to unsuspecting purchasers.[72] If this is right, the same is presumably true of the new offence. It is questionable whether it is within the spirit of either offence. In effect it amounts to liability for preparing to aid and abet an offence by another, which is not a form of liability currently known to the law.[73] Such conduct is more appropriately charged under the Trade Marks Act 1994, s.92.

MAKING OR SUPPLYING ARTICLES FOR USE IN FRAUDS

21–046 FA 2006, s.7(1) provides:

> "A person is guilty of an offence if he makes, adapts, supplies or offers to supply any article[74]—
>
> (a) knowing that it is designed or adapted for use in the course of or in connection with fraud, or
>
> (b) intending it to be used to commit, or assist in the commission of, fraud."

The offence is triable either way, and is punishable on conviction on indictment with 10 years' imprisonment.

21–047 In debate on the Bill, Dominic Grieve MP proposed that it should be necessary for the prosecution to satisfy both paragraph (a) *and* paragraph (b). The Solicitor General explained that this would restrict the scope of the offence too much.

> "[I]t is possible to imagine the supply of an ordinarily innocent article . . . to be used in the commission of a fraud. The example of a credit card reader comes to mind. The device has not been made or adapted with the fraud in mind but could be supplied with the intention of it being used fraudulently. . . .
>
> Conversely, a criminal may make an article specifically for a fraud—for example, a device covertly to copy credit cards—but be ambivalent about

[71] *Hansard,* HL Vol.673, col.1452 (July 19, 2005).
[72] *Re McAngus* [1994] Crim. L.R. 602; see Richard Lawson (1994) 138 S.J. 339.
[73] But see the Serious Crime Bill: above, para.21–024.
[74] Including any program or data held in electronic form: FA 2006, s.8(1).

whether the person to whom it is supplied will use it for fraud. He will not have the intention necessary for clause 7(1)(b) but will fall within clause 7(1)(a)."[75]

[75] *Hansard,* SC Deb.B, cols 47–48 (June 20, 2006).

CHAPTER 22

INTERNATIONAL FRAUD

Fraud often has an international dimension. Can a person be convicted in England and Wales of an offence committed elsewhere? What if some elements of the offence occurred in England and Wales and others occurred elsewhere? These issues are not peculiar to fraud, but are particularly likely to arise in fraud cases.[1] This chapter attempts to set out **22–001**

[1] "A fairly brief perusal of the reported case law will show that cases of fraud or dishonesty have reached the appellate courts, in criminal or extradition proceedings, more frequently than all other types of cross-frontier crime combined": Michael Hirst, *Jurisdiction and the Ambit of the Criminal Law* (2003) at 112.

the principles applicable to cross-border offences generally, and those applicable under the Criminal Justice Act 1993 ("CJA 1993") to certain fraud offences committed on or after June 1, 1999. A few of the other offences discussed in this book have their own rules, and these are explained in the context of the offences in question.[2]

AMBIT OR JURISDICTION?

22–002 This is, inevitably, a complicated subject. In recent years it has become even more complicated, as a result of both judicial activism and messy legislation. These complications have been exacerbated by persistent confusion as to the very nature of the issue under discussion. When certain elements of an offence are alleged to have occurred outside England and Wales—an area conveniently referred to as "the jurisdiction"[3]—practitioners and courts habitually ask whether the English courts *have jurisdiction* to try the alleged offence. Sometimes Parliament provides that an offence committed outside the jurisdiction may be tried in the English courts, as if this were an extension of the courts' jurisdiction. This usage is incorrect. The issue is not one of jurisdiction, but of the ambit of the offence. The question is whether the foreign elements of the alleged offence prevent it from being an offence at all, as a matter of substantive English criminal law.

22–003 In *Treacy v DPP*[4] the defendant posted a blackmailing letter from London to Frankfurt, and the question was whether his conviction of blackmail could stand. The Court of Appeal accepted that there is a "general rule that English criminal law is applied on the territorial principle and no conduct constitutes an offence unless it occurs in the territory of England and Wales". This rule was said to need no authority.[5] However, the court concluded that Treacy had "made" a demand within the meaning of s.21 of the Theft Act 1968 ("TA 1968") when he posted the letter containing the demand. In the House of Lords it was again common ground that the appeal turned on the construction of s.21. Lords Reid and Morris thought that the section applied only to demands made within the jurisdiction, and that the posting of the letter did not constitute the making of a demand within the meaning of the section. Lords Hodson and Guest agreed that the section applied only to demands made within the jurisdiction, but thought that the posting of the letter *was* the making of a demand.

[2] e.g. Financial Services and Markets Act 2000, s.397(6) and (7) (above, paras 13–024, 13–043); CJA 1993, s.62 (above, para.13–081). The rules under the Computer Misuse Act 1990 are included in this chapter for convenience, since they resemble those under CJA 1993.

[3] Also referred to in this chapter, for brevity only and with apologies to any readers in other jurisdictions, as "here". "Abroad" similarly means "outside England and Wales", and includes Scotland and Northern Ireland.

[4] [1971] A.C. 537.

[5] (1971) 55 Cr.App.R. 113 at 116.

Lord Diplock agreed with Lords Hodson and Guest on this point, but **22–004**
also gave what he regarded as an alternative reason[6] for holding that Treacy's conduct fell within the section. He argued that, although the section must be read as being subject to *some* territorial limitation, it was necessary to do this *only* to the extent required by international comity; and comity required *only* that the section be read as excluding conduct outside the jurisdiction which has no harmful consequences within the jurisdiction. For the purpose of this argument he sought to clarify the nature of the point at issue.

> "[T]he Court of Appeal . . . certified that the following point of law of general public importance was involved in the decision: 'Whether, when a person with a view to gain for himself or with intent to cause loss to another makes an unwarranted demand with menaces by letter posted in England and received by the intended victim in West Germany, the person can be tried in England on a charge under section 21 of the Theft Act 1968.' In view of the way in which the question is framed and the wide-ranging argument about 'jurisdiction' before your Lordships' House, I am prompted to state at the outset that the question in this appeal is not whether the Central Criminal Court had jurisdiction to try the defendant on that charge but whether the facts alleged and proved against him amounted to a criminal offence under the English Act of Parliament. . . .
>
> The fact that the appellant was arrested in Greater London and committed for trial at the Central Criminal Court unquestionably gave to that court jurisdiction to determine whether or not he was guilty of the offence for which he was indicted. That offence was the statutory offence of 'blackmail' as defined in section 21 of the Theft Act 1968. . . . The only question for your Lordships' House is what did Parliament mean when it enacted in 1968 that: 'A person is guilty of blackmail if, with a view to gain for himself or another or with intent to cause loss to another, he makes any unwarranted demand with menaces'?"[7]

In *Manning*[8] the Court of Appeal was primarily concerned to counter **22–005**
Lord Diplock's view that the only limitations on the ability of English courts to deal with extra-territorial crime are those imposed by considerations of international comity.[9] But the court also took issue with his analysis of the nature of those limitations.

> "First, that the matter is simply one of the construction of the statute creating the offence was a novel suggestion when it was made, and has not been repeated in any subsequent case, even in those cases . . . that have shown sympathy for Lord Diplock's approach. . . . . Second, the issue had always been

[6] It is not clear why Lord Diplock thought this was an *alternative* ground. If Lords Reid and Morris were right, the prohibited conduct (the making of the demand) took place in Germany; and Lord Diplock did not argue that that conduct had harmful consequences in England. His "alternative" reason *assumes* that the prohibited conduct was the act of posting the letter.

[7] [1971] A.C. 537 at 558–560.

[8] [1999] Q.B. 980.

[9] On this point *Manning* has been overruled by *Smith (Wallace Duncan) (No.4)* [2004] EWCA Crim 631; [2004] Q.B. 1418; below, para.22–062.

thought, before *Reg. v Treacy* . . . , to be indeed one of jurisdiction, and not of the definition of the offence. The English courts had jurisdiction subject to two conditions: that the defendant was physically present before the court (a matter that cannot be affected by construction of the statute) and that he had completed the crime, as defined, within England and Wales. The latter was an overriding requirement that was applied in the light of, rather than which affected the terms of, the definition of the crime charged. Third, Lord Diplock's approach was contrary to existing authority[10] which, although not of course binding on the House of Lords, was in our respectful view too long established to be disturbed save by legislation."[11]

22–006 It is odd that the court thought it necessary to challenge Lord Diplock's analysis on this point: the court might well have accepted that his Lordship was right about this but wrong to say that comity was the only criterion.[12] In any event its criticism is, with respect, misconceived. Since it would be pointless to exclude jurisdiction over conduct which is not an offence anyway, the court's view amounts to saying that the English courts cannot try extra-territorial conduct even if it is criminal under English law. But to say that conduct is criminal under English law *means* that it can be tried and punished in the English legal system. Jurisdictional rules determine whether an alleged offence can be tried by the Crown Court, by a magistrates' court or by either.[13] If *neither* can try it, it is meaningless to say that it is an offence at all.[14]

22–007 Lord Diplock's was not in fact the first judicial analysis to be formulated in terms of ambit rather than jurisdiction.[15] Moreover his analysis was not challenged in the other speeches in *Treacy*. On the contrary, it was implicitly accepted, since it was agreed that the case turned on the construction of TA 1968, s.21(1). That provision creates a substantive offence. It does nothing else. Its construction can only go to the ambit of

[10] i.e. *Harden* [1963] 1 Q.B. 8 (below, para.22–034). In that case the Court of Criminal Appeal simply assumed that the question was where the offence had been committed, rather than considering whether it was Parliament's intention that it should be necessary to ask this question. But Lord Diplock did not suggest that the courts had always *recognised* that the principles they were applying were in fact principles of statutory construction. His approach was not inconsistent with the *decision* in *Harden* at all.

[11] [1999] Q.B. 980 at 995.

[12] Indeed the courts have, paradoxically, been able to reach a position resembling Lord Diplock's comity theory by ignoring his Lordship's observations on the nature of the issue: see below, para.22–014.

[13] If there were a rule that a defendant cannot be tried unless he is physically present before the court, that would also be a rule going to the jurisdiction of the court; but it is clear that there is no such rule. See *Archbold* paras 3–197 *et seq*.

[14] Offences under service law are triable by court-martial (or, once the Armed Forces Act 2006 is in force, the Court Martial), and usually by neither the Crown Court nor a magistrates' court; but these are not criminal offences in the strict sense.

[15] In *Board of Trade v Owen* [1957] A.C. 602, for example, the defendants were convicted of conspiracy to defraud. The alleged fraud took place in Germany, and the House of Lords held that the agreement therefore fell outside the offence of conspiracy—not that it fell within that offence but could not be tried for want of jurisdiction. See also *Cox v Army Council* [1963] A.C. 48 at 67, *per* Viscount Simonds, L.C.: "apart from those exceptional cases in which specific provision is made in regard to acts committed abroad, the whole body of the criminal law of England deals only with acts committed in England."

the offence it creates—that is, the question of what conduct is within the offence and what conduct is not. The provision can be read as if it included the words "in England or Wales". According to Lord Diplock it can be read as if it included words such as "in England and Wales, or elsewhere if there are harmful consequences in England or Wales". But it cannot be read as incorporating a *procedural* rule that, where the offence is committed outside England and Wales, the English courts cannot try it.

Nor is it true that Lord Diplock's analysis had not been repeated in any subsequent case. In *Kelly* the House of Lords construed the Merchant Shipping Act 1894, s.686[16] as extending the substantive ambit of criminal offences so as to include acts done by British subjects on board foreign ships "which if done in England and Wales or Scotland would be offences against the respective criminal law of those countries"[17] but which, by implication, are not in fact offences against those laws. In *DPP v Stonehouse* Lord Keith of Kinkel said: **22–008**

> "My Lords, the general principle of the territoriality of crime is of great importance. The English Courts do not assert jurisdiction to try any person whether a citizen of this country or not, for acts done in a foreign land. The more correct approach is to say that such an act cannot in principle constitute a crime by the law of England rather than that the act is a crime but the court does not have jurisdiction."[18]

And in *R. v Governor of Pentonville Prison, ex p. Osman* the Court of Appeal said:

> "The English court has power to try any defendant who is properly brought before the court. In that sense the court always has jurisdiction over the defendant. But if the defendant is alleged to have committed an offence outside the territorial jurisdiction of the court, then unless the offence is an extra-territorial one, he has committed no offence against English law. The court would have jurisdiction over the defendant, but he could not be indicted."[19]

In *Manning* the court expressed concern that Pt I of CJA 1993, which makes it possible for certain frauds committed outside England and Wales to be punished under English law, had not yet been brought into force.[20] **22–009**

[16] See now Merchant Shipping Act 1995, s.281.

[17] [1982] A.C. 665 at 675–676, *per* Lord Roskill.

[18] [1978] A.C. 55.

[19] [1990] 1 W.L.R. 277 at 289. It would be more accurate to say the defendant could be indicted, but would have to be acquitted.

[20] Part 1 of CJA 1993 was based on the Law Commission's report No.180, *Criminal Law: Jurisdiction over Offences of Fraud and Dishonesty with a Foreign Element*, HC 318. The Commissioner primarily responsible for this report was Brian Davenport Q.C., but by the time it appeared he had been succeeded by Richard Buxton Q.C.—who, as Buxton L.J., delivered the judgment in *Manning*. The report acknowledged that "In one sense, a court always has 'jurisdiction' over a defendant who has been properly brought before it; strictly, it is incorrect to refer to our courts having (or lacking) 'jurisdiction' to try someone for a

The drafting of that Act suggests that Parliament shared Lord Diplock's view. CJA 1993, s.2(3) provides that a person "may be guilty of" specified offences in specified circumstances—not that the Crown Court has jurisdiction to try them in those circumstances.[21] The Computer Misuse Act 1990 similarly treats the matter as one of substantive liability. Sections 4–9 have the cross-heading "Jurisdiction", but the sidenotes to ss.4, 6 and 7 refer to the "territorial scope of offences"; and the drafting of these provisions is in terms of the commission of the offence, or the accused's guilt. There is no suggestion that they relate to the power of an English court to try a charge.

22–010 Section 1A of the Criminal Law Act 1977 ("CLA 1977") seems to be drafted on the same basis. It extends the offence of conspiracy created by s.1 of the Act so as to include conspiracies in relation to which certain conditions are satisfied—broadly, conspiracies in England and Wales to do things abroad which would be offences if done in England or Wales. Section 1A(6) then provides:

> "In the application of this Part of this Act to an agreement in the case of which each of the above conditions is satisfied, a reference to an offence is to be read as a reference to what would be the offence in question but for the fact that it is not an offence triable in England and Wales."

If extra-territoriality deprived the English courts of jurisdiction but did not prevent the conduct in question from being an offence, this provision would be unnecessary.[22]

22–011 The Crown Court is a creature of statute (originally the Courts Act 1971). Its jurisdiction is now governed by the Supreme Court Act 1981,[23] of which s.45(2) provides:

particular offence, since to say that our courts lack jurisdiction to try someone for a particular offences is to say that he has not committed the offence: *R. v Governor of Pentonville Prison, ex p. Osman* [see above, para.22–008] . . . For convenience, however, we refer in this report . . . to 'jurisdiction' as relating to the question whether he is triable in this country for an offence that he has committed somewhere." The second sentence of this passage appears to contradict the first. The question is not whether the person is triable for an offence that he has committed, but whether he has committed an offence at all.

[21] A.P. Simester and G.R. Sullivan, *Criminal Law: Theory and Doctrine*, 2nd edn (2003) at 477 argue that CJA 1993 is defective because it merely confers jurisdiction without extending the territorial scope of the offences to which it relates. But the words "may be guilty of" make it clear that s.2(3) is about substantive liability, not jurisdiction.

[22] See also CJA 1993, s.62(1) and (2) (above, paras 13–081 and 13–082: a person "is not guilty" of certain offences unless there is a connection of a specified kind with the United Kingdom); Financial Services and Markets Act 2000, s.397(6) and (7) (above, paras 13–024, 13–043: certain offence-creating provisions "do not apply" unless there is such a connection; Insolvency Act 1986, s.350(4) (above, para.15–064: "It is not a defence" in proceedings for certain offences that anything relied on as constituting the offence was done outside England and Wales). But cf. Enterprise Act 2002, s.190(3) ("No proceedings may be brought for an offence . . . in respect of an agreement outside the United Kingdom . . ."; above, para.20–017). Sometimes a statute provides *both* that an offence may be committed outside the jurisdiction *and* that, if so committed, it may be tried within the jurisdiction: e.g. Anti-terrorism, Crime and Security Act 2001, s.109(2) (above, para.19–042).

[23] Renamed the Senior Courts Act 1981, with effect from a day to be appointed, by the Constitutional Reform Act 2005.

> "Subject to the provisions of this Act, there shall be exercisable by the Crown Court—
>
> (a) all such appellate and other jurisdiction as is conferred on it by or under this or any other Act . . ."

Section 46(2) provides:

> "The jurisdiction of the Crown Court with respect to proceedings on indictment shall include jurisdiction in proceedings on indictment for offences wherever committed . . .".

If the view expressed in *Manning* is right, this must be read as being subject to a common law exception excluding jurisdiction in the case of offences committed abroad, except where the common law exception has been displaced by statute. It is submitted that it cannot be so read.

22–012 The terminology of jurisdiction is undeniably convenient. By treating extra-territoriality as a separate issue from that of liability, it enables each to be discussed independently of the other. In considering whether a person can be convicted in England and Wales for something done abroad, it is natural to refer to the conduct as "the offence" and to ask whether the English courts "have jurisdiction" over it. Treating the issue as one of substantive law is more accurate, but tends to involve tiresome circumlocutions. And it rarely matters which terminology is used. But sometimes it does. For example, if a trial judge concludes that the defendant has committed no offence because he acted abroad, there is no case to answer. The judge should direct an acquittal, and the acquittal will be final unless set aside. If it were a question of jurisdiction, a purported acquittal would be a nullity.

22–013 Sometimes incorrect terminology leads to fallacious reasoning. In *Atakpu*[24] it was held that a person who disposes of property which he has already stolen does not thereby steal it again, and that if he steals it outside the jurisdiction he does not commit theft by bringing it into the jurisdiction to dispose of it. TA 1968, s.3(1), which provides that a person can "appropriate" property by keeping it or dealing with it as owner where he has come by it *without stealing it,* does not apply where the defendant has already "stolen" it within the meaning of TA 1968; and the fact that the original "theft" took place abroad does not prevent it from being a "stealing" within the meaning of TA 1968, because s.24 (which defines "stolen goods") refers to goods "which have been stolen . . . whether the stealing occurred in England or Wales or elsewhere". This reasoning assumes that "stealing" means the same in TA 1968, s.3(1) as it does in s.24 (where it clearly does include an act done abroad which would be theft if done in England and Wales). But s.24 is clearly intended to *extend* the concept of "stolen goods" *beyond* those that have literally been stolen contrary to s.1(1). It is only for the sake of brevity that it refers to "goods

[24] [1994] Q.B. 69.

which have been stolen" outside England and Wales. This understandably loose drafting does not affect the principle that "stealing" outside England and Wales is not just an offence over which the English courts lack jurisdiction: it is not an offence (under English law) at all. It is submitted with respect that, by overlooking this fundamental principle, the court fell into error.

22–014 A more far-reaching example is the reasoning of the Court of Appeal in *Smith (Wallace Duncan)*[25] and *Smith (Wallace Duncan) (No.4)*,[26] where deception offences were held to include extra-territorial conduct on the basis that "Questions of jurisdiction although they involve substantive law have a strong procedural element and are less immutable than issues of pure substantive law".[27] That may be true of questions of jurisdiction; but the issue under consideration was not one of jurisdiction at all. It was one of "pure substantive law", namely whether the defendant's conduct amounted to a particular offence. In both cases the Court of Appeal was extending the scope of the substantive law with retrospective effect. Indeed it is questionable whether these decisions complied with Art.7 of the European Convention on Human Rights.

SUBSTANTIVE OFFENCES

GROUP A OFFENCES COMMITTED ON OR AFTER JUNE 1, 1999

22–015 Part I of CJA 1993, which is based on recommendations made by the Law Commission,[28] extends a number of substantive offences so as to include certain conduct which would previously have fallen outside those offences on grounds of extra-territoriality. The offences affected are divided into two groups: A and B.[29] The Group A offences are substantive; Group B consists of the inchoate offences of attempt, conspiracy and incitement to commit a Group A offence, and conspiracy to defraud. Pt I of CJA 1993 came into force on June 1, 1999,[30] and does not apply to any act, omission or other event occurring before that date. Even if offences committed before that date can technically be Group A or B offences, this is academic because liability for them falls to be determined without reference to CJA 1993.

[25] [1996] 2 Cr.App.R. 1; below, para.22–061.

[26] [2004] EWCA Crim 631; [2004] Q.B. 1418; below, para.22–062.

[27] [2004] EWCA Crim 631; [2004] Q.B. 1418 at [56].

[28] Law Com. No.180, *Criminal Law: Jurisdiction over Offences of Fraud and Dishonesty with a Foreign Element*.

[29] CJA 1993, s.1. The Secretary of State can add any offence to, or remove any offence from, either group, by order subject to the affirmative resolution procedure: CJA 1993, s.1(4)–(6).

[30] SI 1999/1189 and 1999/1499.

THE GROUP A OFFENCES

The Group A offences are those listed in CJA 1993, s.1(2). Those that fall within the scope of this book[31] are: **22–016**

(1) all the offences under the Fraud Act 2006 ("FA 2006")—i.e.
   - fraud,[32]
   - possession of articles for use in fraud,[33]
   - making or supplying articles for use in fraud,[34]
   - fraudulent trading by sole trader (etc.),[35] and
   - obtaining services dishonestly;[36]

(2) the following offences under TA 1968:
   - theft,[37]
   - false accounting,[38] and
   - false statements by company directors (etc.);[39]

(3) the following offences under the Forgery and Counterfeiting Act 1981:
   - forgery,[40]
   - copying a false instrument,[41]
   - using a false instrument,[42]
   - using a copy of a false instrument,[43] and
   - possessing, or making or possessing materials for the making of, false instruments of the kinds specified in s.5(5);[44] and

(4) cheating the public revenue.[45]

[31] The Group A offences not dealt with in this book are blackmail, handling stolen goods, retaining stolen credits, various counterfeiting offences (added by SI 2000/1878) and possession of false identity documents contrary to the Identity Cards Act 2006, s.25.
[32] Above, Chs 1–6.
[33] Above, para.21–042.
[34] Above, para.21–046.
[35] Above, Ch.8.
[36] Above, Ch.10.
[37] Above, Ch.9.
[38] Above, paras 12–001 *et seq*.
[39] Above, para.12–030.
[40] Above, paras 11–001 *et seq*.
[41] Above, para.11–044.
[42] Above, para.11–046.
[43] Above, para.11–048.
[44] Above, para.11–053.
[45] Above, paras 16–040 *et seq*.

22–017 The following were also Group A offences but are abolished by FA 2006:

- obtaining property by deception,[46]
- obtaining a money transfer by deception,[47]
- obtaining services by deception,[48]
- evasion of liability by deception,[49]
- obtaining a pecuniary advantage by deception,[50] and
- procuring the execution of a valuable security by deception.[51]

The rules in Pt I of CJA 1993 therefore apply to these offences if they were committed between June 1, 1999 and January 14, 2007.[52]

22–018 Among the offences *not* included are fraudulent trading by a company,[53] and all the offences discussed in Chs 13–20 above (except cheating the public revenue).[54]

THE TERRITORIAL SCOPE OF GROUP A OFFENCES

22–019 CJA 1993, s.2(3) is the lynchpin of Pt I of the Act. It provides:

> "A person may be guilty of a Group A offence if any of the events which are relevant events in relation to the offence occurred within the jurisdiction."

The wording of s.2(3) implies that it supplements the rules which had previously applied, and that a person might be guilty of a Group A offence under the old rules even if the condition in s.2(3) is not satisfied. But this does not seem to be possible, since every case which satisfies the old rules will also satisfy the condition in s.2(3). In effect, the new rule *supersedes* the old.

22–020 In order to understand s.2(3) we must examine two issues. First, what is a "relevant event"? And second, how is it determined whether a relevant event occurs within the jurisdiction?

[46] Above, paras 4–095 *et seq.*
[47] Above, paras 4–116 *et seq.*
[48] Above, paras 4–121 *et seq.*
[49] Above, paras 4–134 *et seq.*
[50] Above, paras 4–146 *et seq.*
[51] Above, paras 4–151 *et seq.*
[52] Subject to the transitional provisions of FA 2006: above, para.1–006.
[53] Above, Ch.8. The Law Commission did not include this offence on the grounds that (a) the conduct proscribed is not susceptible of division into two or more distinct events, and (b) it would not be desirable to consider the jurisdictional rules relating to it in isolation from the other offences under the companies legislation: Law Com. No.180, para.3.14. The first ground is unconvincing because it would apply equally to theft; the latter is undermined by the fact that fraudulent trading *is* now a Group A offence if the fraudulent business is not a company.
[54] Some of these offences have their own rules as to territorial ambit, which are given in the chapter dealing with the offence in question.

Relevant events

"Any . . . event . . . proof of which is required for conviction"

Only if an event is a "relevant event" does its occurrence within the jurisdiction satisfy the condition in CJA 1993, s.2(3). In relation to all the Group A offences *except fraud*,[55] a relevant event is defined by CJA 1993, s.2(1) as **22–021**

> "any act or omission or other event (including any result of one or more acts or omissions) proof of which is required for conviction of the offence".

Taking s.2(1) and (3) together, therefore, and with the exception of a charge of fraud, the prosecution must prove that

- every relevant event occurred *somewhere*, and
- at least one relevant event occurred within the jurisdiction.

Elements of the offence which are not events

Where the actus reus of an offence includes the existence of specified circumstances, those circumstances are not a relevant event because they are not an act, omission or other event. The condition in CJA 1993, s.2(3) is therefore not satisfied merely because those circumstances can be said to have existed within the jurisdiction. For example, on a charge of theft the prosecution must prove that the property appropriated belonged to a person other than the defendant. The appropriation is a relevant event, because it is an act proof of which is required for conviction of the offence. The fact that the property belonged to another is a fact proof of which is required for conviction of the offence; but it is not an act, omission or other event, so it cannot be a relevant event. So an appropriation in France of property located in England is not theft under English law.[56] **22–022**

In general the same applies to mens rea. On a charge of theft the prosecution must prove that the defendant intended permanently to deprive of the property the person to whom it belonged. This too is a fact proof of which is required for conviction of the offence; but again it is not an act, omission or other event. It is therefore not sufficient that the defendant intended the permanent deprivation to occur in England or Wales. In the case of fraud, however, it may be sufficient that events intended by the defendant occur within the jurisdiction, although they are not part of the actus reus.[57] **22–023**

Events which need not be proved

If the alleged conduct results in consequences which need not be proved in order to secure a conviction, those consequences are by definition not relevant events. For example, theft of a British company's property abroad **22–024**

[55] In the case of fraud, certain events falling outside the definition in CJA 1993, s.2(1) are also relevant events: below, para.22–030.

[56] But conduct in France might amount to an appropriation in England: below, paras 22–033 *et seq*.

[57] Below, para.22–030.

may result in the company's insolvency; but the insolvency is not a relevant event because it need not be proved to secure a conviction. A dishonest transfer of funds from one bank account to another is not indictable as theft merely because the receiving bank is within the jurisdiction: since the funds are appropriated when they are transferred by the paying bank,[58] it need not be proved that they arrived, and their arrival is therefore not a relevant event. In this respect CJA 1993 is less radical than the "comity theory" advanced by Lord Diplock in *Treacy v DPP*,[59] and accords with the more limited version of that theory developed by the courts in recent years.[60] Indeed, with the exception of fraud,[61] s.2(3) has no real effect on offences (such as theft) whose actus reus consists solely of prohibited conduct as distinct from subsequent events.[62]

Events which are not elements of the offence

22–025 It is arguable that an event may be a relevant event even though it is not an *element* of the offence at all. This is not what the Law Commission meant.

> "Our principal recommendation is quite simply that our courts should have jurisdiction to try a charge of one of the listed offences if any event that is required to be proved in order to obtain a conviction of that offence takes place in England and Wales. That would, in particular, mean that where the definition of the offence forbids conduct producing a certain result our courts would have jurisdiction if any part of that conduct, or any part of the defined specified result, took place here. Similarly, our courts would have jurisdiction over crimes whose definition relates only to the accused's conduct (as has been suggested to be the case with theft) if any part of the conduct forbidden by the definition of the offence took place here.
>
> We regard it as important, however, that jurisdiction should be taken by the courts of this country only if an element *required to be proved for conviction* takes place here. It would in our view be excessive, and would also lead to substantial arguments about jurisdiction of the type that on grounds of economy and efficiency we seek to avoid, if the courts of this country sought jurisdiction merely because a preparatory, or incidental, act or event that happened to form part of the 'narrative' took place here."[63]

The Commission gave an example of this latter point:

> "Armed with documents that contain false statements that he has previously prepared in London, D calls on V in Paris. He there produces the documents to V, in reliance on which V gives him a sum of money. The court would not have jurisdiction, since neither the deception nor the obtaining took place in England and Wales. The fact that D's preparatory act of preparing the documents took place here is immaterial."[64]

[58] If not sooner: above, paras 9–101 *et seq*.
[59] [1971] A.C. 537; below, para.22–060.
[60] Below, paras 22–061 *et seq*.
[61] Below, para.22–030.
[62] But such offences may be affected by CJA 1993, s.4: see below, paras 22–033 *et seq*.
[63] Law Com. No.180, paras 2.27–2.28 (italics in original).
[64] Law Com. No.180, para.2.29(d). The example relates to the offence of obtaining property by deception, which has since been abolished.

CJA 1993 arguably goes further than the Commission intended. In practice the prosecution may allege the occurrence of an event which is not part of the definition of the offence, but which *in this case* must be proved before there can be a conviction. Consider, for example, the case put by the Commission (assuming that the old law of deception applies). Suppose it is accepted that the person who swindled V was the person who prepared the documents; but D denies being that person. There is no evidence that it was D who swindled V, other than the evidence that it was D who prepared the documents. In these circumstances the jury might well be directed that they could not convict unless they were satisfied that it was D who prepared the documents. The preparing of the documents is, literally, an act "proof of which is required for conviction of the offence". If the Act is read literally it achieves precisely what the Commission thought it important to avoid. **22–026**

If the courts are willing to construe the Act in the light of the Commission's report, there is no difficulty. The intention is clear, not only from the passages quoted above but also from the description of the recommended solution as being "along the lines" of New Zealand's Crimes Act 1961, s.7.[65] Section 6 of that Act provides that no act done or omitted outside New Zealand is an offence. But s.7 provides: **22–027**

> "For the purpose of jurisdiction, where any act or omission forming part of any offence, or any event necessary to the completion of any offence, occurs in New Zealand, the offence shall be deemed to be committed in New Zealand, whether the person charged with the offence was in New Zealand or not at the time of the act, omission, or event."

There is no ambiguity here. The question is simply what forms part of, or is necessary to the completion of, the *offence*. That is a matter of substantive criminal law. Under CJA 1993, by contrast, the question is what must be *proved*; and that arguably varies from case to case.

Alternative elements

There is a similar difficulty even if the Law Commission's intention prevails. Some of the Group A offences can be committed in more than one way. The prime example is fraud, which can be committed by false representation, by failing to disclose information or by abuse of position. On a charge which alleges (for example) false representation and failing to disclose information in the alternative, is the alleged false representation a relevant event? On a literal reading it would seem not: the making of a false representation is not an act proof of which is *required* for a conviction, because a failure to disclose will do instead; and vice versa. This would drive a coach and horses through the legislation. It is submitted that, if the prosecution can secure a conviction by proving any one of two or more events, each of those events is an event "proof of which is required for **22–028**

[65] Law Com. No.180, para.2.26.

conviction of the offence" within the meaning of CJA 1993, s.2(1), and is therefore a relevant event. Again this interpretation would accord with the New Zealand model, since alternative ways of committing an offence can fairly be described as "forming part of" the offence.

Secondary participation

22–029 Suppose A, in England, aids and abets conduct by B in France which would be theft if it occurred in England. Is the aiding and abetting a relevant event? It is no part of the definition of theft; but, in relation to A, the prosecution must prove it (as well as the appropriation) in order to secure a conviction. Arguably, therefore, it *is* a relevant event. In that case A is guilty under English law even if, because the appropriation occurred in France, B is not. But it is doubtful whether it is possible to aid and abet an offence which (under English law) is not committed.[66] If B were in fact guilty of theft and the Crown Court merely lacked jurisdiction to try him, the problem would not arise; but this is not the case.[67]

Other relevant events in the case of fraud

22–030 In relation to fraud, an event of the kind described in CJA 1993, s.2(1) is always a relevant event. But, by virtue of s.2(1A), certain events falling outside s.2(1) are *also* relevant events. If the fraud involves an intention to make a gain, and the gain occurs, the occurrence of the gain is a relevant event. If the fraud involves an intention to cause a loss or to expose another to a risk of loss, and the loss occurs, the occurrence of the loss is a relevant event. Since it is possible to secure a conviction of the offence without proving that a gain or a loss occurred, the occurrence of gain or loss is not a relevant event within s.2(1); but, if gain or loss does occur, that is a relevant event anyway, by virtue of s.2(1A).

22–031 Section 2(1A) applies only if the defendant succeeds in making a gain or causing a loss. If he makes a false representation in France with intent to make a gain or cause a loss in England or Wales, he commits the offence only if he succeeds in that intention. If no gain or loss in fact occurs, he is guilty of an attempt only.[68] If his intention is to expose another to a *risk* of loss, s.2(1A) does not apply unless the loss actually occurs. It is not sufficient that he succeeded in his intention and someone in England or Wales was in fact exposed to a risk of loss.

Place of occurrence immaterial

22–032 CJA 1993, s.2(2) provides that, for the purpose of determining whether a particular event is a relevant event, it is immaterial where it occurs. This rule applies to all Group A offences, including fraud. Under s.2(3) the

[66] See David Ormerod (ed.), *Smith and Hogan, Criminal Law*, 11th edn (2005) at 205–207.
[67] See above, paras 22–002 *et seq*.
[68] It is immaterial that the attempt is committed abroad: below, para.22–068.

place where the event occurs may be crucial in determining whether there is an offence, if the event *is* a relevant event (and no other relevant event occurs in England or Wales); but, in determining whether the event is a relevant event, we must disregard the place where it occurred. It is not clear why this provision was thought necessary. Even if the definition of a relevant event in s.2(1) could somehow be read as excluding events that occur outside the jurisdiction, a relevant event thus excluded would not satisfy the condition in s.2(3) anyway.

The location of an event

Under CJA 1993, s.2(3), a Group A offence is committed only if a relevant event occurs within the jurisdiction. Once a relevant event has been identified, it may therefore be necessary to determine where it occurred. Under the old law this was sometimes difficult. In the case of Group A offences, CJA 1993, s.4 resolves most of the difficulties by providing that certain cross-border events are taken to have occurred in England and Wales. Section 4 seems to have this effect even if the event in question is not a relevant event, though this does not appear to have been the Law Commission's intention;[69] but, since the condition in s.2(3) is not satisfied by the occurrence within the jurisdiction of an event other than a relevant event, the point seems academic. Certainly s.4 does not turn non-relevant events into relevant events: it merely deems certain events to occur in England and Wales even if they actually occur elsewhere. This becomes significant only if the event in question is a relevant event (and no *other* relevant event occurs in England or Wales). **22–033**

Obtaining property

Until recently it was accepted that the offence of obtaining property by deception (now abolished) was committed where the property was obtained, not where the deception was practised. There was no offence under English law unless the property was "obtained" within the jurisdiction. If the property was sent from one jurisdiction to another, identifying the jurisdiction in which it was "obtained" sometimes involved subtle distinctions. In *Harden*[70] the defendant, in England, deceived a Jersey company into sending him cheques. His letters to the company stated that the offers they contained could be accepted by sending a cheque. It was held that he obtained the cheques when they were posted in Jersey, because it was agreed that their receipt by the Jersey postmaster should be equivalent to receipt by Harden himself.[71] In *Tirado*[72] the defendant **22–034**

[69] The Commission's recommendation was that the rules in what is now CJA 1993, s.4 should apply for the purpose of what is now CJA 1993, s.2(3): Law Com. No.180, para.2.32.

[70] [1963] 1 Q.B. 8.

[71] cf. *Stoddart* (1909) 2 Cr.App.R. 217, where the posting in England of letters containing postal orders was held to be an obtaining of the postal orders in England even though the letters were addressed to Holland, because the Post Office received them on behalf of the addressee.

[72] (1974) 59 Cr.App.R. 80.

similarly induced his victims to post money from Morocco; but there was no basis for inferring any agreement that the posting amounted to receipt,[73] so the money was obtained in England. In *R. v Governor of Pentonville Prison, ex p. Herbage (No.3)*[74] the applicant induced investors to send him money on standard terms which provided that all such payments should be lodged at an address in Holland; but there was evidence that the investors were in practice expected to send the money by post. The court applied *Harden* to the extent of holding that, prima facie, the money was obtained in the country where it was posted; but ultimately it was a question of fact for the jury, who might reasonably attach more significance to what was expected of the investors than to what was technically required. The standard terms were not thought to be crucial.

22–035 CJA 1993, s.4(a) is designed to avoid these difficulties. It provides that, in relation to a Group A offence,

> "there is an obtaining of property in England and Wales if the property is either despatched from or received at a place in England and Wales".

So a person to whom property is despatched from abroad is treated, like Harden, as obtaining it when it is despatched; but, unlike Harden, he is also treated as obtaining it *in England and Wales*.

22–036 On the face of it, this is so even if he never *receives* it at all—just as Harden would still have obtained the cheques (in Jersey) if they had not arrived in England. Indeed it seems to be so even if he is abroad at the time. This does not appear to have been the Law Commission's intention. The Commission's recommendation referred only to "property which is despatched from outside, *but received within*, England and Wales or vice versa".[75] The Commission described the recommendation as applying to "cases in which money or property is despatched from *or* received in England and Wales",[76] but went on to explain that it

> "would give the court jurisdiction . . . to try some cases where an essential part of the criminal activity has taken place in this country. It would also obviate the present need for the jury to determine the highly technical question, that arises where property is despatched abroad *but received here* (or vice versa), of whether or not the property is to be treated as obtained in England and Wales."[77]

22–037 These inconsistencies suggest that the Commission did not address its mind to the question of property which is despatched but not received. But CJA 1993, s.4(a) arguably applies to property despatched from abroad *only*

[73] The court was not referred to *Baxter* [1972] 1 Q.B. 1, in which *Harden* was apparently treated (wrongly) as authority for a general rule that property sent by post is "obtained" in the place where it is posted.
[74] (1987) 84 Cr.App.R. 149.
[75] Law Com. No.180, para.2.32 (italics supplied).
[76] Law Com. No.180, para.2.30 (italics supplied).
[77] Law Com. No.180, para.2.30 (italics supplied).

if (a) it was received in England and Wales, or (b) although it was not received, it was in fact (that is, without the help of s.4(a)) obtained when it was despatched. On this view, Harden would be deemed to have obtained the cheques here even if they were lost in the post, because he did in fact obtain them when they were posted; but Tirado would not be deemed to have obtained the money at all (let alone to have done so here) merely because it was posted, if it never arrived. This interpretation might be supported by analogy with s.4(b), which more plainly contains a drafting error along similar lines.[78]

22–038 The offence of obtaining property by deception, at which CJA 1993, s.4(a) is primarily aimed, was abolished by FA 2006. In relation to that offence, s.4(a) will bite only if the property is despatched from or received in England and Wales before January 15, 2007, or on or after that date as a result of a deception before that date.[79] But s.4(a) applies to any Group A offence, and can affect any Group A offence for whose purposes the obtaining of property is a relevant event. Suppose D, in France, dishonestly induces V to send him property from England. D is charged with theft of the property.[80] The only relevant event is the appropriation. Where did the appropriation occur? It depends which event constituted the appropriation. If the property was appropriated by D when V sent it,[81] the appropriation occurred in England. If the property was appropriated by D when D received it, the appropriation occurred in France; but in this case s.4(a) seems to apply. D in fact obtained the property in France, but is deemed to have obtained the property in England (and thus to have appropriated it in England) when it was despatched in England. This seems to have been the Law Commission's intention. The recommendation implemented by s.4(a) was that, for the purpose of what is now s.2(3), there should be a rule that "property which is despatched from outside, but received within, England and Wales or vice versa is *appropriated or* obtained in England and Wales".[82]

Communication

22–039 CJA 1993, s.4(b) provides that, in relation to a Group A offence,

> "there is a communication in England and Wales of any information, instruction, request, demand or other matter if it is sent by any means—
>
> (i) from a place in England and Wales to a place elsewhere; or
>
> (ii) from a place elsewhere to a place in England and Wales."

[78] Below, para.22–040.
[79] See above, para.1–006.
[80] Fraud would now be a more appropriate charge. V's parting with the property in England would be a relevant event by virtue of CJA 1993, s.2(1A): above, para.22–030.
[81] See above, paras 9–113 *et seq*.
[82] Law Com. No.180, para.2.32 (italics supplied).

22–040 If this is read literally, its effect is surprising. When any information (etc.) is sent to England and Wales from abroad or vice versa on or after June 1, 1999, for the purposes of a Group A offence the information is deemed to have been communicated in England and Wales. The main object, clearly, is to ensure that the condition in CJA 1993, s.2(3) is satisfied, because a relevant event (the communication of the information) will have occurred within the jurisdiction. But s.4(b) also seems to say that the information is deemed to be communicated (within the jurisdiction) even if it is not in fact communicated at all. One would expect it to say that the information is communicated within the jurisdiction if it is sent to or from England and Wales *and is communicated* (somewhere); but it does not. It is arguable that a person does not "make" a false representation within the meaning of FA 2006, s.2 unless the representation is communicated to the intended representee.[83] If the representation does not arrive, there is only an attempt. But, even if the courts accept this view, on a literal reading of CJA 1993, s.4(b) it does not matter, because once the representation is sent it is deemed to have been communicated anyway. This does not appear to have been the intention. The Law Commission's recommendation was that the rule should apply to information "the communication of which is initiated outside, but received [*sic*] within, England and Wales or vice versa".[84]

22–041 Indeed, on a literal reading s.4(b) does not seem to achieve its objective in the case of a Group A offence which *can* be committed by sending matter without communicating it. One such offence is blackmail. The House of Lords held in *Treacy v DPP* that a person "makes" a demand with menaces within the meaning of TA 1968, s.21 if he posts a blackmailing letter from England to Germany. The offence is complete even if the letter never arrives. Arguably it follows that, if the letter were posted from Germany to England, the demand would be "made" in Germany even if the letter did arrive. CJA 1993, s.4(b) is apparently intended to ensure that, on those facts, the demand would be deemed to have been made in England, thus satisfying the condition in s.2(3). But s.4(b) does not help if the communication is not a relevant event anyway. Where an account is falsified in Germany, for example, it is not deemed to have been falsified merely because it is sent to head office in England: the sending of the account is not a relevant event, so deeming it to have occurred within the jurisdiction does not help to satisfy the condition in s.2(3).[85] According to *Treacy*, communication of the demand is not an event "proof of which is required for conviction" of blackmail; so it is not a relevant event. CJA 1993, s.4(b) deems it to have occurred within the jurisdiction; but that does

[83] See above, paras 4–080 *et seq*.

[84] Law Com. No.180, para.2.32. See also para.2.31: "[T]he act of transmitting 'information' across national boundaries should be regarded as occurring both in the place where it is originated and in the place where it is received."

[85] cf. *R. v Governor of Pentonville Prison, ex p. Osman* [1990] 1 W.L.R. 277 at 297; Michael Hirst, *Jurisdiction and the Ambit of the Criminal Law* (2003) at 171–172.

not help with s.2(3) because the only relevant event is the posting of the letter, and that occurred in Germany.

A literal reading of s.4(b) would thus ensure both that it does not have the intended effect, and that it does have an effect which was apparently not intended. Part I of CJA 1993 is about the territorial scope of offences. It extends the scope of the offences to which it applies, so that they can be committed by conduct which previously would not have been sufficient because of the place where it occurred. It is not intended to extend the scope of offences by including conduct which previously would not have been sufficient at all, irrespective of where it occurred. This suggests that CJA 1993, s.4(b) should be construed as meaning that **22–042**

(a) there is a *sending* in England and Wales of any information (etc.) not only if it is sent abroad from England and Wales, but also if it is sent to England and Wales from abroad (even if it does not arrive); and

(b) there is a *communication* in England and Wales of any information (etc.) not only if it is communicated in England and Wales after being sent from abroad, but also if it is communicated abroad after being sent from England and Wales.

Limb (a) applies where the sending of the information (etc.) is a relevant event, as in the case of blackmail. Limb (b) applies where the communication of the information (etc.) is a relevant event, which is probably so in the case of fraud by false representation. In this chapter it is assumed that the courts will adopt this construction.

CJA 1993, s.4(b) does not appear to be confined to cases where the offence-creating provision expressly requires a sending or communication of information (etc.) as an element of the offence, and thus as a relevant event. Suppose D, in France, instructs a bank in England to transfer funds. According to *R. v Governor of Pentonville Prison, ex p. Osman*,[86] he appropriates the funds by sending the instructions. He therefore appropriates them in France. But, under s.4(b), instructions sent from France to England are deemed to be sent in England. Arguably, therefore, the appropriation (which in this case consists in the sending of the instructions) is deemed to have occurred in England. **22–043**

Other relevant events

CJA 1993, s.4 applies only to two kinds of event—the obtaining of property, and the "communication" (i.e. sending or communication) of information, etc. If a relevant event is neither of those things, s.4 does not apply. The event is not deemed to have occurred in any place in which it did not in fact occur. So, for the purposes of the rule in CJA 1993, s.2(3), the question is where it did in fact occur. **22–044**

[86] [1990] 1 W.L.R. 277.

Things done abroad regarded as including consequences here

22–045 In the case of human conduct, it might seem that the answer to this question would be obvious, because a person's conduct can only occur in the place where he is. But this is true only of his physical acts or omissions. His conduct may also be regarded as including the consequences of those acts or omissions. And these consequences may occur far from the place where he is. If they occur in England and Wales, he may be regarded as having acted in England and Wales even if he is abroad at the time.

22–046 In *Baxter*,[87] for example, the defendant sent fraudulent football pool claims from Northern Ireland to England. It was held that, although his attempt to obtain money by deception had begun when he posted the claims, it continued until they were delivered, and was therefore committed in England too. In *DPP v Stonehouse*[88] the defendant, a well-known public figure, faked his own death while in Miami, intending to enable his wife to obtain the proceeds of life insurance policies in England. It was held that he too had committed an attempt in England by ensuring that his death would be reported here. These decisions proceeded on the basis that an attempt is not indictable in England and Wales unless committed within the jurisdiction. It has now been held that there is no such rule;[89] and, even if there were, CJA 1993 abrogates it in the case of attempts to commit Group A offences.[90] But these cases illustrate a general point, not confined to the law of attempts—that a person's conduct can sometimes be regarded as occurring in a country other than the one he is in.[91] This principle may be relevant to Group A offences which are defined in such a way that CJA 1993, s.4 has no application.

22–047 The definition of forgery, for example, suggests that there is only one relevant event: the making of a false instrument. Forgery is committed in the place where the false instrument is made.[92] If a person in France sends instructions or data so as to cause a computer in England to generate a false instrument, the analogy of *Baxter* and *Stonehouse* suggests that he has made a false instrument in England. It seems to follow that, if he were in England and the computer in France, he would *not* have made a false instrument in England, and therefore would not be guilty of forgery. The courts would undoubtedly try to avoid this conclusion. One approach would

[87] [1972] 1 Q.B. 1.

[88] [1978] A.C. 55.

[89] *Latif* [1996] 1 W.L.R. 104.

[90] CJA 1993, s.3(3); below, para.22–068.

[91] See also *Treacy v DPP* [1971] A.C. 537 at 558, where Lord Hodson suggested that a blackmail demand posted from another country to England might be "made" in England on the basis that it was a continuing demand, subsisting until the victim received it. In *Forsyth* [1997] 2 Cr.App.R. 299 the defendant sent stolen money from Geneva with instructions that it be credited to an account in London, and was held to have undertaken or assisted in the disposal or realisation of the money (within the meaning of TA 1968, s.22) in England on the basis that the disposal or realisation continued until the money arrived in the account in England.

[92] This need not be the place where the maker of the instrument intends it to be used: *Hornett* [1975] R.T.R. 256; *El-Hakkaoui* [1975] 1 W.L.R. 396.

be to argue that an offence may be committed in England and Wales even if no relevant event occurs here, provided that the defendant's physical acts or omissions occur here. This would be consistent with the approach recently evolved by the courts for offences to which CJA 1993 does not apply. But it would mean that CJA 1993, s.2(3) had to be supplemented by other criteria not stated in the legislation—which, given the complexity of the legislation, is not an appealing prospect. Alternatively it might be argued that the words "makes a false instrument" conceal two distinct events: the conduct that results in a false instrument coming into being, and the coming into being of the false instrument. Both are relevant events, because both must be proved. So it is sufficient under s.2(3) if *either* event occurs within the jurisdiction. It is submitted that this is the better view.

In the case of theft there is only one relevant event, namely the appropriation. A person can appropriate funds in a bank account by securing their transfer to another account. This appears to be so whether he sends instructions which are acted upon by the bank[93] or he accesses the bank's computer and gives it the necessary instructions directly.[94] On this basis, a person in France commits theft in England if he dishonestly secures the transfer of funds from an account in England. But it is arguable that he would *already* have committed theft, by doing the acts in France that result in the transfer: those acts are deemed under CJA 1993, s.4(b) to have been done in England.[95] And, having stolen the funds once, he cannot steal them again.[96] **22–048**

Things done abroad regarded as done here through an agent

Sometimes a person abroad can be regarded as having acted within the jurisdiction because an agent within the jurisdiction acted on his behalf. In *Secretary of State for Trade v Markus*[97] a company with offices in London obtained money from investors in Germany by arranging for salesmen to call on them and show them brochures relating to a bogus investment trust. A director of the company was charged with conniving at the offence of fraudulently inducing a person to take part in an investment arrangement.[98] Under the law as it was then understood, the offence had to be *completed* in England and Wales. It was not completed until the victims took part in the arrangement. The victims were in Germany throughout. It was therefore argued that they took part in the arrangement in Germany. The House of Lords held that they did so in England, by proxy. Although they handed over their application forms and their money in Germany, the documents were sent to London for processing by the company. In carrying out this **22–049**

[93] As in *Tomsett* [1985] Crim. L.R. 369: above, para.9–103.

[94] As in *R. v Governor of Brixton Prison, ex p. Levin* [1997] Q.B. 65: above, para.9–104.

[95] Above, para.22–039.

[96] *Atakpu* [1994] Q.B. 69; above, para.9–110.

[97] [1976] A.C. 35.

[98] Prevention of Fraud (Investments) Act 1958, s.13(1)(b). See now Financial Services and Markets Act 2000, s.397(2): above, para.13–002.

processing the company was acting as the investors' agent. They had, through the company, taken part in the arrangement in England.

22–050 The offence charged in *Markus* is not a Group A offence, but the principle might be adapted to Group A offences. In *Oliphant*[99] the defendant was employed in the Paris office of a London firm. It was his duty to send regular accounts of his receipts so that they could be entered in the cash-book in London, but he sent accounts which were incomplete. It was held that he had omitted material particulars from the cash-book within the jurisdiction. It was immaterial that he had not personally made the entries in London, but had made them through the innocent agency of the clerk. On this basis it seems likely a person "makes" a false instrument within the meaning of the Forgery and Counterfeiting Act 1981, s.1,[100] or "falsifies" an account within the meaning of TA 1968, s.17,[101] if, while abroad, he induces an innocent agent in England to do so.[102] Arguably a person holding a fiduciary position in France can commit fraud if his agent in England acts on instructions from the fiduciary in a way which amounts to an abuse of the fiduciary's position; but this might be academic, since the fiduciary would presumably be deemed to have sent the instructions (and thus abused his position) in England by virtue of CJA 1993, s.4(b).[103]

Obtaining of services

22–051 CJA 1993, s.4(a) applies to an obtaining of property but not to an obtaining of services. Suppose D, in England, downloads valuable data from a computer in the USA without making payment as required. This is an obtaining of services within the meaning of FA 2006, s.11, but where does it occur? Does a person obtain a service in the place where he is when he obtains it, or in the place where the thing is done that constitutes the service?[104] By analogy with the cases on appropriation, the courts are likely to say that he does so in *both* places.

Omissions

22–052 Some Group A offences (including fraud,[105] false accounting[106] and cheating the revenue)[107] can be committed by failing to disclose information that ought to be disclosed. If the defendant, in Paris, dishonestly omits to

[99] [1905] 2 K.B. 67; cf. *Shuck* [1992] Crim. L.R. 209.
[100] Above, para.11–001.
[101] Above, para.12–001.
[102] If the agent were not innocent but were aware of the falsity, the agent would be guilty of the offence and the principal would be guilty of aiding and abetting it: see below, para.22–137.
[103] It would in any event be sufficient if an intended gain or loss occurred in England and Wales: above, para.22–030.
[104] This assumes that the provision of services must involve the doing of a thing, if only by an inanimate object. See above, para.10–007.
[105] Above, Ch.5.
[106] Above, para.12–001.
[107] *Dimsey* [2000] Q.B. 744; above, para.16–044.

disclose information to someone in London, CJA 1993, s.4(b) does not apply directly because it applies only to communications—not to a *failure* to communicate. So the question is simply: where did the omission occur? Arguably a person can only omit to do something in the place where he is at the relevant time. But on the basis of *Oliphant*[108] it might be arguable that a failure to disclose occurs in the place where the information would have been disclosed if it had been disclosed as it should have been. Even if that place would not have been London, it could (in this hypothetical scenario) be *deemed* to be London, by virtue of s.4(b).[109]

Immaterial matters

A person may be guilty of a Group A offence whether or not he was a British citizen[110] (unless "jurisdiction is given to try the offence in question by an enactment which makes provision by reference to the nationality of the person charged"),[111] and whether or not he was in England and Wales at any material time. So a foreign national can commit an offence under English law without entering the jurisdiction, for example by doing an act abroad which amounts to an appropriation of property in England.[112] **22–053**

Although there is no express provision to this effect, it seems that a person may be guilty of a Group A offence by virtue of a relevant event occurring within the jurisdiction even if he did not intend it to occur here. For example, CJA 1993, s.2(1A) would seem to apply to a false representation made in France with intent to make a gain or cause a loss in France, if the gain or loss unexpectedly resulted in England or Wales. The words "the gain" in s.2(1A)(a) and "the loss" in s.2(1A)(b) clearly refer to the gain that the defendant intended to make, or the loss that he intended to cause (or to a risk of which he intended to expose another). If the gain or loss that occurred were otherwise the same as the gain or loss that he intended, it seems unlikely that its occurrence in an unexpected location would prevent it from being the gain or loss that he intended, and therefore from being a relevant event. But, if he did not suspect that the desired consequences might occur anywhere but in France, it is not obvious why their unexpected occurrence in England should render him liable under English law. **22–054**

OTHER SUBSTANTIVE OFFENCES

In this section we examine the territorial scope of substantive offences which are not Group A offences within the meaning of CJA 1993, or are Group A offences but were committed before Pt I of CJA 1993 came into force on June 1, 1999. **22–055**

[108] [1905] 2 K.B. 67; above, para.22–050.
[109] It would in any event be sufficient that the intended gain or loss occurred in England and Wales: above, para.22–030.
[110] CJA 1993, s.3(1)(a).
[111] CJA 1993, s.3(4).
[112] Above, para.22–048.

COMMON LAW OFFENCES

22–056 Until recently, at least, the common law principle was clear. Nothing done outside England and Wales was an offence at common law.

> "[T]he common law of England did not originally apply beyond the shores of the realm. At common law, criminal courts had jurisdiction only over things done within their own counties . . . The common law had no conception of territorial waters or of crimes committed abroad. These are all the creation of legislation."[113]

As Viscount Simonds pointed out in *Cox v Army Council*,[114] "the whole body of the criminal law of England deals only with acts committed in England" except where statute provides otherwise. So, for example, a person whose conduct in France in 1998 was a fraud on the Inland Revenue cannot be charged with cheating the revenue unless his conduct can somehow be regarded as having occurred in England or Wales, without the assistance of CJA 1993, s.4.

STATUTORY OFFENCES

22–057 With the exception of offences of cheating the revenue committed before June 1, 1999, all the offences with which we are here concerned are statutory. Parliament has the competence to make it an offence under English law for a Frenchman to smoke in the streets of Paris. Determining the territorial scope of a statutory offence is, in principle, a matter of construing the provision that creates it. And it is a principle of statutory interpretation that criminal offences are not intended to have extra-territorial effect unless that intention is clearly expressed.[115] Taken to its logical conclusion, this principle would suggest that there would be no offence under English law if a British company entered into a transaction abroad which would be prohibited if effected within the jurisdiction, such as the provision of financial assistance towards the acquisition of its shares.[116] But it may be arguable that, in view of the mischief at which the offence is aimed, Parliament cannot have intended that it should be possible to evade the prohibition merely by arranging for the transaction to be effected through a foreign bank account. It is ultimately a question of construction.

22–058 In practice, however, the courts have tended to ignore this point. Until recently they treated statutory offences as having extra-territorial ambit only where the statute *expressly* so provides. In the absence of such provision it was therefore necessary to determine whether an alleged

[113] Michael Hirst, *Jurisdiction and the Ambit of the Criminal Law* (2003) at 5.
[114] [1963] A.C. 48 at 67.
[115] *Gold Star Publications Ltd v DPP* [1981] 1 W.L.R. 732 at 737, *per* Lord Simon of Glaisdale (dissenting); *BBC Enterprises Ltd v Hi-Tech Xtravision Ltd* [1990] 2 W.L.R. 1123 at 1127 (affirmed [1991] 2 A.C. 327), *per* Staughton L.J.
[116] Above, paras 14–049 *et seq*.

offence was committed within the jurisdiction. For this purpose a distinction was sometimes drawn between those offences that consist simply of the prohibited conduct ("conduct crimes") and those that are not committed unless specified events ensue ("result crimes").[117] Obtaining property by deception was a result crime, because deception alone was not sufficient: the deception had to result in an obtaining of property. Theft is a conduct crime, because it is complete once the property is appropriated with the necessary intent. A conduct crime was, obviously, committed in the place where the prohibited conduct occurred. A result crime, by contrast, was committed in the place where the result which *completed* the offence occurred. In *Harden*,[118] for example, it was held that the defendant did not commit an offence under English law when by false pretences he induced a company to post cheques from Jersey, because the offence was completed when the cheques were posted in Jersey.[119] This "terminatory theory"[120] did not treat conduct crimes and result crimes as fundamentally different. It followed logically from the principle that the place in which an offence is committed must necessarily be the place in which the event occurs which completes the commission of the offence. That principle had different effects when applied to result crimes and to conduct crimes; but it was the same principle.

In recent years the courts have come to regard the terminatory theory as **22–059**
unduly restrictive in permitting a conviction *only* where the offence is completed within the jurisdiction, and have adopted a more flexible approach. On this view, the rule against extra-territorial offences is based solely on considerations of international comity. The rule therefore applies *only* to the extent that comity so requires. Comity is infringed *neither* by a rule that it is sufficient if the offence is completed within the jurisdiction (even if the prohibited conduct occurs elsewhere) *nor* by a rule that it is sufficient if the prohibited conduct occurs within the jurisdiction (even if the offence is completed elsewhere). This view resembles the approach now adopted in Pt I of CJA 1993, under which it is sufficient that any relevant event (that is, any event proof of which is required for conviction) occurs within the jurisdiction. It may thus enable the courts to achieve results similar to those which CJA 1993 was designed to achieve, in relation to events occurring before the legislation came into force on June 1, 1999.

[117] But it may be an element of the offence that an event should occur, without any requirement that it should occur as a result of the defendant's conduct: e.g. Domestic Violence, Crime and Victims Act 2004, s.5.

[118] [1963] 1 Q.B. 8.

[119] Cases in which this approach was assumed to be correct include *R. v Pentonville Prison, ex p. Khubchandani* (1980) 71 Cr.App.R. 241; *Thompson* (1984) 79 Cr.App.R. 191; *Beck* (1985) 80 Cr.App.R. 355; *Nanayakkara* [1987] 1 W.L.R. 265; *Re Nagdhi* [1990] 1 W.L.R. 317.

[120] The test is sometimes referred to as one of where the "gist" of the offence occurred; but it seems to be assumed that the gist of the offence is the event that completes it, which is not obviously so.

22–060 The "comity theory" was advanced by Lord Diplock in *Treacy v DPP.*[121] The question for the House of Lords was whether the posting of a blackmailing letter from England to Germany amounted to the offence of blackmail under English law. The other Law Lords assumed that the answer turned solely on whether, by posting the letter, the appellant had "made" a demand within the meaning of TA 1968, s.21. The majority (including Lord Diplock) concluded that he had. But Lord Diplock thought that this was not crucial, because the question ought to be approached in a different way.

> "The source of any presumption that Parliament intended that the right created by the Act to punish conduct should be subject to some territorial limitation upon where the conduct takes place or its consequences take effect can, in my view, only be the rules of international comity, and the extent of the limitation, where none has been expressed in words, can only be determined by considering what compliance with those rules requires. . . . [T]he rules of international comity, in my view, do not call for more than that each sovereign state should refrain from punishing persons for their conduct within the territory of another sovereign state where that conduct has had no harmful consequences within the territory of the state which imposes the punishment. I see no reason for presuming that Parliament in enacting the Theft Act 1968 intended to make the offences which it thereby created subject to any wider exclusion than this. In my view, where the definition of any such offence contains a requirement that the described conduct of the accused should be followed by described consequences the implied exclusion is limited to cases where *neither* the conduct *nor* its harmful consequences took place in England or Wales."[122]

22–061 Although this approach found no support in *Treacy* itself,[123] Lord Diplock's suggestion that the position should be determined by the requirements of international comity has since received broad acceptance. First it was invoked as justifying the extension of attempt and conspiracy to conduct outside the jurisdiction which is directed at the commission of an offence within the jurisdiction.[124] This was relatively easy, since it was obviously unsatisfactory that English law should be powerless against those trying or planning to commit crimes here. But in *Smith (Wallace Duncan)*[125] the Court of Appeal went further, holding that there was an offence under TA 1968, s.15[126] when the defendant, in London, secured by deception a transfer of funds between accounts in New York. This involved departing from *Harden*,[127] where it was assumed that an obtaining of property outside the jurisdiction could not be the offence of obtaining by false pretences under the Larceny Act 1916. The court did not doubt the correctness of *Harden*, and purported to treat the issue as turning on the construction of

121 [1971] A.C. 537.
122 [1971] A.C. 537 at 564 (italics in original).
123 It was however cited with apparent approval in *Baxter* [1972] 1 Q.B. 1 at 11.
124 *Somchai Liangsiriprasert v Government of the USA* [1991] 1 A.C. 225; *Sansom* [1991] 2 Q.B. 130; *Latif* [1996] 1 W.L.R. 104; below, paras 22–085 *et seq*.
125 [1996] 2 Cr.App.R. 1.
126 Now repealed by FA 2006.
127 [1963] 1 Q.B. 8; above, para.22–034.

TA 1968. But its conclusion was based primarily on the absence of any reasons of international comity for the English courts to decline jurisdiction. It is questionable how much bearing this had on the question of what Parliament intended in 1968. Indeed the court revealingly observed that jurisdiction depended on *common law*[128]—which was plainly untrue, since the offence in question was statutory.

This approach was accepted, *obiter*, in *Caresana*.[129] In *Manning*[130] a differently constituted Court of Appeal held that *Smith* was wrongly decided, and followed *Harden* instead. But when *Smith* was reconsidered as *Smith (Wallace Duncan) (No.4)*[131] (following a reference by the Criminal Cases Review Commission), *Manning* was held to be wrong and *Smith (No.1)* right. On this view it is sufficient not only if the last required event occurred within the jurisdiction, but also if substantial activities constituting the crime took place within the jurisdiction and there is no reason of comity why it should not be tried by the English courts. The court that decided *Smith (No.1)* had been entitled to develop the common law in the way that it had. **22–062**

Fundamental to the court's reasoning in *Smith (No.4)* is the assumption that *Smith (No.1)* was a decision about a common law rule restricting the jurisdiction of the English courts. For example, the court accepted the assertion in *Smith (No.1)* that "Questions of jurisdiction, though involving substantive law, contain a strong procedural element"; but in neither case did the court explain what this "procedural element" is. As we have pointed out,[132] the extent to which extra-territorial conduct may be criminal is a matter of substantive law. It has nothing to do with procedure. The idea that it does is a reflection of the myth that extra-territoriality goes to jurisdiction. Had the court in *Smith (No.1)* been right in thinking that the issue turned on a procedural rule of common law, it arguably *would* have been entitled to develop the common law in the way it purported to do. But what it in fact did was to extend the territorial ambit of the deception offences, retrospectively, and without considering Parliament's intention in creating them. It is submitted with respect that *Manning* is right on this point[133] and the *Smith* decisions wrong. **22–063**

The *Smith* decisions do not go as far as the view advanced by Lord Diplock in *Treacy*. Whereas Lord Diplock thought it sufficient if conduct abroad has harmful *consequences* within the jurisdiction, the *Smith* decisions emphasise the fact that substantial parts of the alleged *conduct* occurred here. Since the courts seem untroubled by the existence of earlier authority in this area, they might yet go further and embrace Lord **22–064**

128 [1996] 2 Cr.App.R. 1 at 16–17.
129 [1996] Crim. L.R. 667.
130 [1999] Q.B. 980.
131 [2004] EWCA Crim 631; [2004] Q.B. 1418.
132 Above, paras 22–002 *et seq*.
133 But not as regards the court's view that extra-territoriality goes to jurisdiction rather than ambit.

Diplock's approach in its entirety. But this would go even further than CJA 1993,[134] and therefore seems unlikely.

INCHOATE OFFENCES

THE GROUP B OFFENCES

22–065 Part I of CJA 1993 also extends the extra-territorial ambit of certain inchoate offences, described as Group B offences. The Group B offences are

- attempting to commit a Group A offence;
- conspiracy to commit a Group A offence;
- conspiracy to defraud; and
- incitement to commit a Group A offence.[135]

The new rules do not apply to a conspiracy, attempt or incitement before June 1, 1999,[136] even if the intention was that a Group A offence should be committed on or after that date.

THE LOCATION OF AN EVENT

22–066 CJA 1993, s.4, which deems certain events to have occurred in England and Wales even if they actually occurred elsewhere, applies in relation to Group B offences.

CONDUCT ABROAD AIMED AT FRAUD HERE

GROUP B OFFENCES

22–067 When CJA 1993 was passed it was generally thought that inchoate offences were not indictable unless committed within the jurisdiction, though a person might sometimes be regarded as having committed an offence within the jurisdiction despite being abroad at the relevant time.[137] The courts have since abandoned this rule,[138] but in the case of Group B offences committed on or after June 1, 1999 it is abrogated by CJA 1993.

[134] A harmful consequence of the defendant's conduct is not a "relevant event" within the meaning of the Act unless the prosecution must prove it to secure a conviction: above, para.22–024.

[135] CJA 1993, s.1(3).

[136] CJA 1993, s.78(5).

[137] Above, paras 22–045 *et seq*.

[138] *Somchai Liangsiriprasert v Government of the USA* [1991] 1 A.C. 225; *Sansom* [1991] 2 Q.B. 130; *Latif* [1996] 1 W.L.R. 104; below, paras 22–085 *et seq*.

Attempt to commit a Group A offence

CJA 1993, s.3(3) provides: 22–068

> "On a charge of attempting to commit a Group A offence, the defendant may be guilty of the offence whether or not—
>
> (a) the attempt was made in England and Wales;
>
> (b) it has an effect in England and Wales."

So an attempt to commit a Group A offence is indictable even if it occurs abroad and has no effect in England and Wales, provided that the Group A offence would itself have been indictable—which in turn depends on whether a relevant event would have occurred within the jurisdiction.

Attempts indictable by virtue of Criminal Attempts Act 1981, section 1A

CJA 1993, s.3(3) is subject to an exception. Section 1A of the Criminal Attempts Act 1981 ("CAA 1981"), inserted by CJA 1993, enables a person in certain circumstances to be convicted of attempting to commit a Group A offence if he attempts in England and Wales to do something abroad which would be a Group A offence if done here.[139] But CJA 1993, s.3(3) does not apply where the charge is brought by virtue of CAA 1981, s.1A.[140] If the thing attempted would not be a Group A offence because no relevant event would have occurred here, the attempt is not *in fact* an attempt to commit a Group A offence. It may nonetheless be indictable *as* an attempt to commit a Group A offence, by virtue of CAA 1981, s.1A—but *only* if it is committed in England and Wales. In this case CJA 1993, s.3(3) does not apply. In order to determine whether the attempt *is* committed in England and Wales, it may be necessary to apply the principles applicable in cases that are not governed by CJA 1993 at all.[141] 22–069

It is only s.3(3) of CJA 1993 that is disapplied where the charge is brought by virtue of CAA 1981, s.1A: CJA 1993, s.4 still applies.[142] It may be arguable, for example, that the sending of a message from France to England counts as an act done in England (by virtue of CJA 1993, s.4(b)), and may therefore constitute an attempt to commit a Group A offence (by virtue of CAA 1981, s.1A) although the Group A offence would not itself be indictable because no relevant event would have occurred here. 22–070

Conspiracy to commit a Group A offence

CJA 1993, s.3(2) provides: 22–071

[139] Below, para.22–099.
[140] CJA 1993, s.3(6).
[141] See above, paras 22–045 *et seq*.
[142] Above, paras 22–033 *et seq*. Cf. CLA 1977, s.1A(11), which makes express provision broadly corresponding to CJA 1993, s.4(b): below, para.22–00. In this case CJA 1993, s.4(b) alone would not achieve the desired result because CLA 1977, s.1A is not confined to conspiracy to commit Group A offences. It does not follow that CJA 1993, s.4(b) would not apply (together with CLA 1977, s.1A(11)) where the conspiracy *is* to commit a Group A offence.

> "On a charge of conspiracy to commit a Group A offence . . . the defendant may be guilty of the offence whether or not—
>
> (a) he became a party to the conspiracy in England and Wales;
>
> (b) any act or omission or other event in relation to the conspiracy occurred in England and Wales."

So a conspiracy to commit a Group A offence is indictable even if it is entered into abroad and nothing is done in England and Wales in pursuance of it, provided that the Group A offence would itself have been indictable had it been committed—which depends whether a relevant event would have occurred within the jurisdiction.

22–072 CLA 1977, s.1A, inserted by CJA 1993, enables a person in certain circumstances to be convicted of conspiracy to commit an offence if he conspires in England and Wales to do something abroad which would be an offence if done here.[143] But CJA 1993, s.3(2) does not apply where the charge is brought by virtue of CLA 1977, s.1A.[144] If the agreed course of conduct would not involve the commission of a Group A offence because no relevant event would have occurred here, the agreement is not *in fact* a conspiracy to commit a Group A offence. It may nonetheless be indictable *as* a conspiracy to commit a Group A offence, by virtue of CLA 1977, s.1A—but *only* if there is some act or omission in relation to it in England and Wales. CJA 1993, s.3(2) does not apply. In this case it is expressly provided that an act done by means of a message counts as an act done in England and Wales if the message is sent or received here.[145]

Conspiracy to defraud

22–073 CJA 1993, s.3(2) applies equally to a charge of conspiracy to defraud in England and Wales. Such a conspiracy is therefore indictable even if it is entered into abroad and nothing happens here in relation to it. But this applies only if the conspiracy is to defraud *in England and Wales*. Indeed, if it is not a conspiracy to defraud in England and Wales, it is not indictable at common law at all, even if it is entered into here and carried out here.[146] Determining whether a conspiracy falls within this description may involve two issues: (a) what kinds of event amount to defrauding in England and Wales, and (b) what constitutes an agreement to bring about such an event.

Defrauding in England and Wales

22–074 A person can be defrauded in a variety of ways,[147] and in some cases it may be debatable whether the defrauding occurs in England and Wales. Sir John Smith thought it arguable that, just as a person can be killed or

[143] See below, para.22–109.
[144] CJA 1993, s.3(5).
[145] CLA 1977, s.1A(11).
[146] *Board of Trade v Owen* [1957] A.C. 602.
[147] See above, Ch.7.

wounded only in the place where he is, so he can be defrauded only in the place where he is.[148] This argument was rejected in *Naini*,[149] where it was held that a person resident abroad is defrauded within the jurisdiction if property is obtained from him here. This seems questionable. Lord Radcliffe said in *Welham v DPP*:

> "I think that there are one or two things that can be said with confidence about the meaning of this word 'defraud'. It requires a person as its object: that is, defrauding involves doing something to someone. Although in the nature of things it is almost invariably associated with the obtaining of an advantage for the person who commits the fraud, it is the effect upon the person who is the object of the fraud that ultimately determines its meaning."[150]

In principle, therefore, it would seem that a person is defrauded when he is dishonestly induced to part with his property (which might arguably occur either in the place where he is or in the place where the property is before he parts with it), not when the fraudster obtains the property as a result. If the defrauding consists in a direct infringement of his proprietary rights, on the other hand (such as an appropriation of his property without his consent), the defrauding presumably occurs in the place where the infringement occurs. This might arguably be either the place where the property is[151] or the place where the infringer is. If the defrauding consists in preventing the victim from getting something that he might otherwise have got, it may be arguable that he is defrauded either in the place where he is (or, perhaps, the place where he would have been when he got the thing in question, had he done so) or in the place where the fraudster is when he does the act that prevents the victim from getting the thing. The law is hopelessly unclear about all this. **22–075**

In *Tarling (No.1) v Government of the Republic of Singapore*[152] it was alleged that Tarling, the chairman of a Singapore company, had purchased shares from it at a considerable undervalue. In extradition proceedings brought by the Singapore government, the crucial question was whether he could have been committed for trial in England and Wales if the events alleged to have occurred in Singapore had occurred in England and Wales. One of the charges alleged a conspiracy to defraud the shareholders by concealing the transaction from them and thus inducing them to refrain from demanding an account of the proceeds. It would have been simpler to allege that they were defrauded by the purchase itself, but that took place **22–076**

148 [1979] Crim. L.R. 220 at 223.
149 [1999] 2 Cr.App.R. 398.
150 [1961] A.C. 103 at 123.
151 Which in turn may not be clear. Choses in action are generally regarded as situated in the country where they are properly recoverable and can be enforced: *Dicey, Morris & Collins on the Conflict of Laws*, 14th edn (2006), Rule 120. But there may be more than one such country. Moreover the question can arise in various contexts, and it cannot be assumed that the criterion is the same in all contexts: ibid., para.22–025.
152 (1978) 70 Cr.App.R. 77. See J.C. Smith, "Theft, Conspiracy and Jurisdiction: Tarling's Case" [1979] Crim. L.R. 220.

in Hong Kong. The possibility of alleging that they were defrauded in Singapore because *they* were in Singapore was presumably rejected. The effect of focusing on the alleged deception was that the fraud could more plausibly be presented as having occurred in Singapore. It was unnecessary to decide the point because a majority of the House of Lords held that there was no evidence of the alleged conspiracy anyway, but Lord Salmon thought that if there had been a fraud it would have been committed in Hong Kong.[153] The minority thought that there was evidence of the alleged conspiracy and that the fraud would have been committed in Singapore. This view is implicit in Lord Edmund-Davies' dissent[154] and was expressly stated by Viscount Dilhorne.[155]

22–077 It is not clear whether CJA 1993, s.4, which deems certain events to occur within the jurisdiction even if they in fact occur abroad, applies for the purpose of determining whether a conspiracy entered into on or after June 1, 1999 is a conspiracy to defraud in England and Wales. If the agreement is to obtain property by inducing the victim to send it here from abroad, for example, is the agreement deemed under CJA 1993, s.4(a) to be an agreement to obtain the property here? CJA 1993, s.4 is expressed to apply to Group B offences, which includes conspiracy to defraud. On the other hand it provides that there *is* an obtaining (etc.) in England and Wales if specified events *do* occur. It does not follow that there is an *agreement* to obtain in England and Wales if there is an agreement that those events *should* occur. But, since it seems that the receipt of the property would in fact be a defrauding in England and Wales anyway,[156] the point is probably academic.

Agreement to defraud in England and Wales

22–078 There is a further difficulty where the agreement, if carried out, would involve defrauding in England and Wales *and* defrauding abroad, or might involve either or both. Is there, in such a case, an agreement to defraud in England and Wales?

22–079 In *Attorney-General's Reference (No.1 of 1982)* it was held that a scheme to pass whisky off as a well-known English brand was not a conspiracy to defraud in England and Wales because the whisky was to be sold in Lebanon.

> "The real question must in each case be what was the true object of the agreement entered into by the conspirators? In our judgment, the object here was to obtain money from prospective purchasers of whisky in the Lebanon by falsely representing that it was the X Co's whisky. It may well be that if the

[153] (1978) 70 Cr.App.R. 77 at 132.

[154] He would have allowed the Singapore government's appeal on the charges of conspiracy to defraud. He appears to have been under the impression that the only issue dividing the House on these charges was that of dishonesty: (1978) 70 Cr.App.R. 77 at 134.

[155] (1978) 70 Cr.App.R. 77 at 124.

[156] *Naini* [1999] 2 Cr.App.R. 398.

> plan had been carried out, some damage could have resulted to the X Co. But that would have been a side effect or incidental consequence of the conspiracy, and not its object."[157]

This is confusing because it fails to distinguish between intention and purpose. Clearly the defendants *intended* to defraud both the English company and the purchasers in Lebanon, because the scheme would inevitably cause loss to both. But in neither case was this the *object* of the agreement. The object was to make money.

In *McPherson*[158] the defendants presented to banks in Germany stolen **22–080** cheques issued by a bank in England, backing them with stolen guarantee cards so that the English bank had to honour them. Convictions of conspiracy to defraud were quashed because, although the effect of carrying out the agreement would undoubtedly be to defraud the English bank, the jury were not asked to decide whether that was the *object* of the agreement. Had they been asked, they might have accepted that the defendants "had never really thought beyond the defrauding of the German banks", though the court thought they would probably have concluded that the defendants knew that the English bank would inevitably be defrauded. This implies that, had the jury taken the latter view, it would have been sufficient. But according to the *Attorney-General's Reference* (which the court purported to follow) it would *not* have been sufficient: the jury would have to be satisfied not just that the defendants foresaw the defrauding of the English bank as an inevitable consequence of carrying out the agreement, but that that was the *object* of the agreement. In principle the *McPherson* approach seems preferable.

In *Levitz*[159] the defendants arranged for telephone calls to be made from **22–081** abroad without being registered by the meters of the foreign exchanges. They were convicted of conspiracy to defraud British Telecom, on the basis that, while the main victims of the fraud were the foreign telecommunications companies who were deprived of payment for the calls, British Telecom was also defrauded because its lines, equipment and electricity were used without authority or payment. The convictions were quashed on other grounds, so it was unnecessary to decide whether an argument based on the *Attorney-General's Reference* was sound; but the court expressed the tentative view that it was not, because the question referred in that case had been about a conspiracy "to be carried out abroad". In *Levitz*, by contrast, the conspiracy was to be carried out by attaching the devices to telephones in England and Wales. It was only the interference with the meters and the ensuing financial gain that were intended to take place abroad. On this view there would be a conspiracy to defraud in England and Wales if *either* (1) the object of the agreement were to defraud within the jurisdiction, *or* (2) the agreement was intended to defraud within the jurisdiction (though that was not the object) *and* was to be carried out within the jurisdiction.

157 [1983] Q.B. 751 at 757.
158 [1985] Crim. L.R. 508.
159 (1990) 90 Cr.App.R. 33.

22–082 It seems that there is a conspiracy to defraud in England and Wales if the terms of the agreement are such that a victim *might* be defrauded in England and Wales, even if all the defrauding might equally occur abroad.[160] But this is presumably subject to the rules above. The possibility that a defrauding might occur in England and Wales would be insufficient unless such a defrauding would be within the object of the agreement *or* (if *Levitz* is right) the agreement was to be carried out within the jurisdiction.

Incitement to commit a Group A offence

22–083 CJA 1993 does not expressly provide that a person can be guilty of incitement to commit a Group A offence even if the incitement does not occur in England and Wales,[161] but in view of the case law on conspiracy and attempt[162] this is probably the position at common law in any event. The offence of incitement will be abolished and replaced by wider statutory offences if the Serious Crime Bill currently before Parliament is passed.[163]

Immaterial matters

22–084 A person may be guilty of a Group B offence whether or not he is a British citizen[164] (unless "jurisdiction is given to try the offence in question by an enactment which makes provision by reference to the nationality of the person charged"),[165] and whether or not he was in England and Wales at any material time.

OTHER INCHOATE OFFENCES

Conspiracy to defraud

22–085 These provisions of CJA 1993 were thought necessary because inchoate offences are "conduct crimes"[166]—that is, they do not require the actual occurrence of the intended consequences. It was formerly accepted that an inchoate offence is therefore indictable only if committed within the jurisdiction—though the courts sometimes found ways of holding that this condition was satisfied despite the defendant's being outside the jurisdiction at the relevant time.[167] In *Stonehouse* Lord Diplock suggested that this was unnecessary, because comity would not preclude the English courts from

[160] *Kohn* (1864) 4 F. & F. 68; *Cox* [1968] 1 W.L.R. 88; *Naini* [1999] 2 Cr.App.R. 398.

[161] CJA 1993, s.3(1)(b) provides that he may be guilty of incitement to commit a Group A offence whether or not he is *in* England and Wales at any material time, but it does not follow that the incitement need not *occur* in England and Wales.

[162] *Somchai Liangsiriprasert v Government of the USA* [1991] 1 A.C. 225; *Sansom* [1991] 2 Q.B. 130; *Latif* [1996] 1 W.L.R. 104; below, paras 22–085 *et seq*.

[163] See below, para.22–088.

[164] CJA 1993, s.3(1)(a).

[165] CJA 1993, s.3(4).

[166] See above, para.22–058.

[167] See above, paras 22–045 *et seq*.

punishing conduct abroad intended to cause harm in England and Wales.[168] His view found no support at the time,[169] but has since been accepted. In *Somchai Liangsiriprasert v Government of the USA*[170] the Privy Council held that there is a conspiracy under the law of Hong Kong (which in this respect is the same as the common law of England and Wales) if there is an agreement outside the jurisdiction to commit an offence within it. No overt act within the jurisdiction is required.

> "In the case of conspiracy in England the crime is complete once the agreement is made and no further overt act need be proved as an ingredient of the crime. The only purpose of looking for an overt act in England in the case of a conspiracy entered into abroad can be to establish the link between the conspiracy and England or possibly to show the conspiracy is continuing. But if this can be established by other evidence, . . . it defeats the preventative purpose of the crime of conspiracy to have to wait until some overt act is performed in pursuance of the conspiracy . . . Their Lordships can find nothing in precedent, comity or good sense that should inhibit the common law from regarding as justiciable in England inchoate crimes committed abroad which are intended to result in the commission of criminal offences in England."[171]

Since the decision in *Somchai Liangsiriprasert* was on the common law of conspiracy, the effect is that a conspiracy to defraud in England and Wales is indictable at common law even if it is entered into abroad and no overt act is done here. Thus the position is broadly the same in the case of conspiracies entered into before June 1, 1999 as in the case of those that are entered into on or after that date and are therefore subject to CJA 1993, s.3(2). The question of what constitutes a conspiracy to defraud in England and Wales is discussed in the context of s.3(2).[172] **22–086**

Attempt, conspiracy and incitement

CJA 1993, s.3 does not apply to attempts, conspiracies or incitements committed before June 1, 1999, or to attempt, conspiracy or incitement to commit an offence which is not a Group A offence. However, the decision in *Somchai Liangsiriprasert* was extended in *Sansom*[173] to statutory conspiracy under CLA 1977, and in *Latif*[174] to attempt. It presumably applies *a fortiori* to the common law offence of incitement. The effect is that, as far **22–087**

[168] [1978] A.C. 55 at 67.

[169] Lord Keith expressly disagreed: [1978] A.C. 55 at 93.

[170] [1991] 1 A.C. 225. It had already been suggested in *R. v Governor of Pentonville Prison, ex p. Osman* [1990] 1 W.L.R. 277 that there might be jurisdiction over an agreement abroad to make corrupt payments as an inducement or reward for favour shown within England and Wales.

[171] [1991] 1 A.C. 225 at 251.

[172] Above, paras 22–073 *et seq.*

[173] [1991] 2 Q.B. 130.

[174] [1996] 1 W.L.R. 104. The case concerned the offence under the Customs and Excise Management Act 1979, s.170(2) of being knowingly concerned in a fraudulent attempt at evasion of a prohibition, rather than attempt under CAA 1981, but this does not appear to have been thought significant.

as conduct abroad directed at fraud in England and Wales is concerned, there is little or no difference between Group B offences and others, or between offences committed before and after June 1, 1999.

ENCOURAGING OR ASSISTING AN OFFENCE

22–088 Part 2 of the Serious Crime Bill, if enacted, would replace the common law offence of incitement with three new and wider offences of encouraging or assisting the commission of an offence. At the time of writing, these offences appear in cls 39, 40 and 41 of the Bill. Clause 48(1) provides that, if a person knows or believes that the offence he anticipates might take place wholly or partly in England or Wales, he may be guilty of one of these offences no matter where he is at any relevant time. So D, who is in France, could be guilty of encouraging or assisting the commission of a crime by E in England. D would also be guilty if he encouraged or assisted E to do something in a place *outside* England and Wales which, if done *by D* in that place, would be an offence triable in England and Wales.[175]

UNAUTHORISED ACCESS TO A COMPUTER

22–089 The offence under s.2 of the Computer Misuse Act 1990 ("CMA 1990") consists of the offence under s.1 (causing a computer to perform a function with intent to secure unauthorised access to programs or data) plus the additional intention of committing or facilitating the commission of a further offence. It is essentially an offence of *attempting* to commit or facilitate the further offence (minus the requirement that the act done be more than merely preparatory), and much the same issues arise as in the context of attempts in the strict sense. But it is neither a Group A offence nor a Group B offence for the purposes of CJA 1993.

22–090 By virtue of CMA 1990, s.4(1) and (2), the offence under CMA 1990, s.1 may be committed abroad, provided that there is a "significant link with domestic jurisdiction". If the defendant is abroad when he does the act that causes the computer to perform the function, this means that the computer to which he thereby secures or intends to secure unauthorised access[176] must be in England and Wales.[177] If that computer is also abroad, there is no offence under CMA 1990, s.1; but this is not fatal to a charge under s.2. CMA 1990, s.4(3) provides:

> "There is no need for any [significant link with domestic jurisdiction] to exist for the commission of an offence under section 1 above to be established in

[175] If the offence in question can only be committed in that place by certain kinds of person (such as UK nationals), D is assumed for this purpose to be such a person.

[176] Or, when the amendments to CMA 1990 made by the Police and Justice Act 2006 are in force, the computer to which he thereby enables or intends to enable unauthorised access to be secured.

[177] CMA 1990, s.5(2).

proof of an allegation to that effect in proceedings for an offence under section 2 above."

So if D, while abroad, accesses a computer which is also abroad, but does so with the intention of committing or facilitating the commission of an offence punishable with five years' imprisonment, he is guilty under CMA 1990, s.2 though not under s.1. Whether he intends to commit or facilitate the commission of a particular offence depends whether that offence would be committed if his intentions were carried out, which in turn depends on the rules for substantive offences explained above. If the offence he intends to commit, or the commission of which he intends to facilitate, is a Group A offence, it will depend whether a relevant event would occur within the jurisdiction. 22–091

Conspiracy

CMA 1990, s.6(1) provides: 22–092

"On a charge of conspiracy to commit an offence under section 1, 2 or 3 above[178] the following questions are immaterial to the accused's guilt—

(a) the question where any party became a party to the conspiracy; and

(b) the question whether any act, omission or other event occurred in [England and Wales]."

The position is thus similar to that under CJA 1993.[179]

Incitement

CMA 1990, s.6(3) provides: 22–093

"On a charge of incitement to commit an offence under section 1, 2 or 3 above[180] the question where the incitement took place is immaterial to the accused's guilt."

This is probably the same as the position under CJA 1993.[181]

Attempt

CMA 1990, s.6(2) makes provision for attempts which is comparable to that made for conspiracy and incitement by s.6(1) and (3). But it applies only to a charge of attempting to commit the offence under CMA 1990, s.3 22–094

[178] The current wording is "under this Act": it is amended by the Police and Justice Act 2006 so that CMA 1990, s.6(1) does not apply to the new offence under s.3A: above, para.21–041.

[179] Above, para.22–071.

[180] The current wording is "under this Act": it is amended by the Police and Justice Act 2006 so that CMA 1990, s.6(3) does not apply to the new offence under s.3A: above, para.21–041.

[181] Above, para.22–083.

(which is broadly an offence of impairing the operation of a computer)—*not* to a charge of attempting to commit the offence under s.2 (or, when it becomes indictable, the offence under s.1). It would be surprising if Parliament, while relaxing the default rules in the case of extra-territorial attempts to interfere with computers, decided not to do so in the case of extra-territorial attempts to use computers for criminal purposes. An alternative explanation is that the possibility of attempting to commit the offence under CMA 1990, s.2 was thought too remote to require provision, because the actus reus of the offence is simply causing a computer to perform a function. If a person causes a computer to perform a function with intent to secure unauthorised access and thereby to commit an offence of dishonesty, he commits the full offence under s.2 (not just an attempt) even if he fails to secure access. On the other hand he does not commit the full offence if he fails to cause the computer to perform a function at all. In this case there would seem to be an attempt, if his act is "more than merely preparatory"; but CMA 1990 makes no special provision for it, so it is presumably governed by the default rules above.[182]

Immaterial matters

22–095 In proceedings for any offence under CMA 1990, it is immaterial whether or not the defendant was a British citizen at the time of any act, omission or other event proof of which is required for conviction of the offence.[183]

CONDUCT HERE AIMED AT FRAUD ABROAD

22–096 At common law, inchoate offences involve conduct intended to bring about the commission of an offence under English law, and therefore the commission of an offence in England or Wales (or, in the case of conspiracy to defraud, a defrauding in England and Wales). If the intended fraud would not be an offence under English law because it would be committed abroad, conduct directed towards the fraud is not an offence at common law either. This rule is relaxed by CJA 1993 in the case of attempt or incitement (on or after June 1, 1999) to commit a Group A offence, and conspiracy to defraud, and by the Criminal Justice (Terrorism and Conspiracy) Act 1998 in the case of conspiracy to commit an offence (not just a Group A offence).

ATTEMPT

22–097 Where the changes made by CJA 1993 do not apply (either because the offence attempted is not a Group A offence or because the attempt occurred before June 1, 1999), the offence of attempt requires an intention

[182] Para.22–087.
[183] CMA 1990, s.9(1).

to commit an offence which, if completed, would be indictable in England and Wales.[184] In *Re Nagdhi*[185] it was held that this precluded a conviction of attempting to obtain property by deception if the property would have been obtained abroad, because there would not have been an offence indictable here even if the attempt had succeeded. It now appears that there *would* have been an offence indictable here,[186] but this does not affect the principle: the attempt is indictable only if the full offence would have been indictable. Under CAA 1981, s.1(2), an attempt may be committed even though the facts are such that the commission of the full offence is impossible; but this does not seem to include a person who would not commit an offence under English law if he achieved his objective, even if he thinks he would.

Attempt to commit a Group A offence

CJA 1993 extends the reach of CAA 1981 so as to catch attempts within the jurisdiction (on or after June 1, 1999) to commit frauds elsewhere. To some extent this is consequential on the extension of the Group A offences by CJA 1993, s.2(3).[187] Even if the Group A offence attempted would have been committed outside the jurisdiction, under s.2(3) it would still have been indictable if a relevant event would have occurred within the jurisdiction. So an act may be an attempt to commit an indictable offence, and therefore itself indictable under CAA 1981, whereas under the old law it would not have been. The scope of CAA 1981 is indirectly extended by extending the scope of the substantive offences to which it refers. **22–098**

CJA 1993 also inserts a new s.1A into CAA 1981. This provides, in part: **22–099**

> "(1) If this section applies to an act, what the person doing the act had in view shall be treated as an offence to which section 1(1) above applies.
>
> (2) This section applies to an act if—
>
> (a) it is done in England and Wales, and
>
> (b) it would fall within section 1(1) above as more than merely preparatory to the commission of a Group A offence[188] but for the fact that that offence, if completed, would not be an offence triable in England and Wales. . . .
>
> (5) Where a person does any act to which this section applies, the offence which he commits shall for all purposes be treated as the offence of attempting to commit the relevant Group A offence."

The drafting of this provision is defective. Under CAA 1981, s.1(1), attempt requires an intent to commit an offence to which s.1 applies, coupled with an act which is more than merely preparatory to the **22–100**

[184] CAA 1981, s.1(1), (4).
[185] [1990] 1 W.L.R. 317.
[186] *Smith (Wallace Duncan) (No.4)* [2004] EWCA Crim 631; [2004] Q.B. 1418; above, para.22–62.
[187] Above, para.22–19.
[188] "Group A offence" has the same meaning as in CJA 1993, Pt I: CAA 1981, s.1A(3).

commission of that offence. CAA 1981, s.1 applies (with certain exceptions) to "any offence which, if it were completed, would be triable in England and Wales as an indictable offence".[189] CAA 1981, s.1A is clearly aimed at attempts, within the jurisdiction, to do things abroad which would be Group A offences if done here. But this is not what it says. On the face of it, it applies to an attempt to do something abroad which *would in fact* be a Group A offence but would not be "an offence triable in England and Wales" (with the result that the attempt falls outside s.1). This does not make sense, because Group A offences are, by definition, offences triable in England and Wales. Section 1A needs to be read as applying where

(a) a person intends to do an act, or to cause an event;

(b) he does, in England or Wales,[190] an act which is more than merely preparatory to the doing of that act or the causing of that event;

(c) if the intended act or event occurred, it would occur outside the jurisdiction; but

(d) if it occurred in England or Wales (but otherwise in the circumstances in which it is intended to occur) it would be a Group A offence.

22–101 It is not easy to think of circumstances in which these conditions would be satisfied. For example, a person who posts a letter containing false statements probably does not commit fraud by false representation if the letter never arrives, but only attempted fraud.[191] What if the addressee is in France, so that the false representation is intended to be made in France? This is the kind of situation at which CAA 1981, s.1A appears to be aimed. But it is probably not needed for this purpose. Since the relevant event is the making of the false representation, which is a communication, the position is governed by CJA 1993, s.4(b).[192] If the letter arrives, the full offence will have been committed, because under s.4(b) the representation is deemed to have been made within the jurisdiction. So the posting of the letter is an attempt to do something which *would in fact* be the full offence. It falls within CAA 1981, s.1, and s.1A is not required.

22–102 Professor Michael Hirst has argued that CAA 1981, s.1A can *never* apply, because the act done by way of attempt will be a relevant event for the purpose of the Group A offence. The attempt will necessarily be an attempt to do something that *would in fact* be indictable in England and Wales, if only by virtue of CJA 1993, s.2(3).[193] This assumes that an event is a relevant event not only if it is an element of the offence (which an attempt

[189] CAA 1981, s.1(4).

[190] CJA 1993, s.3(3), under which an attempt to commit a Group A offence is triable in England and Wales even if the attempt is made elsewhere, does not apply in relation to a charge brought by virtue of CAA 1981, s.1A: CJA 1993, s.3(6); above, para.22–069.

[191] See above, paras 4–080 *et seq*.

[192] Above, para.22–039.

[193] *Jurisdiction and the Ambit of the Criminal Law* (2003) at 173–174.

normally is not) but also if it forms part of the prosecution case. This is a possible construction but, as we have seen,[194] does not appear to have been the intention. If D, in England, attempts to steal funds located in France, in such circumstances that the intended appropriation would occur in France,[195] it is submitted that the attempt in England would not be a relevant event in relation to the intended theft. There is only one relevant event, namely the appropriation in France.

Hirst continues: 22–103

> "This does not merely make section 1A a useless provision; it makes it a dangerous trap for unwary prosecutors or courts, who may be tempted to rely upon it instead of section 1, in cases where it is, in fact, inapplicable and in which any conviction obtained at trial would fall to be quashed on appeal."[196]

The risk envisaged seems to be that prosecutors might charge an offence under CAA 1981, s.1A in circumstances in which s.1 applies and s.1A does not. But a charge laid under s.1A will always be bad, because s.1A creates no offence: it merely extends the circumstances in which s.1 applies. If a prosecutor charges an offence under s.1 thinking that s.1A applies, whereas in fact it is not needed because s.1 applies anyway, no great harm will be done. The charge under s.1 will still be good.

Criminality under local law

CJA 1993, s.6(2) provides: 22–104

> "A person is guilty of an offence triable by virtue of section 1A of the Criminal Attempts Act 1981 . . . only if what he had in view would involve the commission of an offence under the law in force where the whole or any part of it was intended to take place."

Thus an attempt here to do something abroad will be indictable if the thing attempted

(1) would be an indictable offence (with the help of CJA 1993, s.2(3) if necessary), in which case CAA 1981, s.1 applies without the help of s.1A; or

(2) would be a Group A offence if it occurred here, *and* would be an offence under the law of the place where it was intended to occur if it occurred there.

It is only the thing attempted that must be an offence under the law of the place where it was intended to occur, not the attempt itself.[197] For this

[194] Above, para.22–025.

[195] In some circumstances the defendant's act in England would itself be an appropriation: cf. *R. v Governor of Pentonville Prison, ex p. Osman* [1990] 1 W.L.R. 277; above, para.9–104.

[196] *Jurisdiction and the Ambit of the Criminal Law*, at 174.

[197] cf. Law Com. No.180, para.5.12.

purpose conduct is an offence under the local law if it is punishable under that law, however that law may describe it.[198]

22–105 CJA 1993, s.6 prescribes a procedure for determining whether the relevant conduct[199] would have been an offence under the foreign law in question. The presumption is that it would, unless the defence serve on the prosecution a notice stating their opinion that it would not, showing their grounds for that opinion, and requiring the prosecution to show that it would.[200] Rules of court lay down time limits for the service of such a notice, but this can be waived if the court thinks fit.[201] The issue is to be decided by the judge alone,[202] and may be determined at a preparatory hearing held under the Criminal Justice Act 1987.[203]

Immaterial matters

22–106 Provided that one of the conditions at para.22–104 is satisfied, it is immaterial whether the defendant is a British citizen[204] and whether he is in England and Wales at any material time.[205]

CONSPIRACY TO COMMIT AN OFFENCE

22–107 CLA 1977, s.1(1) provides:

> "Subject to the following provisions of this Part of this Act, if a person agrees with any other person or persons that a course of conduct shall be pursued which, if the agreement is carried out in accordance with their intentions, either—
>
> (a) will necessarily amount to or involve the commission of any offence or offences by one or more of the parties to the agreement, or
>
> (b) would do so but for the existence of facts which render the commission of the offence or any of the offences impossible,
>
> he is guilty of conspiracy to commit the offence or offences in question."

22–108 "Offence" means an offence triable in England and Wales.[206] So a conspiracy here to commit a fraud abroad is not indictable by virtue of

[198] CJA 1993, s.6(3).
[199] i.e. what the defendant had in view: CJA 1993, s.6(5)(b).
[200] CJA 1993, s.6(4), (5).
[201] CJA 1993, s.6(6).
[202] CJA 1993, s.6(7). It was said in *Ditta* [1988] Crim. L.R. 42 that an issue of foreign law had been rightly left to the jury; but the point was apparently not argued, and the court appears to have overlooked the decision in *Hammer* [1923] 2 K.B. 786 that the Administration of Justice Act 1920, s.15, which provides that questions of foreign law are to be decided by the judge, extends to criminal trials.
[203] Criminal Justice Act 1987, s.9(3)(aa). For preparatory hearings, see below, paras 24–061 *et seq*.
[204] CJA 1993, s.3(1)(a). This does not apply if the enactment conferring jurisdiction to try the offence in question makes provision by reference to the nationality of the person charged: CJA 1993, s.3(4).
[205] CJA 1993, s.3(1)(b).
[206] CLA 1977, s.1(4).

CLA 1977, s.1(1) unless the intended fraud would have been an offence triable in England and Wales despite being committed abroad. This was also the position at common law.[207] If the agreement were that the fraud might be committed either within the jurisdiction or outside it, depending on the circumstances, the conspiracy would have been indictable at common law;[208] but this possibility appears to be ruled out by the wording of s.1(1), since the agreed course of conduct will not *necessarily* involve the commission of an offence in England and Wales. Nor would it make any difference whether the conspirators *thought* they would be committing an offence triable in England and Wales: it could not fairly be said that the course of conduct would involve such an offence "but for the existence of facts which render the commission of the offence . . . impossible".

CJA 1993, s.5(1) was intended to extend the offence under CLA 1977, s.1 **22–109** so as to include certain conspiracies to commit frauds outside the jurisdiction. It inserted a new s.1A into CLA 1977, which would have extended CLA 1977, s.1 in much the same way that CAA 1981, s.1A extends CAA 1981, s.1. However, before Pt I of CJA 1993 was brought into force, Parliament enacted the Criminal Justice (Terrorism and Conspiracy) Act 1998, which inserts a new and wider s.1A into CLA 1977. CJA 1993, s.5(1) was never brought into force, and was repealed by the 1998 Act. The new s.1A of CLA 1977 extends CLA 1977, s.1 so as to include certain agreements entered into on or after the date on which the 1998 Act was passed[209] (September 4, 1998).

The drafting of CLA 1977, s.1A has been criticised on the ground that **22–110** there is no overlap between ss.1 and 1A: if the agreed course of conduct would involve an offence under English law despite being carried out abroad, the conspiracy must be charged under s.1 and not s.1A.[210] But s.1A does not create an offence at all, and *any* indictment charging an offence under s.1A would therefore be defective.[211] Section 1A provides that, where the conditions are satisfied, Pt I of CLA 1977 "has effect in relation to the agreement as it has effect in relation to an agreement falling within section 1(1)". Pt I of CLA 1977 includes s.1. So the effect of s.1A, where it applies, is that s.1 applies to the agreement in question as if it were an agreement of the kind described in s.1. The agreement is therefore an offence under s.1.

The four conditions

CLA 1977, s.1A has this effect if four conditions are satisfied. In that **22–111** case, references in Pt I of CLA 1977 to an offence are to be read as a reference to what would be the offence in question but for the fact that it is

[207] *Board of Trade v Owen* [1957] A.C. 602; *R. v Governor of Brixton Prison, ex p. Rush* [1969] 1 W.L.R. 165.

[208] *Kohn* (1864) 4 F. & F. 68; *Board of Trade v Owen* [1957] A.C. 602 at 629, *per* Lord Tucker.

[209] CLA 77, s.1A(14)(a).

[210] Michael Hirst, *Jurisdiction and the Ambit of the Criminal Law* (2003) at 146–147.

[211] CLA 1977, s.4(5) refers to an offence *triable by virtue of* s.1A, but this is not the same as an offence *under* s.1A. The offence falls within s.1 by virtue of s.1A—i.e. because s.1A says so.

not an offence triable in England and Wales;[212] and references in any other enactment, or any instrument or document, to an offence of conspiracy to commit an offence include an offence triable as such a conspiracy by virtue of s.1A.[213]

Agreement to be pursued outside the United Kingdom

22–112 CLA 1977, s.1A(2) provides:

> "The first condition is that the pursuit of the agreed course of conduct would at some stage involve—
>
> (a) an act by one or more of the parties, or
>
> (b) the happening of some other event,
>
> intended to take place in a country or territory outside the United Kingdom."

22–113 CLA 1977, s.1A does not apply to an agreement in England and Wales to commit a fraud in Scotland or Northern Ireland. Such an agreement is indictable under CLA 1977, s.1 only if the fraud would involve the commission of an offence under English law—for example, a Group A offence in relation to which a relevant event would occur in England and Wales.

Criminality under local law

22–114 CLA 1977, s.1A(3) provides:

> "The second condition is that that act or other event constitutes an offence under the law in force in that country or territory."

Conduct is an offence for this purpose if it is punishable under the law of the country or territory in question, however it is described in that law.[214]

22–115 CLA 1977, s.1A goes on to make provision for the application of this condition, in terms broadly similar to those of CJA 1993, s.6 (which makes analogous provision for attempt, incitement and conspiracy to defraud). The condition is presumed to be satisfied unless the defence serve on the prosecution a notice stating their opinion that it is not, showing their grounds for that opinion, and requiring the prosecution to show otherwise.[215] Rules of court lay down time limits for the service of such a notice, but this can be waived if the court thinks fit.[216] The issue is to be decided by the judge alone,[217] and can be determined at a preparatory hearing as if it were a question of law.[218]

[212] CLA 1977, s.1A(6).
[213] CLA 1977, s.1A(13).
[214] CLA 1977, s.1A(7).
[215] CLA 1977, s.1A(8).
[216] CLA 1977, s.1A(9).
[217] CLA 1977, s.1A(10). See above, fn.202.
[218] CLA 1977, s.1A(10). This seems to mean that there is an interlocutory right of appeal against the judge's ruling, although there is no such appeal against a ruling under CJA 93, s.6: see below, para.24–103.

Criminality under English law

CLA 1977, s.1A(4) provides: 22–116

> "The third condition is that the agreement would fall within section 1(1) above as an agreement relating to the commission of an offence but for the fact that the offence would not be an offence triable in England and Wales if committed in accordance with the parties' intentions."

The words "the offence" presumably mean the thing that the parties agree to do, although that would not in fact be an offence: if it would, CLA 1977, s.1 applies and s.1A is not needed. On the other hand, s.1A is clearly not intended to apply to an agreement to do something which, though an offence under the law of the place where it is to be done, would not be an offence under English law even if it were done here. So the third condition is that the agreement would fall within CLA 1977, s.1(1) but for the fact that some or all of what the parties agree to do is to be done abroad and therefore would not be an offence.

Act or omission in England and Wales

CLA 1977, s.1A(5) provides: 22–117

> "The fourth condition is that—
>
> (a) a party to the agreement, or a party's agent, did anything in England and Wales in relation to the agreement before its formation, or
>
> (b) a party to the agreement became a party in England and Wales (by joining it either in person or through an agent), or
>
> (c) a party to the agreement, or a party's agent, did or omitted anything in England and Wales in pursuance of the agreement."

This ensures that, as under the old law, there must still be a nexus between the agreement itself (as distinct from the conduct agreed upon) and England and Wales. In the case of conspiracy to commit a Group A offence, CJA 1993, s.3(2) dispenses with the need for any such nexus; but CJA 1993, s.3(2) does not apply to a charge brought by virtue of CLA 1977, s.1A.[219] If the fourth condition is not satisfied, therefore, the agreement is not indictable under CLA 1977, s.1 unless it is *in fact* an agreement to commit an offence—for example because it is an agreement to commit a Group A offence in relation to which a relevant event would occur here.

The location of an act

CLA 1977, s.1A(11) provides: 22–118

> "Any act done by means of a message (however communicated) is to be treated for the purposes of the fourth condition as done in England and Wales if the message is sent or received in England and Wales."

[219] CJA 1993, s.3(5); above, para.22–072.

This rule corresponds to CJA 1993, s.4(b).[220] It is debatable whether s.4(b) would apply in any event if the offence to be committed were a Group A offence, but this would seem to be academic.[221]

22–119 CJA 1993, s.4(a), by contrast, has no counterpart in CLA 1977, s.1A; but there seems no reason why it should not apply for the purposes of determining whether the fourth condition is satisfied and there is therefore a conspiracy to commit a Group A offence. If one of the parties to the agreement obtains property in France (under the *Harden*[222] principle) by securing its despatch to England, he is deemed under CJA 1993, s.4(a) to have obtained it here; and, since CJA 1993, s.4 is not expressed to apply only for the purposes of CJA 1993 itself, the obtaining is presumably deemed to have occurred in England for the purposes of CLA 1977, s.1A(5)(c).

Nationality

22–120 Where the four conditions are satisfied, it is immaterial to guilt whether the defendant was a British citizen at the time of any act or other event proof of which is required for conviction of the offence.[223]

Crown servants

22–121 CLA 1977, s.1A does not apply to any person acting on behalf of, or holding office under, the Crown.[224]

Consent to proceedings

22–122 Proceedings for an offence which is triable by virtue of CLA 1977, s.1A may only be instituted by or with the consent of the Attorney-General.[225] If in doubt as to whether the agreed course of conduct would have involved an offence under English law (for example, because it is not clear whether an event intended by the conspirators would have been a relevant event for the purposes of CJA 1993),[226] it may be prudent to seek consent anyway.

CONSPIRACY TO DEFRAUD

22–123 At common law, a conspiracy to defraud is not indictable unless it is a

[220] Above, para.22–039.
[221] Unless CJA 1993, s.4(b) were read as applying to a message which is sent but not received: see above, para.22–040. The words "however communicated" make it clear that CLA 1977, s.1A(11) does not apply to such a message.
[222] [1963] 1 Q.B. 8; above, para.22–034.
[223] CLA 1977, s.1A(12). CLA 1977 does not say that it is immaterial whether the defendant was *in* England and Wales at any material time—cf. CJA 1993, s.3(1)(b)—but this must be implied.
[224] CLA 1977, s.1A(14).
[225] CLA 77, s.4(5). The functions of the Attorney-General may be exercised by the Solicitor General: Law Officers Act 1997, s.1(1).
[226] See Michael Hirst, *Jurisdiction and the Ambit of the Criminal Law* (2003) at 147.

conspiracy to defraud *in England and Wales*.[227] We have discussed above what constitutes a conspiracy to defraud in England and Wales.[228]

CJA 1993, s.5(3) provides: 22–124

> "A person may be guilty of conspiracy to defraud if—
>
> (a) a party to the agreement constituting the conspiracy, or a party's agent, did anything in England and Wales in relation to the agreement before its formation, or
>
> (b) a party to it became a party in England and Wales (by joining it either in person or through an agent), or
>
> (c) a party to it, or a party's agent, did or omitted anything in England and Wales in pursuance of it,
>
> and the conspiracy would be triable in England and Wales but for the fraud which the parties had in view not being intended to take place in England and Wales."

So, if any of the conditions in s.5(3)(a)–(c) is satisfied, it is immaterial that the defrauding was to occur abroad. But this is subject to CJA 1993, s.6, which is discussed below.

Nothing in CJA 1993, s.5 applies to any act, omission or other event 22–125 occurring before June 1, 1999.[229] In order to rely on s.5(3), therefore, the prosecution must show that one of the events mentioned in s.5(3)(a)–(c) occurred on or after that date. It would not be sufficient that a party to the conspiracy did something in relation to it in England in 1998, even if it continued in existence after June 1, 1999.

Criminality under local law

CJA 1993, s.6(1) provides: 22–126

> "A person is guilty of an offence triable . . . by virtue of section 5(3), only if the pursuit of the agreed course of conduct would at some stage involve—
>
> (a) an act or omission by one of the parties, or
>
> (b) the happening of some other event,
>
> constituting an offence under the law in force where the act, omission or other event was intended to take place."

So a conspiracy in England to defraud in France is indictable as a conspiracy to defraud if, but only if, the defrauding would involve an offence under French law. The procedure for determining whether the agreed conduct would have constituted an offence under the local law is the same as for a charge of attempt.[230]

[227] *Board of Trade v Owen* [1957] A.C. 602.
[228] Paras 22–073 *et seq.*
[229] CJA 1993, s.78(5).
[230] Above, para.22–105.

22–127 The rule in CJA 1993, s.6(1) is somewhat illogical, since there is no requirement that the defrauding would involve an offence under *English* law if it occurred here. By the same token, s.6(1) does not apply where the defrauding is to occur in England and Wales. It applies only where the prosecution needs to invoke s.5(3), because the agreement is not *in fact* a conspiracy to defraud in England and Wales.

INCITEMENT

22–128 There is a dearth of authority on the extent of the territorial jurisdiction of the English courts over offences of incitement, and there is no statutory definition to offer guidance: like conspiracy to defraud, incitement is still (for the time being)[231] a common law offence. In principle, however, and by analogy with the rules on attempt and conspiracy, a person probably commits no offence in England and Wales if he incites another to do an act elsewhere which would not be an offence under English law, even if that act would be an offence if done in England and Wales. The relevant provisions of CJA 1993 appear to assume that this is the case, as do certain other statutes making it an offence to incite the commission of an offence outside the jurisdiction.[232]

Incitement to commit a Group A offence

22–129 Part I of CJA 1993 extends the law of incitement so as to catch incitement within the jurisdiction to commit frauds elsewhere. It does this, first, by extending the territorial ambit of the Group A offences; and, secondly, in s.5(4). This provides:

> "A person may be guilty of incitement to commit a Group A offence if the incitement—
>
> (a) takes place in England and Wales; and
>
> (b) would be triable in England and Wales but for what the person charged had in view not being an offence triable in England and Wales."

This is subject to CJA 1993, s.6(2), which provides in effect that a person is not guilty of incitement by virtue of s.5(4) unless the act incited would be an offence under the law of the place where it was intended to occur.[233]

22–130 Like CAA 1981, s.1A,[234] s.5(4) of CJA 1993 is hard to make sense of. It ostensibly enables the offence of incitement to be committed in a case where the act incited is not an offence triable in England and Wales, but *is* a Group A offence. This is contradictory, unless we accept that acts done

[231] It will be abolished if the Serious Crime Bill is passed.

[232] e.g. Sexual Offences (Conspiracy and Incitement) Act 1996, s.2; Terrorism Act 2000, s.59.

[233] The procedure for determining whether the act incited would have been an offence under the law of that place is set out above, para.22–105.

[234] See above, para.22–100.

abroad are offences under English law which no English court has jurisdiction to try.[235] What is meant, presumably, is that the offence of incitement can be committed by inciting a person to do something which, if done within the jurisdiction, would be a Group A offence, *and*, if done in the place where the inciter intends it to be done, would be an offence under the law of that place.

ENCOURAGING OR ASSISTING AN OFFENCE

Part 2 of the Serious Crime Bill, if enacted, would abolish the common law offence of incitement and replace it with three new offences of encouraging or assisting the commission of an offence. If D's behaviour takes place in England and Wales but he knows or believes that what he anticipates might occur in a place outside England and Wales, he could be guilty of one of these offences if what he anticipates would be an offence under English law[236] *or* the law of that place. The procedure for determining whether the latter condition is satisfied would be similar to that under CJA 1993, s.6.[237] In the Crown Court, the question would be decided by the judge alone; but, since the question is one of fact and the Bill neither deems it to be one of law nor amends the provisions relating to preparatory hearings, it appears that there would be no power to give a ruling at a preparatory hearing. **22–131**

UNAUTHORISED ACCESS TO A COMPUTER

The offence under CMA 1990, s.2 consists of the offence under s.1 (causing a computer to perform a function with intent to secure unauthorised access to programs or data) plus the additional intention of committing or facilitating the commission of a further offence. The offence under s.1 requires a "significant link with domestic jurisdiction",[238] which means that either the defendant or the computer to which he secures or intends to secure unauthorised access[239] must be within the jurisdiction.[240] **22–132**

CMA 1990, s.4(4) provides: **22–133**

> "Subject to section 8 below, where—
>
> (a) any [significant link with domestic jurisdiction] does in fact exist in the case of an offence under section 1 above; and

[235] See above, paras 22–002 *et seq*.

[236] Or, where the offence can be committed outside England and Wales only by a person who satisfies a condition as to his citizenship, nationality or residence, if what D anticipates would be that offence if done by a person who satisfies that condition.

[237] See above, para.22–105.

[238] CMA 1990, s.4(2).

[239] Or, when the amendments to CMA 1990 made by the Police and Justice Act 2006 are in force, the computer to which he thereby enables or intends to enable unauthorised access to be secured.

[240] CMA 1990, s.5(2).

(b) commission of that offence is alleged in proceedings for an offence under section 2 above;

section 2 shall apply as if anything the accused intended to do or facilitate in any place outside [England and Wales] which would be an offence to which section 2 applies if it took place in [England and Wales] were the offence in question."

So if D, while in England, accesses a computer in France with the intention of stealing property in France, he is treated for the purposes of CMA 1990, s.2 as if he intended to commit theft in England.

22–134 But CMA 1990, s.8(1) imposes a requirement of "double criminality":

> "A person is guilty of an offence triable by virtue of section 4(4) above only if what he intended to do or facilitate would involve the commission of an offence under the law in force where the whole or any part of it was intended to take place."

The procedure for determining whether the intended conduct would involve an offence under the foreign law is similar to that laid down by CJA 1993, s.6.[241]

22–135 A conspiracy here to do something abroad which would be an offence if done here is indictable if the agreed course of conduct would also involve an offence under the law of the country in question,[242] and this applies equally where the offence planned would be one under CMA 1990. An incitement here to do something abroad which would be an offence under CMA 1990, s.1, 2 or 3 if done here is indictable if the conduct incited would also be an offence under the law of the country in question.[243] There is no provision for an attempt here to do something abroad which would be an offence under CMA 1990 if done here; but if the defendant is here there will be a "significant link with domestic jurisdiction", so the attempt will in fact be an attempt to commit an offence under CMA 1990.

22–136 In proceedings for any offence under CMA 1990, it is immaterial whether or not the defendant was a British citizen at the time of any act, omission or other event proof of which is required for conviction of the offence.[244]

SECONDARY LIABILITY

SECONDARY LIABILITY FOR CONDUCT HERE

22–137 A person who aids, abets, counsels or procures an offence committed within the jurisdiction is guilty of that offence, even if the aiding, abetting, counselling or procuring occurs elsewhere. In *Robert Millar (Contractors)*

[241] CMA 1990, s.8(5)–(9); see above, para.22–105.
[242] CLA 1977, s.1A; above, paras 22–109 *et seq*.
[243] CMA 1990, s.7(4), 8(3).
[244] CMA 1990, s.9(1).

Ltd[245] the managing director of a haulage company based in Scotland instructed an employee to drive a vehicle which both knew to be in an unsafe condition. A fatal accident resulted in England. The managing director was held liable for counselling and procuring the driver's offence of causing death by dangerous driving. One way of reaching this conclusion, advanced by Fisher J. at trial[246] and approved on appeal, was that the counselling and procuring was a continuous act which persisted while the employee was driving in England. A simpler explanation, also accepted on appeal, is that the accessory's liability is parasitic on that of the principal offender. He commits no offence unless and until the principal does. His offence is necessarily committed in the same place as that of the principal.[247]

SECONDARY LIABILITY FOR CONDUCT ABROAD

Conversely, and for similar reasons, in the absence of statutory provision **22–138**
there is no liability for aiding, abetting, counselling or procuring conduct by another which is not an offence under English law because it occurs abroad. The prosecution must show either that the principal did commit an offence under English law despite acting abroad (for example, a Group A offence in relation to which a relevant event occurred here) or that the person who acted here was actually a principal offender. For example, if D's accomplice in France steals property and sends it to D in England, it may be arguable that D has himself stolen the property by virtue of CJA 1993, s.4(a).[248]

245 [1970] 2 Q.B. 54.

246 [1969] 3 All E.R. 247 at 255.

247 The same principle applies to offences of being knowingly concerned in fraudulent evasion of duty, etc., contrary to the Customs and Excise Management Act 1979, s.170(2): *Wall* [1974] 1 W.L.R. 930.

248 Above, para.22–035.

CHAPTER 23

THE SERIOUS FRAUD OFFICE

In 1983 the Lord Chancellor and the Home Secretary appointed a Fraud Trials Committee under the chairmanship of Lord Roskill to address concerns which had been expressed as to the difficulties of investigating and prosecuting complex fraud. The Committee made 112 recommendations, not all of which were implemented. But its principal recommendation, that the "need for a new unified organisation responsible for all the functions of detection, investigation and prosecution of serious fraud cases should be examined forthwith", gave rise to the creation of the Serious Fraud Office by the Criminal Justice Act 1987 ("CJA 1987"). **23–001**

The Director of the SFO is empowered by CJA 1987, s.1(3) to investigate any suspected offence which appears to him on reasonable grounds to involve serious or complex fraud,[1] and by s.1(5) to institute or take over any **23–002**

[1] The Director may, if he thinks fit, conduct any such investigation in conjunction either with the police or with any other person who is, in the opinion of the Director, a proper person to be concerned in it: CJA 1987, s.1(4).

criminal proceedings which appear to him to relate to such fraud. CJA 1987 is silent on what makes a fraud "serious" or "complex"; but certain procedural provisions apply to proceedings for serious or complex fraud,[2] and those provisions are commonly invoked in proceedings brought by bodies other than the SFO.[3] The SFO's criteria for selecting cases for investigation may be found in its annual report.

THE SECTION 2 POWERS

23–003 CJA 1987, s.2 gives the Director of the SFO extensive powers

- to require a person to answer questions, or otherwise furnish information, with respect to any matter relevant to the investigation,[4]
- to require the production of documents, to take copies of them and to demand explanations,[5] and
- to search for and seize documents.[6]

Provided that the powers are exercised for the purposes of an investigation under CJA 1987, s.1—that is, an investigation of a suspected offence which appears to the Director on reasonable grounds to involve serious or complex fraud—they can be exercised in any case in which it appears to the Director that there is good reason to do so for the purpose of investigating the affairs, or any aspect of the affairs, of any person.[7]

23–004 The s.2 powers can also be exercised on a request made by

- the Attorney-General of the Isle of Man, Jersey or Guernsey, acting under legislation corresponding to CJA 1987, s.1, or
- the Secretary of State acting under the Crime (International Co-operation) Act 2003, s.15(2) in response to a request received by him from a person mentioned in s.13(2) of that Act (an "overseas authority"), provided that it appears to the Director on reasonable grounds that the offence[8] in respect of which he has been requested to obtain evidence involves serious or complex fraud.[9]

[2] See below, Ch.24.

[3] e.g. the Fraud Prosecution Service (part of the Crown Prosecution Service), the Revenue and Customs Prosecution Office and the Department of Trade and Industry.

[4] CJA 1987, s.2(2); below, paras 23–008 *et seq.*

[5] CJA 1987, s.2(3); below, paras 23–015 *et seq.*

[6] CJA 1987, s.2(4)–(7); below, paras 23–064 *et seq.*

[7] CJA 1987, s.2(1).

[8] "The offence" must be read in the light of the Crime (International Co-operation) Act 2003, s.14(2), under which the Secretary of State may arrange for the obtaining of evidence if satisfied that there are reasonable grounds for suspecting that an offence under the law of the requesting country has been committed, and that an investigation into that (suspected) offence is being carried on there. It cannot be intended that the Director should be able to act upon a letter of request only where it appears to him on reasonable grounds that an offence involving serious or complex fraud has in fact been committed.

[9] CJA 1987, s.2(1), (1A), (1B).

In *R. v Secretary of State for the Home Department, ex p. Fininvest SpA*[10] the Home Secretary's referral of a letter of request to the SFO was challenged on the ground (inter alia) that the letter of request described the documents sought so widely that it was merely a fishing expedition. The Divisional Court rejected this argument. Where action was taken by the domestic authorities on an application from a foreign jurisdiction in the context of a criminal investigation, it was inevitable that the permissible area of search would be wide and would encompass more material than would ultimately be used as evidence at any trial. The request was as precise and focused as it could sensibly be in the circumstances. *Fininvest* was relied upon in *R. (Evans) v Director of SFO*,[11] where the claimants were refused permission to challenge by way of judicial review the SFO's decision to issue a s.2(2) notice requiring them to answer questions and provide information in connection with a criminal investigation in the United States. It was held that the SFO's powers in such a case were as extensive as in the case of an investigation into offences in England and Wales. **23–005**

SECTION 2 NOTICES

The SFO makes extensive use of its powers under CJA 1987, s.2(2) and (3) to require answers to questions and the production of documents. In the year 2005–06 it issued a total of 1215 notices, of which 265 (22 per cent) required answers to questions, 828 (68 per cent) required the production of documents and 122 (10 per cent) required both.[12] In earlier years the great majority of notices required both, so there has been a shift towards a purely document-oriented use of the powers.[13] 488 (40 per cent) of the notices were issued to banks. The latest annual report does not break down the other 60 per cent, but earlier reports suggest that the recipients will have included companies, liquidators, solicitors and accountants as well as individuals. **23–006**

In many cases the SFO will first make an informal request for information or documentation. Only if that request is refused, or it is felt that co-operation is not as full as it might be, is a s.2 notice served. It is not unusual for persons from whom information or documents are informally sought to *request* the service of a s.2 notice. This may be of particular importance to professional persons or employees who may, for example, owe a duty of confidentiality to clients or employers and may wish it to be made clear that they were compelled to co-operate. Persons who are concerned that they **23–007**

[10] [1997] 1 W.L.R. 743.

[11] [2002] EWHC 2304; [2003] 1 W.L.R. 299.

[12] SFO Annual Report 2005–06 at 20.

[13] This may be to some extent connected with the difficulties that can arise in a joint trial where any of the defendants have been interviewed under CJA 1987, s.2(2): see below, para.23–033.

may themselves become the subject of investigation may also require the service of a s.2 notice so that any statement they provide is inadmissible against them.[14]

ANSWERING QUESTIONS AND FURNISHING INFORMATION

23–008 CJA 1987, s.2(2) provides:

> "The Director may by notice in writing require the person whose affairs are to be investigated . . . or any other person whom he has reason to believe has relevant information to answer questions or otherwise furnish information with respect to any matter relevant to the investigation at a specified place and either at a specified time or forthwith."

23–009 The scope of this power was considered by the House of Lords in *R. v Director of SFO, ex p. Wallace Smith*.[15] On April 30, 1991 the police charged the applicant with fraudulent trading. The Director of the SFO formed the opinion that the matter was suitable for investigation under CJA 1987, and on June 24, 1991 a s.2(2) notice was served upon the applicant, requiring him to attend and answer questions. The applicant applied for judicial review. He sought an order of certiorari to quash the s.2 notice and an order prohibiting the Director from (inter alia) requiring him to comply with it without causing him to be cautioned in accordance with para.16.5 of Code C of the Codes of Practice issued under the Police and Criminal Evidence Act 1984 ("PACE"). The Divisional Court granted a declaration that the Director was entitled to ask him questions after he had been charged only if a fresh caution was administered, and that if such a caution were given it would amount to a "reasonable excuse" for refusing to answer questions. The Director appealed.

23–010 In the House of Lords, the leading speech was given by Lord Mustill. He rejected the applicant's contention that, as a matter of construction of CJA 1987, s.2, the Director's power to require a person under investigation to answer questions ceased at the moment when he was charged. Lord Mustill said that the powers conferred by s.2(2) and (3) extended to "any matter relevant to the investigation", and that the investigation did not cease when a suspect was charged.

> "If 'the investigation' has ceased for the purpose of enabling the Director to question the suspect, then they [*sic*] must equally have ceased so as to terminate all her other powers. This means that even as regards third parties who neither have nor need the protection of Code C, and who have never had such protection in the past, the police officer [*sic*] cannot demand the production of a document relevant to the suspected offence. Nor can he demand of such persons answers to the kind of questions to which . . . he could have demanded answers before the suspect was charged. Such a result would

[14] CJA 1987, s.2(8) and (8AA); below, para.23–028.

[15] [1993] A.C. 1.

> be so illogical, and so much out of tune with the extensive inquisitorial powers which are undeniably created by the Act, that [Counsel] accepted that this could not be the meaning of section 2. Yet if 'the investigation' continues after charge as regards some of the Director's powers, how can it cease as regards others? As a matter of interpretation the only possible answer is that it cannot."[16]

Lord Mustill also rejected the applicant's second contention that, whatever the wording of CJA 1987 might indicate, the conflict with Code C and the "right of silence" was so acute that s.2 must be read as being subject to an implied exception in the case of persons who have been charged. He analysed the right of silence and the history of para.16.5 of Code C, which prohibits questioning after charge save in exceptional circumstances, and concluded that that prohibition was not linked to the privilege against self-incrimination: it was concerned to see that any confessions made were made *voluntarily*. Questioning after charge was prohibited because of the risk that answers given at that time might not be voluntary and reliable. Lord Mustill reasoned that, as s.2 was plainly not concerned with whether answers were given voluntarily, and statements made in compliance with a requirement made under it would not normally be admissible against the suspect,[17] neither history nor logic demanded that any qualification should be placed upon its terms. The SFO was entitled to use its coercive powers against a suspect even after he had been charged. 23–011

Ex p. Smith leaves it unclear at what point, if any, the SFO must *cease* questioning a person who has been charged. Lord Mustill had no doubt that if the SFO were to seek to question a defendant during the *trial* there would be 23–012

> "ample remedies to ensure that the Director's powers are not abused, either at long range through the medium of judicial review, or in a more peremptory manner through the power of the trial judge to ensure that the conduct of the trial is fair. Other than in a most exceptional case, I doubt whether a judge who heard that a defendant in the charge of a jury was being interrogated under compulsory powers would have a moment's hesitation about what to do."[18]

But it is not clear what a judge *could* do in these circumstances. In *Nadir*[19] the SFO sought to re-interview prosecution witnesses after the defendants had served their case statements in accordance with orders made by the trial judge under CJA 1987, s.9(5).[20] The defence objected, and the trial judge sought to fetter the Director's investigative powers by requiring the prosecution to draw up a list of questions and submit them to him for consideration. The SFO appealed, contending that the trial judge 23–013

16 [1993] A.C. 1 at 39–40.
17 See below, para.23–028.
18 [1993] A.C. 1 at 43.
19 [1993] 1 W.L.R. 1322.
20 See below, para.24–093.

had no power to curtail the Director's powers or to circumscribe his exercise of them. The defence submitted that, while CJA 1987 itself gave the judge no power to limit or supervise the Director's powers, the judge's inherent power to control the trial gave him jurisdiction to make the order he had made. The Court of Appeal held that the judge had no power to make the order. This suggests that, as far as the trial judge is concerned, the "ample remedies" referred to in *Ex p. Smith* are limited to excluding evidence obtained as a result of a late s.2 interview, rather than preventing such an interview from being held at all. If the interview led to the discovery of admissible evidence, the judge's discretion under PACE, ss.78 and 82(3) would be a difficult one to exercise.

23–014 Where a s.2 notice requires the recipient to attend for interview, the SFO is not obliged to provide a list of questions which it is intended to ask, or even an indication of the areas to which the questions may relate. In *R. v SFO, ex p. Maxwell (Kevin)*[21] it was argued that the Director was under a duty to act fairly in conducting an investigation, and that fairness required that documents available to the interviewer should also be available to the interviewee. The Divisional Court rejected the argument, and said it was important to appreciate that s.2 created an inquisitorial regime and not a judicial one. An investigator was not obliged to give information on the questions to be asked, though an abuse of his powers could be the subject of judicial review.

PRODUCTION AND EXPLANATION OF DOCUMENTS

23–015 CJA 1987, s.2(3) provides:

> "The Director may by notice in writing require the person under investigation or any other person to produce at such place as may be specified in the notice and either forthwith or at such time as may be so specified any specified documents which appear to the Director to relate to any matter relevant to the investigation or any documents of a specified description which appear to him so to relate; and—
>
> (a) if any such documents are produced, the Director may—
>
> (i) take copies or extracts from them;
>
> (ii) require the person producing them to provide an explanation of any of them;
>
> (b) if any such documents are not produced, the Director may require the person who was required to produce them to state, to the best of his knowledge and belief, where they are."

THE SPECIFICITY OF THE REQUIREMENT

23–016 The notice may require the recipient to produce either "specified documents" or "documents of a specified description". Specific documents are generally identified if their identity is known. In relation to banks, the

[21] *The Times*, October 7, 1992.

request for information and documents will often be simply for all information and documentation relating to certain identified bank accounts between stated dates. Professional advisers may simply be asked for "all records of dealings with X" or "all files, papers and other documents relating to X".

However, a notice might be challenged on the basis that the documents requested are inadequately particularised. By contrast with certain other statutory provisions which empower an investigator to require the production of documents of such description as the investigator may specify,[22] CJA 1987, s.2(3) applies only to documents which appear to the Director to relate to any matter relevant to the investigation. A general request for any documents relating to the affairs of the person under investigation would smack of a fishing expedition.[23] In an appropriate case, the proper procedure would be for the recipient of the s.2 notice to apply by way of judicial review for an order quashing the notice on the ground that the Director had no power to issue a notice which insufficiently identified the documents of which production was sought.[24] One would expect the SFO to contend that any obligation on it to show the relevance of the documents sought was a minimal one, and that, in the absence of bad faith or evidence that the power was being abused, a genuine belief that the general category of documents sought was relevant to the investigation would be sufficient to justify the exercise of the power. The s.2 powers are an *investigative* tool: often the SFO will not know exactly what documents exist. **23–017**

PRODUCTION OF DOCUMENTS AFTER CHARGE

The SFO's power under CJA 1987, s.2(3) extends to requiring the production of documents after charges have been laid. In *R. v Director of SFO, ex p. Saunders*[25] the SFO had served s.2(3) notices on Guinness plc requiring it to produce documents which the applicant had disclosed to it in civil proceedings. Guinness was subject to an undertaking not to disclose information or documents disclosed to it by the applicant without the leave of the court, which leave had been refused. The applicant sought a declaration that the notices were *ultra vires* the Director and an injunction to restrain him from taking further steps to enforce them. It was held that the SFO's right to require the production of documents, by third parties at least, continued after charges had been laid. The charging of a suspect did not bring to an end the power to investigate. After *Ex p. Smith*, the same would clearly apply to a notice requiring the *defendant* to produce documents. **23–018**

[22] e.g. Companies Act 1985, s.447(3)(a); but cf. Financial Services and Markets Act 2000, s.173(3).

[23] See *Miailhe v France* (1993) 16 E.H.R.R. 332, in which the European Court of Human Rights expressed concern in relation to powers permitting the "indiscriminate" seizure of documents.

[24] See below, para.23–060.

[25] [1988] Crim L.R. 837.

PRODUCTION OF INTERVIEW TRANSCRIPTS

23–019 In *Re Arrows Ltd (No.4)*[26] the House of Lords was required to consider, after *Ex p. Smith*, the impact of CJA 1987, s.2(3) on the privilege against self-incrimination. Naviede was a director and principal shareholder of Arrows Ltd. When it collapsed he was examined by the company's liquidators under the Insolvency Act 1986, s.236, and transcripts made of those interviews. The SFO informally requested from the liquidators copies of the transcripts, it being clear that in the event of a refusal a s.2(3) notice would be served. The SFO intended to use the transcripts as evidence in criminal proceedings against Naviede. The liquidators applied to the Companies Court for directions. At first instance, Vinelott J. held that he had a discretion under the Insolvency Rules 1986, r.9.5(4), whether to let the SFO have copies of the transcripts.[27] In the exercise of that discretion he refused to make such an order unless the Director undertook not to use the transcripts in evidence against Naviede, thus effectively putting the SFO in the position it would have been in had it interviewed Naviede under CJA 1987, s.2(2).[28]

23–020 On the Director's appeal, the Court of Appeal held[29] that CJA 1987, s.2(3) authorised the Director to require office-holders under compulsion to produce transcripts and affirmations relating to examinations, and that the court had no discretion in relation to the discharge of the office-holder's functions and could not fetter the exercise of the Director's powers. Further, Dillon and Steyn L.JJ. stated that the civil court had no power, either directly or indirectly, to impose restrictions on the evidence to be adduced in criminal proceedings by a prosecuting authority.

23–021 In the House of Lords, argument proceeded on the basis that the Director could validly serve a s.2(3) notice on the liquidators requiring production of the transcripts. Accordingly, Lord Browne-Wilkinson said, the liquidators were bound to produce the transcripts unconditionally unless there was a court order restricting production *and* such order provided a "reasonable excuse" (within the meaning of CJA 1987, s.2(13)) for the failure to comply.[30] Lord Browne-Wilkinson, with whom the other members of the House agreed, held that although Vinelott J. had a discretion by virtue of the Insolvency Rules 1986, r.9.5 whether to authorise the unconditional release of the transcripts, it was an improper exercise of his discretion to prevent their use by the SFO in criminal proceedings. Rule 9.5 conferred on the court a discretion to decide who could inspect the records of a s.236 examination. The issue of the admissibility of the transcripts in any trial was a matter for the trial judge, in the light of all the circumstances known to him.

[26] [1995] 2 A.C. 75 (also known as *Hamilton v Naviede*).
[27] [1993] B.C.L.C. 424.
[28] See below, para.23–028.
[29] [1993] Ch. 452.
[30] See below, paras 23–034 *et seq*.

SAFEGUARDS

The powers conferred by CJA 1987, s.2 are wide, and are counter-balanced by several safeguards. **23–022**

LEGAL PROFESSIONAL PRIVILEGE

Under CJA 1987, s.2(9), a person may not be required under s.2 to disclose any information or produce any document which he would be entitled to refuse to disclose or produce on grounds of legal professional privilege in proceedings in the High Court, except that a lawyer may be required to furnish the name and address of his client. This imports the common law relating to legal professional privilege, rather than the definition in PACE, s.10. It should be noted in particular that communications between a solicitor and his client for the purpose of facilitating or assisting the commission of a crime are not covered by legal professional privilege.[31] But, if the privilege exists, it is that of the client and cannot be waived by the solicitor. **23–023**

BANKING CONFIDENTIALITY

Under CJA 1987, s.2(10), a person may not be required to disclose information or produce a document in respect of which he owes an obligation of confidence by virtue of carrying on any banking business unless **23–024**

(a) the person to whom the obligation of confidence is owed consents to the disclosure or production; or

(b) the Director (or, if it is impracticable for him to act personally, a member of the SFO designated by him for the purpose) has authorised the making of the requirement.

ADMISSIBILITY OF MATERIAL OBTAINED

The powers conferred by CJA 1987, s.2, coupled as they are with a criminal sanction for non-compliance,[32] may compel a person to provide information or documents which incriminate him. The use of such material in criminal proceedings against him might infringe his right to a fair trial under Art.6 of the European Convention on Human Rights, which includes the privilege against self-incrimination.[33] **23–025**

[31] *Cox* (1884) 14 Q.B.D. 153; *Banque Keyser Ullmann SA v Skandia (UK) Insurance Co Ltd* [1986] 1 Lloyd's Rep. 336.

[32] CJA 1987, s.2(13). The existence of the defence of "reasonable excuse" to a s.2(13) charge does not prevent compliance from being compulsory for the purpose of the privilege against self-incrimination, because the fact that compliance would incriminate the recipient of the s.2 notice is not a reasonable excuse for non-compliance: see below, para.23–046.

[33] See also the United Nations International Covenant on Civil and Political Rights 1966, cl.14(3): "In the determination of any criminal charge against him, everyone shall be entitled to the following minimum guarantees, in full equality: . . . (g) Not to be compelled to testify against himself or to confess guilt."

Statements adduced by the prosecution

23–026 This argument was accepted by the European Court of Human Rights, in relation to analogous provisions of the Companies Act 1985, in *Saunders v United Kingdom*.[34] The Court held that the use in the first Guinness trial of interviews given by Saunders to DTI inspectors infringed his right to a fair trial because the interviews were held under compulsory powers, backed by the sanction of imprisonment if he failed to comply. Those accused of fraud were as entitled to the privilege against self-incrimination as those accused of other kinds of offence. There could be no legitimate aim in depriving someone of the guarantees necessary to secure a fair trial. The House of Lords nevertheless held that the Guinness defendants' convictions were safe, because at the time of the trial the Companies Act had expressly provided that the evidence was admissible.[35] The Human Rights Act 1998 did not assist the appellants because it was not enacted until after the trial.[36]

23–027 In response to the European Court's decision in *Saunders* the Attorney-General issued guidance to the effect that statements obtained under compulsory powers should not normally be adduced in evidence against their maker or put to him in cross-examination.[37] The guidance was given statutory effect by the Youth Justice and Criminal Evidence Act 1999. A number of provisions conferring compulsory powers, and creating exceptions to the privilege against self-incrimination, were amended so that statements obtained under them are, subject to certain exceptions, inadmissible against their maker.

23–028 In the case of CJA 1987, s.2 the amendment required was somewhat less radical, because s.2(8) already shielded the recipient of a s.2 notice from having his answers used against him. Section 2(8) provides:

> "A statement by a person in response to a requirement imposed by virtue of this section may only be used in evidence against him—
>
> (a) on a prosecution for an offence under subsection (14) below;[38] or

[34] (1997) 23 E.H.R.R. 313. In *I.J.L. v United Kingdom* (2000) 9 B.H.R.C. 222 the Court came to a similar conclusion in respect of the other Guinness defendants.

[35] *Lyons* [2002] UKHL 44; [2003] 1 A.C. 976. The relevant provisions of the Companies Act had since been amended (below, para.23–027), but the amendments were not retrospective.

[36] *Lambert* [2001] UKHL 37; [2002] 2 A.C. 545; *Kansal (No.2)* [2001] UKHL 62; [2002] 2 A.C. 69.

[37] In *Faryab* [2000] Crim. L.R. 180 a conviction was quashed where the prosecution had adduced such statements in ignorance of the guidelines. In *Lyons* [2002] UKHL 44; [2003] 1 A.C. 976 at [42] Lord Hoffmann reserved his position on the correctness of *Faryab*. Lord Hutton pointed out at [66] that the court had been largely influenced by the Crown's concession that the evidence would probably not have been adduced if counsel had known of the guidelines at the time of the trial, but reserved his opinion as to the correctness of the decision if it went beyond that.

[38] i.e. deliberately or recklessly making a false or misleading statement.

(b) on a prosecution for some other offence where in giving evidence he makes a statement inconsistent with it."[39]

The first exception does not encroach on the privilege against self-incrimination because the proceedings are brought on the basis that the statement was exculpatory but untruthful. The second exception does encroach on the privilege if the defendant gives exculpatory evidence at the trial and an incriminating statement elicited under s.2 is adduced as evidence of guilt.[40] *Saunders* made it clear that the admission of a statement under the second exception could infringe Art.6. The 1999 Act therefore cut down the second exception by inserting CJA 1987, s.2(8AA). This provides: **23–029**

> "However, the statement may not be used against that person by virtue of paragraph (b) of subsection (8) unless evidence relating to it is adduced, or a question relating to it is asked, by or on behalf of that person in the proceedings arising out of the prosecution."

The assumption is that Art.6 is not infringed if the defendant chooses to expose himself to evidence of the incriminating statement by adducing evidence about it or asking a question about it.

Other evidence adduced by the prosecution

That may be a reasonable assumption. But there are other ways in which material obtained under the powers conferred by CJA 1987, s.2 may be used against the person compelled to provide it, and some of them would arguably infringe the privilege against self-incrimination and thus render the trial unfair under Art.6. Where incriminating but inadmissible information has been obtained from a suspect under s.2, the SFO usually has little difficulty in locating other, admissible evidence against him. Such evidence often comes from documents which he is required to produce under s.2(3) (and to which s.2(8) and (8AA) do not apply), or from statements taken from potential witnesses identified by him in the course of his s.2 interviews. A person under investigation may thus be required to incriminate himself by providing information which will assist in the preparation of a case against him. In *Funke v France*[41] the European Court of Human Rights appeared to accept that this might in itself infringe Art.6. **23–030**

In *Saunders v United Kingdom*, however, the Court resiled from this view. The majority said: **23–031**

> "The right not to incriminate oneself is primarily concerned . . . with respecting the will of an accused person to remain silent. As commonly understood in

[39] It might formerly have been arguable that s.2(8) could apply where a witness other than a defendant gives evidence inconsistent with a statement he has previously made in response to a s.2 notice; but s.2(8AA) seems to assume that the maker of the statement will be a party to the proceedings.

[40] Not just as going to the credibility of the defendant's evidence: Criminal Justice Act 2003, s.119.

[41] (1993) 16 E.H.R.R. 297.

> the legal systems of the Contracting Parties to the Convention and elsewhere, it does not extend to the use in criminal proceedings of material which may be obtained from the accused through the use of compulsory powers but which has an existence independent of the will of the suspect such as, inter alia, documents acquired pursuant to a warrant, breath, blood and urine samples and bodily tissue for the purposes of DNA testing."[42]

In his dissenting judgment,[43] Judge Martens subjected this distinction to powerful criticism and suggested that the majority were implicitly overruling *Funke*; but the majority view was repeated when the Court came to deal with the other Guinness defendants.[44] In *Attorney-General's Reference (No.7 of 2000)*[45] the Court of Appeal accordingly held that documents obtained from a bankrupt under the compulsory powers in the Insolvency Act 1986 were admissible against him without any infringement of Art.6. In the court's view the distinction drawn in *Saunders* was not only one to which the court should have regard, but was also "jurisprudentially sound".

23–032 It therefore seems that documents obtained under a s.2 notice are admissible against the recipient of the notice. It does not follow that *all* evidence obtained as a result of the recipient's compliance with the notice (other than statements made by him) will be admissible. Where he is compelled to give information which leads the SFO to other witnesses who are willing to testify against him, or to documents in the possession of others which incriminate him, this would seem to be self-incrimination even under the *Saunders* distinction. The information provided by the recipient of the notice can be extracted from him only by failing to respect his "will . . . to remain silent". The admission, as evidence against him, of evidence thus obtained might arguably infringe his right to a fair trial.

Statements adduced by a co-defendant

23–033 In the first of the Wickes trials in 2002,[46] Mitting J. ruled that admissions made by a defendant in interviews under CJA 1987, s.2 were admissible at the instance of his co-defendant if they were relevant to the co-defendant's case.[47] CJA 1987, s.2(8) protected the first defendant from the use of the admissions by the prosecution, but not by a co-defendant. It is submitted that this was correct: although evidence adduced in support of the co-defendant's cut-throat defence might reasonably be described as evidence "against" the first defendant,[48] that construction would infringe the co-

[42] (1997) 23 E.H.R.R. 313 at para.69.
[43] At para.12.
[44] *I.J.L. v United Kingdom* (2000) 9 B.H.R.C. 222.
[45] [2001] EWCA Crim 888; [2001] 1 W.L.R. 1879.
[46] *Sweetbaum*, Southwark C.C.
[47] See *Myers* [1998] A.C. 124. PACE, s.76A (inserted by the Criminal Justice Act 2003) now provides that a defendant's confession may be given in evidence for a co-defendant in so far as it is relevant to a matter in issue. It may be excluded if the co-defendant cannot prove that it was not obtained by oppression or in consequence of anything said or done that was likely to render it unreliable.
[48] cf. *Murdoch v Taylor* [1965] A.C. 574, on what constituted giving evidence "against" a co-defendant for the purposes of the Criminal Evidence Act 1898, s.1(f)(iii).

defendant's right to a fair trial. So the Human Rights Act 1998, s.3 requires an alternative construction—namely that CJA 1987, s.2(8) applies only to evidence adduced by the prosecution. But, on the basis of *Saunders v United Kingdom*, the admission of the interviews would probably[49] have infringed the *first* defendant's right to a fair trial; so the judge had no option but to sever the first defendant from the indictment. It has been suggested that this will discourage the SFO from using s.2 interview powers except in the unusual case where there is only one suspect, so as to avoid costly separate trials.[50]

Reasonable Excuse for Non-Compliance

The powers conferred by CJA 1987, s.2(2) and (3) are given teeth by s.2(13), under which failure to comply with a s.2 notice is an offence. But the offence is not committed if there is a "reasonable excuse" for such failure. The scope of this defence is of considerable practical importance. **23–034**

The recipient of a s.2 notice will often wish to know whether, if he refuses to comply with it, he will be committing an offence under s.2(13). It will often be difficult to advise him with any certainty: it seems that he cannot even seek judicial review of the s.2 notice on the ground that he has a reasonable excuse for failing to comply with it.[51] He is in a dilemma. If he refuses to comply, he risks prosecution. If he complies, he may help the SFO to secure his own conviction, or break professional obligations or confidences and incur other sanctions. Unfortunately CJA 1987 provides no machinery for the question of "reasonable excuse" to be resolved before the recipient decides whether to comply. In contrast, both the Companies Act 1985[52] and the Financial Services and Markets Act 2000[53] provide regimes whereby inspectors appointed to investigate may certify to the High Court the refusal of a person to comply with a requirement imposed upon him; the court may then enquire into the case and, if appropriate, punish the offender as if for contempt of court. In practice what often happens is that, when the court regards a refusal to co-operate as unjustified, the offender is given an opportunity to appear again before the inspectors, and comply with their requirements, before it is decided whether he will be punished. **23–035**

There is no statutory definition of "reasonable excuse" for failing to comply with a s.2 notice. In the context of the Banking Act 1987, s.42 (which set up a similar regime for the production of documents and the **23–036**

[49] It may be arguable that Art.6 is not infringed in this situation, because the statement does not form part of the case against the defendant who made it. But, if it is inconsistent with evidence given by that defendant, it seems to be admissible against him as if he had made it in giving oral evidence: Criminal Justice Act 2003, s.119(1).

[50] Nigel Hood, "Compulsory Questions" (2003) 153 N.L.J. 1141.

[51] See below, para.23–061.

[52] s.436. The section does not expressly require that the refusal be without "reasonable excuse", though that would seem to be implied since the court has a discretion whether to punish the defaulter.

[53] Part XI; see below, para.23–044.

furnishing of information, and created an offence of non-compliance without reasonable excuse) it was said that "reasonable excuse" would include such matters as "physical inability to comply with a requirement for information or documents arising from illness or accidental destruction of papers etc."[54] This is a very restrictive interpretation, and is clearly not an exhaustive definition of what constitutes a reasonable excuse for the purposes of CJA 1987, s.2.

23–037 However, it is now established that a number of factors do *not* constitute a reasonable excuse. They include the fact that

- the person under investigation has been charged;[55]
- the recipient of the notice has not had the opportunity to apply for legal aid, or has not been legally advised and is not legally represented;[56]
- the SFO has not disclosed to the interviewee the nature of its inquiries or the areas upon which it seeks to question him, or has not given him advance disclosure;[57]
- the information or documentation sought is confidential;[58]
- the recipient of the notice is subject to a court order securing compliance with an obligation, the existence of which does not, of itself, amount to a reasonable excuse;[59]
- the recipient is the spouse of the person under investigation and is therefore not a compellable witness for the prosecution;[60] or
- the recipient is the solicitor of the person under investigation.[61]

Orders of the court

23–038 In *R. v Director of SFO, ex p. Saunders*[62] the SFO had served s.2(3) notices on Guinness plc requiring it to produce documents which the applicant had disclosed to it in civil proceedings. Guinness was subject to an undertaking not to disclose information or documents disclosed to it by the applicant without the leave of the court, which leave had been refused. The

[54] *Bank of England v Riley* [1992] Ch. 475 at 482, *per* Ralph Gibson L.J. (approving Morritt J. at first instance). This formulation was adopted by Steyn L.J. in *Re Arrows Ltd (No.4)* [1993] Ch. 452. The Banking Act 1987 is now replaced by the Financial Services and Markets Act 2000: see below, para.23–044.

[55] *R. v Director of SFO, ex p. Wallace Smith* [1993] A.C. 1; above, para.23–009; *R. v Metropolitan Stipendiary Magistrate, ex p. Director of SFO*, *The Independent*, June 24, 1994.

[56] *R. v Director of SFO, ex p. Wallace Smith* [1993] A.C. 1.

[57] *R. v SFO, ex p. Maxwell (Kevin)*, *The Times*, October 7, 1992; above, para.23–014.

[58] *Re Arrows Ltd (No.4)* [1995] 2 A.C. 75.

[59] *Re Arrows Ltd (No.4)* [1995] 2 A.C. 75; *Marlwood Commercial Inc v Kozeny* [2004] EWCA Civ 798; [2005] 1 W.L.R. 104.

[60] *R. v Director of SFO, ex p. Johnson* [1993] C.O.D. 58.

[61] *Marlwood Commercial Inc v Kozeny* [2004] EWCA Civ 798; [2005] 1 W.L.R. 104.

[62] [1988] Crim. L.R. 837.

court said that, so long as Guinness's undertaking remained in force, Guinness had a reasonable excuse for failing to comply with the notice. Similarly it was said in *Marlwood Commercial Inc v Kozeny*[63] that, if a litigant needs permission under CPR, r.31.22 to comply with a notice requiring the disclosure of documents disclosed to him, and that permission would not be granted, he would have a reasonable excuse for failing to comply.

In *Re Arrows Ltd (No.4)*,[64] where the SFO sought production of interview transcripts held by liquidators, it submitted that even if the Companies Court could make an order prohibiting disclosure of the transcripts to it, that would not give the liquidators a reasonable excuse for failing to produce to it the copies in their possession. Lord Browne-Wilkinson rejected this argument. **23–039**

> "Section 2(3) . . . does not expressly limit the documents in relation to which production can be demanded to documents which are in the possession or under the control of the recipient of the notice. But it must be clear that, if the recipient of the notice cannot, directly or indirectly, procure the production of a document he must have a 'reasonable excuse' for not producing them. Insolvency is a process conducted by, or under the control of, the court, the court acting through its officers, the liquidators. Documents held by liquidators are held by them to the order of the court. In my judgment a statute would need to use very clear words if it intended to override the powers of the court to control the use of property under the administration of the court, including documents. If the court acting properly under a discretion, directs that its officers shall not produce documents, this must provide a reasonable excuse to those officers for failure to do so.[65]"

This reasoning seems to apply only to documents *in the custody* of the court, not to every document held subject to an order of the court. Lord Browne-Wilkinson considered *A v B Bank (Bank of England intervening)*.[66] In that case, A had obtained an injunction restraining B Bank from disclosing documents and information. The Bank of England had served on B Bank a notice under the Banking Act 1987, s.39, which conferred on the Bank of England powers similar to those conferred on the SFO by CJA 1987, s.2. Hirst J. held that the injunction did not give B Bank a reasonable excuse for failure to comply with the s.39 notice. Lord Browne-Wilkinson distinguished that decision on the ground that the documents in question belonged to A or to B Bank: they were not in the custody of the court. But he also said that the purpose of the injunction had been to secure compliance with a banking duty of confidence which was itself overridden by the Banking Act 1987. **23–040**

It therefore appears that, in certain limited circumstances, if the documents whose production is required by a s.2 notice are within the custody of the court, that may provide the recipient of the notice with a reasonable **23–041**

63 [2004] EWCA Civ 798; [2005] 1 W.L.R. 104 at [43].
64 [1995] 2 A.C. 75; above, para.23–019.
65 [1995] 2 A.C. 75 at 104.
66 [1993] Q.B. 311.

excuse for failing to comply with it. There is still some doubt as to whether, in other cases where the use of documents (or information) is restrained by court order, the existence of such an injunction provides a reasonable excuse. But it seems clear that there is no reasonable excuse where the order was made for the purpose of ensuring compliance with an obligation whose existence would not of itself amount to a reasonable excuse. In cases of doubt, the appropriate course would be to apply to the court that made the original order and seek its variation to permit compliance with the s.2 notice.

Obligations of secrecy

23–042 CJA 1987, s.3(3) provides:

> "Where any information is subject to an obligation of secrecy imposed by or under any enactment other than an enactment contained in the Taxes Management Act 1970, the obligation shall not have effect to prohibit the disclosure of that information to any person in his capacity as a member of the Serious Fraud Office . . .".

23–043 This has the effect of overriding statutory obligations of secrecy, even if they are expressed in absolute terms. A person is *not prohibited* from disclosing information in pursuance of a s.2 notice by the fact that some other statute says he may not do so. It does not follow that he *must* disclose it: it might be argued that the obligation of secrecy gives him a "reasonable excuse" for non-compliance, if he chooses to rely on it. But this possibility appears to be closed off by *Re Arrows Ltd (No.4)*.[67] Lord Browne-Wilkinson rejected the submission advanced on behalf of Naviede that a private law right to confidentiality gave Vinelott J. a discretion to refuse to order the handing over of the transcripts.

> "In my view there are many reasons why this argument must fail . . . Subject to limited exceptions the Act of 1987 expressly overrides any duty of confidence 'imposed by or under' any statute other than the Taxes Management Act 1970: section 3(3) of the Act of 1987. Similarly, the fact that section 2(9) and (10) of the Act of 1987 expressly preserves two specific duties of confidence (legal professional privilege and banking confidence) shows that all other common law duties of confidence are overridden. Therefore even if [Counsel] could demonstrate a private law duty of confidence owed by the liquidators to Mr Naviede, such duty would provide no excuse to the liquidators for their failure to comply with a notice under section 2(3)."[68]

It therefore seems clear that the fact that the recipient of a s.2 notice is bound by an obligation of secrecy or confidence, other than legal professional privilege or banking confidentiality, is not a reasonable excuse for failing to comply with the notice.

[67] [1995] 2 A.C. 75; above, para.23–019.
[68] [1995] 2 A.C. 75 at 99.

Prohibition against disclosure under foreign law

Part XI of the Financial Services and Markets Act 2000 sets up a regime for the investigation of (inter alia) suspected offences of insider dealing and market manipulation.[69] Section 173 defines the powers of an investigator appointed for this purpose, and is comparable to CJA 1987, s.2. By contrast with CJA 1987, however, a refusal to co-operate is not itself an offence. Instead, s.177(1) enables the inspector to certify the refusal to the High Court. Section 177(2) provides that, if satisfied that there is no reasonable excuse for the refusal, the court may deal with the defaulter as if he had been guilty of contempt of court. No guidance is given as to what constitutes a reasonable excuse. 23–044

For the purposes of the corresponding provision in the Financial Services Act 1986, however, "reasonable excuse" was partially defined, in exclusionary terms at least. Section 178(6) of the 1986 Act provided: 23–045

> "A person shall not be treated . . . as having a reasonable excuse for refusing to comply with a request or answer a question in a case where the contravention or suspected contravention being investigated relates to dealing by him on the instructions or for the account of another person, by reason that at the time of the refusal—
>
> (a) he did not know the identity of that other person; or
>
> (b) he was subject to the law of a country or territory outside the United Kingdom which prohibited him from disclosing information relating to the dealing without the consent of that other person, if he might have obtained that consent or obtained exemption from that law."

This implied that the person *would* have a reasonable excuse if a foreign law prohibited him from disclosing the information without his principal's consent and he could *not* obtain that consent or exemption from that law. This situation may arise, for example, in relation to multi-national companies or banks which may be subject to non-disclosure obligations enforceable by criminal sanctions within their own jurisdiction. It would probably amount to a reasonable excuse for the purposes of s.177 of the 2000 Act, despite the absence of a provision corresponding to s.178(6) of the 1986 Act. It is arguable that, by analogy, the recipient of a notice under CJA 1987, s.2 has a reasonable excuse for refusing to comply if the law of another country prohibits him from complying and he cannot be released from that prohibition. The argument would be strengthened if breach of the prohibition would be a criminal offence in the other jurisdiction. However, the argument is somewhat weakened by the disappearance of s.178(6) of the 1986 Act. It is not entirely clear that the foreign prohibition would be a reasonable excuse even under the 2000 Act.

Self-incrimination

CJA 1987, s.2(8) expressly protects the recipient of a s.2 notice against the possibility of statements made by him in response to the notice being used in evidence against him.[70] The fact that compliance with the notice 23–046

[69] See above, Ch.13.

[70] See above, para.23–028.

would incriminate him, therefore, is clearly not intended to be a reasonable excuse for failing to comply. This has been held to be so in relation to analogous powers conferred by the Banking Act 1987,[71] the Companies Act 1985[72] and the Insolvency Act 1986.[73] In *Bishopsgate Investment Management Ltd v Maxwell* Dillon L.J. said:

> "[I]f Parliament, in the public interest, sets up by statute special investigatory procedures to find out if the affairs of a company have been conducted fraudulently, with the possibility of special remedies in the light of an inspector's report, or to find out if there have been infringements of certain sections of the Banking Act which have been enacted for the protection of members of the public who make deposits, Parliament cannot have intended that anyone questioned under those procedures should be entitled to rely on the privilege against self-incrimination, since that would stultify the procedures and prevent them achieving their obvious purpose."[74]

Similar considerations clearly apply to CJA 1987, s.2.

23–047 These decisions pre-date the Human Rights Act 1998, and it might now be argued that a conviction for refusing to provide incriminating evidence under a s.2 notice would infringe the recipient's rights under Art.6 of the European Convention on Human Rights. In *Funke v France*[75] customs officers required the applicant to produce three years' statements for a variety of bank accounts held outside France. He refused, and was prosecuted and fined for his refusal. He was also made subject to a daily fine which was to continue until he provided the documentation sought. It was held by the European Court that this violated his right under Art.6(1) of the Convention to remain silent and not to incriminate himself. The customs had secured his conviction in order to obtain evidence of offences which they suspected him of having committed. Being unable or unwilling to procure the evidence by other means, for example by seeking international assistance, they had tried to make him provide it himself. The fact that the French Customs Code allowed this did not justify the infringement of the right to remain silent and of the privilege against self-incrimination.

23–048 In *R. v Herts C.C., ex p. Green Environmental Industries Ltd* Lord Hoffmann said, with reference to this finding in *Funke*:

> "I am bound to say that there are obscurities in this reasoning. What were the criminal proceedings in which Mr Funke was deprived of the right to a fair trial? They could not have been the prosecution for the offences suspected by the customs officers, since that was never brought. The only proceedings against him were for failure to produce his bank statements. In those proceedings, however, he was not obliged to incriminate himself. There was no need, because his guilt under French law was established by his failure to produce the bank statements. Perhaps the case is best regarded as an example

[71] *Bank of England v Riley* [1992] Ch. 475.
[72] *Re London United Investments plc* [1992] Ch. 578.
[73] *Bishopsgate Investment Management Ltd v Maxwell* [1993] Ch. 1.
[74] [1993] Ch. 1 at 20.
[75] (1993) 16 E.H.R.R. 297.

> of Lord Mustill's principle[76] that without some good reason everyone has the right to tell other people, even customs officers, to mind their own business."[77]

It is submitted with respect that the criticism is justified. Punishing a person for an offence of failing to provide information is quite different from punishing him for an offence which can only be proved by the use of information which he has been compelled to provide.

But *Funke* has been applied by the European Court in other cases. In *Heaney v Ireland*[78] it was held that Art.6 was infringed where the applicants were sentenced to imprisonment for the offence of failing to give the police an account of their movements. Indeed this was an extension of *Funke*, because the continuing fine imposed on Funke was more obviously intended to force him to comply than the single prison sentences imposed in *Heaney*. In *J.B. v Switzerland*[79] there was held to be a violation of Art.6 where the applicant was the subject of tax evasion proceedings and was fined for failing to submit documents which could have incriminated him. And in *Shannon v United Kingdom*[80] there was held to be a violation where the applicant was fined for refusing to attend an interview with financial investigators at which he would have been compelled to answer questions in connection with events in respect of which he had already been charged. **23–049**

It seems clear that a person required to answer questions or furnish information would not have a reasonable excuse for failing to do so simply because truthful answers to the questions, or the information sought, would tend to suggest that he had committed an offence. This is because any statement made by him in response to the s.2 notice would not be admissible evidence of such an offence.[81] Such a statement might lead the SFO to conclude that he was guilty, but could not be used to prove it. If the notice required him to produce documents, on the other hand, compliance might involve handing over evidence which *could* be used against him, and might thus require him to incriminate himself directly. But, if he does hand over the documents, it seems that there is no breach of Art.6 if they are used against him.[82] The law cannot consistently say that, while Art.6 is not infringed if he hands over the documents and they are used against him, it *is* infringed if he is punished for refusing to hand them over on the ground that they might be used against him. **23–050**

That leaves the case where compliance with the notice would not directly provide the SFO with evidence of guilt, but might lead to the discovery of other evidence which would be admissible against the recipient of the **23–051**

[76] In *Ex p. Wallace Smith* [1993] A.C. 1 at 31.
[77] [2000] 2 A.C. 412 at 424.
[78] [2000] E.C.H.R. 684.
[79] [2001] Crim. L.R. 748.
[80] (2006) 42 E.H.R.R. 31.
[81] CJA 1987, s.2(8), (8AA); above, para.23–028. The events in *Shannon v UK* (2006) 42 E.H.R.R. 31 occurred before the relevant Northern Ireland legislation was amended in the light of *Saunders* so as to prevent the use of the applicant's answers against him if he merely gave evidence inconsistent with them.
[82] *Att-Gen's Reference (No.7 of 2000)* [2001] EWCA Crim 888; [2001] 1 W.L.R. 1879; above, para.23–031.

notice. In this case it is not clear whether the admission of the evidence thus found would violate Art.6.[83] But this uncertainty does not seem to affect the question whether the recipient would have a reasonable excuse for non-compliance. If the courts conclude that evidence found as a result of compliance would be inadmissible because its admission would infringe Art.6, it will follow that the possibility of compliance revealing such evidence will not be a reasonable excuse for non-compliance, because compliance would not incriminate the recipient in any practical sense. The case would be on all fours with the case where he is required to make a statement which would incriminate him if it were admissible, but it is not admissible because of CJA 1987, s.2(8). If, on the other hand, the courts conclude that evidence found through compliance with a s.2 notice *is* admissible against the recipient of the notice without violating Art.6, the possibility of compliance revealing such evidence will *still* not be a reasonable excuse for non-compliance, because treating it as a reasonable excuse would be inconsistent with the view that the evidence (if found) could properly be admitted. The case would be on all fours with the case where the notice requires the recipient to produce documents that will incriminate him. The conclusion seems to be that it is *never* a reasonable excuse for non-compliance that compliance would tend to incriminate the recipient of an offence under the law of any part of the United Kingdom.[84]

23–052 The position is arguably otherwise if compliance would incriminate the recipient under the law of some other country. CJA 1987, s.2(8) and (8AA) protect him against the possibility that a statement made by him in response to the notice might be used in proceedings against him in the United Kingdom. They do not protect him against the possibility that such a statement might be used in proceedings against him in another country. It is therefore arguable that, where a s.2 notice is issued in pursuance of a request by the authorities of another country,[85] the recipient could claim to have a reasonable excuse for failing to comply with it on the ground that the information or documents required of him would be admissible against him in proceedings in the country making the request. It is fundamental to the legislation that the recipient of a notice is afforded the protection of s.2(8) and (8AA). If he cannot be guaranteed that protection, he should be entitled to refuse to comply. It would seem objectionable that he should be required to incriminate himself for the purposes of an investigation in another jurisdiction, or proceedings in a foreign court, when the same evidence would not normally be admissible against him in proceedings in a domestic court. It seems, however, that in practice such an objection is overcome by an undertaking being sought from the requesting overseas authority that any information provided will be used only for the purposes of the investigation for which it is sought and will not be used in evidence

[83] See above, para.23–032.
[84] CJA 1987, s.2 extends to Scotland and Northern Ireland: s.17(2), (3). It can be extended by Order in Council to any of the Channel Islands (s.17(6)), but no such order has been made.
[85] See above, para.23–004.

against the recipient of the notice, other than in the circumstances contemplated by s.2(8)(b) and (8AA).[86]

Privacy, etc.

23–053 In some cases, for example where the production of personal correspondence is required, a notice under CJA 1987, s.2 will engage the recipient's right to respect for privacy, family life, home and correspondence under Art.8 of the European Convention on Human Rights. In such a case it may be arguable that forcing him to comply with the notice would infringe that right and would thus be unlawful under the Human Rights Act 1998. If that were so, a court hearing proceedings under CJA 1987, s.2(13) for non-compliance with the notice would presumably be obliged by the Human Rights Act to find that the recipient had a reasonable excuse for refusing to comply. Whether Art.8 is infringed will depend whether the interference with the recipient's rights is "necessary in a democratic society" in the interests of one of the legitimate aims set out in Art.8(2). One of those aims is "the prevention of . . . crime", but this does not appear to include the investigation and prosecution of crime.[87] Another is "the economic well-being of the country". It might perhaps be said that all fraud investigations are directed towards that end, among others. Even so, it might be questionable whether the interference with the recipient's rights is "necessary" in the sense of being proportionate to this legitimate aim.

The public interest

23–054 The possibility that compliance with a notice under CJA 1987, s.2 might be contrary to the public interest, and that this may constitute a reasonable excuse for non-compliance, has been considered in several cases. In *Re Arrows Ltd (No.4)*[88] it was contended that public interest immunity attached to the interview transcripts, and that Vinelott J. therefore had a discretion to decide whether such interest was overridden by the public interest in ensuring that all admissible evidence should be available in criminal proceedings. The claim to public interest immunity was advanced on two grounds. First it was said that there was a public interest in ensuring that information obtained under statutory powers is used only for the purposes for which those powers were conferred. Information obtained under the Insolvency Act 1986, it was contended, could be used only for the purposes of the liquidation. Secondly it was submitted that there was a public interest in ensuring that persons required to assist office-holders by providing information could be assured that that information would not be communicated to others. In the absence of such confidentiality the free and speedy

[86] See *R. (Evans) v Director of SFO* [2002] EWHC 2304; [2003] 1 W.L.R. 299 at [24].

[87] In *Funke v France* (1993) 16 E.H.R.R. 297 (above, para.23–047) the Court appeared not to accept the French government's arguments that the customs officers' powers could be justified on this basis.

[88] [1995] 2 A.C. 75; above, para.23–019.

flow of information would be impeded, and the proper winding up of the company's affairs rendered more difficult.

23–055 The SFO contended that any public interest immunity based on the confidentiality of information obtained under statutory powers was overridden by CJA 1987, s.3(3), which disapplies obligations of secrecy.[89] Lord Browne-Wilkinson rejected that contention on the ground that s.3(3) overrides only obligations of secrecy imposed *by statute*, and does not affect considerations of public policy which may justify non-disclosure. He agreed with Hoffmann J., who in *Re Arrows Ltd (No.1)* had said:

> "The reason, in my judgment, why section 3(3) overrides most statutory obligations of secrecy is that these are expressed in absolute terms, or at any rate in terms which permit no exception for the needs of the SFO. But the doctrine of public policy, which may well underlie some of the statutory provisions, permits a balance to be struck between the public interest in preserving secrecy and the public interest in the investigation of fraud. There was no reason why these heads of public policy should have to be excluded from the concept of 'reasonable excuse' and in my judgment section 3(3) does not have this effect."[90]

It would seem, therefore, that a head of public policy justifying a refusal to disclose under the general law, such as public interest immunity or national security, *may* amount to a reasonable excuse for non-compliance. Whether it *does* amount to a reasonable excuse will depend on a balancing exercise between the public interest in preserving secrecy and the public interest in the investigation of fraud.

23–056 The SFO also maintained that the public interest contended for, namely the free flow of information based on the assurance of confidentiality, did not exist, as the machinery established by the Insolvency Act 1986 permitted wide disclosure of information obtained under s.236 of that Act. Lord Browne-Wilkinson agreed. After setting out the wide range of authorities to whom liquidators might be required to disclose information, he said:

> "The statutory framework thus imposes a wide range of duties on liquidators to report, directly or indirectly, to the DTI and prosecuting authorities cases of suspected criminal and dishonest conduct and to furnish them with all documents and information they may require . . . The liquidator cannot be under any duty of confidence which will prevent the performance of these statutory duties. Therefore liquidators cannot in any event give any assurance to a person examined under section 236 that his answers will not be disclosed to prosecuting authorities. In the absence of such assurance there cannot be any maintainable claim that such answers enjoy public interest immunity on the grounds either of the public interest in preserving confidentiality or the public interest in giving an assurance to witnesses that their information will be confidential."[91]

[89] See above, para.23–042.
[90] [1992] Ch. 545 at 552.
[91] [1995] 2 A.C. 75 at 103.

In *Re an Inquiry under the Company Securities (Insider Dealing) Act 1985*[92] the question was whether a journalist, Jeremy Warner, had a "reasonable excuse" within the meaning of the Financial Services Act 1986, s.178(2)[93] for refusing to answer questions put to him by an inspector. He invoked the statutory privilege under the Contempt of Court Act 1981, s.10 on the basis that answering the questions would disclose his sources. In the Court of Appeal, Slade L.J. said: 23–057

> "The following propositions appear to me clearly correct and indeed, I think, have been more or less common ground in this appeal. (1) If Mr Warner would have been able successfully to invoke section 10 of the Act of 1981 as a good ground for refusing to answer the inspectors' questions if the inspectors had been a court of law, he would now have a 'reasonable excuse' for having refused to answer those questions within the meaning of section 178(2). He cannot be in a worse position because the inspectors are not a court of law . . ."[94]

Similarly, in the House of Lords, Lord Griffiths said:

> "The parties to this appeal are rightly agreed that whether or not Mr Warner has a 'reasonable excuse' to refuse to answer the inspectors' questions depends upon whether he is entitled to rely upon the public interest in protecting his source and that the test to be applied must be the same whether that question arises in judicial proceedings or in the course of an inquiry such as this."[95]

It seems implicit in these dicta that a recognised head of privilege may amount to a reasonable excuse. This appears to be consistent with Lord Browne-Wilkinson's distinction between statutory obligations of secrecy, which are overridden by CJA 1987, and considerations of public policy justifying non-disclosure, which require a balancing exercise.

In *Marlwood Commercial Inc v Kozeny*[96] the Court of Appeal examined the conflict between the public interest in the investigation of serious fraud and the public interest in the due administration of civil justice. The SFO sought the production of documents disclosed by the suspect in civil proceedings brought against him. It was held that CJA 1987 does not override the public interest reflected in r.31.22 of the Civil Procedure Rules (which prohibits the collateral use of documents disclosed), any more than it does those cited by Hoffmann J. in *Re Arrows Ltd (No.1)*. The public interests capable of affording a reasonable excuse for non-compliance with a s.2 notice are not confined to the examples given by Hoffmann J. ("national security, diplomatic relations and the administration of central government"). Moreover the obligation under r.31.22 was owed to the court, not the disclosing party. 23–058

[92] [1988] A.C. 660.
[93] See now Financial Services and Markets Act 2000, s.177(2); above, para.23–044.
[94] [1988] A.C. 660 at 673.
[95] [1988] A.C. 660 at 702.
[96] [2004] EWCA Civ 798; [2005] 1 W.L.R. 104.

23–059 In general, however, the court thought that

> "the public interest in the investigation or prosecution of a specific offence of serious or complex fraud should take precedence over the merely general concern of the courts to control the collateral use of compulsorily disclosed documents".[97]

That general concern did not in itself amount to a reasonable excuse for non-compliance. If permission for disclosure were needed and would not be granted, that would be a reasonable excuse; but permission normally *would* be granted. There might be special factors which might make it unjust to require compliance in a particular case. But in *Kozeny* the only special factor was the fact that the suspect was a foreign litigant whose documents had only come within the jurisdiction under the compulsion of the rules relating to English jurisdiction and disclosure; and that fact did not amount to a reasonable excuse either. There were adequate safeguards within the statutory scheme to prevent arbitrary exercise of the powers in question. Moreover, serious or complex fraud can often be investigated only with co-operation between nations.

CHALLENGING A SECTION 2 NOTICE

23–060 It seems clear that the validity of a notice under CJA 1987, s.2 can be challenged by way of judicial review. In *Ex p. Saunders*[98] the Divisional Court entertained an application to quash a notice served on Guinness plc. In *Ex p. Wallace Smith*[99] it does not appear to have been suggested that judicial review was not the appropriate means by which to challenge the Director's decision to issue notices after charges had been laid. Steyn L.J. appeared to believe in *Re Arrows Ltd (No.4)*[100] that the court had jurisdiction to restrain an abuse of the s.2 powers by declaring a notice invalid. In *R. (Evans) v Director of SFO*[101] the court refused permission to challenge a notice on the ground that the SFO's powers were narrower when exercised in pursuance of a letter of request, but only because the argument was clearly bad. In *R. v SFO, ex p. K.M. and S.*[102] the court quashed search warrants obtained under s.2. Applications of this kind involve consideration of the extent of the SFO's powers or the manner in which they are exercised. The function of the Administrative Court is to see that the authority exercised is lawful and that it is not being abused.

[97] [2004] EWCA Civ 798; [2005] 1 W.L.R. 104 at [52].
[98] [1988] Crim. L.R. 837. The court also said that Guinness had a reasonable excuse for refusing to comply with the notice, but it is questionable whether the court had jurisdiction to consider the point: see below, para.23–061.
[99] [1993] A.C. 1; above, para.23–009.
[100] [1993] Ch. 452 at 473.
[101] [2002] EWHC 2304; [2003] 1 W.L.R. 299.
[102] April 7, 1998.

But the issue of a s.2 notice cannot normally be reviewed solely on the ground that the recipient has a reasonable excuse for failing to comply with the notice. In *Ex p. Johnson,*[103] where the applicant challenged the service of a s.2 notice on his wife, Auld J. said that the question whether she had a reasonable excuse for failure to comply was not an appropriate issue for judicial review: it would have to be determined if and when proceedings for non-compliance were brought against her.[104] A similar approach was adopted in *R. v Director of SFO, ex p. Nadir.*[105] The applicant sought judicial review of the SFO's refusal to give him short particulars of the transactions in respect of which they suspected he might have been guilty of criminal conduct. Steyn J. held, on the application for leave, that he had no right to this information, and observed that the structure of the scheme created by CJA 1987 did not appear to contemplate judicial intrusion into the investigative process. By contrast with the statutory schemes under the Companies Act 1985 and the Financial Services Act 1986,[106] there was no supervising court to which aggrieved interviewees could turn for a ruling.[107] **23–061**

However, the distinction between a challenge to the validity of the s.2 notice and an argument based on the existence of a reasonable excuse may not be watertight. It may sometimes be arguable that the existence of a reasonable excuse not only gives the recipient a defence in any proceedings for non-compliance but invalidates the notice itself. For example, we have argued that a recipient might have a reasonable excuse for refusing to produce personal documents on the ground that the intrusion into his private life would be disproportionate and would thus infringe his rights under Art.8 of the European Convention on Human Rights.[108] If that were so, it would seem to follow that the issue of the notice was itself unlawful under the Human Rights Act 1998, and that the recipient could therefore challenge the notice by judicial review without waiting to be prosecuted for non-compliance. **23–062**

There may also be collateral ways of challenging the validity of a s.2 notice. In *Re Arrows Ltd (No.4),*[109] on the facts of that case, it was possible to make an application for directions to the Companies Court. Similarly, if documents are held subject to an undertaking or order imposed in existing proceedings it may be possible to apply for directions in those proceedings.[110] In addition, it may be possible to commence proceedings which have the effect of resolving the issues raised by the s.2 notice. In *Price* **23–063**

103 [1993] C.O.D. 58.

104 Auld J. also thought that the applicant had no *locus standi* to make the application, as he was not the recipient of the notice and it imposed no requirement upon him.

105 *The Times*, November 5, 1990.

106 Now the Financial Services and Markets Act 2000: see above, para.23–044.

107 Taylor L.J. and Morland J. subsequently granted leave on a renewed *inter partes* application: November 1, 1990. The reasons for granting leave are not entirely clear from the short transcript.

108 Above, para.23–053.

109 [1995] 2 A.C. 75; above, para.23–039.

110 See above, para.23–038.

Waterhouse v BCCI Holdings (Luxembourg) SA,[111] which arose out of the SFO investigation following the collapse of BCCI, Price Waterhouse was served with s.2 notices requiring it to produce certain documents. Those documents were potentially the subject of legal professional privilege. Price Waterhouse therefore sought directions, in proceedings commenced by originating summons, to establish whether it was precluded from complying with the s.2 notice by reason of the claim to legal professional privilege.

SEARCH AND SEIZURE

23–064 CJA 1987, s.2 also enables the SFO to apply to a justice of the peace for a warrant to search for, and seize, documents which it appears may be relevant to the investigation. Section 2 provides:

> "(4) Where, on information on oath laid by a member of the Serious Fraud Office, a justice of the peace is satisfied, in relation to any documents, that there are reasonable grounds for believing—
>
> (a) that—
>
> (i) a person has failed to comply with an obligation under this section to produce them;
>
> (ii) it is not practicable to serve a notice under subsection (3) above in relation to them; or
>
> (iii) the service of such a notice in relation to them might seriously prejudice the investigation; and
>
> (b) that they are on premises specified in the information,
>
> he may issue such a warrant as is mentioned in subsection (5) below.
>
> (5) The warrant referred to above is a warrant authorising any constable—
>
> (a) to enter (using such force as is reasonably necessary for the purpose) and search the premises, and
>
> (b) to take possession of any documents appearing to be documents of the description specified in the information or to take in relation to any documents so appearing any other steps which may appear to be necessary for preserving them and preventing interference with them."

It appears that the general provisions relating to search warrants in Pt II of PACE apply to warrants issued under CJA 1987, s.2(4).[112]

ALTERNATIVES TO A WARRANT

23–065 A search warrant is a last resort. In *Kent Pharmaceuticals Ltd v SFO* Lord Woolf C.J. said:

[111] [1992] B.C.L.C. 583.

[112] Lord Woolf C.J. was prepared to assume this in *Kent Pharmaceuticals Ltd v SFO* [2002] EWHC 3023.

"The structure of section 2 is clear. It is intended that the powers that are given to the Director under subsection (3) should be used to obtain documents, if it is appropriate to do so, and it is only in cases that do not lend themselves to being dealt with under subsection (3) that the powers contained in subsections (4) and (5) . . . can be used."[113]

In *Energy Financing Team Ltd v Director of SFO* Kennedy L.J. gave an example of circumstances in which the service of a notice under s.2(3) might be possible but not practicable.

"If [a notice under section 2(3)] will not suffice, for example because the documents may be destroyed, consideration should be given to the possibility of obtaining the documents from an alternative untainted source, such as a bank, but where that would involve many enquiries of many institutions which might or might not be willing and able to produce the information required, the need to assist the investigating authority to make progress with its overall investigation may well, as in this case, render resort to alternative sources impracticable."[114]

THE SPECIFICITY OF THE WARRANT

CJA 1987, s.2(5)(b) envisages that the documents sought will be specified by "description" in the information. This may be contrasted with PACE, s.15(2)(c) and (6)(b), which require an application for a warrant and a warrant to "identify, so far as is practicable, the articles . . . to be sought". In *Energy Financing Team Ltd v Director of SFO* it was argued that, if the Director of the SFO does resort to a warrant rather than a notice under s.2(3), the warrant can only relate to documents which could have been adequately described for the purposes of s.2(3).[115] Kennedy L.J. said: **23–066**

"When there is an ongoing investigation into, for example, the affairs of a company . . . which appears to have been at the centre of a fraud, it will always be difficult to say precisely what documentation of value to the inquiry may be recovered from those who are justifiably suspected of being in contact with the main target company, but nevertheless the warrant needs to be drafted with sufficient precision to enable both those who execute it and those whose property is affected by it to know whether any individual document or class of documents falls within it. If that is done it seems to me that the specificity required will be no less than would be required for a notice under section 2(3) were it practicable to serve such a notice, and although the terms of the warrant may be wide it will not simply be fishing if it is directed to support an investigation which has apparent merit."[116]

Crane J. added that a warrant should be capable of being understood by those carrying out the search, and by those whose premises are being searched, without reference to any other document.[117] A warrant authorising the seizure of "all documents which appear to relate to any matter **23–067**

[113] [2002] EWHC 3023 at [20].
[114] [2005] EWHC 1626 at [24].
[115] As to the extent to which documents sought under s.2(3) must be identified, see above, para.23–017.
[116] [2005] EWHC 1626 at [24].
[117] [2005] EWHC 1626 at [37].

relevant to" a specified investigation would be objectionable if those persons had insufficient information about the investigation to be able to tell whether a particular document was relevant to it.

23–068 When the SFO seeks a warrant pursuant to a letter of request,[118] the warrant need not precisely reflect the wording of the letter of request. The Director has a duty to decide for himself how best to give effect to the request in furtherance of the overall investigation, and if that means going further than the letter of request he is entitled to do so.[119]

EXECUTION OF THE WARRANT

23–069 CJA 1987, s.2(6) requires the constable executing the warrant to be accompanied by a member of the SFO or a person authorised by the Director. The Criminal Justice Act 2003 inserts a new s.2(6A), under which the accompanying civilian can exercise the powers of search and seizure himself. The SFO has welcomed this development on the ground that searches will be made more effective by the direct involvement of civilians with specialist expertise in gathering evidence. It will also help compensate for the decline in police resources available to the SFO in recent years.

23–070 PACE, s.19(3) allows a constable who is lawfully on premises to seize anything on the premises, but only if he has reasonable grounds for believing that it is evidence in relation to an offence *and* that it is necessary to seize it in order to prevent it from being concealed, lost, altered or destroyed. But, where a warrant is obtained under CJA 1987, s.2(4) on the ground that the issue of a s.2(3) notice might result in the concealment (etc.) of the evidence, the second condition is likely to be satisfied in relation to any evidence that satisfies the first.[120]

23–071 Where documents are held on the hard drives of computers on the premises, those executing the warrant may take electronic copies of the documents. Since printing all the documents out is unlikely to be practicable, the alternative would be to seize the computers, which would be absurd.[121]

23–072 In *R. v Chesterfield Justices, ex p. Bramley*,[122] the Divisional Court identified certain difficulties in the application of the search powers conferred by PACE to material which is potentially privileged. In the court's view, common sense dictated that a constable ought to be able to carry out a preliminary sift of the material at the premises and then take it away elsewhere to sort properly, with the owner of the material entitled to be present; but PACE did not permit this. The difficulty is now met by the Criminal Justice and Police Act 2001, s.50, which applies to the search

[118] See above, para.23–004.
[119] *Energy Financing Team Ltd v Director of SFO* [2005] EWHC 1626 at [24], *per* Kennedy L.J.
[120] *Kent Pharmaceuticals Ltd v SFO* [2002] EWHC 3023 at [32].
[121] *Kent Pharmaceuticals Ltd v SFO* [2002] EWHC 3023 at [27].
[122] [2000] Q.B. 576.

powers under CJA 1987, s.2 as well as those under PACE and similar statutes. Search officers are permitted to seize articles and remove them for examination elsewhere if the bulk of material is so great that it is not reasonably practicable to determine immediately whether it contains privileged information, or to separate the privileged material from the remainder (for example because it is all on the same hard disk). In assessing whether it would be reasonably practicable to do either of these things, the following factors (only) are to be taken into account:

- the length of time it would take to examine or separate material;
- the manpower required;
- any possible damage to property;
- any equipment or apparatus required; and
- in the case of separation, the likelihood of prejudicing the proper use of material separated.

A notice must be served on the occupier of the premises searched stating that the s.50 power has been exercised, and to what extent.[123] The material seized must be sifted as soon as reasonably practicable.[124] Items subject to legal privilege must be returned unless they cannot be separated from the remainder.[125] A purported exercise of the power may be challenged before a Crown Court judge.[126]

R. v Commissioners of Customs and Excise, ex p. Popely[127] concerned the judicial review of a decision of the Customs and Excise to search and seize materials and to continue to retain them. It was decided before the reforms, but, given the skeletal nature of the obligations imposed by the 2001 Act, probably remains relevant to the question of how to carry out the sifting process once the materials have been removed from the premises which are the subject of the search warrant. The Divisional Court approved the system devised by the Commissioners of referring documents seized to independent counsel before a decision was made as to which should be retained. This protected the solicitor involved, as well as the Commissioners, and reduced the areas of dispute. 23–073

THE RIGHT TO PRIVACY, ETC.

The execution of a search warrant may sometimes engage the right to respect for privacy, family life, home and correspondence under Art.8 of the European Convention on Human Rights. In *Funke v France*[128] customs 23–074

[123] Criminal Justice and Police Act 2001, s.52.
[124] Criminal Justice and Police Act 2001, s.53.
[125] Criminal Justice and Police Act 2001, s.54.
[126] Criminal Justice and Police Act 2001, s.59.
[127] [1999] S.T.C. 1016.
[128] (1993) 16 E.H.R.R. 297. See also *Miailhe v France* (1993) 16 E.H.R.R. 332 and *Cremieux v France* (1993) 16 E.H.R.R. 357.

officers accompanied by a police officer went to the applicant's house to seek details of his assets abroad. The applicant, a German national, admitted having, or having had, several bank accounts abroad for professional and family reasons but said that he did not have any bank statements at his home. The customs officers searched his home and discovered statements and cheque books from foreign banks. These (and other items) were seized. The European Court of Human Rights held that Art.8 had been infringed.

23–075 However, the Court thought it important that no judicial warrant was required. In view of the need for a warrant under CJA 1987, s.2(4), and the safeguards provided by Pt II of PACE, it is unlikely that a search by the SFO which complied with the statutory requirements would be held unlawful under the Human Rights Act 1998. In *Kent Pharmaceuticals Ltd v SFO* Lord Woolf C.J. said:

> "[O]n any showing there is an intrusion into the protection provided by Article 8(1) where searches of the sort that took place in this case, and the removal of material as happened here, occur. However, Article 8(1) does not stand by itself; it stands subject to Article 8(2). It is my view that in drawing the legislation contained in PACE in the terms that it has, Parliament is endeavouring to give statutory effect to the same principles which Article 8 is designed to protect. The need to consider Article 8 only arises if sections 15 and 16 [of PACE] do not provide sufficient protection in themselves. In my judgment they do. Article 8 in a case of this sort does not add anything to what has been the position hitherto."[129]

This was endorsed by Kennedy L.J. in *Energy Financing Team Ltd v Director of SFO*:

> "The remedy which is available to a person or persons affected by a warrant is to seek judicial review. It is an adequate remedy because the statutory provisions have to be read in the light of those Articles of the European Convention which are now part of English law. In fact, as was said by the Lord Chief Justice in the *Kent* case if the statutory provisions are satisfied the requirements of Article 8 of the Convention will also be satisfied, and at least since the implementation of the Human Rights Act an application for judicial review is not bound to fail if, for example, the applicant cannot show that the Director's decision to seek a warrant in a particular form was irrational, but in deciding whether to grant permission to apply for judicial review the High Court will always bear in mind that the seizure of documents pursuant to a warrant is an investigative step, perhaps best reconsidered either at or even after the trial."[130]

23–076 In the earlier case of *R. v SFO, ex p. K.M. and S.*,[131] however, the Divisional Court had reminded the prosecuting authorities that the exercise of these powers required "skilful planning and execution". On the facts of

[129] [2002] EWHC 3023 at [30].
[130] [2005] EWHC 1626 at [24].
[131] April 7, 1998.

the case the court described the SFO's conduct as having fallen "far below what must be expected when this very serious interference with the liberty of the subject is involved". The court quashed the search warrants on the grounds that important information had not been disclosed when obtaining them. The court also held that there was a debt-collecting element to the application for the warrants, some of them had been drawn in excessively wide terms, and the issue of legal professional privilege had not been considered in a satisfactory manner.

OFFENCES

FAILING TO COMPLY

CJA 1987, s.2(13) creates a summary offence of failing, without reasonable excuse, to comply with a requirement imposed under s.2. We have already considered what might amount to a reasonable excuse for non-compliance.[132] **23–077**

MAKING A FALSE STATEMENT

Under CJA 1987, s.2(14), a person commits an offence if, in purported compliance with a requirement under s.2, he knowingly or recklessly makes a statement which is false or misleading in a material particular. The offence is triable either way, and is punishable on conviction on indictment with two years' imprisonment.[133] **23–078**

FALSIFICATION OR DESTRUCTION OF DOCUMENTS

CJA 1987, s.2(16) creates a further and more serious offence designed to prevent the SFO's investigations from being hindered by the destruction of documentary evidence or the falsification of evidence. It provides: **23–079**

> "Where any person—
>
> (a) knows or suspects that an investigation by the police or the Serious Fraud Office into serious or complex fraud is being or is likely to be carried out; and
>
> (b) falsifies, conceals, destroys or otherwise disposes of, or causes or permits the falsification, concealment, destruction or disposal of documents which he knows or suspects are or would be relevant to such an investigation, he shall be guilty of an offence unless he proves that he had no intention of concealing the facts disclosed by the documents from persons carrying out such an investigation."

[132] Above, paras 23–034 *et seq*.

[133] CJA 1987, s.2(15).

This offence is triable either way, and is punishable on conviction on indictment with seven years' imprisonment.[134]

23–080 The defendant need not *know* that an investigation is being undertaken: he need only suspect it. An investigation need not have actually commenced: it is sufficient if the defendant knows or suspects that an investigation is *likely* to be carried out. And the investigation (actual or potential) need not be one undertaken by the SFO, though it must be an investigation into serious or complex fraud. "Documents" is widely defined so as to include information recorded in any form.[135]

23–081 It is a defence for the defendant to prove that he had no intention of concealing the facts disclosed by the documents from persons carrying out such an investigation. Read literally, this would probably infringe the presumption of innocence under Art.6(2) of the European Convention on Human Rights. If so, s.3 of the Human Rights Act 1998 would require it to be read down as imposing only an evidential burden.[136]

SECTION 2 AND SUBSTANTIVE CHARGES

23–082 Although the SFO is likely to be the prosecuting authority in a case where charges are laid under CJA 1987, s.2, a charge under s.2(14) or (16) is unlikely to be transferred to the Crown Court under CJA 1987, s.4[137] because it will rarely reveal "a case of fraud of such seriousness or complexity that it is appropriate that the management of the case should without delay be taken over by the Crown Court".

23–083 Where an investigation results in fraud charges being laid against a person alleged to have committed a s.2 offence in the course of (or prior to) the investigation, the s.2 charges will probably form the subject of a separate trial, as it is unlikely that they could properly be tried with the substantive fraud charges. In such an event, it will have to be decided which trial should take place first. The prosecution may wish to have the shorter and less complex s.2 charges disposed of first. The defence will be concerned that trying the lesser charges first may prejudice the trial of the main charges, in that it may compel them to disclose evidence that they might not otherwise have to reveal. The effect of a conviction on the s.2 charges may also be to inhibit the defendant in the conduct of his defence in the main trial, by restricting his ability to cross-examine prosecution witnesses or preventing him from asserting his own good character—though, under the Criminal Justice Act 2003, the conviction would probably be admissible anyway.[138]

[134] CJA 1987, s.2(17).

[135] CJA 1987, s.2(18).

[136] *Lambert* [2001] UKHL 37; [2002] 2 A.C. 545; *Johnstone* [2003] UKHL 28; [2003] 1 W.L.R. 1736; *Sheldrake v DPP* [2004] UKHL 43; [2005] 1 A.C. 264.

[137] Or, when the Criminal Justice Act 2003 is fully in force, sent to the Crown Court under the Crime and Disorder Act 1998, s.51 in pursuance of a notice under s.51B of that Act: see below, para.24–005.

[138] See below, paras 27–021 *et seq*.

CHAPTER 24

THE PROSECUTION OF SERIOUS OR COMPLEX FRAUD

In this chapter we examine the procedures put in place by the Criminal Justice Act 1987 ("CJA 1987") for the prosecution of cases of serious or complex fraud. The principal changes introduced by the Act were **24–001**

- the creation of the process of "transfer", by which a case can be transferred from the magistrates' court to the Crown Court without committal proceedings; and
- the provision for "preparatory hearings"—pre-trial hearings in which both prosecution and defence can be required to disclose

their cases, and issues of law and the admissibility of evidence resolved, before the jury is sworn and witnesses called.

Both of these innovations have since been extended to other kinds of case, but CJA 1987 still contains provisions applicable to fraud cases alone.

TRANSFER AND SENDING

24–002 The transfer procedure was intended to reduce the scope for the abuse of committal proceedings in cases of complex fraud. The Roskill committee recognised that the committal procedure had serious drawbacks which were often exploited by defendants.[1] Before 1988, committal proceedings were often prolonged and expensive. The complexity of the evidence and the legal issues was not suited to determination by lay magistrates. Few magistrates' courts, in London at least, had the time or the space to accommodate a big committal hearing.

24–003 The overall scheme of CJA 1987 is that certain prosecuting authorities are authorised to transfer a case to the Crown Court without the need for committal proceedings, subject to the defendant's right to apply to have the charges dismissed on the ground that there is insufficient evidence against him. Upon service of the notice of transfer, the magistrates' court ceases to have jurisdiction (except for certain ancillary matters such as bail, legal aid and witness orders), the case is removed to the jurisdiction of the Crown Court, and the prosecution can prefer a bill of indictment.

24–004 The transfer system set up by CJA 1987 no longer applies to fraud cases triable only on indictment, such as those in which conspiracy is charged.[2] Following the recommendations of the Narey report,[3] such cases are now "sent" to the Crown Court (again without committal proceedings, but subject to the defendant's right to apply to have the charges dismissed) under s.51 of the Crime and Disorder Act 1998 ("CDA 1998"). So the transfer system now applies only to cases in which all the charges are triable either way. The procedure under CDA 1998, s.51 applies to indictable-only offences generally, and is not discussed in this chapter.

24–005 Schedule 3 to the Criminal Justice Act 2003 ("CJA 2003") repeals CJA 1987, ss.4–6 altogether. In fraud cases, a designated authority will instead be able to give notice to the magistrates' court under a new s.51B of CDA 1998, and the case will then be sent to the Crown Court forthwith under a new version of CDA 1998, s.51. Fraud charges triable either way will thus be subject to the same procedure as charges triable only on indictment. CDA 1998, s.51B will apply *only* to cases of serious or complex fraud, and is discussed in this chapter alongside the corresponding provisions in CJA 1987. At the time of writing these reforms are not yet in force.

[1] *Report of the Fraud Trials Committee* (1986), para.4.33.
[2] CJA 1987, s.4(4).
[3] *Review of Delay in the Criminal Justice System* (1997).

DESIGNATED AUTHORITIES

The power to transfer a case of serious or complex fraud under CJA 1987 is not confined to the Director of the SFO: CJA 1987, s.4(2) also confers that power on the DPP, the Commissioners for Revenue and Customs[4] and the Secretary of State. These persons are collectively referred to in CJA 1987 as "designated authorities".[5] Under CDA 1998, s.51B(9), the same bodies can operate the new sending procedure, except that the Director of Revenue and Customs Prosecutions is substituted for the Commissioners. **24–006**

CONDITIONS

CJA 1987, s.4(1) sets out the conditions for the exercise of the power to transfer a case. The power can be exercised only if **24–007**

- the defendant has been charged with an indictable offence, but is not an adult charged with an offence triable *only* on indictment;[6] and
- the designated authority (or one of his officers acting on his behalf) is of the opinion that the evidence of the offence charged
    - would be sufficient for the defendant to be committed for trial, and
    - reveals a case of fraud of such seriousness or complexity that it is appropriate that the management of the case should without delay be taken over by the Crown Court.

The new power to give notice under CDA 1998, s.51B will be available in respect of any indictable offence, whether triable either way or only on indictment. Since committal for trial will no longer exist, the test will be whether the designated authority is of the opinion that the evidence is sufficient for the defendant to be "put on trial for the offence"; but this seems to be effectively the same test, namely whether there is a case to answer. **24–008**

Not every case of serious or complex fraud is suitable for the transfer procedure, or will be suitable for the sending procedure. The case can only be transferred or sent if, in the opinion of the designated authority (or his officer), the case is *so* serious or[7] complex that the management of the case **24–009**

[4] Commissioners for Revenue and Customs Act 2005, s.50(1).

[5] CJA 1987, s.4(2).

[6] In which case CDA 1998, s.51 applies and CJA 1987, s.4 does not: CJA 1987, s.4(4).

[7] As originally enacted, CJA 1987, s.4(1)(b)(ii) required the alleged fraud to be both serious *and* complex. This was an anomaly, since CJA 1987, s.1(3) allows the SFO to investigate a suspected fraud which is either serious *or* complex. Section 4(i)(b)(ii) was amended by the Criminal Justice and Public Order Act 1994. However, a case which is serious but not complex is less likely to satisfy the requirement that it be appropriate that the management of the case should without delay be taken over by the Crown Court. Indeed it is not clear how such a case could *ever* satisfy that requirement: see below, para.24–070.

should be taken over by the Crown Court without delay. The kind of factors that determine whether transfer or sending is appropriate may include

- the number of defendants and charges;
- the nature and seriousness of the charges laid;
- the complexity of the factual and legal issues involved;
- the volume of documentation (in terms of both witness statements and exhibits); and
- listing considerations—for example, the prosecution will wish to avoid the case being delayed in the magistrates' court.

Under the transfer system it may also be relevant that there is a combination of fraud charges and other charges which cannot be transferred, so that a transfer of the fraud charges would result in fragmentation of the case.[8] This consideration will not arise under the new system, since the magistrates' court will be able to send the defendant to the Crown Court for trial for any indictable offence related to the offence in respect of which notice is given under CDA 1998, s.51B.[9]

CHALLENGING THE DECISION

24–010 CJA 1987, s.4(3) and CDA 1998, s.51B(8) provide that a decision to give a notice of transfer or a notice under CDA 1998, s.51B "shall not be subject to appeal or liable to be questioned in any court". These provisions are intended to ensure that the defence cannot delay the proceedings by challenging the decision to transfer or send. However, they do not provide a complete bar to all proceedings questioning the exercise of the power. In *R. v Salford Magistrates' Court, ex p. Gallagher*[10] it was held that a designated authority's decision to transfer a case was subject to judicial review. This would seem correct. Ouster clauses of this nature have been held in other contexts not to prevent a decision being questioned on the grounds that it was made without (or in excess of) jurisdiction, in bad faith, on the basis of irrelevant considerations or without taking account of those that were relevant, or in breach of the rules of natural justice.

24–011 In practice, however, a decision to transfer or send a case will rarely be susceptible to a successful application for judicial review. Certainly the *merits* of the decision will not be questioned: for that, the appropriate procedure is to apply for dismissal of the charges transferred or sent.[11] Moreover, as the designated authority is not required to state its reasons

[8] But it may be possible to reunite the charges in a single indictment: *Townsend* [1997] 2 Cr.App.R. 540.
[9] CDA 1998, s.51(3)(a) (as substituted by CJA 2003).
[10] [1994] Crim. L.R. 374.
[11] See below, paras 24–040 *et seq*.

for deciding to transfer, it will be difficult to challenge the decision on the ground that the designated authority acted in bad faith, took into account an irrelevant or improper consideration or failed to consider the statutory criteria.[12] Given the structure of the provisions, and the procedure for applying to dismiss charges transferred or sent, it also seems unlikely that the designated authority is expected to observe the rules of natural justice when making the decision. Had it been intended that a person charged should have a right to make representations to the designated authority as to whether the case ought to be transferred or sent, express provision would have been made.

But it is only the designated authority's decision to give the notice at all that may not be questioned. Arguably this does not prevent a challenge to the contents of the notice, or (in the case of a transfer under CJA 1987) the statement of the evidence—for example if it were insufficient to enable the defendant to understand how the evidence was said to support the charges transferred. **24–012**

TIME LIMIT FOR GIVING NOTICE

Under CJA 1987, s.4, the notice of transfer must be given before the magistrates' court begins to inquire into the case as examining justices. Under the new system the court will not inquire into the case as examining justices at all, but will be required to send the case to the Crown Court in any event once it has decided that the case is more suitable for trial on indictment.[13] So CDA 1998, s.51B merely requires a notice under that section to be given before any summary trial begins.[14] **24–013**

DOCUMENTS

NOTICE OF TRANSFER OR SENDING

The process of transfer is effected when a notice of transfer is served on the magistrates' court seised of the case. This procedure is regulated by CJA 1987, s.5 and the Notice of Transfer Regulations.[15] A notice of transfer must be in Form 1 in the Schedule to the regulations, or in a form to the like effect.[16] In particular it must certify that the designated authority (or **24–014**

[12] In *Ex p. Gallagher* [1994] Crim. L.R. 374 it was contended by the applicant that the designated authority had decided to transfer the case because one of the defendants had expressed a wish to hear the oral evidence of all 85 witnesses at the committal hearing. The Divisional Court concluded that the Head of the relevant CPS Fraud Division had applied his mind exclusively to the statutory criteria.

[13] Magistrates' Courts Act 1980, s.21 (as substituted by CJA 2003).

[14] CDA 1998, s.51B(5).

[15] Criminal Justice Act 1987 (Notice of Transfer) Regulations 1988 (SI 1988/1691).

[16] Notice of Transfer Regulations, reg.3.

his officer) is of opinion that the statutory criteria are satisfied.[17] There will be a similar requirement under the new system.[18]

24–015 The notice must identify the proposed place of trial. In selecting that place, the designated authority is at present required to have regard to the considerations to which the Magistrates' Courts Act 1980, s.7 requires a magistrates' court committing a person for trial to have regard in selecting the place of trial,[19] namely

(a) the convenience of the defence, the prosecution and the witnesses,

(b) the expediting of the trial, and

(c) any practice directions given.[20]

Under the new system, CDA 1998, s.51D(4) will require a magistrates' court sending a defendant for trial under the new s.51 (including a court doing so in pursuance of a notice under s.51B) to have regard to the same criteria when selecting the place of trial, and s.51B(3) will require the designated authority to have regard to those criteria when selecting the place of trial to be proposed in a notice under that section. The magistrates' court will have no power to select a place other than that proposed in the notice.[21]

24–016 The notice must also state the position in relation to the defendant's bail, and must be accompanied by a Schedule of Proposed Witnesses indicating the witnesses whom the Crown intends to call at trial and the witnesses whose attendance the Crown considers unnecessary.

DOCUMENTS FOR THE DEFENCE

24–017 The Notice of Transfer Regulations,[22] reg.4 currently requires the designated authority (or someone acting on his behalf) to give to any person to whom the notice of transfer relates (or his solicitor)

- a copy of the notice of transfer,
- a notice in Form 2 in the Schedule (or in a form to the like effect), and

[17] CJA 1987, s.4(1)(c). For the criteria, see above, para.24–007.
[18] CDA 1998, s.51B(2).
[19] CJA 1987, s.5(1).
[20] The Consolidated Criminal Practice Direction, para.III.21.3 requires the magistrates' court to have regard to the location or locations of the Crown Court designated by a presiding judge as the location to which cases should normally be committed from that magistrates' court. Paragraph III.21.10 requires the proposed place of trial specified in a notice of transfer to be one of the Crown Court centres designated by the senior presiding judge.
[21] CDA 1998, s.51D(1)(b).
[22] SI 1988/1691.

- "a statement of the evidence on which any charge to which the notice of transfer relates is based".[23]

In practice, the SFO provides each defendant with a bundle containing the notice of transfer, the Form 2 notice, a schedule of all the charges laid against each defendant, the statement of the evidence, an index to the witness statements relied upon, and an index to the documentary exhibits. Further bundles are supplied containing the witness statements and, separately, the documents.

Form 2 notice, etc.

The Form 2 notice contains details of the proposed venue for trial and informs the defendant of his right to apply to the Crown Court to vary the place of trial, to apply for bail, and to apply for all or any of the charges to be dismissed. It also contains details of his bail position and an alibi warning. In addition, it must contain a list of the witnesses (together with copies of the statements or other documents outlining their evidence) on whom the prosecution intends to rely, indicating in each case whether the magistrates' court is to be invited to make the witness fully or conditionally bound. **24–018**

For the purposes of the transfer documents, the prosecution has some flexibility as to the way in which its evidence is prepared. It need not serve its evidence in the form of witness statements, although in practice it usually does. It can serve unsigned statements, documents prepared by persons other than the witnesses and "outlining" their evidence,[24] or transcripts of interviews conducted under CJA 1987, s.2[25] or by DTI inspectors. But full details of the evidence must be provided: a "bare outline" will not suffice.[26] **24–019**

Under the new system the designated authority will not be required to serve a copy of the notice on the person to whom it relates. CDA 1998, s.51D will instead require the magistrates' court to specify in a notice the offence or offences for which the person is sent for trial, and the place at which he is to be tried, and to serve a copy of that notice on him. **24–020**

Statement of evidence

Under the current system, when giving notice of transfer the prosecution must also serve on the defence a statement of the evidence on which any charge to which the notice of transfer relates is based. This is, in effect, a **24–021**

[23] The regulations are required by CJA 1987, s.5(9)(a) to include this requirement. CPIA 1996 replaced the words "statement of the evidence" in CJA 1987, s.5(9)(a) with "copies of the documents containing the evidence (including oral evidence)", and inserted a s.5(9A) to the effect that the regulations could dispense with the requirement for copies of documents to accompany the copy of the notice of transfer if they were referred to, in documents sent with the notice of transfer, as having already been supplied; but the amendments have not been brought into force (in relation to transfers under CJA 1987) and the regulations have not been amended.

[24] *Cheung* [1999] 8 Archbold News 3.

[25] i.e. interviews with witnesses and not defendants, as the records of s.2 interviews with defendants will not be admissible: above, para.23–028.

[26] *Cheung* [1999] 8 Archbold News 3.

precursor to the prosecution case statement that will normally be ordered at the preparatory hearing.[27] It is usually a detailed document which sets out the background to the alleged offences and indicates how the evidence relates to each of the defendants and each of the charges (or groups of charges), cross-referenced to the relevant pages of the witness statements and documentary exhibits. It sets out the chronology of the events on which the case is based, and identifies the material characters. It gives the defence and the court, at an early stage, an indication of the way in which the case is being put, and enables the defence to begin to identify points as to the admissibility of evidence which need to be resolved in the preparatory hearing before the service of the prosecution's case statement. It also serves as an aide-mémoire for the prosecution in the compilation of the transfer bundles, and is a useful source document for all parties during applications to dismiss transferred charges.

24–022 The legislation does not dictate how the statement is to be prepared, and gives the prosecution a free hand in its drafting and structure. It must, however, contain only such evidence as will be admissible at trial. It may not contain evidence which the prosecution hopes to adduce but which is, as yet, unavailable, since the evidence relied upon at the time of transfer must itself be sufficient to disclose a case to answer in relation to each charge laid and against each defendant charged. It is permissible, and indeed advisable, for the prosecution to indicate the inferences that it suggests should be drawn from the direct evidence. In *X*[28] Henry J. said:

> "In serious fraud cases the case is always likely to depend to a greater or lesser extent on inference, and it seems to me to be not only not prejudicial but positively desirable that the inferences which the prosecution say should be drawn from the direct evidence should be included in their statement of evidence so that, first, the defendant may make a fully informed decision whether to apply to dismiss and, second, that in his written submissions or material he originally files in support of an oral application [to dismiss transferred charges] he may deal with the whole of the case against him at that stage and not have to foresee the inferences that will be sought to be drawn."

24–023 Although the statement of the evidence and the prosecution case statement[29] serve different purposes, Henry J. said in *Saunders*[30] that he thought it desirable that the statement of evidence should be "as close to the case statement as can be achieved" at the time of transfer. In practice, a well-drafted statement of evidence will have been prepared with a view to its forming the basis of the part of the case statement that deals with the principal facts of the prosecution case, the witnesses who will speak to those facts and the exhibits relevant to those facts.[31] If this is done, it enables the

[27] See below, paras 24–087 *et seq*.
[28] [1989] Crim. L.R. 726.
[29] See below, para.24–087.
[30] November 6, 1989.
[31] CJA 1987, s.9(4)(a)(i)–(iii); below, para.24–088.

prosecution, after transfer, promptly to invite the judge to order a preparatory hearing and to order it to serve a case statement,[32] thus maintaining the momentum of the case.

Under the new system, and already in the case of offences triable only on indictment, a statement of the evidence is not required at the stage when the case is sent for trial. CDA 1998, Sch.3 para.1 merely requires regulations to provide for the service, on a person sent for trial under s.51, of copies of the documents containing the evidence on which the charges are based. The Crime and Disorder Act 1998 (Service of Prosecution Evidence) Regulations 2005[33] require these documents to be served no later than 70 days (or, in the case of a person committed to custody under CDA 1998, s.52(1)(a), 50 days) of the person being sent for trial.[34] In practice, primary disclosure and a draft indictment are usually served at the same time. A "courtesy bundle" containing a brief case summary and some witness statements may have been served at the magistrates' court as a matter of good practice. **24–024**

DOCUMENTS FOR THE CROWN COURT

The Notice of Transfer Regulations,[35] reg.5 requires the prosecution to give copies of the notice of transfer, the Form 2 notice and the statement of the evidence to the Crown Court venue specified in the notice of transfer as the proposed place of trial. **24–025**

Under the new system, the magistrates' court will be required to give the Crown Court a copy of the notice under CDA 1998, s.51D.[36] The Service of Prosecution Evidence Regulations[37] require "copies of the documents containing the evidence" to be given to the Crown Court. **24–026**

DOCUMENTS FOR PRISON, ETC.

The Notice of Transfer Regulations,[38] reg.6 requires a copy of the notice of transfer and the Form 2 notice to be served on any person having custody of the defendant. There is no corresponding requirement under the new system. **24–027**

THE ROLE OF THE MAGISTRATES' COURT

Where a case is to be transferred under CJA 1987, the defendant makes his first appearance at the magistrates' court as a result of being summoned to appear or (more likely) being arrested, charged and brought to court. At **24–028**

[32] CJA 1987, s.7(3).
[33] SI 2005/902, reg.2.
[34] The time limit can be extended even after it has expired: *Fehily v Governor of Wandsworth Prison* [2002] EWHC 1295; [2003] 1 Cr.App.R. 10 (p.153).
[35] SI 1988/1691.
[36] See above, para.24–020.
[37] SI 2005/902, reg.2.
[38] SI 1988/1691.

the first hearing, questions of bail are considered, and it is usual for the prosecution to give an indication as to when the transfer bundle is likely to be ready. Ancillary applications, for example relating to representation orders, are also considered. Until the notice of transfer is served, the magistrates' court remains seised of the case and retains all its functions in relation to it, and it is to that court that all applications must be made. The court may entertain applications relating to delays, dismissal on the grounds of abuse of process, or the variation of bail conditions.

24–029 Once the designated authority serves the notice of transfer, however, the functions of the magistrates' court cease, save for issues relating to bail, representation and witness orders.[39] Since the issue of a notice of transfer is an administrative act on the part of the designated authority, it does not take place during a court hearing, and at least one further hearing will therefore be required after the giving of the notice to deal with some or all of these outstanding issues.

24–030 Under the new system, most defendants facing allegations of serious fraud will have a single hearing in the magistrates' court when the case will be sent forthwith to the Crown Court under CDA 1998, s.51 (as substituted) following the giving of notice by the designated authority under s.51B. On the giving of the notice, the functions of the magistrates' court will cease except for the requirement to issue a notice under s.51D[40] and the power to deal with representation and bail.[41] The magistrates' court also has the power to adjourn the proceedings under s.51,[42] for example where the prosecuting authority wishes to review its case against the accused and consider amendment of the charges.

BAIL

24–031 The rules relating to bail after transfer under CJA 1987 are convoluted, and depend upon whether the defendant was in custody or on bail when the notice of transfer was issued.

- If the defendant has been remanded on bail to appear before the magistrates' court on an appointed day, that requirement ceases on the giving of the notice of transfer unless the notice states that it is to continue.[43] The Form 2 notice given to the defendant on transfer gives him notice either to attend at the Crown Court on a date to be notified or to appear at the magistrates' court on the date to which he was remanded on bail, as the case may be.[44]
- If the Form 2 notice states that the defendant's obligation to attend at the magistrates' court continues, he remains under an

[39] CJA 1987, s.4(1).
[40] See above, para.24–020.
[41] CDA 1998, s.51B(6).
[42] CDA 1998, s.52(5).
[43] CJA 1987, s.5(6).
[44] Notice of Transfer Regulations (SI 1988/1691) reg.4 and Sch., Form 2.

obligation to do so on the appropriate date. On that date, the court has power either to remand him in custody or to bail him. It also has power, in the absence of a surety, to enlarge a recognizance previously given, so that the surety is bound to secure the defendant's attendance before the Crown Court.[45]

- If the defendant has been remanded in custody, the magistrates' court may, when he next appears before it, either remand him in custody or bail him to appear before the Crown Court for trial.[46] It may exercise these powers in his absence if he has given his written consent and the court is satisfied that, when he gave his consent, he knew that the notice of transfer had been issued.[47] If he does not consent he must be brought back before the magistrates' court.

The legislation does not indicate whether transfer is a change of circumstances requiring the court to reconsider the bail position.[48] In *R. v Reading Crown Court, ex p. Malik*[49] the Divisional Court expressed the view, *obiter*, that when committal has taken place there will usually be a clear change of circumstances warranting a full review of the bail position. By that stage the prosecution will have completed its investigations, the court will be in a better position to assess the nature and seriousness of the offence, and the strength of the prosecution's case can be fully evaluated by the court and the defendant's advisers for the first time.[50] We would suggest that the position after transfer ought to be the same as that which used to exist following a committal. The fact of committal *could* amount to a change of circumstances justifying a fresh consideration of bail. Whether it *did* would depend on the facts of the case. **24–032**

Under the new system, CDA 1998, s.52(1) will simply allow the magistrates' court to send the defendant to the Crown Court in custody or on bail, subject to the usual restrictions on the court's discretion. **24–033**

AFTER TRANSFER OR SENDING

THE INDICTMENT

Time limit

Where the case is transferred under CJA 1987, a draft indictment must be served within 28 days of the transfer.[51] Where the defendant is sent for trial under CDA 1998, s.51, it must be served within 28 days of the service **24–034**

[45] CJA 1987, s.5(7A).
[46] CJA 1987, s.5(3).
[47] CJA 1987, s.5(4), (5). See also para.3 of the Form 2 notice, and Form 3 (consent form for person remanded in custody).
[48] See *R. v Nottingham JJ., ex p. Davies* [1981] Q.B. 38.
[49] [1981] Q.B. 451.
[50] But cf. *R. v Slough JJ., ex p. Duncan* (1982) 75 Cr.App.R. 384.
[51] CPR 2005 (SI 2005/384) r.14.1(1)(d). An application can be made for an extension of time: r.14.1(2).

of copies of the documents containing the evidence on which the charge or charges are based.[52]

Counts that may be included

24–035 Where the case is transferred under CJA 1987, the evidence relied upon at the time of transfer was formerly of crucial importance in determining the future shape of the case. This is because the counts in the indictment had to be based upon the evidence contained in the transfer documents. The Administration of Justice (Miscellaneous Provisions) Act 1933, s.2(2), proviso (iA) currently allows the indictment to include *only* counts specified in the notice of transfer or founded on material that accompanied the copy of the transfer notice given to the defendant under the Notice of Transfer Regulations.[53] The effect of this is that, while the prosecution can serve additional evidence in support of charges which have been transferred, it cannot include in the indictment counts not founded on the transfer material.[54] But r.14.2(5) of the Criminal Procedure Rules 2005 ("CPR 2005") now provides that an indictment may contain any count charging "substantially the same offence" as one specified in the notice of transfer, or any other count based on the prosecution evidence already served which the Crown Court may try. This gives the prosecution a much freer hand; but it appears to be inconsistent with the primary legislation, which, though prospectively repealed by CJA 2003, is still in force.

24–036 Where the case was sent for trial under CDA 1998, s.51, the 1933 Act allows the indictment to include not only a count charging an offence specified in the notice issued by the magistrates' court under CDA 1998, s.51(7) (or, under the new system, s.51D(1))[55] but also any count founded on material subsequently served on the defendant under the Service of Prosecution Evidence Regulations.[56] CPR 2005, r.14.2(5) allows the indictment to contain any count charging "substantially the same offence" as one specified in the notice under CDA 1998, s.51, or any other count based on the prosecution evidence already served which the Crown Court may try.

[52] CPR 2005, r.14.1(1)(a).

[53] See above, para.24–017.

[54] In *R. v Central Criminal Court, ex p. Director of SFO* [1993] 1 W.L.R. 949 at 954 Woolf L.J. said that if a count were added to the indictment which was not supported by the material that accompanied the notice of transfer it could be challenged by a motion to quash the indictment. In *Osieh* [1996] 2 Cr.App.R. 145 it was said that an indictment can be *amended* by the addition of a count which is not disclosed in the committal evidence but only in evidence subsequently served; and the same would presumably apply to a case transferred under CJA 1987. But the contrary had often been assumed: see J.C. Smith, "Adding Counts to an Indictment" [1996] Crim. L.R. 889. *Archbold 2000* criticised the dicta on the basis that an indictment is not "defective" within the meaning of the Indictments Act 1915, s.5(1) because it does not include a count which could not lawfully have been included in it when it was preferred; but see now *Hemmings* [2000] 1 Cr.App.R. 360, and *Archbold 2007* para.1–149.

[55] See above, para.24–020. The amendment made to the Administration of Justice (Miscellaneous Provisions) Act 1933 by CJA 2003, Sch.3 para.34 refers to a notice under CDA 1998, s.57D(1), but this appears to be an error.

[56] Administration of Justice (Miscellaneous Provisions) Act 1933, proviso (iB) to s.2(2), and proviso (i) as substituted by CJA 2003, Sch.3 para.34.

It is permissible to join counts founded on separate committals and transfers in one indictment, provided that none of the defendants are prejudiced by the joinder.[57] **24–037**

THE FIRST HEARING IN THE CROWN COURT

After a case has been transferred or sent, the Crown Court assigns a judge to deal with the case and it is listed "for mention".[58] This is distinct from any preparatory hearing that may later be held.[59] The judge and the parties consider the future timetable of the case, having regard to **24–038**

- whether any applications to dismiss transferred or sent charges are to be made;[60]
- whether a preparatory hearing ought to be ordered (and, if so, when it should commence, how long it is likely to last and whether case statements are likely to be ordered); and
- the start date and likely length of the trial (or, if there is to be a preparatory hearing, the trial proper).

If the judge orders a preparatory hearing, he has power at this first hearing (or independently of it) to order the prosecution to serve a case statement.[61] At this hearing, questions of bail, representation and any other ancillary applications can be dealt with.[62] If the defence wishes to object to the proposed venue for the trial, this is an appropriate time to do so. **24–039**

APPLICATIONS TO DISMISS

While the Roskill Committee was concerned to eliminate the delay caused by the abuse of committal proceedings, it recognised that the defendant must be given an opportunity to apply for charges to be dismissed on the ground that the evidence does not disclose a case to answer. The framework within which such applications are made is established by CJA 1987, s.6 for cases transferred; CDA 1998, Sch.3 para.2 for cases sent; and, in either case, Pt 13 of the CPR 2005. The onus lies on the defence to make the application. Unless it does so, the prosecution is not required to satisfy the court that there is a prima facie case. **24–040**

[57] *Townsend* [1997] 2 Cr.App.R. 540.

[58] Where the defendant is sent for trial under CDA 1998, s.51, r.12.2 of CPR 2005 requires the first hearing to be listed in accordance with any directions given by the magistrates' court.

[59] See below, paras 24–061 *et seq*.

[60] See below, paras 24–040 *et seq*. At this first hearing, consideration may be given to the listing of such applications and the timetable for serving applications and responses.

[61] CJA 1987, s.9A; below, para.24–073. The prosecution may wish to force the pace by seeking these orders at an early stage.

[62] It is good practice for prosecuting counsel to prepare and circulate to all parties an agenda of matters expected to be raised at this hearing.

24–041 CJA 1987, s.6(1) provides that, where a notice of transfer has been given, any person to whom it relates, at any time before he is arraigned (and whether or not an indictment has been preferred), may apply, orally or in writing, to the Crown Court sitting at the proposed place of trial for the transferred charges (or any of them) to be dismissed. CDA 1998, Sch.3 para.2(1) makes similar provision for a person who has been sent for trial under s.51, except that he cannot apply until he has been served with copies of the documents containing the evidence on which the charge or charges are based.

24–042 Once the defendant has been arraigned—which, if there is a preparatory hearing, will be at the start of that hearing—it is too late to make an application to dismiss. Arguably this means that the defence must wait until the close of the prosecution case and then make a submission of no case. If this were right, it would be unfortunate.[63] It may be that in the course of the preparatory hearing rulings are made, for example as to admissibility, which have the effect of excluding certain evidence and, in the view of the defence, of reducing the evidence to a point where it is insufficient for a jury properly to convict. But the judge does have power, at a preparatory hearing, to determine "any . . . question of law relating to the case".[64] In *Saunders*[65] Henry J. ruled that this did not enable him to rule on a submission of no case. In *Hedworth*[66] it was similarly held that there was no power, at a preparatory hearing, to quash an amended indictment on the basis that the charges as amended were not supported by the evidence served, and in *Van Hoogstraten*[67] that there was no power to rule at a preparatory hearing that the jury could not properly convict even if the facts alleged were proved.

24–043 Since the House of Lords' decision in *H.*,[68] however, it seems that such rulings can be made within a preparatory hearing if they involve the determination of a question of law. This would presumably include a ruling under the first limb of *Galbraith*[69] that there is no case to answer because there is no evidence of an essential element of the offence, but not a ruling under the second limb that there is no case because the evidence is so weak that a jury could not properly convict. Moreover, even if the judge cannot make such a ruling within the preparatory hearing, there is nothing to stop him doing so (assuming that he would have power to do so during the trial proper) in a "parallel" hearing which is not part of the preparatory

[63] See *R. v Central Criminal Court, ex p. Director of SFO* [1993] 1 W.L.R. 949 at 954, *per* Woolf L.J.

[64] CJA 1987, s.9(3)(c).

[65] November 6, 1989.

[66] [1997] 1 Cr.App.R. 421.

[67] [2003] EWCA Crim 3642; [2004] Crim. L.R. 498.

[68] [2007] UKHL 7; *The Times*, March 2, 2007; below, para.24–085.

[69] [1981] 1 W.L.R. 1039.

hearing.[70] The main difference is that only rulings made within the preparatory hearing are appealable under CJA 1987, s.9(11).[71]

ORAL APPLICATIONS

Written notice of intention to apply

An application to dismiss, under CJA 1987 or CDA 1998, may be argued orally or made in writing. A defendant wishing to make an oral application must give written notice of his intention to do so.[72] Where the case was transferred under CJA 1987, the notice must be given in the form prescribed in the Consolidated Criminal Practice Direction,[73] not later than 28 days after the date on which the notice of transfer was given.[74] Where the case was sent for trial under CDA 1998, notice must be given within 14 days of service of the prosecution case.[75] Time may be extended, in either case, upon application to the Crown Court.[76] Notice of the application must also be given to the prosecution and any person to whom the notice of transfer relates or with whom the applicant is jointly charged.[77] **24–044**

The notice of intention to make an application must specify the charges to which it relates, and state whether the leave of the judge is sought to adduce oral evidence on the application, indicating which witnesses it is proposed to call at the hearing.[78] **24–045**

The notice must be accompanied by "a copy of any material upon which the applicant relies".[79] This clearly means material on which he relies in support of his argument that the case should be dismissed because the prosecution evidence would not be sufficient for him to be properly convicted: it does not require him to disclose his own case. In *R. (Snelgrove) v Woolwich Crown Court* it was said that "material" may be anything, whether admissible evidence or not. The judge has a discretion as to the use he makes of such material. **24–046**

> "The judge could, for example, on the strength of some inadmissible material that has a potential for being turned into relevant and otherwise admissible evidence or for testing admissible prosecution evidence on which the prosecution relies, adjourn the application to enable the accused's representatives to do whatever is necessary to that end. Or perhaps, on the strength of such

[70] See below, para.24–078.

[71] But a ruling that there is no case to answer is appealable under CJA 2003, s.58 if made outside a preparatory hearing. This does not apply to a dismissal under CJA 1987, s.6: see below, para.24–060.

[72] CJA 1987, s.6(2); CDA 1998, Sch.3 para.2(3).

[73] CPR 2005, r.13.2(1).

[74] CPR 2005, r.13.2(2)(a).

[75] CPR 2005, r.13.2(2)(c). In this case there is no prescribed form.

[76] CPR 2005, r.13.2(3), (4).

[77] CPR 2005, r.13.2(2).

[78] CPR 2005, r.13.2(6).

[79] CPR 2005, r.13.2(6).

> material, he could direct certain enquiries if he considers that the interests of justice require it. He has a discretion—one that he should exercise one way or the other in the light of the prosecution evidence and other material put before him, having regard always to the statutory test whether the prosecution evidence before him considered in its context is sufficient for a jury properly to convict the accused."[80]

24–047 The legislation does not require the defendant to state the grounds of his application. Indeed, the form prescribed in the Practice Direction contains the pre-printed statement that the grounds of the application are that "The evidence which has been disclosed would not be sufficient for a jury to properly convict", and there is no room to say anything else. In practice, however, detailed grounds are set out in skeleton arguments which either accompany the notice of intention to make an application or are provided before the hearing. If leave to call oral evidence is sought it is prudent to provide detailed grounds.[81]

Oral evidence

24–048 Oral evidence may be given only if the judge gives leave or orders it of his own volition.[82] An application for leave to adduce oral evidence can be made by either the defence or the prosecution. If the defence wishes to call oral evidence, it must say so in its notice of intention to make an application to dismiss.[83] If the prosecution wishes to do so it must make a written application for leave, indicating what witnesses it intends to call,[84] not later than seven days from the date of service upon it of the defence's notice of intention to make the application.[85] But the judge may grant leave for a witness to give oral evidence, on either side, even if notice of intention to call the witness has not been given.[86]

24–049 There is no provision for the parties to be heard upon an application to adduce oral evidence. The rules appear to assume that the judge will decide the application on the papers. But in many cases the judge will wish to hear representations from both parties, and it would seem that he has an inherent jurisdiction to do so. Since he can grant leave at the hearing even if no written application has been made at all,[87] he must *a fortiori* have power to reserve his decision on a written application.

[80] [2004] EWHC 2172; [2005] 1 W.L.R. 3223 at [17], *per* Auld L.J.

[81] In determining whether to grant leave, the judge is currently required to have regard to any matters stated in the application for leave: CJA 1987, s.6(3); CDA 1998, Sch.3 para.2(4). This requirement is removed by CJA 2003 from a date to be appointed.

[82] CJA 1987, s.6(3); CDA 1998, Sch.3 para.2(4); CPR 2005, r.13.2(6)(b), (7). At present the judge may not grant leave unless it appears to him that the interests of justice require him to do so, but this restriction is removed by CJA 2003 from a date to be appointed.

[83] CPR 2005, r.13.2(6)(b).

[84] There is no longer any requirement to specify the grounds of the application, though it is probably prudent to do so.

[85] CPR 2005, r.13.4(1). Time may be extended: CPR 2005, r.13.4(6), (7).

[86] CPR 2005, r.13.5(1). CJA 1987, s.6(4) and CDA 1998, Sch.3 para.2(5) refer to the possibility of the judge's making an order *requiring* a person to give oral evidence, which implies that there is power to make such an order; but these provisions are repealed by CJA 2003 from a date to be appointed.

[87] CPR 2005, r.13.5(1).

WRITTEN APPLICATIONS

Where the case was transferred under CJA 1987 and the defendant wishes to make his application for dismissal without an oral hearing, he must make it in the prescribed form,[88] not later than 28 days after the date on which the notice of transfer was given.[89] Where the case was sent for trial under CDA 1998, a written application must be made within 14 days of service of the prosecution case.[90] Time may be extended, in either case, on application to the Crown Court.[91] The written application must be sent to the Crown Court, and must "be accompanied by a copy of any statement or other document, and identify any article, on which the applicant for dismissal relies".[92] A copy of the application and accompanying documents must be given at the same time to the prosecution and to any other person to whom the notice of transfer relates or with whom the applicant for dismissal is jointly charged.[93] **24–050**

The prosecution can apply for the application to be determined at an oral hearing. Such an application must be made in writing (and, if made under CJA 1987, in the prescribed form)[94] within seven days from service of the application to dismiss.[95] The application must state whether leave to adduce oral evidence is sought and, if so, what witnesses it is proposed to call.[96] **24–051**

SERVICE OF FURTHER PROSECUTION MATERIAL

In resisting an application to dismiss transferred charges, the prosecution is not restricted to the evidence disclosed in the documents that accompanied the notice of transfer or the evidence served since the defendant was sent for trial. It can, and often does, adduce additional evidence or other material in response to the defendant's application. Where it proposes to do so, CPR 2005, r.13.4(5) requires it to serve on the Crown Court any written comments, copies of statements or other documents outlining the evidence of any proposed witnesses, and copies of any further documents, within 14 days of receiving the application to dismiss or notice of intention to make an oral application. Time may be extended on application to the **24–052**

[88] CPR 2005, r.13.3(1).
[89] CPR 2005, r.13.3(4)(a).
[90] CPR 2005, r.13.3(4)(c).
[91] CPR 2005, r.13.3(4).
[92] CPR 2005, r.13.3(2). In *R. (Snelgrove) v Woolwich Crown Court* [2004] EWHC 2172; [2005] 1 W.L.R. 3223 at [16] Auld L.J. said that, although this wording is more specific than the reference to "any material" in r.13.2(6) (above, para.24–046), they mean the same—viz. "anything", whether admissible evidence or not.
[93] CPR 2005, r.13.3(3).
[94] CPR 2005, r.13.4(3).
[95] CPR 2005, r.13.4(2). Time may be extended: r.13.4(6), (7).
[96] CPR 2005, r.13.4(3). The rules no longer require reasons to be given, but the prescribed form for an application under CJA 1987 does.

court.[97] Copies of the new material must at the same time be served on any other person to whom the notice of transfer relates or with whom the applicant is jointly charged.

TACTICAL CONSIDERATIONS

24–053 Rule 13.4(5) marks a significant departure from the procedure at committal proceedings, where the defence could "ambush" the prosecution with arguments after the prosecution had closed its case. The structure of the rules governing applications to dismiss, by requiring the defence to disclose its hand to some extent, has the effect of enabling the prosecution to put its house in order. This may deter some defendants from making an application to dismiss, and persuade them that their arguments are best left to the close of the prosecution's case. Whether to make an application to dismiss will therefore be a matter of tactics. If the application is to be made on the basis of a technicality or a lacuna in the prosecution's evidence, the defence may wish to keep its powder dry until after the close of the prosecution's case, when it will be too late to correct the defect. This involves a risk that the prosecution may discover the lacuna before it closes its case; but, if an application is made to dismiss the charges, the prosecution will be put on notice at that stage and can supplement its evidence for the purpose of resisting the application. This dilemma will not arise where it appears that the prosecution's case is fundamentally flawed (legally or evidentially) in a way which the prosecution will not be able to rectify, or that the evidence is too weak or inconsistent for the defendant to be convicted on it. In such a case there is no reason not to make an application to dismiss.

24–054 It will be appropriate to make an application orally where the defence wishes to adduce evidence in support of its application, or where it is thought that oral argument will be necessary. In most cases, even those where the application could be argued in writing, the defence will wish to make it orally in order to be able to deal with any concerns which the judge may have as a result of the arguments advanced.

THE TEST TO BE APPLIED

24–055 Whether the application is made orally or in writing, it will succeed only if, in relation to any charge, it appears to the judge that "the evidence against the applicant would not be sufficient for him to be properly convicted".[98] This is the same test as that laid down in *Galbraith*[99] for ruling

[97] CPR 2005, r.13.4(6), (7).

[98] CDA 1998, Sch.3 para.2(2). Under CJA 1987, s.6(1) the test is whether the evidence would be sufficient for a *jury* properly to convict, but this is no longer appropriate since there may be no jury: see below, Ch.26.

[99] [1981] W.L.R. 1039.

on a submission of no case.[100] The *Galbraith* test is particularly difficult to apply in the context of serious fraud, where much will depend upon the inferences drawn from largely undisputed facts. In *R. (Inland Revenue Commissioners) v Kingston Crown Court* it was pointed out that, according to the legislation,

> "the judge will decide not only whether there is any evidence to go to a jury, but whether that evidence is sufficient for a jury properly to convict. That exercise requires the judge to assess the weight of the evidence. This is not to say that the judge is entitled to substitute himself for the jury. The question for him is not whether the defendant should be convicted on the evidence put forward by the prosecution, but the sufficiency of that evidence. Where the evidence is largely documentary, and the case depends on the inferences or conclusions to be drawn from it, the judge must assess the inferences or conclusions that the prosecution propose to ask the jury to draw from the documents, and decide whether it appears to him that the jury could properly draw those inferences and come to those conclusions."[101]

THE EFFECT OF A SUCCESSFUL APPLICATION

Where an application to dismiss a charge is successful, the judge must quash any count relating to that charge,[102] and no further proceedings may be brought on that charge except by preferring a voluntary bill of indictment.[103] The Roskill Committee recommended that a successful application to dismiss should entitle the defendant to plead *autrefois acquit* to any subsequent charge based on the same facts, but this recommendation was not implemented. A refusal by examining magistrates to commit for trial did not have the effect of an acquittal:[104] the prosecution could apply to a differently constituted bench to commit the defendant, or apply to a High Court judge for a voluntary bill of indictment. The effect of the legislation is that, if the prosecution wishes to include a dismissed *charge* in any indictment, it cannot apply to the magistrates' court for the same charge to be transferred or sent again, but must apply for a voluntary bill. But if the success of the application to dismiss convinces the prosecution that it chose the wrong charges, the legislation does not appear to preclude it from applying to transfer or send *different* charges based on the same facts. 24–056

[100] [1989] Crim. L.R. 726 (Henry J.); *Thompson* [2006] EWCA Crim 2849; [2007] Crim. L.R. 387 at [6].

[101] [2001] EWHC 581; [2001] 4 All E.R. 721 at [16].

[102] CJA 1987, s.6(1); CDA 1998, Sch.3 para.2(2). CDA 1998, Sch.3 paras 7–15 make provision for occasions where only either-way offences remain before the Crown Court following a successful application to dismiss an indictable-only charge. The Crown Court will need to hold a mode of trial hearing in that situation.

[103] CJA 1987, s.6(5); CDA 1998, Sch.3 para.2(6). See *R. v Central Criminal Court, ex p. Director of SFO* [1993] 1 W.L.R. 949 at 953.

[104] *R. v Manchester City Stipendiary Magistrate, ex p. Snelson* [1977] 1 W.L.R. 911.

24–057 The circumstances in which it will be appropriate to proceed by way of a voluntary bill are considered in para.IV.35.3 of the Practice Direction, which provides:

> "The preferment of a voluntary bill is an exceptional procedure. Consent should only be granted where good reason to depart from the normal procedure is clearly shown and only where the interests of justice, rather than considerations of administrative convenience, require it."

The application of this guidance to cases in which there has been a successful application to dismiss has yet to be explored. It is possible to envisage circumstances in which it would be appropriate to apply for a voluntary bill, for example where the application had succeeded on a technicality, or where fresh evidence had become available and the interests of justice required a prosecution. A voluntary bill might seem inappropriate where the prosecution simply disagrees with the judge's decision on the application to dismiss; but it now seems that the prosecution cannot challenge the judge's decision directly, either by way of appeal or by judicial review,[105] so a voluntary bill would seem the only option. A voluntary bill would probably be inappropriate where the prosecution accepts the judge's decision but now seeks to rely on further evidence which it could have adduced at the hearing of the application to dismiss.

CHALLENGING THE OUTCOME

24–058 CJA 1987 and CDA 1998 provide no right of appeal for a party aggrieved by the judge's decision to dismiss, or refuse to dismiss, transferred or sent charges. Indeed, it was clearly Parliament's intention that there should be no right of appeal.[106] As originally enacted, CJA 1987, s.9(3)(a) permitted the judge conducting a preparatory hearing to entertain an application to dismiss transferred charges.[107] Although s.9(11) made provision for interlocutory appeals in respect of other matters decided under s.9(3),[108] that power of appeal did not extend to the determination under s.9(3)(a) of an application under s.6.

24–059 It was held in *R. v Central Criminal Court, ex p. Director of SFO*[109] that the judge's decision on an application to dismiss could be challenged by way of judicial review.[110] That decision was difficult to reconcile with the view

[105] See below, paras 24–058 *et seq*.

[106] Whether that intention was overtaken by the provisions for prosecution appeals in CJA 2003 is more questionable: see below, para.24–060.

[107] That provision was repealed before CJA 1987 came into force, as it was inconsistent with other provisions of the Act: the application must be made before arraignment (s.6(1)), and the preparatory hearing starts when the defendant is arraigned (s.8(2)).

[108] See below, para.24–102.

[109] [1993] 1 W.L.R. 949.

[110] This was assumed to be so in *R. v Snaresbrook Crown Court, ex p. Director of SFO*, *The Times*, October 26, 1998; *R. v Snaresbrook Crown Court, ex p. A.*, *The Times*, July 12, 2001; *R. (Inland Revenue Commissioners) v Kingston Crown Court* [2001] EWHC 581; [2001] 4 All E.R. 721.

subsequently taken by the House of Lords that neither a decision whether to stay the proceedings as an abuse of process[111] nor a decision on whether to quash the indictment[112] was reviewable, because both kinds of decision related to the Crown Court's jurisdiction in "matters relating to trial on indictment" and were therefore excluded by the Supreme Court Act 1981,[113] s.29(3). In *R. (Salubi) v Bow Street Magistrates' Court*[114] the Divisional Court expressed the view that *Ex p. Director of SFO* had been overtaken by these decisions, and that a judge's decision on an application to dismiss charges transferred under CJA 1987 or sent under CDA 1998 would equally be caught by the exclusionary words of s.29(3). This view was subsequently confirmed in *R. (Snelgrove) v Woolwich Crown Court*.[115] The underlying purpose of the transfer and sending procedures was to speed up the criminal justice process. The availability of judicial review would inject delay and uncertainty into the process, and this cannot have been Parliament's intention.

The effect is that a defendant aggrieved at the judge's refusal to dismiss the case under CJA 1987, s.6 or CDA 1998, Sch.3 para.2 cannot challenge that decision at all, but must wait until the close of the prosecution's case at the trial. Where the prosecution seeks to challenge the judge's decision to dismiss the case, there is a further possibility. CJA 2003, s.58 enables the prosecution to appeal against a ruling[116] in relation to a trial on indictment which is made before the start of the summing-up, whether before or after the commencement of the trial.[117] At first sight this would seem wide enough to include a decision on an application to dismiss. In *Thompson*,[118] however, it was held to be impossible to appeal under CJA 2003, s.58 against the dismissal of a charge under CDA 1998, Sch.3 para.2. The decision rested primarily on the fact that a s.58 appeal, if unsuccessful, results in an acquittal; and an acquittal is impossible if the relevant count has been quashed. Moreover, CDA 1998, Sch.3 para.2(6)(a) makes it clear that the only way in which the prosecution can challenge a dismissal is by preferring a voluntary bill, and in the court's view CJA 2003 could not be read as creating an implied exception to that. The court was also influenced by the fact that this was not one of the many examples given to Parliament of rulings to which the proposed right of appeal would apply. The Law **24–060**

[111] *Ashton* [1994] 1 A.C. 9.

[112] *R. v Manchester Crown Court, ex p. DPP* (1994) 98 Cr.App.R. 461.

[113] Renamed the Senior Courts Act by the Constitutional Reform Act 2005, from a date to be appointed.

[114] [2002] EWHC 919; [2002] 2 Cr.App.R. 40 at [48]–[49], *per* Auld L.J.

[115] [2004] EWHC 2172; [2005] 1 W.L.R. 3223. *Snelgrove* was followed in *O. v Central Criminal Court* [2006] EWHC 256, where an additional argument based on Art.5(4) of the European Convention on Human Rights was rejected.

[116] Defined as including a decision, determination, direction, finding, notice, order, refusal, rejection or requirement: CJA 2003, s.74(1).

[117] CJA 2003, s.58(13).

[118] [2006] EWCA Crim 2849; [2007] Crim. L.R. 387.

Commission, in the report implemented by Pt 9 of CJA 2003,[119] seems to have overlooked the point.[120]

PREPARATORY HEARINGS

24–061 Before CJA 1987 the resolution of issues before a fraud trial was generally conducted at a pre-trial review, before the trial judge, at which prosecution and defence counsel canvassed matters affecting the conduct of the trial such as the pleas to be tendered, issues of severance, the witnesses who were required to be called, the documents and other exhibits, additional evidence, admissions of fact and points of law. When properly conducted and with the co-operation of the defence, pre-trial reviews were of great assistance in identifying issues and shortening trials. But the pre-trial review was a creature of practice rather than statute. It depended on the co-operation of the defence. Nothing decided at the pre-trial review was enforceable, and, while counsel would be expected to honour promises and undertakings given, if their client subsequently gave contrary instructions their obligation was to follow those instructions unless the circumstances demanded their withdrawal from the case. Nothing said or done could be used in evidence. No additional powers were conferred on the judge.[121]

24–062 Against this background, CJA 1987 introduced what was then a radical new procedure, the preparatory hearing. This procedure is a creature of statute with its own rules and sanctions. It is a part of the trial process: it starts when the defendant is arraigned.[122] The object of the procedure is to identify the issues in dispute before the trial "proper" begins, to resolve issues of law and issues as to the admissibility of evidence, and to prepare the case in a manner which will assist the jury's comprehension of the remaining issues,[123] expedite the proceedings and assist the judge's management of the trial. The power to order preparatory hearings is available in serious or complex fraud cases generally: it is not limited to cases prosecuted by the SFO or another designated authority, or to cases which have been transferred to the Crown Court under CJA 1987 or sent under CDA 1998. While it has been doubted whether there are many cases in which a preparatory hearing will produce a significant saving in time and money overall,[124] preparatory hearings have in practice replaced the pre-trial review in most fraud cases of any complexity.

119 Law Com. No.267, *Double Jeopardy and Prosecution Appeals*, Cm.5048, Pt VII.

120 On the other hand, CJA 2003, s.57(2) expressly excludes certain kinds of ruling which might otherwise have been thought to be included. The absence from s.57(2) of any mention of dismissals under CDA 1998, Sch.3 para.2 might have been regarded as meaning that they are included, whether or not those responsible for the proposals positively intended to include them.

121 The strengths and weaknesses of the pre-trial review system were discussed in *Hutchinson* (1986) 82 Cr.App.R. 51 at 56.

122 CJA 1987, s.8.

123 Assuming that there is to be a jury: see below, Ch.26.

124 *Re Kanaris* [2003] UKHL 2; [2003] 1 W.L.R. 443 at [15], *per* Lord Hope of Craighead.

The conduct of preparatory hearings in serious fraud cases is regulated by CJA 1987, ss.7–10 and Pt 15 of CPR 2005. The procedure was extended by Pt III of the Criminal Procedure and Investigations Act 1996 ("CPIA 1996") to non-fraud cases which are complex or likely to give rise to a long trial, and more recently to non-fraud cases which are merely serious;[125] but the procedure under CJA 1987 is left intact. Indeed, CPIA 1996, s.29(3) ensures that the CJA 1987 provisions take precedence. In a fraud case, the judge must *first* consider whether the case qualifies for a preparatory hearing under CJA 1987. If it does, and he decides to order such a hearing, the CPIA 1996 procedure does not apply. If it does qualify for a hearing under CJA 1987 but he decides not to order one, he cannot order one under CPIA 1996 either.[126] Only if it does not qualify for a CJA 1987 hearing does he have a discretion to order one under CPIA 1996. This could in theory happen in the unlikely event of his considering that a preparatory hearing, though not justified by the seriousness or complexity of the case, *is* justified by the likely length of the trial—a consideration which is sufficient under CPIA 1996 but not under CJA 1987. For practical purposes, preparatory hearings in fraud cases are hearings under CJA 1987, and this section is concerned only with that procedure. **24–063**

APPLICATION FOR A PREPARATORY HEARING

The judge can order a preparatory hearing on an application by the prosecution or any defendant, or on his own motion.[127] An application must be made in writing in the prescribed form, including "a short explanation of the reasons for applying" (which will necessarily be based on the purposes for which CJA 1987, s.7(1) allows a preparatory hearing to be held).[128] It must be served on the other parties,[129] who have seven days to make written representations.[130] **24–064**

The application must be made not more than 28 days after the committal, the consent to the preferment of a bill of indictment, the service of a notice of transfer or (where the case was sent for trial under CDA 1998, s.51) the service of the prosecution case.[131] Since CJA 1987, s.7 refers **24–065**

125 See below, para.24–071.

126 Unless the case involves terrorism and he is therefore *required* by CPIA 1996, s.29(1B) or (1C) to hold a preparatory hearing.

127 CJA 1987, s.7(2). If the prosecution wants the judge to order a trial without a jury under CJA 2003, ss.43 or 44 (see below, Ch.26), it must apply for a preparatory hearing even if a defendant has already done so: CPR 2005, r.15.1(2).

128 See below, para.24–067.

129 CPR 2005, r.15.1(1).

130 CPR 2005, r.15.3.

131 CPR 2005, r.15.2(1). Time may be extended, even after it has expired: r.15.2(3). The Criminal Justice Act 1987 (Preparatory Hearings) Rules 1997 (SI 1997/1051) formerly allowed an application to be made within seven days of an application for dismissal of transferred charges being rejected, even if this is more than 28 days after transfer. CPR 2005 make no provision for this situation. While time might be extended, it may be prudent for a party seeking a preparatory hearing to apply for one within the 28–day limit rather than wait and see whether the application to dismiss is successful.

to "the evidence on an indictment", a preparatory hearing cannot be *ordered* until an indictment is in existence.[132] In practice, an application is usually made by the prosecution when the draft indictment is served, and representations from the parties are heard at the first hearing "for mention" before the judge.[133]

24–066 It is important that the judge allocated to the case should deal with it throughout. In *R. v Southwark Crown Court, ex p. Customs and Excise Commissioners*[134] the Divisional Court emphasised that, in the absence of exceptional circumstances such as death or serious illness, in a case of serious and complex fraud the judge who presides at the preparatory hearing should conduct the trial. Administrative convenience is not a sufficient reason for the judge to be changed once the preparatory hearing has begun. In *H.*[135] Lord Hope pointed out that this follows from CJA 1987, s.8, under which the preparatory hearing is part of the trial.

POWER TO ORDER A PREPARATORY HEARING

24–067 Under CJA 1987, s.7(1), the judge has a discretion to order a preparatory hearing if it appears to him that the evidence on an indictment reveals a case of fraud of such seriousness or complexity that substantial benefits are likely to accrue from such a hearing for the purpose of

> "(a) identifying issues which are likely to be material to the determinations and findings which are likely to be required during the trial,
>
> (b) if there is to be a jury,[136] assisting their comprehension of those issues and expediting the proceedings before them,
>
> (c) determining an application to which section 45 of the Criminal Justice Act 2003 applies,[137]
>
> (d) assisting the judge's management of the trial, or
>
> (e) considering questions as to the severance or joinder of charges".

24–068 A pre-trial hearing cannot be declared to be a preparatory hearing where the case does not meet these requirements, simply in order to give the

[132] If, therefore, the service of the draft indictment is delayed, the entire process will be also be held up. It is questionable whether the defence can technically *apply* for a preparatory hearing before the draft indictment is signed, since CJA 1987, s.7(2) refers to "the application . . . of the person indicted"; but the point seems academic, since the judge can order a hearing of his own motion anyway.

[133] See above, para.24–038.

[134] [1993] 1 W.L.R. 764.

[135] [2007] UKHL 7; *The Times*, March 2, 2007, at [19].

[136] See below, Ch.26. If there is to be no jury, CJA 1987, s.7(1)(b) does not allow the judge to hold a preparatory hearing solely for the purpose of assisting his *own* comprehension of the issues; but, if he thinks he might need such assistance, anything that might provide it would presumably assist his management of the trial, and would thus justify a preparatory hearing under s.7(1)(d).

[137] i.e. an application for the trial to be conducted without a jury: see below, Ch.26. Such an application *must* be determined at a preparatory hearing: CJA 2003, s.45(2); CPR 2005, r.15.4(1).

parties a right to an interlocutory appeal.[138] Neither should a preparatory hearing be ordered as a matter of convenience or by agreement between the parties.[139] If the judge purports to order a preparatory hearing where the statutory conditions are not satisfied, the Court of Appeal will have no jurisdiction to hear an interlocutory appeal.[140] But the s.7(1) purposes are to be construed broadly, in the light of the reasons for which the preparatory hearing procedure was introduced.[141]

> "What the judge has to consider . . . is whether substantial advantages in respect of one or more of those purposes are likely to accrue if he holds a preparatory hearing rather than leaving everything to be dealt with at the trial proper—by which I mean the trial when the jury are sworn.
>
> When a judge is considering this question, he must naturally have regard to the powers which he will be entitled to exercise in such a hearing if he does decide to order one."[142]

Moreover the question is whether it appears *to the judge* that substantial benefits are likely to accrue from holding a hearing for any of the s.7(1) purposes. Where the Court of Appeal has to consider whether the judge was entitled to reach the conclusion he did, that question must be considered without the benefit of hindsight. If he has considered the relevant factors and ordered a hearing on the basis that the potential advantages outweigh the disadvantages, the Court of Appeal will be reluctant to set his decision aside.[143] **24–069**

The criterion is not simply whether substantial benefits would be likely to accrue from holding a preparatory hearing for the specified purposes. It is whether such benefits would be likely to accrue because of the seriousness or complexity of the case. The *complexity* of the case can obviously make it useful to consider the specified matters before a jury is sworn. It is by no means obvious how this might be useful because the case is *serious*, if it is not also complex. Indeed, under s.7(1) as originally enacted the case had to be both serious *and* complex. The current wording was substituted by the Criminal Justice and Public Order Act 1994, when the condition for transferring a case under CJA 1987, s.4 was similarly amended. The fact that this made the s.7(1) criterion incoherent appears to have been overlooked.[144] **24–070**

[138] *M.* [2001] EWCA Crim 2024; [2002] 1 W.L.R. 824; *Ward* [2003] EWCA Crim 814; [2003] 2 Cr.App.R. 20 (p.315); *Loizou* [2005] EWCA Crim 1579; [2005] Cr.App.R. 37 (p.618).

[139] *Att-Gen's Reference (No.1 of 2004),* sub nom. *Edwards* [2004] EWCA Crim 1025; [2004] 1 W.L.R. 2111 at [58].

[140] But it may be prepared to express a view anyway, as in *Loizou* [2005] EWCA Crim 1579; [2005] Cr.App.R. 37 (p.618).

[141] *H* [2007] UKHL 7; *The Times*, March 2, 2007 at [7], *per* Lord Nicholls; at [32], *per* Lord Scott; at [91], *per* Lord Mance.

[142] *H* [2007] UKHL 7, *The Times*, March 2, 2007 at [50]–[51], *per* Lord Rodger. For the powers that the judge can exercise at a preparatory hearing, see below, para.24–077.

[143] *Pennine Acute Hospitals NHS Trust* [2003] EWCA Crim. 3436; [2004] 1 All E.R. 1324 at [61].

[144] It arguably made the s.4(1) criterion incoherent too, since it is not clear why the seriousness of a case should make it appropriate for the Crown Court to take over the management of the case sooner than it otherwise would.

24–071 In 2001, however, the Law Commission regarded the fact that seriousness was sufficient in a fraud case as justifying the extension of preparatory hearings under CPIA 1996, s.29 to *non*-fraud cases which are serious but not complex[145]—an amendment duly made by CJA 2003, s.309. Surprisingly, the Commission found it unnecessary to explain how or why it might be more desirable to hold a preparatory hearing for the purposes mentioned in CJA 1987, s.7(1) and CPIA 1996, s.29(2) where a case is serious than where it is not. It did however quote a retired Lord Justice of Appeal as having pointed out that, because preparatory hearings under CPIA 1996 were not then available for non-fraud cases which were serious but not complex, erroneous pre-trial rulings in such cases which did not bring the proceedings to an end would not be subject to interlocutory appeal even if there were a prosecution right of appeal against terminating rulings (as the Commission recommended there should be).[146] This suggests that the Commission saw the justification for preparatory hearings in serious but non-complex cases as lying primarily if not solely in the interlocutory right of appeal against rulings made in such hearings. It may indeed be arguable that it is more important for such a right of appeal to be available in serious cases than in others. But the fact that rulings given in a preparatory hearing would be appealable is not a valid reason for holding such a hearing. The right of appeal is a side-effect of the decision to hold a preparatory hearing, and that decision may only be taken for the purposes specified in CJA 1987, s.7(1) or CPIA 1996, s.29(2). The connection between those purposes and the seriousness of the case remains elusive.

24–072 Although it is usually appropriate for a preparatory hearing to take place in respect of all defendants charged in the same indictment, the judge can order a separate preparatory hearing in respect of one defendant if circumstances so require.[147]

PRE-PREPARATORY HEARING POWERS

24–073 The preparatory hearing cannot commence until any applications for the dismissal of transferred or sent charges have been determined, since the trial formally begins when the preparatory hearing commences, and arraignment takes place at the start of the preparatory hearing.[148] As there may be some delay in determining such applications, the judge has power, once he has ordered that a preparatory hearing should take place, to order the prosecution and the defence to prepare and serve any documents that appear to him to be relevant and whose service could be ordered at the preparatory hearing.[149] It is not unusual for the service of prosecution and

[145] Law Com. No.267, *Double Jeopardy and Prosecution Appeals*, Cm.5048, para.7.34.

[146] Law Com. No.267, para.7.27. The recommendation for a right of appeal against terminating rulings was implemented by CJA 2003, s.58.

[147] *Re Kanaris* [2003] UKHL 2; [2003] 1 W.L.R. 443.

[148] CJA 1987, s.8(1), (2).

[149] CJA 1987, s.9A.

defence case statements to be ordered at an early stage, since the preparation of these documents may take some considerable time. It is good practice for the prosecution to have its case statement prepared (or in an advanced state of preparation) at or shortly after transfer or sending, so that it can invite the judge at the first "mention" hearing to order its service and to set a time for service of the defence case statements. This will maintain the momentum of the case and enable the important issues to be identified and timetabled for resolution in the preparatory hearing.

Where a defendant is in custody, there is a further reason for making full **24–074**
use of the pre-preparatory hearing powers. Once the preparatory hearing begins, the trial will have begun, and the defendant will therefore lose the protection of the custody time limits. In *Re Kanaris* Lord Hope said that the judge should therefore be careful not to take this step until it becomes necessary to do so.[150] In the meantime, proper use of the pre-preparatory hearing powers will enable considerable progress to be made. Lord Hutton (with whom the other members of the House agreed) did not dissent from this advice, but pointed out that the defendant can still apply for bail after the custody time limit has ceased to apply, and that on such an application the judge would have to take into account the period likely to elapse before the start of the trial proper. There is therefore no inflexible rule that a judge should not start a preparatory hearing until he is certain that he is in a position to proceed expeditiously with the trial.[151] In *H.*[152] Lord Nicholls pointed out that, because a preparatory hearing is part of the trial,[153]

> "the underlying object of a preparatory hearing is to conduct *part of the trial* before the jury is sworn because of the benefits this course is likely to have. The preparatory hearing procedure is not intended to be the means for deciding questions which can and should be decided *in advance of the trial*. I emphasise this distinction because ordering a preparatory hearing has custody time limit consequences. As a general rule a judge should not order a preparatory hearing where the court has adequate powers to decide the matters in dispute before the trial takes place."

THE PREPARATORY HEARING

The commencement of the preparatory hearing is the start of the trial, **24–075**
and it commences with arraignment. It is therefore essential that all defendants attend in person to tender their pleas. Not only will their absence delay the start of the hearing, but it will probably be a breach of their bail obligations. It may also be necessary, depending on the terms in which bail was granted or continued, to re-take sureties. Once the defendants have had their pleas taken, however, it is not unusual for the judge, on application being made to him, to excuse their attendance while

[150] [2003] UKHL 2; [2003] 1 W.L.R. 443 at [17].
[151] [2003] UKHL 2; [2003] 1 W.L.R. 443 at [41], [42].
[152] [2007] UKHL 7; *The Times*, March 2, 2007, at [7].
[153] CJA 1987, s.8(1).

the business of the preparatory hearing is dealt with, and from future adjourned hearings of the preparatory hearing whenever their attendance is not strictly required.[154]

24–076 Given that the legislation provides scope for interlocutory appeals against rulings made in the preparatory hearing, it is important that a realistic timetable and trial date should be set at the outset which provides leeway for such appeals, and that that timetable should be adhered to. In addition, it is essential for the proper conduct of the preparatory hearing that an agenda be set (usually by the prosecution) for each hearing, and circulated in advance so that all parties are aware of the issues to be raised. Provision should also be made for the exchange and submission of skeleton arguments on issues of any substance. The Court of Appeal has pointed out that the new case management powers under CPR 2005 permit the judge to make rulings at a preparatory hearing exclusively by reference to written submissions, or to limit oral submissions to a specified length. The necessary public element of any hearing is sufficiently achieved if the defendants and any media representatives present are supplied with copies of written submissions.[155]

QUESTIONS THAT MAY BE DETERMINED

24–077 CJA 1987, s.9(1) provides that the powers specified in s.9 may be exercised at a preparatory hearing. Section 9(3) provides that the judge may determine

> "(aa) a question arising under section 6 of the Criminal Justice Act 1993 (relevance of external law to certain charges of conspiracy, attempt and incitement);[156]
>
> (b) any question as to the admissibility of evidence;[157] and
>
> (c) any other question of law relating to the case; and
>
> (d) any question as to the severance or joinder of charges."

24–078 In *H.*[158] there was a difference of opinion in the House of Lords as to whether s.9 is an *exhaustive* statement of the powers exercisable at a preparatory hearing. Lords Hope, Rodger and Mance[159] thought that it is,

[154] CJA 1987, s.9(2) makes it clear that the preparatory hearing may be adjourned from time to time.

[155] *K.* [2006] EWCA Crim 724; [2006] 2 All E.R. 552n.

[156] See above, para.22–105.

[157] "Admissibility" includes the question of whether admissible evidence should be excluded as a matter of discretion: *Claydon* [2001] EWCA Crim 1359; [2004] 1 W.L.R. 1575; *H.* [2007] UKHL 7; *The Times*, March 2, 2007 at [86], *per* Lord Mance.

[158] [2007] UKHL 7; *The Times*, March 2, 2007.

[159] "[T]here seems to me little room for doubt that the powers stated in section 9 represent the full range of powers intended to be capable of exercise as part of any preparatory hearing": [2007] UKHL 7 at [83].

Lords Nicholls[160] and Scott that it is not.[161] But the point is somewhat academic, because, even on the majority view, the judge does not lose any power that he would otherwise have merely because a preparatory hearing is in progress. Powers which (on the majority view) he cannot exercise in the preparatory hearing can be exercised in a "parallel" hearing, outside the preparatory hearing.

> "There is . . . no reason in principle why two hearings should not be held on the same occasion provided that all concerned keep clearly in mind the distinction between the two hearings and between the issues which the judge can determine in each."[162]

The main reason why the preparatory and the parallel hearing would need to be differentiated (assuming that the parallel hearing is needed at all) is that not every order or ruling made on the occasion of a preparatory hearing can be the subject of an interlocutory appeal. CJA 1987, s.9(11) provides an interlocutory right of appeal *only* against the determination of a question within s.9(3)(b)–(d), or the judge's decision on an application for the trial to be conducted without a jury. The defence will be well advised to ensure that issues which *can* be determined within the preparatory hearing are raised and dealt with before the start of the trial proper, since, if they are not and are subsequently raised during the course of the trial, the defendant will have lost his interlocutory right of appeal. **24–079**

EXERCISE OF DISCRETION

In *H.*[163] the House of Lords unanimously held that the judge's determination of a matter requiring an exercise of discretion (such as an application for disclosure) is not, of itself, the determination of a "question of law" within the meaning of CJA 1987, s.9(3)(c). Lord Rodger said: **24–080**

[160] "Section 9 enables the judge, at a preparatory hearing, to exercise the powers set out in that section. This enabling provision cannot be interpreted as exhaustive of the judge's powers during a preparatory hearing. It cannot be, for example, that the judge's case-management powers exercisable at a preparatory hearing ordered pursuant to section 7(1)(d) are limited to those set out expressly in section 9": [2007] UKHL 7 at [8].

[161] It clearly is not *completely* exhaustive, because it does not expressly confer a power to make an order under CJA 2003, s.43 for the trial to be conducted without a jury (though s.9(11) does provide a right of appeal against the judge's decision on an application for such an order). That power is conferred by CJA 2003, s.43(3). The power to make such an order *at a preparatory hearing* derives not from CJA 1987, s.9 but from CJA 2003, s.45(2), which *requires* an application for such an order to be determined at a preparatory hearing. Moreover Lord Scott pointed out that "An application that would assist the judge's management of the trial would clearly fall within the section 7(1) purposes but it might well not fall within any of the sub-sections of section 9 that say what the judge at a preparatory hearing 'may' do. To produce a construction of sections 7 to 9 that allowed a particular proposed application to be a sufficient ground for ordering a preparatory hearing to be held but excluded that application from the business that could be transacted at the preparatory hearing would, to my mind, be absurd. I do not see how one could attribute to Parliament an intention to produce such a result": [2007] UKHL 7 at [36]. With respect, this seems unanswerable.

[162] [2007] UKHL 7 at [57], *per* Lord Rodger of Earlsferry.

[163] [2007] UKHL 7, *The Times*, March 2, 2007.

> "An application for disclosure is not a question of law. In my view, therefore, in any normal use of the English language it cannot be said that a judge who sits to determine an application for disclosure is sitting to determine 'a question of law relating to the case'. The mere fact that, when considering such an application, the judge must correctly identify the scope of his powers and duties and apply the correct test cannot mean that, when he orders or declines to order disclosure, he is determining a 'question of law relating to the case' in terms of section 9(3)(c). Such a broad interpretation would not only make paragraphs (aa), (b) and (d) redundant but would also turn any application to a judge, whatever its nature and whether under statute or at common law, into a question of law for the purposes of paragraph (c)."[164]

24–081 In *Re Saunders*[165] it had been held that a refusal to make an order under the Contempt of Court Act 1981, s.4(2) would not involve a question of law unless the discretion was exercised on a basis that was fundamentally flawed. In *Jennings*[166] the same view was taken in relation to the judge's refusal of an application for severance (though s.9(3)(d) now makes express provision for decisions on such applications). On the basis of *H.*, however, it seems likely that an exercise of discretion would not fall within s.9(3)(c), and (unless it fell within s.9(3)(b) or (d), or was a decision on whether to order a non-jury trial) would therefore not be appealable even it *were* fundamentally flawed. Even if legally unsound, it would still not be a determination of a question of law.

THE SECTION 9(3) POWERS AND THE SECTION 7(1) PURPOSES

24–082 The right of appeal under CJA 1987, s.9(11) is available only in respect of orders and rulings made under CJA 1987, s.9(3)(b)–(d) (which specify questions that may be determined at a preparatory hearing)[167] or the determination of an application under CJA 2003, s.45 (which must be done at a preparatory hearing).[168] Until recently the courts took the view that an order or ruling is not necessarily made under CJA 1987, s.9(3) merely because it is the kind of order or ruling that s.9(3) permits the judge to make at a preparatory hearing, and a preparatory hearing is in progress. It must in addition be made for one or more of the purposes for which CJA 1987, s.7(1) allows a preparatory hearing to be held.[169] This was established in *Re Gunawardena*,[170] where the defence sought leave to appeal against the

[164] [2007] UKHL 7 at [59]. The words "any other question of law" in CJA 1987, s.9(3)(c) imply that a question as to the admissibility of evidence (which is covered by s.9(3)(b)) is a question of law; and questions falling within s.9(3)(b) are often (perhaps usually) matters of discretion. But some of them—e.g. questions as to the construction of CJA 2003, Pt 11—are questions of law. So the word "other" in s.9(3)(c) does not imply that an exercise of discretion is a determination of a question of law.

[165] *The Times*, February 8, 1990.

[166] (1993) 98 Cr.App.R. 308.

[167] CJA 1987, s.9(1).

[168] CJA 2003, s.45(2).

[169] See above, para.24–067.

[170] [1990] 1 W.L.R. 703.

judge's refusal to stay the proceedings as an abuse of process. The defence argued that, once a preparatory hearing was under way, any ruling on a question of law fell within the ambit of the preparatory hearing even if it was unrelated to the purposes for which CJA 1987, s.7(1) allowed such a hearing to be ordered. The court thought this could not have been Parliament's intention. Since an application to stay the proceedings was outside the purposes envisaged in CJA 1987, s.7(1), the judge's decision on the application was not a determination made "at the preparatory hearing" within the meaning of CJA 1987, s.9(1). There was therefore no jurisdiction to grant leave to appeal against it.

Gunawardena was a troublesome decision in at least two ways. First, it was not clear what relationship had to be established between the s.7(1) purposes and the ruling against which it was sought to appeal. Did the application have to made for a s.7(1) purpose, or was it sufficient that the judge's determination of the application was made for such a purpose? In *Moore*[171] it was said that a motion to quash a count was not made for the purpose of expediting the trial proper (though, if successful, it might incidentally have that effect) but to prevent the defendant having to stand trial on that count. This reasoning suggested that it was the applicant's purpose that was crucial rather than the judge's. But in *Maxwell*[172] it was said that the relevant purpose was that of the court. In *Hedworth*[173] the court purported to follow *Maxwell*, but also said that the test was objective rather than subjective. This made no sense because purposes are subjective by nature: there is no such thing as an objective purpose. In *W.*[174] the court agreed that "the matter has to be looked at objectively" and that "the subjective purpose of the judge, the defendant or anyone else is irrelevant". But in *G., S. and N.*[175] it was said (wrongly) to be clear from *Hedworth* that the relevant purpose is the judge's purpose. **24–083**

Secondly, in the light of *Gunawardena* an awkward distinction emerged between applications whose only possible purpose is to prevent the trial from going ahead, either at all or in relation to a particular count, and applications which could in theory be conducive to the effective management of the trial but are in fact made with a view to preventing the trial from going ahead. Rulings on the latter kind of application were appealable; rulings on the former were not. The former category included an application for a stay on grounds of abuse of process,[176] an application for a ruling that a CPS prosecution for tax evasion was barred by the Inland Revenue's acceptance of a settlement,[177] a motion to quash,[178] an application to quash an amended indictment on the basis that the charges as **24–084**

171 February 4, 1991.
172 February 9, 1995.
173 [1997] 1 Cr.App.R. 421.
174 [1998] S.T.C. 550.
175 [2001] EWCA Crim 442; [2002] 1 Cr.App.R. 15 (p.147) at [32].
176 *Re Gunawardena* [1990] 1 W.L.R. 703.
177 *W.* [1998] S.T.C. 550.
178 *Moore*, February 4, 1991.

amended were not supported by the evidence served,[179] an application for a ruling that the jury could not properly convict even if the facts alleged were proved,[180] and an application for an order putting the prosecution to its election as between a conspiracy count and substantive counts.[181] The latter category included an application for evidence to be excluded, either on grounds of inadmissibility or in the exercise of the judge's discretion,[182] and an application for a ruling as to the construction of the indictment which had the effect of confining it to a much smaller conspiracy than intended and rendering 80 per cent of the prosecution's evidence irrelevant.[183] Even if the evidence in question was crucial, and a ruling in favour of the defence would therefore put an end to the case, this did not mean that the judge was not determining the matter for a purpose within s.7(1). Even if the grounds on which the defence sought to have the evidence excluded were essentially the same as those on which the defence sought to have the proceedings stayed as an abuse of process, the judge's decision would be appealable on the former point but not the latter.

24–085 In *H.*[184] the House of Lords agreed that it was "impossible to find a coherent path"[185] through the "maze"[186] of the existing case law and that they should instead "take a chain-saw to the impenetrable thicket of interpretation that has grown up and . . . start again"[187] from "first principles".[188] They also agreed that there should now be a less restrictive interpretation of the right to appeal conferred by CJA 1987, s.9(11). Unfortunately they did not speak with one voice about what the new approach should be. There were five reasoned speeches, and on this point their Lordships divided into three camps.

- Lord Rodger, with whom Lord Hope agreed,[189] said that at a preparatory hearing the judge can (but, by implication, can *only*) exercise those of his powers under s.9 that he thinks are likely to achieve the benefits for which s.7(1) allows him to order such a hearing. It is immaterial whether the party *raising* the issue in question does so in order to achieve one of those benefits.[190]
- Lord Scott, with whose speech Lord Nicholls "substantially" agreed,[191] said that, because in his view the s.7(1) purposes should be broadly construed, he could not conceive of an order or ruling

[179] *Hedworth* [1997] 1 Cr.App.R. 421.
[180] *Van Hoogstraten* [2003] EWCA Crim 3642; [2004] Crim. L.R. 498.
[181] *Moore*, February 4, 1991.
[182] *Claydon* [2001] EWCA Crim 1359; [2004] 1 W.L.R. 1575.
[183] *G., S. and N.* [2001] EWCA Crim 442; [2002] 1 Cr.App.R. 15 (p.147).
[184] [2007] UKHL 7; *The Times*, March 2, 2007.
[185] [2007] UKHL 7 at [32], *per* Lord Scott.
[186] [2007] UKHL 7 at [50], *per* Lord Rodger.
[187] [2007] UKHL 7 at [32], *per* Lord Scott.
[188] [2007] UKHL 7 at [91], *per* Lord Mance; at [16], *per* Lord Hope.
[189] [2007] UKHL 7 at [26].
[190] [2007] UKHL 7 at [53], [54].
[191] [2007] UKHL 7 at [15].

under s.9(3)(b)–(d) that would not be for one of the purposes set out in s.7(1).[192]

- Lord Mance thought that the s.9 powers were independent of s.7; but, even if he were wrong about that, there was no need for a "direct or immediate link", and the s.9 powers were not confined to circumstances where a ruling would promote (rather than preclude) an efficient trial.[193]

Overall, *H.* seems to be authority for the following propositions: 24–086

- The s.7(1) purposes should be broadly construed.[194]
- In view of that, it is virtually inconceivable that an order or ruling made under s.9 might not be made for one of the s.7(1) purposes (even if Lords Rodger and Hope were right in thinking that it has to be so made).
- If an order or ruling is made for one of the s.7(1) purposes, it may be made under s.9 even if the application it determines was made for some other purpose (such as securing an acquittal).
- It is therefore immaterial that the order or ruling is one which would effectively put an end to the proceedings (or to the proceedings on a particular count), or that it is a refusal to do so. This is so even if it is made in response to a challenge to the validity of the indictment.

But none of these propositions were essential to the decision, which ultimately turned on the construction of the words "He may determine . . . any . . . question of law" in s.9(3).

ORDERS THAT MAY BE MADE

ORDERS AGAINST THE PROSECUTION

The prosecution case statement

One of the most significant innovations introduced by CJA 1987 was the case statement. Section 9(4)(a) enables the the judge to order the prosecution to supply the court and the defendants with a "case statement" setting out 24–087

- the principal facts of the prosecution case;
- the witnesses who will speak to those facts;

[192] [2007] UKHL 7 at [45].
[193] [2007] UKHL 7 at [91].
[194] [2007] UKHL 7 at [7], *per* Lord Nicholls; at [32], *per* Lord Scott; at [91], *per* Lord Mance.

- any exhibits relevant to those facts;
- any proposition of law on which the prosecution proposes to rely; and
- the consequences, in relation to any count, that appear to the prosecution to flow from the matters stated under any of the heads above.

24–088 The prosecution case statement is usually a detailed exposition of the way in which the prosecution puts its case in relation to each count against each defendant. It often comprises three distinct sections:

- an account of the factual background upon which the counts in the indictment are based, cross-referenced to the witness statements and documentary exhibits that support the factual assertions set out;
- a series of propositions of law, supported by references to authorities; and
- a section in which the evidence and propositions of law are combined to indicate how each count is to be established.

24–089 In *Re Case Statements made under Section 9 of the Criminal Justice Act 1987* the Court of Appeal stressed the importance of the case statement setting out the case against each defendant in such a way as to make it readily accessible to each defendant, thus enabling each defendant to respond effectively to it.

> "It is quite wrong for one of a number of defendants to be expected to wade through a large document such as a Case Statement and to endeavour to extract matters of evidence and documents which may relate to him and upon which he has to make up his mind as to whether he would agree them or otherwise provide some reasons in accordance with the Act for not agreeing."[195]

The court also stressed the importance of the prosecution's ensuring that the defence is provided with copies of the case statement in sufficient time to enable it to argue such points as may be raised at the preparatory hearing with regard to the provision of case statements and other documents by the defence.

24–090 CJA 1987, s.9(4)(d) gives the judge power to order the prosecution to make any amendments to its case statement which appear appropriate having regard to objections made by a defendant. This clearly presupposes that the defence has a right to make representations to the judge as to, for example, inadequacies or inaccuracies in the prosecution case statement.

[195] (1993) 97 Cr.App.R. 417 at 420.

Presentation of evidence

The judge also has power to order the prosecution to prepare its evidence and other explanatory material in a form likely to aid comprehension by the jury[196] and to supply it in that form to the court and the defence.[197] The prosecution may be ordered to produce a draft jury bundle (or an index to the jury bundle) on which the defence's comments as to the inclusion or exclusion of documents can be sought. In practice, orders of this kind appear rarely to be made, although the SFO, of its own initiative, aims to prepare the evidence in a readily accessible format. Depending upon the nature of the case, this may include flow charts, time lines, graphs of share price movements, schedules of transactions and computer generated graphics to illustrate complex company structures. 24–091

Admissions

The judge also has power to require the prosecution to give the court and the defence notice of documents the truth of whose contents ought in the prosecution's view to be admitted, and of any other matters which in the prosecution's view ought to be agreed.[198] The exercise of this power is intended to reduce the number of factual issues to be determined, crystallise the real issues in the case and thereby reduce the length and complexity of the trial proper. The power is frequently exercised, usually at the request of the prosecution, which will be anxious to ensure that as many factual matters are admitted as possible. In *Re Case Statements made under Section 9 of the Criminal Justice Act 1987*[199] the Court of Appeal emphasised the importance of the prosecution's identifying clearly and in relation to *each* defendant the matters that it requires him to admit. In *P.*[200] an order requiring the defence to respond to the prosecution case statement was quashed where the case statement invited the defence to admit some matters which were irrelevant and others which were outside the defendants' knowledge. The court said that if the guidance in *Re Case Statements* had been followed the matter would not have needed to be appealed. 24–092

ORDERS AGAINST THE DEFENCE

Perhaps the most radical innovation of the preparatory hearing procedure was the vesting in the judge of a power to require each defendant, after service of a prosecution case statement, to serve a statement in writing setting out in general terms the nature of his defence and indicating the principal matters on which he takes issue with the prosecution.[201] This 24–093

196 If there is to be no jury (see below, Ch.26) the judge seems to have no power to order the prosecution to prepare its evidence in a form likely to aid the judge's own comprehension.
197 CJA 1987, ss.7(3), 9(4)(b).
198 CJA 1987, s.9(4)(c).
199 (1993) 97 Cr.App.R. 417.
200 February 25, 2004, Lawtel no.AC9800285.
201 CJA 1987, s.9(5)(i).

power has now been superseded by the general obligation to provide a defence statement under CPIA 1996, s.5, and no longer appears in CJA 1987, s.9(5).[202] But s.9(5) still enables the judge to require the defence to respond to the prosecution case statement by giving notice of any objections that it has to the case statement.[203]

24–094 The judge can also order the defence to give notice stating the extent to which it agrees with the prosecution as to documents and other matters in respect of which the prosecution has sought agreement, and the reason for any disagreement.[204] This power is particularly useful in reducing the volume of evidence required to be called at the trial by requiring the defendant to admit (for example) the authenticity of documents, or transactions such as movements between bank accounts or share purchases. Such matters, once admitted, can be reduced to a format in which they are more readily comprehensible. This can save considerable time at the trial by obviating the need to call numerous witnesses simply to prove routine matters which ought properly to be admitted. But the defence should only be expected to admit matters which are relevant and are within the knowledge of the defendant.[205]

24–095 If a defendant is not prepared to admit matters which the prosecution invites him to admit, and it appears that his reasons are inadequate, the judge can require him to give further or better reasons.[206]

ORDER FOR TRIAL WITHOUT A JURY

24–096 Where an application is made for the trial to be conducted without a jury,[207] the application must be determined at a preparatory hearing.[208] At present a non-jury trial can be ordered only if there is a risk of jury tampering, but, if and when CJA 2003, s.43 is brought into force, it will be possible to make such an order in any fraud case transferred under CJA 1987 (or, when CDA 1998, s.51B is brought into force, sent to the Crown Court in pursuance of a notice under that section). This possibility is examined in Ch.26.

EFFECT OF DEPARTURE FROM CASE AND NON-COMPLIANCE WITH REQUIREMENTS

24–097 CJA 1987, s.10(1) provides that any party may depart from the case he disclosed in pursuance of a requirement imposed under s.9. But s.10(2) adds that, where a party does so, the judge or (with the leave of the judge)

[202] CJA 1987, s.9(6) still provides that, with certain exceptions, a summary required by virtue of s.9(5) need not disclose who will give evidence; but there is no longer any power to require a "summary" of anything under s.9(5).
[203] CJA 1987, s.9(5)(ii).
[204] CJA 1987, s.9(5)(iv).
[205] *P.*, February 25, 2004, Lawtel no.AC9800285; above, para.24–092.
[206] CJA 1987, s.9(8).
[207] See below, Ch.26.
[208] CJA 2003, s.45(2).

any other party may make such comment as appears appropriate and the jury (or, if there is no jury, the judge)[209] may draw such inference as appears proper. In commenting, deciding whether to grant leave to comment, or (if there is no jury) deciding whether to draw inferences and if so what inferences to draw, the judge must have regard to the extent of the departure and to whether there is any justification for it.[210]

CJA 1987, s.10 refers to departures by "any party" from his case statement, because it originally applied to a defence statement as well as the prosecution case statement. Now that defence statements are required by CPIA 1996, s.5 rather than by CJA 1987, s.9(5), it seems that s.10 can only apply to departures by the prosecution, because the defence cannot be required to disclose its case *under s.9* at all. The sanctions for departing from a defence statement are provided by CPIA 1996, s.11. Under CPIA 1996, the judge may direct that the jury (if any) be given a copy of a defence statement if he thinks this would help the jury to understand the case or to resolve any issue in the case.[211] But the defence is protected from any further disclosure to the jury of information elicited under CJA 1987, s.9. Under CJA 1987, s.10(4), except as provided by that section, neither a statement given under s.9(5) nor any other information relating to the case for a defendant and given in pursuance of a requirement under s.9 may be disclosed to the jury without the consent of that defendant. The reference to a statement given under s.9(5) no longer has anything to bite on, since there is no longer power under s.9(5) to order a defence statement at all. Section 10(4) seems to apply only to information given by the defence in response to a requirement under s.9(5) to state any objections to the prosecution case statement or the extent to which the defence is prepared to admit documents and other matters. **24–098**

CJA 1987, s.10 does not expressly permit the disclosure of a case statement to the jury (if any). In *Mayhew*[212] the Court of Appeal thought this was permissible but was not to be encouraged. **24–099**

> "[W]e share the learned judge's general view that it would be undesirable for case statements to be put as a matter of course before juries as if they were projections of the indictment or particulars thereof. The object of ordering a case statement is to inform the opposing party of the case that it is intended to be put forward so as to facilitate preparation for trial and avoid surprise. If there is a significant departure, then subject to the judge's discretion under section 10, the jury may be apprised of it. But to provide the jury with pleadings and raise pleadings arguments would tend to confusion and diversion from the factual issues."

CJA 1987, s.10(2) similarly allows the judge or (with the leave of the judge) any party to comment on a failure to comply with a requirement imposed under s.9, and allows the jury (or, if there is no jury, the judge) to **24–100**

[209] See below, Ch.26.
[210] CJA 1987, s.10(2).
[211] CPIA 1996, s.6E(4)(a), (5)(b).
[212] November 18, 1991.

draw such inference as appears proper. This power would appear to be of most use to the prosecution, and will be of particular use in cases where the defence has failed to admit matters which it ought properly to have admitted.

INTERLOCUTORY APPEALS

24–101 CJA 1987, s.9(11)–(14) and CPR 2005, Pt 65 provide a machinery for challenging, by way of interlocutory appeal, an order or ruling made during a preparatory hearing. These provisions are now supplemented by Pt 9 of CJA 2003. CJA 2003, s.58 gives the prosecution (but not the defence) an interlocutory right of appeal against most orders and rulings made in relation to a trial on indictment.[213] CJA 2003, s.62 will give the prosecution a further right of appeal against an *evidentiary* ruling which "significantly weakens the prosecution's case",[214] but has not been brought into force. Neither of these rights of appeal is available in respect of an order or ruling made in a preparatory hearing, because there is already a right of appeal under CJA 1987, s.9(11).[215] Their significance in the present context is that they do apply to orders and rulings in favour of the defence which are made when a preparatory hearing is in progress but are outside the scope of that hearing.[216] The main disadvantage of the CJA 2003, s.58 route is that an unsuccessful appeal under that section results in the defendant's acquittal, even if the prosecution could have fought on had it not appealed.[217] This consideration obviously has no force if the order or ruling is one that makes it impossible for the prosecution to fight on anyway, such as a stay of proceedings.

THE RIGHT OF APPEAL

24–102 Under CJA 1987, s.9(11) a right of appeal lies to the Court of Appeal, with the leave of the judge or of the Court of Appeal, from

- any order or ruling by the judge in the preparatory hearing determining
  - any question as to the admissibility of evidence,
  - any other question of law relating to the case, or
  - any question as to the severance or joinder of charges; or
- the judge's granting or refusal of an application under CJA 2003 s.45 for the trial to be conducted without a jury.[218]

[213] But not against the granting of an application to dismiss: *Thompson* [2006] EWCA Crim 2849; [2007] Crim. L.R. 387; above, para.24–060.
[214] CJA 2003, s.63.
[215] CJA 2003, s.57(2)(b).
[216] See above, para.24–079.
[217] CJA 2003, s.58(8).
[218] See below, Ch.26. Until CJA 2003, s.43 is brought into force, the only ground on which such an application can be made is that there is a risk of jury tampering.

There is no right of appeal against an order made under CJA 1987, s.9(4).[219]

24–103 There is also no right of appeal under CJA 1987, s.9(11) against a ruling on a question arising under the Criminal Justice Act 1993, s.6, although such a ruling can be made within the preparatory hearing.[220] Section 6 of the 1993 Act ensures that, where a person is charged with conspiracy to defraud, attempt or incitement, but the conduct he had in view would have occurred outside England and Wales and would therefore not be indictable in England and Wales, he can be convicted only if the judge rules that the conduct he had in view would be an offence under the law of the place where it was to be done.[221] If the charge is one of conspiracy to commit an *offence*, however, the position is governed not by the 1993 Act but by s.1A of the Criminal Law Act 1977; and s.1A(10) of that Act provides that the issue of whether the agreed course of conduct would be an offence under the law of the place in question is to be treated for the purposes of CJA 1987, s.9(3) as one of law. So a ruling on that issue is to be treated as a ruling under CJA 1987, s.9(3)(c); and a ruling under s.9(3)(c) is appealable under s.1A(10) of the 1977 Act even if it is not in fact a ruling on a question of law. It seems to follow that, where the charge is one of statutory conspiracy, either side can appeal against the ruling under CJA 1987, s.9(11); but, where it is one of conspiracy to defraud, attempt or incitement, an appeal by the prosecution must be under CJA 2003, s.58, and the defence has no interlocutory right of appeal at all. If this is right, it is a curious anomaly.

PROCEDURE

24–104 The rules governing interlocutory appeals from preparatory hearings (whether held under CJA 1987, s.7 or CPIA 1996, s.29) are set out in CPR 2005, Pt 65. The timetable of an appeal is as follows:

(1) An application for leave to appeal may be made orally to the judge on the occasion of the order or ruling.

(2) If it is not made on that occasion, and leave is to be sought from the judge, an application must be made within two days of the making of the order or ruling to which it relates.[222] The applicant must serve a written notice, specifying the grounds of the application, on the Crown Court and all parties directly affected by the order or ruling in question.[223]

(3) Within seven days of the date of the order or ruling, the appellant must (if he has obtained leave) serve notice of appeal or (if he has

[219] *Smithson* [1994] 1 W.L.R. 1052.
[220] CJA 1987, s.9(3)(aa).
[221] See above, para.22–104.
[222] CPR 2005, r.65.1(1). It appears that an application does not have to be made to the judge, but can be made directly to the Court of Appeal.
[223] CPR 2005, r.65.1(2).

not obtained leave) notice of an application to the Court of Appeal for leave. These notices are to be in the form prescribed by the Practice Direction and must be served on the Registrar of Criminal Appeals, the Crown Court and the parties directly affected by the order or ruling, together with any additional documents required by the rules to be served.[224]

(4) The notice of appeal, or the application for leave to appeal, must be accompanied by any documents or other things necessary for the proper determination of the appeal or the application,[225] and must

(a) specify any question of law in respect of which the appeal is brought, and, where appropriate, such facts of the case as are necessary for its proper consideration;

(b) summarise the arguments intended to be put to the Court of Appeal; and

(c) specify any authorities intended to be cited.[226]

(5) Within seven days of receiving the notice of appeal or application for leave, the respondent, if he wishes to oppose the appeal, must serve a notice in the prescribed form on the Registrar of Criminal Appeals, the Crown Court and the appellant and any parties directly affected by the order or ruling.[227]

24–105 Leave to appeal may be granted by a single judge.[228] If the single judge refuses leave to appeal, the appellant can apply to a full court of the Court of Appeal by serving the appropriate notice (in the prescribed form) on the Registrar of Criminal Appeals within seven days from the date on which notice of refusal was served on him. If no such notice is served the application is treated as having been refused by the full Court of Appeal.[229]

POSTPONING THE APPEAL

24–106 CJA 1987, s.9(10) provides that an order or ruling made under s.9 has effect during the trial unless it appears to the judge, on application made to him during the trial,[230] that the interests of justice require him to vary or discharge it. One can envisage situations where, for example, a ruling of law

[224] CPR 2005, r.65.1(3), (4), (6). Time for giving these notices may be extended by the Court of Appeal: r.65.1(5). However, given the urgent nature of these appeals, time is unlikely to be extended unless satisfactory grounds are made out.

[225] CPR 2005, r.65.1(10).

[226] CPR 2005, r.65.1(8).

[227] CPR 2005, r.65.2(1). Time may be extended: r.65.2(2).

[228] CPR 2005, r.65.6. The single judge also has the power to grant ancillary applications, e.g. to extend time.

[229] CPR 2005, r.65.7. There are provisions for time to be extended.

[230] But apparently not of his own motion.

made during the preparatory hearing is shown to be wrong by a subsequent decision in another case, which requires the judge to discharge his previous order. But the existence of this power suggests that a party aggrieved with an order or ruling made is not *required* to appeal against it.

In practice, if the prosecution believes that an order or ruling in favour of the defence is appealable under CJA 1987, s.9(11) it will wish to appeal, since it will have no right of appeal at the conclusion of the trial if the defendant is acquitted as a result of that ruling. A defendant, on the other hand, might for tactical reasons prefer to reserve his position and appeal against conviction if necessary. Such a course would not be without risk. In *Hunt*[231] the defendant obtained leave to appeal against a ruling made in the preparatory hearing, but abandoned that appeal. It was held that he was estopped from challenging the ruling in an appeal against conviction. If that were right, the same must arguably be true where no attempt is made to bring an interlocutory appeal at all, since an abandoned appeal cannot have a greater effect than no appeal at all. But in *Hedworth* the court pointed out that any such rule would be an incentive to the bringing of interlocutory appeals, with consequential delay to the trial proper, and expressed the "strong hope" that no such rule should be read into *Hunt*. **24–107**

> "We would record merely the following three considerations: (1) Any order which is made at the preparatory hearing can be reconsidered in the course of the trial, section 9(10) so provides. What takes place at the trial therefore determines how and on what basis the matter is left to the jury. (2) Leave to appeal might be refused on discretionary grounds and the Court would therefore not consider the substantive issue. It would be clearly inappropriate and unjust if the defendant was prevented from challenging the substantive decision at the post-conviction stage. (3) It might well be the case that there was no appeal because a refusal of leave on discretionary grounds was anticipated. The same comment would then apply."[232]

REPORTING RESTRICTIONS

CJA 1987, s.11 imposes restrictions on the reporting of an unsuccessful application to dismiss transferred charges under s.6, a preparatory hearing under s.7, and any interlocutory appeal or application for leave to appeal in relation to such a hearing. It provides that, with the exception of certain limited information,[233] it shall not be lawful, save with the leave of the trial judge (or, in relation to an appeal, the Court of Appeal) to publish reports of those proceedings until the conclusion of the trial.[234] Section 11A makes it a summary offence to contravene s.11, but the consent of the Attorney-General is required for the institution of proceedings. CDA 1998, Sch.3 **24–108**

[231] [1994] Crim. L.R. 747.
[232] [1997] 1 Cr.App.R. 421 at 431.
[233] CJA 1987, s.11(12).
[234] CJA 1987, s.11(2), (3).

para.3 imposes similar restrictions on the reporting of an application under para.2 to dismiss charges sent for trial under s.51.

24–109 Where an application is made in open court after the start of the preparatory hearing, but the determination of that application falls outside the scope of the preparatory hearing,[235] the restrictions in CJA 1987, s.11 will not apply. If the reporting of the application would create a substantial risk of prejudice to the administration of justice in the trial proper, an application should be made for reporting restrictions to be imposed under the Contempt of Court Act 1981, s.4(2). It is therefore important for the parties and the court to be clear whether the matter under consideration is or is not being dealt with as part of the preparatory hearing. This will normally depend on whether the order or ruling sought is *capable* of being made within the preparatory hearing.[236] At the conclusion of the preparatory hearing in the first Guinness trial Henry J. stated:

> "The parties and I were the first to tread the virgin territory of [CJA 1987]. The preparatory hearings before me have been conducted in exemplary fashion, in an atmosphere of trust combined with business-like informality (which I happily acquiesced in). When we embarked on these hearings I do not believe that anyone involved had foreseen all of the arguable difficulties that the novel procedure would create. With the wisdom of hindsight, it would perhaps have been better had there been a greater degree of formality, certainly in order to identify which applications were within and which applications (if any) were outside the scope of the preparatory hearing, as such a determination could affect reporting, the rights of appeal, and when the jury could be sworn."[237]

[235] See above, paras 24–077 *et seq*.

[236] Even if the judge could have made it in the preparatory hearing, he presumably has a discretion to make it outside that hearing, provided he makes it clear that he is doing so; but it is doubtful whether there would ever be good reasons for doing so. A desire to avoid an interlocutory appeal would not seem to be such a reason.

[237] *Saunders*, February 5, 1990.

CHAPTER 25

THE PROSECUTION OF MULTIPLE OFFENDING

Few fraudsters commit just one offence. They tend either to have multiple victims (as in an investment fraud) or to commit many offences against the same victim (such as their employer). Where there is evidence that a person has committed hundreds of separate offences, an indictment charging all of them would be unmanageable. Dividing them between several trials would be both oppressive and expensive. Charging only a selection of them would mean that, even if the defendant is convicted of all the offences charged, those convictions will not adequately reflect the full criminality of his conduct, and it may not be possible to pass an appropriate sentence. **25–001**

Two quite different approaches to this problem have been developed. One involves treating a number of offences as a single offence, and "rolling them up" into a single count. The other involves charging a representative sample of the offences. Neither approach has proved entirely satisfactory, and both are the subject of recent legislation which at the time of writing has yet to be tested. **25–002**

ROLLED-UP COUNTS

The rule against duplicity prohibits the charging of more than one offence in a single count. A duplicitous count is bad in law and will be quashed. But an apparently major exception to the rule has been introduced by r.14.2(2) of the Criminal Procedure Rules 2005 ("CPR 2005"): **25–003**

"More than one incident of the commission of the offence may be included in a count if those incidents taken together amount to a course of conduct having regard to the time, place or purpose of commission."

25–004 If this provision is taken at face value, the exception it creates is so wide that there is not much left of the original rule. But it cannot be understood, or its likely effect assessed, without some grasp of the law as it previously stood. Lord Diplock pointed out in *DPP v Merriman* that

"The rule against duplicity . . . has always been applied in a practical, rather than in a strictly analytical, way for the purpose of determining what constituted one offence. Where a number of acts of a similar nature committed by one or more defendants were connected with one another, in the time and place of their commission or by their common purpose, in such a way that they could fairly be regarded as forming part of the same transaction or criminal enterprise, it was the practice, as early as the eighteenth century, to charge them in a single count of an indictment."[1]

There are two main ways in which rolled-up counts have been justified, though the line between them is blurred. One involves treating the individual offences as constituting a single, composite offence, so that the rule against duplicity is in theory not infringed. The other allows separate offences to be charged as a single offence, by way of exception to the rule, on the ground that it is impracticable to charge them in separate counts.

CONTINUING OFFENCES

25–005 Certain offences are by nature continuing: they consist in a number of acts committed over a period of time.[2] The definition of fraudulent trading,[3] for example, clearly envisages that the offence may be committed over a period. Cheating the public revenue[4] is another example: tax evasion over a period may be charged as a single offence, notwithstanding that there is a periodic duty to account for tax and a series of actual losses to the revenue.[5] The Value Added Tax Act 1994, s.72(8) enables a number of offences of fraudulent tax evasion under s.72(1) or (3) during a specified period to be charged as a single offence, even if the particulars of those offences are known.[6] Although there is no corresponding provision in relation to the offence of fraudulently evading duty under s.170(2) of the Customs and Excise Management Act 1979, that offence too can consist in multiple transactions.[7] In practice, conspiracy charges often serve the same purpose.[8]

[1] [1973] A.C. 584 at 607.
[2] *Hodgetts v Chiltern District Council* [1983] 2 A.C. 120 at 128, *per* Lord Roskill.
[3] See above, Ch.8.
[4] Above, paras 16–040 *et seq*.
[5] *Hunt* [1994] Crim. L.R. 747.
[6] See above, para.16–010.
[7] *Martin* (1998) 2 Cr.App.R. 385; above, para.16–017.
[8] See below, paras 28–013 *et seq*. But conspiracy charges have disadvantages too: see above, Ch.21.

It seems likely that fraud by abuse of position[9] will be similarly regarded as a continuing offence.

Other offences are defined in such a way as to suggest that their commission is necessarily instantaneous. The classic example is theft. But it has long been permissible in some circumstances to treat a succession of thefts on different occasions as a single theft, and thus to charge them in a single count. In *Henwood*,[10] for example, the defendant had been in the service of the prosecutor for nine years and was found to have a number of articles belonging to the prosecutor in a box at his own lodgings. Although the articles were different in kind, there was no evidence as to when they had been stolen. One count alleging theft of all of them was held good. Bovill C.J. said that it would have made no difference had there been evidence of distinct takings. In *DPP v McCabe*[11] it was held that the appropriation of 76 library books from up to 32 different branch libraries, over a period of up to a year or more, could properly be charged as one theft. **25–006**

In *Barton v DPP*[12] the defendant had stolen a total of £1,338 from his employer on 94 separate and identifiable occasions. The Divisional Court held that it was appropriate to charge a single theft because the defence was the same in each case. But, since duplicity renders a count formally invalid,[13] it is not clear how the nature of the defence can be relevant. The Law Commission regarded *Barton* as "stretching the concept of what constitutes a single continuous offence capable of being charged in a single count about as far as it can properly be taken".[14] In *Tovey*[15] the Court of Appeal regarded the *Barton* approach as acceptable provided that there is no unfairness to the defendant. **25–007**

GENERAL DEFICIENCY COUNTS

Alternatively, where property has been stolen over a period of time but it cannot be proved what was stolen when, it may be possible to charge a single theft of all the property on the basis of a "general deficiency". In *Tomlin*[16] the defendant was bound to account on a particular day for monies received by him in small amounts over a period. There was no evidence as to when any individual amount had been taken, or what the total deficiency was at any one time. An aggregate count was upheld on appeal because it was impossible for the Crown to particularise further. Similarly in *Cain*[17] it was said that it would affront common sense to require **25–008**

9 Above, Ch.6.
10 (1870) 11 Cox C.C. 526.
11 [1992] Crim. L.R. 885.
12 [2001] EWHC 223; 165 J.P. 779.
13 See *Archbold*, para.1–135.
14 Law Com No.277, *The Effective Prosecution of Multiple Offending*, Cm.5609, para.3.9.
15 [2005] EWCA Crim 530; *The Times*, April 19, 2005.
16 [1954] 2 Q.B. 278.
17 [1983] Crim. L.R. 802.

the prosecution to give particulars which it could not give. The justification for a general deficiency count is not that there is in fact a single, continuing appropriation, but that the individual appropriations cannot be charged separately because the prosecution does not have enough information to do so, and the law does not require the prosecution to do the impossible. This might have been a better explanation for some of the cases treated as involving a continuing offence, such as *Henwood*. It is difficult to regard the theft of different *types* of articles as a continuous appropriation.

"COURSE OF CONDUCT"

25–009 The Law Commission examined the problem of multiple offences as part of its review of the law of fraud, though it eventually recognised that the problem was not confined to fraud and therefore published a separate report. In a consultation paper published in 1999 it floated the idea of making it possible for multiple offences to be charged in a single count if, taken together, they amount to a fraudulent "scheme".[18] By the time it circulated an informal consultation document in 2000 this had evolved into a suggestion that it should be possible to charge multiple offences in a single count if they constitute a "course of conduct". The response persuaded the Commission to drop the idea when it came to publish its report on multiple offending.

> "Principally the concerns relate to the concept of a course of conduct. It was thought that this might be difficult to establish, could lead to vague and uncertain charging and lead to a defendant having to be acquitted in some cases where the jury are sure of some offences but not of others. In addition, without special measures, the judge might not be able to determine the basis for sentencing from the verdict of the jury."[19]

25–010 In view of this conclusion, and particularly the fact that the Commission was driven to it by the concerns of the profession and the judiciary, it is surprising that the Criminal Procedure Rule Committee should have settled on "course of conduct" as the criterion in the new r.14.2(2) of CPR 2005.[20] This expression is essentially vacuous: the repetition of any offence by the same person is, by definition, a course of conduct. Clearly the rule cannot be read literally. But it is not clear what kind of limitation is to be implied, or, in particular, how far the rule is intended to depart from the position as it was previously understood.

25–011 The explanatory memorandum to the statutory instrument introducing r.14.2(2)[21] states:

[18] Consultation Paper No.155, *Legislating the Criminal Code: Fraud and Deception*, paras 7.60 *et seq*.

[19] Law Com. No.277, para.5.4.

[20] Above, para.25–003.

[21] SI 2007/699.

"The new rule allows a prosecutor in certain circumstances to bring a single charge against a defendant even though that includes more than one incident of the offence alleged—for example, where the defendant has laundered the proceeds of drug trafficking in comparatively small weekly sums for week after week, or has assaulted the same victim in the same way repeatedly over a period of time. The Committee took account among other things of the potential under the old rules for a perceived unfairness to a victim of multiple offending where out of many alleged offences only a few are prosecuted as examples, giving the impression that the victim's distress has been underestimated or that he or she has not been believed. The Committee was satisfied that the new rule reflects what judgments of the House of Lords in the past have found consistent with fundamental principles of fairness."

The memorandum does not identify the judgments of the House of Lords that the Committee had in mind, and it may be doubted whether they do provide much support for the criterion in r.14.2(2).[22] Indeed, since the House is generally concerned with what the law *is* rather than how it might properly be changed, it is difficult to see how any such judgments *could* support the new criterion, unless it is intended merely as a restatement of the previous law. And the rest of the passage quoted suggests that the rule is intended as a departure from "the old rules".

The Consolidated Criminal Practice Direction, para.IV.34.8 provides guidance on when r.14.2(2) can properly be invoked. **25–012**

"The circumstances in which such a count may be appropriate include, but are not limited to, the following:

(a) the victim on each occasion was the same, or there was no identifiable individual victim as, for example, in a case of the unlawful importation of controlled drugs or of money laundering;

(b) the alleged incidents involved a marked degree of repetition in the method employed or in their location, or both;

(c) the alleged incidents took place over a clearly defined period, typically (but not necessarily) no more than about a year;

(d) in any event, the defence is such as to apply to every alleged incident without differentiation. Where what is in issue differs between different incidents, a single 'multiple incidents' count will not be appropriate, though it may be appropriate to use two or more such counts according to the circumstances and to the issues raised by the defence."

These conditions are apparently intended to be cumulative (though the **25–013** words "in any event" in para.(d) imply that only *that* condition is essential). For example, it can hardly be sufficient that the defendant is alleged to have committed theft many times against the same victim, if he is alleged to

[22] The words "having regard to the time, place or purpose of commission" in r.14.2(2) suggest that one of the authorities referred to is Lord Diplock's dictum in *DPP v Merriman* [1973] A.C. 584 at 607; above, para.25–004. But, even if that dictum is assumed to be literally correct (see below, fn.25), it requires that the different acts should form part of "the same transaction or criminal enterprise"—not merely a "course of conduct".

have stolen many kinds of property in many different ways and locations over many years. And it is presumably not intended that r.14.2(2) should apply where the defendant is alleged to have defrauded *different* victims over a period of time, albeit in a similar way: the Attorney-General himself has doubted that it would be appropriate to charge a single count in such a case.[23]

25–014 If that is right, r.14.2(2) seems to go little further than the previous law, in relation to fraud cases at any rate. Where *all* the conditions in para.IV.34.8 of the Practice Direction are satisfied, it might be permissible to charge the offences as a single, continuing offence even under the old rules. That is certainly so in the case of theft. It seems to have been assumed that repeated obtainings by *deception* could not be charged as a single obtaining, even if the victim is the same in each case;[24] but there seems to be no obvious reason why the continuing offence device should not equally be available. If a person dishonestly obtains £10 from his employer 100 times, *Barton* suggests that he could be charged with a single theft even under the old rules, and it would be anomalous if he could be charged with a single theft but not with a single obtaining by deception. The Law Commission argued, on the somewhat flimsy basis of Lord Diplock's remarks in *DPP v Merriman*,[25] that the continuing offence device is available if two or more similar offences are "connected by time and place of commission or common purpose (typically, the same act committed against the same victim)" so that "they can fairly be regarded as forming part of the same transaction or criminal enterprise", *and* "having regard to the allegations made and the defence put forward . . . , save for particular marginal issues, it may fairly be said to be an 'all or nothing' case".[26] The Commission pointed out that in *Barton* "the fact that numerous transactions of the same type were committed against the same victim provided the crucial connecting factor", and added: "For cases of dishonesty that would, in our view, almost invariably be the case."[27] This appears to mean

[23] *Hansard*, HL Vol.658, cols 1426–1427 (March 11, 2004).

[24] In *Donnelly* [1998] Crim. L.R. 131 the defendant was charged in one count with obtaining £32,068 in unemployment benefit from the DHSS by deception over a period of more than five years. The Court of Appeal held that the count was not duplicitous in *form*, because the fact that the money had been obtained in many instalments could only be discovered on examining the evidence or by requiring particulars; but it seems to have been assumed that a motion to quash the count would have succeeded. The perceived need for s.111A of the Social Security Administration Act 1992 (above, Ch.17) seems to have been based on a similar assumption.

[25] See above, para.25–004. In its consultation paper on fraud, the Law Commission had pointed out that "in *Merriman* the appeal was not directly concerned with the application of the rule against duplicity, and this dictum cannot be taken literally. Where the defendant obtains money from 20 victims by identical deceptions, it may be fair to describe those acts as 'forming part of the same . . . criminal enterprise'; but we think it unlikely that, under the present law, a count charging the 20 obtainings as one offence would survive challenge": Consultation Paper No.155, para.7.65. In its report on multiple offending the Commission seems to have forgotten this, grandly describing Lord Diplock's dictum as "[t]he test for a single continuous offence, enunciated by the House of Lords": Law Com. No.277, para.6.2. The dictum is similarly taken out of context at *Archbold* para.1–136a.

[26] Law Com. No.277, para.6.7.

[27] Law Com. No.277, para.6.8.

that it would almost invariably be *sufficient* that all the frauds are committed against the same victim, though it might also be possible to find the necessary nexus between a number of frauds against different victims. On this view, the old rules were at least as permissive as para.IV.34.8 of the Practice Direction (assuming that the conditions there set out are intended to be cumulative).

Obtaining property by deception has now been abolished anyway: in future, the most pressing question will be whether multiple instances of the new fraud offence can be charged in a single count. It is impossible to say whether this would have been possible under the old rules. Although the Law Commission's report on multiple offending appeared shortly after the report recommending the new fraud offence, it is surprisingly reticent about how the position might be affected by the implementation of that recommendation. Where similar false representations are made to the same victim over a "clearly defined period", and the defendant's justification for making them does not vary from one case to another, para.IV.34.8 of the Practice Direction suggests that r.14.2(2) could be invoked. Where similar representations are made to *different* victims, condition (a) is not satisfied; but that is arguably not fatal, even if the conditions in para.IV.34.8 are cumulative, because para.IV.34.8 says that a count under r.14.2(2) may be appropriate even if the conditions are not satisfied. We are therefore thrown back on the essentially meaningless criterion of whether the alleged instances amount to a "course of conduct". The position is likely to be uncertain for some time to come. **25–015**

SENTENCING

Where a defendant is convicted on a single rolled-up count after a contested trial, it may be unclear whether the jury were satisfied of his guilt in relation to *all* the instances alleged. It may therefore be difficult for the judge to know how to sentence. Paragraph IV.34.11 of the Practice Direction provides: **25–016**

> "In some cases, such as money laundering or theft, there will be documented evidence of individual incidents but the sheer number of these will make it desirable to cover them in a single count. Where the indictment contains a count alleging multiple incidents of the commission of such offences, and during the course of the trial it becomes clear that the jury may bring in a verdict in relation to a lesser amount than that alleged by the prosecution, it will normally be desirable to direct the jury that they should return a partial verdict with reference to that lesser amount."

The Law Commission had recommended a new procedure which would involve asking the jury, when convicting on a rolled-up count, to give a special verdict indicating whether there are any aspects of the alleged offending as respects which the jury are not satisfied of the defendant's guilt. This recommendation was rejected by the Government on the ground that the proposed procedure was "complicated and cumbersome" as well as unnecessary.[28] While the former criticism may be justified,[29] it is not clear how the "partial verdict" procedure differs from that envisaged by the Law Commission, or why it is needed if the Commission's procedure is not.[30]

TRIAL BY JUDGE ALONE AFTER CONVICTION ON SAMPLE COUNTS

25–017 Where it is not possible to roll up all the alleged offences in a single count, and there are too many to charge individually, a solution commonly adopted in the past has been to charge a selection of the offences in specimen counts. Following conviction on those counts, the judge would sentence on the basis that those counts were only a selection and did not reflect the full criminality of the defendant's conduct. This practice was "thrown into disarray"[31] in *Kidd*,[32] where the Court of Appeal held that a defendant may be sentenced only for an offence of which he has been convicted or which he has asked the court to take into consideration. The court recognised that, as a result of its decision, indictments would in future be likely to include more counts, but did not think this need be "unduly burdensome or render the trial unmanageable". In relation to fraud cases, at least, this forecast has proved optimistic. For example, the SFO reported to the Law Commission that a recent case of advance fee fraud involved losses of more than £1m, but no victim lost more than £7,000. The SFO thought it unsafe to include more than 10 counts in the indictment.[33]

25–018 The Law Commission recommended a radical solution, based on the idea of the *Newton* hearing. It involves a two-stage trial process in which the jury try only some of the counts in the indictment; if they convict on those counts, the judge tries the rest. The recommendation was broadly implemented by the Domestic Violence, Crime and Victims Act 2004 ("DVCVA 2004"), ss.17–20. Section 17 enables a Crown Court judge to make an order, on application by the prosecution, for a trial on indictment to take place "on the basis that the trial of some, but not all, of the counts included in the indictment may be conducted without a jury". The drafting of the legislation to some extent follows the model of Pt 7 of the Criminal Justice

[28] *Hansard*, HL Vol.658, col.1427 (March 11, 2004).

[29] It is difficult to be sure, since the Law Commission did not follow its usual practice of annexing draft legislation to its report. The ostensible purpose of this omission was to facilitate the feeding of the Commission's recommendations into the Government's work on developing the White Paper *Justice for All* into legislative form, and to avoid duplication of resources: Law Com. No.277, para.1.3. The existence of draft legislation would certainly have enabled the Government to reach a more informed decision on the recommendation.

[30] Arguably neither is needed, because the judge is free to form his own view as long as it is not inconsistent with the jury's verdict: see the remarks of Buxton L.J. quoted in Law Com. No.277, para.3.15.

[31] Law Com. No.277, para.2.2.

[32] [1998] 1 W.L.R. 604, sometimes known as *Canavan*.

[33] Law Com No.277, para.2.11.

Act 2003, which enables certain cases to be tried by a judge without a jury being involved at all.[34]

ELIGIBILITY

There is no restriction on the types of case in which an application under DVCVA 2004, s.17 may be made. It is immaterial that some or all of the alleged offences were committed before s.17 came into force on January 8, 2007.[35] However, s.17 does not apply where the defendant was committed for trial, a notice of transfer was given or (in a case sent for trial under s.51 of the Crime and Disorder Act 1998) the prosecution evidence was served on the defendant before that date. It is conceivable that there may be cases in which the prosecuting authority has deliberately delayed committal, service of a notice of transfer or service of the evidence in order to take advantage of the new provisions. If it could be shown that this had occurred, it might well be a valid objection to an application under s.17. Indeed it would arguably be an abuse of process, and might lead to the proceedings being stayed altogether.[36] **25–019**

SUITABILITY

Whether a case is *suitable* for a s.17 application is another matter. The Law Commission described a number of features which it would expect to see in cases attracting the new procedure: **25–020**

> "The type of case that we would regard as suited to this procedure is where it would be unthinkable that any judge would order separate trials in relation to the activity covered in the schedule [sc. of the 'linked' offences proposed for trial by the judge alone] for any reason other than overloading of the indictment, or where it would be inconceivable that a judge might direct a jury that they should disregard the evidence relating to the sample offence when considering liability in respect of the linked offences in the schedule. The specimen count on the indictment ought to be a true sample of the linked offences. The two stage process is intended for use in respect of cases of frequently repeated offending of a similar nature, rather than wide ranging, complex and factually differentiated cases. It will thus only be used in those cases where the similarity between the specimen and the linked charges is such that the evidence will be susceptible to being presented in schedule form, or given by a small number of witnesses or, if given by a number of individuals, gone through relatively rapidly."[37]

In *Tovey* the Court of Appeal said that **25–021**

> "the Act's beneficial effects should not be overestimated. There are strict conditions for its use and it does deprive the defendant of his right to have a

[34] See below, Ch.26.
[35] SI 2006/3423.
[36] See *Archbold*, para.4–60.
[37] Law Com No.277, para.7.8.

> jury trial. In addition, it involves two trials, one by a jury and the other by a judge. Unless the normal approach to framing an indictment is abandoned, it could require a massive indictment, which would waste Court time if all the identical offences have to be put separately to the defendant and a verdict taken on each count."[38]

This seems to be a thinly-veiled warning to prosecutors not to seek s.17 orders in inappropriate cases. But the court added, somewhat inconsistently: "We suspect the threat of reliance by the prosecution on the provisions of the new Act will usually result in the defendant holding up his hand and pleading guilty to the additional counts." That is of course exactly the beneficial effect that the new procedure is primarily intended to achieve.

25–022 It may be that a case would formerly have been suitable for the s.17 procedure because it would have required a large number of similar counts, but is no longer suitable because under CPR 2005, r.14.2(2) many or all of the alleged offences can be charged in a single count on the basis that they form a "course of conduct".[39] The Law Commission appears to have regarded the s.17 procedure as an *alternative* to the possibility (which it rejected) of allowing incidents forming a "course of conduct" to be charged in one count.[40] If r.14.2(2) is widely construed, it may render the s.17 procedure largely redundant.

THE INDICTMENT

25–023 The indictment has to be in existence before an order under DVCVA 2004, s.17 can be made;[41] but the prosecution must decide whether to apply for such an order before drafting the indictment. This is because, if an application is to be made, the indictment must be drafted in a prescribed form[42] which reflects the relationship between the sample counts that the prosecution proposes to put before a jury and the linked counts which the prosecution proposes should if necessary be tried by the judge. Paragraph IV.34.6 of the Practice Direction provides, in part:

> "The draft indictment served under Criminal Procedure Rule 14.1(1) should be in the form appropriate to such a trial [sc. under the DVCVA 2004 procedure]. . . . It is undesirable for a draft indictment in the usual form to be served where the prosecutor expects to apply for a two stage trial and hence, of necessity, for permission to amend the indictment at a later stage in order that it may be in the special form."

25–024 In drafting the indictment with a view to an application under s.17, the prosecution must decide not only which counts are to be samples and which

[38] [2005] EWCA Crim 530; *The Times*, April 19, 2005 at [32].
[39] See above, paras 25–003 *et seq*.
[40] See above, para.25–009.
[41] DVCVA 2004, s.17(3) refers to "the number of counts included in the indictment".
[42] Form 6412a.

are to be linked to the samples, but also which of the linked counts relates to which of the samples. This will naturally depend on the subject matter of the counts in question, since the judge cannot make an order under s.17 unless satisfied that each sample count "can be regarded as a sample of" the linked counts.[43]

The indictment is divided into Part 1 and Part 2. Part 1 contains the sample counts which the prosecution proposes to put before a jury. Those counts are numbered in the usual way: "Count 1, Count 2", etc. Part 2 contains the linked counts which the prosecution proposes should if necessary be tried by the judge. It is divided into groups, each of which contains counts associated with a particular sample count. The linked counts are numbered 1.1, 1.2, 1.3; 2.1, 2.2, 2.3; and so on. For each linked count, the first number is that of the sample count with which the count is associated. It must be clear which of the linked counts are associated with which of the sample counts, because a linked count cannot be tried by the judge unless the defendant is convicted on the associated sample count. **25–025**

DVCVA 2004, s.17(4) refers to the possibility of a *group* of counts, rather than a single count, being regarded as a sample of other counts. It is not clear what scenario is envisaged here. Perhaps it is the possibility of the prosecution's hedging its bets by putting forward (for example) counts 1–5 as a sample of a number of other counts, with the effect that a conviction by the jury on (say) count 1 could result in a trial by the judge of all those other counts even if the jury acquit on counts 2–5. On the other hand, s.19(1) provides that the judge can try counts only where the jury convict "on a count which can be regarded as a sample of other counts"—*not* "on a count which is one of a group of counts which can be regarded as a sample of other counts". The reference in s.17(4) to a group of counts is left hanging in the air: nothing seems to turn on it. **25–026**

In *Tovey* the Court of Appeal repeated earlier advice on the drafting of an indictment in a case of multiple offending: **25–027**

> "In preparing the indictment, the prosecution should always have in mind in a situation of multiple offending, the need to provide the sentencing judge, assuming that the defendant pleads or is found guilty, with sufficient examples (and no more) of the offending to enable the judge to impose a sentence which properly reflects the offender's criminal behaviour. For this purpose, in the case of multiple offending, there will usually be no need to have counts reflecting every offence. Indeed, the presence of more counts than necessary will only result in concurrent sentences."[44]

While this guidance was offered in relation to cases to which s.17 does not apply, or for which the s.17 procedure is unsuitable, it seems equally applicable to cases in which a s.17 application is to be made. There need only be enough counts to ensure that the defendant can be properly

[43] DVCVA 2004, s.17(4). As to the circumstances in which one count can be regarded as a sample of others, see below, paras 25–036 *et seq*.

[44] [2005] EWCA Crim 530; *The Times*, April 19, 2005 at [33].

sentenced if the application is successful and the defendant is convicted (whether by jury or judge) on all counts. The court also warned of the difficulty of arraigning a defendant on such a "massive indictment" as would be expected in a s.17 case unless "the normal approach to framing an indictment is abandoned". It may be that a new approach to taking pleas will be required; perhaps the defence could be asked to provide a written indication of pleas which would then be confirmed by the defendant in open court.

THE APPLICATION PROCEDURE

25–028 By contrast with applications for the whole trial to be conducted without a jury,[45] an application for an order under DVCVA 2004, s.17 may be made to any judge of the Crown Court.[46] But the application must be determined at a preparatory hearing.[47] A prosecutor wanting to make a s.17 application must apply for a preparatory hearing, whether or not the defendant has already applied for one,[48] and a preparatory hearing must be held.[49]

25–029 Paragraph IV.34.6 of the Practice Direction provides, in part:

> "The draft indictment served under Criminal Procedure Rule 14.1(1) . . . should be accompanied by an application under Criminal Procedure Rule 15.1 for a preparatory hearing. On receipt of such a draft indictment Crown Court staff should not sign it before consulting a judge, who is likely to direct under Criminal Procedure Rule 14.1(3) that it should not be signed before the prosecutor's application is heard."

Only if the application is allowed does the Practice Direction envisage that the draft indictment in DVCVA 2004 form will be signed.[50] But there is a contradiction here. The application must be determined at a preparatory hearing, which begins with arraignment,[51] which cannot take place until there is an indictment. There is no indictment until the draft indictment is signed,[52] so there is no power to determine the application until then.[53] The

[45] See below, para.26–010.
[46] DVCVA 2004, s.17(1).
[47] DVCVA 2004, s.18(1). For preparatory hearings, see above, paras 24–061 *et seq*. The Criminal Justice Act 1987, s.7(1) and the Criminal Procedure and Investigations Act 1996, s.29(2), which specify the purposes for which a preparatory hearing may be held, have effect as if the purposes there mentioned included the purpose of determining an application under DVCVA 2004, s.17: DVCVA 2004, s.18(2). It is not clear why these provisions were not textually amended so that the specified purposes *do* include the determination of a s.17 application, as was done by the Criminal Justice Act 2003 in the case of applications under s.45 of that Act for the whole trial to be conducted without a jury.
[48] CPR 2005, r.15.1(2).
[49] CPR 2005, r.15.4(1).
[50] Practice Direction, para.IV.34.7.
[51] Criminal Justice Act 1987, s.8(2); Criminal Procedure and Investigations Act 1996, s.30(b).
[52] CPR 2005, r.14.1(3)(a).
[53] The Law Commission appears to have envisaged that the defendant would not be arraigned until after the determination of the application (Law Com. No.277, para.7.9), but did not explain how this could be reconciled with the rule that the preparatory hearing begins with arraignment.

primary legislation seems to dictate that the indictment be signed in advance of the hearing of the application, so that the defendant can be arraigned on it and the application can then be determined. If the application is refused, a draft indictment in the usual form will have to be served instead. The Practice Direction seems to be inconsistent with the primary legislation.

A defendant wishing to oppose the application may (but need not)[54] 25–030
make written representations to that effect within seven days of receiving a copy of the application for a preparatory hearing.[55] At the preparatory hearing, all parties (whether or not directly affected by the application) must be given an opportunity to make representations with respect to the application.[56]

THE CONDITIONS

The judge may not make the order unless satisfied that 25–031

- "the number of counts included in the indictment is likely to mean that a trial by jury involving all of those counts would be impracticable";[57]
- "if an order . . . were made, each count or group[58] of counts which would accordingly be tried with a jury can be regarded as a sample of counts which could accordingly be tried without a jury";[59] and
- it is in the interests of justice for an order to be made.[60]

JURY TRIAL ON ALL COUNTS IMPRACTICABLE

There is no precise limit on the number of counts that it is practicable for 25–032
a jury to try. Although the first condition refers only to the *number* of counts, whether it is practicable for a jury to try them must depend largely on their nature, as well as that of the evidence and possibly the defence. Judges considering this point are likely to apply the case law which has already developed on the topic of overloaded indictments.[61]

The number of counts is likely to affect the length of the trial, and this 25–033
too will presumably be a relevant factor in determining whether it would be impracticable for a jury to try them all. Indeed it is difficult to see how it

[54] CPR 2005, r.15.3(2), which *requires* a defendant to serve written representations if he wants to oppose an application for the whole trial to be conducted without the jury, does not apply to an application under DVCVA 2004, s.17.

[55] CPR 2005, r.15.3(1).

[56] DVCVA 2004, s.18(4).

[57] DVCVA 2004, s.17(3).

[58] See above, para.25–026.

[59] DVCVA 2004, s.17(4).

[60] DVCVA 2004, s.17(5).

[61] See below, paras 28–002 *et seq*.

could ever be said that the *number* of counts in itself made jury trial impracticable if the counts, albeit numerous, could all be tried by a jury within a reasonable time. So this form of trial may become a compromise in cases where the prosecution might otherwise apply (or does in fact apply, but without success) for a serious and complex fraud trial to be heard in its entirety by a judge sitting alone.[62] The Law Commission envisaged that the s.17 procedure would not be available in all cases of serious fraud, but only those that until *Kidd* would have been charged in specimen counts.[63] Indeed it seems likely that, if the provisions for trials without juries are brought into force, they will be used only in cases which are very complex indeed.[64] The s.17 procedure, by contrast, seems to be intended for cases which are relatively straightforward apart from involving an unfeasibly large number of counts.

25–034 In deciding whether to make an order for trial of some of the counts without a jury,[65] the judge must have regard to any steps which might reasonably be taken to facilitate a trial by jury on the whole indictment.[66] But a step is not to be regarded as reasonable if it could lead to any defendant in the trial (not necessarily one to whom the application directly relates) receiving a lesser sentence than he otherwise would:[67] this would defeat the object of the legislation. The Lord Chief Justice's Protocol for the Control and Management of Heavy Fraud and Other Complex Criminal Cases,[68] and Pt 3 of the Criminal Procedure Rules, provide guidance as to the steps that may properly be taken.

25–035 There may be a temptation for the prosecution deliberately to overload the indictment so as to *make* it impracticable for the whole indictment to be tried by a jury, in order to secure an order under s.17. This would arguably be an abuse of process, if it could be shown to have occurred. But the real remedy in such a case would be for the judge to take steps to make jury trial practicable, by ordering the indictment to be cut down to a manageable number of counts. If the indictment was overloaded to begin with (even taking account of the fact that it was drafted with a view to a s.17 application), it must be possible to cut it down without the risk of rendering the judge's sentencing powers inadequate.

[62] See below, Ch.26.

[63] Law Com No.277, para.7.6.

[64] See below, para.26–025.

[65] Logically one would expect the possibility of facilitating a jury trial on all counts to be relevant to whether the first condition is fulfilled, rather than whether an order should be made if all three conditions are fulfilled. But, since the third condition is that it is in the interests of justice for an order to be made, it is inconceivable that the judge might refuse to make an order despite being satisfied that all the conditions are fulfilled.

[66] DVCVA 2004, s.17(6).

[67] DVCVA 2004, s.17(7). The actual wording is "if it could lead to *the possibility of* a defendant ... receiving a lesser sentence" (italics supplied). It is not clear in what circumstances it might be said that a step could lead to the possibility of a defendant receiving a lesser sentence, but not that that step could lead to the defendant's actually receiving a lesser sentence.

[68] See below, para.28–008.

SAMPLE COUNTS

The legislation provides no guidance on the circumstances in which one count "can be regarded as a sample of" others, except that a count may not be so regarded "unless the defendant in respect of each count is the same person".[69] Even in the absence of express provision, it is hardly likely that a count against A alone could have been regarded as a sample of counts against B alone. And, since the singular includes the plural unless a contrary intention appears,[70] a count against both A and B could presumably be a sample of other counts against both A and B (though neither could be convicted on the linked counts unless convicted on the sample count). But the wording suggests that a count against both A and B could not be a sample of counts against A alone. That would seem logical, since the reason for not charging B on the other counts would presumably reflect a material difference in the evidence. 25–036

The Law Commission envisaged that a count could only be a sample of other counts if the evidence on it or conviction of it (or both) would be admissible on each of the other counts, and vice versa.[71] This suggestion was somewhat circular, since cross-admissibility is likely to turn on the degree of similarity between the counts, and was rejected by the Government. 25–037

> "Evidence admissible in respect of sample counts is likely to be admissible in respect of the subsidiary counts because they will be extremely similar. It is important that the prosecution should be able to rely on evidence adduced in that part of the trial that was heard by a jury. However, it would not be appropriate to use admissibility . . . as a criterion for whether counts were similar enough for one to be a sample of another. The question as to what can be regarded as a sample count is best left to judicial discretion.
>
> There is also the practical problem that it may not be clear at the time of the preparatory hearing whether evidence in respect of a count is admissible in respect of another count.[72] We believe that in cases of this type, where a judge is considering whether a count is a sample of another, the judge can be relied upon to know what a sample count is."[73]

Given the ease with which evidence of similar offences can now be adduced under the Criminal Justice Act 2003,[74] it seems unlikely that a s.17 order would ever be made where the evidence was *not* cross-admissible.

[69] DVCVA 2004, s.17(9).
[70] Interpretation Act 1978, s.6(c).
[71] Law Com No.277, para.7.7.
[72] But the preparatory hearing continues until the jury is sworn. There seems to be nothing to prevent the judge from postponing the decision on the s.17 application until he has determined questions of cross-admissibility (which he is expressly given power to do in the preparatory hearing).
[73] *Hansard*, HL Vol.659, cols 832–833 (March 25, 2004), Baroness Scotland of Asthal.
[74] See below, paras 27–021 *et seq*.

INTERESTS OF JUSTICE

25–038 The legislation gives no guidance as to how the judge should determine whether a s.17 order would be in the interests of justice, or in what circumstances the first two conditions might be fulfilled while the third is not. The Law Commission suggested that one relevant factor would be whether the case was one which could have been dealt with by way of sample counts before *Kidd*;[75] but it is not clear what this would add to the second condition. *Kidd* did not affect the question of what counts can be regarded as sample counts, but only the way in which a defendant convicted on sample counts could be sentenced.

25–039 There is no express requirement that the number of counts tried without a jury should be the minimum necessary to ensure that a jury trial of the remainder is practicable. But it may be arguable that it would be contrary to the interests of justice to make an order in respect of more counts than is strictly necessary.

THE ORDER

25–040 If the judge does make an order for trial of some counts without a jury, the order must specify *which* counts may be tried without a jury.[76] The judge clearly has a discretion to make an order in respect of only some of the counts proposed by the prosecution, in which case the indictment will need to be amended accordingly. There is no express requirement that the order should specify which of the sample counts relate to which of the linked counts; but, if the judge disagrees with the linkages shown in the indictment, he will presumably require the indictment to be amended so as to show linkages that he regards as appropriate.

APPEAL AGAINST THE DETERMINATION

25–041 All parties have a right of appeal against the judge's determination of a s.17 application.[77] The Law Commission thought that the judge would need to provide a reasoned judgment for this purpose.[78]

EFFECT OF REFUSAL

25–042 Where the judge declines to make an order under s.17 on the basis that a jury trial on all counts would not be impracticable, the prosecution can presumably proceed to jury trial on the original indictment (except that it

[75] Law Com No.277, para.7.7.
[76] DVCVA 2004, s.17(8).
[77] DVCVA 2004, s.18(5).
[78] Law Com. No.277, para.7.40.

will need to be recast into the form of an ordinary indictment). If the judge agrees that a jury trial on all counts would be impracticable but does not agree that some counts can properly be regarded as samples of others, or agrees that some counts can be regarded as samples but for some reason considers that a two-stage trial would not be in the interests of justice, the prosecution will have to amend the indictment so that it is not too overloaded to be placed before a jury. It might be possible to do this by way of severance.

PROCEDURE AT THE TRIAL

Trial Before the Jury

Where an order under DVCVA 2004, s.17 is made, the trial proceeds before a jury in the ordinary way, on all the counts which the judge has not agreed may be tried without a jury (not all of which will necessarily be samples of other counts). The Law Commission envisaged that evidence in respect of alleged linked offences which were not to be tried by the jury might be admissible as similar fact evidence in the same way as in a pre-*Kidd* trial on sample counts.[79] Under the bad character provisions of the Criminal Justice Act 2003 it is almost inevitable that evidence of the linked offences will be admissible on the sample counts. But, if it is practicable to adduce evidence of the linked offences before the jury, it would presumably have been practicable for the jury to try them. Bringing them into the first stage of the trial is likely to defeat the object of the exercise. For similar reasons it would seem undesirable to let the jury have copies of the whole indictment, including the linked counts. 25–043

Conviction by the Jury

The decision whether to proceed

If a defendant is found guilty by a jury on any count which can be regarded as a sample of other counts to be tried in those proceedings, those other counts (but only those) *may* be tried without a jury.[80] The effect of this appears to be merely to create an exception to the rule that a trial on indictment must be conducted before a jury, rather than giving the judge a discretion whether to proceed to the second stage at all. Abuse of process aside, the prosecution usually has a right to proceed to trial, whether or not the judge thinks this appropriate.[81] The Law Commission's intention was that this rule should not apply where the judge considers it inappropriate to 25–044

[79] Law Com. No.277, para.7.9.
[80] DVCVA 2004, s.19(1).
[81] *Att-Gen's Reference (No.2 of 2000)* [2001] 1 Cr.App.R. 36 (p.503).

proceed to the second stage of a s.17 trial, either because this would not affect the sentence or because he would be unlikely to convict;[82] but there is no provision to that effect. In practice the prosecution is unlikely to insist on proceeding to the second stage if the judge indicates that his view of the case makes this pointless. The Commission suggested that, if the judge decided not to proceed to the second stage, the remaining offences should be left to lie on the file;[83] and this may be equally appropriate where the prosecution chooses not to insist on proceeding to the second stage.

25–045 One of the benefits that the Law Commission expected to result from the new procedure was an increase in admissions of guilt. There will no incentive for a defendant to contest a trial on sample counts rather than pleading guilty to a limited number and asking for the rest to be taken into consideration.[84] The Commission also hoped that defendants convicted on sample counts before a jury might decide to plead guilty to the remaining linked counts with a view to receiving at least a small reduction in their sentence.[85] The prosecution might even agree to accept guilty pleas to only some of the linked offences, thus leaving the defendant with a reduction in sentence attributable to his guilty plea and the fewer convictions.

25–046 The Law Commission did not envisage that the judge should, at the end of the jury stage, give an early indication of sentence on the matters for which the defendant has been convicted, because such an indication might turn out to be misleading if the defendant is then convicted of some or all of the linked offences.[86] It remains to be seen whether it would be appropriate for the judge to provide a *Goodyear*[87] indication at this stage, relating to the likely sentence for the offences of which the defendant has been convicted *and* the linked offences to which he might be tempted to plead guilty. The Court of Appeal might consider such an indication to be capable of putting undue pressure on a defendant, when the judge who provides it will be the fact-finder at the second stage of the proceedings and, having heard all the evidence in relation to the sample counts, may already have formed a provisional opinion on the defendant's guilt of the related matters.

Trial before judge of remaining counts

25–047 The second stage of the trial, if it occurs, will normally be heard by the judge who presided over the first stage.[88] This will make the second stage shorter and less expensive, and will help to ensure consistency. The Law Commission acknowledged concerns that this might be disadvantageous to the defendant, but was confident that the ability of the judge to recuse

[82] Law Com. No.277, paras 7.16 *et seq*.
[83] Law Com. No.277, para.7.27.
[84] Law Com. No.277, para.7.89.
[85] Law Com. No.277, paras 7.14, 7.65.
[86] Law Com. No.277, para.7.15.
[87] [2005] EWCA Crim 888; [2005] 1 W.L.R. 2532.
[88] Law Com. No.277, para.7.43.

himself would provide a sufficient safeguard.[89] In any event, the prosecution would undoubtedly seek to adduce the convictions from the first stage of the trial as evidence in the second stage, so they would become known to any new judge taking over the case at the second stage even if he decided that they were inadmissible (which, under the bad character provisions of the Criminal Justice Act 2003, is unlikely).

The judge will need to take an active role in case management at the start of the second stage. The Law Commission did not expect the second stage to take very long.[90] There will probably be no need for witnesses to be called to give evidence which has already been given in the first stage, though some witnesses may need to be recalled to give evidence on matters which were not covered in the first stage.[91] **25–048**

In the second stage, the court has all the powers of both judge and jury.[92] Unless the context otherwise requires, any reference in an enactment to a jury or to the verdict or finding of a jury is to be read as a reference to the court or to the verdict or finding of the court.[93] **25–049**

Where the judge convicts a defendant on any of the remaining counts, he must provide a reasoned judgment at the time of conviction or as soon as reasonably practicable thereafter.[94] There is a similar requirement where a judge convicts in a serious fraud trial conducted entirely without a jury,[95] and Auld L.J.'s suggestion in that context that the judge use specimen directions and case summaries as a framework for his judgment[96] may be equally relevant here. **25–050**

Appeal against conviction

Time for an appeal against conviction by the jury does not run until the date on which the whole proceedings (including that part of the proceedings that takes place before the judge alone) end.[97] But the sentencing stage does not count for this purpose.[98] The Law Commission proposed that the judge should be able to adjourn the proceedings to allow the defence to appeal against the jury convictions before proceeding to the second stage;[99] but this would be technically an interlocutory appeal and would need legislative authority, which has not been provided. **25–051**

[89] Law Com. No.277, para.7.52.
[90] Law Com. No.277, para.7.89.
[91] Law Com. No.277, para.7.59.
[92] DVCVA 2004, s.19(2).
[93] DVCVA 2004, s.19(3).
[94] DVCVA 2004, s.19(4)(a).
[95] Criminal Justice Act 2003, s.48(5)(a).
[96] *Review of the Criminal Courts of England and Wales*, Ch.5, para.188.
[97] DVCVA 2004, s.19(5).
[98] DVCVA 2004, s.19(6); see also *Hansard*, HL Vol.658, col.1410 (March 11, 2004), the Attorney-General (Lord Goldsmith).
[99] Law Com. No.277, para.7.30.

25–052 Time for serving notice of appeal, or an application for leave to appeal, against conviction in the second stage of the trial runs from the date when the judge gives his reasoned judgment, not the date of the conviction itself.[100]

25–053 The Law Commission assumed that any apparent inconsistencies between the verdicts of the jury and of the judge would be approached by the Court of Appeal in the same way that it normally approaches verdicts attacked on grounds of inconsistency.[101]

ACQUITTAL BY THE JURY

25–054 The Law Commission's intention was that, where a defendant is acquitted on a sample count, the judge would normally direct an acquittal on the counts linked to that count;[102] but, in exceptional circumstances only (for example, where the Crown's case before the jury had been hampered by a witness's absence due to illness), the remaining counts might be allowed to lie on the file. In such circumstances, the Crown would not be permitted to return to court and commence the second stage of the proceedings before the trial judge, but would have to start a fresh trial before a jury, having obtained leave to proceed.[103] The Law Commission proposed that there should be express provision to the effect that the judge may not allow the prosecution to bring fresh proceedings on the linked allegations on the basis that he considers the jury acquittal to be perverse or erroneous.[104] No such provision has been made, but fresh proceedings brought in these circumstances would probably be an abuse of process anyway.

[100] DVCVA 2004, s.19(4)(b).

[101] Law Com. No.277, para.7.69. See *Archbold*, paras 7–70 to 7–72.

[102] This would presumably involve the judge directing himself to acquit, though he could direct the jury to do so if they have not yet been discharged.

[103] Law Com. No.277, paras 7.11, 7.12.

[104] Law Com. No.277, para.7.11.

Chapter 26

FRAUD TRIALS WITHOUT A JURY

Fraud trials without juries were first proposed by the Roskill Committee **26–001**
in 1986. A majority of the committee proposed a Fraud Trials Tribunal, consisting of a judge and a small number of specially qualified lay members. The proposal was not adopted because it was hoped that the changes made by the Criminal Justice Act 1987 ("CJA 1987") would alleviate the problems that Roskill had identified. In 1993 the Royal Commission on Criminal Justice, chaired by Lord Runciman, pointed to continuing problems with fraud trials, but declined to make recommendations in relation to jury trial without the benefit of research.

The proposals for non-jury trials were revived in a Home Office **26–002**
consultation paper in 1998,[1] and the baton was picked up by the Auld review in 2001.[2] Auld L.J. identified two compelling reasons for pressing ahead with this reform: the burdensome length of serious fraud trials, and their increasing speciality and complexity. Both, in his view, put justice at risk. He recommended that, in serious and complex fraud cases, the judge should have power to direct trial by himself sitting with lay members (subject to the defendant's right, also recommended by Auld L.J., to opt for trial by judge alone). This recommendation was supported by the prosecuting authorities, but was rejected by the government for practical reasons relating to the selection of panel members.[3] The Criminal Justice Act 2003 ("CJA 2003"), s.43 enables fraud cases in certain circumstances to be tried by a judge alone, without the consent of the defendant.

[1] *Juries in Serious Fraud Trials.*
[2] *Review of the Criminal Courts of England and Wales*, Ch.5.
[3] *Justice for All*, CM 5563.

COMMENCEMENT OF CRIMINAL JUSTICE ACT 2003, SECTION 43

26–003 At the time of writing, the Government has not succeeded in bringing CJA 2003, s.43 into force. At the insistence of the House of Lords, CJA 2003, s.330(5)(b) requires the approval by both Houses of a commencement order bringing s.43 into force. A draft order was laid in October 2005 but was eventually abandoned, the Attorney-General admitting that the Government would have lost the vote in the Lords.

26–004 The Government then announced its intention of breaking the deadlock by amending CJA 2003. The Fraud (Trials without a Jury) Bill was introduced on November 16, 2006, and passed by the House of Commons on January 25, 2007. On March 20, 2007, the House of Lords in effect declined to give it a Second Reading. The Attorney-General had made it clear that the Government would if necessary resort to the Parliament Acts in order to force the Bill through in the following session. If it is eventually passed in its current form, it will come into force two months after Royal Assent, and will repeal CJA 2003, s.330(5)(b). The effect will be that CJA 2003, s.43 can be brought into force without further Parliamentary approval.[4]

26–005 If enacted in its current form, the Bill will have two further effects. First, CJA 2003, ss.43(2) and 48(1) will be amended so that, instead of any Crown Court judge being able to order a trial without a jury under s.43 and to conduct such a trial, these powers will be confined to High Court judges and Crown Court judges nominated for the purpose by the Head of Criminal Justice.

26–006 Secondly, a transitory amendment will be made to CJA 2003, s.43 so that, pending the introduction of the new procedure for sending serious or complex fraud cases to the Crown Court in pursuance of a notice under the Crime and Disorder Act 1998, s.51B, it will be possible to hold a trial without a jury where the case has been transferred to the Crown Court under CJA 1987, s.4.[5] So the commencement of s.43 will not have to await the commencement of s.51B of the 1998 Act.

26–007 The rest of this chapter is written as if CJA 2003, s.43 were already in force, subject to the amendments that the Fraud (Trials without a Jury) Bill would make if passed in its current form.

DECIDING WHETHER TO MAKE AN ORDER

ELIGIBILITY

26–008 A case is eligible for non-jury trial if one or more defendants are to be tried on indictment for one or more offences, and notice of transfer or sending has been given under CJA 1987, s.4 or the Crime and Disorder Act

[4] CJA 2003, s.330(7).

[5] See above, paras 24–002 *et seq.*

1998, s.51B. It follows that the procedure is available only in cases prosecuted by one of the authorities empowered to give such notices, namely the DPP, the Director of the SFO, the Commissioners for Revenue and Customs[6] or the Director of Revenue and Customs Prosecutions, and the Secretary of State.

THE APPLICATION PROCEDURE

Only the prosecution may apply. It is not obvious why a defendant who believes that a judge is more likely to acquit (perhaps because the defendant is innocent and a judge is more likely to understand the case) should be barred from applying. It may even be arguable that this rule infringes Art.6 of the European Convention on Human Rights, on the basis that it fails to ensure "equality of arms". Perhaps the justification lies in the statutory criterion for determining the application, which relates *only* to the burden on the jury of a long or complex trial.[7] Defendants are not usually expected to be concerned with the welfare of jurors. **26–009**

The application must be made to a High Court judge exercising the jurisdiction of the Crown Court or a judge of the Crown Court nominated for the purposes of s.43 by the Head of Criminal Justice, and must be determined at a preparatory hearing.[8] A prosecutor wanting to apply for a trial without a jury must apply for a preparatory hearing, whether or not the defendant has already applied for one,[9] and a preparatory hearing must be held.[10] A defendant wishing to oppose the application must make written representations to that effect within seven days of receiving a copy of the application for a preparatory hearing, including a short explanation of the reasons for opposing the application.[11] At the preparatory hearing, all parties must be given an opportunity to make representations with respect to the application.[12] **26–010**

[6] Commissioners for Revenue and Customs Act 2005, s.50(1).

[7] See below, para.26–012. But it is not clear that a non-jury trial can only be *ordered* (as against considered) on this ground: see below, para.26–022.

[8] CJA 2003, s.45(2). For preparatory hearings, see above, paras 24–061 *et seq*. The preparatory hearing could in theory be held under either CJA 1987 or Pt 3 of the Criminal Procedure and Investigations Act 1996, but the likelihood of the hearing being held under the 1996 Act in a fraud case is remote: see above, para.24–063.

[9] CPR 2005, r.15.1(2).

[10] CPR 2005, r.15.4(1). This rule applies where "an application has been made under rule 15.1(2)", which is puzzling because r.15.1(2) does not confer a power to make an application at all: it *requires* an application to be made under r.15.1(1) if the prosecution wants the court to order that the trial be conducted without a jury. Presumably r.15.4(1) is intended to apply where the prosecution states in its application for a preparatory hearing, as one of the reasons for making that application, that it wants the court to order a non-jury trial. The prescribed application form requires the prosecution not only to state its reasons for applying for a preparatory hearing but also, where one of those reasons is that it wants the court to order a non-jury trial, a summary of its reasons for wanting the court to do so.

[11] CPR 2005, r.15.3(2).

[12] CJA 2003, s.45(3).

26–011 Although the application must be determined in the course of the preparatory hearing, it need not be determined in advance of the other matters arising in that hearing. The decision on the application may well be affected by, for example, the defence's willingness to admit facts alleged, or applications for severance. While it would create administrative difficulties if the decision on the application were left until the last possible moment, the judge will equally not want to make it in a state of uncertainty about matters relevant to it.

THE CONDITION

26–012 The judge to whom the application is made must first consider whether he is satisfied that the condition in CJA 2003, s.43(5) is fulfilled—namely that

> "the complexity of the trial or the length of the trial (or both) is likely to make the trial so burdensome to the members of a jury hearing the trial that the interests of justice require that serious consideration should be given to the question of whether the trial should be conducted without a jury."[13]

If he is not so satisfied, he must refuse the application.[14] This is so even if the parties are agreed that the trial should be heard without a jury.[15]

26–013 One proposal put forward by Auld L.J. was that the criterion for a trial by judge alone in serious fraud cases should be modelled on that for trial without a jury in civil proceedings for fraud, libel, slander, malicious prosecution or false imprisonment.[16] The test in those circumstances is whether "the trial requires any prolonged examination of documents or accounts or any scientific or local investigation which cannot conveniently be made with a jury".[17] The Court of Appeal has said that, in applying this test, four main factors should be considered:[18]

(a) the physical problem of handling the documentation;

(b) the fact that jury trial inevitably takes longer, thus using more court and judge time and adding to the costs burden for the parties;

(c) the extra expense caused by both the added length of the trial and the cost of copying documents;[19] and

[13] CJA 2003, s.43(3), (5).

[14] CJA 2003, s.43(3).

[15] Auld L.J. suggested that this would be an important factor for the judge to consider in reaching his decision: *Review of the Criminal Courts of England and Wales*, Ch.5, para.193. But s.43 does not seem to envisage that it might be relevant, let alone important.

[16] *Review of the Criminal Courts of England and Wales*, Ch.5, para.200.

[17] Supreme Court Act 1981, s.69. The Act is renamed the Senior Courts Act by the Constitutional Reform Act 2005 with effect from a date to be appointed.

[18] *Beta Construction Ltd v Channel Four Television Ltd* [1990] 1 W.L.R. 1042 at 1049B, *per* Stuart-Smith L.J.

[19] Since the court regarded the additional expense as the main drawback of a longer trial, there seems to be little difference between factors (b) and (c).

(d) the risk that the jury may not understand the case, coupled with the impossibility of identifying any such misunderstanding and correcting the verdict.

These are rational concerns, though the force of some of them may have been diminished by advances in the technology available for presenting a case. But they bear only a distant resemblance to the criterion in CJA 2003, s.43(5). That criterion relates *only* to the possibility of a long or complex trial being "burdensome" to the jury themselves.

The extra *expense* of a long trial, whether in terms of court resources or legal costs, is wholly irrelevant. The likely length of a jury trial will not justify a trial without a jury unless it would be burdensome for the jury. No guidance has yet been given as to how long a trial time estimate might need to be before this criterion is likely to be satisfied. The Lord Chief Justice's Protocol for the Control and Management of Heavy Fraud and Other Complex Criminal Cases states that "in most cases 3 months should be the target outer limit, but there will be cases where a duration of 6 months, or in exceptional circumstances, even longer may be inevitable".[20] It seems unlikely that a trial lasting less than six months would be regarded as unduly burdensome for the jury by virtue of its length alone.[21] **26–014**

Moreover, throughout its efforts to get s.43 enacted and into force, the Goverment has for the most part[22] been at pains to dissociate itself from any suggestion that juries cannot understand complex cases. This stance is reflected in the wording of s.43(5). Any perceived risk that jurors might not understand the case is irrelevant, except to the extent that such incomprehension would be likely to make the trial burdensome to them. The issue is not the intelligence of jurors, but their stamina and resilience. On the other hand it is presumably legitimate to assume that any jury sworn to try the case would be conscientious, and that a conscientious juror would find it burdensome to be trying a case which he does not fully understand—partly because he will make strenuous efforts to understand it better, and partly because he will be distressed by the responsibility of having to reach a decision despite his confusion. Indeed, the reference to "the complexity of the trial or the length of the trial (or both)" makes it clear that a jury trial might be sufficiently burdensome by virtue of its complexity even if it **26–015**

[20] Para.1(i)(a).

[21] See *Hansard*, HC Vol.455, col.1633 (January 25, 2007), where the Solicitor General implied that only trials lasting more than six months would be likely to qualify.

[22] But see *Hansard*, HL Vol.651, col.808 (July 15, 2003), Baroness Scotland of Asthal: "A number of noble Lords have said that the Government have given up on complexity. I say, 'Not entirely'. Some cases are now extraordinarily complex, and it is that very complexity that cloaks sometimes the inequity that lies beneath. To have a successful prosecution we need to rip away that cloak and to lay bare the inequity that lies beneath it. That cannot be done quickly and it cannot always be done easily and simplistically. We advocates believe that all is possible. We are the communicators. We can make that which is cloudy seem clear. We can hone an issue so that those who do not understand will understand. Sometimes that is true, but the tragedy is that sometimes it is not." This seems to imply that a perceived lack of comprehension is indeed part of the mischief at which s.43 is aimed.

were relatively short. It is difficult to see how this could be, unless it is assumed that jurors might be burdened by their own lack of comprehension.

26–016 The likely length and complexity of the trial, and the extent to which the trial would therefore be burdensome for a jury, may be affected by factors other than the volume and complexity of the evidence. One such factor might be the nature of the charges. For example, on a charge alleging dishonesty, the defence may be entitled to adduce voluminous evidence which goes only to that issue. This consideration will not arise if the offence charged is one which does not require dishonesty. It is debatable whether the Fraud Act 2006 is likely to make fraud cases more or less suitable for jury trial. On the one hand, the new law is ostensibly simpler than the old. A case which would previously have had to be charged as theft, relying on s.5(3) of the Theft Act 1968 and thus involving questions of civil law,[23] might now be charged as fraud by abuse of position, to which questions of civil law seem to be irrelevant.[24] But this apparent simplicity does not come without a cost. Its cost is that the scope of the offence is unclear. Juries will in effect have to decide not only what happened, but also whether what happened is properly within the definition of the offence. Indeed this may well be the main or sole issue in the case. And this additional responsibility may make trials *more* burdensome for juries, not less.

26–017 One of the main concerns that gave rise to the proposals is the difficulty that is often encountered in finding 12 jurors who are available to serve for the length of time that many fraud trials take, which in turn means that many juries are not representative of the wider community.[25] However, given that this issue must be decided at the preparatory hearing, there is no scope for attempting to empanel a jury first, before deciding whether the trial would be too burdensome for the individual jurors available. The judge has to assess how burdensome the trial would be for a *hypothetical* jury—presumably one of average resilience.

MAKING THE TRIAL LESS BURDENSOME

26–018 In deciding whether he is satisfied that the condition in CJA 2003, s.43(5) is fulfilled, the judge must have regard to any steps which might reasonably be taken to reduce the complexity or length of the trial.[26] Measures set out in the Lord Chief Justice's Protocol for the Control and Management of Heavy Fraud and Other Complex Criminal Cases[27] are likely to come into play here, together with the Criminal Procedure Rules and the Consolidated Criminal Practice Direction. For example, electronic presentation of

[23] See above, paras 9–039 *et seq*.
[24] See above, Ch.6.
[25] *Review of the Criminal Courts of England and Wales*, Ch.5, paras 174, 181, 183.
[26] CJA 2003, s.43(6).
[27] See below, para.28–008.

evidence, the extensive editing of self-serving interviews and the employment of LiveNote transcribers may all facilitate a jury trial.[28] Severance of defendants or charges may be an option. Where the trial is likely to be long and complex because of the number of counts in the indictment, another possibility is the new procedure under which a jury tries sample counts and (in the event of conviction) the judge tries the rest.[29]

However, one of the Government's reasons for introducing non-jury fraud trials was that **26–019**

> "the complexity and unfamiliarity of sophisticated business processes means prosecutions [*sic*] often pare down cases to try and make them more manageable and comprehensible to a jury. This means the full criminality of such a fraud is not always exposed, and there are risks of a double standard between easy to prosecute 'blue-collar' crime and difficult to prosecute 'white-collar' crime."[30]

CJA 2003, s.43(7) therefore provides that a step is not to be regarded as reasonable if it would significantly disadvantage the prosecution—for example by limiting the evidence to be called, or the issues to be explored, or by severing defendants or charges to the detriment of the prosecution. If the only steps possible would significantly disadvantage the prosecution, the judge must assume that the complexity and length of the trial cannot be reduced at all. If some of them would significantly disadvantage the prosecution and some would not, the judge must take account only of those that would not.

CJA 2003 does not expressly provide that a step is not to be regarded as reasonable if it would significantly disadvantage the *defence*, and the fact that s.43(7) mentions only the prosecution might suggest that this is not the intention. But the judge is only required to have regard to steps that might *reasonably* be taken. A step which would significantly disadvantage the defence might for that reason be unreasonable. Indeed it might infringe the defendant's right to a fair trial under Art.6 of the European Convention on Human Rights, and render a conviction unsafe. **26–020**

Although CJA 2003, s.43 does not say so, presumably the judge should also have regard to any steps that might reasonably be taken to make the trial less burdensome to the jury, even without making the trial shorter or less complex. For example, the burden on the jury can be lessened by the use of "Maxwell hours", which involve starting early and finishing by 2pm, thus enabling the jury to get on with the rest of their lives to a limited extent. For this purpose, the views expressed by the jurors in the notorious Jubilee Line trial should be required reading.[31] **26–021**

[28] Lord Chief Justice's Protocol for the Control and Management of Heavy Fraud and Other Complex Criminal Cases, para.6(vi), (vii), (ix) and (x).

[29] Domestic Violence, Crime and Victims Act 2004, s.17; see above, Ch.25.

[30] *Justice for All*, para.4.29.

[31] Sally Lloyd-Bostock, "The Jubilee Line Jurors: Does their Experience Strengthen the Argument for Judge-only Trial in Long and Complex Fraud Cases?" [2007] Crim. L.R. 255.

THE DISCRETION

26–022 Even if the judge is satisfied that the condition in CJA 2003, s.43(5) is fulfilled, he has a discretion whether to order that the trial be conducted without a jury. If the condition were simply that the interests of justice require the trial to be conducted without a jury because trial by jury would be too burdensome, the possibility of the judge deciding not to make an order despite the condition being satisfied would be theoretical. But the question under s.43(5) is merely whether the trial would be likely to be so burdensome to a jury that the interests of justice require *serious consideration of whether* the trial should be conducted without a jury. Once the judge has decided that serious consideration of that question is justified, the test for determining that question is not whether the interests of justice *require* a trial without a jury, but simply whether the trial *should be* conducted without a jury. This seems to be a somewhat lower hurdle. The judge is apparently entitled to make the order if, having given the matter the "serious consideration" it requires, he concludes that, on balance, the advantages of jury trial are outweighed by those of a non-jury trial—even if a jury trial would not be incompatible with the interests of justice.

26–023 CJA 2003 gives the judge no guidance about what factors he can take into account at this stage. He does not have a discretion at all unless he is satisfied that serious consideration of the question is justified by the likely burdensomeness of a jury trial; but the Act does not say that the likely burdensomeness of a jury trial is the only factor that can militate in favour of a non-jury trial when, having decided that he has a discretion, he comes to decide whether to exercise it. On a literal reading of the section, he could at this stage take account of any of the factors mentioned at para.26–013 above. But this would seem to be contrary to the spirit of the section. Since the judge cannot even consider making an order if the only reason for doing so is (for example) the likely cost of a jury trial, it would be anomalous if, having decided that he can *consider* making an order because a jury trial would be burdensome, he could then *make* the order partly on grounds of cost.

26–024 On the other hand there is clearly no restriction on the factors that may militate *against* the making of an order. These factors are likely to include many of the considerations ventilated in the debates on whether s.43 should be enacted or brought into force, such as the greater democratic legitimacy of jury trial. One factor which would seem highly relevant—and is indeed difficult to reconcile with the whole idea of non-jury fraud trials—is the increasing prominence in substantive fraud offences of the requirement of dishonesty. In some offences (particularly theft, conspiracy to defraud, fraudulent trading, cheating the revenue, and arguably fraud by abuse of position) dishonesty is the main distinction between conduct that is lawful and conduct that is criminal. Senior judges are not particularly representative of the community as a whole, or especially well qualified to pronounce upon the moral standards of ordinary people. In our view, a judge should never agree to conduct a trial without a jury if it appears that most of the facts are agreed and that the main issue will be whether the defendant's conduct was dishonest.

A possibly useful measure of how the discretion is likely to be exercised (and possibly also of how "burdensome" a jury trial would have to be in order to satisfy the s.43(5) condition) is the number of cases in which the Government expects the new procedure to be used. The Home Office estimated in 1998 that, if the procedure were available whenever a case is transferred to the Crown Court under CJA 1987, s.4[32] *or* a preparatory hearing is ordered,[33] a total of 80–85 cases would be eligible every year.[34] But the Government has said that it does not expect more than 15–20 trials without juries to be actually *held* each year, and that its best estimate is more like six.[35] Even the Jubilee Line case would not necessarily have qualified.[36] It seems safe to assume that only in exceptional cases is trial without a jury likely to be ordered. **26–025**

APPROVAL OF THE LORD CHIEF JUSTICE

The judge must seek the approval of the Lord Chief Justice or a judge nominated by him (probably the president of the Queen's Bench Division) before ordering a trial without a jury.[37] Whether oral representations are heard at this point, or the matter is decided on the basis of the judge's notes of the arguments advanced at the hearing, is a matter of judicial discretion.[38] **26–026**

RIGHT OF APPEAL

As in the case of other orders made at a preparatory hearing, there is an interlocutory right of appeal against a judge's order that the trial be conducted without a jury or his refusal of an application for such an order.[39] **26–027**

32 The figure would now include indictable-only cases sent to the Crown Court under the Crime and Disorder Act 1998, s.51, which was not in force when the Home Office consultation paper was published.

33 Under CJA 2003, s.43, the procedure is not available if the case is neither transferred under CJA 1987, s.4 nor sent to the Crown Court in pursuance of a notice under the Crime and Disorder Act 1998, s.51B, even if a preparatory hearing is ordered; but the Home Office thought that the number of such cases would be "very limited".

34 *Juries in Serious Fraud Trials*, paras 3.3–3.7.

35 *Hansard*, HC Vol.455, col.1633 (January 25, 2007), the Solicitor General; HL Vol.690, col.1149 (March 20, 2007), the Attorney-General.

36 *Review of the Investigation and Criminal Proceedings relating to the Jubilee Line Case*, p.8; *Hansard*, HC Vol.455, col.1594 (January 25, 2007), the Solicitor General.

37 CJA 2003, s.43(4).

38 *Hansard*, HC Public Bill Committee on the Fraud (Trials without a Jury) Bill, cols 74–75 (December 12, 2006), the Solicitor General.

39 CJA 1987, s.9(11).

THE EFFECT OF THE ORDER

26–028 An order for trial by judge alone applies to all defendants tried on the same indictment. But it would seem to be possible for the judge at the preparatory hearing to order separate trials and then make a s.43 order in relation to one trial but not another.

26–029 A trial without a jury must be conducted either by a judge of the High Court exercising the jurisdiction of the Crown Court, or a judge of the Crown Court nominated for the purposes of s.43 by the Head of Criminal Justice[40]—that is, a judge who is qualified to *order* a non-jury trial. Normally the trial judge will be the one who conducts the preparatory hearing,[41] and therefore the one who makes the s.43 order.

26–030 Where a s.43 order is made, the court has

> "all the powers, authorities and jurisdiction which the court would have had if the trial had been conducted . . . with a jury (including power to determine any question and to make any finding which would be required to be determined or made by a jury."[42]

Unless the context otherwise requires, any reference in an enactment to a jury or to a verdict or finding of a jury is to be read as a reference to the court or a verdict[43] or finding of the court.[44] It seems, therefore, that the trial judge will be both the fact-finder and the arbiter of all matters of law arising in the course of the trial. There are no special arrangements in place for voir dires, public interest immunity applications and so on: it seems that, where the judge encounters prejudicial material which would be withheld from a jury, he is expected to perform the kind of mental gymnastics demanded of magistrates.[45]

26–031 As soon as reasonably practicable after convicting a defendant, the judge must give a reasoned judgment.[46] No judgment is required where a defendant is acquitted. Where a defendant is convicted on some counts but acquitted on others, the judgment presumably need not refer to the counts on which he has been acquitted unless it is necessary to draw a distinction. The same seems to be true if some defendants are convicted and others are acquitted.

[40] CJA 2003, s.48(1), as substituted by the Fraud (Trials without a Jury) Bill.
[41] *R. v Southwark Crown Court, ex p. Customs and Excise Commissioners* [1993] 1 W.L.R. 764.
[42] CJA 2003, s.48(3). This provision is virtually identical to the Domestic Violence, Crime and Victims Act 2004, s.19(2), which relates to trials of sample counts by a judge sitting alone: see above, para.25–049. A jury will still be required in the circumstances in which the Criminal Procedure (Insanity) Act 1064 requires a special jury to be sworn: CJA 2003, s.48(6).
[43] The judge will deliver a "verdict" of guilty or not guilty, followed by a "judgment" if the verdict is one of guilty: below, para.26–031.
[44] CJA 2003, s.48(4).
[45] *Hansard*, HC Vol.455, col.1636 (January 25, 2007), the Solicitor General.
[46] CJA 2003, s.48(5)(a).

The time limit for giving notice of appeal against conviction, or of an application for leave to appeal against conviction, runs from the date on which the reasoned judgment is given.[47] **26–032**

[47] CJA 2003, s.48(5)(b). If the judgment takes more than a day to deliver, time presumably runs from the date on which the judgment is concluded.

CHAPTER 27

EVIDENCE

It would be impossible to deal in one chapter with every type of evidential problem that may arise in the course of a fraud trial. We examine here a selection of points that are particularly likely to arise, namely: **27–001**

- On a conspiracy charge, may general evidence of the conspiracy be admitted before the defendant's adherence to the agreement is proved?
- Are all acts or declarations by one conspirator in furtherance of a conspiracy admissible against all conspirators? Does this rule apply equally to all joint offences? Does it entail the admissibility of hearsay evidence?
- When is documentary evidence admissible, and how can it be proved?
- What is the status of previous statements by witnesses and defendants?

- When is evidence admissible of a defendant's similar conduct on other occasions?

The Court of Appeal has said that points as to the admissibility of evidence should be taken less readily in fraud trials than in trials of "more conventional crime".[1] But, where such points properly arise, counsel's duty to take them cannot be affected by the nature of the case.

GENERAL EVIDENCE OF CONSPIRACY

27–002 In any joint crime, an act or declaration of one defendant may prove his intention to commit the crime charged, but not the intentions of others. If he is tried with others, the jury will need direction on the probative force, if any, of the evidence against those others. If the others are tried separately, the question will arise whether the evidence is admissible at all.

27–003 In *Queen Caroline's case* the judges were asked the following question by the House of Lords:

> "Supposing that, according to the rules of law, evidence of a conspiracy against a Defendant for any indictable offence ought not to be admitted to convict or criminate him, unless as it may apply to himself or to an agent employed by him, may not general evidence, nevertheless, of the existence of the conspiracy charged upon the record, be received in the first instance; though it cannot affect such Defendant, unless brought home to him, or to an agent employed by him . . .?"[2]

To that question Abbott C.J. delivered the followed unanimous opinion of the judges:

> "We are of opinion, that on a prosecution for a crime to be proved by conspiracy, general evidence of an existing conspiracy may in the first instance be received, as a preliminary step to that more particular evidence, by which it is to be shewn that the individual Defendants were guilty participators in such conspiracy. This is often necessary to render the particular evidence intelligible, and to show the true meaning and character of the acts of the individual defendants; and, on that account, we presume it is permitted. But, it is to be observed, that, in such cases, the general nature of the whole evidence intended to be adduced is previously opened to the Court, whereby the Judge is enabled to form an opinion as to the probability of affecting the individual Defendants by particular proof applicable to them, and connecting them with the general evidence of the alleged conspiracy; and if, upon such opening, it should appear manifest, that no particular proof sufficient to affect the Defendants is intended to be adduced, it would become the duty of the judge to stop the case in limine, and not to allow the general evidence to be received, which, even if attended with no other bad effect, as exciting an unreasonable prejudice, would certainly be a useless waste of time."[3]

[1] *Kellard* [1995] 2 Cr.App.R. 134 at 147.
[2] (1820) 2 Br. & B. 284 at 303.
[3] (1820) 2 Br. & B. 284 at 310.

This general principle should be approached with some caution. The notion that the Crown may prove (i) that there is an agreement between A and B to do *x*, and (ii) that C was party to that agreement, is logically impeccable. But there is a danger that, because A and B agreed to do *x*, and C was associated with them or shared some of their objectives, a jury may be too ready to assume that C was party to that agreement. He may not have been party to any agreement at all, or only to a subsidiary agreement. The opinion of the judges in the Queen's case recognises the power of a trial judge to stop a case if need be; but it omits an intermediate position which is probably more important, namely that evidence of what other conspirators agreed may be more prejudicial than probative, and may therefore be excluded at the judge's discretion. In the example given, the real question is: to what did C agree? What A and B agreed will generally be of limited relevance to this, and its prejudicial effect may be considerable. 27–004

That is not to say that there may not be cases where the evidence of the general conspiracy is sufficiently relevant to be admitted. In *Esdaile*[4] there was a conspiracy to defraud the shareholders of a bank. The defendants were alleged to have fraudulently represented that the bank was solvent when it was not. Some (but not all) of the defendants were party to a new share issue. The evidence of the issue was held admissible against all of them to show the object of the conspiracy. Obviously the misrepresentation of solvency would not be fraudulent unless it were made with a dishonest purpose. If it could be shown that A and B intended to profit from the proceeds of the new issue which shareholders were to be induced to purchase, and that C was party to the misrepresentation, it might be inferred that C must have known the dishonest purpose of the misrepresentation (namely the new issue). The fact of the new issue could therefore be evidence against him. It could not prove his guilt, however, unless the jury were satisfied that he must have known it was the purpose of the misrepresentation. If he did not know that, the fact that A and B had profited independently would prove nothing against him. 27–005

ACTS IN FURTHERANCE OF CONSPIRACY

It is often stated that any act or declaration in furtherance of a conspiracy is admissible against all the conspirators. In this section we explore the ramifications of this supposed rule. 27–006

IS THERE A DISTINCTION BETWEEN CONSPIRACY AND JOINT OFFENCES?

A distinction was formerly drawn in this context between conspiracies and joint substantive offences. In *Griffiths* the Court of Criminal Appeal said: 27–007

[4] (1858) 1 F. & F. 213.

> "The practice of adding what may be called a rolled-up conspiracy charge to a number of counts of substantive offences has become common. We express the very strong hope that this practice will now cease and that the courts will never again have to struggle with this type of case, where it becomes almost impossible to explain to a jury that evidence inadmissible against the accused on the substantive count may be admissible against him on the conspiracy count once he is shown to be a conspirator. We do not believe that most juries can ever really understand the subtleties of the situation . . . [I]n two counts upon which the appellant Bishop was convicted, there was literally no receivable evidence at all against him, the evidence being entries in Griffiths' books of account, evidence in the conspiracy count once Bishop is brought into a conspiracy but not evidence upon which he can be brought into the conspiracy."[5]

It is not only juries who may find this proposition difficult to understand. There can be no reason in principle why evidence should be admissible on a charge of conspiracy to commit an offence but not on a joint charge of committing that offence. Conspiracies are often charged where substantive offences can be proved. It would be absurd if the prosecution could circumvent the ordinary rules of evidence by charging a conspiracy to commit an offence rather than the offence itself. Plainly the rule ought to be the same for all joint offences.

27–008 *Gray*[6] was an unusual case which at first sight seemed to confirm that different rules apply. The prosecution's case was that five people, working in different parts of the financial services industry, had established an informal network for the exchange of price-sensitive information which enabled them individually to make, or help others to make, lucrative deals in securities. The original indictment contained two conspiracy counts alleging that they had agreed to communicate such information in breach of the Company Securities (Insider Dealing) Act 1985.[7] There were a large number of substantive counts under the same Act, alleging either communication of price-sensitive information or dealing in securities with knowledge of such information. A few of these counts were joint counts. At the start of the trial the Crown was put to its election and chose to proceed on the substantive counts.[8] At the close of the prosecution case the trial judge ruled that there was no case to answer on any of the joint counts. The trial then continued on a number of counts, each against a single defendant. The prosecution nevertheless sought to rely on the evidence of a general network to prove guilt on the individual counts. The Court of Appeal held that this was not permissible. The prosecution was in effect seeking to

[5] [1966] 1 Q.B. 589 at 594.

[6] [1995] 2 Cr.App.R. 100.

[7] See now Criminal Justice Act 1993, Pt V; above, paras 13–046 *et seq*.

[8] It may be that it should not have been compelled to elect. This may have been a case where the evidence was such that it was difficult to prove complicity on particular joint counts, but it was possible to prove a more general agreement: see below, para.28–028. The addition of individual substantive counts would have been justifiable in case the prosecution failed to prove the general agreement but the jury were satisfied of individual offences: see below, paras 28–034 *et seq*.

allege joint enterprise although there was no count alleging this. Most of the evidence objected to consisted of telephone conversations between pairs of defendants, with coded references to price-sensitive information. Had there been a conspiracy charge, those conversations might have been admissible on the basis that the jury might infer from them the existence of a general agreement.

However, it is now clear that *Gray* is not authority for any distinction between conspiracy charges and joint substantive charges. In *Murray*[9] the joint enterprise involved the supply of heroin. Murray was convicted on both conspiracy counts and a joint substantive count. His co-accused on the substantive count was not a party to either of the conspiracies. On one of the conspiracy counts, evidence was adduced of an incriminating telephone call made by an admitted conspirator; on the substantive count, of calls made by Murray's co-accused. It was conceded that the first call was admissible to prove Murray's part in the conspiracy; but it was argued, on the basis of *Gray*, that the calls made by his co-accused on the substantive count were inadmissible against him. The argument was rejected. There was other evidence from which the jury could infer that there was a joint enterprise and that Murray was party to it. Since the calls were made in furtherance of that common purpose, they were admissible against Murray. *Gray* was held to have turned, not on the fact that the defendants were charged with substantive offences, but on the fact that the common enterprise was either not proved at all or was at best ill-defined. 27–009

A HEARSAY EXCEPTION?

The rule is commonly regarded as allowing the admission of hearsay evidence. If this is true, it is a common law exception to the hearsay rule, and has survived the revision of that rule by the Criminal Justice Act 2003 ("CJA 2003"). Section 118(1), para.7 preserves 27–010

> "Any rule of law under which in criminal proceedings a statement made by a party to a common enterprise is admissible against another party to the enterprise as evidence of any matter stated."

But this merely ensures that, in so far as the rule is an exception to the rule against hearsay, it is unaffected by CJA 2003. It does not tell us whether the rule *is* an exception to the hearsay rule.

On this point it may be illuminating to examine the case on which the supposed rule is founded. In *Blake*[10] the defendants were charged with various conspiracies which in sum amounted to agreements to evade the payment of customs dues on certain goods imported into the United Kingdom. The second defendant, Tye, was the agent for the importer. He 27–011

[9] [1997] 2 Cr.App.R. 136.
[10] (1844) 6 Q.B. 126.

was under a statutory duty to record in official customs records the quantity and value of goods imported. He had to take an official copy of that entry to Blake, who was a landing waiter. Blake had to certify the correctness of the entry. The prosecution case was that the defendants had agreed to understate, and had in fact understated, the value of the goods so that Tye need only account for a limited amount of customs duty. Tye, it was alleged, then passed the goods to the importer, charging him the true amount of duty, and split the difference with Blake. Tye failed to appear on trial and Blake was tried alone. The entries made by Tye and acknowledged by Blake in official records were admitted without objection. Blake's acknowledgement made them an admission. Even if he had not acknowledged them they might have been admissible, not as hearsay but as establishing the declared value of goods as a fact. That was truly an act in furtherance of the conspiracy. It was admitted not to prove the truth of its contents (on the contrary, it was alleged to be false), but to prove the fact of the undervaluation by Tye to which it was alleged Blake was party. There will be many occasions when an entry in a document will be admissible for a similar purpose.

27–012 But the prosecution went further. It sought to prove that Tye had made an entry in his day book showing the true value of the goods he passed to the importer. The case does not suggest that the day book was any form of official record. As against Tye it would have been an admission; as against Blake it must have been hearsay. The fact that a greater quantity of goods was supplied to the importer would have been relevant, and could have been proved by calling the importer. Could it equally be proved, against Blake, by the entry in Tye's day book?

27–013 The prosecution also sought to prove an entry on a cheque counterfoil by Tye, purporting to show that he had made out a cheque to Blake for an amount equal to half the difference between the duty paid to customs and that acquired from the importer. The payment of a sum equal to half the proceeds would again have been relevant, and might have been proved by direct evidence. Could it be proved against Blake by Tye's entry on the cheque stub?

27–014 At the trial both these items of disputed evidence were admitted. Motion was made to the Court of Queen's Bench for a new trial on the ground that the evidence was inadmissible. The court held that the evidence as to the entry on the cheque counterfoil was not properly admitted, and granted the motion. The ground for the rejection of the evidence was that the paying of the cheque was not an act in furtherance of the conspiracy, since the conspiracy was to evade the payment of customs dues, and that evasion was already complete at the time the counterfoil was written. Hearsay evidence was not admissible to prove an act that was not done in furtherance of the conspiracy. Lord Denman C.J. said:

> "The conspiracy was fully effected before that was done. The evidence, therefore, is on the same footing as evidence that Tye told some other party that he had paid Blake money on account of the fraud . . . If we received every

> statement of a party shewn to be a conspirator, we should often find ourselves embarrassed by a party relying upon a statement of his own, to exonerate himself."[11]

The other judges concurred in this reasoning, Coleridge J. adding the observation that the note was simply made out for Tye's own use.[12] Lord Denman C.J. put forward the classic objection to hearsay evidence, namely that it may be fabricated. However, to say (as Coleridge J. did) that the division of plunder was not part of the common object seems to fly in the face of common sense. The whole purpose of the agreement was the eventual division of plunder, and it must have continued until that was effected.[13]

The question of the admissibility of the day book was never fully argued. Counsel for the applicant was stopped in argument, and Coleridge J. in his judgment made it plain that counsel had not been heard on this issue. The court nevertheless made observations, *obiter*, to the effect that the entry in the day book was admissible. It is upon these observations that the supposed rule is founded. Lord Denman C.J. said: 27–015

> "The day book was evidence of something done in the course of the transaction, and was properly laid before the jury as a step in the proof of the conspiracy."[14]

Patteson J. said:

> "[T]he concert may be shewn by either direct or indirect evidence. The day book here was evidence of what was done towards the very acting in concert which was to be proved. It was receivable as a step in the proof of the conspiracy."[15]

Williams J. said:

> "[T]he existence of a conspiracy may be shewn by the detached acts of the individual conspirators. Therefore, the entry made by Tye in his day book was admissible, in order to shew one act done with the common purpose."[16]

Coleridge J. indicated that he thought the entry was probably admissible.[17]

So far as the report shows, the day book was merely Tye's private record. 27–016
He was under no statutory obligation to make it. He did not show it to the customs officers or to Blake to secure payment of the full dues. Had he

[11] (1844) 6 Q.B. 126 at 137.
[12] (1844) 6 Q.B. 126 at 140.
[13] But *Blake* "remains authority for the proposition that a narrative statement or its equivalent by one co-conspirator *after* the completion of the common design alleged is not admissible": *Williams* [2002] EWCA Crim 2208 at [58].
[14] (1844) 6 Q.B. 126 at 137.
[15] (1844) 6 Q.B. 126 at 138–139.
[16] (1844) 6 Q.B. 126 at 139.
[17] (1844) 6 Q.B. 126 at 140.

done so, it might have been admissible to show the fact that it was made, though not the truth of its contents. Moreover, in all probability, it was made after the goods had entered. In principle, therefore, it seems to be in no different position from the cheque counterfoil. It is possible that the judges' observations confuse two issues. The fact that Tye had given the importer higher value than he had declared to the customs, and charged greater dues than he had paid, was clearly relevant: these acts would have been a necessary part of the conspiracy, or acts in its furtherance. The real question was how they could be proved. They could clearly be proved by the direct evidence of the importer, or by admission against an individual defendant. But a hearsay statement ought to be just as objectionable in this case as in the case of the cheque counterfoil. Conspiracy may be inferred from the detached acts of conspirators, but those acts must be properly proved by admissible evidence.

27–017 The rationale for the admission of evidence of acts which further the conspiracy is set out in the judgment of Dixon C.J. in *Tripodi*:

> "The basic reason for admitting the evidence of the acts or words of one against the other is that the combination or preconcert to commit the crime is considered as implying an authority to each to act or speak in furtherance of the common purpose on behalf of the others. From the nature of the case it can seldom happen that anything said by one which is no more than a narrative statement or account of some event that has already taken place, that is to say some statement which would be receivable in evidence against the man who made it as an admission and not otherwise, can become admissible under principle against his companions in the common enterprise. Usually the question of admissibility will relate to directions, instructions or arrangements, or to utterances accompanying acts."[18]

This passage appears to distinguish between statements admissible as direct evidence of the offence and those inadmissible as hearsay.[19] The rule applies to acts which are themselves *part* of the conspiracy, not acts which merely show that the conspiracy is taking place or has taken place.

27–018 Thus in *Steward*[20] the defendant was convicted of conspiring to defraud by doping racehorses. A fellow conspirator gave evidence that another conspirator had told him that the defendant had doped horses. This statement was held inadmissible because it was not made in furtherance of the conspiracy. Similarly, an account in a private diary which records the progress of a conspiracy, but does not itself advance the conspiracy, is not admissible (except against its maker, as an admission); but a record kept of payments made or goods delivered as *part* of the conspiracy is admissible.

> "[A]n entry 'A asked me to remind X to have the money available to fund the drugs' would be an act in furtherance, because it would be open to the

[18] (1961) 104 C.L.R. 1 at 6–7, cited with approval in *Gray* [1995] 2 Cr.App.R. 100.

[19] See Jeremy Roberts Q.C., "Some Procedural Problems in Criminal Fraud Cases" in Peter Birks (ed.), *Pressing Problems in the Law—Vol.1: Criminal Justice and Human Rights* (1995) at 59.

[20] [1963] Crim. L.R. 697.

> legitimate inference that it was to be used by the author to remind him to convey that message from A to X. To characterise such an entry as an 'aide mémoire' would be quite correct. But because it was made for the stated purpose, it is also capable of being an act in furtherance of the agreement."[21]

The prosecution has sometimes found it necessary to argue for a common law exception to the hearsay rule because according to *Kearley*[22] a statement which implied the existence of a fact was hearsay even if that fact was already known to the hearer. The point may now be of less importance, because CJA 2003, s.115 has reversed *Kearley* and thus narrowed the scope of the hearsay rule.[23] For example, in *Jones*[24] conversations between the co-accused were held admissible because they were "capable of being regarded as words spoken in pursuit of, and for the purpose of advancing the common enterprise"; they were "the enterprise in operation" and "an intrinsic part of the illegal activity". It would have been otherwise if the conversations had merely imparted information about what had already been done: in that case, as the law then stood, they would have been inadmissible hearsay. Since CJA 2003, the conversations would probably not be hearsay on either view. So, even if the rule about acts and declarations in furtherance of conspiracy was originally an exception to the rule against hearsay, it may be that it is no longer an exception to that rule, because the kind of evidence to which it applies is no longer hearsay evidence. **27–019**

EVIDENCE IMPLICATING A CONSPIRATOR

In its application to conspiracy, there is a risk of the rule becoming fallaciously circular. All conspirators are responsible for all acts done in furtherance of the conspiracy, whether they knew about them or not. By agreeing to an end, one is responsible for what is done to that end (though not, of course, for acts outside the contemplation of the agreement). But acts done in furtherance of the conspiracy by others do not prove that one is party to the conspiracy: that must be achieved independently. Since all conspirators are responsible in law for the acts of their fellow conspirators, the point at issue in a conspiracy trial is never to which acts an individual defendant was party, but whether he was a party to the general agreement at all. **27–020**

SIMILAR CONDUCT

The law on the admissibility of conduct other than that charged has been significantly changed by CJA 2003. The common law rules are abolished,[25] and the Court of Appeal has said that it is wrong to approach a case by first **27–021**

[21] *Reeves* December 4, 1998.
[22] [1992] 2 A.C. 228.
[23] See below, para.27–061.
[24] [1997] 2 Cr.App.R. 119; see Sir John Smith, "More on Proving Conspiracy" [1997] Crim. L.R. 333.
[25] CJA 2003, s.99(1). There is a saving for the exception to the hearsay rule which permits evidence of reputation to prove character: CJA 2003, ss.99(2), 118(1).

asking what would have been the position before the Act.[26] But the underlying principles are actually quite similar,[27] and authorities on the common law may still be helpful in so far as they throw light on those principles.

27–022 The kind of evidence regulated by the new provisions is defined by CJA 2003, s.98:

> "References in this Chapter to evidence of a person's 'bad character' are to evidence of, or of a disposition towards, misconduct on his part, other than evidence which—
>
> (a) has to do with the alleged facts of the offence with which the defendant is charged, or
>
> (b) is evidence of misconduct in connection with the investigation or prosecution of that offence."

27–023 "Misconduct" is itself defined by s.112 as "the commission of an offence or other reprehensible behaviour". Although this makes a wide range of evidence potentially inadmissible as evidence of "bad character",[28] in the case of defendants[29] it is matched by a wide range of grounds on which such evidence can nonetheless be admitted. We consider the two gateways to admissibility that are most likely to be pertinent in a fraud case.

IMPORTANT EXPLANATORY EVIDENCE

27–024 Under CJA 2003, s.101(1)(c) evidence of a defendant's bad character is admissible if it is "important explanatory evidence". This gateway is open to a co-defendant as well as the prosecution. Evidence is "important explanatory evidence" if

> "(a) without it, the court or jury would find it impossible or difficult properly to understand other evidence in the case, and
>
> (b) its value for understanding the case as a whole is substantial".[30]

27–025 Section 101(1)(c) is aimed at cases where the evidence of misconduct on other occasions is so inextricably bound up with that relating to the occasion charged, so closely associated with it in time and place, that it is

[26] *Chopra* [2006] EWCA Crim 2133; [2007] Crim. L.R. 380.

[27] See below, para.27–047.

[28] It is sometimes supposed that the wider the definition of "bad character", the easier it is to adduce evidence falling within the definition. This is a misapprehension. Where evidence of bad character is admissible, it is admissible *although* (not because) it is evidence of bad character. Unfortunately the provisions are drafted in such a way as to disguise this fact.

[29] Unlike the previous law, CJA 2003 restricts the admissibility of evidence of the bad character of non-defendants as well as defendants, and indeed restricts it to a greater extent. This is reflected in the fact that evidence of the bad character of a non-defendant cannot be adduced without the leave of the court.

[30] CJA 2003, s.102.

impossible to understand the position without hearing the whole story: the other conduct is an essential part of the background to the case.[31] A hypothetical example was given by the Law Commission.

> "X sets up a company, as sole shareholder and executive director. Its ostensible purpose is to make investments on behalf of clients. X asks D to be a non-executive director. X tells D that the company will seek to 'minimise' corporation tax payments, and D will occasionally be asked to sign off on misleading accounting documents to that end. Over a number of months, both X and D sign off on false accounting documents. Then X disappears overnight. The company's client account has been cleaned out. D is charged with false accounting and conspiracy to defraud the company's clients. D pleads guilty to the false accounting charges, and the convictions are recorded. However, D pleads not guilty to conspiracy, claiming to have been unaware of X's fraud on the clients. At D's conspiracy trial, the prosecution will need to refer to D's previous convictions and the wrong-doing that lay behind them, because the false accounting documents were used to effect the fraud on the clients."[32]

EVIDENCE RELEVANT TO AN IMPORTANT MATTER IN ISSUE

Under CJA 2003, s.101(1)(d) evidence of a defendant's bad character is **27–026** admissible if it is "relevant to an important matter in issue between the defendant and the prosecution". This applies only to evidence adduced by the prosecution.[33] The evidence need not be of behaviour which has resulted in a conviction. It follows that the evidence on one count may be admissible on another.[34] But s.101(1)(d) is subject to s.101(3), which provides:

> "The court must not admit evidence under subsection (1)(d) . . . if, on an application by the defendant to exclude it, it appears to the court that the admission of the evidence would have such an adverse effect on the fairness of the proceedings that the court ought not to admit it."[35]

Where the prosecution seeks to adduce evidence under s.101(1)(d), **27–027** therefore, the court must consider three questions:

[31] cf. *Pettman* May 2, 1985, cited in many subsequent cases including *Fulcher* [1995] 2 Cr.App.R. 251 and *Stevens* [1995] Crim. L.R. 649.

[32] Law Com. No.273, *Evidence of Bad Character in Criminal Proceedings*, Cm.5257, p.136.

[33] CJA 2003, s.103(6).

[34] CJA 2003, s.112(2); *Chopra* [2006] EWCA Crim 2133; [2007] Crim. L.R. 380; *Francis-Macrae* [2006] EWCA Crim 2635; below, para.27–036.

[35] CJA 2003, s.112(2) provides that, where a defendant is charged with two or more offences in the same proceedings, the bad character provisions of the Act (except s.101(3)) have effect as if each offence were charged in separate proceedings. The exception for s.101(3) seems to mean that if a defendant is charged on two counts, and the prosecution seeks to adduce evidence of his bad character under s.101(1)(d) or (g) in relation to count 1 only, and he makes an application under s.101(3) for that evidence to be excluded, the question for the court is whether the admission of the evidence would have such an adverse effect on the fairness of the whole proceedings (*including* the proceedings on count 2) that the court ought not to admit it. It cannot mean that in these circumstances s.101(3) does not apply at all.

(1) Is the evidence relevant to a matter in issue? Matters in issue may include whether certain acts or events occurred, whether the defendant did those acts or caused those events, whether certain circumstances existed, and what the defendant knew or intended. Whether the defendant has a propensity to act in the manner alleged, and whether he has a propensity to be untruthful, are deemed to be matters in issue in nearly every case.[36]

(2) Is the matter in issue to which the evidence is relevant (or, if the evidence is relevant to more than one such matter, any of them) an *important* matter in issue? It is presumably sufficient for this purpose that the defendant cannot be convicted unless the issue is determined in favour of the prosecution; but this cannot be essential, or the Act would have said so.

(3) Assuming that the defence applies to exclude the evidence, would the admission of the evidence have such an adverse effect on the fairness of the proceedings that the evidence should be excluded?

PROOF OF PARTICULAR KNOWLEDGE

27–028 In a fraud case the defendant will often admit the acts alleged, but deny that he acted with the necessary mens rea. If he denies knowledge of certain relevant information, evidence of previous transactions may serve to refute his denial. If he is charged with misrepresenting the quality of goods sold, and claims to have believed that the goods were as he described them, it will clearly be relevant that he had already received complaints from other customers about similar goods.

27–029 In *Patel*[37] the defendant was charged with being knowingly concerned in taking steps with a view to the fraudulent evasion of purchase tax, which was payable on stockings purchased for resale within the United Kingdom. He financed the purchase by a company of large quantities of nylon stockings and paid for their transport to unregistered traders within the United Kingdom, to whom they were sold on for further sale on the UK market. His defence was that he had been deceived by a director of the company, and did not know to whom the stockings were sold or that they were sold on for eventual sale in the United Kingdom. Evidence was admitted that six months earlier he had purchased a large quantity of nylon stockings as agent on behalf of another firm, saying that the stockings were bound for Pakistan. Evidence of the earlier transactions was held admissible.

> "Since [the defendant's] business apparently consisted of financing other companies with which he was not directly concerned in cases in which those

[36] See below, paras 27–037 *et seq*.
[37] (1951) 35 Cr.App.R. 62.

> companies were placing orders for nylon stockings which purported to be orders for export, could the jury believe that in the cases charged he in fact made no inquiries and took no interest in what became of the goods ordered and paid for by him?"[38]

It was not in fact suggested that he had made no inquiries, but that he had been deceived. Even so, his knowledge of the trade, and of the workings of purchase tax, was plainly relevant to his state of mind in the second series of transactions: it cast doubt on his assertion that he did not know what was going on. It does not appear to have been alleged that the previous transaction had been illegal or that the stockings had not gone to Pakistan, and indeed some of them were unsuitable for the British market. The earlier transaction cannot therefore have been relevant as showing a propensity to commit frauds of the kind alleged, but only as showing knowledge of a particular trade.

This case may be contrasted with *Porter*.[39] The defendant was charged with obtaining money by falsely representing that a business carried on by him under the name Approved Hotels, Cafés and Restaurants of Great Britain was a bona fide association honestly carried on to offer advantages to subscribers. He denied intent to defraud. Two years earlier he had carried on a business that was remarkably similar, and had been convicted of obtaining by false pretences. He was cross-examined about that previous business. He was not asked about the conviction, though he volunteered it. It was held that the evidence of the earlier business was admissible to show that he must have known from his experience that carrying on such a business would only result in its failure and in subscribers being defrauded of their money. This reasoning is unconvincing. There was no reason to suppose that a business of that description was necessarily doomed to failure even if it were carried on in good faith. No doubt the second business was equally likely to fail if the defendant made no attempt to give the subscribers value for money; but the issue was whether he intended to do so, not whether he appreciated the commercial realities of running such a business. The evidence might have been admissible as tending to prove that he made a habit of running bogus businesses of this kind, but it should have been justified on that basis rather than as showing proof of particular knowledge. **27–030**

Similar confusion may be detected in *Ollis*.[40] The defendant had a bank account that had lain dormant for three years. On July 5 he drew a cheque on the account for £5. It was dishonoured, and he was charged with obtaining money by false pretences. His defence was that he had expected money to be paid into the account. He was acquitted. The next day he was put on trial for obtaining property by drawing bad cheques on June 24, June 26 and July 6. At this trial the prosecution was allowed to adduce **27–031**

[38] (1951) 35 Cr.App.R. 62 at 67–68.
[39] (1935) 25 Cr.App.R. 59.
[40] [1900] 2 Q.B. 758.

evidence of the transaction on July 5. The Court for Crown Cases Reserved held that this evidence was admissible, but the reasoning is obscure: much of it is directed to the question whether the evidence was inadmissible because of the acquittal in the first trial, rather than the logically prior question of whether it was relevant at all. Lord Russell C.J. said "it was relevant as shewing a course of conduct on the part of the accused, and a belief on his part that the cheques would not be met".[41] Wright J. said: "The evidence tended to shew that the conduct of the prisoner, in tendering drafts on a bank at which he had no living account, was not inadvertent or accidental, but was part of a systematic fraud . . .".[42] But it is hard to see how the writing of several bad cheques could be evidence of a "systematic fraud", when the defence was that the defendant was expecting money to be paid into his account;[43] if that were true, and the aggregate of the cheques drawn did not exceed the amount that he expected to be paid in, there was no reason why he should not write as many cheques as he liked.

27–032 The alternative reason for holding the evidence to be relevant was that it proved the defendant's knowledge of the state of his account. Darling J. said:

> "[T]his evidence . . . was material, for it went some way to shew that the defendant knew he had no assets at the bank on which he gave a cheque, as this had already been brought to his notice in regard to another cheque given by him but a very short time before."[44]

If it had been proved that the defendant knew that one of his cheques had been dishonoured, this would certainly have been relevant to the issue of whether he knew the state of the account.[45] But two of the cheques which were the subject matter of the second trial had been drawn before the one on which the defendant had been acquitted; and according to Bruce J. (who dissented) there was no evidence that when the defendant wrote the cheque on July 6 he knew that the cheque written on July 5 had been dishonoured.[46] It is submitted that, on the facts as reported, the evidence of the transaction on July 5 was irrelevant to any issue before the court.

PROOF OF SYSTEM

27–033 Where a person is alleged to have committed offences on more than one occasion, the combined probative force of the allegations will derive from their number, the similarities between them, and the degree to which they

[41] [1900] 2 Q.B. 758 at 764.
[42] [1900] 2 Q.B. 758 at 768.
[43] Bruce J. thought it could be assumed that the defence was the same as in the first trial: [1900] 2 Q.B. 758 at 772.
[44] [1900] 2 Q.B. 758 at 779.
[45] cf. [1900] 2 Q.B. 758 at 783, *per* Channell J.
[46] [1900] 2 Q.B. 758 at 778.

are independent of each other. The jury may be invited to conclude that the number and nature of the allegations is such that the only reasonable explanation is that they are true. In a fraud case the issue is usually one of intention rather than identity, and proof of other transactions similar to the one charged may tend to suggest that the defendant acted dishonestly throughout. To disappoint one customer may be regarded as a misfortune; to have disappointed a hundred looks suspiciously like fraud. Evidence suggesting a propensity to act in accordance with a particular pattern or system may have greater probative value than evidence of a general propensity to act dishonestly, and even at common law would have been more likely to be admitted.

In *Wyatt*,[47] for example, the defendant was charged with obtaining board and lodging at a boarding house by an implied representation that he intended to pay. In the period immediately preceding this incident he had left other boarding houses without paying. It was held that evidence of the earlier transactions was rightly admitted to prove a system practised by him. In *Francis*[48] the defendant was charged with attempting to obtain an advance from a pawnbroker in Northampton on the security of a ring, by the false pretence that it was a diamond ring. His defence was that his employer had instructed him to pawn the ring and had told him that it was a diamond ring. Evidence was admitted that two days earlier he had obtained an advance from a pawnbroker in Bedford on a chain which he falsely represented to be gold, and had attempted to do the same in Leicester with a ring which he falsely represented to be a diamond ring. This evidence was held admissible. Lord Coleridge C.J. said: 27–034

> "It seems clear upon principle that when the fact of the prisoner having done the thing charged is proved, and the only remaining question is, whether at the time he did it he had guilty knowledge of the quality of his act or acted under a mistake, evidence of the class received must be admissible. It tends to shew that he was pursuing a course of similar acts, and thereby it raises a presumption that he was not acting under a mistake. It is not conclusive, for a man may be many times under a similar mistake, or may be many times the dupe of another; but it is less likely he should be so often, than once, and every circumstance which shews he was not under a mistake on any one of these occasions strengthens the presumption that he was not on the last . . . Evidence that he, . . . at Bedford, obtained money from another pawnbroker on the pledge of a chain which he represented to be gold, when it in fact was not gold, was surely matter from which the jury might infer that he was in a course of cheating pawnbrokers by knowingly passing off on them false articles under the pretence that they were genuine . . ."[49]

EVIDENCE OF PROPENSITY

Even if the other conduct relied upon is not sufficiently similar to the offence charged to justify that kind of reasoning, it may still be admissible on the basis that it goes to propensity. In *Rance*[50] the managing director of 27–035

[47] [1904] 1 K.B. 188.
[48] (1874) L.R. 2 C.C.R. 128.
[49] (1874) L.R. 2 C.C.R. 128 at 131–132.
[50] (1976) 62 Cr.App.R. 118.

a building company was alleged to have bribed a councillor. He had signed both the cheque and a certificate necessary to justify the expense in the company's accounts. His defence was that he must have been tricked into signing the certificate. He was also implicated in two similar, though not identical, bribes which were not charged in the same proceedings. In each case he had signed false documents justifying the bribes, though his explanations were different in each case. The evidence of the other bribes was held admissible at common law. It showed a propensity to bribe councillors and use bogus documents to cover his tracks.

27–036 In *Francis-Macrae*,[51] a case decided under CJA 2003, the defendant was charged on two counts of fraudulent trading, each relating to a different business. The first related to a business which involved obtaining payment in advance for the registration of internet domain names with the suffix "eu" (for Europe), which had been proposed but did not yet exist. It was alleged that the defendant never intended to carry out the registrations. His defence was that he did intend to do so if possible, and if it proved impossible he would have repaid the money. Left at that, the defence would have been plausible. The second count related to a business which involved inviting the holders of existing domain names to pay for the renewal of their registrations. In this case the evidence of dishonesty was stronger. The defendant had no relationship with a registrar. He sent out official-looking letters headed "domain expiration notice, do not ignore this notice", proposing to renew the registrations for far longer than would have been possible. Again his defence was that the business was an honest one: he was mistaken about the period for which a registration could be renewed. It was conceded that the evidence of dishonesty on the second count was admissible as evidence of propensity on the first count.

> "The appellant's honesty was at the heart of the issue between the Crown and the defence. If at the time the appellant was soliciting applications for registration on the yet to be introduced eu domain, he was dishonestly inviting applications for renewal on an existing top level domain, that was relevant to the consideration of the honesty of his intention to register customers on the eu domain, or of his intention to repay subscriptions."[52]

27–037 In the case of evidence of propensity, CJA 2003, s.101(1)(d) (which, subject to s.101(3), makes evidence of a defendant's bad character admissible if it is relevant to an important matter in issue) is supplemented by s.103. Section 103 ensures that the question whether the defendant has certain propensities will normally be a matter in issue. It does not follow that this will be an *important* matter in issue; and, even if it is, the evidence going to it may not be sufficiently probative to pass the test in s.101(3). The prosecution may be on stronger ground if it argues that the evidence goes to some other and more important matter in issue, such as the defendant's

[51] [2006] EWCA Crim 2635.
[52] [2006] EWCA Crim 2635 at [18].

knowledge or intentions. In other words there may be no need to rely on s.103 at all.

Propensity to commit offences of the kind charged

CJA 2003, s.103(1) provides, in part: 27–038

> "For the purposes of section 101(1)(d) the matters in issue between the defendant and the prosecution include—
>
> (a) the question whether the defendant has a propensity to commit offences of the kind with which he is charged, except where his having such a propensity makes it no more likely that he is guilty of the offence . . ."

This makes it clear that a defendant's propensity to commit the kind of offence with which he is charged can be, and virtually always is, a matter in issue. The exception for evidence which does not make it any more likely that he is guilty seems to add nothing: such evidence would be inadmissible anyway, because it would be irrelevant. CJA 2003 does not allow irrelevant evidence to be admitted merely because it is evidence of bad character.[53]

The Act does not say that a general tendency to be anti-social, or even to 27–039
commit offences, is a matter in issue. The only propensity deemed by s.103(1)(a) to be a matter in issue is a propensity to commit offences *of the kind charged*. This phrase is not defined, but s.103(2) gives some guidance by allowing such a propensity to be established by proof of a previous conviction. It provides:

> "Where subsection (1)(a) applies, a defendant's propensity to commit offences of the kind with which he is charged may (without prejudice to any other way of doing so) be established by evidence that he has been convicted of—
>
> (a) an offence of the same description as the one with which he is charged, or
>
> (b) an offence of the same category as the one with which he is charged."[54]

This is subject to s.103(3), which provides that s.103(2)

> "does not apply in the case of a particular defendant if the court is satisfied, by reason of the length of time since the conviction or for any other reason, that it would be unjust for it to apply in his case".

For the purposes of s.103(2)(a), two offences are of the same "descrip- 27–040
tion" as each other if the statement of offence would be in the same terms[55]—that is, they are the same offence in law. So, if the charge is theft

[53] See above, fn.28.

[54] PACE, s.74(3) allows a conviction to serve as proof that an offence was committed unless the contrary is proved. Where commission of an offence may be proved under s.74, s.75(1) allows the "contents of the information, complaint, indictment or charge-sheet" to be admitted.

[55] CJA 2003, s.103(4)(a).

of £10m by means of a complex computer fraud, a previous conviction for shoplifting shows a propensity to commit offences of the kind charged—though a court would presumably decline under s.103(3) to apply s.103(2) in such a case.[56]

27–041 For the purposes of s.103(2)(b), two offences are of the same "category" as each other if they fall within the same Part of the Schedule to the Criminal Justice Act 2003 (Categories of Offences) Order 2004,[57] made under s.103(4)(b). Part I of the Schedule includes theft, but none of the other offences discussed in this book.[58] There is no fraud category. The rationale for the selection of the offences in Pt I is obscure. It is remarkable, for example, that taking a conveyance (which does not even require dishonesty), should be regarded as more akin to theft than the old offence of obtaining property by deception (which by definition was nearly always theft too)[59] or the new offences of fraud by false representation (which will usually involve theft if the fraud succeeds) and obtaining services dishonestly (which was designed as a "theft-like" offence).[60] The effect is that s.103(2)(b) will be irrelevant in a fraud case unless the charge is theft and the defendant happens to have a conviction for one of the other offences listed in the order.[61]

27–042 But that is not the end of the matter. Section 103(2) is without prejudice to any other way of establishing a defendant's propensity to commit offences of the kind with which he is charged. One alternative way of establishing such a propensity would be to prove that he has committed other offences, of the same kind as the offence charged, of which he has not been convicted[62]—for example, another offence of the same kind which is charged in another count.[63] Another way would be to prove that he has been convicted of other offences which are of the same kind as the offence

[56] See *Hanson* [2005] EWCA Crim 824; [2005] 1 W.L.R. 3169 at [9].

[57] SI 2004/3346.

[58] Except going equipped for stealing (but not possession of articles for use in fraud): above, para.21–043. The other offences in Pt 1 of the Schedule are robbery, certain forms of burglary and aggravated burglary, taking a conveyance and aggravated vehicle-taking, handling stolen goods and making off without payment, and attempt and incitement (but not conspiracy) to commit any of these. Offences of aiding, abetting, counselling or procuring the commission of any such offence are also included, though this is unnecessary because a person guilty of aiding, abetting, etc. is guilty of the same offence as the principal offender.

[59] See above, para.9–123.

[60] Law Com. No.276, *Fraud*, Cm.5560, para.8.7.

[61] Even then, the court would probably exercise the discretion under s.103(3) to disapply s.103(2). The fact that the previous conviction is for an offence of the same category as the offence charged is not conclusive: *Hanson* [2005] EWCA Crim 824; [2005] 1 W.L.R. 3169 at [10].

[62] And of which he may even have been acquitted: *Z.* [2000] 2 A.C. 483. It may even be possible to establish that a defendant has a propensity to commit offences of a particular kind by proving that he is psychologically *inclined* to commit offences of that kind, without proving that he has ever actually done so except on the occasion charged; but this is more likely to be relevant in the context of sexual offences than that of dishonesty. Most people have a propensity for trying to acquire money.

[63] CJA 2003, s.112(2); *Chopra* [2006] EWCA Crim 2133; [2007] Crim. L.R. 380; *Francis-Macrae* [2006] EWCA Crim 2635; above, para.27–036.

charged, though not of the same description or category. For example, conspiracy to defraud is presumably the same kind of offence as fraud. But almost any two of the offences discussed in this book will be similar in some ways and dissimilar in others, and it will usually be debatable whether they are the same kind of offence within the meaning of the Act. Is making a deceptive statement to induce another to enter into an investment agreement[64] the same kind of offence as fraud by false representation, because they both involve misrepresentation? Or is it a different kind of offence because it does not require dishonesty? Arguably it depends on the way the case is put. Fraud by false representation is, in law, the same offence as fraud by abuse of position. Perhaps fraud is the same kind of offence as making a deceptive statement if the case is presented as one of fraud by false representation, but not if it is presented as fraud by abuse of position.

A possible clue is that two offences cannot be included in a *category* (in an order made under s.103(4)(b)) unless they are of the same *type*.[65] Since the effect of including them in the same category is that they are regarded as offences of the same *kind*, this implies that two offences may be of the same type without being of the same kind. And, since the two words are in ordinary usage virtually synonymous, it seems to follow either that "type" is intended to have an unusually wide meaning or that "kind" is intended to have an unusually narrow one. **27–043**

Section 103(3), which provides that s.103(2) "does not apply . . . if the court is satisfied . . . that it would be unjust for it to apply", is irrelevant if the prosecution does not rely on s.103(2) because it seeks to establish propensity by proving an offence of the same kind which is not of the same description or category. But in this case the court has a similar discretion under s.101(3), which prohibits the admission of evidence under s.101(1)(d) if "it appears to the court that the admission of the evidence would have such an adverse effect on the fairness of the proceedings that the court ought not to admit it". Unlike s.103(3), this applies in relation to *any* evidence which the prosecution seeks to adduce on the ground that it shows the defendant's propensity to commit the offence charged. It applies even if s.103(3) applies too. It may be queried what significance lies in the difference of wording. A literal reading might suggest that s.101(3) permits a little bit of injustice (but not too much) whereas s.103(3) permits none, but that seems unlikely to be the intention. It is submitted that if there is any difference it lies in the focus: under s.103(3) the court must consider the fairness of the conviction as an item of evidence, whereas under s.101(3) the court must consider the fairness of the proceedings as a whole. It is doubtful whether either provision adds anything to PACE, s.78, which applies in any event.[66] **27–044**

[64] Financial Services and Markets Act 2000, s.397(2); above, para.13–002.

[65] CJA 2003, s.103(5).

[66] The wording of s.101(3) echoes that of PACE, s.78—though, as the Court of Appeal noted in *Hanson* [2005] EWCA Crim 824; [2005] 1 W.L.R. 3169 at [10], "must not admit" is stronger than "may refuse to allow".

27–045 In *Hanson* the Court of Appeal gave the following guidance on the approach to be taken when deciding whether to admit evidence of other offences:

> "Where propensity to commit the offence is relied upon there are . . . essentially three questions to be considered:
>
> (1) Does the history of conviction(s) establish a propensity to commit offences of the kind charged?
>
> (2) Does that propensity make it more likely that the defendant committed the offence charged?
>
> (3) Is it unjust to rely on the conviction(s) of the same description or category; and, in any event, will the proceedings be unfair if they are admitted?"[67]

On the face of it this applies only where the prosecution seek to rely on s.103(2), but it is clear from the judgment that a similar approach is appropriate where s.103(2) does not apply and the discretion to be exercised is that under s.101(3).

27–046 The court scotched any idea that there was any need to reintroduce the concept of "striking similarity" (which had featured in the earlier case law), but accepted that the degree of similarity between the previous offences and that charged could be taken into account.[68] The fewer the previous offences, the weaker the evidence of propensity; a single conviction may not show propensity at all.[69]

> "The judge may also take into consideration the respective gravity of the past and present offences. He or she must always consider the strength of the prosecution case. If there is no or very little other evidence against a defendant, it is unlikely to be just to admit his previous convictions, whatever they are."[70]

27–047 It is commonly assumed that CJA 2003 has radically changed the law on the admissibility of evidence of propensity. But it is questionable whether the legislation actually departs from the common law position as laid down by the House of Lords in *DPP v P.*,[71] namely that evidence of propensity is admissible if (but only if) its probative value is so great as to outweigh the prejudice likely to result from admitting it. CJA 2003, s.101(3), in particular,[72] seems to be simply another way of saying the same thing. The Court

[67] [2005] EWCA Crim 824; [2005] 1 W.L.R. 3169 at [7].

[68] [2005] EWCA Crim 824; [2005] 1 W.L.R. 3169 at [10].

[69] [2005] EWCA Crim 824; [2005] 1 W.L.R. 3169 at [9]. Strictly speaking this appears to be inconsistent with s.103(2): the court presumably meant that in such a case s.103(2) should be disapplied under s.103(3). The court accepted that a single conviction might suffice in certain circumstances, but this is unlikely to be so in a fraud case if the conviction is relied on as evidence of propensity rather than system.

[70] [2005] EWCA Crim 824; [2005] 1 W.L.R. 3169 at [10].

[71] [1991] 2 A.C. 447.

[72] The same is true of CJA 2003, s.103(3) (when it applies) and PACE, s.78 (which always applies).

of Appeal has said that, whereas evidence of the defendant's propensity to offend in the manner now charged was prima facie inadmissible at common law, under CJA 2003 it is prima facie admissible.[73] This is true in the somewhat theoretical sense that s.101(3) does not require the court to consider the justice of admitting the evidence unless the defence applies to exclude it. But such an application is likely to be made in nearly every case.[74] The real issue is the criterion to be applied by the court in determining such an application; and it is not clear how, if at all, the new criterion differs from the old. Section 101(3) does not, on its face, create any presumption in favour of admissibility.[75] Indeed it appears that it was not intended to do so. In debate on the Bill, the Minister (Hilary Benn MP) said in relation to what is now s.101(3):

> "The test for the court to apply is designed to reflect the existing position under the common law as section 78 of the Police and Criminal Evidence Act 1984 does. Under that, the judge balances the probative value of the evidence against the prejudicial effect of admitting it and excludes the evidence where the prejudice exceeds the probative value. The Government's intention is for the courts to apply the fairness test in this Bill in the same way and that is the intended effect of the clause. In applying the test to evidence of a conviction for the same offence, or one of the same category, the court will balance the probative value of the convictions, that is, the extent to which they are relevant to the case . . . against any prejudicial effect of admitting them."[76]

Propensity to be untruthful

Section 103(1) further provides: **27–048**

> "For the purposes of section 101(1)(d) the matters in issue between the defendant and the prosecution include—
>
> . . .
>
> (b) the question whether the defendant has a propensity to be untruthful, except where it is not suggested that the defendant's case is untruthful in any respect."

Section 103(1)(b) is not concerned with evidence which points *directly* to **27–049**
guilt—for example where the charge is fraud by false representation, and the issue is whether the defendant knew that the representation was false, and there is evidence that he has made similar false representations on other occasions. In this case the evidence suggests a propensity to commit offences of the kind charged, and the question whether the defendant has such a propensity is a matter in issue by virtue of s.103(1)(a). Section

[73] *Chopra* [2006] EWCA Crim 2133; [2007] Crim. L.R. 380.

[74] Except where the evidence on one of the offences charged is relied upon as relevant to another. In that case there is no question of excluding the evidence altogether: the question is how it may be used.

[75] It does not even require the court to be "satisfied" that the admission of the evidence would be unfair (cf. s.103(3)), but only that this should "appear" to the court to be the case.

[76] *Hansard*, SC Deb.B, cols 590–591 (January 23, 2003).

103(1)(b) is aimed at evidence which suggests that the defendant's version of events is less likely to be true because he is an untruthful person. His truthfulness (or otherwise) becomes a matter in issue if he challenges the truthfulness of the prosecution's evidence, whether orally at the trial or in pre-trial statements.[77] The only case in which it is *not* a matter in issue is where all the facts are agreed and the only issue is the interpretation to be put on those facts—for example, whether what the defendant is agreed to have done, if done in the state of mind in which he is agreed to have done it, is dishonest by ordinary standards.

27–050 But s.103(1)(b) does not itself make evidence of untruthfulness admissible: it merely ensures that a defendant's propensity to be untruthful counts as a matter in issue for the purposes of s.101(1)(d). The evidence will not be admissible under s.101(1)(d) unless that propensity is an *important* matter in issue. It is arguable that this will rarely, if ever, be so. Most people are sometimes truthful and sometimes untruthful. A person who lies in one situation will not necessarily do so in another. Knowing that the defendant sometimes tells lies is unlikely to help the jury much in deciding whether he is telling the truth on this occasion—especially since he has a strong incentive to lie if he thinks that this will improve his chances of being acquitted.

27–051 Assuming that the defendant's propensity to be untruthful *is* an important matter in issue, however, any evidence which is relevant to it is admissible under s.101(1)(d) unless excluded under s.101(3).[78] In this case, by contrast with evidence showing a propensity to commit offences of the same kind, CJA 2003 is silent about the kind of evidence that may be relevant to the issue. The explanatory notes on the Act state that s.103(1)(b)

> "is intended to enable the admission of a limited range of evidence such as convictions for perjury or other offences involving deception . . . as opposed to the wider range of evidence that will be admissible where the defendant puts his character in issue by, for example, attacking the character of another person".[79]

This suggests that lies which have not resulted in convictions are intended to be excluded under s.101(3) even if they do suggest that the defendant has a propensity to be untruthful. Even a conviction for perjury does not necessarily say much about whether the defendant is likely to be lying on *this* occasion.

27–052 In *Hanson*, however, the Court of Appeal said:

> "Previous convictions, whether for offences of dishonesty or otherwise, are . . . only likely to be capable of showing a propensity to be untruthful where, in the

[77] cf. *Butterwasser* [1948] 1 K.B. 4.

[78] See above, para.27–026.

[79] The case in which the defendant attacks another person's character is a separate gateway to admissibility of the defendant's own bad character (CJA 2003, ss.101(1)(g) and 106), not discussed here.

present case, truthfulness is an issue and, in the earlier case, either there was a plea of not guilty and the defendant gave an account, on arrest, in interview, or in evidence, which the jury must have disbelieved, or the way in which the offence was committed shows a propensity for untruthfulness, for example, by the making of false representations."[80]

Truthfulness will virtually *always* be an issue in the present case, because of s.103(1)(b). As to the earlier case, if it is sufficient *either* that the jury must have disbelieved the defendant *or* that the offence itself was one of untruthfulness, it seems likely that a wide range of convictions will be admissible under s.101(1)(d) (subject to s.101(3)) by virtue of s.103(1)(b).

Warning the jury

In *Hanson* the court said that it would not interfere with a ruling on the **27–053** admissibility of evidence of propensity unless the judge's assessment of the evidence's probative value was "plainly wrong" or the exercise of the discretion was unreasonable in the *Wednesbury*[81] sense.[82] But, in any case where past convictions are admitted to show propensity (whether to commit the offence charged or to be untruthful), the judge should warn the jury against placing "undue reliance" on them.

"Evidence of bad character cannot be used simply to bolster a weak case, or to prejudice the minds of a jury against a defendant. In particular, the jury should be directed: that they should not conclude that the defendant is guilty or untruthful merely because he has these convictions; that, although the convictions may show a propensity, this does not mean that he has committed this offence or been untruthful in this case; that whether they in fact show a propensity is for them to decide; that they must take into account what the defendant has said about his previous convictions; and that, although they are entitled, if they find propensity as shown, to take this into account when determining guilt, propensity is only one relevant factor and they must assess its significance in the light of all the other evidence in the case."[83]

SUBSEQUENT CONDUCT

The prosecution occasionally seeks to rely on similar conduct occurring **27–054** *after* the conduct charged. For some purposes, for example to establish the defendant's knowledge at the time of the alleged offence, subsequent conduct is clearly irrelevant;[84] but it may be relevant as tending to prove a dishonest course of conduct. On principle there would seem to be no reason why subsequent conduct should not be admissible in the same way as previous conduct, provided it is relevant to a matter in issue. This was probably the position at common law.[85] Under CJA 2003, the question is

[80] [2005] EWCA Crim 824; [2005] 1 W.L.R. 3169 at [13].
[81] *Associated Provincial Picture Houses Ltd v Wednesbury Corp* [1948] 1 K.B. 223.
[82] [2005] EWCA Crim 824; [2005] 1 W.L.R. 3169 at [15].
[83] [2005] EWCA Crim 824; [2005] 1 W.L.R. 3169 at [18].
[84] In *Ollis* [1900] 2 Q.B. 758 this point was apparently overlooked: see above, para.27–032.
[85] e.g. *Rhodes* [1899] 1 Q.B. 77; *Mason* (1914) 10 Cr.App.R. 169; but cf. *Boothby* (1933) 24 Cr.App.R. 112.

simply whether the misconduct is relevant to an important matter in issue. In *Adenusi* the issue was whether the trial judge had been right to admit evidence of offences committed five days after the conduct which was the subject of the charges before the court. The Court of Appeal said:

> "What the jury have to concentrate on is of course the defendant's propensity at the time that he is alleged to have committed the offences with which he is being tried. We can see no justification for saying that as a matter of law one is not entitled to determine propensity at the time of committing the offences by reference to offences committed thereafter. Whether or not offences committed thereafter assist the jury to decide on the issue of propensity is a matter for the jury subject always to the duty of the judge to ensure a fair trial (eg under s 101(3))."[86]

DOCUMENTARY EVIDENCE

27–055 In a typical fraud trial, most of the evidence will be in documentary form. The law relating to such evidence is a large subject, and we make no attempt at a comprehensive account. What follows is a brief outline of the main points to bear in mind. These questions should be asked:

- What fact does the document tend to prove?
- Is it permissible to prove that fact *at all*? For example, that fact may be wholly irrelevant to the issues in the case; or it may be inadmissible because it is evidence of bad character.[87]
- Is the document a permissible *way* of proving that fact? For example, the document may be hearsay; or it may have been produced by a machine in such circumstances that its accuracy depends on information supplied by a person.[88]
- How can it be proved what the document says, or said?

DOCUMENTARY HEARSAY

27–056 Suppose a party seeks to prove a fact by documentary evidence. The other party objects that, while that fact might itself be admissible, the document is only hearsay evidence of that fact. In these circumstances it may have to be determined

- whether the evidence is hearsay, and
- if so, whether it is nevertheless admissible under one of the exceptions to the rule against hearsay.

[86] [2006] EWCA Crim 1059; [2006] Crim. L.R. 929 at [13].
[87] See above, paras 27–021 *et seq*.
[88] See below, para.27–082.

The former question may be a difficult one. But, even if the evidence is hearsay, in a fraud case it will usually fall within one of the exceptions to the hearsay rule.

When is a Document Hearsay?

CJA 2003, s.114 provides for the admissibility of a statement "as evidence of any matter stated". A statement is defined as "any representation of fact or opinion made by a person by whatever means".[89] A matter is "stated" if, and only if, **27–057**

> "the purpose, or one of the purposes, of the person making the statement appears to the court to have been—
>
> (a) to cause another person to believe the matter, or
>
> (b) to cause another person to act or a machine to operate on the basis that the matter is as stated."[90]

Whether a document is hearsay therefore depends partly on the purpose for which it is adduced, and partly on how and why it came into being.

The purpose for which the document is adduced

A document is hearsay if it is adduced as evidence of the truth of a fact stated in it. It is not hearsay if its contents are **27–058**

- themselves a fact in issue (for example where they include allegedly false representations made by the defendant; or where the document is an agreement in respect of property allegedly stolen, and the question whether that property "belongs to another" depends on the construction of that agreement);
- real evidence of a fact in issue "as an original and independent fact"[91] (such as a printout from an automatic recording device,[92] a live recording of an incident,[93] a record from a calculating device,[94] or a screen shot of activity on a computer);[95] or
- circumstantial evidence of a fact in issue.

[89] CJA 2003, s.115(2).
[90] CJA 2003, s.115(3).
[91] *Romeo* (1982) 30 S.A.S.R. 243 at 262, *per* Cox J.; see *Lydon* (1987) 85 Cr.App.R. 221 at 224.
[92] *Neville* [1991] Crim. L.R. 288; *Spiby* (1990) 91 Cr.App.R. 186.
[93] *Dodson* (1984) 79 Cr.App.R. 220.
[94] *Wood* (1983) 76 Cr.App.R. 23, though evidence may be needed of the facts on which the calculations were based. In *McCarthy* [1998] R.T.R. 374 the document was hearsay to the extent that it depended on human input, but real evidence to the extent that it was generated automatically.
[95] *Skinner* [2005] EWCA Crim 1439; [2006] Crim. L.R. 56.

27–059 Circumstantial evidence can be particularly hard to distinguish from hearsay. If the existence of the document, in the form in which it exists or existed, tends to suggest that a fact in issue is more or less likely to be true, the document is not hearsay but is direct evidence of that fact. For example, the terms of a document may justify the drawing of inferences as to the state of mind of the person who produced it, or of a person who received it, at that or some later time. It may show that a false statement made by the defendant was false to his knowledge, or that the alleged victim was not misled by it because he had seen a document which stated the truth. The document is not hearsay unless the court is being invited to infer that a fact is true because it is stated in the document. But, in the case of a document which appears to record a fact, it may be true *both* that the document states that fact *and* that the document would not have said what it does if the fact were not true. The question whether the document is hearsay then depends which of these propositions is selected for emphasis.[96]

27–060 A similar problem can arise where reliance is placed on the fact that a document does *not* mention a fact which it might be expected to mention if that fact were true; but in this case it is easier to argue that the document is circumstantial evidence than that it states a negative. In *Shone*[97] employees gave evidence that, if certain motor parts had been legitimately supplied by their employer, that fact would have been recorded. The absence of any such record was therefore circumstantial evidence that the parts had been stolen.

The character of the document

27–061 Whether a document is hearsay also depends in part on the character of the document itself—the way in which it was created, and the purpose for which it was created. By virtue of CJA 2003, s.115, a document is not hearsay if

(a) it has been automatically generated without any human input (because in that case it will not be a representation "made by a person"),[98] or

(b) the matter stated in the document was not stated by a person with the purpose of causing another to believe the matter, or to cause another person or a machine to operate on the basis that the matter is as stated.[99]

The effect of (b) is to reverse the rule in *Kearley*[100] that an assertion implicit in an out-of-court statement was hearsay even if the maker did not intend

[96] e.g. *Miller v Howe* [1969] 1 W.L.R. 1510, where a label on a breath-testing device was held to be circumstantial evidence that the device was one approved by the Home Secretary.

[97] (1983) 76 Cr.App.R. 72.

[98] CJA 2003, s.115(2).

[99] CJA 2003, s.115(3).

[100] [1992] 2 A.C. 228. In *Singh* [2006] EWCA Crim 660; [2006] 1 W.L.R. 1564 an argument that CJA 2003 had failed to reverse *Kearley* was rejected.

to make any such assertion. An unintentional implied assertion is now circumstantial evidence rather than hearsay, so no exception to the hearsay rule is required.

WHEN IS A HEARSAY DOCUMENT ADMISSIBLE?

Even if a document is hearsay it will often be admissible under an exception to the hearsay rule. Some common law exceptions are preserved by CJA 2003, s.118.[101] The most important statutory exceptions are those contained in CJA 2003, ss.114(1)(d), 116 and 117, and (for present purposes) particularly the last. A further exception is created by the Bankers' Books Evidence Act 1879. **27–062**

The "safety-valve"

If the court is satisfied that it is in the interests of justice for a statement to be admissible, CJA 2003, s.114(1)(d) allows it to be adduced (by the prosecution or the defence) even if no other exception applies. This exception was conceived by the Law Commission as a last resort (a "safety-valve"), but there is nothing in the Act to say that it is available only where no other exception applies. It offers a flexibility not found in the others. The maker of the statement need not be identified;[102] he need not have been competent to give evidence; the statement may be a previous statement of a witness who is before the court,[103] or (so long as it is sufficiently relevant)[104] a confession by a third party. In deciding whether to admit a statement under this exception, the court is required to have regard to a number of factors listed in s.114(2), including the apparent reliability of the statement and the difficulty involved in challenging it. **27–063**

Unavailable witness

CJA 2003, s.116 permits the admission of a statement (whether contained in a document or not) made by a person who is unavailable to give oral evidence because **27–064**

- he is dead;
- he is unfit to be a witness because of his bodily or mental condition;
- he is outside the United Kingdom and it is not reasonably practicable to secure his attendance;

[101] The rule allowing evidence of acts in furtherance of a common enterprise is one of those preserved by s.118, but *quaere* whether it is actually a hearsay exception at all: see above, paras 27–010 *et seq*.
[102] cf. CJA 2003, s.116(1)(b).
[103] *Xhabri* [2005] EWCA Crim 3135; [2006] 1 All E.R. 776.
[104] See *Blastland* [1986] 1 A.C. 41; *Greenwood* [2004] EWCA Crim 1388; [2005] 1 Cr.App.R. 7 (p.99).

- he cannot be found, although such steps as it is reasonably practicable to take to find him have been taken; or
- he is too frightened.

Business documents

27–065 CJA 2003, s.117(1) provides:

> "In criminal proceedings a statement contained in a document[105] is admissible as evidence of any matter stated[106] if—
>
> (a) oral evidence given in the proceedings would be admissible as evidence of that matter, [and]
>
> (b) the requirements of subsection (2) are satisfied . . ."

This is subject to s.117(4).[107] The requirements of subsection (2) are satisfied if

> "(a) the document or the part containing the statement was created or received by a person in the course of a trade, business, profession or other occupation, or as the holder of a paid or unpaid office,
>
> (b) the person who supplied the information contained in the statement (the relevant person)[108] had or may reasonably be supposed to have had personal knowledge of the matters dealt with, and
>
> (c) each person (if any) through whom the information was supplied from the relevant person to the person mentioned in paragraph (a) received the information in the course of a trade, business, profession or other occupation, or as the holder of a paid or unpaid office."

27–066 So, if a fact can be proved at all, it can be proved by adducing a documentary statement of it if the conditions in s.117(2) are satisfied.[109] The document need not be *created* in the course of a trade, business, profession, etc: it is sufficient if it is *received* in that capacity from a private individual, provided that the supplier of the information may reasonably be supposed to have had personal knowledge of the matters dealt with. This is wide enough to cover nearly all of the documentary evidence adduced in a typical fraud trial.

27–067 The information may have passed through a number of hands between the person supplying it and the person making the document in which it is stated. But s.117 does not apply if a person in the chain receives the information in a purely personal capacity. In *Maher*,[110] A witnessed an

[105] "Document" means "anything in which information of any description is recorded": CJA 2003, s.134(1).
[106] See above, para.27–057.
[107] Below, para.27–068.
[108] The persons mentioned in paras (a) and (b) may be the same person: CJA 2003, s.117(3).
[109] Subject to CJA 2003, s.117(4): below, para.27–068.
[110] [2006] EWHC 1271; 2006 WL 1546690.

accident in which B's car was damaged. A made a note of the registration number of the car responsible, and gave it to B. B telephoned the police and gave them the number, which was entered in the Police Incident Log. The original note was lost. The s.117(2) conditions were not satisfied in relation to the log entry because the clerk who created it received the information from someone (B) who neither had personal knowledge of it nor was acting in a business capacity.[111]

If the statement was prepared for the purposes of criminal proceedings or a criminal investigation,[112] CJA 2003, s.117(4) imposes further requirements. In this case the statement is not admissible unless, in addition to the conditions in s.117(2) being satisfied, *either* the "unavailable witness" exception applies[113] *or* the maker of the statement **27–068**

> "cannot reasonably be expected to have any recollection of the matters dealt with in the statement (having regard to the length of time since he supplied the information and all other circumstances)".[114]

The wording of s.117 suggests that extrinsic evidence must be called in order to prove that the requirements of the section are met; but this may be unnecessary. In *Dobson*[115] records of the Driver and Vehicle Licensing Centre were held admissible (under the predecessor of s.117) without such extrinsic evidence: the judge was entitled to rely on his knowledge of the Centre and to draw inferences from the document and its contents. Similarly in *Foxley*[116] it was held that documents purporting to emanate from foreign companies, and representing corrupt payments by those companies, were admissible although the only evidence relating to them was that of the police officer who had seized them. It was said that the purpose of the legislation was to enable a document to speak for itself, and this aim would be defeated if oral evidence were required in every case from either the creator or keeper of the document or the supplier of the information contained in it.[117] **27–069**

Even if the requirements of s.117 are satisfied, s.117(6) and (7) give the judge a discretion to exclude the statement if satisfied that its reliability as evidence for the purpose for which it is tendered is doubtful in view of **27–070**

> "(a) its contents,

[111] But the log entry was held admissible under the "safety-valve" exception: above, para.27–063.

[112] But was not obtained pursuant to a request under the Crime (International Co-operation) Act 2003, s.7 or an order under the Criminal Justice Act 1988, Sch.13 para.6: CJA 2003, s.117(4)(b).

[113] CJA 2003, s.117(5)(a); see above, para.27–064.

[114] CJA 2003, s.117(5)(b).

[115] November 12, 1993.

[116] [1995] Crim. L.R. 636.

[117] But the documents in question were not hearsay anyway: they were direct evidence of a fact in issue. "These were not documents in which the creator of the documents recorded that another had told him that . . . a payment had been made. These documents were copies of the payments themselves." See J.C. Smith's commentary at [1995] Crim. L.R. 637.

(b) the source of the information contained in it,

(c) the way in which or the circumstances in which the information was supplied or received, or

(d) the way in which or the circumstances in which the document concerned was created or received."

Bankers' books

27–071 The Bankers' Books Evidence Act 1879, s.3 provides:

> "Subject to the provisions of this Act, a copy of any entry in a banker's book[118] shall in all legal proceedings be received as prima facie evidence of such entry, and of the matters, transactions, and accounts therein recorded."

A copy of an entry in a banker's book is admissible under s.3 whether the customer and bank agree to the inspection and copying of the entry or an order is obtained under s.7 of the 1879 Act[119] to enable a party to make the inspection and take the copy.[120]

27–072 Sections 4 and 5 of the 1879 Act qualify s.3. Section 4 provides:

> "A copy of an entry in a banker's book shall not be received in evidence under this Act unless it be first proved that the book was at the time of the making of the entry one of the ordinary books of the bank, and that the entry was made in the usual and ordinary course of business, and that the book is in the custody or control of the bank.
>
> Such proof may be given by a partner or officer of the bank, and may be given orally or by an affidavit sworn before any commissioner or person authorised to take affidavits."

Section 5 provides:

> "A copy of an entry in a banker's book shall not be received in evidence under this Act unless it be further proved that the copy has been examined with the original entry and is correct.
>
> Such proof shall be given by some person[121] who has examined the copy with the original entry, and may be given either orally or by an affidavit sworn before any commissioner or person authorised to take affidavits."

Cumulative use of hearsay exceptions

27–073 CJA 2003, s.121(1) restricts the extent to which exceptions to the hearsay rule may be combined. It provides:

[118] Including ledgers, day books, cash books, account books and other records used in the ordinary business of the bank, whether in written form or on microfilm, magnetic tape or any other form of mechanical or electronic data retrieval mechanism: Bankers' Books Evidence Act 1879, s.9(2). This does not appear to include correspondence: *Dadson* (1983) 77 Cr.App.R. 91. "Bank" and "banker" are now defined by reference to the Financial Services and Markets Act 2000: Bankers' Books Evidence Act 1879, s.9(1)–(1C).

[119] Section 7 provides: "On the application of any party to a legal proceeding a court or judge may order that such party be at liberty to inspect and take copies of any entries in a banker's book for any of the purposes of such proceedings. . . ."

[120] *Wheatley v Commissioner of Police of the British Virgin Islands* [2006] UKPC 24; [2006] 1 W.L.R. 2383.

[121] Not necessarily an officer of the bank: *Albutt* (1910) 6 Cr.App.R. 55.

> "A hearsay statement[122] is not admissible to prove the fact that an earlier hearsay statement was made unless—
> (a) either of the statements is admissible under section 117, 119 or 120,[123]
> (b) all parties to the proceedings so agree, or
> (c) the court is satisfied that the value of the evidence in question, taking into account how reliable the statements appear to be, is so high that the interests of justice require the later statement to be admissible for that purpose."

Section 121(1)(a) ensures that, where a hearsay statement is admissible under s.117 because it is in a business document, s.121 does not make it inadmissible even if the party who seeks to adduce it must rely on another hearsay exception in order to do so—for example where the only evidence of what the business document said is a statement made by a person who is not available to testify. Even if neither statement is admissible under s.117, s.121(1)(c) provides a catch-all exception to the rule against multiple hearsay. In *Maher*[124] the police log did not fall within s.117, but it did fall within s.114(1)(d),[125] and it was not rendered inadmissible by s.121 because s.121(1)(c) applied. 27–074

DISCRETION TO EXCLUDE

CJA 2003, s.117(6) and (7) confer a discretion to exclude evidence which would otherwise be admissible under s.117. But there are more general discretions to exclude hearsay, not confined to s.117. Under CJA 2003, s.126 the court may refuse to admit a hearsay statement if satisfied that 27–075

> "the case for excluding the statement, taking account of the danger that to admit it would result in undue waste of time, substantially outweighs the case for admitting it, taking account of the value of the evidence".

The discretion under s.78 of the Police and Criminal Evidence Act 1984 ("PACE") to exclude prosecution evidence where it would be unfair to admit it, and the general common law discretion to exclude prosecution evidence whose probative value is outweighed by its potentially prejudicial effect, are also available.

One of the factors which a court will take into account when exercising these discretions will be the efforts made by the party tendering the statement to secure the attendance of a witness, or to adduce the evidence in a less objectionable form. In *C. and K.*[126] a witness in South Africa refused to attend or to give evidence via a videolink. The prosecution 27–076

[122] Defined by CJA 2003, s.121(2) as "a statement, not made in oral evidence, that is relied on as evidence of a matter stated in it".
[123] Sections 119 and 120 relate to the admissibility of previous statements made by witnesses.
[124] [2006] EWHC 1271; 2006 WL 1546690; above, para.27–067.
[125] Above, para.27–063.
[126] [2006] EWCA Crim 197.

sought to have his statement admitted on the grounds that it was not reasonably practicable to secure his attendance. It was said that in considering whether to exclude a statement under PACE, s.78 or CJA 2003, s.126 the court should take into account what efforts have been made to secure the attendance of the witness, or at least "to arrange a procedure whereby the contents of the statement can be clarified and challenged".[127]

27–077 In exercising the discretions available to it, the court will be concerned to ensure that the trial is fair when looked at as a whole. With regard to hearsay evidence adduced against a defendant, the court will take particular notice of Art.6(3) of the European Convention on Human Rights, which provides that "Everyone charged with a criminal offence has the following minimum rights: . . . (d) to examine or have examined witnesses against him . . .". The court may take into account the possibility of controverting prosecution evidence by means other than oral evidence from the defendant, such as cross-examining witnesses, calling evidence, or attacking the credibility of the maker of the hearsay statement.[128] But in *Arnold* the Court of Appeal warned:

> "Very great care must be taken in each and every case to ensure that attention is paid to the letter and spirit of the Convention and judges should not easily be persuaded that it is in the interests of justice to permit evidence to be read. Where that witness provides the sole or determinative evidence against the accused, permitting it to be read may well, depending on the circumstances, jeopardise infringing the defendant's Article 6(3)(d) rights; even if it is not the only evidence, care must be taken to ensure that the ultimate aim of each and every trial, namely a fair hearing, is achieved."[129]

ATTACKING THE MAKER'S CREDIBILITY

27–078 Where a hearsay statement is admitted, CJA 2003, s.124 enables the credibility of its maker to be attacked as if he had given oral evidence. Section 124(2) provides:

> "In such a case—
>
> (a) any evidence which (if he had given such evidence) would have been admissible as relevant to his credibility as a witness is so admissible in the proceedings;
>
> (b) evidence may with the court's leave be given of any matter which (if he had given such evidence) could have been put to him in cross-examination as relevant to his credibility as a witness but of which evidence could not have been adduced by the cross-examining party;
>
> (c) evidence tending to prove that he made (at whatever time) any other statement inconsistent with the statement admitted as evidence is admissible for the purpose of showing that he contradicted himself."

[127] [2006] EWCA Crim 197 at [24].
[128] *Gokal* [1997] 2 Cr.App.R. 266.
[129] [2004] EWCA Crim 1293; [2005] Crim. L.R. 56.

Section 124(2)(c) must be read in conjunction with CJA 2003, s.119(2), which provides: **27–079**

> "If in criminal proceedings evidence of an inconsistent statement by any person is given under section 124(2)(c), the statement is admissible as evidence of any matter stated in it of which oral evidence by that person would be admissible."

So, if a person makes two inconsistent statements, and either of them is admitted under an exception to the hearsay rule, the other is admissible not just to undermine the first statement but as evidence of the facts stated.

FURTHER SAFEGUARDS

CJA 2003, s.125 requires the judge to direct the jury[130] to acquit (or to discharge the jury if the judge thinks there should be a retrial) where the case against the defendant depends in whole or in part on a hearsay statement and **27–080**

> "the evidence provided by the statement is so unconvincing that, considering its importance to the case against the defendant, his conviction of the offence would be unsafe".

In *Joyce*[131] it was accepted that this does not require a higher standard than that required by *Galbraith*.[132]

Where the case is left to the jury, a careful direction is essential. **27–081**

> "It is necessary to remind the jury, however obvious it may be to them, that such a statement has not been verified on oath nor the author tested by cross-examination. But the direction should not stop there: the judge should point out the potential risk of relying on a statement by a person whom the jury have not been able to assess and who has not been tested by cross-examination, and should invite the jury to scrutinise the evidence with particular care. . . . It is desirable to direct the jury to consider the statement in the context of all the other evidence, but again the direction should not stop there. If there are discrepancies between the statement and the oral evidence of other witnesses, the judge (and not only defence counsel) should direct the jury's attention specifically to them. It does not follow of course that the omission of some of these directions will necessarily render a trial unfair, but because the judge's directions are a valuable safeguard of the defendant's interests, it may."[133]

DOCUMENTS PRODUCED BY MACHINES

CJA 2003, s.129(1) provides: **27–082**

[130] If any: see above, Ch.26.
[131] [2005] EWCA Crim 1785.
[132] [1981] 1 W.L.R. 1039.
[133] *Grant v The State* [2006] UKPC 2; [2006] 2 W.L.R. 835 at [21].

"Where a representation of any fact—

(a) is made otherwise than by a person, but

(b) depends for its accuracy on information supplied (directly or indirectly) by a person,

the representation is not admissible in criminal proceedings as evidence of the fact unless it is proved that the information was accurate."

Where a document is produced by a machine and does *not* depend on human input (such as an automatically generated record of telephone calls made), it is not hearsay but real evidence, and s.129(1) is not relevant.

27–083 There is no longer any special requirement for documents produced by computers.[134] As in the case of any other device, the law presumes that the computer is reliable unless there is evidence to the contrary. If there is evidence to the contrary, it goes only to the weight of the evidence.

PROOF OF STATEMENTS IN DOCUMENTS

27–084 If the contents of a document are an admissible way of proving a fact, but the original document is not available for production, how can it be proved what the contents of the document are or were? Is it permissible to adduce a copy of the document, or other (for example, oral) evidence of the document's contents? The common law rule is that if the original document is available, or could be produced without difficulty, it should be produced, and failure to do so will result in the exclusion of the copy;[135] but it is doubtful how rigorously this principle is applied today. Subject to this, oral evidence of the document's contents is admissible if a copy would have been admissible.

27–085 CJA 2003, s.133 provides:

"Where a statement in a document is admissible as evidence in criminal proceedings, the statement may be proved by producing either—

(a) the document, or

(b) (whether or not the document exists) a copy of the document or of the material part of it,

authenticated in whatever way the court may approve."

27–086 This does not displace the common law rules,[136] but misleadingly restates them in part only. It does not refer to the possibility of proving the statement by oral evidence, though that is permissible at common law. And

[134] PACE, s.69 was repealed by the Youth Justice and Criminal Evidence Act 1999.

[135] *Kajala v Noble* (1982) 75 Cr.App.R. 149 at 152; *Wayte* (1983) 76 Cr.App.R. 110 at 116; *R. v Governor of Pentonville Prison, ex p. Osman* (1990) 90 Cr.App.R. 281 at 309.

[136] CJA 2003, s.118(2) abolishes only the common law on the admissibility of hearsay statements—not on how a statement may be proved, if it is admissible.

it applies only to *statements*,[137] not (for example) predictions or promises made in documents. But, if the probative value of the document lies in something other than a statement made in it, the fact that it says what it does is real or circumstantial evidence, and at common law that fact can be proved by adducing a copy[138] or by oral evidence. In *Foxley*,[139] for example, copies were admitted of documents which did not contain statements, but were themselves the medium by which corrupt payments had been made. But if the document is relied upon for a statement contained in it, and the fact that it contains that statement is admissible, s.133 applies even if that fact is not admissible as evidence of the matter stated (that is, as hearsay) but for some other purpose. For example, it would apply to a false representation which the defendant is alleged to have made in a document which is now lost.

PREVIOUS STATEMENTS

ADMISSIBILITY OF STATEMENTS MADE UNDER COMPULSION

A number of statutory provisions indirectly reflect the privilege against self-incrimination by requiring a suspect to answer questions but prohibiting the use in evidence against him of the answers thus obtained. An example is the Criminal Justice Act 1987, s.2(8), which applies to statements obtained by the SFO.[140] **27–087**

The Fraud Act 2006, s.13(1) similarly prevents a person from refusing to answer a question or comply with an order in "proceedings relating to property"[141] on the grounds that to do so might incriminate him, or his spouse or civil partner, of a fraud offence; but s.13(2) prevents any statement or admission made in answering such a question or complying with such an order from being admitted as evidence against its maker, or the maker's spouse or civil partner (unless they married or became civil partners after the statement or admission was made), in proceedings for an offence under the Fraud Act 2006 or for a "related offence". Related offences are conspiracy to defraud and "any other offence involving any form of fraudulent conduct or purpose".[142] This would include, for example, fraudulent trading contrary to the Companies Act 2006, s.993,[143] and any **27–088**

137 For the definition of a statement, see above, para.27–057.

138 cf. PACE, s.71, which provides that any contents of a document (not just statements) may be proved by producing an enlargement of a microfilm copy, authenticated in such manner as the court may approve.

139 [1995] Crim. L.R. 636.

140 See above, para.23–028.

141 Defined as "any proceedings for (a) the recovery or administration of any property, (b) the execution of a trust, or (c) an account of any property or dealings with property": Fraud Act 2006, s.13(3). "Property" means money or other property, whether real or personal (including things in action and other intangible property).

142 Fraud Act 2006, s.13(4).

143 Fraudulent trading by a sole trader is an offence under the Fraud Act 2006, s.9: see above, Ch.8.

offence defined as requiring an intent to defraud or using the word "fraudulently". Arguably it also includes any offence of dishonesty which, if proved, would amount to fraud at common law.[144] Surprisingly, s.13(2) appears to apply even if the statement or admission was made before s.13(1) came into force on January 15, 2007, and the maker could therefore have refused to make it.

THE STATUS OF PREVIOUS STATEMENTS

27–089 CJA 2003 changed the status of previous statements made by a person called to give evidence. Where such a statement is admitted, it is evidence of its truth and not merely as going to the witness's credibility. This applies both to previous inconsistent statements which are admissible under CJA 2003, s.119 (including those of a hostile witness) and to previous consistent statements which are admissible under s.120. A previous consistent statement is evidence of its truth where

- it is admitted to show that the witness's evidence has not been fabricated;[145]
- it is in a document which the witness uses to refresh his memory, he is cross-examined on it and it is therefore received in evidence;[146]
- it identifies or describes a person, object or place, and the witness adopts it;[147]
- it was made when the matters stated were fresh in the witness's memory, he cannot reasonably be expected to remember them well enough to give oral evidence of them, and he adopts the statement;[148] or
- it is a "recent complaint".[149] Recent complaint is no longer restricted to sexual offences. The complaint need not be made soon after the alleged offence, provided it is made as soon as could reasonably be expected. Clearly a victim of fraud cannot reasonably be expected to make a complaint until he realises that the fraud has been committed, even if he should have realised this earlier than he did.

[144] For common law fraud, see above, paras 7–005 *et seq*.
[145] CJA 2003, s.120(2).
[146] CJA 2003, s.120(3).
[147] CJA 2003, s.120(5), (5).
[148] CJA 2003, s.120(4), (6).
[149] CJA 2003, s.120(4), (7).

CHAPTER 28

PRESENTING A FRAUD CASE

Fraud cases vary enormously in complexity. This chapter is concerned **28–001** principally with the presentation of a case alleging large-scale fraud, though much of what is said will apply to fraud cases in general.

CURBING THE LENGTH OF A TRIAL

Fraud trials are often inevitably long; the photocopier has made them **28–002** longer. There is often a tension between prosecution and defence which the court has to resolve. The prosecution feels that its best chance of achieving a conviction of the maximum number of defendants is to try them all together and subject them to a mass of evidence. If they are tried separately, those in one trial may blame those in another; if only part of the picture is presented, the jury are less likely to be convinced of overall fraud. For precisely corresponding reasons, defendants will want to be tried separately, with as little evidence as possible called against them. Their fears may be not just the natural trepidation of the guilty, but the genuine concern of the innocent. Trying a large number of people together, with a vast amount of evidence, may make it difficult for the tribunal (particularly a lay one) to distinguish the guilty from the innocent, and may present it with the difficult task of considering certain evidence against some of the defendants but not against all.

28–003 In a number of modern cases the courts have stressed the need to curb the length of trials. Some are fraud cases, others are not; the principle remains good throughout. The courts do recognise that, where serious large-scale crime is involved, a long trial may be a necessity. Since the danger to the community is great, the community must be prepared to undertake the burden of averting it. In *Simmonds* the court said, in relation to a purchase tax fraud:

> "[T]he ever-mounting intricacy of the legislation imposing taxes has been followed by every-increasing ingenuity on the part of numbers of persons conspiring together fraudulently to evade the taxation. Such are the complexities of these fraudulent schemes and the devices used in them that only too often the only way that the interests of justice can be served is by presenting to a jury with the aid of schedules an overall picture of the scheme and charging a conspiracy to cheat and defraud. Obviously every effort should be made to present instead to the jury a relatively small series of substantive offences—but that cannot always be done and this case is one of those where only a conspiracy charge can provide for the protection of the interests of the community when once the legislature produces intricate laws."[1]

28–004 On the other hand the courts discourage long trials whenever they can be avoided. In *Novac* the court said:

> "We cannot conclude this judgment without pointing out that, in our opinion, most of the difficulties which have bedevilled this trial, and which have led in the end to the quashing of all convictions except on the conspiracy and related counts, arose directly out of the overloading of the indictment. . . . Quite apart from the question whether the prosecution could find legal justification for joining all these counts in one indictment and resisting severance, the wider and more important question has to be asked whether in such a case the interests of justice were likely to be better served by one very long trial, or by one moderately long and four short separate trials. We answer unhesitatingly that whatever advantages were expected to accrue from one long trial, the precise character of which has never been apparent to us, they were heavily outweighed by the disadvantages. A trial of such dimensions puts an immense burden on both judge and jury. In the course of a four or five day summing-up the most careful and conscientious judge may so easily overlook some essential matter. Even if the summing-up is faultless, it is by no means cynical to doubt whether the average juror can be expected to take it all in and apply all the directions given. Some criminal prosecutions involve consideration of matters so plainly inextricable and indivisible that a long and complex trial is an ineluctable necessity. But we are convinced that nothing short of the criterion of absolute necessity can justify the imposition of the burdens of a very long trial on the Court. . . .
>
> It is quite wrong for prosecuting authorities to charge, in a single indictment, numerous offenders and offences, simply because some nexus may be discoverable between them, leaving it to the Court to determine any application to

[1] [1969] 1 Q.B. 685 at 689.

sever which may be made by the defence. If multiplicity of defendants and charges threatens undue length and complexity of trial then a heavy responsibility must rest on the prosecution in the first place to consider whether joinder is essential in the interests of justice or whether the case can reasonably be sub-divided or otherwise abbreviated and simplified. In jury trial brevity and simplicity are the hand-maidens of justice, length and complexity its enemies."[2]

In serious fraud trials the Criminal Justice Act 1987 provides for preparatory hearings, which are designed to identify and narrow the issues.[3] Although these have been extensively used, they have not succeeded in shortening trials to the extent predicted in the Roskill report.[4] There have been a number of trials of exceptional length, and preliminary hearings have often seemed to obey Parkinson's law that work expands to fill the time available for its completion. In *Cohen*[5] the convictions were quashed at the end of a trial which lasted over a year and which in the Court of Appeal's view had got out of control. The court was particularly critical of the wide time-scale embraced by the prosecution case and the large number of issues originally put before the jury, reduced to manageable proportions only after counsel's speeches. **28–005**

"The awesome time-scale of the trial, the multiplicity of the issues, the distance between evidence, speeches and retirement and not least the two prolonged periods of absence by the jury (amounting to 126 days) could be regarded as combining to destroy a basic assumption. This assumption is that a jury determine guilt or innocence upon evidence which they are able as humans both to comprehend and remember, and upon which they have been addressed at a time when the parties can reasonably expect the speeches to make an impression upon the deliberations . . ."

The trial in *Kellard*[6] bore "the ignoble distinction of being the longest criminal jury trial in English history" at that time,[7] occupying 252 working days over a period of 17 months. At a preparatory hearing seven months before it began it had been estimated at three months by the prosecution and six by the defence. The Court of Appeal thought that it could have been shortened if its likely length had been re-assessed when it eventually got under way. **28–006**

"Had this been done on a detailed basis, projecting specific periods for speeches and individual witnesses, it must quickly have been apparent that the trial could not have been anywhere near completed within six months. This, in turn, would have required the Crown to give serious consideration as to how the case might be shortened. A further advantage of a detailed project estimate is that when slippage occurs, it quickly becomes apparent to everybody."[8]

[2] (1976) 65 Cr.App.R. 107 at 118; cf. *Thorne* (1978) 66 Cr.App.R. 6 at 13–14.
[3] Above, paras 24–061 *et seq*.
[4] *Report of the Fraud Trials Committee* (1986).
[5] (1992) 142 N.L.J. 1267 (the Blue Arrow case).
[6] [1995] 2 Cr.App.R. 134 (the Britannia Park case).
[7] It is believed that that distinction is currently held by the Jubilee Line trial, which began in June 2003 and collapsed in March 2005.
[8] [1995] 2 Cr.App.R. 134 at 142.

28–007 The court referred to the passage from *Cohen* quoted above, and went on:

> "These dicta show that in a potentially long criminal case a heavy responsibility lies upon the trial judge and counsel, in particular prosecution counsel, to ensure that it remains manageable and of a dimension that enables it to be presented clearly to a jury. The judge's powers in this area are restricted. The Indictments Act 1915 gives him the right to sever the indictment in an appropriate case, but he cannot prevent the prosecution calling relevant evidence, save for the well known common law and statutory exceptions. It is for prosecution counsel to decide what evidence he should call and it is for this reason that he is in the best position to decide the shape of the case. The difficulty over recent years, as appears from the authorities, has been the reluctance of prosecution counsel to cut down the size of the case by failing to agree to the severance of certain counts and by calling evidence, which although admissible on the remaining counts, is not essential to prove them. Presumably counsel fear that if they do not call all the relevant evidence available to them, the accused may be unjustly acquitted. However, in our judgment, it is the duty of prosecution counsel to review the evidence in a long case and decide how much of it, even though relevant, can be withheld in the interests of time and clarity.
>
> Furthermore, when the judge is minded to sever the indictment, it is not appropriate for prosecution counsel to frustrate the judge's purpose by calling the evidence supporting the severed count or counts, on the basis that it is relevant to those remaining."[9]

As the court conceded, it is easy to be wise with hindsight. In other serious fraud cases where severance has occurred, the prosecution has failed to achieve results which it regarded as satisfactory. It may be unfortunate if a fraudster severs an important area of evidence which in a smaller trial would have been admitted. Speaking anecdotally, juries have continued to show seriousness of purpose and care in the way they approach long fraud trials, and a surprising willingness to undertake the burden.[10]

THE PROTOCOL

28–008 On March 22, 2005 the Lord Chief Justice issued a Protocol on the Control and Management of Heavy Fraud and other Complex Criminal Cases. Its aim is to keep the length of all trials within manageable limits, bearing in mind the need both to ensure that the jury can retain and assess the evidence and to make proper use of limited public resources. It regards three months as the target outer limit for most cases, though it recognises that there will be cases where a duration of six months or, in exceptional circumstances, even longer may be inevitable. Timetables are encouraged, and advocates should be kept to them. Abuse of process applications should be dealt with in a day. Limits should not be set to cross-examination, but conciseness is encouraged.

[9] [1995] 2 Cr.App.R. 134 at 145.

[10] See Sally Lloyd-Bostock, "The Jubilee Line Jurors: Does their Experience Strengthen the Argument for Judge-only Trial in Long and Complex Fraud Cases?" [2007] Crim. L.R. 255.

The Protocol encourages the nomination of an experienced judge to try complex cases and continuously handle the pre-trial process. He is given a strongly interventionist role, though he is advised to consider carefully how heavily he needs to weigh in. The Protocol encourages the instruction of counsel at an early stage in the investigation process, and the shortening of interviews of suspects. The lead advocate must not commit the Crown in policy matters without discussing the issue with the Director of the prosecuting authority. 28–009

From the first directions hearing the court, prosecution and defence must appoint a progression officer. A trial date should be fixed and worked to, once the issues are fully understood at a directions hearing. For this purpose the prosecution must provide a simple outline of its case and the key facts and evidence on which it relies. At the first case management hearing each defence advocate should be asked to outline the defence. The Protocol encourages co-operation between all sides to result in an expeditious trial, though a defence advocate may wish to limit himself to what he is bound to give under a defence case statement. The judge is encouraged to use his statutory powers to ensure that defence case statements are adequate.[11] Early identification and exchange of expert evidence is encouraged. The prosecution is encouraged to disclose only relevant material, rather than giving the defence a "warehouse key" to vast quantities of documents. 28–010

The Protocol recognises the propriety of severing indictments for case management purposes. Before ordering severance, the judge should consider any representations that it would weaken the prosecution's case. The Protocol also recognises that there may be particular difficulties over severance when there is a cut-throat defence, or where some defendants say they relied on the advice of a co-defendant who is a professional adviser. 28–011

SELECTION OF CHARGES

THE NEED FOR PRECISION

A criminal trial should seek to convict the guilty and acquit the innocent. In order to ensure the latter it has long been recognised that the charges should be precise, so that a defendant may know in advance exactly what it is he has to meet. But if the indictment is too precise, the guilty may escape on a technicality. The tension between the need for precision and the desire to avoid over-technicality is frequently present in a fraud trial. The prosecution has usually accumulated evidence which on the face of it reveals dishonest conduct and which calls for an answer. Often, however, it lacks inside information that would reveal the precise nature of the fraud. It 28–012

[11] See above, para.24–093.

may, and in a complicated case often will, have drawn a false inference in a particular area. It may be right in the inference of dishonest conduct but wrong in its deductions about the method employed. Whilst, therefore, it must formulate its charges with reasonable precision, it will also wish to stretch them as wide as possible, so as to allow itself room for manoeuvre during the trial. The defence, on the other hand, will want in most cases to pin the prosecution down to as narrow and precise a charge as possible. It will be conscious that the adversarial system offers it distinct advantages. It need not show its hand until the prosecution has committed itself to a particular charge. Once that is done, it may escape because the prosecution has chosen the wrong charge; or it may succeed in excluding evidence which, while possibly indicating fraud, is irrelevant to the particular offence charged.

SUBSTANTIVE CHARGES AND CONSPIRACY

28–013 Very often in a fraud case there are a multiplicity of charges that the prosecution might bring. To bring them all would be oppressive and would over-complicate the trial. The prosecution has a number of ways of meeting this problem. It may choose sample charges, adducing evidence of other criminal acts as evidence of dishonesty; but there are disadvantages to this approach.[12] It may now be possible to charge a number of similar offences in a single count.[13] Alternatively, instead of charging the actual offences committed, it may charge a conspiracy to commit them. The acts alleged to constitute substantive offences then become evidence from which the antecedent criminal agreement may be inferred. Sometimes the prosecution tries to have its cake and eat it by charging both a conspiracy *and* substantive offences. In general the courts have discouraged both the use of a conspiracy charge where substantive charges will do, and the inclusion of conspiracy *and* substantive charges in one indictment.

28–014 Before considering the cases in which these rules have evolved, it may be useful to consider in general the advantages and disadvantages, to either side, of conspiracy and substantive charges. Defendants generally prefer to meet substantive charges. The word "conspiracy" has a sinister ring which many defendants fear. It is more difficult for a defendant in a conspiracy trial to sever his trial from that of other defendants. On a joint trial co-defendants who might exculpate a particular defendant may choose not to give evidence, whereas in a separate trial they could be compelled to do so. If the prosecution elects substantive charges, there is always the chance that it may choose the wrong one. If it picks sample counts, it may choose an instance for which the defence happens to have an explanation. On the other hand, if there has been fraudulent conduct and the prosecution picks a sufficiently wide selection of sample counts, conviction ought to ensue in

[12] Above, para.25–017.
[13] CPR 2005, r.14.2(2); above, para.25–003.

at least some instances. If sample counts are chosen, a defendant may be able to argue successfully that other conduct is inadmissible because it lacks the similarity necessary for its admission in evidence or because it is irrelevant to any issue raised by the substantive charges. A defendant in a conspiracy case may be exposed to evidence which would not be admissible on a substantive charge. For instance, it is frequently held that in a conspiracy case the act of any conspirator in furtherance of the conspiracy is the act of all conspirators.[14]

For similar reasons, prosecutors often favour a conspiracy charge. Such a charge gives them the maximum room for manoeuvre during the trial. The fact that they fail to prove one part of their case is immaterial if they adduce other evidence which still goes to prove the general agreement. No difficulties as to similar fact evidence are likely to arise, since all relevant conduct goes to the conspiracy. Evidence inadmissible on a substantive charge may become admissible on a conspiracy. Where the organisers of crimes have deliberately kept themselves in the background, a jury may more readily understand their guilt of conspiracy than their involvement in individual offences committed by others. If sample counts are laid, the defendant can only be sentenced on the basis of those counts (unless he asks for other offences to be taken into consideration).[15] If a conspiracy count is included, the agreement will cover all the offences committed in pursuance of it, and the trial judge can form his own view whether to sentence on the basis that the defendant committed all or only some of them. But a conspiracy count has its disadvantages. The prosecutor must define his conspiracy precisely and particularise it. He must not charge two conspiracies in one count. He may find that the defendants can take advantage of technicalities even more easily on a conspiracy charge than on substantive counts.[16] **28–015**

The court may have interests of its own, independent of both prosecution and defence. In a jury trial, a conspiracy verdict may be too wide to be an adequate guide to sentence, and the judge may prefer to avoid any vital fact-finding exercise independent of the jury's verdict. The court will also want to ensure that the trial is kept within reasonable bounds, and that the jury is not overburdened with detail or the public with expense. In any event, on a conviction for conspiracy to commit a number of identical substantive offences, the maximum sentence available is the maximum for one of the substantive offences.[17] The court may regard this as inadequate. **28–016**

The choice between conspiracy and substantive counts involves two separate questions: **28–017**

- Should there be a conspiracy count at all?
- If so, should it co-exist with substantive counts or be tried alone?

[14] See above, paras 27–006 *et seq*.
[15] See above, para.25–017.
[16] See above, Ch.21.
[17] Criminal Law Act 1977, s.3(3).

SUBSTANTIVE CHARGES PREFERABLE

28–018 In *Selsby*[18] Lord Cranworth (then Rolfe B.) expressed the view that where possible it was more satisfactory to indict for a substantive offence rather than conspiracy. This view was adopted, and greatly reinforced, by Cockburn C.J. in *Boulton*,[19] a case so weak it required six counsel (including two Law Officers) to prosecute it to acquittal. Two men were found walking in public in women's clothing. A medical examination produced some evidence of buggery.[20] At their lodgings were found letters from a number of other men with apparent references to dressing in women's clothing. There was also evidence that some of the defendants had lived in the same premises and had occasionally shared a bed. They were indicted with a general conspiracy to commit felonious and unnatural crime (presumably buggery), a general conspiracy to incite persons unknown to commit the same offence, and, in a series of twelve other counts, a number of smaller conspiracies to commit the same crime (these last being based principally upon the letters that passed from one to another). Cockburn C.J. was strongly critical of the way the police had behaved in the investigation. As to the form of the indictment, he said:

> "I am clearly of opinion that where the proof intended to be submitted to a jury is proof of the actual commission of crime, it is not the proper course to charge the parties with conspiring to commit it; for that course operates, it is manifest, unfairly and unjustly against the parties accused; the prosecutors are thus enabled to combine in one indictment a variety of offences, which, if treated individually, as they ought to be, would exclude the possibility of giving evidence against one defendant to the prejudice of others, and deprive defendants of the advantage of calling their co-defendants as witnesses."[21]

He nevertheless left the counts to the jury, though his comments on the facts must have contributed to the defendants' acquittal.

28–019 In *West* the Court of Criminal Appeal quashed a count of conspiracy as duplicitous, and added:

> "The most serious aspect of the present case was the creation of false documents brought into being and used for the purpose of deceiving the Board of Trade. The law of this country is not so futile that such conduct, if proved, cannot be criminally punished without recourse to a vaguely worded general charge of conspiracy extending over six years. There is a growing tendency to charge persons with criminal conspiracy rather than with the specific offences which the evidence shows them to have committed. It is not to be encouraged."[22]

28–020 In *Cooper*[23] two police officers were charged with conspiracy to steal and in four substantive counts of robbery and four alternative counts of larceny.

[18] (1851) 5 Cox C.C. 495n. at 497.
[19] (1871) 12 Cox C.C. 87.
[20] The report is somewhat coy about the "unnatural act".
[21] (1871) 12 Cox C.C. 87 at 93.
[22] [1948] 1 K.B. 709 at 720.
[23] (1947) 32 Cr.App.R. 102.

The allegation against them was that they had used their position as police officers to force four named witnesses to hand over property under threats of police action of one sort or another against them. Their defence was that in three of the four cases they had not taken any property, and that in the fourth they had done so but only at the request of the complainant. The jury convicted them of conspiracy but acquitted them on the substantive counts. The Court of Criminal Appeal quashed the conviction as unreasonable, because the only material on which it could be based was the evidence on the four incidents, and the jury had acquitted the defendants on the substantive charges relating to those incidents. The court added:

> "In this case it appears to us that there was no necessity from any point of view for the insertion of any charge of conspiracy. A verdict of Guilty could be supported only if the jury believed the general story, and the general story was one told by four different persons, each of whom, if he was believed, proved conclusively a charge of stealing . . . Counsel for the prosecution was doing his duty in considering whether it was desirable or not to insert a count for conspiracy in this indictment. He thought that it was. In a similar case in future counsel for the prosecution will probably think, and think very long, before he clogs a perfectly simple case of stealing in one or more instances with a count for conspiracy, because it is so well known that juries not infrequently fail to understand what the lawyer finds so simple to understand, the difference between conspiracy and larceny."[24]

In *Verrier v DPP*[25] the House of Lords confirmed the general rule that, **28–021**
where there is an effective and sufficient charge of a substantive offence, the addition of a charge for conspiracy is undesirable. These cases, and others which followed them, were also concerned with the inclusion of conspiracy and substantive counts in the same indictment and with rolled-up or duplicitous conspiracy counts. To these topics we shall return.[26] But these cases do discourage the use of conspiracy counts which do no more than rehearse, in different form, allegations which could as well be made in substantive counts, or which amount to an improper attempt to launch a prosecution on evidence too nebulous to support substantive counts. It is to be noted, however, that while the use of conspiracy counts in such circumstances is discouraged, in none of these cases was a count quashed on that ground alone.

CIRCUMSTANCES WHERE CONSPIRACY CHARGES MAY PROPERLY BE LAID

There is in any event another side to the coin. The courts have **28–022**
recognised that the conspiracy charge has a legitimate place in an indictment for fraud. In many cases it is the organisation of crime that is the greater evil than the individual crimes committed under its aegis, and a

[24] (1947) 32 Cr.App.R. 102 at 111.
[25] [1967] 2 A.C. 195 at 223–224, *per* Lord Pearson.
[26] Below, paras 28–031 *et seq*.

conspiracy charge may legitimately aim at that. In *Verrier v DPP*[27] the House of Lords approved two passages from R.S. Wright J. on Conspiracy.

> "There may be cases in which the agreement or concurrence of several persons in the execution of a criminal design is a proper ground for aggravation of their punishment beyond what would be proper in the case of a sole defendant. Such would be cases in which the co-operation of several persons at different places is likely to facilitate the execution or the concealment of a crime, or in which the presence of several persons together is intended to increase the means of force or to create terror, or cases of fraud in which suspicion and ordinary caution are likely to be disarmed by the increased credibility of a representation made by several persons. . . .
>
> To permit two persons to be indicted for a conspiracy to make a slide in the street of a town, or to catch hedge sparrows in April, would be to destroy that distinction between crimes and minor offences which in every country it is held important to preserve. On the other hand, there may be cases in which the concurrence of several persons for committing an offence may essentially change its character, and so enhance its mischief that the joint act may properly be treated as a crime."[28]

28–023 *Verrier* was a case in which the substantive offence had not been consummated, so that conspiracy had to be charged. Their Lordships nevertheless expressed the view that it was only in exceptional cases that conspiracy should be substituted for substantive counts.[29] Moreover they held that the sentence for conspiracy could be greater than for the substantive offence or offences which it was agreed to commit. This rule is now reversed by the Criminal Law Act 1977, s.3, but the general observations of R. S. Wright J. are still apt in this context. Lord Coleridge C.J. made a similar point in *Mogul Steamship Co. Ltd v McGregor, Gow and Co*, drawing a distinction between the tort of conspiracy, for which damage must be proved, and the *crime* of conspiracy, for which proof of the agreement is sufficient.

> "[I]n an indictment it suffices if the combination exists and is unlawful, because it is the combination itself which is mischievous, and which gives the public an interest to interfere by indictment."[30]

28–024 There are other criminal cases in which the courts have pointed out that the fact of combination may make a crime more serious. Like *Verrier*, they were concerned with the appropriate sentence in conspiracy cases, and should now be read subject to s.3 of the Criminal Law Act 1977. In *Morris* the defendant had been engaged in the wholesale smuggling of watches over an eight month period. The court observed:

> "Where the evidence showed that the only matter in which the defendant had been concerned was one definite offence, it would obviously be wrong, by

[27] [1967] 2 A.C. 195.

[28] *The Law of Criminal Conspiracies and Agreements* (1873) at 81–83; cf. *Blamires Transport Services Ltd* [1964] 1 Q.B. 278 at 282–283.

[29] [1967] 2 A.C. 195 at 223–224, *per* Lord Pearson.

[30] (1888) 21 Q.B.D. 544 at 549.

means of indicting him for conspiracy, to impose on him a longer sentence than he could have received if he had been indicted merely for the substantive offence. But in the present case the appellant has been engaged in a traffic which obviously has been going on for many months; he has had four motor-cars fitted so that this traffic can be carried on, and was smuggling on a very extensive scale. Those considerations do not therefore apply to this case."[31]

Similarly in *Field* it was argued that the defendants, who had conspired to obstruct the course of justice, had in effect done no more than wilfully obstruct the police and should be sentenced on that basis. The court disagreed. **28–025**

"Even if the object of the conspiracy had been the obstruction of the police, which it was not, in the circumstances of this case the fact of the unlawful combination of these appellants to achieve that end would have changed its character and so enhanced its mischief that the joint act might properly be treated as a different and more serious crime."[32]

The seriousness of conspiracy may lie not only in the organisation involved, but also in the aggregate of the acts committed in pursuance of the agreement. In *Jones*[33] this was described as the "overall criminality" of the acts alleged. The six defendants were union shop stewards in the building trade and members of a strike action committee. They organised a picket of 250 people at five building sites in Shrewsbury and three sites in the nearby town of Telford. Their intention was to bring about a stoppage of work at all the building sites, some of which were themselves extensive in area. At each site there was a terrifying display of force and violence, committed or threatened, against buildings, plant and equipment; at some sites there were also acts and threats of personal violence. The indictment charged conspiracy to intimidate, unlawful assembly and affray. In addition there were 39 substantive counts against some of the defendants, some being for offences of intimidation. The defence sought to quash the conspiracy count on the ground that it was unnecessary, the intimidation involved being sufficiently covered by the substantive counts. The Court of Appeal said: **28–026**

"It is not desirable to include a charge of conspiracy which adds nothing to an effective charge of a substantive offence. But where charges of substantive offences do not adequately represent the overall criminality, it may be appropriate and right to include a charge of conspiracy . . . In the present case the alleged criminality disclosed by the witness statements could not be represented by charges of substantive offences alone, the Crown case could not be adequately presented in the interests of justice by preferring a small number of charges of substantive offences of intimidation, and the task of the judge and the jury was simplified by proceeding upon one count of conspiracy instead of a large number of counts alleging substantive offences."[34]

31 [1951] 1 K.B. 394 at 399.
32 [1965] 1 Q.B. 402 at 423.
33 (1974) 59 Cr.App.R. 120.
34 (1974) 59 Cr.App.R. 120 at 124.

28–027 Three separate points are involved in this judgment.

- The nub of the case against the defendants was their overall organisation of the picketing at all the sites involved. It was that organisation that distinguished their culpability from that of the other pickets who had merely acted on their orders.
- The aggregate of violence at all six sites was a truly aggravating aspect of the case.
- Those propositions established, it was simpler to represent the overall criminality in one conspiracy count.

These propositions are often applicable in fraud cases. Very often it is the organisation of the fraud that is the nub of the case. Frequently the organisers ensure that they remain in the background while the front men commit the substantive offences. Usually the fraud consists of a very large number of identically repeated substantive offences. It is their aggregate that makes the fraud serious, not their individuality.

28–028 There may be cases where the evidence that a defendant committed substantive offences is thin, but, taken as a whole, the evidence clearly indicates that he conspired with others to do so. In *Cooper*[35] the example was given of conspiracy to steal being a proper count where the evidence supporting individual thefts is nebulous, but the jury are likely to infer the existence of a general conspiracy.

28–029 In *Greenfield*[36] the defendants were charged with a general conspiracy to cause explosions and with a number of substantive counts of possessing explosive substances and firearms. There had been 25 explosions which, on the basis of scientific evidence, were alleged to have had one source. One group of explosions was declared to be the work of the Angry Brigade, one group was aimed at Spanish targets and another at Italian. There was a good deal of argument at the trial as to whether all the explosions could be attributed to a common source. Beyond the general pattern of explosions and explosive devices, the prosecution had evidence that the defendants had all lived together in premises where explosive substances were found, together with publicity material for the Angry Brigade. They had all been associated over a long period. The fingerprints of two of them linked them to particular explosions. The defence contended that the conspiracy count made the trial unfair and that the defendants should have been charged with substantive counts. Only in this way would the judge and the defendants have known which overt acts had been proved against which defendant. The court rejected that argument, although acknowledging that there was some substance in it.

> "If there has been a series of criminal overt acts which can be shown by clear evidence to be the acts of identifiable individuals, in most cases there is no

[35] (1947) 32 Cr.App.R. 102 at 109–110.
[36] [1973] 1 W.L.R. 1151.

> need for a charge of conspiracy. But in some cases there may be clear evidence of conspiracy but little evidence that any of the conspirators committed any of the criminal overt acts. Those who instigated the criminal acts can only be brought to justice by means of a charge of conspiracy. In such cases a charge of conspiracy is both justifiable and necessary . . . Between those extremes there are cases in which there is evidence that some of the defendants, but not all, committed a few, but not all, of the criminal overt acts. [Counsel for the Crown] submitted that this was just such a case and that a conspiracy charge was justified. We agree."[37]

Although *Greenfield* was not a fraud case, the principles there enunciated are often relevant to fraud cases, which frequently consist of a very large number of individual instances. In some instances it will be unclear at the outset—indeed it may never become clear at all—which defendant committed the individual frauds, while it is plain that some of the defendants committed some of them. Usually the organisers distance themselves from the public and are not involved directly in the individual instances of fraud. What is plain is that all are members of the same organisation, bent to a greater or lesser degree on the same fraudulent ends. In the same way it mattered not in *Greenfield* that only two of the defendants could be directly implicated in only two of the explosions. To have charged only those two with those two offences would (as the jury's verdict demonstrated) not have adequately represented the true criminality of all the defendants' actions. What mattered was not the particular identity of a particular actor, but the fact that all were prepared to join an organisation bent on causing explosions, thereby giving encouragement and succour to those who committed the individual acts. By joining, they technically made themselves guilty of all the acts of the organisation. That, the defence said, was unfair. The court rejected that criticism. **28–030**

> "[W]hat usually matters when assessing what sentence to pass is not when a defendant joined a conspiracy but what part he played in furthering it. Many a dangerous conspiracy has been near to ending when a man of strong personality has joined and given it more vigour."[38]

In this context it should be borne in mind that where confiscation is ordered a conspirator may be liable for the benefits received by co-conspirators.

TRIAL OF CONSPIRACY AND SUBSTANTIVE CHARGES TOGETHER DISCOURAGED

If a conspiracy count is properly laid, it may be accompanied by other counts, either substantive or conspiracy. Should the conspiracy count or counts be tried alone, or together with substantive counts? The Consolidated Criminal Practice Direction, para.IV.34.3 provides, in part: **28–031**

[37] [1973] 1 W.L.R. 1151 at 1158.
[38] [1973] 1 W.L.R. 1151 at 1158.

> "Where an indictment contains substantive counts and one or more related conspiracy counts the court will expect the prosecution to justify the joinder. Failing justification the prosecution should be required to choose whether to proceed on the substantive counts or on the conspiracy counts."

28–032 In *Griffiths*,[39] where a general conspiracy count was held to be bad for duplicity, the court expressed the view that except in simple cases a conspiracy count should be tried separately from substantive counts. Not only should there not have been a general conspiracy count in that case, but in the court's view there should not have been a single trial either. There were in all 25 counts involving 78 verdicts. The court's reasons for urging the separate trial of conspiracy and substantive counts were, first, that the sum of the two over-complicated the trial, and secondly that juries found it difficult to comprehend that evidence admissible on a conspiracy count was inadmissible on substantive counts.

28–033 It is plainly undesirable to include a conspiracy count if its ambit is no wider than substantive counts in the same indictment. To do so risks the problems that arose in *Cooper*,[40] where a conspiracy to steal depended on allegations of four separate thefts which were covered by substantive counts in the same indictment. Sometimes the prosecution seeks to include sample substantive counts and a general conspiracy which covers a whole course of fraud, including other instances of fraudulent conduct which could have been the subject of identical substantive counts. Technically a conspiracy verdict might be justified on the basis that the jury, though not satisfied of guilt in relation to the particular instances charged, were so satisfied in relation to other instances. Where the conduct relied upon is identical, however, the same dangers of confusion and inconsistency will arise, and it will generally be better that the prosecution be put to its election. In other instances the prosecution may seek to include in a conspiracy count subsidiary examples of fraud which are different in kind from those charged in the substantive counts. As long as it is clear that the conspiracy count embraces only matters different in kind, it may be justifiable to join it with substantive counts. But in a complicated case it is probably better to simplify the issues and, again, put the prosecution to its election.

CIRCUMSTANCES WHERE CONSPIRACY AND SUBSTANTIVE CHARGES MAY BE TRIED TOGETHER

28–034 There are plainly cases where joinder of a conspiracy count with substantive counts is justified. The clearest instance is where the conspiracy and substantive counts are truly alternatives. In many cases there are matters of form or substance which might warrant an acquittal on one charge without precluding a conviction on another. This was recognised in *Cooper* itself.

[39] [1966] 1 Q.B. 589.
[40] (1947) 32 Cr.App.R. 102; above, para.28–020.

"In a great many cases there is no doubt at all that a verdict of Guilty of conspiracy but Not Guilty of the particular acts charged is a perfectly proper and reasonable one. In such cases it would be very wrong not to insert in the indictment a charge of conspiracy. Criminal lawyers know that often while a general conspiracy, for example, a conspiracy to steal, is likely to be inferred by the jury from the evidence, it may be that the evidence of the particular acts forming the larcenies, which are charged in the indictment, are supported by rather nebulous evidence. In such a case the jury may say, and very likely will say, Not Guilty of larceny, but Guilty of conspiracy to commit larceny."[41]

This line of reasoning was followed in *Greenfield*,[42] where there was **28–035** evidence (a) that two of the defendants had been involved in causing an explosion or explosions, (b) that a number of the defendants had been involved in a general conspiracy to cause 25 explosions (though it was possible that a jury might at the end of a trial acquit some or all of the defendants of that allegation), and (c) that certain of the defendants had explosives (namely firearms) in their possession. The Crown charged all the defendants with a general conspiracy to cause explosions. It did not charge any substantive counts of causing explosions, but did charge substantive counts of possessing firearms and explosives. The Court of Appeal approved that course. It did not give detailed reasons, but it is clear that the possession counts (being different in kind) were true alternatives, and that their joinder was justified by the danger that the defendants, though acting illegally, might not have been convicted on the general conspiracy.

Similarly in *Jones*[43] the defendants were indicted for a general conspiracy **28–036** to intimidate persons working on a number of building sites, unlawful assembly, affray and a large number of substantive counts of intimidation. The substantive counts of intimidation were severed but the other counts remained joined. Clearly the three remaining counts were different in kind from one another. They might have been open to the objection that they all covered precisely the same ground, but on the other hand there might have been grounds to acquit on one and convict on another: the jury might have found that there was unlawful fighting but not intimidation, or that there was unlawful assembly but not fighting, or that there was fighting but it was not to the terror of the public. There was also legal argument as to the correct definition of intimidation. The trial proceeded on all three counts and in the event the jury convicted on all three. The prosecution may often be tempted to hedge its bets with alternative counts in this way, and the extent to which it should be allowed to do so will always be a question of degree. *Jones* may well have been a case where three alternative counts were too many: in a complicated case the jury should be presented with simple issues. However, the Court of Appeal said nothing to disapprove the course taken.

41 (1947) 32 Cr.App.R. 102 at 109–110.
42 [1973] 1 W.L.R. 1151; above, para.28–029.
43 (1974) 59 Cr.App.R. 120; above, para.28–026.

28–037 It is not difficult to think of other examples where joinder of a conspiracy and a substantive count would be justified. If there is a charge of attempt but it is doubtful whether the acts alleged are sufficiently proximate, and more than two are involved, an alternative conspiracy count should be charged. If there are only two conspirators a substantive count may be necessary, in case the jury take the view that one is guilty and the other is not.

SIMPLIFICATION OF ISSUES

28–038 It is clearly desirable that the issues left to the jury should be as few and as simple as possible. Issues which it is right that the prosecution should cover at the outset may prove to be non-issues; if so, they may properly be abandoned at the close of the evidence. In *Jones* it is unlikely that three alternatives were really required, and they could probably have been pruned. If the jury are asked to consider a number of alternatives covering substantially the same ground, it may be oppressive to take verdicts on all of them. The jury can be told that if they convict on alternative no.1, they need not consider no.2, and that they should go on to no.2 only if they have acquitted on no.1 on a specified ground which does not apply to no.2. If they then convict on no.1, they can be discharged from giving a verdict on no.2.

28–039 Another way to simplify the alternatives is for the prosecution to charge them all but to elect to proceed on only one, with the warning that if at the close of its case (or even later) a specific point is taken, it will fall back on a count included in the indictment but not immediately proceeded upon. Yet another possibility is to put all the alternatives before the jury, but to tell them that some are there for technical reasons which in the event may not arise, and that they should therefore concentrate their minds on one particular count.

GENERAL AND SEPARATE CONSPIRACIES

28–040 A problem that frequently arises when conspiracy is charged is the exact description of the particular conspiracy. On a general conspiracy charge defendants often argue that, even if it be proved that they have acted fraudulently in association with the general conspirators, they are not party to the general conspiracy but only to some separate and subsidiary conspiracy. If a conspiracy count on its face alleges two separate agreements it is bad for duplicity and will be quashed;[44] but duplicity is a matter of form, not substance.[45] If a count on its face charges only one conspiracy,

[44] *West* [1948] 1 K.B. 709; *Davey* [1960] 1 W.L.R. 1287. It is assumed that two conspiracies could not be two "incidents" of the same offence amounting to a "course of conduct" within the meaning of CPR 2005, r.14.2(2): see above, para.25–003.

[45] *Greenfield* [1973] 1 W.L.R. 1151 at 1156.

it cannot be quashed at the outset of the trial, though a submission of no case will succeed if the evidence shows that a defendant is guilty not of the agreement charged but of a separate (though associated) one.[46] The Crown may guard against this eventuality by including *alternative* conspiracy counts. If the defence wishes to quash a count at the outset which on its face alleges only one agreement, it may force the prosecution to reveal that it in fact alleges two by obtaining particulars of it.[47] If the prosecution fails to deliver particulars when it should, it may be permissible for the judge to regard the depositions as constituting particulars. On the other hand it may be to the advantage of the defence to allow the count to run in the hope of escaping on a submission of no case; but this tactic may fail if the judge allows the count to be amended, or an additional count added, at the close of the prosecution case.

Griffiths[48] illustrates the dangers involved in a failure to analyse the true nature of an agreement. Griffiths and his accountant were alleged to have devised a scheme to defraud the Ministry of Agriculture, which had instituted a scheme to give subsidies to farmers who spread agricultural lime on their fields. It was alleged that in a number of instances Griffiths had greatly exaggerated the quantity of lime which had been spread. Seven farmers were allegedly induced to take part in this scheme, but there was no evidence that any one farmer knew that any of the others were involved, or knew that Griffiths was doing this with other farmers or at all. The prosecution charged a general conspiracy to defraud. **28–041**

The Court of Criminal Appeal held that there was no general agreement, but a central agreement between Griffiths and his accountant and a series of separate agreements with each farmer. **28–042**

> "[A]ll must join in the one agreement, each with the others, in order to constitute one conspiracy. They may join in at various times, each attaching himself to that agreement; any one of them may not know all the other parties but only that there are other parties; any one of them may not know the full extent of the scheme to which he attaches himself. But what each must know is that there is coming into existence, or is in existence, a scheme which goes beyond the illegal act or acts which he agrees to do . . .
>
> The matter can be illustrated quite simply. I employ an accountant to make out my tax return. He and his clerk are both present when I am about to sign the return. I notice an item in my expenses of £100 and say: 'I don't remember incurring this expense.' The clerk says: 'Well, actually I put it in. You didn't incur it, but I didn't think you would object to a few pounds being saved.' The accountant indicates his agreement to this attitude. After some hesitation I agree to let it stand. On those bare facts I cannot be charged with 50 others in a conspiracy to defraud the Exchequer of £100,000 on the basis that this accountant and his clerk have persuaded 500 other clients to make false returns, some being false in one way, some in another, or even all in the same way. I have not knowingly attached myself to a general agreement to defraud.

[46] *Griffiths* [1966] 1 Q.B. 589; *Greenfield* [1973] 1 W.L.R. 1151 at 1156–1157.
[47] Below, paras 28–053 *et seq*.
[48] [1966] 1 Q.B. 589.

> Similarly, the Post Office clerk who agrees to alter a date stamp in a case where a bookmaker has been swindled must know that the alteration is to be used for a fraudulent purpose. He therefore joins a scheme to defraud that bookmaker, of whom he may not have heard, but he cannot be indicted, merely because he has agreed to alter that stamp, on a charge of a conspiracy to alter date stamps and cheat bookmakers all over the country.
>
> We venture to say that far too often this principle is forgotten and accused persons are joined in a charge of conspiracy without any real evidence from which a jury may infer that their minds went beyond committing with one or more other persons the one or more specific acts alleged against them in the substantive counts, or went beyond a conspiracy to do a particular act or acts."[49]

28–043 The court distinguished the earlier case of *Meyrick*,[50] where the defendants were the owners of separate clubs in Soho. Each had bribed the same police officer to give a falsely favourable report to his superiors on the conduct of the defendant's club. They were charged in substantive counts, and also with a conspiracy to obstruct the police and prevent the due administration of the law. The judge directed the jury that they should not convict on the conspiracy count unless they were satisfied that the defendants had entered into an agreement with a common design. The convictions were upheld on appeal. In *Griffiths* this case was distinguished on the ground that the incidents had occurred in the small geographical area of Soho, in circumstances which indicated that night-club proprietors in that district well knew what was happening generally in relation to the police. It may be doubted whether this is a valid ground of distinction. If I make an agreement with A, the mere fact that I know A has made similar agreements with B, C and D does not make me party to those agreements. If I buy a suit from a West End store, my knowledge that the same store has sold many suits to other customers does not make me party to those other contracts of sale. To speak of a common design may be misleading: a number of different agreements may all have an object in common, but that does not make them one agreement.

WHAT CONSTITUTES A GENERAL AGREEMENT

28–044 What then is required, beyond knowledge of the conduct of other conspirators, to make a defendant party to a general agreement? In order to answer this question we must bear in mind some basic principles of the law of conspiracy. All conspirators are guilty of any criminal acts committed in pursuance of the conspiracy.[51] A conspirator need not be party to the agreement at its inception, but may join it at some later stage.[52] To become

[49] [1966] 1 Q.B. 589 at 597–599.

[50] (1929) 21 Cr.App.R. 94.

[51] *Hawkins' Pleas of the Crown*, Book II, p.442; applied in *Greenfield* [1973] 1 W.L.R. 1151 at 1158.

[52] *Murphy* (1837) 8 C. & P. 297; *Simmonds* [1969] 1 Q.B. 685 at 696; *Greenfield* [1973] 1 W.L.R. 1151 at 1158.

a party to a general agreement, a defendant must be party to the *same* criminal plan or agreement as his fellow conspirators. Since this requirement is a matter of agreement, its fulfilment must depend upon the common intention of the conspirators; and that intention may be inferred from the surrounding circumstances. Thus in *Parnell* Fitzgerald J. said:

> "It may be that the alleged conspirators have never seen each other, and have never corresponded, one may have never heard the name of the other, and yet by the law they may be parties to the same common criminal agreement. Thus in some of the Fenian cases tried in this country, it frequently happened that one of the conspirators was in America, the other in this country, that they had never seen each other, but that there were acts on both sides which led the jury to the inference, and they drew it, that they were engaged in accomplishing the same common object, and, when they had arrived at this conclusion, the acts of one became evidence against the other."[53]

In the case of a political conspiracy it is easy to see that an individual who joins in to commit a specific act will also intend to subscribe to the aims of the entire conspiracy: he will intend by his modest part to further the general aim of the organisation. A similar line of argument may be applied in fraud cases. Knowledge of the acts of fellow conspirators is not in itself enough to make a defendant party to a general agreement, but knowledge may be one of the facts from which the necessary intent can be inferred. To take some examples: **28–045**

- A conspirator may know that his limited act is essential to the success of the conspiracy: without him it will fail. If he commits the act, he plainly intends to further the general scheme.
- He may know that a general scheme exists and that, though his act is not crucial to its success, the scheme is nevertheless dependent on a number of persons like himself subscribing to it. He may thus intend to further the general scheme.
- He may know that the success of his individual fraud depends in part on a large number of people doing the same thing under the general scheme. For example, it may further the general scheme if a particular fraudulent form is supplied many times to the party defrauded, who is likely thereby to be deluded into thinking that the scheme is not fraudulent.
- Although his interest is primarily in his individual benefit, he may know that the effect of his joining in the scheme will be to aid the perpetrators. In this way he may intend to further the ends of the scheme, particularly if there is a possibility that he may join in again later.

These examples might be multiplied. They all come down to the same question, which must be answered on the facts of the individual case: did

[53] (1881) 14 Cox C.C. 508 at 515.

the defendant intend to become party to the general agreement or only a particular one? On this point it may be doubted whether the facts of *Meyrick*,[54] as reported, were sufficient to justify the inference that was drawn.

28–046 If the alleged conspirators have quite different objects, there will clearly be more than one agreement—if indeed there is an agreement at all. In *Dawson*[55] a man was alleged to have conspired with 12 other men, of whom six were charged and three convicted, to cheat and defraud. The subject matter of the alleged agreement was orange juice, buses, bogies, landing vehicles and bills of exchange. It was held that on the facts there were several separate agreements relating to the various types of goods. In *Jackson*[56] there was alleged a conspiracy to take over two separate companies in a fraudulent manner. There were differences in the method employed in each case. It was held that there were two separate agreements. In *Davey*[57] a count was brought against seven persons for conspiracy to defraud the creditors of a large number of companies over a period of 11 years. Some of those charged had had nothing to do with the affairs of some of the companies involved, and indeed some of the companies had been wound up before some of the defendants appeared on the scene. It was held that this constituted more than one agreement.

28–047 It must always be a question of fact whether a general agreement can be inferred from particular details in the case. The fact that the conspirators have different objects at different times may not matter if the essence of the fraud is a single method employed in differing circumstances. On the other hand if a particular defendant is interested in only one of these objects, he may be party only to an agreement relating to that object. Similarly it is not uncommon for fraudsters to employ, either at one and the same time or in succession, a series of companies which effectively exist only to disguise the fraud or give substance to it. If the methods used are the same, the existence of the individual companies does not negate the general agreement. The case of *Jones*[58] is an example, where a common agreement to intimidate workmen on a number of building sites at different times was properly indicted as one agreement.

Change in Law Resulting in Separate Agreements

28–048 It may be that a change in the law results in an inference of separate agreements. In *West*[59] the defendants were charged with conspiracy to contravene reg.55 of the Defence Regulations 1939. Between 1940 and 1946, which were the pleaded limits of the conspiracy, the Board of Trade

[54] (1929) 21 Cr.App.R. 94; above, para.28–043.
[55] (1960) 44 Cr.App.R. 87.
[56] [1959] Crim. L.R. 839.
[57] [1960] 1 W.L.R. 1287.
[58] (1974) 59 Cr.App.R. 120; above, para.28–026.
[59] [1948] 1 K.B. 709.

made a number of orders under the regulation controlling (inter alia) the manufacture of toilet preparations. The orders were successive and were not in force at the same time. The later orders were obviously not in force at the inception of the conspiracy. In one instance an order replaced its predecessor in virtually identical terms. Other orders substantially altered the system of control which the conspirators contravened. It was held that this was not one agreement but successive agreements relating to the different orders. If the substance of the law had remained the same throughout and only the form had changed, a general conspiracy to contravene such orders as were from time to time in force might perhaps have been alleged; but the court did not encourage this view. Where there is a change in the substance of the law, adjustments in the method may be vital even if the overriding object of the fraud remains the same. It may be prudent for the prosecution at least to include counts alternative to a general conspiracy.

SUBSIDIARY AGREEMENTS

On the facts of a particular case there may be a general agreement between certain conspirators, but separate and subsidiary agreements between them and other defendants. An example is *Griffiths*,[60] where Griffiths and his accountant entered into a general agreement between themselves to defraud the Ministry of Agriculture but then entered into a series of individual agreements with different farmers to defraud the Ministry in particular cases. In such circumstances a general conspiracy count can be preferred against the principal conspirators, with separate and smaller conspiracies alleged against the others. The principals may be charged as defendants in the subsidiary counts, or simply named as persons with whom the subsidiary defendants conspired. If the former course is adopted and the principal conspirators are convicted on the main conspiracy, the jury can be discharged from giving a verdict in the case of the principals on the lesser conspiracies.[61] **28–049**

CORE AGREEMENT

It matters not that the prosecution fails to prove the entire conspiracy alleged against all the alleged conspirators, as long as there is a core conspiracy to which all are shown to be party. Thus in *Greenfield*[62] the prosecution alleged a general agreement to cause 25 explosions. There was argument at the trial as to whether, even if it were shown that the defendants were involved in some explosions, there was sufficient proof **28–050**

[60] [1966] 1 Q.B. 589; above, para.28–041.
[61] cf. above, para.28–038.
[62] [1973] 1 W.L.R. 1151; above, para.28–029.

that they were involved in all. The Court of Appeal endorsed the view that it was enough if there were a core of explosions for which they were all responsible.

ALTERNATIVE CONSPIRACY COUNTS

28–051 In some cases the prosecution may wish to insert alternative conspiracy counts, for example to cover the possibility that a general conspiracy count will fail because the jury take the view that there were in fact separate agreements. Such an eventuality might also be covered by alternative *substantive* counts, but the point is probably made more clearly with alternative conspiracies. There is nothing wrong in principle with charging alternative conspiracies in an appropriate case.

PARTICULARS

OVERT ACTS

28–052 In cases of treason the law formerly required proof of an overt act of the defendant to ground a conviction, and these overt acts were commonly set out in the indictment. In conspiracy cases proof of overt acts was not necessary in law, but if the prosecution relied upon them to prove the conspiracy it became the custom to particularise them or provide particulars on request.[63] The advent of depositions rendered such particulars largely unnecessary but they continued to be ordered, and it is now usual to provide particulars of a conspiracy under the Indictments Act 1915. A particular is not the same as an overt act (though in many cases particulars will *describe* overt acts): a particular is a reasonably precise assertion of the prosecution's case. It need not refer to an *act* at all. The provision of particulars dispenses with the need to set out overt acts, but they are referred to in some of the earlier cases cited below and for this reason they are explained here.

THE NEED FOR PARTICULARS

28–053 The Indictments Act 1915, s.3(1) provides:

> "Every indictment shall contain, and shall be sufficient if it contains, a statement of the specific offence or offences with which the accused person is charged, together with such particulars as may be necessary for giving reasonable information as to the nature of the charge."

[63] See Jeremy Roberts Q.C., "Some Procedural Problems in Criminal Fraud Cases" in Peter Birks (ed.), *Pressing Problems in the Law—Vo.1: Criminal Justice and Human Rights* (1995) at 62–63.

Rule 14.2(1)(b) of the Criminal Procedure Rules 2005 ("CPR 2005") requires a count to contain

> "such particulars of the conduct constituting the commission of the offence as to make clear what the prosecutor alleges against the defendant".

Particular counts should be linked to particular incidents.[64] Where on a single count the Crown puts its case in more than one way, it should give (and the defence should seek) particulars. If the defence fails to ask for particulars in these circumstances, the prosecution's failure to provide them will not necessarily cause the conviction to be quashed. In any event the judge should not leave a count to the jury on a basis that has not been canvassed in evidence.[65]

In substantive counts it has long been customary to provide particulars of, for instance, deceptions alleged. In conspiracy cases it became customary, on application for particulars, for the Crown to reply that sufficient particularity was to be found in the depositions and counsel's opening address. This practice was sanctioned by the courts until the Court of Appeal indicated in *Landy*[66] that particulars of fraud ought to be supplied as a matter of course. It gave two reasons for requiring particulars: first to enable the defendants and the trial judge to know precisely, and on the face of the indictment itself, the nature of the prosecution's case, and secondly to stop the prosecution shifting its ground during the trial without leave of the judge and the making of an amendment. **28–054**

THE DRAFTING OF PARTICULARS

The Court of Appeal stressed in *Landy* that the indictment should not resemble a civil statement of claim: what is required is conciseness and clarity. In particular the court discouraged the use of phrases such as "falsely representing"[67] and "to the prejudice of" and forbade the use of a general allegation of "divers other false and fraudulent devices". The draft particulars suggested by the court as appropriate to the facts of *Landy* itself warrant detailed scrutiny. They read as follows: **28–055**

> "[A, B and C] on divers days between _______ and _______ conspired together and with [X, Y and Z] to defraud such corporations, companies, partnerships, firms and persons as might lend funds to or deposit funds with Israel British Bank (London) Ltd ('the bank') by dishonestly
>
> (i) causing and permitting the bank to make excessive advances to insubstantial and speculative trading companies incorporated in Liechtenstein and

[64] *Ferrugia*, *The Times*, January 8, 1988; cf. *Shore* (1988) 89 Cr.App.R. 32.
[65] *Warburton-Pitt* (1990) 92 Cr.App.R. 136.
[66] [1981] 1 W.L.R. 355.
[67] But it is no longer possible to avoid this phrase in deception cases, which now have to be charged as "fraud by false representation": above, Ch.4.

Switzerland, such advances being inadequately secured, inadequately guaranteed and without proper provision for payment of interest

(ii) causing and permitting the bank to make excessive advances to its parent company in Tel Aviv, such advances being inadequately secured, inadequately guaranteed and without proper provision for payment of interest

(iii) causing and permitting the bank to make excessive advances to individuals and companies connected with [X] and his family, such advances being inadequately guaranteed and without proper provision for payment of interest

(iv) causing and permitting the bank's accounts and Bank of England returns to be prepared in such a way as (a) to conceal the nature, constitution and extent of the bank's lending and (b) to show a false and misleading financial situation as at the ends of the bank's accounting years

(v) causing and permitting the bank to discount commercial bills when (a) there was no underlying commercial transaction, (b) the documents evidencing the supposed underlying transactions were false and (c) the transactions were effected in order to transfer funds to the bank's parent company in Tel Aviv."[68]

28–056 It will be noted that the particulars suggested are relatively short, given that the trial lasted some 90 days. They nevertheless state the essential allegations in some detail. Those allegations all related to dealing in funds deposited with the bank without any of the normal safeguards for the protection of those funds. In that sense particulars (i), (ii), (iii) and (v) are homogeneous. Particular (iv) is an allegation of cooking the books to disguise the alleged fraudsters' operations. In fraud cases there will often be a wide variety of fraudulent methods, sometimes very different in kind, though with a common aim. The particulars suggested in *Landy* do not encourage the insertion of a long list of fraudulent devices in the hope that some will stick. The inclusion of too many particulars may cause difficulty when it comes to a verdict.

28–057 It is particularly noticeable that the *Landy* particulars include no allegation of false representation or deception. No doubt the investors who were alleged to have been defrauded were deceived into thinking that the bank intended to operate in accordance with normal prudent banking practice, and may in particular have been deceived by false or misleading accounts. Some of the transactions are alleged to have been false; others are merely alleged to have been insufficiently secured. A simple departure from normal commercial standards might be evidence of fraud, but would not necessarily be so. The various under-secured advances are all alleged to have been excessive; the alleged departure from normal practice is gross. The absence of an allegation of deception, and the presence of an allegation of gross departure from standard practice, put great weight on the word "dishonestly". Where a man persistently deals in a manner which he knows would in ordinary commercial terms be wholly unacceptable to

[68] [1981] 1 W.L.R. 355 at 362.

those who entrust money to him, he will usually be dishonest. He puts himself forward as a banker, receives money from people who naturally expect that he will follow certain prudent commercial practices, and deliberately drives a coach and horses through those practices. Whether he is dishonest or not may depend on the *extent* to which he departs from normal practice. If he were dealing with his own money he could act as he chose; when he deals with monies which others have entrusted to him, those others can reasonably expect a certain minimum standard of conduct. A slight departure from that standard would not warrant a finding of dishonesty; a substantial departure would. It must always be a matter of degree.

MUST ALL THE PARTICULARS BE PROVED?

Some particulars are essential to the proof of a charge: for instance, appropriation must be proved to establish theft. In other cases there may be particulars the proof of which is not essential. In *O'Connell*[69] a number of defendants were indicted for a conspiracy which was alleged to have had a large number of objects. The jury convicted some defendants of conspiring to effect all the objects, some of conspiring to effect some and not others, and one with conspiring to effect an even smaller number. At the invitation of the House of Lords, the judges of the Queen's Bench indicated that in their opinion the verdicts were bad. Tindal C.J. gave their reasons: **28–058**

> "[T]hough it was competent to the jury to find one conspiracy on each count, and to have included in that finding all or any number of the defendants, yet it was not competent for them to find some of the defendants guilty of a conspiracy to effect one or more of the objects stated, and others of the defendants guilty of a conspiracy to effect others of the objects stated, because that is, in truth, finding several conspiracies on a count which charges only one."[70]

Such difficulties may often arise on a conspiracy charge in a fraud case. Over the full period of the conspiracy numerous fraudulent devices may be used. Whether or not all the defendants are guilty will depend upon the proof of a core agreement to which they are all party. Provided there is such a core agreement, the various devices used may be evidence from which the individual defendants' guilt may be inferred, or evidence of the general intent of the agreement, or evidence from which it may be inferred that a particular device was within the general contemplation of the agreement. In *Esdaile*[71] there was a conspiracy to defraud shareholders of the Royal British Bank. The defendants were alleged to have represented that the bank was solvent when it was not. Thereafter there was a new share **28–059**

[69] (1844) 1 Cox C.C. 365.
[70] (1844) 1 Cox C.C. 365 at 473–474.
[71] (1858) 1 F. & F. 213; see above, para.27–005.

issue to which shareholders subscribed on the basis of the misrepresentation. Only some of the defendants could be shown to be party to that issue. It was objected that it could not in those circumstances be an overt act of the conspiracy. It was held that an overt act, laid and proved against some of the conspirators but not all, may be admissible to prove the object or intent of the conspiracy.

28–060 The prosecution should in any event take care to ensure that the particulars define an agreement to which all are party. The fact that an act or device is not particularised does not make it inadmissible in evidence: it may be relevant in any of the ways described above. If it is particularised but it cannot be shown to be part of the agreement which all the defendants joined, the particular may be regarded as surplusage (if it is inessential to guilt) and evidence of it as relevant in some subsidiary manner.

CHANGING THE INDICTMENT

SEVERANCE OF DEFENDANTS

28–061 The joinder of defendants is governed by common law.[72] The alleged wrongdoing of the individual defendants must be sufficiently related that the interests of justice will best be served by trying them together. The *relationship* between the offenders rarely presents a problem in a fraud case, since there is usually alleged some joint offence or some form of participation in a fraudulent organisation. The difficulty that does arise is the number of defendants who ought to be in the dock at one time in order to produce a fair trial. On the one hand the case must be presented in a form which a jury can reasonably be expected to understand.[73] If the jury are asked to consider the case against too many defendants, they may be unable to distinguish sufficiently between them, and an innocent man may be sucked down with the guilty.[74] There may be evidence which is admissible against one defendant, but inadmissible and prejudicial against another.[75]

28–062 In *Kellard* the Court of Appeal emphasised the importance of severance as a way of keeping the trial manageable.

> "In any large fraud case . . . it is the duty of the prosecutor to consider carefully before the preparatory hearing whether the case can properly be tried in parts rather than as a whole. A solution can often be found by a consultation with counsel who has been instructed by the defence, and then an agreed proposal for severance can be submitted to the trial judge. Prosecution counsel

[72] *DPP v Merriman* [1973] A.C. 584; *Assim* [1966] 2 Q.B. 249.

[73] Unless there is to be no jury: above, Ch.26.

[74] *Novac* (1976) 65 Cr.App.R. 107; *Thorne* (1978) 66 Cr.App.R. 6; *Dawson* [1960] 1 W.L.R. 163.

[75] *Griffiths* [1966] 1 Q.B. 589; above, para.28–041.

> must be reconciled to the fact that their case may be weaker as a result of being split into a number of trials, but that is the price that must be paid to avoid the situation that arose in the present case. Severance may not be possible in all cases but a determined effort to do so should be made where it will best serve the interests of justice and the tax payer."[76]

The danger for the prosecution in following this advice is that the absence of one defendant may enable another to cast all the blame on him, and so escape justice.[77] A jury may speculate unwisely on the reasons for the absence of a potential defendant.

In the absence of agreement, the court has to strike a balance between these rival considerations. As these are matters of practice, the court has a complete discretion to sever defendants either on application or of its own motion. In *Miller* Devlin J. said that only in rare cases would it be proper to try alleged conspirators separately. 28–063

> "Take the case of two prisoners, A and B, who are said to have been engaged in a common illegal enterprise, and one desires to say that he was made use of by the other, that he was innocent and was misled. If a separate trial be granted, the result would be that in the first case the prisoner A might go into the witness-box and give evidence of all sorts of things said by B and of the conduct of B which would pass necessarily without any denial, and might represent B as being a man of obvious criminality, and the result would be that the jury, hearing only A's side and not B's, might think it proper to acquit A. Then the trial of B takes place before another jury and the same procedure happens in reverse, and the jury in that case might think it proper to acquit B. The result of granting a separate trial might, therefore, be that there was a miscarriage of justice. And the same result would, I think, apply if one assumes, contrary to the assumption that I have made, that one of the accused is innocent. The result might be that the jury in such a case, hearing only the innocent accused and not having had the advantage of seeing the other accused, not being able to form any opinion about his character, not hearing him cross-examined, might come to the conclusion that there was not enough in the story that they had heard, in the absence of hearing the other side and of it being tested, to justify an acquittal."[78]

But there would seem to be no reason in principle why alleged conspirators should not be severed if a joint trial would be unmanageable. The same considerations would apply to joint substantive counts.

The position as to severance may change in the course of a trial. In *O'Boyle*[79] a defendant's alleged confession was excluded. A co-defendant sought to cross-examine him as to its contents, and was given permission to do so. The Court of Appeal held that the trial judge ought at that stage to have granted a separate trial to the defendant who was alleged to have confessed.[80] 28–064

[76] [1995] 2 Cr.App.R. 134 at 161.
[77] *Moghal* (1977) 65 Cr.App.R. 56.
[78] [1952] 2 All E.R. 667 at 670.
[79] (1990) 92 Cr.App.R. 202.
[80] See also above, para.23–033.

SEVERANCE OF COUNTS

28–065 Joinder of counts is governed by the Indictments Act 1915, s.4 and CPR 2005, r.14.2(3), which allow counts to be joined in the same indictment if they are founded on the same facts, or form or are a part of a series of offences of the same or a similar character. This plainly leaves a wide discretion; but again there are practical limits to the scope of an indictment. In *King* Hawkins J. said:

> "The defendant was tried for obtaining and attempting to obtain goods by false pretences upon an indictment containing no fewer than forty counts; and I pause here to express my decided opinion that it is a scandal that an accused person should be put to answer such an array of counts containing, as these do, several distinct charges. Though not illegal, it is hardly fair to put a man upon his trial on such an indictment, for it is almost impossible that he should not be grievously prejudiced as regards each one of the charges by the evidence which is being given upon the others. In such a case it would not be unreasonable for the defendant to make an application that each count or each set of counts should be taken separately."[81]

If an indictment contains counts misjoined in contravention of the rules, the trial will be a nullity.[82]

28–066 In addition to any inherent power to sever counts as a matter of practice, there is specific statutory authority for such severance. The Indictments Act 1915, s.5(3) provides:

> "Where, before trial, or at any stage of a trial, the court is of opinion that a person accused may be prejudiced or embarrassed in his defence by reason of being charged with more than one offence in the same indictment, or that for any other reason it is desirable to direct that the person should be tried separately for any one or more offences charged in an indictment, the court may order a separate trial of any count or counts of such indictment."

28–067 Section 5(3) appears to be aimed at the severance of counts rather than defendants, though severance of a count may *result* in severance of defendants. The relationship between s.5(3) and the predecessor of CPR 2005, r.14.2(3) was considered in *Ludlow v Metropolitan Police Commissioner*.[83] Lord Pearson, with whom the other members of the House agreed, stated the following propositions:

- If counts are not based on the same facts, to be capable of joinder they must be part of a series of offences of the same or a similar nature.
- Two offences can constitute a series.
- Whether the nature of offences is similar is a question of both law and fact.

[81] [1897] 1 Q.B. 214 at 216.
[82] *Newland* [1988] Q.B. 402; cf. *Lombardi* [1989] 1 W.L.R. 73.
[83] [1971] A.C. 29.

- For the similarity to be sufficient there must be a nexus between the offences. The offences should exhibit such similar features as to establish a prima facie case that they can properly and conveniently be tried together.
- The fact that evidence in relation to one count is admissible on others may be a ground for joining it with them, but joinder is not restricted to such a situation.
- Section 5(3) gives the trial judge power to sever even when counts are properly joined.

These propositions leave the nature of the required nexus rather vague. **28–068**
The fact that both or all offences are alleged to have been committed by the same person is a nexus of a kind, but is obviously not enough. The House of Lords approved the decision in *Clayton-Wright*,[84] where the defendant was charged with arson, arson with intent to defraud insurers, and attempting to obtain money from insurers by false pretences. All three counts were concerned with an attempted fraud on insurers by burning a boat. There was added a count which alleged that some nine months earlier the defendant had obtained money from insurers by the false pretence that a mink coat had been stolen from his car. It was held that both frauds involved swindling underwriters and that they were properly joined. The decision in *Ludlow* itself, however, makes it plain that the required nexus need not be this close. The defendant had gone into the private part of a public house where, it was alleged, he had attempted to steal. Sixteen days later he entered another public house, had an argument with a barman, punched him and snatched money from him. He was charged on two counts, one of attempted theft and one of robbery. The House of Lords held that they were properly joined because they had the common ingredient of actual or attempted theft, and they involved stealing or attempting to steal in neighbouring public houses at a interval of only 16 days.

The authorities on joinder tend to be concerned with sexual offences, but **28–069**
some of them may have implications for fraud. In *Wilmot* the defendant was alleged to have made various attacks on prostitutes in circumstances which, it was held, were sufficiently similar to make the evidence of each attack admissible on the counts relating to the others. The court added:

> "Theoretically, even if evidence in relation to one offence is inadmissible in relation to another, the judge has a discretion nevertheless not to sever the indictment, in other words, to allow counts alleging the separate offences to be tried together. Clearly such a course falls within rule 9 of the Indictments Rules 1971.[85] But in our view where evidence in relation to one matter is clearly inadmissible to prove another, it is normally right in such circumstances to sever the trial of the different offences."[86]

[84] [1948] All E.R. 763.
[85] The precursor of CPR 2005, r.14.2(3).
[86] (1988) 89 Cr.App.R. 341 at 345.

28–070 In *Cannan*, however, convictions were affirmed where the trial judge had refused to sever the counts despite ruling that the evidence on them was not inter-admissible. The Court of Appeal said:

> "[T]he Indictments Act 1915 gives the judge a discretion, and it is a well-known fact, and a well-known principle, . . . that that is not a matter with which this Court will interfere, unless it is shown that the judge has failed to exercise his discretion upon the usual and proper principles, namely, taking into account all things he should, and not taking into account anything which he should not."[87]

This approach was endorsed by the House of Lords in *Christou*.[88]

POWER OF THE COURT TO ORDER OTHER CHANGES

28–071 Beyond the court's powers to order an indictment to be quashed or severed or amended on the application of the prosecution, it is an open question whether the court can order the prosecution to amend the indictment in a particular way. Suppose, for example, that the prosecution indicts for conspiracy: can the judge order it to substitute substantive counts if he considers the conspiracy count unfair to the defendants? Can he order the prosecution to include in an indictment counts which are not there but which in his opinion *ought* to be there? Can he quash a count which is in proper form but which he considers inappropriate? If he has such powers, it must follow that the defence can ask him to exercise them. In *Simmonds* the Court of Appeal said:

> "If upon examination of material before him the judge considers that the presentation of the case in the way proposed by the prosecution involves undue burdens on the court in general and jurors in particular, and is for this or other reasons contrary to the interests of justice, he has a right and, indeed, a duty to ask that the prosecution recast their approach in those interests, even if a considerable adjournment is entailed."[89]

But this does not make it entirely clear whether the prosecution can only be *requested* to alter its approach, or can be *ordered* to do so.

28–072 The House of Lords has on a number of occasions considered *obiter* the existence and extent of any general discretion in the judge to secure a fair trial. There are powerful dicta in support of such a general discretion from (among others) Lord Pearce in *Connelly*[90] and *Selvey*,[91] Lord Devlin in *Connelly*,[92] Lord Salmon in *Humphrys*[93] and *Sang*[94] and Lord Scarman in

[87] (1990) 92 Cr.App.R. 16 at 23.
[88] [1997] A.C. 117.
[89] [1969] 1 Q.B. 685 at 692.
[90] [1964] A.C. 1254 at 1361.
[91] [1970] A.C. 304 at 360.
[92] [1964] A.C. 1254 at 1347, 1354.
[93] [1977] A.C. 1 at 45–46.
[94] [1980] A.C. 402 at 444.

Sang.[95] Viscount Dilhorne in *Humphrys*[96] was less willing to recognise its existence.

The jurisdiction was exercised in *Riebold*,[97] a fraud case in which the defendants were indicted on two conspiracy counts and 27 counts of larceny and obtaining by false pretences. The Crown elected to proceed on the conspiracies, and the defendants were convicted. Subsequently both defendants' convictions were quashed: the trial judge had wrongly refused to let one cross-examine the other as to character, and once his conviction was quashed there was, on the facts, no-one left for the other defendant to have conspired with. The prosecution then sought to proceed on the substantive counts, but the trial judge refused to let them and quashed the remaining counts. **28–073**

In *Smith*[98] the defendants were charged with manslaughter in one indictment and offences of dishonesty in another. Glyn Jones J. took the view that the two indictments ought to be tried together, and granted a voluntary bill combining them in one. It is not entirely clear whether this was done of his own motion (though this would seem technically possible). But it was simply a matter of combining existing counts in one indictment: it was not a case of forcing the prosecution to proceed on counts which it had not drawn. **28–074**

If there is any general power to compel the prosecution to proceed on certain counts or in a certain manner, it should be exercised with caution. In *DPP v Humphrys* Viscount Dihorne said: **28–075**

> "A judge must keep out of the arena. He should not have or appear to have any responsibility for the institution of a prosecution. The functions of prosecutors and of judges must not be blurred."[99]

Lord Salmon concurred in that view.

> "[A] judge has not and should not appear to have any responsibility for the institution of prosecutions; nor has he any power to refuse to allow a prosecution to proceed merely because he considers that, as a matter of policy, it ought not to have been brought. It is only if the prosecution amounts to an abuse of the process of the court and is oppressive and vexatious that the judge has the power to intervene."[100]

[95] [1980] A.C. 402 at 457.
[96] [1977] A.C. 1 at 23–24.
[97] [1967] 1 W.L.R. 674.
[98] [1958] 1 W.L.R. 312.
[99] [1977] A.C. 1 at 26.
[100] [1977] A.C. 1 at 46.

INDEX

This index has been prepared using Sweet and Maxwell's Legal Taxonomy. Main index entries conform to keywords provided by the Legal Taxonomy except where references to specific documents or non-standard terms (denoted by quotation marks) have been included. These keywords provide a means of identifying similar concepts in other Sweet & Maxwell publications and online services to which keywords from the Legal Taxonomy have been applied. Readers may find some minor differences between terms used in the text and those which appear in the index. Suggestions to *sweetandmaxwell.taxonomy@thomson.com*.

(All references are to paragraph numbers)